C000205783

angel Trains

www.angeltrains.com

# BRITISH RAILWAYS
# LOCOMOTIVES & COACHING STOCK
# 2006

The Complete Guide to all
Locomotives & Coaching Stock which
operate on National Rail & Eurotunnel

Robert Pritchard, Peter Fox & Peter Hall

ISBN 1 902336 50 X

© 2006. Platform 5 Publishing Ltd., 3 Wyvern House, Sark Road, Sheffield,
   S2 4HG, England.

All rights reserved. No part of this publication may be reproduced in any form
or transmitted in any form by any means electronic, mechanical, photocopying,
recording or otherwise without the prior permission of the publisher.

# CONTENTS

# CONTENTS

## SECTION 5 – NON-PASSENGER COACHING STOCK

## SECTION 6 – SERVICE STOCK

## SECTION 7 – CODES

## COVER PHOTOGRAPHS

**Front Cover:** EWS-liveried 92031 "The Institute of Logistics and Transport" passes Abington with 6M12 12.58 Mossend–Carlisle Yard Enterprise on 22 August 2005.
**Ian Lothian**

**Rear Cover:** The first Class 175s are now emerging in a revised Arriva Trains livery. On 10 February 2006 175 008 arrives at Rhyl with the 10.30 Holyhead–Cardiff.
**Robert Pritchard**

**Keep this book up to date with official stock changes published every month in Today's Railways UK magazine.**

**Today's Railways UK** is the only magazine to publish official Platform 5 stock changes for Locomotives, Coaching Stock, Diesel Multiple Units and Electric Multiple Units, presented in the same clear format used in this book. Keeping your book up to date couldn't be easier!

And of course every issue of **Today's Railways UK** also contains the very latest news, interesting articles and regular features. Please see pages 356 & 357 for further details.

**Today's Railways UK – The UK railway magazine from Platform 5 Publishing On sale 2nd Monday of every month.**

# PROVISION OF INFORMATION

This book has been compiled with care to be as accurate as possible, but in some cases official information is not available and the publisher cannot be held responsible for any errors or omissions. We would like to thank the companies and individuals which have been co-operative in supplying information to us. The authors of this book will be pleased to receive notification of any inaccuracies readers may find in the series, and also any additional information to supplement our records and thus enhance future editions. Please send comments to:

Robert Pritchard, Platform 5 Publishing Ltd., 3 Wyvern House, Sark Road, Sheffield, S2 4HG, England.

**Tel:** 0114 255 2625 **Fax:** 0114 255 2471
**e-mail:** robert@platform5.com

Both the author and the staff of Platform 5 regret they are unable to answer specific queries regarding locomotives and rolling stock.

This book is updated to 1 January 2006.

# ACKNOWLEDGEMENTS

The author would like to thank all Train Operating Companies, Freight Companies and Leasing Companies that have helped with the compilation of this book.

Thanks are also due to the following individuals for their reports of changes observed during 2005 (for the **entrain/Today's Railways UK** magazine "Stock Changes" column) and for corrections given to the "pocket book" series:

Brian Loughlin, Tony Russell, Keith Foster, Nick Lawford, John Patston, Jason Rogers, John Hall, Ian Lothian, Allan Staite, Martin Haywood, Peter Hintz, Andrew Macfarlane, Brian Ovington, Andrew Marsh, Adrian Jackson, Jon Barlow, Phil Wright, John Henley, Steve Taylor, Edward Tucker, Roger Templeman, Donald J. Bishop, Alan Costello, Mark Beal, David Haydock, Mike Stone, Mark Allatt, J. Bogucki, Brian Garvin, Ian Hardy, Ben Williams, Kevin Lee, Gwot, Doug Crawford, Rowland Pittard, Steve Revill, Mick Tindall, Ken Brunt, Mark Bearton, Robin Ralston, SJ Ralph, Andrew Mist, Rodney Lissenden, Kevin Lee, John Atkinson, John Chalcraft, Graham Lee, Gary Lennon, Duncan Anderson, Dafydd Whyles, Nick Tooth, Mick Barstow and many others – keep the observations coming!

# BRITAIN'S RAILWAY SYSTEM

## INFRASTRUCTURE & OPERATION

Britain's national railway infrastructure is owned by a "not for dividend" company, Network Rail. Many stations and maintenance depots are leased to and operated by Train Operating Companies (TOCs), but some larger stations remain under Network Rail control. The only exception is the infrastructure on the Isle of Wight, which is nationally owned and is leased to the Island Line franchisee.

Trains are operated by TOCs over Network Rail, regulated by access agreements between the parties involved. In general, TOCs are responsible for the provision and maintenance of the locomotives, rolling stock and staff necessary for the direct operation of services, whilst Network Rail is responsible for the provision and maintenance of the infrastructure and also for staff needed to regulate the operation of services.

## DOMESTIC PASSENGER TRAIN OPERATORS

The large majority of passenger trains are operated by the TOCs on fixed term franchises. Franchise expiry dates are shown in parentheses in the list of franchisees below:

| Franchise | Franchisee | Trading Name |
|---|---|---|
| Central Trains[1] | National Express Group plc (until 11 November 2007) | Central Trains |
| Chiltern Railways | M40 Trains Ltd. (until July 2021) | Chiltern Railways |
| Cross-Country[2] | Virgin Rail Group Ltd. (until 11 November 2007) | Virgin Trains |
| Gatwick Express[3] | National Express Group plc (until 27 April 2011) | Gatwick Express |
| Great Western Trains[4] | First Group plc (until 31 March 2006) | First Great Western |
| Greater Anglia[5] | National Express Group plc (until 31 March 2014) | "One" |
| InterCity East Coast[6] | GNER Holdings Ltd. (until 30 April 2012) | Great North Eastern Railway |
| InterCity West Coast | Virgin Rail Group Ltd. (until 8 March 2012) | Virgin Trains |
| Island Line[7] | Stagecoach Holdings plc (until 3 February 2007) | Island Line |
| LTS Rail | National Express Group plc (until 25 May 2011) | c2c |
| Merseyrail Electrics[8] | Serco/NedRail (until 20 July 2028) | Merseyrail Electrics |
| Midland Main Line[9] | National Express Group plc (until 27 April 2008) | Midland Mainline |

| | | |
|---|---|---|
| North London Railways[10] | National Express Group plc (until 17 October 2006) | Silverlink Train Services |
| Northern Rail[11] | Serco/NedRail (until 11 September 2013) | Northern |
| ScotRail | First Group plc (until 16 October 2011) | First ScotRail |
| South Central | GoVia Ltd. (Go-Ahead/Keolis) (until December 2009) | Southern |
| South Eastern[12] | (until 31 March 2006) | South Eastern Trains |
| South Western[7] | Stagecoach Holdings plc (until 3 February 2007) | South West Trains |
| Thames[4] | First Group plc (until 31 March 2006) | First Great Western Link |
| Thameslink[13] | GoVia Ltd. (until 31 March 2006) | Thameslink Rail |
| Trans-Pennine Express | First Group/Keolis (until 31 January 2012) | First Trans-Pennine Express |
| Wales & Borders | Arriva Trains Ltd. (until 6 December 2018) | Arriva Trains Wales |
| Wessex Trains[4] | National Express Group plc (until 31 March 2006) | Wessex Trains |
| Great Northern[13] | National Express Group plc (until 31 March 2006) | WAGN |

## Notes:

[1] Due to be abolished on expiry. Services expected to be split between Chiltern, Trans-Pennine Express and the new East Midlands (also incorporating the existing Midland Main Line franchise and part of Cross-Country) and West Midlands franchises (including all existing West Midlands area Central Trains and Silverlink services).

[2] On 31 October 2005 the Department for Transport gave Virgin Rail Group two years' notice to give up the Cross-Country franchise. This franchise is currently being operated under a "letter agreement" drawn up in July 2002, giving the DfT the right to terminate it before the original end date in 2012. A new expanded Cross-Country franchise will be created in 2007, also including the existing Central Trains Birmingham–Stansted Airport and Nottingham–Hereford/Cardiff services.

[3] Gatwick Express has been proposed for possible absorption by Southern as part of the DfT's Brighton Main Line Route Utilisation Strategy. This could take place before the expiry of the current Gatwick Express franchise.

[4] Due to transfer to the new Greater Western franchise (to be run by First Group) on 1 April 2006.

[5] Incorporates the former Anglia and Great Eastern franchises and the West Anglia half of West Anglia Great Northern. Awarded for seven years with a likely extension for a further three.

[6] The new East Coast franchise started on 1 May 2005 for an initial period of seven years, to be extended by a further three if performance targets are met.

[7] These two franchises will be combined to form a new South Western franchise to start in February 2007.

[8] Now under control of Merseytravel PTE instead of the DfT. Franchise due to be reviewed after seven years and then every five years to fit in with Merseyside Local Transport Plan.

[9] Due to be replaced by a new East Midlands franchise, incorporating all existing Midland Mainline and East Midlands area Central Trains services.

[10] Due to be abolished on expiry. Services expected to be split between the new North London Railway franchise (control of which will be transferred to Transport for London) and the new West Midlands franchise.

[11] Urban and rural services previously run by Arriva Trains Northern and First North Western were transferred to the new Northern franchise on 12 December 2004. Trans-Pennine services formerly run by these operators were taken over by the new Trans-Pennine Express franchise on 1 February 2004. The Northern franchise runs for up to 8¾ years.

[12] Currently run by an interim management company known as South Eastern Trains (SET) formed on 9 November 2003. SET was established as a subsidiary of the SRA. Due to be replaced by the new Integrated Kent Franchise (IKF) on 1 April 2006, run by GoVia. The IKF will also run domestic services via the Channel Tunnel Rail Link.

[13] To be absorbed by the new Thameslink franchise from 1 April 2006, run by First Group and branded First Capital Connect. This will include the existing Great Northern and Thameslink services. Until now Great Northern has been branded WAGN because it formerly also included West Anglia services, now part of Greater Anglia ("One").

A major reorganisation of franchises is under way. See **Today's Railways UK** magazine for developments.

The following operators run non-franchised services only:

| Operator | Trading Name | Route |
|---|---|---|
| British Airports Authority | Heathrow Express | London Paddington–Heathrow Airport |
| Hull Trains§ | Hull Trains | London King's Cross–Hull |
| West Coast Railway Company | West Coast Railway | Birmingham Snow Hill–Stratford-on-Avon<br>Fort William–Mallaig*<br>York–Scarborough* |

\* Special summer-dated services only.
§ Owned by First Group.

# INTERNATIONAL PASSENGER OPERATIONS

Eurostar (UK) operates international passenger-only services between the United Kingdom and continental Europe, jointly with French National Railways (SNCF) and Belgian National Railways (SNCB/NMBS). Eurostar (UK) is a subsidiary of London & Continental Railways, which is jointly owned by National Express Group plc and British Airways.

In addition, a service for the conveyance of accompanied road vehicles through the Channel Tunnel is provided by the tunnel operating company, Eurotunnel.

# FREIGHT TRAIN OPERATIONS

The following operators operate freight train services under "Open Access" arrangements:

English Welsh & Scottish Railway Ltd (EWS).
Freightliner Ltd.
GB Railfreight Ltd. (owned by First Group)
Direct Rail Services Ltd.
FM Rail
Advenza (Cotswold Rail)

# PLATFORM 5 MAIL ORDER

## PRESERVED LOCOMOTIVES OF BRITISH RAILWAYS 11th edition

The definitive guide to all ex-British Railways, London Transport and Ministry of Defence steam, diesel and electric locomotive and multiple unit vehicles, published in December 2002 is still available.

160 pages including 32 pages in colour **£10.75.**

**Also Available:**
**Preserved Coaching Stock Part 1:**
**BR Design Stock** (Published 1994) .................................................... **£7.95**

**Preserved Coaching Stock Part 2:**
**Pre-Nationalisation Stock** (Published 1996) .................................... **£8.95**

Please add postage: 10% UK, 20% Europe, 30% Rest of World.

**Telephone, fax or send your order to the Platform 5 Mail Order Department. See inside front cover of this book for details.**

# 1. LOCOMOTIVES

# INTRODUCTION

## SCOPE

This section contains details of all locomotives which can run on Britain's national railway network, plus those of Eurotunnel. Locomotives which are owned by EWS and Freightliner which have been withdrawn from service and awaiting disposal are now listed in the main list, as are those owned by companies such as FM Rail, Harry Needle and DRS which are awaiting possible restoration to service. Only preserved locomotives which are currently used or are likely to be used on the national network in the foreseeable future are included. Others, which may be Network Rail registered but not at present certified for use, are not included, but will be found in the Platform 5 book, "Preserved locomotives and Multiple Units". Locos already at scrapyards are not generally included, unless they are there for storage purposes and not for disposal.

## LOCO CLASSES

Loco classes are listed in numerical order of class. Principal details and dimensions are quoted for each class in metric and/or imperial units as considered appropriate bearing in mind common UK usage.

**Builders:** These are shown in class headings. Abbreviations used are found in section 7.8.

All dimensions and weights are quoted for locomotives in an "as new" condition with all necessary supplies (e.g. oil, water and sand) on board. Dimensions are quoted in the order length x width. Lengths quoted are over buffers or couplers as appropriate. All widths quoted are maxima. Where two different wheel diameter dimensions are shown, the first refers to powered wheels and the second refers to non-powered wheels.

## NUMERICAL LISTINGS

Locomotives are listed in numerical order. Where numbers actually carried are different from those officially allocated, these are noted in class headings where appropriate. Where locomotives have been recently renumbered, the most immediate previous number is shown in parentheses. Each locomotive entry is laid out as in the following example:

| RSL No. | Detail | Livery | Owner | Pool | Allocn. | Name |
|---------|--------|--------|-------|------|---------|------|
| 47813 | + | **CD** | CD | CRRH | MM | John Peel |

In some cases where few members of a class are named, names are appended as a separate list at the end of the class listings to save space.

**Detail Differences**. Only detail differences which currently affect the areas and types of train which locomotives may work are shown. All other detail differences are specifically excluded. Where such differences occur within a class or part class, they are shown in the "Detail" column alongside the individual locomotive number.

Standard abbreviations used are:

| | |
|---|---|
| a | Train air brake equipment only. |
| b | Drophead buckeye couplers. |
| c | Scharfenberg couplers. |
| d | Fitted with retractable Dellner couplers. |
| k | Fitted with Swinghead Automatic "buckeye" combination couplers. |
| p | Train air, vacuum and electro-pneumatic brakes. |
| r | RETB fitted |
| s | Slow Speed Control equipment. |
| v | Train vacuum brake only. |
| x | Train air and vacuum brakes ("Dual brakes"). |
| + | Additional fuel tank capacity. |
| § | Sandite laying equipment. |

In all cases use of the above abbreviations indicates the equipment indicated is normally operable. Meaning of non-standard abbreviations and symbols is detailed in individual class headings.

**Codes**. Codes are used to denote the livery, owner, pool and depot of each locomotive. Details of these will be found in section 7 of this book.

**Names**. Only names carried with official sanction are listed. As far as possible names are shown in UPPER/lower case characters as actually shown on the name carried on the locomotive.

# GENERAL INFORMATION

## CLASSIFICATION AND NUMBERING

All locomotives are classified and allocated numbers by the Rolling Stock Library under the TOPS numbering system, introduced in 1972. This comprises a two-digit class number followed by a three-digit serial number. Where the actual number carried by a locomotive differs from the allocated number, or where an additional number is carried to the allocated number, this is shown by a note in the class heading.

For diesel locomotives, class numbers offer an indication of engine horsepower as shown in the table below.

| Class No. Range | Engine h.p. |
|---|---|
| 01–14 | 0–799 |
| 15–20 | 800–1000 |
| 21–31 | 1001–1499 |
| 32–39 | 1500–1999 |
| 40–54, 57 | 2000–2999 |
| 55–56, 58–69 | 3000+ |

For electric locomotives class numbers are allocated in ascending numerical order under the following scheme:

Class 70–80     direct current and DC/diesel dual system locomotives.
Class 81 onwards     alternating current and AC/DC dual system locos.

Numbers in the 89xxx series (except 89001) are allocated by the Rolling Stock Library to locomotives which have been de-registered but subsequently re-registered for use on the Network Rail network and whose original number has already been re-used. 89xxx numbers are normally only carried inside locomotive cabs and are not carried externally in normal circumstances.

## WHEEL ARRANGEMENT

For main line locomotives the number of driven axles on a bogie or frame is denoted by a letter (A = 1, B = 2, C = 3 etc.) and the number of non-powered axles is denoted by a number. The use of the letter 'o' after a letter indicates each axle is individually powered, whilst the '+' symbol indicates bogies are inter-coupled.

For shunting locomotives, the Whyte notation is used. In this notation the number of leading wheels are given, followed by the number of driving wheels and then the trailing wheels.

# HAULAGE CAPABILITY OF DIESEL LOCOMOTIVES

The haulage capability of a diesel locomotive depends upon three basic factors:

1. Adhesive weight. The greater the weight on the driving wheels, the greater the adhesion and more tractive power can be applied before wheelslip occurs.

2. The characteristics of its transmission. To start a train the locomotive has to exert a pull at standstill. A direct drive diesel engine cannot do this, hence the need for transmission. This may be mechanical, hydraulic or electric. The present British Standard for locomotives is electric transmission. Here the diesel engine drives a generator or alternator and the current produced is fed to the traction motors. The force produced by each driven wheel depends on the current in its traction motor. In other words, the larger the current, the harder it pulls. As the locomotive speed increases, the current in the traction motor falls, hence the *Maximum Tractive Effort* is the maximum force at its wheels the locomotive can exert at a standstill. The electrical equipment cannot take such high currents for long without overheating. Hence the *Continuous Tractive Effort* is quoted which represents the current which the equipment can take continuously.

3. The power of its engine. Not all power reaches the rail, as electrical machines are approximately 90% efficient. As the electrical energy passes through two such machines (the generator or alternator and the traction motors), the *Power at Rail* is approximately 81% (90% of 90%) of the engine power, less a further amount used for auxiliary equipment such as radiator fans, traction motor blowers, air compressors, battery charging, cab heating, Electric Train Supply (ETS) etc. The power of the locomotive is proportional to the tractive effort times the speed. Hence when on full power there is a speed corresponding to the continuous tractive effort.

# HAULAGE CAPABILITY OF ELECTRIC LOCOMOTIVES

Unlike a diesel locomotive, an electric locomotive does not develop its power on board and its performance is determined only by two factors, namely its weight and the characteristics of its electrical equipment. Whereas a diesel locomotive tends to be a constant power machine, the power of an electric locomotive varies considerably. Up to a certain speed it can produce virtually a constant tractive effort. Hence power rises with speed according to the formula given in section three above, until a maximum speed is reached at which tractive effort falls, such that the power also falls. Hence the power at the speed corresponding to the maximum tractive effort is lower than the maximum speed.

# BRAKE FORCE

The brake force is a measure of the braking power of a locomotive. This is shown on the locomotive data panels so operating staff can ensure sufficient brake power is available on freight trains.

# ELECTRIC TRAIN SUPPLY (ETS)

A number of locomotives are equipped to provide a supply of electricity to the train being hauled to power auxiliaries such as heating, cooling fans, air conditioning and kitchen equipment. ETS is provided from the locomotive by means of a separate alternator (except Class 33 locos, which have a DC generator). The ETS index of a locomotive is a measure of the electrical power available for train supply.

Similarly, most loco-hauled coaches also have an ETS index, which in this case is a measure of the power required to operate equipment mounted in the coach. The sum of the ETS indices of all the hauled vehicles in a train must not exceed the ETS index of the locomotive.

ETS is commonly (but incorrectly) known as ETH (Electric Train Heating), which is a throwback to the days before loco-hauled coaches were equipped with electrically powered auxiliary equipment other than for train heating.

# ROUTE AVAILABILITY (RA)

This is a measure of a railway vehicle's axle load. The higher the axle load of a vehicle, the higher the RA number on a scale from 1 to 10. Each Network Rail route has a RA number and in general no vehicle with a higher RA number may travel on that route without special clearance.

# MULTIPLE & PUSH-PULL WORKING

Multiple working between vehicles (i.e. two or more powered vehicles being driven from one cab) is facilitated by jumper cables connecting the vehicles. However, not all types are compatible with each other, and a number of different systems are in use, each system being incompatible with any other.

**Association of American Railroads (AAR) System:** Classes 59, 66, and 67.
**Blue Star Coupling Code:** Classes 20, 25, 31, 33, and 37.
**DRS System:** Classes 20/3, 37 and 47.
**Green Circle Coupling Code:** Class 47 (not all equipped).
**Orange Square Coupling Code:** Class 50.
**Red Diamond Coupling Code:** Classes 56 and 58.
**SR System:** Classes 33/1, 73 and various electric multiple units.
**Within Own Class only:** Classes 43 and 60.

Many locomotives use a time-division multiplex (TDM) system for push-pull and multiple working which utilises the existing RCH jumper cables fitted to coaching stock vehicles. Previously these cables had only been used to control train lighting and public address systems.

Class 47 locos 47701–47717 were equipped with an older non-standard TDM system.

**IAN ALLAN BOOKSHOPS**

Choose from our extensive range for the transport & military enthusiast:

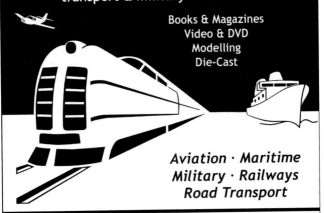

Books & Magazines
Video & DVD
Modelling
Die-Cast

*Aviation · Maritime*
*Military · Railways*
*Road Transport*

**BIRMINGHAM** 47 Stephenson Street, Birmingham. B2 4DH
Tel: 0121 643 2496  Fax: 0121 643 6855  Email: bcc@ianallanpublishing.co.uk
**BIRMINGHAM INTERNATIONAL AIRPORT** The Aviation Experience,
3rd Floor, Main Terminal, Birmingham International Airport. B26 3QJ
Tel: 0121 781 0921  Fax: 0121 781 0928  Email: bia@ianallanpublishing.co.uk
**CARDIFF** 31 Royal Arcade, Cardiff. CF10 1AE
Tel: 029 2039 0615  Fax: 029 2039 0621  Email: cardiff@ianallanpublishing.co.uk
**LONDON** 45/46 Lower Marsh, Waterloo, London. SE1 7RG
Tel: 020 7401 2100  Fax: 020 7401 2887  Email: waterloo@ianallanpublishing.co.uk
**MANCHESTER** 5 Piccadilly Station Approach, Manchester. M1 2GH
Tel: 0161 237 9840  Fax: 0161 237 9921  Email: manchester@ianallanpublishing.co.uk

*Mail Order from:* MIDLAND COUNTIES PUBLICATIONS
4 Watling Drive, Sketchley Industrial Estate, Hinckley, Leics. LE10 3EY
Tel: 01455 254 450  Fax: 01455 233 737  Email: midlandbooks@compuserve.com
www.midlandcountiessuperstore.com

# *MDS BOOK SALES*

We stock the widest range of railway books and videos.

All the latest Venture Publications, Platform 5, Ian Allan, Middleton Press, Irwell Press, Wild Swan, Capital Transport, OnLine books and videos available plus those from many smaller publishers. We stock titles from around 500 publishers and video producers.

Write to us at
**Freepost SK2162**
**Glossop SK13 8YF**

Call in the shop at
**128 Pikes Lane Glossop**

visit the website
**www.mdsbooks.co.uk**

email
**mdsbooksales@aol.com**

or  phone **01457 861508**

# 1.1 DIESEL LOCOMOTIVES

## CLASS 03          BR/GARDNER          0–6–0

**Built:** 1962 by BR at Swindon Works.
**Engine:** Gardner 8L3 of 152 kW (204 h.p.) at 1200 r.p.m.
**Transmission:** Mechanical. Fluidrive type 23 hydraulic coupling to Wilson-Drewry CA5R7 gearbox with SCG type RF11 final drive.
**Maximum Tractive Effort:** 68 kN (15300 lbf).
**Continuous Tractive Effort:** 68 kN (15300 lbf) at 3.75 m.p.h.
**Train Brakes:** Air & vacuum.
**Brake Force:** 13 t.
**Weight:** 31.3 t.
**Design Speed:** 28.5 m.p.h.
**Fuel Capacity:** 1364 litres.
**Train Supply:** Not equipped.

**Dimensions:** 7.93 x 2.59 m.
**Wheel Diameter:** 1092 mm.
**Maximum Speed:** 28.5 m.p.h.
**RA:** 1.
**Multiple Working:** Not equipped.

Originally numbered D 2179.

| 03179 | WN | WN | HQXX | HE | CLIVE |

## CLASS 08          BR/ENGLISH ELECTRIC          0-6-0

**Built:** 1955–1962 by BR at Crewe, Darlington, Derby Locomotive, Doncaster or Horwich Works.
**Engine:** English Electric 6KT of 298 kW (400 h.p.) at 680 r.p.m.
**Main Generator:** English Electric 801.
**Traction Motors:** Two English Electric 506.
**Maximum Tractive Effort:** 156 kN (35000 lbf).
**Continuous Tractive Effort:** 49 kN (11100 lbf) at 8.8 m.p.h.
**Power At Rail:** 194 kW (260 h.p.).
**Brake Force:** 19 t.
**Weight:** 49.6–50.4 t.
**Design Speed:** 20 m.p.h.
**Fuel Capacity:** 3037 litres.
**Train Supply:** Not equipped.

**Train Brakes:** Air & vacuum.
**Dimensions:** 8.92 x 2.59 m.
**Wheel Diameter:** 1372 mm.
**Maximum Speed:** 15 m.p.h.
**RA:** 5.
**Multiple Working:** Not equipped.

**Notes:** † – Equipped with remote control (Hima Sella system) for working at Celsa (formerly Allied Steel & Wire), Cardiff.

§ – Equipped with remote control (Cattron system) for evaluation purposes.

### Non-standard liveries/numbering:

08350 Carries number D3420.
08414 As **DG**, but with BR & Railfreight Distribution logos and large bodyside numbers. Carries number D3529.
08442 Dark grey lower bodyside with light grey upper bodyside.
08460 Light grey with black underframe, cab doors, window surrounds & roof. Carries number D3575.
08480 Yellow with a red bodyside band. Carries number "TOTON No 1".

08499 Pullman Rail blue & white.
08527 White with a black roof, blue bodyside stripe & "Ilford Level 5" branding.
08568 and 08730 Special Alstom (Springburn) livery. Dark grey lower bodyside with a light grey upper bodyside. Red solebar stripe.
08613 Blue with a white bodyside stripe & BOMBARDIER TRANSPORTATION branding.
08616 Carries number 3783.
08629 Red with italic numbers.
08642 London & South Western Railway style black. Carries number D3809.
08648 Yellow with black cabsides & roof.
08649 Grey with blue, white & red stripes & Alstom logo. Carries number D3816.
08678 Glaxochem grey & blue.
08682 Dark blue with a grey roof.
08699 All-over mid blue.
08701 Carries number "Tyne 100".
08715 "Day-glo" orange.
08721 As **B**, but with a black roof & "Express parcels" branding with red & yellow stripe.
08824 Carries number IEMD01.
08834 RFS(E) livery of blue with silver lining.
08883 Caledonian Railway style blue.
08928 As **FO** with large bodyside numbers & light blue solebar.

Originally numbered in series D3000–D4192.

**Class 08/0. Standard Design.**

| 08077 | | **FL** | P | DFLS | FD | |
|---|---|---|---|---|---|---|
| 08308 | a | **CS** | RT | MOLO | ZB | |
| 08331 | | **GN** | WA | RFSH | ZB | |
| 08350 | | **G** | LW | MBDL | CP | |
| 08375 | a | **RT** | RT | MOLO | TV | |
| 08389 | a | **E** | E | WSWM | BS | NOEL KIRTON OBE |
| 08393 | a | **E** | E | WSEM | TO | |
| 08397 | a | **E** | E | WZTS | AN | |
| 08401 | a | **DG** | E | WZTS | IM | |
| 08402 | a | **E** | E | WNXX | ML | |
| 08405 | a | **E** | E | WSWR | OC | |
| 08410 | a | **GL** | FG | HJXX | PZ | |
| 08411 | a | **B** | E | WNYX | AN | |
| 08414 | a | **0** | E | WNYX | TO | |
| 08417 | a | **SB** | SO | CDJD | ZA | |
| 08418 | a | **E** | E | WZTS | BS | |
| 08428 | a | **B** | E | WSEM | TO | |
| 08441 | a | **E** | E | WNYX | ML | |
| 08442 | a | **0** | E | WSXX | EH | |
| 08451 | | **GB** | VW | ATLO | WN | |
| 08454 | | **SL** | VW | ATLO | WN | |
| 08460 | a | **0** | E | WZTS | AN | |
| 08466 | a† | **E** | E | WSEM | TO | |
| 08472 | a | **WA** | WA | RFSH | EC | |
| 08480 | a | **0** | E | WSXX | TO | |

| | | | | | |
|---|---|---|---|---|---|
| 08482 a | E | E | WRLN | TD | |
| 08483 a | GL | FG | HJXX | OO | DUSTY Driver David Miller |
| 08484 a | DG | AM | ARZN | ZN | |
| 08485 a | B | E | WZTS | CU | |
| 08489 a | E | E | WZTS | MH | |
| 08492 a | B | HN | HNRS | ML | |
| 08493 a | B | RT | MOLO | DW (S) | |
| 08495 | E | E | WSNE | TE | |
| 08499 a | O | E | WSXX | CF | |
| 08500 | E | E | WSSC | ML | |
| 08506 a | B | E | WNXX | OC | |
| 08507 a | HN | HN | HNRL | CZ | |
| 08509 a | F | E | WNYX | IM | |
| 08510 a | B | E | WZTS | EH | |
| 08511 a | E | E | WNYX | AY | |
| 08512 a | E | E | WSEM | TO | |
| 08514 a | E | E | WSNE | TE | |
| 08516 a | E | E | WSXX | BK | |
| 08523 | ML | RT | MOLO | SB | |
| 08525 | MA | MA | HISL | NL | |
| 08526 | E | E | WSGW | MG | |
| 08527 | O | BT | KCSI | ZI (S) | |
| 08528 | DG | E | WNTS | BS | |
| 08529 | B | RT | MOLS | ZB | |
| 08530 | FL | P | DFLS | FD | |
| 08531 a | DG | P | DFLS | FD | |
| 08535 | DG | RT | MOLS | CP | |
| 08536 | B | MA | HISE | DY (S) | |
| 08538 | DG | E | WRWM | BS | |
| 08540 | E | E | WNTR | TO | |
| 08541 | DG | HN | HNRS | OC | |
| 08543 | DG | E | WNYX | BS | |
| 08561 | B | E | WNXX | TD | |
| 08567 | E | E | WNYX | AN | |
| 08568 a | O | AM | ARZH | ZH | St. Rollox |
| 08569 | E | E | WNYX | DR | |
| 08571 a | WA | WA | HBSH | BN | |
| 08573 | RT | RT | MOLO | IS | |
| 08575 | FL | P | DFLS | FD | |
| 08577 | E | E | WNTR | BS | |
| 08578 | E | E | WSWM | BS | |
| 08580 | E | E | WNYX | BS | |
| 08582 a | DG | E | WNXX | DR | |
| 08585 | FL | P | DFLS | FD | Vicky |
| 08587 | E | E | WSAW | MG | |
| 08588 | RT | RT | MOLO | MY | |
| 08593 | E | E | WSWM | BS | |
| 08596 a† | WA | WA | RFSH | ZB | |
| 08597 | E | E | WNTR | DR | |
| 08599 | E | E | WNTR | IM | |
| 08605 | E | E | WSSC | ML | |

| | | | | | |
|---|---|---|---|---|---|
| 08611 | **V** | VW | ATLO | MA | |
| 08613 | **0** | RT | KCSI | ZI | |
| 08615 | **WA** | WA | RFSH | EC | |
| 08616 | **GW** | MA | HGSS | TS | COOKIE |
| 08617 | **VP** | VW | ATLO | WB | |
| 08623 | **E** | E | WNTR | TD | |
| 08624 | **FL** | P | DFLS | FD | |
| 08629 | **0** | AM | ARZN | ZN | |
| 08630 | **E** | E | WSGW | MG | |
| 08631 | **N** | FM | SDFR | DF | EAGLE |
| 08632 | **E** | E | WSWM | BS | |
| 08633 | **E** | E | WSEM | TO | |
| 08635 | **B** | E | WNYX | TO | |
| 08641 | **GL** | FG | HJSL | LA | |
| 08642 | **0** | P | DHLT | LD | |
| 08644 | **GL** | FG | HJSL | LA | |
| 08645 | **GL** | FG | HJSL | LA | |
| 08646 | **F** | E | WNXX | TD | |
| 08648 | **0** | RT | MOLO | NW | |
| 08649 | **0** | AM | ARZG | ZG | G.H. Stratton |
| 08651 a | **DG** | E | WNYX | BS | |
| 08653 | **E** | E | WRWM | BS | |
| 08662 | **E** | E | WSGW | MG | |
| 08663 a | **GL** | FG | HJSL | PM | |
| 08664 | **E** | E | WSLS | OC | DON GATES 1952-2000 |
| 08665 | **E** | E | WNYX | HM | |
| 08669 a | **WA** | WA | RFSH | ZB | |
| 08670 a | **E** | E | WNYX | ML | |
| 08676 | **E** | E | WSWR | OC | |
| 08678 a | **0** | WC | MBDL | CS | ARTILA |
| 08682 | **0** | BT | KDSD | ZF | Lionheart |
| 08683 | **E** | E | WNXX | TO | |
| 08685 | **E** | E | WSNE | TE | |
| 08689 a | **E** | E | WSWR | OC | |
| 08690 | **MA** | MA | HISE | DY | |
| 08691 | **FL** | WA | DFLS | FD | Terri |
| 08694 a | **E** | E | WNXX | OC | |
| 08695 a | **E** | E | WNYX | AY | |
| 08696 a | **G** | VW | ATXX | MA | LONGSIGHT TMD |
| 08697 | **B** | MA | HISE | DY (S) | |
| 08698 a | **E** | E | WNTS | ML | |
| 08699 | **0** | CD | CREL | TM | |
| 08701 a | **RX** | E | WSXX | TY | |
| 08703 a | **E** | E | WSEM | TO | |
| 08706 | **E** | E | WSWM | BS | |
| 08709 | **E** | E | WSWM | BS | MOLLY'S DAY |
| 08711 k | **RX** | E | WSEM | TO | |
| 08714 | **E** | E | WSGW | MG | Cambridge |
| 08715 v | **0** | E | WNXX | CU | |
| 08720 a | **E** | E | WNYX | ML | |
| 08721 | **0** | VW | ATLO | MA | STARLET |

| | | | | | |
|---|---|---|---|---|---|
| 08724 | **WA** | WA | HBSH | NL | |
| 08730 | **O** | AM | ARZH | ZH | The Caley |
| 08735 | **E** | E | WSEM | TO | |
| 08737 a | **E** | E | WSWM | BS | |
| 08738 | **E** | E | WNXX | CU | |
| 08742 | **RX** | E | WNXX | BS | |
| 08743 | **EN** | EN | MBDL | WI | Bryan Turner |
| 08745 | **FE** | P | DHLT | SZ | |
| 08750 a | **RT** | RT | MOLO | QU | |
| 08752 † | **E** | E | WNXX | DR | |
| 08754 | **FL** | RT | MOLO | TV | |
| 08756 | **DG** | RT | MOLO | ZB (S) | |
| 08757 | **RG** | E | WSWR | OC | |
| 08762 | **RT** | RT | MOLO | NW | |
| 08765 | **E** | E | WSLS | OC | |
| 08770 a | **DG** | E | WNTR | MG | |
| 08775 | **E** | E | WSWM | BS | |
| 08776 a | **DG** | E | WNTR | KE | |
| 08782 a | **CU** | E | WRWM | BS | CASTLETON WORKS |
| 08783 | **E** | E | WRWM | BS | |
| 08784 | **E** | E | WSEM | TO | |
| 08785 a | **FL** | P | DFLS | FD | |
| 08786 a | **DG** | E | WSLN | TD | |
| 08788 | **RT** | RT | MOLO | IS | |
| 08790 | **B** | VW | ATLO | MA | M.A. Smith |
| 08792 | **F** | E | WNXX | BS | |
| 08795 | **GL** | FG | HJSE | LE | |
| 08798 | **E** | E | WSSC | ML | |
| 08799 a | **E** | E | WSNE | TE | ANDY BOWER |
| 08802 | **RX** | E | WNTS | AN | |
| 08804 | **E** | E | WSWR | OC | |
| 08805 | **B** | MA | HGSS | SI | |
| 08807 | **BR** | E | WZTS | ML | |
| 08809 | **AR** | CD | CREL | LB | |
| 08810 a | **AR** | LW | MBDL | CP | |
| 08813 a | **DG** | HN | HNRS | TE | |
| 08818 | **HN** | HN | HNRL | LM | Molly |
| 08819 | **DG** | RT | MOLO | DW (S) | |
| 08822 | **GL** | FG | HJSE | PM | |
| 08823 a | **B** | BT | KDSD | ZF | |
| 08824 ak | **K** | E | WSXX | CE | |
| 08825 a | **B** | HN | HNRL | LM | |
| 08827 a | **B** | HN | HNRS | BH | |
| 08828 a | **E** | E | WNYX | BS | |
| 08830 | **LW** | AW | HLSV | LD | |
| 08834 | **O** | WA | HBSH | ZB | |
| 08836 | **GL** | FG | HJXX | PM | |
| 08842 | **E** | E | WNTS | TD | |
| 08844 | **E** | E | WRWM | BS | CHRIS WREN 1955–2002 |
| 08847 | **CD** | CD | CREL | NC | |
| 08853 a | **B** | WA | RFSH | BN | |

| | | | | | |
|---|---|---|---|---|---|
| 08854 † | E | E | WNXX | TD | |
| 08856 | B | E | WNXX | DC | |
| 08865 | E | E | WSWR | OC | |
| 08866 | E | E | WSSC | ML | |
| 08868 | B | HN | HNRL | CP | |
| 08869 | G | HN | HNRS | BH | |
| 08870 | RL | RL | MBDL | KE | |
| 08871 | CD | CD | CREL | NC | |
| 08872 | E | E | WZTS | TD | TONY LONG STRATFORD DEPOT 1971–2002 |
| 08873 | RX | HU | | TP | |
| 08874 | SL | RT | MOLO | BY | Catherine |
| 08877 | DG | E | WSXX | SP | |
| 08879 | E | E | WSLS | OC | |
| 08881 | DG | E | WZTS | ML | |
| 08883 | O | E | WNYX | ML | |
| 08884 | B | E | WZTS | BS | |
| 08885 | GB | RT | MOLO | MY | |
| 08886 § | E | E | WNTS | ML | |
| 08887 a | VP | VW | ATLO | LL | |
| 08888 | E | E | WSNE | TE | |
| 08890 | DG | E | WNYX | EH | |
| 08891 | FL | P | DFLS | FD | |
| 08892 | GN | WA | RFSH | DW (S) | |
| 08894 | B | E | WNYX | AN | |
| 08896 | E | E | WNXX | TO | |
| 08897 | E | E | WSWM | BS | |
| 08899 | MM | MA | HISE | DY | |
| 08900 | DG | E | WNTS | MG | |
| 08902 | B | E | WNYX | AN | |
| 08903 | EN | EN | MBDL | WI | John W Antill |
| 08904 | E | E | WSLN | TD | |
| 08905 | E | E | WNTS | BS | |
| 08907 | E | E | WRWM | BS | |
| 08908 | MM | MA | HISL | NL | |
| 08909 | E | E | WREM | TO | |
| 08910 | B | E | WNYX | TO | |
| 08911 | DG | NM | MBDL | YK | |
| 08912 | B | E | WNYX | TO | |
| 08913 | E | E | WNXX | ML | |
| 08915 | F | E | WNXX | TO | |
| 08918 | DG | E | WNTS | OC | |
| 08919 | RX | E | WNYX | OC | |
| 08920 | F | E | WNXX | BS | |
| 08921 † | E | E | WNTR | TD | |
| 08922 | DG | E | WRSC | ML | |
| 08924 | E | E | WSSC | ML | |
| 08925 | B | E | WNXX | DR | |
| 08926 | B | E | WNYX | AN | |
| 08927 | B | E | WNTS | ML | |
| 08928 | O | HN | HNRS | BH | |
| 08933 | E | E | WNTR | ML | |

| 08934 a | **VP** | VW | ATXX | WB |      |
|---------|--------|----|------|----|------|
| 08936   | **HN** | HN | CREL | AS |      |
| 08939   | **E**  | E  | WRWR | OC |      |
| 08941   | **E**  | E  | WSAW | MG |      |
| 08942   | **B**  | E  | WNYX | TO |      |
| 08946   | **FE** | E  | WNYX | AN |      |
| 08947   | **B**  | E  | WNXX | WY |      |
| 08948 c | **EP** | EU | GPSS | NP |      |
| 08950   | **MA** | MA | HISL | NL |      |
| 08951 † | **E**  | E  | WNTS | AN | FRED |
| 08953 a | **DG** | E  | WNXX | DR |      |
| 08954   | **F**  | E  | WNXX | AN |      |
| 08955   | **F**  | E  | WNXX | BS |      |
| 08956   | **SB** | SO | CDJD | ZA |      |

**Class 08/9. Reduced height cab.** Converted 1985–1987 by BR at Landore T&RSMD.

| 08993   | **E** | E | WNTR | BZ | ASHBURNHAM |
|---------|-------|---|------|----|-----------|
| 08994 a | **E** | E | WSEM | TO |           |
| 08995 a | **E** | E | WNTR | MG |           |

# CLASS 09        BR/ENGLISH ELECTRIC        0-6-0

**Built:** 1959–1962 by BR at Darlington or Horwich Works.
**Engine:** English Electric 6KT of 298 kW (400 h.p.) at 680 r.p.m.
**Main Generator:** English Electric 801.
**Traction Motors:** English Electric 506.
**Maximum Tractive Effort:** 111 kN (25000 lbf).
**Continuous Tractive Effort:** 39 kN (8800 lbf) at 11.6 m.p.h.
**Power At Rail:** 201 kW (269 h.p.).    **Train Brakes:** Air & vacuum.
**Brake Force:** 19 t.                   **Dimensions:** 8.92 x 2.59 m.
**Weight:** 50 t.                        **Wheel Diameter:** 1372 mm.
**Design Speed:** 27 m.p.h.              **Maximum Speed:** 27 m.p.h.
**Fuel Capacity:** 3037 litres.          **RA:** 5.
**Train Supply:** Not equipped.          **Multiple Working:** Not equipped.

Class 09/0 were originally numbered D3665–D3671, D3719–3721, D4099–D4114.

**Class 09/0. Built as Class 09.**

| 09001   | **E**  | E | WNTS | TO |                      |
|---------|--------|---|------|----|----------------------|
| 09003   | **E**  | E | WSWR | OC |                      |
| 09005 k | **E**  | E | WRLS | OC |                      |
| 09006   | **E**  | E | WSLS | OC |                      |
| 09007   | **ML** | E | WNTS | DR |                      |
| 09008   | **E**  | E | WNTR | BS |                      |
| 09009   | **E**  | E | WNXX | SL | Three Bridges C.E.D. |
| 09010   | **DG** | E | WNTR | HG |                      |
| 09011   | **DG** | E | WNTS | MG |                      |
| 09012   | **DG** | E | WNXX | HG |                      |
| 09013   | **DG** | E | WSGW | MG |                      |
| 09014   | **DG** | E | WSNE | TE |                      |
| 09015   | **E**  | E | WSGW | MG |                      |

| 09016 |   | **E**  | E  | WNXX | BZ |              |
|-------|---|--------|----|------|----|--------------|
| 09017 |   | **E**  | E  | WRGW | MG |              |
| 09018 |   | **E**  | E  | WNXX | HG |              |
| 09019 |   | **ML** | E  | WSWR | OC |              |
| 09020 |   | **E**  | E  | WSGW | MG |              |
| 09021 |   | **E**  | E  | WNXX | DR |              |
| 09022 | a | **E**  | E  | WSWM | BS |              |
| 09023 | a | **E**  | E  | WSEM | TO |              |
| 09024 |   | **ML** | E  | WSLS | OC |              |
| 09026 |   | **G**  | SN | HWSU | BI | Cedric Wares |

**Class 09/1. Converted from Class 08/0. 110 V electrical equipment.**
**Converted:** 1992–1993 by RFS Industries, Kilnhurst.

| 09101 | (08833) | **DG** | E | WSGW | MG |
|-------|---------|--------|---|------|----|
| 09102 | (08832) | **DG** | E | WNTS | MG |
| 09103 | (08766) | **DG** | E | WSSC | ML |
| 09104 | (08749) | **DG** | E | WNXX | AN |
| 09105 | (08835) | **DG** | E | WSGW | MG |
| 09106 | (08759) | **DG** | E | WSEM | TO |
| 09107 | (08845) | **DG** | E | WRSC | ML |

**Class 09/2. Converted from Class 08. 90 V electrical equipment.**
**Converted:** 1992 by RFS Industries, Kilnhurst.

| 09201 | (08421) | ak | **DG** | E | WSNE | TE |
|-------|---------|----|--------|---|------|----|
| 09202 | (08732) |    | **DG** | E | WNYX | DR |
| 09203 | (08781) |    | **DG** | E | WNYX | CE |
| 09204 | (08717) |    | **DG** | E | WNXX | TY |
| 09205 | (08620) |    | **DG** | E | WSNE | TE |

# CLASS 20           ENGLISH ELECTRIC           Bo-Bo

**Built:** 1957–1968 by English Electric Company at Vulcan Foundry, Newton le Willows or by Robert Stephenson & Hawthorn at Darlington.
**Engine:** English Electric 8SVT Mk. II of 746 kW (1000 h.p.) at 850 r.p.m.
**Main Generator:** English Electric 819/3C.
**Traction Motors:** English Electric 526/5D or 526/8D.
**Maximum Tractive Effort:** 187 kN (42000 lbf).
**Continuous Tractive Effort:** 111 kN (25000 lbf) at 11 m.p.h.
**Power At Rail:** 574 kW (770 h.p.).
**Brake Force:** 35 t.
**Weight:** 73.4–73.5 t.
**Design Speed:** 75 m.p.h.
**Fuel Capacity:** 1727 litres.
**Train Supply:** Not equipped.
**Train Brakes:** Air & vacuum.
**Dimensions:** 14.25 x 2.67 m.
**Wheel Diameter:** 1092 mm.
**Maximum Speed:** 75 m.p.h.
**RA:** 5.
**Multiple Working:** Blue Star.

**Non-standard liveries/numbering:**

20088 RFS grey.
20092 BR Central Services red & grey.
20132 Carries number D8132.
20138 and 20215 As **F0** but with a red solebar stripe.
20906 Carries no number.

Originally numbered in series D8007–D8190, D8315–D8325.

**Class 20/0. Standard Design.**

| | | | | | |
|---|---|---|---|---|---|
| 20016 | **B** | HN | HNRS | LT | |
| 20032 | **B** | HN | HNRS | LT | |
| 20056 | **G** | HN | HNRL | BH | |
| 20057 | **B** | HN | HNRS | LT | |
| 20066 | **B** | HN | HNRS | BH | |
| 20072 | **B** | HN | HNRS | LT | |
| 20073 | **B** | HN | HNRS | BH | |
| 20081 | **B** | HN | HNRS | LT | |
| 20088 | **O** | HN | HNRS | LT | |
| 20092 | **O** | HN | HNRS | LT | |
| 20096 | **F** | HN | HNRL | BH | |
| 20121 | **B** | HN | HNRS | BH | |
| 20132 | **G** | HN | HNRS | BH | |
| 20138 | **O** | HN | HNRS | LT | |
| 20168 | **LA** | HN | HNRL | EA | SIR GEORGE EARLE |
| 20215 | **O** | HN | HNRS | LT | |

**Class 20/3. Direct Rail Services refurbished locos.** Details as Class 20/0 except:

**Refurbished:** 1995–1996 by Brush Traction at Loughborough (20301–20305) or 1997–1998 by RFS(E) at Doncaster (20306–20315). Disc indicators or headcode panels removed.

| | |
|---|---|
| **Train Brakes:** Air. | **Maximum Speed:** 75 m.p.h. |
| **Brake Force:** 31 t. | **Fuel Capacity:** 2900 (+ 4909) litres. |

**Multiple Working:** DRS system.

| | | | | | | |
|---|---|---|---|---|---|---|
| 20301 | (20047) | + | **DR** | DR XHNR | KM | Max Joule 1958–1999 |
| 20302 | (20084) | | **DR** | DR XHMW | LB | |
| 20303 | (20127) | + | **DR** | DR XHMW | LB | |
| 20304 | (20120) | | **DR** | DR XHMW | LB | |
| 20305 | (20095) | | **DR** | DR XHNR | KM | |
| 20306 | (20131) | + | **DR** | DR XHNC | KM | |
| 20307 | (20128) | + | **DR** | DR XHNR | KM | |
| 20308 | (20187) | + | **DR** | DR XHNR | KM | |
| 20309 | (20075) | + | **DR** | DR XHNC | KM | |
| 20310 | (20190) | + | **DR** | DR XHNC | KM | |
| 20311 | (20102) | + | **DR** | DR XHNR | KM | |
| 20312 | (20042) | + | **DR** | DR XHNR | KM | |
| 20313 | (20194) | + | **DR** | DR XHNR | KM | |
| 20314 | (20117) | + | **DR** | DR XHNR | KM | |
| 20315 | (20104) | + | **DR** | DR XHNR | KM | |

**Class 20/9. Harry Needle Railroad Company (former Hunslet-Barclay/DRS) locos.**
Details as Class 20/0 except:

| | |
|---|---|
| **Refurbished:** 1989 by Hunslet-Barclay at Kilmarnock. | |
| **Train Brakes:** Air. | **Fuel Capacity:** 1727 (+ 4727) litres. |

| | | | | | |
|---|---|---|---|---|---|
| 20901 | (20101) | | **DR** | HN HNRS | BQ |
| 20902 | (20060) | + | **DR** | HN HNRS | BH |

| 20903 | (20083) | + | **DR** | HN | HNRS | KM |
|-------|---------|---|--------|----|------|----|
| 20904 | (20041) |   | **DR** | HN | HNRS | BQ |
| 20905 | (20225) | + | **F**  | HN | HNRL | BH |
| 20906 | (20219) |   | **DR** | HN | HNRS | CP |

# CLASS 31 BRUSH/ENGLISH ELECTRIC A1A-A1A

**Built:** 1958–1962 by Brush Traction at Loughborough.
**Engine:** English Electric 12SVT of 1100 kW (1470 h.p.) at 850 r.p.m.
**Main Generator:** Brush TG160-48.       **Traction Motors:** Brush TM73-68.
**Maximum Tractive Effort:** 160 kN (35900 lbf).
**Continuous Tractive Effort:** 83 kN (18700 lbf) at 23.5 m.p.h.
**Power At Rail:** 872 kW (1170 h.p.).     **Train Brakes:** Air & vacuum.
**Brake Force:** 49 t.                     **Dimensions:** 17.30 x 2.67 m.
**Weight:** 106.7–111 t.                   **Wheel Diameter:** 1092/1003 mm.
**Design Speed:** 90 m.p.h.                **Maximum Speed:** 90 m.p.h.
**Fuel Capacity:** 2409 (+ 4820) litres.   **RA:** 5 or 6.
**Train Supply:** Not equipped.            **Multiple Working:** Blue Star.

Originally numbered D5520–D5699, D5800–D5862 (not in order).

**Non-standard livery/numbering:**

31110 Also carries number D5528.
31301 As **F0** but with a red solebar stripe.

**Class 31/1. Standard Design.** RA: 5.

| 31102   | **CE** | NR | QETS | TH |               |
|---------|--------|----|------|----|---------------|
| 31105   | **Y**  | NR | QADD | DF |               |
| 31106   | **FR** | HJ | SDPP | DF | SPALDING TOWN |
| 31107   | **CE** | NR | QETS | DF |               |
| 31110 a | **G**  | E  | WMOC | BH | TRACTION magazine |
| 31128   | **FR** | FM | SDPP | DF | CHARYBDIS     |
| 31154   | **CE** | FM | SDXL | DF |               |
| 31190   | **WS** | FM | SDFR | DF | GRYPHON       |
| 31200   | **F**  | NR | QETS | TH |               |
| 31206   | **CE** | CD | CROL | LB |               |
| 31233 a | **Y**  | NR | QADD | DF |               |
| 31285   | **Y**  | NR | QADD | DF |               |
| 31301   | **0**  | FM | SDXL | MQ |               |
| 31306   | **CE** | HN | HNRS | OC |               |
| 31308   | **CE** | HN | HNRS | OC |               |
| 31319   | **F**  | NR | QETS | TH |               |

**Class 31/4. Electric Train Supply equipment.** RA: 6.
**Class 31/5. Train Heating Equipment isolated.** RA: 6.

| 31407 | **ML** | FM | SDXL | BH |
|-------|--------|----|------|----|
| 31412 | **CE** | FM | SDXL | BH |
| 31415 | **B**  | FM | SDXL | MQ |
| 31420 | **IM** | E  | WNXX | OC |
| 31422 | **IM** | FM | SDXL | TM |
| 31423 | **IM** | FM | SDXL | MQ |

| | | | | | |
|---|---|---|---|---|---|
| 31426 | **CE** | FM | SDXL | MQ | |
| 31427 | **B** | E | WNXX | OC | |
| 31433 | **CE** | FM | SDXL | BH | |
| 31437 | **CE** | FM | SDXL | MQ | |
| 31439 | **RR** | FM | SDXL | MQ | |
| 31452 | **FR** | FM | SDPP | DF | MINOTAUR |
| 31454 | **IC** | FM | SDPP | DF | THE HEART OF WESSEX |
| 31459 | **FR** | FM | SDPP | DF | CERBERUS |
| 31460 | **B** | FM | SDXL | BH | |
| 31461 + | **DG** | FM | SDXL | DF | |
| 31462 | **DG** | FM | SDXL | TM | |
| 31465 | **RR** | HN | HNRS | OC | |
| 31466 a | **E** | E | WNXX | OC | |
| 31468 | **FR** | FM | SDPP | DF | HYDRA |
| 31524 | **CE** | FM | SDXL | BH | |

**Class 31/6. ETS through wiring and controls.** RA: 5.

| | | | | | | |
|---|---|---|---|---|---|---|
| 31601 | (31186) | **WX** | FM | SDPP | DF | THE MAYOR OF CASTERBRIDGE |
| 31602 | (31191) | **FR** | FM | SDPP | DF | CHIMAERA |

# CLASS 33      BRCW/SULZER      Bo-Bo

**Built:** 1960–1962 by the Birmingham Railway Carriage & Wagon Company at Smethwick.
**Engine:** Sulzer 8LDA28 of 1160 kW (1550 h.p.) at 750 r.p.m.
**Main Generator:** Crompton Parkinson CG391B1.
**Traction Motors:** Crompton Parkinson C171C2.
**Maximum Tractive Effort:** 200 kN (45000 lbf).
**Continuous Tractive Effort:** 116 kN (26000 lbf) at 17.5 m.p.h.
**Power At Rail:** 906 kW (1215 h.p.).    **Train Brakes:** Air & vacuum.
**Brake Force:** 35 t.               **Dimensions:** 15.47 x 2.82 (2.64 m. 33/2).
**Weight:** 77.7 t.                **Wheel Diameter:** 1092 mm.
**Design Speed:** 85 m.p.h.        **Maximum Speed:** 85 m.p.h.
**Fuel Capacity:** 3410 litres.      **RA:** 6.
**Train Supply:** Electric, index 48 (750 V DC only).
**Multiple Working:** Blue Star.

Originally numbered in series D6500–D6597 but not in order.

**Non-standard liveries/numbering:**

33046 All over mid-blue. Carries no number.
33109 Carries number D6525.
33208 Carries number D6593.

**Class 33/0. Standard Design.**

| | | | | | |
|---|---|---|---|---|---|
| 33021 | **FR** | FM | SDFR | DF (S) | Eastleigh |
| 33025 | **DR** | WC | MBDL | CS | |
| 33029 | **DR** | WC | MBDL | CS | |
| 33030 | **DR** | WC | MBDL | CS | |
| 33046 | **O** | FM | SDXL | DF | |
| 33053 | **F** | X | MBDL | BH (S) | |

**Class 33/1. Fitted with Buckeye Couplings & SR Multiple Working Equipment for use with SR EMUs, TC stock & Class 73.** Also fitted with flashing light adaptor for use on Weymouth Quay line.

| | | | | | |
|---|---|---|---|---|---|
| 33103 b | **FR** | CM | SDFR | DF | SWORDFISH |
| 33109 b | **B** | MH | MBDL | CP (S) | |

**Class 33/2. Built to former Loading Gauge of Tonbridge–Battle Line.** All equipped with slow speed control.

| | | | | | |
|---|---|---|---|---|---|
| 33202 | **FR** | FM | SDFR | DF | METEOR |
| 33207 | **WS** | WC | MBDL | CS | Jim Martin |
| 33208 | **G** | MH | MBDL | RL | |

# CLASS 37      ENGLISH ELECTRIC      Co-Co

**Built:** 1960–1965 by English Electric Company at Vulcan Foundry, Newton le Willows or by Robert Stephenson & Hawthorn at Darlington.
**Engine:** English Electric 12CSVT of 1300 kW (1750 h.p.) at 850 r.p.m.
**Main Generator:** English Electric 822/10G.
**Traction Motors:** English Electric 538/A.
**Maximum Tractive Effort:** 245 kN (55500 lbf).
**Continuous Tractive Effort:** 156 kN (35000 lbf) at 13.6 m.p.h.
**Power At Rail:** 932 kW (1250 h.p.).      **Train Brakes:** Air & vacuum.
**Brake Force:** 50 t.                        **Dimensions:** 18.75 x 2.74 m.
**Weight:** 102.8–108.4 t.                    **Wheel Diameter:** 1092 mm.
**Design Speed:** 90 m.p.h.                   **Maximum Speed:** 80 m.p.h.
**Fuel Capacity:** 4046 (+ 7678) litres.      **RA:** 5 (§ 6).
**Train Supply:** Not equipped.
**Multiple Working:** Blue Star. († DRS System).

Originally numbered D6600–D6608, D6700–D6999 (not in order).

**Non-standard liveries/numbering:**

37137 Has been used for paint trials.
37351 Carries number 37002 on one side only.
37402 Light grey lower bodyside & dark grey upper bodyside.
37403 Also carries number D6607.
37411 Also carries number D6990.

**Class 37/0. Standard Design.** Details as above.

| | | | | | |
|---|---|---|---|---|---|
| 37010 a | **CE** | HN | HNRS | LM | |
| 37023 | **ML** | DR | XHSS | LB | |
| 37029 § | **DR** | DR | XHBS | KM | |
| 37038 † | **DR** | DR | XHMW | LB | |
| 37042 + | **E** | E | WNTR | DR | |
| 37046 a | **CE** | E | WZKF | TY | |
| 37047 + | **ML** | E | WNTA | HG | |
| 37051 | **E** | DR | XHSS | LB | |
| 37055 + | **ML** | E | WNXX | TE | |
| 37057 + | **E** | E | WNTA | CE | Viking |
| 37058 a+† | **CE** | E | WZKF | TY | |

| 37059 a+ | **DR** | DR | XHNC | KM | |
| 37065 + | **ML** | E | WNTR | TO | |
| 37069 a+† | **DR** | DR | XHNR | KM | |
| 37077 a | **ML** | E | WZKF | BK | |
| 37087 a | **DR** | DR | XHMW | ZH | |
| 37108 + | **WS** | TT | TTTC | CS | |
| 37109 | **E** | E | WNTA | HG | |
| 37114 r+ | **E** | E | WNTA | BS | City of Worcester |
| 37116 + | **B** | E | WNYX | EH | |
| 37137 | **0** | E | WNZX | TT | |
| 37146 a | **CE** | E | WNXX | TY | |
| 37152 | **IC** | JB | MBDL | CS (S) | |
| 37158 | **WS** | WC | MBDL | CS (S) | |
| 37165 a+ | **CE** | PO | MBDL | CS (S) | |
| 37170 a | **CE** | HN | HNRS | LM | |
| 37174 a | **E** | E | WNTS | BS | |
| 37175 a | **CE** | E | WMOC | OC | |
| 37178 + | **F** | HN | HNRS | BH | |
| 37188 | **K** | JB | MBDL | CS (S) | |
| 37194 | **DR** | DR | XHBS | KM | |
| 37196 a | **CE** | E | WZKF | TY | |
| 37197 | **WS** | DR | MBDL | CS | Loch Laidon |
| 37203 | **ML** | E | WNTR | BS | |
| 37214 | **B** | JB | MBDL | CS | |
| 37216 + | **ML** | E | WNTR | ML | |
| 37217 + | **B** | E | WNZX | AY | |
| 37218 † | **DR** | DR | XHNR | KM | |
| 37221 a | **F** | E | WZKF | TY | |
| 37222 | **F** | HN | HNRS | CS | |
| 37229 § | **DR** | DR | XHBS | KM | Jonty Jarvis 8-12-1998 to 18-3-2005 |
| 37235 | **F** | WC | MBDL | CS (S) | |
| 37238 a+ | **F** | E | WZKF | TY | |
| 37248 + | **ML** | TT | TTTC | CS | |
| 37250 a+ | **F** | E | WZKF | TY | |
| 37259 † | **DR** | DR | XHNR | KM | |
| 37261 a+ | **DR** | DR | XHBS | KM | |
| 37293 a+ | **ML** | E | WZKF | TY | |
| 37294 a+ | **CE** | E | WNXX | CD | |
| 37308 + | **B** | E | WNTR | TT | |

**Class 37/3. Re-geared (CP7) bogies.** Details as Class 37/0 except:

**Maximum Tractive Effort:** 250 kN (56180 lbf).
**Continuous Tractive Effort:** 184 kN (41250 lbf) at 11.4 m.p.h.
**Design Speed:** 80 m.p.h.

| 37351 + | **CE** | E | WNXX | CD | |
| 37358 + | **F** | E | WNZX | IM | |
| 37372 | **ML** | E | WNTA | ML | |
| 37375 a+ | **ML** | E | WNTS | TO | |
| 37377 + | **U** | E | WZKF | BK | |
| 37379 a | **ML** | E | WNXX | BK | Ipswich WRD Quality Approved |
| 37383 + | **ML** | RV | RTLS | CP | |

**Class 37/4. Refurbished with electric train supply equipment.** Main generator replaced by alternator. Re-geared (CP7) bogies. Details as Class 37/0 except:
**Main Alternator:** Brush BA1005A.        **Power At Rail:** 935 kW (1254 h.p.).
**Maximum Tractive Effort:** 256 kN (57440 lbf).
**Continuous Tractive Effort:** 184 kN (41250 lbf) at 11.4 m.p.h.
**Weight:** 107 t.
**Design Speed:** 80 m.p.h.
**Fuel Capacity:** 7678 litres.
**Train Supply:** Electric, index 38.

| | | | | | |
|---|---|---|---|---|---|
| 37401 | r | **GS** | E | WKBM | ML |
| 37402 | | **O** | E | WNTR | TO | Bont Y Bermo |
| 37403 | a | **G** | E | WNYX | MG |
| 37405 | | **E** | E | WKCK | MG |
| 37406 | r | **E** | E | WKBM | ML | The Saltire Society |
| 37407 | | **F** | E | WNYX | MO |
| 37408 | | **E** | E | WNYX | TO | Loch Rannoch |
| 37409 | | **F** | E | WNXX | ML |
| 37410 | | **E** | E | WNTA | HM |
| 37411 | | **G** | E | WKCK | MG | CAERPHILLY CASTLE/CASTELL CAERFFILI |
| 37412 | | **F** | E | WNXX | MG | Driver John Elliott |
| 37413 | | **E** | E | WNXX | MG |
| 37415 | | **E** | E | WNXX | MG |
| 37416 | r | **GS** | E | WKBM | ML |
| 37417 | ra | **E** | E | WKBM | ML | Richard Trevithick |
| 37418 | r | **E** | E | WNTR | TO |
| 37419 | | **E** | E | WKCK | MG |
| 37420 | | **RR** | E | WNXX | CD |
| 37421 | r | **E** | E | WNTR | ML |
| 37422 | | **E** | E | WNTS | TO | Cardiff Canton |
| 37423 | | **F** | WC | MBDL | CS (S) |
| 37424 | | **F** | E | WNYX | ML |
| 37425 | | **BL** | E | WKCK | MG | Pride of the Valleys/ |
| | | | | | | Balchder y Cymoedd |
| 37426 | | **E** | E | WNXX | CD |
| 37427 | r | **E** | E | WKBM | ML |
| 37428 | | **GS** | E | WNXX | MG |
| 37429 | | **RR** | E | WNXX | TT |
| 37430 | a | **F** | E | WNYX | ML |

**Class 37/5. Refurbished without train supply equipment.** Main generator replaced by alternator. Re-geared (CP7) bogies. Details as Class 37/4 except:
**Maximum Tractive Effort:** 248 kN (55590 lbf).
**Weight:** 106.1–110.0 t.

| | | | | | |
|---|---|---|---|---|---|
| 37503 | r§ | **E** | E | WNTA | DR |
| 37505 | a§ | **F** | E | WZKF | AY | British Steel Workington |
| 37510 | a | **DR** | DR | XHSS | DW |
| 37513 | as§ | **LH** | E | WNXX | OC |
| 37515 | as | **DR** | DR | XHMW | ZH |
| 37516 | s§ | **LH** | E | WNTA | DR |
| 37517 | as§ | **LH** | E | WNTA | HM |

| | | | | | |
|---|---|---|---|---|---|
| 37518 | a§ **F** | E | WZKF | AY | |
| 37519 | **F** | E | WZKF | EH | |
| 37520 | r§ **E** | E | WNXX | CD | |
| 37521 | r§ **E** | E | WNTA | DR | English China Clays |

**Class 37/6. Originally refurbished for Nightstar services.** Main generator replaced by alternator, re-geared bogies and UIC jumpers. Details as Class 37/5 except:

**Maximum Speed:** 90 m.p.h.     **Train Brake:** Air.
**Train Supply:** Not equipped, but electric through wired.
**Multiple Working:** Blue Star († DRS System).

| | | | | | |
|---|---|---|---|---|---|
| 37601 | **EP** | EU | GPSV | NP | |
| 37602 | † **DR** | DR | XHNR | KM | |
| 37603 | **EP** | EU | GPSV | NP | |
| 37604 | **EP** | EU | GPSV | NP | |
| 37605 | † **DR** | DR | XHNC | KM | |
| 37606 | † **DR** | DR | XHNC | KM | |
| 37607 | † **DR** | DR | XHNC | KM | |
| 37608 | † **DR** | DR | XHNC | KM | |
| 37609 | † **DR** | DR | XHNC | KM | |
| 37610 | † **DR** | DR | XHNC | KM | The MALCOLM Group |
| 37611 | † **DR** | DR | XHNC | KM | |
| 37612 | † **DR** | DR | XHNC | KM | |

**Class 37/5 continued.**

| | | | | | |
|---|---|---|---|---|---|
| 37667 | rs§ **E** | HN | HNRS | BS | |
| 37668 | s§ **E** | E | WNTA | HM | |
| 37669 | r§ **E** | E | WNTS | BS | |
| 37670 | r§ **E** | E | WNTR | TD | St. Blazey T&RS Depot |
| 37671 | a **F** | E | WZKF | TY | |
| 37672 | as **F** | HN | HNRS | TE | |
| 37673 | § **F** | E | WNXX | TE | |
| 37674 | § **F** | E | WNTA | ML | Saint Blaise Church 1445–1995 |
| 37675 | as§ **F** | E | WNTA | MG | Margam TMD |
| 37676 | a§ **F** | E | WNTA | HM | |
| 37677 | a§ **F** | E | WNXX | IM | |
| 37678 | a§ **F** | E | WNXX | BS | |
| 37679 | a§ **F** | E | WZKF | AY | |
| 37680 | a§ **F** | HN | HNRS | TE | |
| 37682 | r§ **E** | E | WNTA | CE | Hartlepool Pipe Mill |
| 37683 | a **F** | E | WNXX | TE | |
| 37684 | ar§ **E** | E | WNTA | MG | Peak National Park |
| 37685 | a§ **IC** | E | WNTA | HM | |
| 37688 | § **E** | DR | XHMW | LB | |
| 37689 | a§ **F** | E | WNTA | HM | |
| 37692 | s§ **F** | E | WNTA | MG | Didcot Depot |
| 37693 | as **F** | E | WZKF | TY | |
| 37694 | § **E** | E | WNTR | TD | |
| 37695 | s§ **E** | E | WNTR | HM | |
| 37696 | as **F** | E | WZKF | BK | |
| 37698 | a§ **LH** | E | WNTA | MG | |

**Class 37/7. Refurbished locos. Main generator replaced by alternator. Re-geared (CP7) bogies. Ballast weights added.** Details as Class 37/5 except:
**Main Alternator:** GEC G564AZ (37796–803) Brush BA1005A (others).
**Maximum Tractive Effort:** 276 kN (62000 lbf).
**Weight:** 120 t.                                    **RA:** 7.

| | | | | | |
|---|---|---|---|---|---|
| 37701 | as | **F** | E | WZKF | OC |
| 37702 | s | **GIF** | E | WZKS | ES |
| 37703 | | **GIF** | E | WZKS | ES |
| 37704 | s | **E** | HN | HNRS | MG |
| 37705 | | **F** | E | WZKF | ML |
| 37706 | | **E** | E | WNTA | HM |
| 37707 | | **E** | E | WNTA | BS |
| 37708 | a | **F** | E | WNXX | HM |
| 37709 | | **F** | E | WNTA | MH |
| 37710 | | **LH** | E | WNTA | HM |
| 37712 | a | **E** | E | WNTA | HM |
| 37713 | | **LH** | HN | HNRS | CD |
| 37714 | a | **GIF** | E | WZKS | ES |
| 37716 | | **GIF** | E | WZKS | ES |
| 37717 | | **E** | E | WNTA | HM |
| 37718 | | **GIF** | E | WZKS | ES |
| 37719 | a | **F** | E | WZKF | OC |
| 37796 | as | **F** | E | WZKF | TY |
| 37798 | | **ML** | E | WNTA | MG |
| 37799 | as | **GIF** | E | WZKS | ES |
| 37800 | a | **GIF** | E | WZKS | ES |
| 37801 | s | **GIF** | E | WZKS | ES |
| 37803 | a | **ML** | E | WNXX | TY |
| 37883 | | **GIF** | E | WZKS | ES |
| 37884 | | **GIF** | E | WZKS | ES |
| 37886 | | **E** | E | WNTA | MH | Sir Dyfed/County of Dyfed |
| 37887 | s | **F** | E | WZKF | IM |
| 37888 | | **GIF** | E | WZKS | ES |
| 37889 | | **F** | HN | HNRS | CD |
| 37890 | a | **F** | E | WNTA | MG |
| 37891 | a | **F** | E | WZKF | TY |
| 37892 | | **F** | E | WZKF | OC | Ripple Lane |
| 37893 | | **E** | E | WNTA | BS |
| 37894 | as | **F** | E | WZKF | TY |
| 37895 | s | **E** | E | WNTA | BS |
| 37896 | s | **F** | E | WNTA | MG |
| 37897 | s | **F** | PO | WNSO | BS |
| 37898 | s | **F** | HN | HNRS | MG |

**Class 37/9. Refurbished loco. New power unit. Main generator replaced by alternator. Ballast weights added.** Details as Class 37/4 except:

**Engine:** Ruston RK270T of 1340 kW (1800 h.p.) at 900 r.p.m.
**Train supply:** Not equipped.
**Main Alternator:** Brush BA1005A.

**Maximum Tractive Effort:** 279 kN (62680 lbf).
**Continuous Tractive Effort:** 184 kN (41250 lbf) at 11.4 m.p.h.
**Weight:** 120 t.                          **RA:** 7.

37906 s **FO**  E   WMOC      KR

---

# CLASS 40          ENGLISH ELECTRIC          1Co-Co1

**Built:** 1958–1962 by the English Electric Co. at Vulcan Foundry, Newton le Willows.
**Engine:** English Electric 16SVT Mk2 of 1490 kW (2000 h.p.) at 850 r.p.m.
**Main Generator:** English Electric 822.
**Traction Motors:** English Electric 526/5D.
**Maximum Tractive Effort:** 231 kN (52000 lbf).
**Continuous Tractive Effort:** 137 kN (30900 lbf) at 18.8 m.p.h.
**Power At Rail:** 1160 kW (1550 h.p.).      **Train Brakes:** Air & vacuum.
**Brake Force:** 51 t.                       **Dimensions:** 21.18 x 2.78 m.
**Weight:** 132 t.                           **Wheel Diameter:** 914/1143 mm.
**Design Speed:** 90 m.p.h.                  **Maximum Speed:** 90 m.p.h.
**Fuel Capacity:** 3250 litres.              **RA:** 6.
**Train Supply:** Steam.                     **Multiple Working:** Not equipped.

40145     **B**   40   MBDL      BQ

---

# CLASS 43          BREL/PAXMAN               Bo-Bo

**Built:** 1976–1982 by BREL at Crewe Works.
**Engine:** Paxman Valenta 12RP200L of 1680 kW (2250 h.p.) at 1500 r.p.m.
(* Paxman 12VP185 of 1680 kW (2250 h.p.) at 1500 r.p.m.).
(§ MTU 16V4000 of 1680kW (2250 h.p.) at 1500 r.p.m.). Experimentally fitted by Angel Trains to two power cars.
**Main Alternator:** Brush BA1001B.
**Traction Motors:** Brush TMH68–46 or GEC G417AZ, frame mounted.
**Maximum Tractive Effort:** 80 kN (17980 lbf).
**Continuous Tractive Effort:** 46 kN (10340 lbf) at 64.5 m.p.h.
**Power At Rail:** 1320 kW (1770 h.p.).      **Train Brakes:** Air.
**Brake Force:** 35 t.                       **Dimensions:** 17.79 x 2.71 m.
**Weight:** 70.25 t.                         **Wheel Diameter:** 1020 mm.
**Design Speed:** 125 m.p.h.                 **Maximum Speed:** 125 m.p.h.
**Fuel Capacity:** 4500 litres.              **RA:** 5.
**Train Supply:** Three-phase electric.
**Multiple Working:** Within class, jumpers at non-driving end only.

**Notes:** † Buffer fitted.

43013, 43014 and 43062 are fitted with measuring apparatus & front-end cameras.

**Non-standard livery:** 43101 All over black with a red cab.

**Advertising livery:** 43087 Hornby red with yellow decals.

| 43002 |   | FG | A | IWRP | PM | TECHNIQUEST |
| 43003 |   | FG | A | IWRP | PM |   |
| 43004 | § | FG | A | IWRP | PM | First for the future/ |
|   |   |   |   |   |   | First ar gyfer y dyfodol |
| 43005 |   | FG | A | IWRP | PM |   |
| 43006 |   | GN | A | IECP | EC | Kingdom of Fife |
| 43007 |   | MN | A | IMLP | NL |   |
| 43008 |   | GN | A | IECP | EC | City of Aberdeen |
| 43009 | § | FG | A | IWRP | PM | First transforming travel |
| 43010 |   | FG | A | IWRP | PM |   |
| 43012 |   | FG | A | IWRP | PM |   |
| 43013 | † | Y | P | QCAR | EC |   |
| 43014 | † | Y | P | QCAR | EC |   |
| 43015 |   | FG | A | IWRP | PM |   |
| 43016 |   | FG | A | IWRP | PM | Peninsula Medical School |
| 43017 |   | FG | A | IWRP | PM |   |
| 43018 |   | FG | A | IWRP | PM | The Red Cross |
| 43020 |   | FG | A | IWRP | LA | John Grooms |
| 43021 |   | FG | A | IWRP | LA |   |
| 43022 |   | FG | A | IWRP | PM |   |
| 43023 |   | FG | A | IWRP | PM | County of Cornwall |
| 43024 |   | FG | A | IWRP | PM |   |
| 43025 |   | FG | A | IWRP | PM | Exeter |
| 43026 |   | FG | A | IWRP | PM | City of Westminster |
| 43027 |   | FG | A | IWRP | PM | Glorious Devon |
| 43028 |   | FG | A | IWRP | PM |   |
| 43029 |   | FG | A | IWRP | PM |   |
| 43030 |   | FG | A | IWRP | PM | Christian Lewis Trust |
| 43031 |   | FG | A | IWRP | PM |   |
| 43032 |   | FG | A | IWRP | PM | The Royal Regiment of Wales |
| 43033 |   | FG | A | IWRP | PM | Driver Brian Cooper |
|   |   |   |   |   |   | 15 June 1947–5 October 1999 |
| 43034 |   | FG | A | IWRP | PM | The Black Horse |
| 43035 |   | FG | A | IWRP | PM |   |
| 43036 |   | FG | A | IWRP | PM |   |
| 43037 |   | FG | A | IWRP | PM | PENYDARREN |
| 43038 |   | GN | A | IECP | EC | City of Dundee |
| 43039 |   | GN | A | IECP | EC | The Royal Dragoon Guards |
| 43040 |   | FG | A | IWRP | PM | Bristol St. Philip's Marsh |
| 43041 |   | FG | A | IWRP | PM | City of Discovery |
| 43042 |   | FG | A | IWRP | PM |   |
| 43043 | * | MN | P | IMLP | NL |   |
| 43044 | * | MN | P | IMLP | NL |   |
| 43045 | * | MN | P | IMLP | NL |   |
| 43046 |   | MM | P | IMLP | NL | Royal Philharmonic |
| 43047 | * | MN | P | IMLP | NL |   |
| 43048 | * | MN | P | IMLP | NL |   |
| 43049 | * | MN | P | IMLP | NL | Neville Hill |
| 43050 | * | MM | P | IMLP | NL |   |
| 43051 |   | MN | P | IMLP | NL |   |
| 43052 | * | MN | P | IMLP | NL |   |

| 43053 |   | MN | P | IMLP | NL |  |
|---|---|---|---|---|---|---|
| 43054 |   | MN | P | IMLP | NL |  |
| 43055 | * | MN | P | IMLP | NL |  |
| 43056 |   | MN | P | IMLP | NL |  |
| 43057 |   | MN | P | IMLP | NL |  |
| 43058 |   | MN | P | IMLP | NL |  |
| 43059 | * | MN | P | IMLP | NL |  |
| 43060 | * | MM | P | IMLP | NL | COUNTY OF LEICESTERSHIRE |
| 43061 | * | MN | P | IMLP | NL |  |
| 43062 |   | Y | P | QCAR | EC |  |
| 43063 |   | FG | P | IWRP | LA |  |
| 43064 |   | MN | P | IMLP | NL |  |
| 43065 | † | V | P | SBXL | LM |  |
| 43066 |   | MN | P | IMLP | NL |  |
| 43067 | † | Y | P | SBXL | LM |  |
| 43068 | † | V | P | SBXL | LE |  |
| 43069 |   | MN | P | SBXL | LM | Rio Enterprise |
| 43070 |   | CD | P | CRRH | MM |  |
| 43071 |   | FG | P | IWRP | LA |  |
| 43072 | * | MN | P | IMLP | NL |  |
| 43073 | * | MM | P | IMLP | NL |  |
| 43074 | * | MN | P | IMLP | NL |  |
| 43075 | * | MM | P | IMLP | NL |  |
| 43076 | * | MN | P | IMLP | NL |  |
| 43077 |   | MM | P | IMLP | NL |  |
| 43078 |   | GN | P | SBXL | EC |  |
| 43079 |   | FG | P | IWRP | LA |  |
| 43080 | † | GN | P | SBXL | LM |  |
| 43081 |   | MN | P | IMLP | NL |  |
| 43082 | * | MN | P | IMLP | NL |  |
| 43083 |   | MM | P | IMLP | NL |  |
| 43084 | † | V | P | SBXL | LM |  |
| 43085 |   | MN | P | IMLP | NL |  |
| 43086 |   | MN | P | SBXL | LM | Rio Talisman |
| 43087 |   | AL | P | CRRH | MM |  |
| 43088 |   | FG | P | IWRP | LA |  |
| 43089 |   | MN | P | SBXL | LB | Rio Thunderer |
| 43090 |   | V | P | SBXL | LM |  |
| 43091 |   | FG | P | IWRP | LA |  |
| 43092 |   | V | FG | FGXP | LE |  |
| 43093 |   | V | FG | FGXP | LB |  |
| 43094 |   | V | FG | FGXP | LE |  |
| 43095 |   | GN | A | IECP | EC | Perth |
| 43096 |   | GN | A | IECP | EC | Stirling Castle |
| 43097 |   | V | FG | FGXP | LB |  |
| 43098 |   | V | FG | FGXP | LB |  |
| 43099 |   | GN | P | IECP | EC |  |
| 43100 |   | V | P | SBXL | LM |  |
| 43101 |   | O | P | SBXL | LB |  |
| 43102 |   | GN | P | IECP | EC |  |
| 43103 |   | V | P | SBXL | LM |  |

| 43104 | **MN** | A  | IMLP | NL |                                |
|-------|--------|----|------|----|--------------------------------|
| 43105 | **GN** | A  | IECP | EC | City of Inverness              |
| 43106 | **GN** | A  | IECP | EC | Fountains Abbey                |
| 43107 | **GN** | A  | IECP | EC | Tayside                        |
| 43108 | **GN** | A  | IECP | EC | Old Course St. Andrews         |
| 43109 | **GN** | A  | IECP | EC | Leeds International Film Festival |
| 43110 | **GN** | A  | IECP | EC | Stirlingshire                  |
| 43111 | **GN** | A  | IECP | EC | Scone Palace                   |
| 43112 | **GN** | A  | IECP | EC | Doncaster                      |
| 43113 | **GN** | A  | IECP | EC | The Highlands                  |
| 43114 | **GN** | A  | IECP | EC | East Riding of Yorkshire       |
| 43115 | **GN** | A  | IECP | EC | Aberdeenshire                  |
| 43116 | **GN** | A  | IECP | EC | The Black Dyke Band            |
| 43117 | **GN** | A  | IECP | EC | Bonnie Prince Charlie          |
| 43118 | **GN** | A  | IECP | EC | City of Kingston upon Hull     |
| 43119 | **GN** | A  | IECP | EC | Harrogate Spa                  |
| 43120 | **GN** | A  | IECP | EC | National Galleries of Scotland |
| 43121 | **V**  | P  | SBXL | LM |                                |
| 43122 | **V**  | FG | FGXP | LA |                                |
| 43123 † | **V** | P  | SBXL | LM |                                |
| 43124 | **FG** | A  | IWRP | LE |                                |
| 43125 | **FG** | A  | IWRP | LE | Merchant Venturer              |
| 43126 | **FG** | A  | IWRP | LE | City of Bristol                |
| 43127 | **FG** | A  | IWRP | LE | Sir Peter Parker 1924–2002     |
|       |        |    |      |    | Cotswold Line 150              |
| 43128 | **FG** | A  | IWRP | LE |                                |
| 43129 | **FG** | A  | IWRP | LE |                                |
| 43130 | **FG** | A  | IWRP | LE | Sulis Minerva                  |
| 43131 | **FG** | A  | IWRP | LE | Sir Felix Pole                 |
| 43132 | **FG** | A  | IWRP | LE |                                |
| 43133 | **FG** | A  | IWRP | LE |                                |
| 43134 | **FG** | A  | IWRP | LE | County of Somerset             |
| 43135 | **FG** | A  | IWRP | LE | QUAKER ENTERPRISE              |
| 43136 | **FG** | A  | IWRP | LE |                                |
| 43137 | **FG** | A  | IWRP | LE | Newton Abbot 150               |
| 43138 | **FG** | A  | IWRP | LE |                                |
| 43139 | **FG** | A  | IWRP | LE | Driver Stan Martin             |
|       |        |    |      |    | 25 June 1960 – 6 November 2004 |
| 43140 | **FG** | A  | IWRP | LE |                                |
| 43141 | **FG** | A  | IWRP | LE |                                |
| 43142 | **FG** | A  | IWRP | LE |                                |
| 43143 | **FG** | A  | IWRP | LE | Stroud 700                     |
| 43144 | **FG** | A  | IWRP | LE |                                |
| 43145 | **FG** | A  | IWRP | LE |                                |
| 43146 | **FG** | A  | IWRP | LE |                                |
| 43147 | **FG** | A  | IWRP | LE |                                |
| 43148 | **FG** | A  | IWRP | LE |                                |
| 43149 | **FG** | A  | IWRP | LE | B.B.C. Wales Today             |
| 43150 | **FG** | A  | IWRP | LE | Bristol Evening Post           |
| 43151 | **FG** | A  | IWRP | LE |                                |
| 43152 | **FG** | A  | IWRP | LE |                                |

| | | | | | |
|---|---|---|---|---|---|
| 43153 | **V** | FG | FGXP | RG | |
| 43154 | **Y** | FG | FGXP | LE | |
| 43155 | **V** | FG | FGXP | RG | |
| 43156 | **FG** | P | IWRP | LA | |
| 43157 | **V** | P | CRRH | MM | |
| 43158 | **V** | FG | FGXP | LE | |
| 43159 | **MN** | P | SBXL | LM | Rio Warrior |
| 43160 | **V** | P | SBXL | LB | |
| 43161 | **FG** | P | IWRP | LA | |
| 43162 | **FG** | P | IWRP | LA | |
| 43163 | **FG** | A | IWRP | LA | |
| 43164 | **FG** | A | IWRP | LA | |
| 43165 * | **FG** | A | IWRP | LA | |
| 43166 | **MN** | A | IMLP | NL | |
| 43167 | **GN** | A | IECP | EC | DELTIC 50 1955–2005 |
| 43168 * | **FG** | A | IWRP | LA | |
| 43169 * | **FG** | A | IWRP | LA | THE NATIONAL TRUST |
| 43170 * | **FG** | A | IWRP | LA | Edward Paxman |
| 43171 | **FG** | A | IWRP | LA | |
| 43172 | **FG** | A | IWRP | LA | |
| 43173 | **FG** | A | IWRP | LA | Bristol–Bordeaux |
| 43174 | **FG** | A | IWRP | LA | |
| 43175 | **FG** | A | IWRP | LA | |
| 43176 | **FG** | A | IWRP | LA | |
| 43177 * | **FG** | A | IWRP | LA | University of Exeter |
| 43178 | **MN** | A | IMLP | NL | |
| 43179 * | **FG** | A | IWRP | LA | Pride of Laira |
| 43180 | **FG** | P | IWRP | LA | |
| 43181 | **FG** | A | IWRP | LA | Devonport Royal Dockyard 1693–1993 |
| 43182 | **FG** | A | IWRP | LA | |
| 43183 | **FG** | A | IWRP | LA | |
| 43184 | **MN** | A | IMLP | NL | |
| 43185 | **FG** | A | IWRP | LA | Great Western |
| 43186 | **FG** | A | IWRP | LA | Sir Francis Drake |
| 43187 | **FG** | A | IWRP | LA | |
| 43188 | **FG** | A | IWRP | LA | City of Plymouth |
| 43189 | **FG** | A | IWRP | LA | RAILWAY HERITAGE TRUST |
| 43190 | **FG** | A | IWRP | LA | |
| 43191 * | **FG** | A | IWRP | LA | Seahawk |
| 43192 | **FG** | A | IWRP | LA | City of Truro |
| 43193 | **MN** | P | CRRH | MM | Rio Triumph |
| 43194 | **V** | FG | FGXP | BR | |
| 43195 | **FG** | P | IWRP | LA | |
| 43196 | **Y** | P | QCAR | EC | |
| 43197 | **GN** | P | IECP | EC | |
| 43198 | **MN** | FG | FGXP | LB | Rio Victorious |

## CLASS 45      BR/SULZER      1Co-Co1

**Built:** 1963 by BR at Derby Locomotive Works.
**Engine:** Sulzer 12LDA28B of 1860 kW (2500 h.p.) at 750 r.p.m.
**Main Generator:** Crompton-Parkinson CG426 A1.
**Traction Motors:** Crompton-Parkinson C172 A1.
**Maximum Tractive Effort:** 245 kN (55000 lbf).
**Continuous Tractive Effort:** 134 kN (31600 lbf) at 22.3 m.p.h.
**Power At Rail:** 1490 kW (2000 h.p.).    **Train Brakes:** Air & vacuum.
**Brake Force:** 63 t.      **Dimensions:** 20.70 x 2.78 m.
**Weight:** 140 t.      **Wheel Diameter:** 914/1143 mm.
**Design Speed:** 90 m.p.h.      **Maximum Speed:** 90 m.p.h.
**Fuel Capacity:** 3591 litres.      **RA:** 7.
**Train Supply:** Electric.      **Multiple Working:** Not equipped.

Originally numbered D61.

| 45112 | **B** | FM | SDMS | DF | THE ROYAL ARMY ORDNANCE CORPS |

## CLASS 46      BR/SULZER      1Co-Co1

**Built:** 1963 by BR at Derby Locomotive Works.
**Engine:** Sulzer 12LDA28B of 1860 kW (2500 h.p.) at 750 r.p.m.
**Main Generator:** Brush TG160-60.    **Traction Motors:** Brush TM73-68 Mk3.
**Maximum Tractive Effort:** 245 kN (55000 lbf).
**Continuous Tractive Effort:** 141 kN (31600 lbf) at 22.3 m.p.h.
**Power At Rail:** 1460 kW (1960 h.p.).    **Train Brakes:** Air & vacuum.
**Brake Force:** 63 t.      **Dimensions:** 20.70 x 2.78 m.
**Weight:** 140 t.      **Wheel Diameter:** 914/1143 mm.
**Design Speed:** 90 m.p.h.      **Maximum Speed:** 75 m.p.h.
**Fuel Capacity:** 3591 litres.      **RA:** 7.
**Train Supply:** Not equipped.      **Multiple Working:** Not equipped.

| 46035 | **B** | WH | MBDL | CQ |

## CLASS 47      BR/BRUSH/SULZER      Co-Co

**Built:** 1963–1967 by Brush Traction, at Loughborough or by BR at Crewe Works.
**Engine:** Sulzer 12LDA28C of 1920 kW (2580 h.p.) at 750 r.p.m.
**Main Generator:** Brush TG160-60 Mk4 or TM172-50 Mk1.
**Traction Motors:** Brush TM64-68 Mk1 or Mk1A.
**Maximum Tractive Effort:** 267 kN (60000 lbf).
**Continuous Tractive Effort:** 133 kN (30000 lbf) at 26 m.p.h.
**Power At Rail:** 1550 kW (2080 h.p.).    **Train Brakes:** Air.
**Brake Force:** 61 t.      **Dimensions:** 19.38 x 2.79 m.
**Weight:** 111.5–120.6 t.      **Wheel Diameter:** 1143 mm.
**Design Speed:** 95 m.p.h.      **Maximum Speed:** 95 m.p.h. (*75 m.p.h.).
**Fuel Capacity:** 3273 (+ 5550).
**Train Supply:** Not equipped.
**Multiple Working:** Green Circle (n – not equipped, † DRS System).

Originally numbered in series D1100–D1111, D1500–D1999 but not in order.

**Non-standard liveries/numbering:**

47004 Also carries number D1524.
47145 Dark blue with Railfreight Distribution logos.
47803 BR experimental Infrastructure livery. Yellow & white with a red stripe.
47812 Also carries number D1916.
47815 Also carries number D1748.
47829 "Police" livery of white with a broad red band outlined in yellow.
47851 Also carries number D1648.
47853 "XP64 blue" with red cabside panels. Also carries number D1733.
47972 BR Central Services red & grey.

**Class 47/0 (Dual-braked locos) or Class 47/2 (Air-braked locos). Standard Design.** Details as above.

| | | | | | |
|---|---|---|---|---|---|
| 47004 | xn | **GG** | E | WMOC | OC |
| 47033 | | **CD** | CD | CRUR | DW |
| 47053 | + | **FE** | FM | SDXL | BH |
| 47145 | | **0** | FM | SDFL | DF | MYRDDIN EMRYS |
| 47150 | *+ | **FL** | FL | DFLH | FD |
| 47186 | + | **FE** | FM | SDXL | KT |
| 47194 | | **F** | WC | MBDL | CS (S) |
| 47197 | n* | **FF** | P | DHLT | BA |
| 47200 | + | **CD** | CD | CRRH | GL | The Fosse Way |
| 47201 | + | **FE** | FM | SDXL | KT |
| 47219 | + | **FE** | FM | SDXL | KT |
| 47224 | xn* | **F** | P | DHLT | CP |
| 47226 | + | **F** | FM | SDXL | KT |
| 47228 | + | **FE** | FM | SDXL | KT |
| 47229 | + | **F** | FM | SDXL | BH |
| 47236 | + | **FE** | FM | SDXL | CS |
| 47237 | +† | **DR** | DR | XHKM | KM |
| 47245 | + | **WS** | WC | MBDL | CS |
| 47270 | *n | **FL** | P | DHLT | BA | Cory Brothers 1842–1992 |
| 47279 | *+ | **FL** | P | DHLT | BA |
| 47280 | + | **F** | FM | SDXL | KT |
| 47289 | *+ | **FF** | P | DHLT | BA |
| 47292 | *+ | **FL** | P | DHLT | BA |
| 47293 | + | **FE** | FM | SDXL | KT |
| 47298 | +† | **DR** | DR | XHKM | KM |

**Class 47/3 (Dual-braked locos) or Class 47/2 (Air-braked locos).**
Details as Class 47/0 except: **Weight: 113.7 t.**

| | | | | | |
|---|---|---|---|---|---|
| 47302 | + | **FF** | FL | DHLT | BA |
| 47303 | *+ | **FF** | P | DHLT | BA | Freightliner Cleveland |
| 47306 | + | **FE** | E | WMOC | BZ | The Sapper |
| 47307 | + | **FE** | FM | SDXL | KT |
| 47309 | *+ | **FF** | FL | DHLT | SZ | European Rail Operator of The Year |
| 47313 | + | **F** | FM | SDXL | KT |
| 47314 | + | **F** | FM | SDXL | KT |
| 47316 | + | **CD** | CD | CRRH | GL | Cam Peak |

| 47326 | + | **FE** | CD | CROL | DW | |
|---|---|---|---|---|---|---|
| 47335 | + | **F** | FM | SDXL | KT | |
| 47338 | + | **FE** | CD | CRUR | DW | |
| 47345 | n | **FF** | P | SBXL | LB | |
| 47348 | + | **FE** | FM | SDXL | MQ | |
| 47355 | | **FB** | FM | SDFL | DF | AVOCET |
| 47358 | *+ | **FF** | P | DHLT | SZ | IVANHOE |
| 47360 | + | **FE** | FM | SDXL | KT | |
| 47363 | | **F** | FM | SDXL | CS | |
| 47365 | + | **FE** | CD | CRUR | CO | |
| 47368 | xn | **F** | FM | SDXL | CS | |
| 47370 | *+ | **FF** | P | DHLT | IP | |
| 47375 | + | **FB** | FM | SDFL | DF (S) | |

**Class 47/4. Electric Train Supply equipment.**
Details as Class 47/0 except:

**Weight:** 120.4–125.1 t.                    **Fuel Capacity:** 3273 (+ 5887) litres.
**Train Supply:** Electric. ETH 66.       **RA:** 7.
**Multiple Working:** Not equipped except † DRS System.

| 47475 | x | **RX** | E | WNZX | HM | |
|---|---|---|---|---|---|---|
| 47484 | x | **GW** | WC | MBDL | ZH | |
| 47488 | x | **GG** | FM | SDFR | BH (S) | |
| 47489 | x | **RG** | FM | SDXL | CS | |
| 47492 | x | **RX** | GD | MBDL | CS (S) | |
| 47501 | x† | **DR** | DR | XHKM | KM | |
| 47525 | x | **FE** | FM | SDXL | CS | |
| 47526 | x | **BL** | FM | SDXL | CS | |
| 47528 | x | **IM** | CD | CRUR | DW | |
| 47550 | x | **IM** | FM | SDXL | IR | |
| 47575 | x | **RG** | RV | RTLS | BQ | |
| 47635 | x | **BL** | E | WNTR | OC | The Lass O' Ballochmyle |

**Class 47/7. Previously fitted with an older form of TDM.**

Details as Class 47/4 except:
**Weight:** 118.7 t.                           **Fuel Capacity:** 5887 litres.
**Maximum Speed:** 100 m.p.h.
**Multiple Working:** Not equipped except m= Green Circle.

| 47701 | x | **FR** | WF | SDFR | LU (S) | Waverley |
|---|---|---|---|---|---|---|
| 47703 | x | **FR** | FM | SDFR | DF | HERMES |
| 47704 | x | **RX** | FM | SDXL | TH | |
| 47707 | x | **RX** | FM | SDXL | BH | |
| 47709 | x | **BP** | FM | SDFR | DF | DIONYSOS |
| 47710 | x | **FR** | FM | SDFR | DF (S) | |
| 47712 | x | **BP** | FM | SDFR | DF | ARTEMIS |
| 47714 | xm | **AR** | CD | CRRH | NC | |
| 47715 | | **FR** | FM | SDXL | YK | POSEIDON |
| 47717 | x | **RG** | FM | SDXL | BH | |

**Class 47/7. Former Railnet dedicated locos.** All have twin fuel tanks and are fitted with RCH jumper cables for operation with Propelling Control Vehicles (PCVs).

| | | | | | |
|---|---|---|---|---|---|
| 47721 | **RX** | E | WNXX | TT | Saint Bede |
| 47722 | **V** | E | WNXX | TT | |
| 47726 | **RX** | E | WNXX | TT | Manchester Airport Progress |
| 47727 | **E** | E | WNTR | WN | Castell Caerffili/Caerphilly Castle |
| 47732 x | **RX** | E | WNTR | HM | |
| 47733 | **RX** | E | WNTR | HM | |
| 47734 | **RX** | E | WNTR | HM | |
| 47736 | **RX** | E | WNXX | CD | Cambridge Traction & Rolling Stock Depot |
| 47737 | **RX** | E | WNSS | HM | |
| 47739 | **RX** | E | WNSS | ML | Resourceful |
| 47741 | **V** | E | WNXX | TT | Resilient |
| 47742 | **RX** | E | WNXX | TT | The Enterprising Scot |
| 47744 | **E** | FM | SDXL | BH | |
| 47746 | **RX** | E | WNTR | CD | |
| 47747 | **E** | E | WNTR | MH | Florence Nightingale |
| 47749 | **RX** | E | WNXX | CE | Atlantic College |
| 47750 | **V** | E | WNXX | HM | |
| 47756 | **RX** | HN | WNSO | OC | |
| 47758 x | **E** | E | WNXX | TT | |
| 47759 | **RX** | E | WNXX | CD | |
| 47760 | **E** | E | WNTR | CE | |
| 47761 | **RX** | E | WNTR | MG | |
| 47767 | **E** | FM | SDXL | AS | |
| 47769 | **V** | RV | RTLS | BH | |
| 47770 | **RX** | E | WNXX | BS | Reserved |
| 47772 x | **RX** | E | WNTR | MG | |
| 47773 | **E** | E | WNXX | HM | |
| 47776 x | **RX** | E | WNXX | HM | |
| 47780 | **RX** | FM | SDXL | BH | |
| 47781 | **RX** | E | WNXX | TT | Isle of Iona |
| 47782 | **RX** | E | WNXX | OC | |
| 47783 | **RX** | E | WNXX | CD | Saint Peter |
| 47784 | **RX** | E | WNXX | CD | Condover Hall |
| 47785 | **E** | E | WNTR | ML | |
| 47786 | **E** | E | WNXX | HM | |
| 47787 | **E** | E | WNXX | HM | |
| 47789 | **RX** | E | WNSS | TT | |
| 47790 | **E** | E | WNTR | HM | |
| 47791 | **RX** | E | WNXX | SY | |
| 47792 | **E** | E | WNTR | HM | |
| 47793 | **E** | E | WNTR | HM | |

**Class 47/4 continued.** RA6.

| | | | | | |
|---|---|---|---|---|---|
| 47798 | **RP** | NM | MBDL | YK | Prince William |
| 47799 | **RP** | E | WNXX | FB | Prince Henry |
| 47802 +† | **DR** | DR | XHKM | KM | |
| 47803 | **0** | FM | SDXL | AS | |
| 47805 + | **V** | RV | RTLO | CP | |

| | | | | | |
|---|---|---|---|---|---|
| 47810 + | **V** | CD | CREL | NC | PORTERBROOK |
| 47811 + | **GL** | P | DFLH | FD | |
| 47812 + | **GG** | RV | RTLO | CP | |
| 47813 +m | **CD** | CD | CRRH | GL | John Peel |
| 47815 + | **GG** | RV | RTLO | CP | GREAT WESTERN |
| 47816 + | **GL** | P | DFLH | FD | |
| 47818 + | **1** | CD | CRRH | GL | |
| 47826 + | **IC** | WC | MBDL | CS | Springburn |
| 47828 +m | **CD** | CD | CRRH | GL | Joe Strummer |
| 47829 + | **0** | RV | RTLO | CP | |
| 47830 + | **GL** | P | DFLH | FD | |
| 47832 + | **FM** | FM | SDFR | DF | DRIVER TOM CLARK O.B.E. |
| 47839 + | **RV** | RV | RTLO | CP | |
| 47840 + | **B** | P | GBZZ | OO | NORTH STAR |
| 47841 + | **V** | P | DFLH | FD | |
| 47843 + | **V** | RV | RTLO | CP | VULCAN |
| 47847 + | **BL** | RV | RTLO | CP | Railway World Magazine/Brian Morrison |
| 47848 + | **V** | RV | RTLO | CP | Newton Abbot Festival of Transport |
| 47851 + | **GG** | WC | MBDL | CS | Traction Magazine |
| 47853 + | **0** | RV | RTLO | CP | RAIL EXPRESS |
| 47854 + | **WS** | WC | MBDL | CS | |
| 47972 | **0** | FM | SDXL | CS | |

# CLASS 50          ENGLISH ELECTRIC          Co-Co

**Built:** 1967–1968 by English Electric at Vulcan Foundry, Newton-le-Willows.
**Engine:** English Electric 16CVST of 2010 kW (2700 h.p.) at 850 r.p.m.
**Main Generator:** English Electric 840/4B.
**Traction Motors:** English Electric 538/5A.
**Maximum Tractive Effort:** 216 kN (48500 lbf).
**Continuous Tractive Effort:** 147 kN (33000 lbf) at 23.5 m.p.h.
**Power At Rail:** 1540 kW (2070 h.p.).          **Train Brakes:** Air & vacuum.
**Brake Force:** 59 t.                              **Dimensions:** 20.88 x 2.78 m.
**Weight:** 116.9 t.                                **Wheel Diameter:** 1092 mm.
**Design Speed:** 105 m.p.h.                        **Maximum Speed:** 90 (* 100) m.p.h.
**Fuel Capacity:** 4796 litres.                     **RA:** 6.
**Train Supply:** Electric, index 66.               **Multiple Working:** Orange Square.

Originally numbered D417–D449, D400.

**Non-standard livery/numbering:**

50017 "LMS Coronation Scot" style maroon with four gold bands.
50044 Also Carries number D444.

| | | | | | |
|---|---|---|---|---|---|
| 50017 * | **0** | JK | MBDL | TM (S) | |
| 50031 | **BL** | 50 | MBDL | KR | Hood |
| 50044 | **GG** | 50 | MBDL | KR | |
| 50049 | **BL** | PD | MBDL | KR | Defiance |
| 50050 | **BL** | HS | MBDL | YJ (S) | Fearless |

## CLASS 52             WESTERN          C-C

**Built:** 1961–1964 Swindon Works.
**Engine:** Two Maybach MD655 of 1007 kW (1350 h.p) at 1500 r.p.m.
**Transmission:** Hydraulic. Voith L630rV.
**Maximum Tractive Effort:** 297 kN (66700 lbf).
**Continuous Tractive Effort:** 201 kN (45200 lbf) at 14.5 m.p.h.
**Power At Rail:** 1490 kW (2000 h.p.).     **Train Brakes:** Air & vacuum.
**Brake Force:** 65 t.                   **Dimensions:** 20.7 m x 2.78 m.
**Weight:** 111 t.                    **Wheel Diameter:** 1092 mm.
**Design Speed:** 90 m.p.h.         **Maximum Speed:** 90 m.p.h.
**Fuel Capacity:** 3900 litres.       **RA:** 7.
**Train Supply:** Steam.           **Multiple Working:** Not equipped.

**Non-standard livery:** Golden ochre.

Never allocated a number in the 1972 number series.

| D1015 | **0** | DT | MBDL | OC | WESTERN CHAMPION |

## CLASS 55      ENGLISH ELECTRIC      Co-Co

**Built:** 1961 by English Electric at Vulcan Foundry, Newton-le-Willows.
**Engine:** Two Napier-Deltic D18-25 of 1230 kW (1650 h.p.) each at 1500 r.p.m.
**Main Generators:** Two English Electric 829.
**Traction Motors:** English Electric 538/A.
**Maximum Tractive Effort:** 222 kN (50000 lbf).
**Continuous Tractive Effort:** 136 kN (30500 lbf) at 32.5 m.p.h.
**Power At Rail:** 1969 kW (2640 h.p.).    **Train Brakes:** Air & vacuum.
**Brake Force:** 51 t.                  **Dimensions:** 21.18 x 2.68 m.
**Weight:** 104.7 t.               **Wheel Diameter:** 1092 mm.
**Design Speed:** 105 m.p.h.       **Maximum Speed:** 100 m.p.h.
**Fuel Capacity:** 3755 litres.      **RA:** 5.
**Train Supply:** Electric, index 66.   **Multiple Working:** Not equipped.

Originally numbered D9009–D9019, D9000.

**Non-standard numbering:**

55009 Carries number D9009.
55016 Carries number 9016.

| 55009 | **GG** | DP | MBDL | BH (S) | ALYCIDON |
| 55016 | **GG** | PO | MBDL | TM (S) | GORDON HIGHLANDER |
| 55019 | **B** | DP | MBDL | BH (S) | ROYAL HIGHLAND FUSILIER |
| 55022 | **B** | MW | MBDL | BH | ROYAL SCOTS GREY |

# CLASS 56      BRUSH/BR/PAXMAN      Co-Co

**Built:** 1976–1984 by Electroputere at Craiova, Romania (as sub contractors for Brush) or BREL at Doncaster or Crewe Works.
**Engine:** Ruston Paxman 16RK3CT of 2460 kW (3250 h.p.) at 900 r.p.m.
**Main Alternator:** Brush BA1101A.
**Traction Motors:** Brush TM73-62.
**Maximum Tractive Effort:** 275 kN (61800 lbf).
**Continuous Tractive Effort:** 240 kN (53950 lbf) at 16.8 m.p.h.
**Power At Rail:** 1790 kW (2400 h.p.).      **Train Brakes:** Air.
**Brake Force:** 60 t.      **Dimensions:** 19.36 x 2.79 m.
**Weight:** 125.2 t.      **Wheel Diameter:** 1143 mm.
**Design Speed:** 80 m.p.h.      **Maximum Speed:** 80 m.p.h.
**Fuel Capacity:** 5228 litres.      **RA:** 7.
**Train Supply:** Not equipped.      **Multiple Working:** Red Diamond.

**Note:** All equipped with Slow Speed Control.

**Non-standard liveries:**

56063 As **F**, but with the light grey replaced by a darker grey.
56027 and 56109 Are **LH** but with the Loadhaul branding on one side only.

| | | | | |
|---|---|---|---|---|
| 56006 | **B** | E | WNSS | BH |
| 56007 | **FER** | E | WZGF | FN |
| 56011 | **E** | FM | SDXL | IM |
| 56018 | **FER** | E | WZGF | FN |
| 56021 | **LH** | FM | SDXL | IM |
| 56022 | **F** | FM | SDXL | IR |
| 56025 | **F** | E | WNXX | IM |
| 56027 | **LH** | E | WNXX | IM |
| 56029 | **F** | J | RCJA | LB |
| 56031 | **FER** | E | WZGF | FN |
| 56032 | **FER** | E | WZGF | FN |
| 56033 | **F** | E | WNXX | HM |
| 56034 | **LH** | J | RCJA | LB |
| 56037 | **E** | E | WZTS | OC |
| 56038 | **FER** | E | WZGF | FN |
| 56041 | **E** | E | WNXX | HM |
| 56043 | **F** | E | WNXX | IM |
| 56044 | **F** | X | WNSO | IM |
| 56045 | **LH** | J | RCJA | LB |
| 56046 | **CE** | E | WNXX | TO |
| 56048 | **CE** | E | WZTS | HM |
| 56049 | **FER** | E | WZGF | FN |
| 56051 | **FER** | E | WZGF | FN |
| 56052 | **F** | E | WNXX | IM |
| 56053 | **F** | E | WNXX | HM |
| 56054 | **F** | E | WNXX | FB |
| 56055 | **LH** | E | WNXX | HM |
| 56056 | **F** | E | WNTR | HM |
| 56058 | **FER** | E | WZGF | FN |

| | | | |
|---|---|---|---|
| 56059 | **FER** | E | WZGF | FN |
| 56060 | **FER** | E | WZGF | FN |
| 56061 | **F** | FM | SDXL | BH |
| 56062 | **E** | E | WNSS | MG |
| 56063 | **0** | X | WNSO | LB |
| 56064 | **F** | E | WNXX | IM |
| 56065 | **FER** | E | WZGF | FN |
| 56067 | **E** | E | WNXX | FB |
| 56068 | **E** | E | WNXX | HM |
| 56069 | **FER** | E | WZGF | FN |
| 56070 | **F** | E | WNTR | HM |
| 56071 | **FER** | E | WZGF | FN |
| 56072 | **F** | E | WNSS | HM |
| 56073 | **F** | E | WNXX | TO |
| 56074 | **FER** | E | WZGF | FN |
| 56076 | **F** | E | WNXX | IM |
| 56077 | **LH** | E | WNXX | CD |
| 56078 | **FER** | E | WZGF | FN |
| 56079 | **F** | E | WNXX | HM |
| 56081 | **FER** | E | WZGF | FN |
| 56082 | **F** | E | WNXX | IM |
| 56083 | **LH** | E | WNXX | FB |
| 56084 | **LH** | E | WNXX | IM |
| 56085 | **LH** | E | WNXX | TE |
| 56086 | **F** | E | WNXX | IM |
| 56087 | **FER** | E | WZGF | FN |
| 56088 | **E** | E | WNSS | TE |
| 56089 | **E** | E | WNXX | IM |
| 56090 | **FER** | E | WZGF | FN |
| 56091 | **FER** | E | WZGF | FN |
| 56093 | **F** | E | WNXX | HM |
| 56094 | **FER** | E | WZGF | FN |
| 56095 | **FER** | E | WZGF | FN |
| 56096 | **FER** | E | WZGF | FN |
| 56099 | **F** | E | WNXX | HM |
| 56100 | **LH** | E | WNXX | MG |
| 56101 | **F** | E | WNXX | IM |
| 56102 | **LH** | E | WNXX | TE |
| 56103 | **FER** | E | WZGF | FN |
| 56104 | **FER** | E | WZGF | FN |
| 56105 | **FER** | E | WZGF | FN |
| 56106 | **FER** | E | WZGF | FN |
| 56107 | **LH** | E | WNTR | FB |
| 56108 | **F** | E | WNXX | TE |
| 56109 | **LH** | E | WNXX | FB |
| 56110 | **LH** | E | WNXX | HM |
| 56111 | **LH** | E | WNXX | TE |
| 56112 | **LH** | E | WNXX | HM |
| 56113 | **FER** | E | WZGF | FN |
| 56114 | **E** | E | WNTR | IM |
| 56115 | **FER** | E | WZGF | FN |

| | | | | |
|---|---|---|---|---|
| 56116 | **LH** | E | WNXX | HM |
| 56117 | **FER** | E | WZGF | FN |
| 56118 | **FER** | E | WZGF | FN |
| 56119 | **E** | E | WNTR | HM |
| 56120 | **E** | E | WNXX | FB |
| 56124 | **F** | J | RCJA | LB |
| 56125 | **F** | FM | SDXL | DF |
| 56127 | **F** | E | WNXX | TE |
| 56128 | **F** | HN | HNRS | TO |
| 56129 | **F** | E | WNXX | TE |
| 56131 | **F** | X | WNSO | LB |
| 56133 | **F** | E | WZTS | OC |
| 56134 | **F** | E | WZTS | HM |

# CLASS 57                    BRUSH/GM                    Co-Co

**Built:** 1964–1965 by Brush Traction at Loughborough or BR at Crewe Works as Class 47. Rebuilt 1997–2004 by Brush Traction at Loughborough.
**Engine:** General Motors 645-12E3 of 1860 kW (2500 h.p.) at 900 r.p.m.
**Main Alternator:** Brush BA1101A.
**Traction Motors:** Brush TM68-46.
**Maximum Tractive Effort:** 244.5 kN (55000 lbf).
**Continuous Tractive Effort:** 140 kN (31500 lbf) at ?? m.p.h.
**Power at Rail:** 1507 kW (2025 h.p.).     **Train Brakes:** Air.
**Brake Force:** 80 t.                      **Dimensions:** 19.38 x 2.79 m.
**Weight:** 120.6 t.                        **Wheel Diameter:** 1143 mm.
**Design Speed:** 75 m.p.h.                 **Maximum Speed:** 75 m.p.h.
**Fuel Capacity:** 5550 litres.             **RA:** 6
**Train Supply:** Not equipped.             **Multiple Working:** Not equipped.

**Class 57/0. No Train Supply Equipment. Rebuilt 1998–2000.**

| | | | | | |
|---|---|---|---|---|---|
| 57001 | (47356) | **FL** | P | DFTZ | FD | Freightliner Pioneer |
| 57002 | (47322) | **FL** | P | DFTZ | FD | Freightliner Phoenix |
| 57003 | (47317) | **FL** | P | DFTZ | FD | Freightliner Evolution |
| 57004 | (47347) | **FL** | P | DFTZ | FD | Freightliner Quality |
| 57005 | (47350) | **FL** | P | DFTZ | FD | Freightliner Excellence |
| 57006 | (47187) | **FL** | P | DFTZ | FD | Freightliner Reliance |
| 57007 | (47332) | **FL** | P | DFTZ | FD | Freightliner Bond |
| 57008 | (47060) | **FL** | P | DFTZ | FD | Freightliner Explorer |
| 57009 | (47079) | **FL** | P | DFTZ | FD | Freightliner Venturer |
| 57010 | (47231) | **FL** | P | DFTZ | FD | Freightliner Crusader |
| 57011 | (47329) | **FL** | P | DFTZ | FD | Freightliner Challenger |
| 57012 | (47204) | **FL** | P | DFTZ | FD | Freightliner Envoy |

**Class 57/3. Electric Train Supply Equipment. Virgin Trains locos. Rebuilt 2002–2004.** Details as Class 57/0 except:

**Engine:** General Motors 645-F3B-12 Cylinder of 2050 kW (2750 h.p.).
**Fuel Capacity:** 5887 litres.        **Train Supply:** Electric, index 100.
**Design Speed:** 95 m.p.h.            **Maximum Speed:** 95 m.p.h.
**Brake Force:** 60 t.                 **Weight:** 117 t.

| | | | | | | | |
|---|---|---|---|---|---|---|---|
| 57301 | (47845) | d | **VT** | P | ATTB | MA | SCOTT TRACY |
| 57302 | (47827) | d | **VT** | P | ATTB | MA | VIRGIL TRACY |
| 57303 | (47705) | d | **VT** | P | ATTB | MA | ALAN TRACY |
| 57304 | (47807) | d | **VT** | P | ATTB | MA | GORDON TRACY |
| 57305 | (47822) | d | **VT** | P | ATTB | MA | JOHN TRACY |
| 57306 | (47814) | d | **VT** | P | ATTB | MA | JEFF TRACY |
| 57307 | (47225) | d | **VT** | P | ATTB | MA | LADY PENELOPE |
| 57308 | (47846) | d | **VT** | P | ATTB | MA | TIN TIN |
| 57309 | (47806) | d | **VT** | P | ATTB | MA | BRAINS |
| 57310 | (47831) | d | **VT** | P | ATTB | MA | KYRANO |
| 57311 | (47817) | d | **VT** | P | ATTB | MA | PARKER |
| 57312 | (47330) | d | **VT** | P | ATTB | MA | THE HOOD |
| 57313 | (47371) | d | **VT** | P | ATTB | MA | TRACY ISLAND |
| 57314 | (47372) | d | **VT** | P | ATTB | MA | FIREFLY |
| 57315 | (47234) | d | **VT** | P | ATTB | MA | THE MOLE |
| 57316 | (47290) | d | **VT** | P | ATTB | MA | FAB 1 |

**Class 57/6. Electric Train Supply Equipment. Prototype ETS loco. Rebuilt 2001.** Details as Class 57/0 except:

**Fuel Capacity:** 5887 litres.      **Train Supply:** Electric, index 100.
**Design Speed:** 95 m.p.h.      **Maximum Speed:** 95 m.p.h.
**Weight:** 113 t.

| | | | | | |
|---|---|---|---|---|---|
| 57601 | (47825) | **WC** | WC MBDL | CS | |

**Class 57/6. Electric Train Supply Equipment. First Great Western locos. Rebuilt 2004.** Details as Class 57/3.

| | | | | | | |
|---|---|---|---|---|---|---|
| 57602 | (47337) | **GL** | P | IWLA | LA | Restormel Castle |
| 57603 | (47349) | **GL** | P | IWLA | LA | Tintagel Castle |
| 57604 | (47209) | **GL** | P | IWLA | LA | Pendennis Castle |
| 57605 | (47206) | **GL** | P | IWLA | LA | Totnes Castle |

---

# CLASS 58      BREL/PAXMAN      Co-Co

**Built:** 1983–1987 by BREL at Doncaster Works.
**Engine:** Ruston Paxman 12RK3ACT of 2460 kW (3300 h.p.) at 1000 r.p.m.
**Main Alternator:** Brush BA1101B.      **Traction Motors:** Brush TM73-62.
**Maximum Tractive Effort:** 275 kN (61800 lbf).
**Continuous Tractive Effort:** 240 kN (53950 lbf) at 17.4 m.p.h.
**Power At Rail:** 1780 kW (2387 h.p.).    **Train Brakes:** Air.
**Brake Force:** 62 t.      **Dimensions:** 19.13 x 2.72 m.
**Weight:** 130 t.      **Wheel Diameter:** 1120 mm.
**Design Speed:** 80 m.p.h.      **Maximum Speed:** 80 m.p.h.
**Fuel Capacity:** 4214 litres.      **RA:** 7.
**Train Supply:** Not equipped.      **Multiple Working:** Red Diamond.

**Notes:** All equipped with Slow Speed Control.

Locos in use in The Netherlands currently carry the following numbers: 58039; 5811, 58044; 5812 and 58038; 5814.

**Non-standard liveries:**

58001 As **FO** but with a red solebar stripe.
58038 Vos Logistics (black with a broad orange stripe).

| | | | | | |
|---|---|---|---|---|---|
| 58001 | **O** | E | WNXX | BH | |
| 58002 | **ML** | E | WNXX | EH | |
| 58003 | **F** | E | WNXX | TO | Markham Colliery |
| 58004 | **FER** | E | WZFF | FN | |
| 58005 | **ML** | E | WZTS | LR | |
| 58006 | **F** | E | WZTS | EH | |
| 58007 | **SCO** | E | WZFF | FN | |
| 58008 | **ML** | E | WNXX | TT | |
| 58009 | **SCO** | E | WZFF | FN | |
| 58010 | **FER** | E | WZFF | FN | |
| 58011 | **FER** | E | WZFF | FN | |
| 58012 | **F** | E | WNXX | TO | |
| 58013 | **ML** | E | WZTS | EH | |
| 58014 | **ML** | E | WNXX | TT | |
| 58015 | **FER** | E | WZFF | FN | |
| 58016 | **FER** | E | WZFF | FN | |
| 58017 | **F** | E | WZTS | EH | |
| 58018 | **FER** | E | WZFF | FN | |
| 58019 | **F** | E | WNXX | TO | Shirebrook Colliery |
| 58020 | **GIF** | E | WZFS | ES | |
| 58021 | **FER** | E | WZFF | FN | |
| 58022 | **F** | E | WNXX | CD | |
| 58023 | **ML** | E | WNXX | TT | |
| 58024 | **GIF** | E | WZFS | ES | |
| 58025 | **GIF** | E | WZFS | ES | |
| 58026 | **F** | E | WZTS | EH | |
| 58027 | **SCO** | E | WZFF | FN | |
| 58028 | **F** | E | WNXX | TT | |
| 58029 | **GIF** | E | WZFS | ES | |
| 58030 | **GIF** | E | WZFS | ES | |
| 58031 | **GIF** | E | WZFS | ES | |
| 58032 | **FER** | E | WZFF | FN | |
| 58033 | **TSO** | E | WZFF | FN | |
| 58034 | **FER** | E | WZFF | FN | |
| 58035 | **FER** | E | WZFF | FN | |
| 58036 | **ML** | E | WZFH | TT | |
| 58037 | **E** | E | WNXX | EH | |
| 58038 | **O** | E | WZFH | TB | |
| 58039 | **ACT** | E | WZFH | TB | |
| 58040 | **SCO** | E | WZFF | FN | |
| 58041 | **GIF** | E | WZFS | ES | |
| 58042 | **ML** | E | WNXX | EH | |
| 58043 | **GIF** | E | WZFS | ES | |
| 58044 | **ACT** | E | WZFH | TB | |
| 58045 | **F** | E | WNXX | OC | |
| 58046 | **FER** | E | WZFF | FN | |
| 58047 | **TSO** | E | WZFF | FN | |

| | | | | | |
|---|---|---|---|---|---|
| 58048 | **E** | E | WNXX | TT | |
| 58049 | **TSO** | E | WZFF | FN | |
| 58050 | **TSO** | E | WZFF | FN | |

---

# CLASS 59      GENERAL MOTORS      Co-Co

**Built:** 1985 (59001/59002/59004) or 1989 (59005) by General Motors, La Grange, Illinois, USA or 1990 (59101–59104), 1994 (59201) and 1995 (59202–59206) by General Motors, London, Ontario, Canada.
**Engine:** General Motors 645E3C two stroke of 2460 kW (3300 h.p.) at 900 r.p.m.
**Main Alternator:** General Motors AR11 MLD-D14A.
**Traction Motors:** General Motors D77B.
**Maximum Tractive Effort:** 506 kN (113 550 lbf).
**Continuous Tractive Effort:** 291 kN (65 300 lbf) at 14.3 m.p.h.

| | |
|---|---|
| **Power At Rail:** 1889 kW (2533 h.p.). | **Train Brakes:** Air. |
| **Brake Force:** 69 t. | **Dimensions:** 21.35 x 2.65 m. |
| **Weight:** 121 t. | **Wheel Diameter:** 1067 mm. |
| **Design Speed:** 60 (* 75) m.p.h. | **Maximum Speed:** 60 (* 75) m.p.h. |
| **Fuel Capacity:** 4546 litres. | **RA:** 7. |
| **Train Supply:** Not equipped. | **Multiple Working:** AAR System. |

**Class 59/0. Owned by Foster-Yeoman.**

| | | | | | |
|---|---|---|---|---|---|
| 59001 | **FY** | FY | XYPO | MD | YEOMAN ENDEAVOUR |
| 59002 | **MR** | FY | XYPO | MD | ALAN J DAY |
| 59004 | **FY** | FY | XYPO | MD | PAUL A HAMMOND |
| 59005 | **FY** | FY | XYPO | MD | KENNETH J PAINTER |

**Class 59/1. Owned by Hanson Quarry Products.**

| | | | | | |
|---|---|---|---|---|---|
| 59101 | **HA** | HA | XYPA | MD | Village of Whatley |
| 59102 | **HA** | HA | XYPA | MD | Village of Chantry |
| 59103 | **HA** | HA | XYPA | MD | Village of Mells |
| 59104 | **HA** | HA | XYPA | MD | Village of Great Elm |

**Class 59/2. Owned by EWS.**

| | | | | | | |
|---|---|---|---|---|---|---|
| 59201 | * | **E** | E | WDAG | TD | Vale of York |
| 59202 | * | **E** | E | WDAG | TD | Vale of White Horse |
| 59203 | * | **E** | E | WDAG | TD | Vale of Pickering |
| 59204 | * | **E** | E | WDAG | TD | Vale of Glamorgan |
| 59205 | b* | **E** | E | WDAG | TD | L. Keith McNair |
| 59206 | b* | **E** | E | WDAG | TD | Pride of Ferrybridge |

# *LocoTrack*

## THE BRITISH LOCOMOTIVE DATABASE

### Version 3 - Completely revised and improved format

- Enter full details of *all* your sightings, photo's and haulage
- View your entries linked to historical and TOPS data
- All diesels + electrics since 1948, all DMU's + current EMU's
- All Mk 1 – Mk 4 coaches, GUV's etc. and ~40,000 wagons
- All numbers carried, names, latest TOPS information, etc.
- Link every record to a photograph on your PC

Simple search, filtering and updating - *all core data can be modified.*

*LocoTrack*, 13 Alderley Edge, Waltham, N.E. Lincs, DN37 0UR
£20 including P+P in UK          Website at www.locotrack.co.uk

## Excellent reviews in railway press

---

*Railway books and videos, on the Internet!*
*Browse our on-line shop at*
# www.transportdiversions.com
*Contents, Descriptions, Pictures and Samples*
*Order on-line with our secure Credit Card payment pages*

CLASS 31
PHOTO FILE

MARTIN LOADER and RICH NORRIS

Ticket to Ride..

The Railways of Austria part 1

Amongst
our 4,000
titles:

and we
also stock
other
transport
titles
too(!):

The Mailvan HANDBOOK

TRANSPORT DIVERSIONS

31, Woodlands, Standlake, Witney,
Oxfordshire OX29 7RA United Kingdom
Tel: +44(0)1865 300123  Fax: +44(0)1865 300122

# CLASS 60 BRUSH/MIRRLEES Co-Co

**Built:** 1989–1993 by Brush Traction at Loughborough.
**Engine:** Mirrlees 8MB275T of 2310 kW (3100 h.p.) at 1000 r.p.m.
**Main Alternator:** Brush BA1000.
**Traction Motors:** Brush TM216.
**Maximum Tractive Effort:** 500 kN (106500 lbf).
**Continuous Tractive Effort:** 336 kN (71570 lbf) at 17.4 m.p.h.
**Power At Rail:** 1800 kW (2415 h.p.). **Train Brakes:** Air.
**Brake Force:** 74 (+ 62) t. **Dimensions:** 21.34 x 2.64 m.
**Weight:** 129 (+ 131) t. **Wheel Diameter:** 1118 mm.
**Design Speed:** 62 m.p.h. **Maximum Speed:** 60 m.p.h.
**Fuel Capacity:** 4546 (+ 5225) litres. **RA:** 7.
**Train Supply:** Not equipped.
**Multiple Working:** Within class.

**Notes:** All equipped with Slow Speed Control.

60034, 60038, 60061, 60064, 60066, 60072, 60073, 60077, 60079, 60082, 60084, 60088 and 60090 carry their names on one side only.

60500 used to carry the number 60016.

| 60001 | | E | E | WCAN | IM | The Railway Observer |
| 60002 | + | E | E | WCBN | IM | High Peak |
| 60003 | + | E | E | WCBN | IM | FREIGHT TRANSPORT ASSOCIATION |
| 60004 | + | E | E | WCBN | IM | |
| 60005 | + | E | E | WNTS | TO | BP Gas Avonmouth |
| 60006 | | CU | E | WNTS | TO | Scunthorpe Ironmaster |
| 60007 | + | LH | E | WNTS | IM | |
| 60008 | | E | E | WCAN | IM | |
| 60009 | + | E | E | WCBN | IM | |
| 60010 | + | E | E | WCBN | IM | |
| 60011 | | ML | E | WCAN | IM | |
| 60012 | + | E | E | WNTS | TE | |
| 60013 | | F | E | WCAN | IM | Robert Boyle |
| 60014 | | F | E | WNTS | TE | Alexander Fleming |
| 60015 | + | EG | E | WCBN | IM | Bow Fell |
| 60017 | + | E | E | WCBN | IM | Shotton Works Centenary Year 1996 |
| 60018 | | E | E | WCAN | IM | |
| 60019 | | E | E | WCAN | IM | PATHFINDER TOURS 30 YEARS OF RAILTOURING 1973–2003 |
| 60020 | + | E | E | WNTS | TO | |
| 60021 | + | E | E | WCBN | IM | Star of the East |
| 60022 | + | E | E | WCBN | IM | |
| 60023 | + | E | E | WNTS | TO | |
| 60024 | | E | E | WCAN | IM | |
| 60025 | + | E | E | WCBN | IM | Caledonian Paper |
| 60026 | + | E | E | WCBN | IM | |
| 60027 | + | E | E | WCBN | IM | |
| 60028 | + | EG | E | WNTS | TO | John Flamsteed |
| 60029 | | E | E | WCAN | IM | Clitheroe Castle |

| | | | | | |
|---|---|---|---|---|---|
| 60030 + | E | E | WCBN | IM | |
| 60031 | E | E | WNTS | IM | ABP Connect |
| 60032 | F | E | WCAN | IM | William Booth |
| 60033 + | CU | E | WCBN | IM | Tees Steel Express |
| 60034 | EG | E | WCAN | IM | Carnedd Llewelyn |
| 60035 | E | E | WCAN | IM | |
| 60036 | E | E | WCAN | IM | GEFCO |
| 60037 + | E | E | WNTS | MG | Aberddawan/Aberthaw |
| 60038 + | E | E | WNTS | TO | AvestaPolarit |
| 60039 | E | E | WCAN | IM | |
| 60040 | E | E | WCAN | IM | |
| 60041 + | E | E | WCBN | IM | |
| 60042 | E | E | WCAN | IM | The Hundred of Hoo |
| 60043 | E | E | WCAN | IM | |
| 60044 | ML | E | WCAN | IM | |
| 60045 | E | E | WCAN | IM | The Permanent Way Institution |
| 60046 + | EG | E | WCBN | IM | William Wilberforce |
| 60047 | E | E | WCAN | IM | |
| 60048 | E | E | WCAN | IM | EASTERN |
| 60049 | E | E | WCAN | IM | |
| 60050 | E | E | WCAN | IM | |
| 60051 + | E | E | WNTS | TE | |
| 60052 + | E | E | WCBN | IM | Glofa Twr – The last deep mine in Wales – Tower Colliery |
| 60053 | E | E | WCAN | IM | NORDIC TERMINAL |
| 60054 + | F | E | WCBN | IM | Charles Babbage |
| 60055 + | F | E | WNTS | TO | Thomas Barnardo |
| 60056 + | F | E | WNTS | TO | William Beveridge |
| 60057 | F | E | WCAN | IM | Adam Smith |
| 60058 + | E | E | WCBN | IM | |
| 60059 + | LH | E | WCBN | IM | Swinden Dalesman |
| 60060 | EG | E | WCAN | IM | James Watt |
| 60061 | F | E | WCAN | IM | Alexander Graham Bell |
| 60062 | E | E | WCAN | IM | |
| 60063 | F | E | WCAN | IM | James Murray |
| 60064 + | EG | E | WNTS | IM | Back Tor |
| 60065 | E | E | WCAN | IM | Spirit of JAGUAR |
| 60066 | EG | E | WCAN | IM | John Logie Baird |
| 60067 | EG | E | WCAN | IM | James Clerk-Maxwell |
| 60068 | F | E | WNTS | TO | Charles Darwin |
| 60069 | E | E | WCAN | IM | Slioch |
| 60070 + | F | E | WNTS | IM | John Loudon McAdam |
| 60071 + | E | E | WCBN | IM | Ribblehead Viaduct |
| 60072 | EG | E | WCAN | IM | Cairn Toul |
| 60073 | F | E | WNTS | TO | Cairn Gorm |
| 60074 | EG | E | WCAN | IM | |
| 60075 | E | E | WCAN | IM | |
| 60076 | F | E | WNTS | TO | |
| 60077 + | F | E | WNTS | IM | Canisp |
| 60078 | ML | E | WCAN | IM | |
| 60079 | EG | E | WCAN | IM | Foinaven |

| 60080 | + | E  | E | WCBN | IM | Bispham Drive Junior School, Toton EWS Rail Safety Competition Winners 2004 |
|-------|---|----|---|------|----|---|
| 60081 | + | GW | E | WNTS | TO | ISAMBARD KINGDOM BRUNEL |
| 60082 |   | EG | E | WCAN | IM | Mam Tor |
| 60083 |   | E  | E | WCAN | IM | Mountsorrel |
| 60084 |   | F  | E | WCAN | IM | Cross Fell |
| 60085 |   | E  | E | WCAN | IM | MINI Pride of Oxford |
| 60086 |   | EG | E | WNTS | TO | Schiehallion |
| 60087 |   | E  | E | WNTS | IM | Barry Needham |
| 60088 |   | F  | E | WNTS | TO | Buachaille Etive Mor |
| 60089 | + | E  | E | WNTS | IM | THE RAILWAY HORSE |
| 60090 | + | EG | E | WCBN | IM | Quinag |
| 60091 | + | EG | E | WCBN | IM | An Teallach |
| 60092 | + | EG | E | WCBN | IM | Reginald Munns |
| 60093 |   | E  | E | WCAN | IM | |
| 60094 |   | E  | E | WNTS | TE | Rugby Flyer |
| 60095 |   | EG | E | WCAN | IM | |
| 60096 | + | E  | E | WCBN | IM | |
| 60097 | + | E  | E | WCBN | IM | ABP Port of Grimsby & Immingham |
| 60098 | + | E  | E | WNTS | IM | Charles Francis Brush |
| 60099 |   | EG | E | WNTS | IM | Ben More Assynt |
| 60100 |   | E  | E | WCAN | IM | Pride of Acton |
| 60500 |   | E  | E | WCAN | IM | RAIL Magazine |

# CLASS 66        GENERAL MOTORS/EMD        Co-Co

**Built:** 1998–2006 by General Motors/EMD, London, Ontario, Canada (Model JT42CWR).
**Engine:** General Motors 12N-710G3B-EC two stroke of 2385 kW (3200 h.p.) at 900 r.p.m.
**Main Alternator:** General Motors AR8/C86.
**Traction Motors:** General Motors D43TR.
**Maximum Tractive Effort:** 409 kN (92000 lbf).
**Continuous Tractive Effort:** 260 kN (58390 lbf) at 15.9 m.p.h.
**Power At Rail:** 1850 kW (2480 h.p.).        **Train Brakes:** Air.
**Brake Force:** 68 t.                         **Dimensions:** 21.35 x 2.64 m.
**Weight:** 126 t.                             **Wheel Diameter:** 1120 mm.
**Design Speed:** 87.5 m.p.h.                  **Maximum Speed:** 75 m.p.h.
**Fuel Capacity:** 6550 litres.                **RA:** 7.
**Train Supply:** Not equipped.                **Multiple Working:** AAR System.

**Note:** All equipped with Slow Speed Control.

**Class 66/0. EWS-operated locomotives.**

| | | | | | |
|---|---|---|---|---|---|
| 66001 | | E | A | WBAN | TO |
| 66002 | | E | A | WBAN | TO | Lafarge Quorn |
| 66003 | k | E | A | WBAN | TO |
| 66004 | k | E | A | WBAN | TO |
| 66005 | k | E | A | WBAN | TO |
| 66006 | k | E | A | WBAN | TO |
| 66007 | k | E | A | WBAN | TO |
| 66008 | k | E | A | WBAN | TO |
| 66009 | k | E | A | WBAN | TO |
| 66010 | k | E | A | WBAN | TO |
| 66011 | k | E | A | WBAN | TO |
| 66012 | k | E | A | WBAN | TO |
| 66013 | k | E | A | WBAN | TO |
| 66014 | k | E | A | WBAN | TO |
| 66015 | k | E | A | WBAN | TO |
| 66016 | k | E | A | WBAN | TO |
| 66017 | k | E | A | WBAN | TO |
| 66018 | k | E | A | WBAN | TO |
| 66019 | k | E | A | WBAN | TO |
| 66020 | k | E | A | WBAN | TO |
| 66021 | k | E | A | WBAN | TO |
| 66022 | k | E | A | WBAN | TO | Lafarge Charnwwod |
| 66023 | k | E | A | WBAN | TO |
| 66024 | k | E | A | WBAN | TO |
| 66025 | k | E | A | WBAN | TO |
| 66026 | k | E | A | WBAN | TO |
| 66027 | k | E | A | WBAN | TO |
| 66028 | k | E | A | WBAN | TO |
| 66029 | k | E | A | WBAN | TO |
| 66030 | k | E | A | WBAN | TO |
| 66031 | k | E | A | WBAN | TO |

| 66032 | k | E | A | WBAN | TO | |
|-------|---|---|---|------|----|-|
| 66033 | k | E | A | WBAN | TO | |
| 66034 | k | E | A | WBAN | TO | |
| 66035 | k | E | A | WBAN | TO | |
| 66036 | k | E | A | WBAN | TO | |
| 66037 | k | E | A | WBAN | TO | |
| 66038 | k | E | A | WBAN | TO | |
| 66039 | k | E | A | WBAN | TO | |
| 66040 | k | E | A | WBAN | TO | |
| 66041 | k | E | A | WBAN | TO | |
| 66042 | k | E | A | WBAN | TO | Lafarge Buddon Wood |
| 66043 | k | E | A | WBAN | TO | |
| 66044 | k | E | A | WBAN | TO | |
| 66045 | k | E | A | WBAN | TO | |
| 66046 | k | E | A | WBAN | TO | |
| 66047 | k | E | A | WBAN | TO | |
| 66048 | k | E | A | WBAN | TO | |
| 66049 | k | E | A | WBAN | TO | |
| 66050 | k | E | A | WBAN | TO | |
| 66051 | k | E | A | WBAN | TO | |
| 66052 | k | E | A | WBAN | TO | |
| 66053 | k | E | A | WBAN | TO | |
| 66054 | k | E | A | WBAN | TO | |
| 66055 | k | E | A | WBLN | TO | |
| 66056 | k | E | A | WBLN | TO | |
| 66057 | k | E | A | WBLN | TO | |
| 66058 | k | E | A | WBLN | TO | |
| 66059 | k | E | A | WBLN | TO | |
| 66060 | k | E | A | WBAN | TO | |
| 66061 | k | E | A | WBAN | TO | |
| 66062 | k | E | A | WBAN | TO | |
| 66063 | k | E | A | WBAN | TO | |
| 66064 | k | E | A | WBAN | TO | |
| 66065 | k | E | A | WBAN | TO | |
| 66066 | k | E | A | WBAN | TO | |
| 66067 | k | E | A | WBAN | TO | |
| 66068 | k | E | A | WBAN | TO | |
| 66069 | k | E | A | WBAN | TO | |
| 66070 | k | E | A | WBAN | TO | |
| 66071 | k | E | A | WBAN | TO | |
| 66072 | k | E | A | WBAN | TO | |
| 66073 | k | E | A | WBAN | TO | |
| 66074 | k | E | A | WBAN | TO | |
| 66075 | k | E | A | WBAN | TO | |
| 66076 | k | E | A | WBAN | TO | |
| 66077 | k | E | A | WBAN | TO | Benjamin Gimbert G.C. |
| 66078 | k | E | A | WBAN | TO | |
| 66079 | k | E | A | WBAN | TO | James Nightall G.C. |
| 66080 | k | E | A | WBAN | TO | |
| 66081 | k | E | A | WBAN | TO | |
| 66082 | k | E | A | WBAN | TO | |

| | | | | | |
|---|---|---|---|---|---|
| 66083 | k | E | A | WBAN | TO |
| 66084 | k | E | A | WBAN | TO |
| 66085 | k | E | A | WBAN | TO |
| 66086 | k | E | A | WBAN | TO |
| 66087 | k | E | A | WBAN | TO |
| 66088 | k | E | A | WBAN | TO |
| 66089 | k | E | A | WBAN | TO |
| 66090 | k | E | A | WBAN | TO |
| 66091 | k | E | A | WBAN | TO |
| 66092 | k | E | A | WBAN | TO |
| 66093 | k | E | A | WBAN | TO |
| 66094 | k | E | A | WBAN | TO |
| 66095 | k | E | A | WBAN | TO |
| 66096 | k | E | A | WBAN | TO |
| 66097 | k | E | A | WBAN | TO |
| 66098 | k | E | A | WBAN | TO |
| 66099 | kr | E | A | WBBM | TO |
| 66100 | kr | E | A | WBBM | TO |
| 66101 | kr | E | A | WBBM | TO |
| 66102 | kr | E | A | WBBM | TO |
| 66103 | kr | E | A | WBBM | TO |
| 66104 | kr | E | A | WBBM | TO |
| 66105 | kr | E | A | WBBM | TO |
| 66106 | kr | E | A | WBBM | TO |
| 66107 | kr | E | A | WBBM | TO |
| 66108 | kr | E | A | WBBM | TO |
| 66109 | k | E | A | WBAN | TO |
| 66110 | kr | E | A | WBBM | TO |
| 66111 | kr | E | A | WBBM | TO |
| 66112 | kr | E | A | WBBM | TO |
| 66113 | kr | E | A | WBBM | TO |
| 66114 | kr | E | A | WBBM | TO |
| 66115 | k | E | A | WBAN | TO |
| 66116 | k | E | A | WBAN | TO |
| 66117 | k | E | A | WBAN | TO |
| 66118 | k | E | A | WBAN | TO |
| 66119 | k | E | A | WBAN | TO |
| 66120 | k | E | A | WBAN | TO |
| 66121 | k | E | A | WBAN | TO |
| 66122 | k | E | A | WBAN | TO |
| 66123 | k | E | A | WBAN | TO |
| 66124 | k | E | A | WBAN | TO |
| 66125 | k | E | A | WBAN | TO |
| 66126 | k | E | A | WBAN | TO |
| 66127 | k | E | A | WBAN | TO |
| 66128 | k | E | A | WBAN | TO |
| 66129 | k | E | A | WBAN | TO |
| 66130 | k | E | A | WBAN | TO |
| 66131 | k | E | A | WBAN | TO |
| 66132 | k | E | A | WBAN | TO |
| 66133 | k | E | A | WBAN | TO |

| | | | | | |
|---|---|---|---|---|---|
| 66134 k | E | A | WBAN | TO | |
| 66135 k | E | A | WBAN | TO | |
| 66136 k | E | A | WBAN | TO | |
| 66137 k | E | A | WBAN | TO | |
| 66138 k | E | A | WBAN | TO | |
| 66139 k | E | A | WBAN | TO | |
| 66140 k | E | A | WBAN | TO | |
| 66141 k | E | A | WBAN | TO | |
| 66142 k | E | A | WBAN | TO | |
| 66143 k | E | A | WBAN | TO | |
| 66144 k | E | A | WBAN | TO | |
| 66145 k | E | A | WBAN | TO | |
| 66146 k | E | A | WBAN | TO | |
| 66147 k | E | A | WBAN | TO | |
| 66148 k | E | A | WBAN | TO | |
| 66149 k | E | A | WBAN | TO | |
| 66150 k | E | A | WBAN | TO | |
| 66151 k | E | A | WBAN | TO | |
| 66152 k | E | A | WBAN | TO | |
| 66153 k | E | A | WBAN | TO | |
| 66154 k | E | A | WBAN | TO | |
| 66155 k | E | A | WBAN | TO | |
| 66156 k | E | A | WBAN | TO | |
| 66157 k | E | A | WBAN | TO | |
| 66158 k | E | A | WBAN | TO | |
| 66159 k | E | A | WBAN | TO | |
| 66160 k | E | A | WBAN | TO | |
| 66161 k | E | A | WBAN | TO | |
| 66162 k | E | A | WBAN | TO | |
| 66163 k | E | A | WBAN | TO | |
| 66164 k | E | A | WBAN | TO | |
| 66165 k | E | A | WBAN | TO | |
| 66166 k | E | A | WBAN | TO | |
| 66167 k | E | A | WBAN | TO | |
| 66168 k | E | A | WBAN | TO | |
| 66169 k | E | A | WBAN | TO | |
| 66170 k | E | A | WBAN | TO | |
| 66171 k | E | A | WBAN | TO | |
| 66172 k | E | A | WBAN | TO | Paul Melleney |
| 66173 k | E | A | WBAN | TO | |
| 66174 k | E | A | WBAN | TO | |
| 66175 k | E | A | WBAN | TO | |
| 66176 k | E | A | WBAN | TO | |
| 66177 k | E | A | WBAN | TO | |
| 66178 k | E | A | WBAN | TO | |
| 66179 k | E | A | WBAN | TO | |
| 66180 k | E | A | WBAN | TO | |
| 66181 k | E | A | WBAN | TO | |
| 66182 k | E | A | WBAN | TO | |
| 66183 k | E | A | WBAN | TO | |
| 66184 k | E | A | WBAN | TO | |

| | | | | | |
|---|---|---|---|---|---|
| 66185 k | E | A | WBAN | TO | |
| 66186 k | E | A | WBAN | TO | |
| 66187 k | E | A | WBAN | TO | |
| 66188 k | E | A | WBAN | TO | |
| 66189 k | E | A | WBAN | TO | |
| 66190 k | E | A | WBAN | TO | |
| 66191 k | E | A | WBAN | TO | |
| 66192 k | E | A | WBAN | TO | |
| 66193 k | E | A | WBAN | TO | |
| 66194 k | E | A | WBAN | TO | |
| 66195 k | E | A | WBAN | TO | |
| 66196 k | E | A | WBAN | TO | |
| 66197 k | E | A | WBAN | TO | |
| 66198 k | E | A | WBAN | TO | |
| 66199 k | E | A | WBAN | TO | |
| 66200 k | E | A | WBAN | TO | RAILWAY HERITAGE COMMITTEE |
| 66201 k | E | A | WBAN | TO | |
| 66202 k | E | A | WBAN | TO | |
| 66203 k | E | A | WBAN | TO | |
| 66204 k | E | A | WBAN | TO | |
| 66205 k | E | A | WBAN | TO | |
| 66206 k | E | A | WBAN | TO | |
| 66207 k | E | A | WBAN | TO | |
| 66208 k | E | A | WBAN | TO | |
| 66209 k | E | A | WBAN | TO | |
| 66210 k | E | A | WBAN | TO | |
| 66211 k | E | A | WBAN | TO | |
| 66212 k | E | A | WBAN | TO | |
| 66213 k | E | A | WBAN | TO | |
| 66214 k | E | A | WBAN | TO | |
| 66215 k | E | A | WBEN | TO | |
| 66216 k | E | A | WBAN | TO | |
| 66217 k | E | A | WBAN | TO | |
| 66218 k | E | A | WBAN | TO | |
| 66219 k | E | A | WBAN | TO | |
| 66220 k | E | A | WBAN | TO | |
| 66221 k | E | A | WBAN | TO | |
| 66222 k | E | A | WBAN | TO | |
| 66223 k | E | A | WBAN | TO | |
| 66224 k | E | A | WBAN | TO | |
| 66225 k | E | A | WBAN | TO | |
| 66226 k | E | A | WBAN | TO | |
| 66227 k | E | A | WBAN | TO | |
| 66228 k | E | A | WBAN | TO | |
| 66229 k | E | A | WBAN | TO | |
| 66230 k | E | A | WBAN | TO | |
| 66231 k | E | A | WBAN | TO | |
| 66232 k | E | A | WBAN | TO | |
| 66233 k | E | A | WBAN | TO | |
| 66234 k | E | A | WBAN | TO | |
| 66235 k | E | A | WBAN | TO | |

| 66236 | k | **E** | A | WBAN | TO |
|--------|---|-------|---|------|-----|
| 66237 | k | **E** | A | WBAN | TO |
| 66238 | k | **E** | A | WBAN | TO |
| 66239 | k | **E** | A | WBAN | TO |
| 66240 | k | **E** | A | WBAN | TO |
| 66241 | k | **E** | A | WBAN | TO |
| 66242 | k | **E** | A | WBAN | TO |
| 66243 | k | **E** | A | WBAN | TO |
| 66244 | k | **E** | A | WBAN | TO |
| 66245 | k | **E** | A | WBAN | TO |
| 66246 | k | **E** | A | WBAN | TO |
| 66247 | k | **E** | A | WBAN | TO |
| 66248 | k | **E** | A | WBAN | TO |
| 66249 | k | **E** | A | WBAN | TO |
| 66250 | k | **E** | A | WBAN | TO |

**Class 66/4. Direct Rail Services-operated locomotives. 66401–66410. Porterbrook locos.** Details as Class 66/0.

**Advertising livery:** 66405 WH Malcolm (DRS Blue with WH Malcolm logos).

| 66401 | **DS** | P | XHIM | KM |
|--------|--------|---|------|-----|
| 66402 | **DS** | P | XHIM | KM |
| 66403 | **DS** | P | XHIM | KM |
| 66404 | **DS** | P | XHIM | KM |
| 66405 | **AL** | P | XHIM | KM |
| 66406 | **DS** | P | XHIM | KM |
| 66407 | **DS** | P | XHIM | KM |
| 66408 | **DS** | P | XHIM | KM |
| 66409 | **DS** | P | XHIM | KM |
| 66410 | **DS** | P | XHIM | KM |

**66411–66420. HBOS locos on order for DRS.** New "low emission" engines. Due for delivery June 2006 (66411–415) and September 2006 (66416–420). Details as Class 66/9.

| 66411 | HX |
|--------|-----|
| 66412 | HX |
| 66413 | HX |
| 66414 | HX |
| 66415 | HX |
| 66416 | HX |
| 66417 | HX |
| 66418 | HX |
| 66419 | HX |
| 66420 | HX |

**Class 66/5. Freightliner-operated locomotives.** Details as Class 66/0.

**Advertising livery:** 66522 Shanks Waste (one half of loco Freightliner green and one half Shanks' Waste light green).

| 66501 | **FL** | P | DFGM | FD | Japan 2001 |
|--------|--------|---|------|-----|-----------------------------|
| 66502 | **FL** | P | DFRT | FD | Basford Hall Centenary 2001 |
| 66503 | **FL** | P | DFGM | FD | The RAILWAY MAGAZINE |

| 66504 | **FL** | P | DFGM | FD | |
|-------|--------|---|------|----|---|
| 66505 | **FL** | P | DFRT | FD | |
| 66506 | **FL** | H | DFHH | FD | Crewe Regeneration |
| 66507 | **FL** | H | DFRT | FD | |
| 66508 | **FL** | H | DFGM | FD | |
| 66509 | **FL** | H | DFHH | FD | |
| 66510 | **FL** | H | DFRT | FD | |
| 66511 | **FL** | H | DFRT | FD | |
| 66512 | **FL** | H | DFHH | FD | |
| 66513 | **FL** | H | DFHH | FD | |
| 66514 | **FL** | H | DFRT | FD | |
| 66515 | **FL** | H | DFGM | FD | |
| 66516 | **FL** | H | DFGM | FD | |
| 66517 | **FL** | H | DFGM | FD | |
| 66518 | **FL** | H | DFRT | FD | |
| 66519 | **FL** | H | DFHH | FD | |
| 66520 | **FL** | H | DFRT | FD | |
| 66521 | **FL** | H | SAXL | LD | |
| 66522 | **AL** | H | DFRT | LD | |
| 66523 | **FL** | H | DFRT | FD | |
| 66524 | **FL** | H | DFHH | LD | |
| 66525 | **FL** | H | DFHH | FD | |
| 66526 | **FL** | P | DFRT | LD | Driver Steve Dunn (George) |
| 66527 | **FL** | P | DFRT | LD | Don Raider |
| 66528 | **FL** | P | DFHH | FD | |
| 66529 | **FL** | P | DFHH | FD | |
| 66530 | **FL** | P | DFHH | LD | |
| 66531 | **FL** | P | DFHH | FD | |
| 66532 | **FL** | P | DFGM | FD | P&O Nedlloyd Atlas |
| 66533 | **FL** | P | DFGM | FD | Hanjin Express/Senator Express |
| 66534 | **FL** | P | DFGM | FD | OOCL Express |
| 66535 | **FL** | P | DFGM | FD | |
| 66536 | **FL** | P | DFGM | FD | |
| 66537 | **FL** | P | DFGM | FD | |
| 66538 | **FL** | H | DFIM | FD | |
| 66539 | **FL** | H | DFIM | FD | |
| 66540 | **FL** | H | DFIM | FD | Ruby |
| 66541 | **FL** | H | DFIM | FD | |
| 66542 | **FL** | H | DFIM | FD | |
| 66543 | **FL** | H | DFIM | FD | |
| 66544 | **FL** | P | DFHG | LD | |
| 66545 | **FL** | P | DFHG | FD | |
| 66546 | **FL** | P | DFNR | FD | |
| 66547 | **FL** | P | DFNR | LD | |
| 66548 | **FL** | P | DFHG | LD | |
| 66549 | **FL** | P | DFHG | LD | |
| 66550 | **FL** | P | DFHG | LD | |
| 66551 | **FL** | P | DFHG | LD | |
| 66552 | **FL** | P | DFHG | LD | Maltby Raider |
| 66553 | **FL** | P | DFHG | LD | |
| 66554 | **FL** | H | DFHG | LD | |

| 66555 | FL | H | DFHG | LD | |
|---|---|---|---|---|---|
| 66556 | FL | H | DFHG | LD | |
| 66557 | FL | H | DFHG | FD | |
| 66558 | FL | H | DFHG | FD | |
| 66559 | FL | H | DFNR | LD | |
| 66560 | FL | H | DFHG | FD | |
| 66561 | FL | H | DFHG | FD | |
| 66562 | FL | H | DFHG | LD | |
| 66563 | FL | H | DFHG | FD | |
| 66564 | FL | H | DFHG | LD | |
| 66565 | FL | H | DFHG | LD | |
| 66566 | FL | H | DFHG | LD | |
| 66567 | FL | H | DFIM | FD | |
| 66568 | FL | H | DFIM | FD | |
| 66569 | FL | H | DFIM | FD | |
| 66570 | FL | H | DFGM | FD | |
| 66571 | FL | H | DFGM | FD | |
| 66572 | FL | H | DFIM | FD | |
| 66573 | FL | H | DFIM | FD | |
| 66574 | FL | H | DFIM | FD | |
| 66575 | FL | H | DFIM | FD | |
| 66576 | FL | H | DFIM | FD | Hamburg Sud Advantage |
| 66577 | FL | H | DFIM | FD | |
| 66578 | FL | H | DFIM | FD | |
| 66579 | FL | H | DFGM | FD | |
| 66580 | FL | H | DFGM | FD | |
| 66581 | FL | H | DFHG | FD | |

**Class 66/6. Freightliner-operated locomotives with modified gear ratios.** Details as Class 66/0 except:

**Maximum Tractive Effort:** 467 kN (105080 lbf).
**Continuous Tractive Effort:** 296 kN (66630 lbf) at 14.0 m.p.h.
**Design Speed:** 65 m.p.h. **Maximum Speed:** 65 m.p.h.

| 66601 | FL | P | DFHH | FD | The Hope Valley |
|---|---|---|---|---|---|
| 66602 | FL | P | DFRT | FD | |
| 66603 | FL | P | DFRT | FD | |
| 66604 | FL | P | DFRT | FD | |
| 66605 | FL | P | DFRT | FD | |
| 66606 | FL | P | DFRT | FD | |
| 66607 | FL | P | DFHG | FD | |
| 66608 | FL | P | DFHG | FD | |
| 66609 | FL | P | DFHG | FD | |
| 66610 | FL | P | DFHG | FD | |
| 66611 | FL | P | DFHG | FD | |
| 66612 | FL | P | DFHG | FD | Forth Raider |
| 66613 | FL | H | DFHG | FD | |
| 66614 | FL | H | DFHG | FD | |
| 66615 | FL | H | DFHG | FD | |
| 66616 | FL | H | DFHG | FD | |
| 66617 | FL | H | DFHG | FD | |

| 66618 | **FL** | H | DFHG | FD | Railways Illustrated Annual |
|---|---|---|---|---|---|
| | | | | | Photographic Awards David Gorton |
| 66619 | **FL** | H | DFHG | FD | |
| 66620 | **FL** | H | DFHG | FD | |
| 66621 | **FL** | H | DFHG | FD | |
| 66622 | **FL** | H | DFHG | FD | |

**Class 66/7. GB Railfreight-operated locomotives.** Details as Class 66/0.

**Non-standard/Advertising liveries:**

66705 **GB** livery but with the addition of "Union Jack" bodyside vinyls.
66709 Black & orange with MEDITE branding.

| 66701 | **GB** | H | GBRT | WN | Whitemoor |
|---|---|---|---|---|---|
| 66702 | **GB** | H | GBRT | WN | Blue Lightning |
| 66703 | **GB** | H | GBRT | WN | Doncaster PSB 1981–2002 |
| 66704 | **GB** | H | GBRT | WN | Colchester Power Signalbox |
| 66705 | **GB** | H | GBRT | WN | Golden Jubilee |
| 66706 | **GB** | H | GBRT | WN | Nene Valley |
| 66707 | **GB** | H | GBRT | WN | Sir Sam Fay GREAT CENTRAL RAILWAY |
| 66708 | **GB** | H | GBCM | WN | |
| 66709 | **AL** | H | GBCM | WN | Joseph Arnold Davies |
| 66710 | **GB** | H | GBCM | WN | |
| 66711 | **GB** | H | GBCM | WN | |
| 66712 | **GB** | H | GBCM | WN | |
| 66713 | **GB** | H | GBCM | WN | Forest City |
| 66714 | **GB** | H | GBCM | WN | Cromer Lifeboat |
| 66715 | **GB** | H | GBCM | WN | VALOUR – IN MEMORY OF ALL RAILWAY |
| | | | | | EMPLOYEES WHO GAVE THEIR LIVES FOR |
| | | | | | THEIR COUNTRY |
| 66716 | **GB** | H | GBCM | WN | Willesden Traincare Centre |
| 66717 | **GB** | H | GBCM | WN | |

**66718–66727.** New "low emission" engines. Due for delivery Spring 2006 (66718–722) and late 2006 (66723–727). Details as Class 66/9.

| 66718 | H |
|---|---|
| 66719 | H |
| 66720 | H |
| 66721 | H |
| 66722 | H |
| 66723 | H |
| 66724 | H |
| 66725 | H |
| 66726 | H |
| 66727 | H |

**Class 66/9. Freightliner locos.** New "low emission" engines. Details as Class 66/6 except:
**Fuel Capacity:** 5150 litres.

| 66951 | **FL** | H | DFHG | FD |
|---|---|---|---|---|
| 66952 | **FL** | H | DFHG | FD |

# CLASS 67 ALSTOM/GENERAL MOTORS EMD Bo-Bo

**Built:** 1999–2000 by Alstom at Valencia, Spain, as sub-contractors for General Motors (General Motors model JT42 HW-HS).
**Engine:** General Motors 12N-710G3B-EC two stroke of 2385 kW (3200 h.p.) at 900 r.p.m.
**Main Alternator:** General Motors AR9/HE3/CA6B.
**Traction Motors:** General Motors D43FM.
**Maximum Tractive Effort:** 141 kN (31750 lbf).
**Continuous Tractive Effort:** 90 kN (20200 lbf) at ?? m.p.h.
**Power At Rail:** 1860 kW.
**Brake Force:** 78 t.
**Weight:** 90 t.
**Design Speed:** 125 m.p.h.
**Fuel Capacity:** 4927 litres.
**Train Supply:** Electric, index 66.
**Train Brakes:** Air.
**Dimensions:** 19.74 x 2.72 m.
**Wheel Diameter:** 965 mm.
**Maximum Speed:** 125 m.p.h.
**RA:** 8.
**Multiple Working:** AAR System.

**Note:** All equipped with Slow Speed Control and Swinghead Automatic "Buckeye" Combination Couplers.

**Non-standard livery:** 67029 All over silver with EWS logos (EWS "Special Train").

| | | | | | |
|---|---|---|---|---|---|
| 67001 | E | A | WAAK | TO | |
| 67002 | E | A | WAAK | TO | Special Delivery |
| 67003 | E | A | WAAK | TO | |
| 67004 r | E | A | WABK | TO | Post Haste |
| 67005 | RZ | A | WAAK | TO | Queen's Messenger |
| 67006 | RZ | A | WAAK | TO | Royal Sovereign |
| 67007 r | E | A | WABK | TO | |
| 67008 r | E | A | WABK | TO | |
| 67009 r | E | A | WABK | TO | |
| 67010 | E | A | WNTS | TO | Unicorn |
| 67011 r | E | A | WABK | TO | |
| 67012 | E | A | WAAK | TO | |
| 67013 | E | A | WAAK | TO | |
| 67014 | E | A | WAAK | TO | |
| 67015 | E | A | WAAK | TO | |
| 67016 | E | A | WAAK | TO | |
| 67017 | E | A | WAAK | TO | Arrow |
| 67018 | E | A | WAAK | TO | Rapid |
| 67019 | E | A | WAAK | TO | |
| 67020 | E | A | WAAK | TO | |
| 67021 | E | A | WAAK | TO | |
| 67022 | E | A | WAAK | TO | |
| 67023 | E | A | WAAK | TO | |
| 67024 | E | A | WAAK | TO | |
| 67025 | E | A | WAAK | TO | Western Star |
| 67026 | E | A | WNTR | ML | |
| 67027 | E | A | WAAK | TO | Rising Star |
| 67028 | E | A | WAAK | TO | |
| 67029 | O | A | WAAK | TO | |
| 67030 | E | A | WAAK | TO | |

# PLATFORM 5 MAIL ORDER

## RAILWAYS RESTORED 2006

### Ian Allan

Fully revised and updated edition of the definitive guide to heritage railways, railway museums and preservation centres in the British Isles. Contains essential opening and operating information for over 180 heritage locations, plus details of on-site facilities, disabled access, special events and other useful information. Also includes a locomotive stocklist for most locations and 2006 timetables for over 60 operating railways. Well illustrated. 224 pages. **£14.99.**

## ABC BRITISH RAILWAYS MOTIVE POWER COMBINED VOLUME SPRING 1963

### Ian Allan

Reprint of the classic Ian Allan combined volume from Spring 1963. Contains a full fleet list of all locomotives in service with British Railways or on order in the Spring of 1963. This is a particularly interesting period as steam locomotives were by then rapidly succumbing to modern traction in the form of diesel and electric locomotives and multiple units. Also includes a full list of engine sheds and many black & white illustrations. 348 pages. Hardback. **£12.99.**

**Please add postage: 10% UK, 20% Europe, 30% Rest of World.**

**Telephone, fax or send your order to the Platform 5 Mail Order Department. See page 384 of this book for details.**

▲ EWS-liveried 08703 at Toton on 16/6/04.　　　　　**Paul Robertson**

▼ BR Departmental-liveried 09014 is seen shunting at Healey Mills on 12/05/05.
　　　　　　　　　　　　　　　　　　　　　　　　**Chris Booth**

▲ Unique Lafarge-liveried 20168 "SIR GEORGE EARLE" is seen at Barrow Hill on 05/10/04. This loco is normally used for trip workings between Earles Sidings and Hope Cement Works.                                                    **Robert Pritchard**

▼ Shortly after its overhaul was completed DRS-liveried 33029 is seen at FM Rail, Derby on 10/04/05.                                                                                        **Paul Robertson**

Network Rail yellow-liveried 31105 at Derby on 04/0505.

**Gavin Morrison**

EWS-liveried 37417 "Richard Trevithick" passes Achallader, north of Bridge of Orchy, on 07/06/05 with the 04.50 Edinburgh–Fort William portion of the First ScotRail Highland Sleeper.

Jonathan Allen

First Group-liveried 43169 "The National Trust" passes Pixash near Keynsham with the 14.00 Bristol Temple Meads–London Paddington on 18/04/05. 43042 was on the rear.
— **John Chalcraft**

▲ Ex-works in the new Midland Mainline livery, 43076 leaves Chesterfield with the 16.25 London St. Pancras–Sheffield on 28/05/05. 43075 was on the rear.
**Robert Pritchard**

▼ West Coast Railway Company (Royal Scotsman locos)-liveried 47854 leads 37261 at Plean with the 08.49 Stirling–Edinburgh leg of the luxury train on 21/05/05.
**Ian Lothian**

"One"-liveried 47818 passes Shepreth Branch Jn., south of Cambridge, with the diverted 17.27 Liverpool Street–Norwich on 19/07/04. This loco is owned by Cotswold Rail. **Anthony Kay**

Golden ochre-liveried D1015 "WESTERN CHAMPION" was busy on mainline charter work throughout 2005. On 19/03/05 it is seen leaving Totnes with the 07.04 Ealing Broadway–Plymouth "Western China Clay" railtour. **Charles Woodland**

▲ Virgin's 57310 "KYRANO" is seen near Rainhill on 15/07/05, hauling Pendolino 390 013 on the diverted 10.06 Euston–Liverpool Lime Street. **Andrew Wills**

▼ Foster Yeoman-liveried 59001 "YEOMAN ENDEAVOUR" passes Newbury on 14/07/05 with 7C76 14.17 Acton–Westbury empty stone train. **Robert Pritchard**

▲ 60078, in Mainline blue livery, is seen at Doncaster on 13/04/04 with an Immingham–Doncaster steel working. **Paul Shannon**

▼ Freightliner-liveried 66566 is seen near Barrow upon Soar with 4G40 12.00 West Burton–Daw Mill empty coal working on 04/10/04. **Paul Robertson**

GBRf-liveried 66716 climbs away from Tonbridge with the 05.34 West Burton–Mountfield train of gypsum containers on 13/05/04. **Rodney Lissenden**

▲ Class 67s are used regularly on charter services. On 22/05/04 67025 is seen at Adamsdown, Cardiff with the 08.34 charter from London Euston. **Andrew Mist**

▼ 73205 and 73204 are seen running light engine from Hoo Junction to Tonbridge at Chalk on 16/09/04. **Anthony Kay**

▲ South West Trains "Desiro"-liveried 73235 hauls three Class 423 units as the 10.10 Wimbledon–Bournemouth e.c.s. on 05/04/05, the train passes Eastleigh.
**Chris Booth**

▼ The unique re-geared 86501 passes Cathiron, near Rugby, with 4M87 12.49 Ipswich–Trafford Park Freightliner on 14/04/04.  **Chris Booth**

▲ LNWR black-liveried 87019 "ACoRP Association of Community Rail Partnerships" is seen at Longport with Virgin's 15.24 Manchester–Birmingham service on 07/06/05. This loco is now operated by GBRf. **Cliff Beeton**

▼ 90030 "Crewe Locomotive Works" is seen at Stoke with the 14.24 Manchester–Birmingham on 07/06/05. **Cliff Beeton**

GNER-liveried 91108 "City of Leeds" passes Blindwells, near Prestonpans, with the 07.00 London King's Cross–Glasgow Central on 13/09/04. **Ian Lothian**

▲ EPS grey-liveried 92025 "Oscar Wilde" passes Carpenders Park with 6X77 17.31 Wembley–Mossend loaded cartics on 08/06/05.  **Gavin Morrison**

▼ Unrefurbished Eurotunnel loco 9012 is seen arriving at Cheriton with a train from Folkestone on 23/02/05.  **Hugh Ballantyne**

# 1.2. ELECTRO-DIESEL & ELECTRIC LOCOMOTIVES

## CLASS 73          BR/ENGLISH ELECTRIC          Bo-Bo

Electro-diesel locomotives which can operate either from a DC supply or using power from a diesel engine.

**Built:** 1965–1967 by English Electric Co. at Vulcan Foundry, Newton le Willows.
**Engine:** English Electric 4SRKT of 447 kW (600 h.p.) at 850 r.p.m.
**Main Generator:** English Electric 824/5D.
**Electric Supply System:** 750 V DC from third rail.
**Traction Motors:** English Electric 546/1B.
**Maximum Tractive Effort (Electric):** 179 kN (40000 lbf).
**Maximum Tractive Effort (Diesel):** 160 kN (36000 lbf).
**Continuous Rating (Electric):** 1060 kW (1420 h.p.) giving a tractive effort of 35 kN (7800 lbf) at 68 m.p.h.
**Continuous Tractive Effort (Diesel):** 60 kN (13600 lbf) at 11.5 m.p.h.
**Maximum Rail Power (Electric):** 2350 kW (3150 h.p.) at 42 m.p.h.
**Train Brakes:** Air, vacuum & electro-pneumatic († Air & electro-pneumatic).
**Brake Force:** 31 t.                    **Dimensions:** 16.36 x 2.64 m.
**Weight:** 77 t.                         **Wheel Diameter:** 1016 mm.
**Design Speed:** 90 m.p.h.              **Maximum Speed:** 90 m.p.h.
**Fuel Capacity:** 1409 litres.
**Train Supply:** Electric, index 66 (on electric power only).
**Multiple Working:** SR System.

Formerly numbered E6001–E6020/E6022–E6026/E6028–E6049 (not in order).

**Note:** Locomotives numbered in the 732xx series are classed as 73/2 and were originally dedicated to Gatwick Express services.

**Non-standard numbering:** 73136 Also carries number D6043.

| | | | | | |
|---|---|---|---|---|---|
| 73103 | **IM** | FM | SDXL | MQ | |
| 73107 | **FB** | FM | SDED | DF | SPITFIRE |
| 73109 | **SD** | SW | HYWD | WD | Battle of Britain 50th Anniversary |
| 73117 | **IM** | FM | SDXL | MQ | |
| 73118 †c | **EP** | EU | GPSN | NP | |
| 73130 †c | **EP** | EU | GPSN | NP | |
| 73132 | **IM** | NR | QAED | DF (S) | |
| 73136 | **B** | 73 | MBEL | SL | Perseverance |
| 73141 | **IM** | NR | QAED | YK (S) | |
| 73201 † | **SD** | SW | HYWD | WD | |
| 73202 † | **GX** | P | IVGA | SL | Dave Berry |
| 73203 † | **GX** | GB | GBZZ | PB | |
| 73204 † | **GB** | GB | GBED | DF | Janice |
| 73205 † | **GB** | GB | GBED | DF | Jeanette |
| 73206 † | **GB** | GB | GBED | DF | Lisa |
| 73207 † | **GX** | GB | GBZZ | PB | |

| | | | | | |
|---|---|---|---|---|---|
| 73208 | † | **GX** | GB | GBED | DF | |
| 73209 | † | **GB** | GB | GBED | DF | Alison |
| 73210 | † | **GX** | 73 | MBEL | SL (S) | |
| 73211 | † | **GX** | 73 | MBEL | SL (S) | |
| 73212 | † | **Y** | NR | QAED | DF | |
| 73213 | † | **Y** | NR | QAED | DF | |
| 73235 | † | **SD** | SW | HYWD | WD | |

## CLASS 86   BR/ENGLISH ELECTRIC   Bo-Bo

**Built:** 1965–1966 by English Electric Co. at Vulcan Foundry, Newton le Willows or by BR at Doncaster Works.
**Electric Supply System:** 25 kV AC 50 Hz overhead.
**Train Brakes:** Air.                      **Brake Force:** 40 t.
**Dimensions:** 17.83 x 2.65 m.            **Weight:** 83–86.8 t.
**RA:** 6.                                  **Multiple Working:** TDM system.
**Train Supply:** Electric, index 74.

Formerly numbered E3101–E3200 (not in order).

**Non-standard livery:** 86233 BR "Electric blue" livery.

**Class 86/2. Standard design rebuilt with resilient wheels and Flexicoil suspension.**

**Traction Motors:** AEI 282BZ axle hung.
**Maximum Tractive Effort:** 207 kN (46500 lbf).
**Continuous Rating:** 3010 kW (4040 h.p.) giving a tractive effort of 85 kN (19200 lbf) at 77.5 m.p.h.
**Maximum Rail Power:** 4550 kW (6100 h.p.) at 49.5 m.p.h.
**Wheel Diameter:** 1156 mm.               **Weight:** 85–86.2 t.
**Design Speed:** 125 m.p.h.               **Maximum Speed:** 100 m.p.h.

| | | | | | |
|---|---|---|---|---|---|
| 86205 | **V** | H | SAXL | IR | |
| 86212 | **V** | H | SAXL | EM | |
| 86215 | **AR** | H | SAXL | PY | |
| 86217 | **AR** | H | SAXL | OY | |
| 86218 | **AR** | H | SAXL | IR | |
| 86223 | **AR** | H | SAXL | OY | Norwich Union |
| 86226 | **V** | H | SAXL | IR | |
| 86228 | **IC** | H | SAXL | ZH | Vulcan Heritage |
| 86229 | **V** | H | SAXL | OY | |
| 86230 | **AR** | H | SAXL | PY | |
| 86231 | **V** | H | SAXL | OY | |
| 86232 | **AR** | H | SAXL | IR | |
| 86233 | **0** | H | SAXL | OY | |
| 86234 | **AR** | H | SAXL | IR | |
| 86235 | **AR** | H | SAXL | IR | |
| 86242 | **AR** | H | SAXL | PY | |
| 86245 | **V** | H | SAXL | IR | |
| 86246 | **AR** | H | SAXL | IR | |
| 86247 | **V** | H | SAXL | IR | |

| 86248 | **V**  | H  | SAXL | ZH | Sir Clwyd/County of Clwyd |
| 86250 | **AR** | H  | SAXL | OY |  |
| 86251 | **V**  | H  | SAXL | OY |  |
| 86258 | **V**  | H  | SAXL | LB |  |
| 86260 | **AR** | H  | SAXL | IR |  |

**Class 86/4. Network Rail-owned locomotive.**

**Traction Motors:** AEI 282AZ axle hung.
**Maximum Tractive Effort:** 258 kN (58000 lbf).
**Continuous Rating:** 2680 kW (3600 h.p.) giving a tractive effort of 89 kN (20000 lbf) at 67 m.p.h.
**Maximum Rail Power:** 4400 kW (5900 h.p.) at 38 m.p.h.
**Wheel Diameter:** 1156 mm.        **Weight:** 83–83.9 t.
**Design Speed:** 100 m.p.h.        **Maximum Speed:** 100 m.p.h.

| 86424 | **RX** | NR | SDXL | AS |

**Class 86/5. Regeared locomotive operated by Freightliner.**
Details as Class 86/4 except:

**Continuous Rating:** 2680 kW (3600 h.p.) giving a tractive effort of 117 kN (26300 lbf) at 67 m.p.h.
**Maximum Speed:** 75 m.p.h.        **Train Supply:** Electric, isolated.

| 86501 | (86608) | **FL** | FL | DFGC | FE |

**Class 86/6. Freightliner-operated locomotives.**
Details as Class 86/4 except:
**Maximum Speed:** 75 m.p.h.        **Train Supply:** Electric, isolated.

| 86602 | **FL** | FL | DHLT | BA |  |
| 86604 | **FL** | FL | DFNC | FE |  |
| 86605 | **FL** | FL | DFNC | FE |  |
| 86606 | **FF** | FL | DHLT | CE |  |
| 86607 | **FL** | FL | DFNC | FE |  |
| 86609 | **FL** | FL | DFNC | FE |  |
| 86610 | **FL** | FL | DFNC | FE |  |
| 86612 | **FL** | P  | DFNC | FE |  |
| 86613 | **FL** | P  | DFNC | FE |  |
| 86614 | **FF** | P  | DFNC | FE |  |
| 86615 | **FL** | P  | DHLT | CE | Rotary International |
| 86620 | **FL** | P  | DHLT | CE | Philip G Walton |
| 86621 | **FL** | P  | DFNC | FE |  |
| 86622 | **FF** | P  | DFNC | FE |  |
| 86623 | **FF** | P  | DHLT | BA |  |
| 86627 | **FL** | P  | DFNC | FE |  |
| 86628 | **FL** | P  | DFNC | FE |  |
| 86632 | **FL** | P  | DFNC | FE |  |
| 86633 | **FF** | P  | DHLT | BA |  |
| 86635 | **FL** | P  | DHLT | BA |  |
| 86637 | **FF** | P  | DFNC | FE |  |
| 86638 | **FL** | P  | DFNC | FE |  |
| 86639 | **FL** | P  | DFNC | FE |  |

Class 86/9. Network Rail-owned locomotives. Rebuilt for use as Mobile Load Bank test locos to test Overhead Line Equipment, initially on the WCML. No. 1 end Traction Motors isolated. Can still move under own power.

**Maximum Speed:** 60 m.p.h.

| 86901 | Y | NR | QACL | RU | CHIEF ENGINEER |
| 86902 | Y | NR | QACL | RU | RAIL VEHICLE ENGINEERING |

# CLASS 87        BREL/GEC       Bo-Bo

**Built:** 1973–1975 by BREL at Crewe Works.
**Electric Supply System:** 25 kV AC 50 Hz overhead.
**Traction Motors:** GEC G412AZ frame mounted.
**Maximum Tractive Effort:** 258 kN (58000 lbf).
**Continuous Rating:** 3730 kW (5000 h.p.) giving a tractive effort of 95 kN (21300 lbf) at 87 m.p.h.
**Maximum Rail Power:** 5860 kW (7860 h.p.) at 50.8 m.p.h.
**Train Brakes:** Air.                          **Brake Force:** 40 t.
**Dimensions:** 17.83 x 2.65 m.                 **Weight:** 83.3 t.
**Wheel Diameter:** 1150 mm.                    **Design Speed:** 110 m.p.h.
**Maximum Speed:** 110 m.p.h.                   **Train Supply:** Electric, index 95.
**RA:** 6.                                      **Multiple Working:** TDM system.

**Non-standard livery:** 87019 LNWR-style lined black.

| 87002 | P  | P | IWCA | WB     | The AC Locomotive Group |
| 87003 | V  | P | CRRH | OY (S) | |
| 87004 | V  | P | SBXL | OY     | |
| 87006 | DR | P | GBAC | WB     | |
| 87007 | CD | P | CRRH | OY     | |
| 87008 | V  | P | CRRH | OY     | |
| 87009 | V  | P | SBXL | BR     | |
| 87010 | V  | P | SBXL | OY     | |
| 87011 | V  | P | SBXL | BR     | |
| 87012 | N  | P | GBAC | WB     | The Olympian |
| 87013 | V  | P | SBXL | OY     | |
| 87014 | V  | P | SBXL | OY     | |
| 87017 | V  | P | SBXL | BR     | |
| 87018 | V  | P | SBXL | BR     | |
| 87019 | O  | P | GBAC | WB     | ACoRP Association of Community Rail Partnerships |
| 87020 | V  | P | SBXL | BR     | |
| 87021 | V  | P | CREL | OY (S) | |
| 87022 | DR | P | GBAC | WB     | |
| 87023 | V  | P | CRRH | OY (S) | |
| 87025 | V  | P | CRRH | OY (S) | |
| 87026 | V  | P | IWCA | WB     | |
| 87027 | V  | P | SBXL | NC     | |
| 87028 | DR | P | GBAC | WB     | |
| 87029 | V  | P | SBXL | OY     | |
| 87030 | V  | P | SBXL | OY     | |

| 87031 | V | P | ATXX | WN |
|-------|---|---|------|----|
| 87032 | V | P | SBXL | ZH |
| 87033 | V | P | CREL | OY |
| 87034 | V | P | SBXL | BR |

## CLASS 89                    BRUSH                    Co-Co

**Built:** 1986 by BREL at Crewe Works (as sub-contractors for Brush).
**Electric Supply System:** 25 kV AC 50 Hz overhead.
**Traction Motors:** Brush. Frame mounted.
**Maximum Tractive Effort:** 205 kN (46000 lbf).
**Continuous Rating:** 4350 kW (5850 h.p.) giving a tractive effort of 105 kN (23600 lbf) at 92 m.p.h.

| | |
|---|---|
| **Maximum Rail Power:** | **Train Brakes:** Air. |
| **Brake Force:** 50 t. | **Dimensions:** 19.80 x 2.74 m. |
| **Weight:** 104 t. | **Wheel Diameter:** 1150 mm. |
| **Design Speed:** 125 m.p.h. | **Maximum Speed:** 125 m.p.h. |
| **Train Supply:** Electric, index 95. | **RA:** 6. |
| **Multiple Working:** TDM system. | |

| 89001 | GN | SA | ACXX | BH |
|-------|----|----|------|-----|

## CLASS 90                    GEC                    Bo-Bo

**Built:** 1987–1990 by BREL at Crewe Works (as sub contractors for GEC).
**Electric Supply System:** 25 kV AC 50 Hz overhead.
**Traction Motors:** GEC G412CY frame mounted.
**Maximum Tractive Effort:** 258 kN (58000 lbf).
**Continuous Rating:** 3730 kW (5000 h.p.) giving a tractive effort of 95 kN (21300 lbf) at 87 m.p.h.
**Maximum Rail Power:** 5860 kW (7860 h.p.) at 68.3 m.p.h.
**Train Brakes:** Air.

| | |
|---|---|
| **Brake Force:** 40 t. | **Dimensions:** 18.80 x 2.74 m. |
| **Weight:** 84.5 t. | **Wheel Diameter:** 1156 mm. |
| **Design Speed:** 110 m.p.h. | **Maximum Speed:** 110 m.p.h. |
| **Train Supply:** Electric, index 95. | **RA:** 7. |
| **Multiple Working:** TDM system. | |

**Non-standard livery:** 90036 As **FE** but with a yellow roof.

| 90001 | b | 1 | P | IANA | NC | |
|-------|---|---|---|------|----|----|
| 90002 | b | 1 | P | IANA | NC | |
| 90003 | b | 1 | P | IANA | NC | Raedwald of East Anglia |
| 90004 | b | 1 | P | IANA | NC | |
| 90005 | b | 1 | P | IANA | NC | Vice-Admiral Lord Nelson |
| 90006 | b | 1 | P | IANA | NC | Modern Railways Magazine/ Roger Ford |
| 90007 | b | V | P | IANA | NC | |
| 90008 | b | V | P | IANA | NC | |
| 90009 | b | 1 | P | IANA | NC | |
| 90010 | b | 1 | P | IANA | NC | |

| 90011 | b | V | P | IANA | NC | |
|---|---|---|---|---|---|---|
| 90012 | b | V | P | IANA | NC | |
| 90013 | b | 1 | P | IANA | NC | |
| 90014 | b | V | P | IANA | NC | |
| 90015 | b | 1 | P | IANA | NC | |
| 90016 | | FL | E | DFLC | FE | |
| 90017 | b | E | E | WEFE | CE | |
| 90018 | b | E | E | WEFE | CE | |
| 90019 | b | RX | E | WEFE | CE | Penny Black |
| 90020 | b | E | E | WEFE | CE | Collingwood |
| 90021 | | FE | E | WNTS | CE | |
| 90022 | | EG | E | WEFE | CE | Freightconnection |
| 90023 | | E | E | WNTR | CE | |
| 90024 | | GN | E | WNTS | CE | |
| 90025 | | F | E | WNTR | CE | |
| 90026 | | E | E | WEFE | CE | |
| 90027 | | F | E | WEFE | CE | Allerton T&RS Depot |
| 90028 | | E | E | WEFE | CE | Hertfordshire Rail Tours |
| 90029 | | E | E | WNTR | CE | The Institution of Civil Engineers |
| 90030 | | E | E | WNTS | CE | Crewe Locomotive Works |
| 90031 | | E | E | WEFE | CE | The Railway Children Partnership Working For Street Children Worldwide |
| 90032 | | E | E | WNTR | CE | |
| 90033 | | FE | E | WNTS | CE | |
| 90034 | | E | E | WEFE | CE | |
| 90035 | | E | E | WEFE | CE | |
| 90036 | | 0 | E | WEFE | CE | |
| 90037 | | E | E | WNTS | CE | Spirit of Dagenham |
| 90038 | | FE | E | WNTR | CE | |
| 90039 | | E | E | WEFE | CE | |
| 90040 | | E | E | WEFE | CE | The Railway Mission |
| 90041 | | FL | P | DFLC | FE | |
| 90042 | | FF | P | DFLC | FE | |
| 90043 | | FF | P | DFLC | FE | Freightliner Coatbridge |
| 90044 | | FF | P | DFLC | FE | |
| 90045 | | FF | P | DFLC | FE | |
| 90046 | | FL | P | DFLC | FE | |
| 90047 | | FF | P | DFLC | FE | |
| 90048 | | FF | P | DFLC | FE | |
| 90049 | | FF | P | DFLC | FE | |
| 90050 | | FF | P | WNTS | CE | |

# CLASS 91                    GEC                    Bo-Bo

**Built:** 1988–1991 by BREL at Crewe Works (as sub contractors for GEC).
**Electric Supply System:** 25 kV AC 50 Hz overhead.
**Traction Motors:** GEC G426AZ.            **Maximum Tractive Effort:**
**Continuous Rating:** 4540 kW (6090 h.p.) giving a tractive effort of ?? kN at ?? m.p.h.
**Maximum Rail Power:** 4700 kW (6300 h.p.) at ?? m.p.h.
**Train Brakes:** Air.
**Brake Force:** 45 t.                        **Dimensions:** 19.41 x 2.74 m.
**Weight:** 84 t.                             **Wheel Diameter:** 1000 mm.
**Design Speed:** 140 m.p.h.                  **Maximum Speed:** 125 m.p.h.
**Train Supply:** Electric, index 95.         **RA:** 7.
**Multiple Working:** TDM system.

**Note:** Locos originally numbered in the 910xx series, but renumbered upon completion of overhauls at Bombardier, Doncaster by the addition of 100 to their original number. The exception to this rule was 91023 which was renumbered 91132.

| | | | | | |
|---|---|---|---|---|---|
| 91101 | **GN** | H | IECA | BN | City of London |
| 91102 | **GN** | H | IECA | BN | Durham Cathedral |
| 91103 | **GN** | H | IECA | BN | County of Lincolnshire |
| 91104 | **GN** | H | IECA | BN | Grantham |
| 91105 | **GN** | H | IECA | BN | County Durham |
| 91106 | **GN** | H | IECA | BN | East Lothian |
| 91107 | **GN** | H | IECA | BN | Newark on Trent |
| 91108 | **GN** | H | IECA | BN | City of Leeds |
| 91109 | **GN** | H | IECA | BN | The Samaritans |
| 91110 | **GN** | H | IECA | BN | David Livingstone |
| 91111 | **GN** | H | IECA | BN | Terence Cuneo |
| 91112 | **GN** | H | IECA | BN | County of Cambridgeshire |
| 91113 | **GN** | H | IECA | BN | County of North Yorkshire |
| 91114 | **GN** | H | IECA | BN | St. Mungo Cathedral |
| 91115 | **GN** | H | IECA | BN | Holyrood |
| 91116 | **GN** | H | IECA | BN | Strathclyde |
| 91117 | **GN** | H | IECA | BN | Cancer Research UK |
| 91118 | **GN** | H | IECA | BN | Bradford Film Festival |
| 91119 | **GN** | H | IECA | BN | County of Tyne & Wear |
| 91120 | **GN** | H | IECA | BN | Royal Armouries |
| 91121 | **GN** | H | IECA | BN | Archbishop Thomas Cranmer |
| 91122 | **GN** | H | IECA | BN | Tam the Gun |
| 91124 | **GN** | H | IECA | BN | Reverend W Awdry |
| 91125 | **GN** | H | IECA | BN | Berwick-upon-Tweed |
| 91126 | **GN** | H | IECA | BN | York Minster |
| 91127 | **GN** | H | IECA | BN | Edinburgh Castle |
| 91128 | **GN** | H | IECA | BN | Peterborough Cathedral |
| 91129 | **GN** | H | IECA | BN | Queen Elizabeth II |
| 91130 | **GN** | H | IECA | BN | City of Newcastle |
| 91131 | **GN** | H | IECA | BN | County of Northumberland |
| 91132 | **GN** | H | IECA | BN | City of Durham |

# CLASS 92      BRUSH     Co-Co

**Built:** 1993–1996 by Brush Traction at Loughborough.
**Electric Supply System:** 25 kV AC 50 HZ overhead or 750 V DC third rail.
**Traction Motors:** Brush.
**Maximum Tractive Effort:** 400 kN (90 000 lbf).
**Continuous Rating:** 5040 kW (6760 h.p.) on AC, 4000 kW (5360 h.p.) on DC.
**Maximum Rail Power:**      **Train Brakes:** Air.
**Brake Force:** 63 t.        **Dimensions:** 21.34 x 2.67 m.
**Weight:** 126 t.          **Wheel Diameter:** 1160 mm.
**Design Speed:** 140 km/h (87 m.p.h.).   **Maximum Speed:** 140 km/h (87 m.p.h.).
**Train Supply:** Electric, index 108 (AC), 70 (DC).
**RA:** 7.

| | | | | | |
|---|---|---|---|---|---|
| 92001 | **E** | E | WNTS | CE | Victor Hugo |
| 92002 | **EG** | E | WTAE | CE | H.G. Wells |
| 92003 | **EP** | E | WNTS | CE | Beethoven |
| 92004 | **EP** | E | WNTS | CE | Jane Austen |
| 92005 | **EG** | E | WTAE | CE | Mozart |
| 92006 | **EP** | SF | WTAE | CE | Louis Armand |
| 92007 | **EP** | E | WTAE | CE | Schubert |
| 92008 | **EP** | E | WTAE | CE | Jules Verne |
| 92009 | **EP** | E | WTAE | CE | Elgar |
| 92010 | **EP** | SF | WTAE | CE | Molière |
| 92011 | **EG** | E | WNTS | CE | Handel |
| 92012 | **EP** | E | WTAE | CE | Thomas Hardy |
| 92013 | **EG** | E | WTAE | CE | Puccini |
| 92014 | **EP** | SF | WTAE | CE | Emile Zola |
| 92015 | **EG** | E | WTAE | CE | D.H. Lawrence |
| 92016 | **EG** | E | WTAE | CE | Brahms |
| 92017 | **EP** | E | WNTS | TD | Shakespeare |
| 92018 | **EP** | SF | WTAE | CE | Stendhal |
| 92019 | **EP** | E | WTAE | CE | Wagner |
| 92020 | **EP** | EU | WNWX | CE | Milton |
| 92021 | **EP** | EU | WNWX | CE | Purcell |
| 92022 | **EP** | E | WTAE | CE | Charles Dickens |
| 92023 | **EP** | SF | WTAE | CE | Ravel |
| 92024 | **EP** | E | WTAE | CE | J.S. Bach |
| 92025 | **EP** | E | WTAE | CE | Oscar Wilde |
| 92026 | **EG** | E | WTAE | CE | Britten |
| 92027 | **EG** | E | WTAE | CE | George Eliot |
| 92028 | **EP** | SF | WTAE | CE | Saint Saëns |
| 92029 | **EP** | E | WTAE | CE | Dante |
| 92030 | **EG** | E | WTAE | CE | Ashford |
| 92031 | **E** | E | WTAE | CE | The Institute of Logistics and Transport |
| 92032 | **EP** | EU | WNWX | CE | César Franck |
| 92033 | **EP** | SF | WTAE | CE | Berlioz |
| 92034 | **EG** | E | WTAE | CE | Kipling |
| 92035 | **EP** | E | WNTR | CE | Mendelssohn |
| 92036 | **EG** | E | WTAE | CE | Bertolt Brecht |

| 92037 | **EG** | E  | WTAE | CE | Sullivan |
| 92038 | **EP** | SF | WTAE | CE | Voltaire |
| 92039 | **EP** | E  | WTAE | CE | Johann Strauss |
| 92040 | **EP** | EU | WNWX | CE | Goethe |
| 92041 | **EG** | E  | WTAE | CE | Vaughan Williams |
| 92042 | **EG** | E  | WTAE | CE | Honegger |
| 92043 | **EP** | SF | WTAE | CE | Debussy |
| 92044 | **EP** | EU | WNWX | CE | Couperin |
| 92045 | **EP** | EU | WNWX | CE | Chaucer |
| 92046 | **EP** | EU | WNWX | CE | Sweelinck |

# PLATFORM 5 MAIL ORDER

## RAILWAY TRACK DIAGRAMS
## 3: WESTERN
## 4: MIDLANDS & NORTH WEST

### Track Maps

Each volume of the Quail reference work contains detailed track
diagrams for the former British Rail Regions, plus private
railways, preservation sites and industrial locations. Includes
extensive notation, list of abbreviations, engineers' line
references and an index to stations, lines and selected other
places. New to these volumes is the use of full colour printing to
denote electrification type and voltage. A definitive source of
reference used throughout the railway industry. Published 2005.
**£10.95 & £12.95 respectively.**

**Note:** new editions of other volumes in this series are currently in preparation. If you
would like to be notified when new editions in the series become available, please contact
our Mail Order Department. Alternatively, please see our advertisements in Today's
Railways UK or Today's Railways Europe magazines for up to date publication information.

**Please add postage: 10% UK, 20% Europe, 30% Rest of World**

**Telephone, fax or send your order to the Platform 5 Mail Order
Department. See page 384 of this book for details.**

# 3. EUROTUNNEL LOCOMOTIVES

## DIESEL LOCOMOTIVES

### 0001–0005                    MaK                    Bo-Bo

**Built:** 1992–1993 by MaK at Kiel, Germany (Model DE1004).
**Engine:** MTU 12V 396 Tc of 1180 kW (1580 h.p.) at 1800 rpm.
**Main Alternator:** BBC.                **Traction Motors:** BBC.
**Maximum Tractive Effort:** 305 kN (68600 lbf).
**Continuous Tractive Effort:** 140 kN (31500 lbf) at 20 mph.
**Power At Rail:** 750 kW (1012 h.p.).
**Brake Force:** 120 kN.                  **Dimensions:** 16.50 x ?? x ?? m.
**Weight:** 84 t.                         **Wheel Diameter:** 1000 mm.
**Design Speed:** 120 km/h.               **Maximum Speed:** 120 km/h.
**Fuel Capacity:**                        **Train Brakes:** Air.
**Train Supply:** Not equipped.           **Multiple Working:** Within class.

| | | | |
|---|---|---|---|
| 0001 | **GY** | ET | EU |
| 0002 | **GY** | ET | EU |
| 0003 | **GY** | ET | EU |
| 0004 | **GY** | ET | EU |
| 0005 | **GY** | ET | EU |

### 0031–0042            HUNSLET/SCHÖMA            0-4-0

**Built:** 1989–1990 by Hunslet Engine Company at Leeds as 900 mm. gauge.
**Rebuilt:** 1993-1994 by Schöma in Germany to 1435 mm. gauge.
**Engine:** Deutz of 270 kW (200 h.p.) at ???? rpm.
**Transmission:** Mechanical.            **Maximum Tractive Effort:**
**Cont. Tractive Effort:**               **Power At Rail:**
**Brake Force:**                         **Dimensions:**
**Weight:**                              **Wheel Diameter:**
**Design Speed:** 50 km/h.               **Maximum Speed:** 50 km/h.
**Fuel Capacity:**                        **Train Brakes:** Air.
**Train Supply:** Not equipped.           **Multiple Working:** Not equipped.

| | | | | |
|---|---|---|---|---|
| 0031 | **Y** | ET | EU | FRANCES |
| 0032 | **Y** | ET | EU | ELISABETH |
| 0033 | **Y** | ET | EU | SILKE |
| 0034 | **Y** | ET | EU | AMANDA |
| 0035 | **Y** | ET | EU | MARY |
| 0036 | **Y** | ET | EU | LAWRENCE |
| 0037 | **Y** | ET | EU | LYDIE |
| 0038 | **Y** | ET | EU | JENNY |
| 0039 | **Y** | ET | EU | PACITA |
| 0040 | **Y** | ET | EU | JILL |
| 0041 | **Y** | ET | EU | KIM |
| 0042 | **Y** | ET | EU | NICOLE |

# ELECTRIC LOCOMOTIVES

## 9001–9113 BRUSH/ABB Bo-Bo-Bo

**Built:** 1993–2001 by Brush Traction at Loughborough.
**Supply System:** 25 kV AC 50 Hz overhead.
**Traction Motors:** ABB 6PH.
**Maximum Tractive Effort:** 400kN (90 000lbf).
**Continuous Rating:** 5760 kW (7725 h.p.) giving a TE of 310 kN at 65 km/h.
(\* Fleet being progressively upgraded to 7000 kW (9387 h.p.) and are also
being renumbered into the 98xx number series upon refurbishment).

| | |
|---|---|
| **Maximum Rail Power:** | **Multiple Working:** TDM system. |
| **Brake Force:** 50 t. | **Dimensions:** 22.01 x 2.97 x 4.20 m. |
| **Weight:** 132 t. | **Wheel Diameter:** 1090 mm. |
| **Design Speed:** 175 km/h (100 m.p.h.) | **Maximum Speed:** 160 km/h (87 m.p.h.) |
| **Train Supply:** Electric. | **Train Brakes:** Air. |

**CLASS 9/0 and CLASS 9/8. Mixed traffic locomotives.**

| | | | | |
|---|---|---|---|---|
| 9001 | | EB | ET | EU | LESLEY GARRETT |
| 9002 | | EB | ET | EU | STUART BURROWS |
| 9803 | \* | EB | ET | EU | BENJAMIN LUXON |
| 9804 | \* | EB | ET | EU | VICTORIA DE LOS ANGELES |
| 9005 | | EB | ET | EU | JESSYE NORMAN |
| 9006 | | EB | ET | EU | REGINE CRESPIN |
| 9007 | | EB | ET | EU | DAME JOAN SUTHERLAND |
| 9808 | \* | EB | ET | EU | ELISABETH SODERSTROM |
| 9809 | \* | EB | ET | EU | FRANÇOIS POLLET |
| 9810 | \* | EB | ET | EU | JEAN-PHILIPPE COURTIS |
| 9011 | | EB | ET | EU | JOSÉ VAN DAM |
| 9012 | | EB | ET | EU | LUCIANO PAVAROTTI |
| 9013 | | EB | ET | EU | MARIA CALLAS |
| 9814 | \* | EB | ET | EU | LUCIA POPP |
| 9015 | | EB | ET | EU | LÖTSCHBERG 1913 |
| 9016 | | EB | ET | EU | WILLARD WHITE |
| 9017 | | EB | ET | EU | JOSÉ CARRERAS |
| 9018 | | EB | ET | EU | WILHELMENA FERNANDEZ |
| 9819 | \* | EB | ET | EU | MARIA EWING |
| 9820 | \* | EB | ET | EU | Nicolai Ghiaurov |
| 9821 | \* | EB | ET | EU | TERESA BERGANZA |
| 9022 | | EB | ET | EU | DAME JANET BAKER |
| 9023 | | EB | ET | EU | DAME ELISABETH LEGGE-SCHWARZKOPF |
| 9024 | | EB | ET | EU | GOTTHARD 1882 |
| 9825 | \* | EB | ET | EU | |
| 9026 | | EB | ET | EU | FURKATUNNEL 1982 |
| 9027 | | EB | ET | EU | BARBARA HENDRICKS |
| 9828 | \* | EB | ET | EU | DAME KIRI TE KANAWA |
| 9029 | | EB | ET | EU | THOMAS ALLEN |
| 9031 | | EB | ET | EU | |
| 9032 | | EB | ET | EU | RENATA TEBALDI |

| 9033 |   | **EB** | ET | EU | MONTSERRAT CABALLE |
|------|---|--------|----|-----|--------------------|
| 9834 | * | **EB** | ET | EU | MIRELLA FRENI |
| 9035 |   | **EB** | ET | EU | Nicolai Gedda |
| 9036 |   | **EB** | ET | EU | ALAIN FONDARY |
| 9037 |   | **EB** | ET | EU | GABRIEL BACQUIER |
| 9038 |   | **EB** | ET | EU | HILDEGARD BEHRENS |
| 9040 |   | **EB** | ET | EU | |

**CLASS 9/1. Freight Shuttle dedicated locomotives.**

| 9101 | **EB** | ET | EU |
|------|--------|----|-----|
| 9102 | **EB** | ET | EU |
| 9103 | **EB** | ET | EU |
| 9104 | **EB** | ET | EU |
| 9105 | **EB** | ET | EU |
| 9106 | **EB** | ET | EU |
| 9107 | **EB** | ET | EU |
| 9108 | **EB** | ET | EU |
| 9109 | **EB** | ET | EU |
| 9110 | **EB** | ET | EU |
| 9111 | **EB** | ET | EU |
| 9112 | **EB** | ET | EU |
| 9113 | **EB** | ET | EU |

# 9701-9707   BRUSH/BOMBARDIER   Bo-Bo-Bo

**CLASS 9/7. Increased power freight shuttle dedicated locomotives.**

**Built:** 2001–2002 by Brush Traction at Loughborough.
**Supply System:** 25 kV AC 50 Hz overhead.
**Traction Motors:** ABB 6PH.
**Maximum Tractive Effort:** 400kN (90 000lbf).
**Continuous Rating:** 7000 kW (9387 h.p.).
**Maximum Rail Power:**
**Brake Force:** 50 t.
**Weight:** 132 t.
**Design Speed:** 175 km/h (100 m.p.h.)
**Train Supply:** Electric.

**Multiple Working:** TDM system.
**Dimensions:** 22.01 x 2.97 x 4.20 m.
**Wheel Diameter:** 1090 mm.
**Maximum Speed:** 160 km/h (87 m.p.h.)
**Train Brakes:** Air.

| 9701 | **EB** | ET | EU |
|------|--------|----|-----|
| 9702 | **EB** | ET | EU |
| 9703 | **EB** | ET | EU |
| 9704 | **EB** | ET | EU |
| 9705 | **EB** | ET | EU |
| 9706 | **EB** | ET | EU |
| 9707 | **EB** | ET | EU |

# PLATFORM 5 MAIL ORDER

## FREIGHTMASTER
### Freightmaster Publishing

Freightmaster is the Great Britain National Railfreight Timetable. It contains full timetable listings for over 80 key locations around the country, including dates of operation, train type and booked motive power for every train. Most locations feature 0700-2300 listings, with full 24 hour timetables for busy locations. Also includes a separate analysis of national freight flows. Well illustrated by a series of detailed maps.160 pages. **£12.95.**

**Note:** Freightmaster is published 4 times a year in January, April, July and October. Customers ordering this title will be supplied with the latest edition available unless requested otherwise.

## LINE BY LINE
### Freightmaster Publishing

Line by Line is a series of excellent guidebooks tracing the route of Britain's main line railways. Each page covers a five-mile section of route with gradient profiles, track layout diagrams and a black & white illustration provided for each section. Also includes a general overview of the line, a gallery section of colour photographs, several OS map reproductions and a table of distances in miles & chains. The following volumes are currently available:

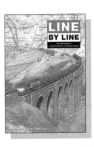

Line by Line: The West Coast Main Line ................................. £14.95
Line by Line: The Great Western Main Line ........................... £14.95
Line by Line: The East Coast Main Line ................................. £14.95
Line by Line: The Midland Route .......................................... £14.95

**Please add postage: 10% UK, 20% Europe, 30% Rest of World.**

**Telephone, fax or send your order to the Platform 5 Mail Order Department. See page 384 of this book for details.**

# 2. LOCO-HAULED PASSENGER COACHING STOCK

# INTRODUCTION

## LAYOUT OF INFORMATION

Coaches are listed in numerical order of painted number in batches according to type.

Each coach entry is laid out as in the following example (former number column may be omitted where not applicable):

| No. | Prev. No. | Notes | Livery | Owner | Operator | Depot/Location |
|-----|-----------|-------|--------|-------|----------|----------------|
| 42348 | (41073) | * | **FG** | A | *GW* | LA |

Note that the operator is the organisation which facilitates the use of the coach and may not be the actual train operating company which runs the train. For example coaches operated by Riviera Trains might run in trains which are operated by Arriva Trains Wales.

## DETAILED INFORMATION & CODES

Under each type heading, the following details are shown:

- 'Mark' of coach (see below).
- Descriptive text.
- Number of first class seats, standard class seats, lavatory compartments and wheelchair spaces shown as F/S nT nW respectively.
- Bogie type (see below).
- Additional features.
- ETH Index.

## TOPS TYPE CODES

TOPS type codes are allocated to all coaching stock. For vehicles numbered in the passenger stock number series the code consists of:

(1) Two letters denoting the layout of the vehicle as follows:

AA  Gangwayed Corridor
AB  Gangwayed Corridor Brake
AC  Gangwayed Open (2+2 seating)
AD  Gangwayed Open (2+1 seating)
AE  Gangwayed Open Brake
AF  Gangwayed Driving Open Brake
AG  Micro-Buffet

| AH | Brake Micro-Buffet |
|---|---|
| AI | As 'AC' but with drop-head buckeye and gangway at one end only |
| AJ | Restaurant Buffet with Kitchen |
| AK | Kitchen Car |
| AL | As 'AC' but with disabled person's toilet (Mark 4 only) |
| AN | Miniature Buffet |
| AP | Pullman First with Kitchen |
| AQ | Pullman Parlour First |
| AR | Pullman Brake First |
| AS | Sleeping Car |
| AT | Royal Train Coach |
| AU | Sleeping Car with Pantry |
| AV | Mark 4 Barrier Vehicle |
| AW | EMU Translator vehicle |
| AX | Generator Van (1000 V DC) |
| AZ | Special Saloon |
| GS | HST Barrier Vehicle |
| NW | Desiro Barrier Vehicle |

(2) A digit denoting the class of passenger accommodation:

| 1 First | 4 Unclassified |
|---|---|
| 2 Standard (formerly second) | 5 None |
| 3 Composite (first & standard) | |

(3) A suffix relating to the build of coach.

| 1 | Mark 1 | C | Mark 2C | G | Mark 3 or 3A |
|---|---|---|---|---|---|
| Z | Mark 2 | D | Mark 2D | H | Mark 3B |
| A | Mark 2A | E | Mark 2E | J | Mark 4 |
| B | Mark 2B | F | Mark 2F | | |

# OPERATING CODES

Operating codes used by train company operating staff (and others) to denote vehicle types in general. These are shown in parentheses adjacent to TOPS type codes. Letters used are:

| B Brake | K Side corridor with lavatory |
|---|---|
| C Composite | O Open |
| F First Class | S Standard Class (formerly second) |

Various other letters are in use and the meaning of these can be ascertained by referring to the titles at the head of each type.

Readers should note the distinction between an SO (Open Standard) and a TSO (Tourist Open Standard) The former has 2+1 seating layout, whilst the latter has 2+2.

# BOGIE TYPES

**BR Mark 1 (BR1).** Double bolster leaf spring bogie. Generally 90 m.p.h., but Mark 1 bogies may be permitted to run at 100 m.p.h. with special maintenance. Weight: 6.1 t.

**BR Mark 2 (BR2).** Single bolster leaf-spring bogie used on certain types of non-passenger stock and suburban stock (all now withdrawn). Weight: 5.3 t.

**COMMONWEALTH (C).** Heavy, cast steel coil spring bogie. 100 m.p.h. Weight: 6.75 t.

**B4.** Coil spring fabricated bogie. Generally 100 m.p.h., but B4 bogies may be permitted to run at 110 m.p.h. with special maintenance. Weight: 5.2 t.

**B5.** Heavy duty version of B4. 100 m.p.h. Weight: 5.3 t.

**B5 (SR).** A bogie originally used on Southern Region EMUs, similar in design to B5. Now also used on locomotive hauled coaches. 100 m.p.h.

**BT10.** A fabricated bogie designed for 125 m.p.h. Air suspension.

**T4.** A 125 m.p.h. bogie designed by BREL (now Bombardier Transportation).

**BT41.** Fitted to Mark 4 vehicles, designed by SIG in Switzerland. At present limited to 125 m.p.h., but designed for 140 m.p.h.

# BRAKES

Air braking is now standard on British main line trains. Vehicles with other equipment are denoted:

v    Vacuum braked.
x    Dual braked (air and vacuum).

# HEATING & VENTILATION

Electric heating and ventilation is now standard on British main-line trains. Certain coaches for use on charter services may also have steam heating facilities, or be steam heated only.

# PUBLIC ADDRESS

It is assumed all coaches are now fitted with public address equipment, although certain stored vehicles may not have this feature. In addition, it is assumed all vehicles with a conductor's compartment have public address transmission facilities, as have catering vehicles.

# COOKING EQUIPMENT

It is assumed that Mark 1 catering vehicles have gas powered cooking equipment, whilst Mark 2, 3 and 4 catering vehicles have electric powered cooking equipment unless stated otherwise.

# ADDITIONAL FEATURE CODES

d       Secondary door locking.
dg     Driver–Guard communication equipment.
f       Facelifted or fluorescent lighting.
k      Composition brake blocks (instead of cast iron).
n      Day/night lighting.
p      Public telephone.
pg     Public address transmission and driver-guard communication.

| pt | Public address transmission facility. |
| q | Catering staff to shore telephone. |
| w | Wheelchair space. |
| z | Disabled persons' toilet. |
| ★ | Blue star multiple working cables fitted. |

Standard class coaches with wheelchair space also have one tip-up seat per space.

# NOTES ON ETH INDICES

The sum of ETH indices in a train must not be more than the ETH index of the locomotive. The normal voltage on British trains is 1000 V. Suffix 'X' denotes 600 amp wiring instead of 400 amp. Trains whose ETH index is higher than 66 must be formed completely of 600 amp wired stock. Class 33 and 73 locomotives cannot provide a suitable electric train supply for Mark 2D, Mark 2E, Mark 2F, Mark 3, Mark 3A, Mark 3B or Mark 4 coaches. Class 55 locomotives provide an e.t.s. directly from one of their traction generators into the train line. Consequently voltage fluctuations can result in motor-alternator flashover. Thus these locomotives are not suitable for use with Mark 2D, Mark 2E, Mark 2F, Mark 3, Mark 3A, Mark 3B or Mark 4 coaches unless modified motor-alternators are fitted. Such motor alternators were fitted to Mark 2D and 2F coaches used on the East Coast main line, but few remain fitted.

# BUILD DETAILS

## Lot Numbers
Vehicles ordered under the auspices of BR were allocated a lot (batch) number when ordered and these are quoted in class headings and sub-headings.

## Builders
These are shown for each lot. Abbreviatios used are shown in section 7.8.

Information on sub-contracting works which built parts of vehicles e.g. the underframes etc. is not shown.

In addition to the above, certain vintage Pullman cars were built or rebuilt at the following works:

Metropolitan Carriage & Wagon Company, Birmingham (Now Alstom)
Midland Carriage & Wagon Company, Birmingham
Pullman Car Company, Preston Park, Brighton
Conversions have also been carried out at the Railway Technical Centre, Derby, LNWR, Crewe and Blakes Fabrications, Edinburgh.

## Vehicle Numbers
Where a coach has been renumbered, the former number is shown in parentheses. If a coach has been renumbered more than once, the original number is shown first in parentheses, followed by the most recent previous number. Where the former number of a coach due to be converted or renumbered is known and the conversion and/or renumbering has not yet taken place, the coach is listed under both current number (with depot allocation) and under new number (without allocation).

**Numbering Systems**

Seven different numbering systems were in use on BR. These were the BR series, the four pre-nationalisation companies' series', the Pullman Car Company's series and the UIC (International Union of Railways) series. BR number series coaches and former Pullman Car Company series are listed separately. There is also a separate listing of 'Saloon' type vehicles which are registered to run on National Rail. Please note the Mark 2 Pullman vehicles were ordered after the Pullman Car Company had been nationalised and are therefore numbered in the BR series.

# THE DEVELOPMENT OF BR STANDARD COACHES

The standard BR coach built from 1951 to 1963 was the Mark 1. This type features a separate underframe and body. The underframe is normally 64 ft. 6 in. long, but certain vehicles were built on shorter (57 ft.) frames. Tungsten lighting was standard and until 1961, BR Mark 1 bogies were generally provided. In 1959 Lot No. 30525 (TSO) appeared with fluorescent lighting and melamine interior panels, and from 1961 onwards Commonwealth bogies were fitted in an attempt to improve the quality of ride which became very poor when the tyre profiles on the wheels of the BR1 bogies became worn. Later batches of TSO and BSO retained the features of Lot No. 30525, but compartment vehicles – whilst utilising melamine panelling in standard class – still retained tungsten lighting. Wooden interior finish was retained in first class vehicles where the only change was to fluorescent lighting in open vehicles (except Lot No. 30648, which had tungsten lighting). In later years many Mark 1 coaches had BR 1 bogies replaced by B4.

In 1964, a new prototype train was introduced. Known as 'XP64', it featured new seat designs, pressure heating & ventilation, aluminium compartment doors and corridor partitions, foot pedal operated toilets and B4 bogies. The vehicles were built on standard Mark 1 underframes. Folding exterior doors were fitted, but these proved troublesome and were later replaced with hinged doors. All XP64 coaches have been withdrawn, but some have been preserved. The prototype Mark 2 vehicle (W 13252) was produced in 1963. This was an FK of semi-integral construction and had pressure heating & ventilation, tungsten lighting, and was mounted on B4 bogies. This vehicle has been preserved by the National Railway Museum and is currently stored at MoD Kineton DM. The production build was similar, but wider windows were used. The TSO and SO vehicles used a new seat design similar to that in the XP64 and fluorescent lighting was provided. Interior finish reverted to wood. Mark 2 vehicles were built from 1964–66.

The Mark 2A design, built 1967–68, incorporated the remainder of the features first used in the XP64 coaches, i.e. foot pedal operated toilets (except BSO), new first class seat design, aluminium compartment doors and partitions together with fluorescent lighting in first class compartments. Folding gangway doors (lime green coloured) were used instead of the traditional one-piece variety.

The following list summarises the changes made in the later Mark 2 variants:

**Mark 2B:** Wide wrap around doors at vehicle ends, no centre doors, slightly longer body. In standard class, one toilet at each end instead of two at one end as previously. Red folding gangway doors.

**Mark 2C:** Lowered ceiling with twin strips of fluorescent lighting and ducting for air conditioning, but air conditioning not fitted.

**Mark 2D:** Air conditioning. No opening top-lights in windows.

**Mark 2E:** Smaller toilets with luggage racks opposite. Fawn folding gangway doors.

**Mark 2F:** Plastic interior panels. Inter-City 70 type seats. Modified air conditioning system.

The Mark 3 design has BT10 bogies, is 75 ft. (23 m.) long and is of fully integral construction with Inter-City 70 type seats. Gangway doors were yellow (red in RFB) when new, although these are being changed on refurbishment. Loco-hauled coaches are classified Mark 3A, Mark 3 being reserved for HST trailers. A new batch of FO and BFO, classified Mark 3B, was built in 1985 with Advanced Passenger Train-style seating and revised lighting. The last vehicles in the Mark 3 series were the driving brake vans built for West Coast Main Line services.

The Mark 4 design was built by Metro-Cammell for use on the East Coast Main Line after electrification and features a body profile suitable for tilting trains, although tilt is not fitted, and is not intended to be. This design is suitable for 140 m.p.h. running, although is restricted to 125 m.p.h. because the signalling system on the route is not suitable for the higher speed. The bogies for these coaches were built by SIG in Switzerland and are designated BT41. Power operated sliding plug exterior doors are standard. All of these coaches and two spare vehicles have now been rebuilt with completely new interiors and are referred to as "Mallard stock" by GNER.

# 2.1. BR NUMBER SERIES STOCK PASSENGER STOCK

## AJ11 (RF)                              RESTAURANT FIRST

Mark 1. Spent most of its life as a Royal Train vehicle and was numbered 2907 for a time. Built with Commonwealth bogies, but B5 bogies substituted. 24/–. ETH 2.

Lot No. 30633 Swindon 1961. 41 t.

| 325 | **PC** | VS | *VS* | SL |

## AP1Z (PFK)        PULLMAN FIRST WITH KITCHEN

Mark 2. Pressure Ventilated. Seating removed and replaced with servery. 2T. B5 bogies. ETH 6.

Lot No. 30755 Derby 1966. 40 t.

| 504 | **PC** | WC | *WC* | CS | ULLSWATER |
| 506 | **PC** | WC | *WC* | CS | WINDERMERE |

## AQ1Z (PFP)                PULLMAN PARLOUR FIRST

Mark 2. Pressure Ventilated. 36/– 2T. B4 bogies. ETH 5.

**Non-standard livery:** 546 is maroon & beige.

Lot No. 30754 Derby 1966. 35 t.

| 546 | **O**  | WC |      | CS | CITY OF MANCHESTER |
| 548 | **PC** | WC | *WC* | CS | GRASMERE |
| 549 | **PC** | WC | *WC* | CS | BASSENTHWAITE LAKE |
| 550 | **PC** | WC | *WC* | CS | RYDAL WATER |
| 551 | **PC** | WC | *WC* | CS | BUTTERMERE |
| 552 | **PC** | WC | *WC* | CS | ENNERDALE WATER |
| 553 | **PC** | WC | *WC* | CS | CRUMMOCK WATER |

## AR1Z (PFB)                    PULLMAN BRAKE FIRST

Mark 2. Pressure Ventilated. 30/– 2T. B4 bogies. ETH 4.

Lot No. 30753 Derby 1966. 35 t.

| 586 | **PC** | WC | *WC* | CS | DERWENTWATER |

## AJ21 (RG)                                        GRIDDLE CAR

Mark 1. Rebuilt from RF. –/30. B5 bogies. ETH 2.

This vehicle was numbered DB975878 for a time when in departmental service for British Railways.

Lot No. 30013 Doncaster 1952. Rebuilt Wolverton 1965. 40 t.

| 1105 | (302) | v | **G** | MH | *MH* | RL |

## AJ1F (RFB)                                 BUFFET OPEN FIRST

Mark 2F. Air conditioned. Converted 1988–9/91 at BREL, Derby from Mark 2F FOs. 1200/1/3/6/11/14–16/20/21/50/2/5/6/9 have Stones equipment, others have Temperature Ltd. 25/– 1T 1W (except 1253 which is 26/– 1T). B4 bogies. d. ETH 6X.

**1200**/**3**/**6**/**11**/**14**/**16**/**20**/**52**/**5**/**6**. Lot No. 30845 Derby 1973. 33 t.
**1201**/**4**/**5**/**7**/**8**/**10**/**12**/**13**/**15**/**19**/**21**/**50**/**1**/**4**/**8**/**60**. Lot No. 30859 Derby 1973–74. 33 t.
**1202**/**9**/**53**/**9**. Lot No. 30873 Derby 1974–75. 33 t.

† Fitted with new m.a. sets.

| 1200 | (3287, 6459) | † | **RV** | H   | *RV* | CP |
| 1201 | (3361, 6445) |   | **V**  | H   |      | TM |
| 1202 | (3436, 6456) | † | **V**  | H   |      | KT |
| 1203 | (3291)       | † |        | H   | *RV* | CP |
| 1204 | (3401)       | † | **V**  | H   |      | PY |
| 1205 | (3329, 6438) | † | **Y**  | AE  |      | ZA |
| 1206 | (3319)       | † | **V**  | H   |      | KT |
| 1207 | (3328, 6422) | † | **V**  | H   |      | KT |
| 1208 | (3393)       |   | **V**  | H   |      | KT |
| 1209 | (3437, 6457) | † | **V**  | H   |      | ZH |
| 1210 | (3405, 6462) | † | **CP** | H   | *SR* | IS |
| 1211 | (3305)       |   |        | H   | *FM* | OY |
| 1212 | (3427, 6453) | † | **V**  | H   | *RV* | CP |
| 1213 | (3419)       | † | **V**  | DM  |      | MQ |
| 1214 | (3317, 6433) |   | **AR** | H   |      | KT |
| 1215 | (3377)       |   | **AR** | H   |      | KT |
| 1216 | (3302)       | † | **V**  | H   | *RV* | CP |
| 1219 | (3418)       |   | **AR** | H   |      | KT |
| 1220 | (3315, 6432) | † | **CS** | H   | *SR* | IS |
| 1221 | (3371)       |   |        | H   | *FM* | OY |
| 1250 | (3372)       | † | **V**  | H   | *RV* | CP |
| 1251 | (3383)       | † | **V**  | H   |      | KT |
| 1252 | (3280)       | † | **V**  | H   |      | KT |
| 1253 | (3432)       | † | **V**  | H   |      | KT |
| 1254 | (3391)       | † | **V**  | H   | *FM* | OY |
| 1255 | (3284)       | † | **V**  | H   |      | KT |
| 1256 | (3296)       | † |        | H   |      | MQ |
| 1258 | (3322)       | † | **V**  | H   | *RV* | CP |
| 1259 | (3439)       | † | **V**  | H   |      | KT |
| 1260 | (3378)       | † | **V**  | H   | *RV* | CP |

## AK51 (RKB)                               KITCHEN BUFFET

Mark 1. No seats. B5 bogies. ETH 1.

Lot No. 30624 Cravens 1960–61. 41 t.

1566      **VN** VS *VS* CP

## AJ41 (RBR)                         RESTAURANT BUFFET

Mark 1. Built with 23 loose chairs. All remaining vehicles refurbished with 23 fixed polypropylene chairs and fluorescent lighting. ETH 2 (2X*). 1683/92/99 were further refurbished with 21 chairs, wheelchair space and carpets.

s Modified for use as servery vehicle with seating removed.

**1646–1699.** Lot No. 30628 Pressed Steel 1960–61. Commonwealth bogies. 39 t.
**1730.** Lot No. 30512 BRCW 1960–61. B5 bogies. 37 t.

**Non-standard liveries:**

1651, 1683 and 1699 are Oxford blue.
1657 is Nanking blue.

| | | | | | | | | | |
|---|---|---|---|---|---|---|---|---|---|
| 1646 | | FM | | ZA | 1680 | *s | **GC** | E | *E* | OM |
| 1651 | **0** | RV | | CO | 1683 | s | **0** | RV | *RV* | CP |
| 1657 | s | **0** | FM | *FM* | EM | 1692 | s | **CH** | RV | *RV* | CP |
| 1658 | **BG** | E | *E* | OM | 1696 | | **G** | E | *E* | OM |
| 1659 | s | **PC** | RA | *WT* | OM | 1698 | s | **GC** | E | *E* | OM |
| 1671 | x* | **M** | E | *E* | OM | 1699 | s | **0** | RV | *RV* | CP |
| 1679 | s | **GC** | E | *E* | OM | 1730 | x | **M** | BK | *BK* | BT |

## AN2F (RSS)              SELF-SERVICE BUFFET CAR

Mark 2F. Air conditioned. Temperature Ltd. equipment. Inter-City 70 seats. Converted 1974 from a Mark 2F TSO as a prototype self-service buffet for APT-P. Sold to Northern Ireland Railways 1983 and regauged to 5'3". Since withdrawn, repatriated to Great Britain and converted back to standard gauge. –/24. B5 bogies. ETH 12X.

Lot No. 30860 Derby 1973–74. 33 t.

1800    (5970, NIR546)    **PC** WT *WT* OM

## AN21 (RMB)               MINIATURE BUFFET CAR

Mark 1. –/44 2T. These vehicles are basically an open standard with two full window spaces removed to accommodate a buffet counter, and four seats removed to allow for a stock cupboard. All remaining vehicles now have fluorescent lighting. Commonwealth bogies. ETH 3.

**1813–1832.** Lot No. 30520 Wolverton 1960. 38 t.
**1840–1842.** Lot No. 30507 Wolverton 1960. 37 t.
**1859–1863.** Lot No. 30670 Wolverton 1961–62. 38 t.
**1882.** Lot No. 30702 Wolverton 1962. 38 t.

1842 is refurbished and fitted with a microwave oven.

| | | | | | | | | | | |
|---|---|---|---|---|---|---|---|---|---|---|
| 1813 | x | **M** | E | *E* | OM | 1860 | x | **M** | WC *WC* | CS |
| 1832 | x | **G** | E | *E* | OM | 1861 | x | **M** | WC *WC* | CS |
| 1840 | v | **G** | FM | *FM* | RL | 1863 | x | **CH** | RV *RV* | CP |
| 1842 | x | **CH** | RV | *RV* | CP | 1882 | x | **M** | WC *WC* | CS |
| 1859 | x | **M** | BK | *BK* | BT | | | | | |

## AJ41 (RBR)      RESTAURANT BUFFET

Mark 1. These vehicles were built as unclassified restaurant (RU). They were rebuilt with buffet counters and 23 fixed polypropylene chairs (RBS), then further refurbished by fitting fluorescent lighting and reclassified RBR. ETH 2X.

s Modified for use as servery vehicle with seating removed.

**1953.** Lot No. 30575 Swindon 1960. B4/B5 bogies. 36.5 t.
**1961.** Lot No. 30632 Swindon 1961. Commonwealth bogies. 39 t.

**Non-standard livery:** 1961 is Nanking blue.

| | | | | | | | | | | |
|---|---|---|---|---|---|---|---|---|---|---|
| 1953 | s | **VN** | VS | *VS* | CP | 1961 | x | **0** | FM *FM* | EM |

## AU51     CHARTER TRAIN STAFF COACHES

Mark 1. Converted from BCKs in 1988. Commonwealth bogies. ETH 2.

Lot No. 30732 Derby 1964. 37 t.

| | | | | | |
|---|---|---|---|---|---|
| 2833 | (21270) | **BG** | E | *E* | OM |
| 2834 | (21267) | **GC** | E | *E* | OM |

## AT5G      HM THE QUEEN'S SALOON

Mark 3. Converted from a FO built 1972. Consists of a lounge, bedroom and bathroom for HM The Queen, and a combined bedroom and bathroom for the Queen's dresser. One entrance vestibule has double doors. Air conditioned. BT10 bogies. ETH 9X.

Lot No. 30886 Wolverton 1977. 36 t.

| | | | | | |
|---|---|---|---|---|---|
| 2903 | (11001) | **RP** | NR | *RP* | ZN |

## AT5G   HRH THE DUKE OF EDINBURGH'S SALOON

Mark 3. Converted from a TSO built 1972. Consists of a combined lounge/dining room, a bedroom and a shower room for the Duke, a kitchen and a valet's bedroom and bathroom. Air conditioned. BT10 bogies. ETH 15X.

Lot No. 30887 Wolverton 1977. 36 t.

| | | | | | |
|---|---|---|---|---|---|
| 2904 | (12001) | **RP** | NR | *RP* | ZN |

## AT5G        ROYAL HOUSEHOLD SLEEPING CAR

Mark 3A. Built to similar specification as SLE 10646–732. 12 sleeping compartments for use of Royal Household with a fixed lower berth and a hinged upper berth. 2T plus shower room. Air conditioned. BT10 bogies. ETH 11X.

Lot No. 31002 Derby/Wolverton 1985. 44 t.

2915                 **RP**      NR      *RP*      ZN

## AT5G HRH THE PRINCE OF WALES'S DINING CAR

Mark 3. Converted from HST TRUK built 1976. Large kitchen retained, but dining area modified for Royal use seating up to 14 at central table(s). Air conditioned. BT10 bogies. ETH 13X.

Lot No. 31059 Wolverton 1988. 43 t.

2916   (40512)      **RP**  NR *RP*      ZN

## AT5G  ROYAL KITCHEN/HOUSEHOLD DINING CAR

Mark 3. Converted from HST TRUK built 1977. Large kitchen retained and dining area slightly modified with seating for 22 Royal Household members. Air conditioned. BT10 bogies. ETH 13X.

Lot No. 31084 Wolverton 1990. 43 t.

2917   (40514)      **RP**  NR *RP*      ZN

## AT5G                          ROYAL HOUSEHOLD CARS

Mark 3. Converted from HST TRUKs built 1976/7. Air conditioned. BT10 bogies. ETH 10X.

Lot Nos. 31083 (31085*) Wolverton 1989. 41.05 t.

2918   (40515)      **RP**  NR            ZN
2919   (40518)   *  **RP**  NR            ZN

## AT5B              ROYAL HOUSEHOLD COUCHETTES

Mark 2B. Converted from BFK built 1969. Consists of luggage accommodation, guard's compartment, workshop area, 350 kW diesel generator and staff sleeping accommodation. B5 bogies. ETH2X.

Lot No. 31044 Wolverton 1986. 48 t.

2920   (14109, 17109)      **RP**  NR *RP*      ZN

Mark 2B. Converted from BFK built 1969. Consists of luggage accommodation, kitchen, brake control equipment and staff accommodation. B5 bogies. ETH7X.

Lot No. 31086 Wolverton 1990. 41.5 t.

2921   (14107, 17107)      **RP**  NR *RP*      ZN

# AT5G HRH THE PRINCE OF WALES'S SLEEPING CAR

Mark 3B. BT10 bogies. Air conditioned. ETH 7X.

Lot No. 31035 Derby/Wolverton 1987.

| 2922 | **RP** | NR | *RP* | ZN |
|------|--------|----|------|-----|

# AT5G                                      ROYAL SALOON

Mark 3B. BT10 bogies. Air conditioned. ETH 6X.

Lot No. 31036 Derby/Wolverton 1987.

| 2923 | **RP** | NR | *RP* | ZN |
|------|--------|----|------|-----|

# AD11 (FO)                                      OPEN FIRST

Mark 1. 42/– 2T. ETH 3. Many now fitted with table lamps.

**3066–3069.** Lot No. 30169 Doncaster 1955. B4 bogies. 33 t.
**3096–3100.** Lot No. 30576 BRCW 1959. B4 bogies. 33 t.

3068 was numbered DB 975606 for a time when in departmental service for BR.

| 3066 | | **RV** | RV | *RV* | CP | | 3097 | | **GC** | E | *E* | OM |
|------|---|--------|----|------|-----|---|------|---|--------|----|------|-----|
| 3068 | | **RV** | RV | *RV* | CP | | 3098 | x | **CH** | RV | *RV* | CP |
| 3069 | | **RV** | RV | *RV* | CP | | 3100 | x | **M** | E | *E* | OM |
| 3096 | x | **M** | BK | *BK* | BT | | | | | | | |

Later design with fluorescent lighting, aluminium window frames and
Commonwealth bogies.

**3105–3128.** Lot No. 30697 Swindon 1962–63. 36 t.
**3130–3150.** Lot No. 30717 Swindon 1963. 36 t.

3128/36/41/3/4/6/7/8 were renumbered 1058/60/3/5/6/8/9/70 when reclassified
RUO, then 3600/5/8/9/2/6/4/10 when declassified to SO, but have since regained
their original numbers. 3136 was numbered DB977970 for a time when in use
with Serco Railtest as a Brake Force Runner.

| 3105 | x | **M** | WC | *WC* | CS | | 3128 | x | **M** | WC | *WC* | CS |
|------|---|-------|----|------|-----|---|------|---|-------|----|------|-----|
| 3107 | x | **CH** | RV | *RV* | CP | | 3130 | v | **M** | WC | *WC* | CS |
| 3110 | x | **M** | E | *E* | OM | | 3131 | x | **M** | E | *E* | OM |
| 3112 | x | **CH** | RV | *RV* | CP | | 3132 | x | **M** | E | *E* | OM |
| 3113 | x | **M** | WC | *WC* | CS | | 3133 | x | **M** | E | *E* | OM |
| 3114 | | **G** | E | *E* | BN | | 3136 | | **M** | WC | *WC* | CS |
| 3115 | x | **M** | BK | | BT | | 3140 | x | **CH** | RV | *RV* | CP |
| 3117 | x | **M** | WC | *WC* | CS | | 3141 | | **GC** | E | *E* | OM |
| 3119 | x | **GC** | E | *E* | OM | | 3143 | | **M** | WC | *WC* | CS |
| 3120 | | **GC** | E | *E* | OM | | 3144 | x | **M** | E | | OM |
| 3121 | | **GC** | E | *E* | OM | | 3146 | | **GC** | E | *E* | OM |
| 3122 | x | **CH** | RV | *RV* | CP | | 3147 | | **GC** | E | *E* | OM |
| 3123 | | **GC** | E | *E* | OM | | 3148 | | **BG** | RV | *RV* | CP |
| 3124 | | **G** | E | *E* | OM | | 3149 | | **GC** | E | *E* | OM |
| 3127 | | **G** | E | *E* | OM | | 3150 | | **G** | BK | | BT |

# AD1D (FO)                                           OPEN FIRST

Mark 2D. Air conditioned. Stones equipment. 42/– 2T. B4 bogies. ETH 5.

† Interior modified to resemble a Pullman Car with new seating, tungsten lighting and table lights for VSOE "Northern Belle".

Lot No. 30821 Derby 1971–72. 34 t.

| | | | | | | | | | |
|---|---|---|---|---|---|---|---|---|---|
| 3174 | † | **VN** | VS | *VS* | CP | 3186 | | MA | DY |
| 3181 | | **RV** | RV | | CD | 3188 | **RV** | RV | CD |
| 3182 | † | **VN** | VS | *VS* | CP | | | | |

# AD1E (FO)                                           OPEN FIRST

Mark 2E. Air conditioned. Stones equipment. 42/– 2T (41/– 2T 1W w, 36/– 2T p). B4 bogies. ETH 5.

r Refurbished with new seats.
u Fitted with power supply for Mk. 1 RBR.
† Interior modified to resemble a Pullman Car with new seating, tungsten lighting and table lights for VSOE "Northern Belle".

3255 was numbered 3525 for a time when fitted with a pantry.

Lot No. 30843 Derby 1972–73. 32.5 t. (35.8 t. †).

| | | | | | | | | | | | |
|---|---|---|---|---|---|---|---|---|---|---|---|
| 3223 | | **RV** | RV | *RV* | CP | 3247 | † | **VN** | VS | *VS* | CP |
| 3228 | du | **RV** | H | *RV* | CP | 3255 | dr | **M** | E | | OM |
| 3229 | d | **RV** | H | *RV* | CP | 3261 | dw | **FP** | H | | CD |
| 3231 | p | **PC** | RA | *WT* | OM | 3267 | † | **VN** | VS | *VS* | CP |
| 3232 | dr | **FP** | H | *GW* | OO | 3269 | dr | **M** | E | *E* | OM |
| 3240 | | **RV** | RV | *RV* | CP | 3273 | † | **VN** | VS | *VS* | CP |
| 3241 | dr | **FP** | H | *GW* | OO | 3275 | † | **VN** | VS | *VS* | CP |
| 3244 | d | **RV** | H | *RV* | CP | | | | | | |

# AD1F (FO)                                           OPEN FIRST

Mark 2F. Air conditioned. 3277–3318/58–81 have Stones equipment, others have Temperature Ltd. 42/– 2T. All now refurbished with power-operated vestibule doors, new panels and new seat trim. B4 bogies. d. ETH 5X.

**3277–3318**. Lot No. 30845 Derby 1973. 33.5 t.
**3325–3426**. Lot No. 30859 Derby 1973–74. 33.5 t.
**3429–3438**. Lot No. 30873 Derby 1974–75. 33.5 t.

r Further refurbished with table lamps, modified seats with burgundy seat trim and new m.a. sets.
s Further refurbished with table lamps and modified seats with burgundy seat trim.
u Fitted with power supply for Mk. 1 RBR.

| | | | | | | | | | | | |
|---|---|---|---|---|---|---|---|---|---|---|---|
| 3277 | | **AR** | H | *1A* | NC | 3285 | s | **BP** | H | *FM* | EM |
| 3278 | r | **BP** | H | *FM* | EM | 3292 | | **M** | E | *E* | OM |
| 3279 | u | **AR** | E | | TO | 3295 | | **AR** | H | *1A* | NC |

| No | | Owner | | | Depot |
|---|---|---|---|---|---|
| 3299 | r | V | H | | KT |
| 3300 | s | V | H | | TH |
| 3303 | | AR | H | 1A | NC |
| 3304 | r | V | H | RV | CP |
| 3309 | | | H | 1A | NC |
| 3312 | | | H | FM | OY |
| 3313 | r | BP | FM | FM | EM |
| 3314 | r | V | H | RV | CP |
| 3318 | | M | E | E | OM |
| 3325 | r | V | H | RV | CP |
| 3326 | r | BP | FM | FM | EM |
| 3330 | r | V | H | RV | CP |
| 3331 | | AR | H | | NC |
| 3333 | r | V | H | RV | CP |
| 3334 | r | V | H | 1A | NC |
| 3336 | u | AR | H | 1A | NC |
| 3337 | r | V | H | | TH |
| 3338 | u | AR | H | | NC |
| 3340 | r | V | H | RV | CP |
| 3344 | r | V | H | RV | CP |
| 3345 | r | V | H | RV | CP |
| 3348 | r | V | H | RV | CP |
| 3350 | r | BP | FM | FM | EM |
| 3351 | | AR | H | 1A | NC |
| 3352 | r | BP | FM | FM | EM |
| 3353 | s | V | DM | | MQ |
| 3354 | s | V | DM | | MQ |
| 3356 | r | V | H | RV | CP |
| 3358 | | AR | E | | TO |
| 3359 | s | V | FM | FM | OY |
| 3360 | s | | FM | FM | OY |
| 3362 | s | | FM | FM | OY |
| 3364 | r | V | H | RV | CP |
| 3366 | s | V | H | FM | OY |
| 3368 | | M | E | E | OM |
| 3373 | | | H | | BR |
| 3374 | | | H | FM | OY |
| 3375 | | AR | H | 1A | NC |
| 3379 | u | AR | H | 1A | NC |
| 3381 | | | H | | Bramley |
| 3384 | r | V | H | RV | CP |
| 3385 | r | V | H | FM | OY |
| 3386 | r | V | H | RV | CP |
| 3387 | s | V | DM | | MQ |
| 3388 | | AR | H | | NC |
| 3390 | r | V | H | RV | CP |
| 3392 | r | BP | FM | FM | EM |
| 3395 | r | V | H | FM | OY |
| 3397 | r | V | H | RV | CP |
| 3399 | u | M | E | E | OM |
| 3400 | | M | E | E | OM |
| 3402 | s | V | DM | | MQ |
| 3408 | s | V | FM | FM | OY |
| 3411 | s | V | DM | | MQ |
| 3414 | | AR | H | | NC |
| 3416 | | | H | 1A | NC |
| 3417 | | AR | H | 1A | NC |
| 3424 | | AR | H | 1A | NC |
| 3425 | s | V | DM | | MQ |
| 3426 | r | V | H | RV | CP |
| 3429 | r | V | H | | TH |
| 3431 | r | BP | FM | FM | EM |
| 3433 | r | V | H | | PY |
| 3438 | s | V | H | | CT |

## AG1E (FO (T))                 OPEN FIRST (PANTRY)

Mark 2E. Air conditioned. Converted from FO. Fitted with pantry containing microwave oven and space for a trolley. 36/– 2T. B4 bogies. d. ETH 5X.

Lot No. 30843 Derby 1972–73. 32.5 t.

| | | | | | | | | | |
|---|---|---|---|---|---|---|---|---|---|
| 3520 | (3253) | FP | H | | BR | 3523 | (3238) | H | BR |
| 3521 | (3271) | AR | H | | BR | 3524 | (3254) | H | BR |
| 3522 | (3236) | FP | H | | BR | | | | |

## AC21 (TSO)                 OPEN STANDARD

Mark 1. These vehicles have 2+2 seating and are classified TSO ('Tourist second open'– a former LNER designation). –/64 2T. ETH 4.

**3766.** Lot No. 30079 York 1953. Commonwealth bogies (originally built with BR Mark 1 bogies). This coach has narrower seats than later vehicles. 36 t.

| | | | | | |
|---|---|---|---|---|---|
| 3766 | x | M | WC | WC | CS |

## AC21 (TSO)                              OPEN STANDARD

Mark 1. These vehicles are a development of the above with fluorescent lighting and modified design of seat headrest. Built with BR Mark 1 bogies. –/64 2T. ETH 4.

**4831–4836.** Lot No. 30506 Wolverton 1959. Commonwealth bogies. 33 t.
**4856.** Lot No. 30525 Wolverton 1959–60. B4 bogies. 33 t.

| | | | | | | | | | | | |
|---|---|---|---|---|---|---|---|---|---|---|---|
| 4831 | x | **M** | BK | *BK* | BT | | 4836 | x | **M** | BK | *BK* | BT |
| 4832 | x | **M** | BK | *BK* | BT | | 4856 | x | **M** | BK | *BK* | BT |

Lot No. 30646 Wolverton 1961. Built with Commonwealth bogies, but BR Mark 1 bogies substituted by the SR. All now re-rebogied. 34 t B4, 36 t C.

| | | | | | | | | | | | |
|---|---|---|---|---|---|---|---|---|---|---|---|
| 4902 | x B4 | **CH** | RV | *RV* | CP | | 4912 | x C | **M** | WC | *WC* | CS |
| 4905 | x C | **M** | WC | *WC* | CS | | | | | | | |

Lot No. 30690 Wolverton 1961–62. Commonwealth bogies and aluminium window frames. 37 t.

| | | | | | | | | | | | |
|---|---|---|---|---|---|---|---|---|---|---|---|
| 4925 | | **G** | E | *E* | OM | | 4994 | x | **M** | WC | *WC* | CS |
| 4927 | x | **CH** | RV | *RV* | CP | | 4996 | x | **M** | E | *E* | OM |
| 4931 | v | **M** | WC | *WC* | CS | | 4998 | | **BG** | E | *E* | OM |
| 4940 | x | **M** | WC | *WC* | CS | | 4999 | | **BG** | E | | CD |
| 4946 | x | **M** | E | *E* | OM | | 5005 | | **BG** | E | *E* | OM |
| 4949 | x | **M** | E | *E* | OM | | 5007 | | **G** | E | *E* | OM |
| 4951 | | **M** | WC | *WC* | CS | | 5008 | x | **M** | E | *E* | OM |
| 4954 | v | **M** | WC | *WC* | CS | | 5009 | x | **CH** | RV | *RV* | CP |
| 4956 | | **BG** | E | *E* | OM | | 5023 | | **G** | E | *E* | OM |
| 4958 | v | **M** | WC | *WC* | CS | | 5027 | | **G** | E | *E* | OM |
| 4959 | | **BG** | E | | OM | | 5028 | x | **M** | BK | *BK* | BT |
| 4960 | x | **M** | WC | *WC* | CS | | 5032 | x | **M** | WC | *WC* | CS |
| 4973 | x | **M** | WC | *WC* | CS | | 5033 | x | **M** | WC | *WC* | CS |
| 4977 | | **G** | E | | BN | | 5035 | x | **M** | WC | *WC* | CS |
| 4984 | x | **M** | WC | *WC* | CS | | 5037 | | **G** | E | *E* | OM |
| 4986 | | **G** | E | *E* | OM | | 5040 | x | **CH** | RV | *RV* | CP |
| 4991 | | **BG** | E | *E* | OM | | 5044 | x | **M** | WC | *WC* | CS |

## AC2Z (TSO)                              OPEN STANDARD

Mark 2. Pressure ventilated. –/64 2T. B4 bogies. ETH 4.

Lot No. 30751 Derby 1965–67. 32 t.

| | | | | | | | | | | | |
|---|---|---|---|---|---|---|---|---|---|---|---|
| 5125 | v | **G** | FM | *FM* | RL | | 5191 | v | **CH** | H | *VT* | TM |
| 5141 | v | **G** | FM | | RL | | 5193 | v | **LN** | H | | TM |
| 5148 | v | **RR** | H | | TM | | 5194 | v | **RR** | H | | TM |
| 5157 | v | **CH** | H | *VT* | TM | | 5198 | v | **CH** | H | *VT* | TM |
| 5171 | v | **G** | FM | *FM* | RL | | 5199 | v | **G** | FM | | RL |
| 5177 | v | **CH** | H | *VT* | TM | | 5200 | v | **G** | FM | *FM* | RL |
| 5179 | v | **RR** | H | | TM | | 5212 | v | **LN** | H | | TM |
| 5183 | v | **RR** | H | | TM | | 5216 | v | **G** | FM | *FM* | RL |
| 5186 | v | **RR** | H | | TM | | 5221 | v | **RR** | H | | TM |

5222 v **G** FM *FM* RL |

## AD2Z (SO)      OPEN STANDARD

Mark 2. Pressure ventilated. –/48 2T. B4 bogies. ETH 4.

Lot No. 30752 Derby 1966. 32 t.

| | | | | | | | | | | |
|---|---|---|---|---|---|---|---|---|---|---|
| 5229 | | **PC** | WT | *WT* | OM | | 5239 | **PC** | WT | *WT* | OM |
| 5236 | v | **G** | FM | *FM* | RL | | 5249 | v **G** | FM | *FM* | RL |
| 5237 | v | **G** | FM | *FM* | RL | | | | | | |

## AC2A (TSO)      OPEN STANDARD

Mark 2A. Pressure ventilated. –/64 2T (–/62 2T w). B4 bogies. ETH 4.

**5276–5341.** Lot No. 30776 Derby 1967–68. 32 t.
**5350–5419.** Lot No. 30787 Derby 1968. 32 t.

f Facelifted vehicles.

| | | | | | | | | | | | |
|---|---|---|---|---|---|---|---|---|---|---|---|
| 5276 | f | **RV** | RV | *RV* | CP | | 5341 | f | **RV** | RV | *RV* | CP |
| 5278 | | **PC** | WT | *WT* | OM | | 5365 | | **RV** | RV | *RV* | CP |
| 5292 | f | **RV** | RV | *RV* | CP | | 5366 | f | **RV** | RV | *RV* | CP |
| 5299 | | **M** | WC | *WC* | CS | | 5376 | | **RV** | RV | *RV* | CP |
| 5309 | | **CH** | RV | | CP | | 5386 | w | **M** | E | | OM |
| 5322 | f | **RV** | RV | *RV* | CP | | 5412 | w | **M** | BK | *BK* | BT |
| 5331 | | **M** | E | | OM | | 5419 | w | **PC** | WT | *WT* | OM |

## AC2B (TSO)      OPEN STANDARD

Mark 2B. Pressure ventilated. –/62 2T. B4 bogies. ETH 4.

Note: 5482 was numbered DB977936 for a time when in departmental service for British Railways.

Lot No. 30791 Derby 1969. 32 t.

| | | | | | | | | | | | |
|---|---|---|---|---|---|---|---|---|---|---|---|
| 5453 | d | **M** | WC | *WC* | CS | | 5482 | | **M** | RP | *E* | OM |
| 5463 | d | **M** | WC | *WC* | CS | | 5487 | d | **M** | WC | *WC* | CS |
| 5478 | d | **M** | WC | *WC* | CS | | 5491 | d | **M** | WC | *WC* | CS |

## AC2C (TSO)      OPEN STANDARD

Mark 2C. Pressure ventilated. –/62 2T. B4 bogies. ETH 4.

Lot No. 30795 Derby 1969–70. 32 t.

| | | | | | | | | | |
|---|---|---|---|---|---|---|---|---|---|
| 5569 | d | **M** | WC | *WC* | CS | | 5600 | **M** | WC | CS |

## AC2D (TSO)      OPEN STANDARD

Mark 2D. Air conditioned. Stones equipment. –/62 2T. B4 bogies. ETH 5.

r Refurbished with new seats and end luggage stacks. –/58 2T.

Lot No. 30822 Derby 1971. 33 t.

| | | | | | |
|---|---|---|---|---|---|
| 5631 | dr | **M** | E | *E* | OM |
| 5632 | dr | **M** | E | *E* | OM |
| 5636 | dr | **FP** | H | *GW* | OO |
| 5647 | | **RV** | RV | | CD |
| 5657 | dr | **M** | E | | OM |
| 5669 | dr | **FP** | H | *GW* | OO |
| 5679 | dr | **FP** | H | *GW* | OO |
| 5700 | dr | **FP** | H | *GW* | OO |
| 5704 | | **M** | WC | | CS |
| 5710 | dr | **FP** | H | *GW* | OO |
| 5714 | | **M** | WC | | CS |
| 5727 | | **M** | WC | | CS |
| 5737 | dr | **FP** | H | *GW* | OO |
| 5740 | dr | **FP** | H | *GW* | OO |

# AC2E (TSO)                                         OPEN STANDARD

Mark 2E. Air conditioned. Stones equipment. –/64 2T (w –/62 2T 1W). B4 bogies. d (except 5756). ETH 5.

**5744–5801.** Lot No. 30837 Derby 1972. 33.5 t.
**5810–5906.** Lot No. 30844 Derby 1972–73. 33.5 t.

r Refurbished with new interior panelling.
s Refurbished with new interior panelling, modified design of seat headrest and centre luggage stack. –/60 2T (w –/58 2T 1W).
t Refurbished with new interior panelling and new seats.

| | | | | | |
|---|---|---|---|---|---|
| 5744 | | **FP** | H | | BR |
| 5745 | s | **V** | H | | KT |
| 5746 | r | **V** | H | | KT |
| 5748 | r pt | | H | *RV* | CP |
| 5750 | s | **V** | H | | KT |
| 5752 | wrpt | | H | *RV* | CP |
| 5754 | ws | **V** | H | | KT |
| 5756 | | **M** | WC | | CS |
| 5769 | r | | H | *RV* | CP |
| 5773 | s pt | **V** | H | *RV* | CP |
| 5775 | s | **V** | H | | KT |
| 5776 | r | | H | *RV* | CP |
| 5778 | | **AR** | H | | KT |
| 5779 | r | | H | *FM* | OY |
| 5780 | | **AR** | H | | CT |
| 5784 | r | **V** | H | | KT |
| 5787 | s | **V** | H | | KT |
| 5788 | r | | H | *FM* | OY |
| 5789 | r pt | | H | *FM* | OY |
| 5791 | wr | | H | *RV* | CP |
| 5792 | r | | H | *RV* | CP |
| 5793 | wspt | **V** | H | | KT |
| 5794 | wr | | H | *RV* | CP |
| 5796 | wr | | H | *RV* | CP |
| 5797 | r★ | | H | *FM* | BH |
| 5800 | | **AR** | H | | CT |
| 5801 | r | **V** | H | | KT |
| 5810 | s | **V** | H | | KT |
| 5812 | wr | | H | *FM* | OY |
| 5814 | r | | H | | CP |
| 5815 | ws | **V** | H | | KT |
| 5816 | r pt | | H | | CP |
| 5821 | r pt | **V** | H | | KT |
| 5822 | wspt | **V** | H | | KT |
| 5824 | rw | | H | *FM* | OY |
| 5827 | r | | H | *FM* | OY |
| 5828 | ws | **V** | H | | KT |
| 5831 | | **AR** | H | | CT |
| 5836 | | **AR** | H | | CT |
| 5843 | rw | | H | *RV* | CP |
| 5845 | s | **V** | H | | KT |
| 5847 | rw | **V** | H | | KT |
| 5852 | | **AR** | H | | CT |
| 5853 | t | **M** | WC | *WC* | CS |
| 5859 | s | **V** | H | | KT |
| 5863 | | **AR** | H | *1A* | NC |
| 5866 | r pt★ | | H | *FM* | BH |
| 5868 | s pt | **V** | H | | KT |
| 5869 | t | **M** | WC | *WC* | CS |
| 5874 | t | **M** | WC | *WC* | CS |
| 5876 | s pt | **V** | H | | KT |
| 5881 | ws | **V** | H | | KT |
| 5886 | s | **V** | H | | KT |
| 5887 | wr | **AR** | H | *1A* | NC |
| 5888 | wr | | H | *FM* | OY |
| 5889 | s | **V** | H | | KT |
| 5893 | s | **V** | H | | KT |
| 5897 | r | | H | *FM* | OY |
| 5899 | s | **V** | H | | KT |
| 5900 | wspt | **V** | H | | KT |
| 5901 | s | **V** | H | | KT |
| 5902 | s | **V** | H | | KT |

| 5903 | s |  | **V** | H |  |  | KT |  | 5906 | wspt★ |  |  | H | *FM* | BH |
|------|---|--|-------|---|--|--|----|--|------|-------|--|--|---|------|----|
| 5905 | s |  | **V** | H | *RV* |  | CP |  |      |       |  |  |   |      |    |

# AC2F (TSO)                                             OPEN STANDARD

Mark 2F. Air conditioned. Temperature Ltd. equipment. Inter-City 70 seats. All were refurbished in the 1980s with power-operated vestibule doors, new panels and new seat trim. –/64 2T. (w –/62 2T 1W) B4 bogies. d. ETH 5X.

**5908–5958.** Lot No. 30846 Derby 1973. 33 t.
**5959–6170.** Lot No. 30860 Derby 1973–74. 33 t.
**6171–6184.** Lot No. 30874 Derby 1974–75. 33 t.

\* Early Mark 2 style seats.

These vehicles have undergone a second refurbishment with carpets and new seat trim.
r Standard refurbished vehicles with new m.a. sets.

**Former Cross-Country vehicles:**

s Also fitted with centre luggage stack. –/60 2T.
t Also fitted with centre luggage stack and wheelchair space. –/58 2T 1W.

**Former West Coast vehicles:**

u As 'r' but with two wheelchair spaces. –/60 2T 2W.
† Standard refurbished vehicles with new seat trim.

| | | | | | | | | | | | |
|------|------|-----|-----|------|----|--|------|------|-----|-----|------|----|
| 5908 | r    | **V** | H  |      | KT |  | 5937 | r    | **V** | H  | *RV* | CP |
| 5910 | u    | **V** | H  | *AW* | CF |  | 5939 | r    | **V** | H  |      | PY |
| 5911 | s    | **V** | RV | *RV* | CP |  | 5940 | u    | **V** | H  |      | KT |
| 5912 | s    | **V** | H  | *FM* | OY |  | 5941 | r    | **V** | H  | *RV* | CP |
| 5913 | s    | **M** | WC | *WC* | CS |  | 5943 | rw   | **V** | H  |      | KT |
| 5914 | u    | **V** | H  |      | KT |  | 5944 |      | **AR** | H | *1A* | NC |
| 5915 | r    | **V** | H  |      | PY |  | 5945 | r    | **V** | H  | *RV* | CP |
| 5916 | t    |      | H  |      | KT |  | 5946 | r    | **V** | H  | *RV* | CP |
| 5917 | s    | **V** | H  |      | KT |  | 5947 | s pt | **V** | H  |      | KT |
| 5918 | t    | **V** | H  |      | KT |  | 5948 | u    | **V** | H  | *FM* | OY |
| 5919 | s pt | **V** | H  | *FM* | OY |  | 5949 | u    | **V** | H  |      | KT |
| 5920 | †    | **V** | DM |      | MQ |  | 5950 |      | **AR** | H | *1A* | NC |
| 5921 |      | **AR** | H | *1A* | NC |  | 5951 | r    | **V** | H  |      | KT |
| 5922 |      | **M** | E  | *E*  | OM |  | 5952 | r    | **V** | H  | *RV* | CP |
| 5924 |      | **M** | E  | *E*  | OM |  | 5954 |      | **AR** | E |      | TO |
| 5925 | s pt★|      | H  |      | MQ |  | 5955 | r    | **V** | H  | *RV* | CP |
| 5926 |      |      | H  |      | NC |  | 5957 | r    | **V** | H  |      | KT |
| 5928 |      | **AR** | H |      | NC |  | 5958 | s★   |      | H  | *FM* | BH |
| 5929 |      | **AR** | H |      | NC |  | 5959 | n    | **AR** | E |      | TO |
| 5930 | t    | **V** | H  |      | KT |  | 5960 | s    | **V** | H  | *FM* | OY |
| 5931 | tw   | **V** | H  | *RV* | CP |  | 5961 | s pt | **V** | RV | *RV* | CP |
| 5932 | r    | **V** | H  | *RV* | CP |  | 5962 | s pt | **V** | H  |      | KT |
| 5933 | r    | **V** | H  |      | KT |  | 5963 | r    | **V** | H  | *RV* | CP |
| 5934 | r    | **V** | H  | *RV* | CP |  | 5964 |      | **AR** | H | *1A* | NC |
| 5935 |      | **AR** | H |      | NC |  | 5965 | t    | **M** | WC | *WC* | CS |
| 5936 |      | **AR** | H |      | NC |  | 5966 |      | **AR** | H | *1A* | NC |

| | | | | | | | | | | | |
|---|---|---|---|---|---|---|---|---|---|---|---|
| 5967 | t | **V** | H | | KT | | 6034 | | **AR** | H | | NC |
| 5968 | | **AR** | H | | NC | | 6035 | t★ | **AV** | E | *AW* | CF |
| 5969 | u | **V** | H | *RV* | CP | | 6036 | * | **M** | E | *E* | OM |
| 5971 | s | **V** | RV | *AW* | CF | | 6037 | | **AR** | H | | OM |
| 5973 | | **AR** | H | | CT | | 6038 | s | **V** | H | | OM |
| 5975 | s | **V** | H | | KT | | 6041 | s | **V** | H | | KT |
| 5976 | t | **V** | RV | *AW* | CF | | 6042 | | **AR** | H | *1A* | NC |
| 5977 | r | **V** | H | | KT | | 6043 | † | **V** | H | *RV* | CP |
| 5978 | r | **V** | H | | KT | | 6045 | †w | **V** | H | *FM* | OY |
| 5980 | r | **V** | H | | KT | | 6046 | s | **V** | H | *FM* | OY |
| 5981 | s★ | | H | | MQ | | 6047 | †n* | **V** | H | | CT |
| 5983 | s | **V** | H | *FM* | OY | | 6049 | r | **V** | H | *FM* | OY |
| 5984 | r | **V** | H | *RV* | CP | | 6050 | s | | H | | KT |
| 5985 | | **AR** | H | *1A* | NC | | 6051 | r | **V** | H | *RV* | CP |
| 5986 | r | **V** | H | *RV* | CP | | 6052 | tw | | H | | KT |
| 5987 | r | **V** | H | *RV* | CP | | 6053 | * | **AR** | H | | NC |
| 5988 | r | **V** | H | | KT | | 6054 | r | **V** | H | *RV* | CP |
| 5989 | t | **V** | H | *FM* | OY | | 6055 | † | **V** | H | | KT |
| 5991 | s | **V** | H | *FM* | OY | | 6056 | † | **V** | H | *RV* | CP |
| 5993 | * | **AR** | H | | KT | | 6059 | s | **V** | H | *FM* | OY |
| 5994 | r | **V** | H | | KT | | 6061 | s pt | **V** | H | | KT |
| 5995 | s | **V** | H | *FM* | OY | | 6062 | † | **V** | H | | KT |
| 5996 | s pt | **V** | H | | KT | | 6064 | s | **V** | RV | *AW* | CF |
| 5997 | r | **V** | H | *RV* | CP | | 6065 | r | **V** | H | | KT |
| 5998 | | **AR** | H | *1A* | NC | | 6066 | s★ | **AV** | E | *AW* | CF |
| 5999 | s | **V** | H | | KT | | 6067 | s pt | **V** | RV | *RV* | CP |
| 6000 | t | **V** | H | | KT | | 6073 | s | **V** | H | | KT |
| 6001 | u | **V** | H | *FM* | OY | | 6100 | †* | **V** | H | | CT |
| 6002 | † | **V** | DM | | MQ | | 6101 | r | **V** | H | *RV* | CP |
| 6005 | r | **V** | H | | KT | | 6103 | | **AR** | H | | NC |
| 6006 | | **AR** | H | *1A* | NC | | 6104 | r | **V** | H | *RV* | CP |
| 6008 | s | **V** | RV | *AW* | CF | | 6105 | tpt | **V** | H | | KT |
| 6009 | r | **V** | H | | KT | | 6107 | r | **V** | H | *AW* | CF |
| 6010 | s | **V** | H | | KT | | 6110 | | **M** | E | *E* | OM |
| 6011 | s | **V** | H | | KT | | 6111 | † | **V** | H | *RV* | CP |
| 6012 | r | **V** | H | | KT | | 6112 | s pt | **V** | H | | KT |
| 6013 | s | **M** | WC | *WC* | CS | | 6113 | † | **V** | H | *RV* | CP |
| 6014 | s pt | | H | | KT | | 6115 | s | **V** | H | | KT |
| 6015 | t | **V** | H | | KT | | 6116 | † | **V** | H | | KT |
| 6016 | r | **V** | H | | KT | | 6117 | t★ | **WX** | H | *WX* | PM |
| 6018 | t | **V** | H | | KT | | 6119 | s | **V** | RV | *AW* | CF |
| 6021 | r | **V** | H | | KT | | 6120 | s | **V** | H | | KT |
| 6022 | s | **V** | H | | KT | | 6121 | † | **V** | H | *FM* | OY |
| 6024 | s | **V** | H | | OM | | 6122 | s★ | **WX** | H | *WX* | PM |
| 6025 | t | **V** | H | | KT | | 6123 | | **AR** | H | *1A* | NC |
| 6026 | s | **V** | H | | KT | | 6124 | s pt★ | **AV** | E | | TO |
| 6027 | u | **V** | H | *AW* | CF | | 6134 | † | **V** | H | *FM* | OY |
| 6028 | | **AR** | H | *1A* | NC | | 6135 | s | | H | | KT |
| 6029 | r | **V** | H | | KT | | 6136 | r | **V** | H | | KT |
| 6030 | t | **V** | H | | KT | | 6137 | s pt | **V** | RV | *AW* | CF |
| 6031 | r | **V** | H | | KT | | 6138 | † | **V** | H | *RV* | CP |

| | | | | | | | | | | |
|---|---|---|---|---|---|---|---|---|---|---|
| 6139 | n* | **M** | E | *E* | OM | 6163 | r | **V** | H | *RV* | CP |
| 6141 | u | **V** | H | *RV* | CP | 6164 | † | **V** | H | *FM* | OY |
| 6142 | †* | **V** | H | *RV* | CP | 6165 | r | **V** | H | | KT |
| 6144 | †* | **V** | H | | CT | 6166 | | | H | | NC |
| 6145 | s pt | **V** | H | | KT | 6167 | | **AR** | H | *1A* | NC |
| 6146 | * | **AR** | H | *1A* | NC | 6168 | s★ | | H | *FM* | BH |
| 6148 | s | | H | | KT | 6170 | s★ | **AV** | E | *AW* | CF |
| 6149 | u | **V** | H | | PY | 6171 | † | **V** | H | *RV* | CP |
| 6150 | s | | H | | KT | 6172 | s | **V** | H | | KT |
| 6151 | †* | **V** | H | *FM* | OY | 6173 | s★ | **WX** | H | *WX* | PM |
| 6152 | * | **M** | E | *E* | OM | 6174 | | **AR** | H | *1A* | NC |
| 6153 | † | **V** | H | | KT | 6175 | r | **V** | H | | KT |
| 6154 | r pt | | H | | KT | 6176 | t | **V** | H | | OM |
| 6155 | * | **AR** | H | | CT | 6177 | s | **V** | RV | *RV* | CP |
| 6157 | s | **V** | H | *RV* | CP | 6179 | r | **V** | H | | KT |
| 6158 | r | **V** | H | *RV* | CP | 6180 | †w | **V** | H | *RV* | CP |
| 6159 | s pt | **V** | H | | KT | 6181 | †wn | **V** | DM | | MQ |
| 6160 | * | **AR** | H | *1A* | NC | 6182 | s | **V** | H | | KT |
| 6161 | †* | **V** | H | | CT | 6183 | s | **V** | RV | *AW* | CF |
| 6162 | s pt | **V** | RV | *AW* | CF | 6184 | s | **V** | H | | KT |

## AC2D (TSO)　　　　　　　　　　　　OPEN STANDARD

Mark 2D. Air conditioned (Stones). Rebuilt from FO with new style 2+2 seats. –/58 1T. B4 bogies. d. ETH 5X. One toilet converted to store room.

Lot No. 30821 Derby 1971–72. 33.5 t.

| | | | | | |
|---|---|---|---|---|---|
| 6202 | (3191) | **FP** | H | KT | |

## AX51　　　　　　　　　　　　　　　GENERATOR VAN

Mark 1. Converted from NEA/NHA in 2003 to generator vans for use on the Southern Region power upgrade project. B5 bogies.

**6260.** Lot No. 30400 Pressed Steel 1957–58.
**6261.** Lot No. 30323 Pressed Steel 1957.
**6262.** Lot No. 30228 Metro-Cammell 1957–58.
**6263.** Lot No. 30163 Pressed Steel 1957.
**6264.** Lot No. 30173 York 1956.

| | | | | | |
|---|---|---|---|---|---|
| 6260 | (81450, 92116) | **NR** | NR | *E* | LU |
| 6261 | (81284, 92988) | **NR** | NR | *E* | LU |
| 6262 | (81064, 92928) | **Y** | NR | *E* | LU |
| 6263 | (81231, 92961) | **Y** | NR | *E* | DY |
| 6264 | (80971, 92923) | **Y** | NR | *E* | DY |

## AX51                      BRAKE GENERATOR VAN

Mark 1. Renumbered 1989 from BR departmental series. Converted from NDA in 1973 to three-phase supply brake generator van for use with HST trailers. Modified 1999 for use with loco-hauled stock. B5 bogies.

Lot No. 30400 Pressed Steel 1958.

6310    (81448, 975325)    **CH**  RV   *RV*        CP

## AX51                            GENERATOR VAN

Mark 1. Converted from NDA in 1992 to generator vans for use on Anglo-Scottish sleeping car services. Now normally used on trains hauled by steam locomotives. B4 bogies. ETH75.

**6311.** Lot No. 30162 Pressed Steel 1958. 37.25 t.
**6312.** Lot No. 30224 Cravens 1956. 37.25 t.
**6313.** Lot No. 30484 Pressed Steel 1958. 37.25 t.

6311    (80903, 92911)    **B**   E    *E*    OM
6312    (81023, 92925)    **PC**  WC   *WC*   CS
6313    (81553, 92167)    **E**   P    *VS*   SL

## NW51          DESIRO EMU BARRIER VEHICLE

Mark 1. Converted from GUVs with bodies removed and B4 bogies for use as Eurostar barrier vehicles but modified in 2003 by LNWR Co., Crewe for current use.

**6321.** Lot No. 30343 York 1957. 40 t.
**6322/23.** Lot No. 30616 Pressed Steel 1959–60. 40 t.
**6324.** Lot No. 30403 Glasgow 1958–60. 40 t.
**6325.** Lot No. 30417 Pressed Steel 1958–59. 40 t.

6321    (86515, 96385)    **B**   SM   *FL*   CP
6322    (86859, 96386)    **B**   SM   *FL*   CP
6323    (86973, 96387)    **B**   SM   *FL*   CP
6324    (86562, 96388)    **B**   SM   *FL*   CP
6325    (86135, 96389)    **B**   SM   *FL*   CP

## GS5 (HSBV)          HST BARRIER VEHICLE

Renumbered from BR departmental series, or converted from various types. B4 bogies (Commonwealth bogies *).

**6330.** Mark 2A. Lot No. 30786 Derby 1968. 32 t.
**6336/38/44.** Mark 1. Lot No. 30715 Gloucester 1962. 31 t.
**6340.** Mark 1. Lot No. 30669 Swindon 1962. 36 t.
**6346.** Mark 2A. Lot No. 30777 Derby 1967. 31.5 t.
**6348.** Mark 1. Lot No. 30163 Pressed Steel 1957. 31.5 t.

6330    (14084, 975629)   **G**   A    *GW*   LA
6336    (81591, 92185)    **G**   A    *GW*   LA

| 6338 | (81581, 92180) |   | **G**  | A | *GW* | LA |
|------|----------------|---|--------|---|------|----|
| 6340 | (21251, 975678) | * | **G**  | A | *GW* | LA |
| 6344 | (81263, 92080) |   | **GN** | A | *GN* | EC |
| 6346 | (9422) |   | **GN** | A | *GN* | EC |
| 6348 | (81233, 92963) |   | **G**  | A | *GW* | LA |

# AV5A/AV5C (MFBV) MARK 4 BARRIER VEHICLE

Mark 2A/2C. Converted from FK* or BSO. B4 bogies.

**6352/3.** Mark 2A. Lot No. 30774 Derby 1968. 33 t.
**6354/5.** Mark 2C. Lot No. 30820 Derby 1970. 32 t.
**6358/9.** Mark 2A. Lot No. 30788 Derby 1968. 31.5 t.

| 6352 | (13465, 19465) | * | **GN** | H | *GN* | BN |
|------|----------------|---|--------|---|------|----|
| 6353 | (13478, 19478) | * | **GN** | H | *GN* | BN |
| 6354 | (9459) |   | **GN** | H | *GN* | BN |
| 6355 | (9477) |   | **GN** | H | *GN* | BN |
| 6358 | (9432) |   | **GN** | H | *GN* | BN |
| 6359 | (9429) |   | **GN** | H | *GN* | BN |

# AW51                            EMU TRANSLATOR VEHICLE

Mark 1. Converted 1992 from BG. BR Mark 1 bogies.

**6364.** Mark 1. Lot No. 30039 Derby 1954. 32 t.
**6365.** Mark 1. Lot No. 30323 Pressed Steel 1957. 32 t.

| 6364 | (80565) | **RR** | MA | *CT* | SI |
|------|---------|--------|----|------|----|
| 6365 | (81296, 84296) | **RR** | MA | *CT* | SI |

# AW51                            EMU TRANSLATOR VEHICLE

Mark 1. Converted 1980 from RUO. Commonwealth bogies.

Lot No. 30647 Wolverton 1959–61. 36 t.

| 6376 | (1021, 975973) | **P** | P | *FL* | ZJ |
|------|----------------|-------|---|------|----|
| 6377 | (1042, 975975) | **P** | P | *FL* | ZJ |
| 6378 | (1054, 975971) | **P** | P | *GB* | WN |
| 6379 | (1059, 975972) | **P** | P | *GB* | WN |

# GS51 (HSBV)                         HST BARRIER VEHICLE

Mark 1. Converted from BG in 1994–5. B4 bogies.

**6392.** Lot No. 30715 Gloucester 1962. 29.5 t.
**6393/96/97.** Lot No. 30716 Gloucester 1962. 29.5 t.
**6394.** Lot No. 30162 Pressed Steel 1956–57. 30.5 t.
**6395.** Lot No. 30484 Pressed Steel 1958. 30.5 t.
**6398/99.** Lot No. 30400 Pressed Steel 1957–58. 30.5 t.

| 6392 | (81588, 92183) | **P** | P | *MM* | NL |
|------|----------------|-------|---|------|----|
| 6393 | (81609, 92196) | **P** | P | *GN* | EC |
| 6394 | (80878, 92906) | **P** | P | *GN* | EC |

| 6395 | (81506, 92148) | **P** | MA | *MM* | NL |
| 6396 | (81607, 92195) | **P** | P | *MM* | NL |
| 6397 | (81600, 92190) | **P** | P | *MM* | NL |
| 6398 | (81471, 92126) | **MA** | MA | *MM* | NL |
| 6399 | (81367, 92994) | **MA** | MA | *MM* | NL |

## AG2C (TSOT)          OPEN STANDARD (TROLLEY)

Mark 2C. Converted from TSO by removal of one seating bay and replacing this by a counter with a space for a trolley. Adjacent toilet removed and converted to steward's washing area/store. Pressure ventilated. –/55 1T. B4 bogies. ETH 4.

Lot No. 30795 Derby 1969–70. 32.5 t.

| 6528 | (5592) | **M** | WC | *WC* | CS |

## AN1F (RLO)          SLEEPER RECEPTION CAR

Mark 2F. Converted from FO, these vehicles consist of pantry, microwave cooking facilities, seating area for passengers, telephone booth and staff toilet. 6703–8 also have a bar. Converted at RTC, Derby (6700), Ilford (6701–5) and Derby (6706–8). Air conditioned. 6700/1/3/5/–8 have Stones equipment and 6702/4 have Temperature Ltd. equipment. 26/– 1T. B4 bogies. d. ETH 5X.

**Advertising Livery:** 6703 is "Visit Scotland" – silver with broad blue tartan stripe down one end.

**6700–2/4/8.** Lot No. 30859 Derby 1973–74. 33.5 t.
**6703/5–7.** Lot No. 30845 Derby 1973. 33.5 t.

| 6700 | (3347) | **CS** | H | *SR* | IS |
| 6701 | (3346) | **CS** | H | *SR* | IS |
| 6702 | (3421) | **CS** | H | *SR* | IS |
| 6703 | (3308) | **AL** | H | *SR* | IS |
| 6704 | (3341) | **CS** | H | *SR* | IS |
| 6705 | (3310, 6430) | **CS** | H | *SR* | IS |
| 6706 | (3283, 6421) | **CS** | H | *SR* | IS |
| 6707 | (3276, 6418) | **CS** | H | *SR* | IS |
| 6708 | (3370) | **CS** | H | *SR* | IS |

## AN1D (RMBF)          MINIATURE BUFFET CAR

Mark 2D. Converted from TSOT by the removal of another seating bay and fitting a proper buffet counter with boiler and microwave oven. Now converted to first class with new seating and end luggage stacks. Air conditioned. Stones equipment. 30/– 1T. B4 bogies. d. ETH 5.

Lot No. 30822 Derby 1971. 33 t.

| 6720 | (5622, 6652) | **M** | E | *E* | OM |
| 6721 | (5627, 6660) | **FP** | H | *GW* | OO |
| 6722 | (5736, 6661) | **FP** | H | *GW* | OO |
| 6723 | (5641, 6662) | **FP** | H | *GW* | OO |
| 6724 | (5721, 6665) | **FP** | H | *GW* | OO |

# AC2F (TSO)                                    OPEN STANDARD

Mark 2F. Renumbered from FO and declassified in 1985–6. Converted 1990 to
TSO with mainly unidirectional seating and power-operated sliding doors. Air
conditioned. 6800–14 were converted by BREL Derby and have Temperature
Ltd. air conditioning. 6815–29 were converted by RFS Industries Doncaster and
have Stones air conditioning. –/74 2T. B4 bogies. d. ETH 5X.

**6800–07. 6810–12. 6813–14. 6819/22/28.** Lot No. 30859 Derby 1973–74. 33 t.
**6808–6809.** Lot No. 30873 Derby 1974–75. 33.5 t.
**6815–18. 6820–21. 6823–27. 6829.** Lot No. 30845 Derby 1973. 33 t.

| | | | | |
|---|---|---|---|---|
| 6800 | (3323, 6435) | **AR** H | | CT |
| 6801 | (3349, 6442) | **AR** H | *1A* | NC |
| 6802 | (3339, 6439) | H | | NC |
| 6803 | (3355, 6443) | **AR** H | *1A* | NC |
| 6804 | (3396, 6449) | H | | CT |
| 6805 | (3324, 6436) | **AR** H | *1A* | NC |
| 6806 | (3342, 6440) | **AR** H | *1A* | NC |
| 6807 | (3423, 6452) | H | | CT |
| 6808 | (3430, 6454) | **AR** H | *1A* | NC |
| 6809 | (3435, 6455) | **AR** H | | CT |
| 6810 | (3404, 6451) | **AR** H | | KT |
| 6811 | (3327, 6437) | **AR** H | *1A* | NC |
| 6812 | (3394, 6448) | **AR** H | *1A* | NC |
| 6813 | (3410, 6463) | H | | CT |
| 6814 | (3422, 6465) | **AR** H | | KT |
| 6815 | (3282, 6420) | **AR** H | | KT |
| 6816 | (3316, 6461) | **AR** H | | CT |
| 6817 | (3311, 6431) | **AR** H | *1A* | NC |
| 6818 | (3298, 6427) | **AR** H | *1A* | NC |
| 6819 | (3365, 6446) | **AR** H | | NC |
| 6820 | (3320, 6434) | **AR** H | *1A* | NC |
| 6821 | (3281, 6458) | **AR** H | | KT |
| 6822 | (3376, 6447) | **AR** H | | NC |
| 6823 | (3289, 6424) | **AR** H | *1A* | NC |
| 6824 | (3307, 6429) | **AR** H | | KT |
| 6825 | (3301, 6460) | **AR** H | | CT |
| 6826 | (3294, 6425) | **AR** H | | NC |
| 6827 | (3306, 6428) | **AR** H | | CT |
| 6828 | (3380, 6464) | **AR** H | *1A* | NC |
| 6829 | (3288, 6423) | **AR** H | *1A* | NC |

# AH2Z (BSOT)
## OPEN BRAKE STANDARD (MICRO-BUFFET)

Mark 2. Converted from BSO by removal of one seating bay and replacing this
by a counter with a space for a trolley. Adjacent toilet removed and converted to
a steward's washing area/store. –/23 0T. B4 bogies. ETH 4.

Lot No. 30757 Derby 1966. 31 t.

| 9101 | (9398) | v | **CH** | H | *VT* | TM |
| 9104 | (9401) | v | **G** | FM | *FM* | RL |

## AE2Z (BSO)                    OPEN BRAKE STANDARD

Mark 2. These vehicles use the same body shell as the Mark 2 BFK and have first class seat spacing and wider tables. Pressure ventilated. –/31 1T. B4 bogies. ETH 4.

Lot No. 30757 Derby 1966. 31.5 t.

| 9391 | **PC** | WT | *WT* | OM | | 9392 | v | **G** | FM | *FM* | RL |

## AE2A (BSO)                    OPEN BRAKE STANDARD

Mark 2A. These vehicles use the same body shell as the Mark 2A BFK and have first class seat spacing and wider tables. Pressure ventilated. –/31 1T. B4 bogies. ETH 4. Modified for use as escort coaches.

**9419**. Lot No. 30777 Derby 1970. 31.5 t.
**9428**. Lot No. 30820 Derby 1970. 31.5 t.

| 9419 | **DR** | DR | *DR* | KM | | 9428 | **DR** | DR | *DR* | KM |

## AE2C (BSO)                    OPEN BRAKE STANDARD

Mark 2C. Pressure ventilated. –/31 1T. B4 bogies. ETH 4.

Lot No. 30798 Derby 1970. 32 t.

| 9440 | d | **M** | WC | *WC* | CS | | 9448 | d | **M** | WC | *WC* | CS |

## AE2D (BSO)                    OPEN BRAKE STANDARD

Mark 2D. Air conditioned (Stones). –/31 1T. B4 bogies. d. pg. ETH 5.

r Refurbished with new interior panelling.
s Refurbished with new seating –/22 1TD.
w Facelifted –/28 1W 1T.

Lot No. 30824 Derby 1971. 33 t.

| 9479 | r |  | H | *FM* | OY | | 9490 | s | **FP** | H | *GW* | OO |
| 9480 | w | **FP** | H | | KT | | 9492 | w | **FP** | DM | | OM |
| 9481 | s | **FP** | H | *GW* | OO | | 9493 | s | **FP** | H | *GW* | OO |
| 9488 | s | **FP** | H | *GW* | OO | | 9494 | s | **M** | E | *E* | OM |
| 9489 | r | **V** | H | | KT | | | | | | | |

## AE2E (BSO)                    OPEN BRAKE STANDARD

Mark 2E. Air conditioned (Stones). –/32 1T. B4 bogies. d. pg. ETH 5.

Lot No. 30838 Derby 1972. 33 t.

r Refurbished with new interior panelling.

s Refurbished with modified design of seat headrest and new interior panelling.
w Facelifted –/28 1W 1T.

| | | | | | | | | | | |
|---|---|---|---|---|---|---|---|---|---|---|
| 9496 | r | | H | *FM* | OY | 9504 | s | **V** | H *RV* | CP |
| 9497 | r★ | | H | *FM* | BH | 9505 | s★ | | H | MQ |
| 9498 | r | **V** | H | | KT | 9506 | s★ | **WX** | H *WX* | PM |
| 9500 | r | | H | *FM* | OY | 9507 | s | **V** | H *AW* | CF |
| 9501 | w | **FP** | DM | | OM | 9508 | s | **V** | H | KT |
| 9502 | s | **V** | H | | KT | 9509 | s | **V** | H *RV* | CP |
| 9503 | s | **V** | H | *RV* | CP | | | | | |

# AE2F (BSO)                    OPEN BRAKE STANDARD

Mark 2F. Air conditioned (Temperature Ltd.). All now refurbished with power-operated vestibule doors, new panels and seat trim. All now further refurbished with carpets and new m.a. sets. –/32 1T. B4 bogies. d. pg. ETH5X.

Lot No. 30861 Derby 1974. 34 t.

| | | | | | | | | | | |
|---|---|---|---|---|---|---|---|---|---|---|
| 9513 | | **BP** | H | *FM* | EM | 9526 | n★ | | H *RV* | CP |
| 9516 | n | **V** | H | *FM* | OY | 9527 | n | **V** | RV *AW* | CF |
| 9520 | n | **V** | RV | *AW* | CF | 9529 | n | **V** | RV *RV* | CP |
| 9521 | ★ | **AV** | E | *AW* | CF | 9531 | | **V** | RV *RV* | CP |
| 9522 | | **V** | H | *FM* | OY | 9537 | n | **V** | H *RV* | CP |
| 9523 | | **V** | H | | KT | 9538 | | **V** | H | KT |
| 9524 | n★ | **AV** | E | | TO | 9539 | | **M** | WC *WC* | CS |
| 9525 | | **WX** | H | *WX* | PM | | | | | |

# AF2F (DBSO) DRIVING OPEN BRAKE STANDARD

Mark 2F. Air conditioned (Temperature Ltd.). Push & pull (t.d.m. system). Converted from BSO, these vehicles originally had half cabs at the brake end. They have since been refurbished and have had their cabs widened and the cab-end gangways removed. –/30 1W 1T. B4 bogies. d. pg. Cowcatchers. ETH 5X.

**9701–9710.** Lot No. 30861 Derby 1974. Converted Glasgow 1979. Disc brakes. 34 t.
**9711–9713.** Lot No. 30861 Derby 1974. Converted Glasgow 1985. 34 t.
**9714.** Lot No. 30861 Derby 1974. Converted Glasgow 1986. Disc brakes. 34 t.

| | | | | | | | | | |
|---|---|---|---|---|---|---|---|---|---|
| 9701 | (9528) | **AR** | H *1A* | NC | 9709 | (9515) | **AR** | H *1A* | NC |
| 9702 | (9510) | **AR** | H | NC | 9710 | (9518) | **1** | H | NC |
| 9703 | (9517) | **AR** | H *1A* | NC | 9711 | (9532) | **AR** | H *1A* | NC |
| 9704 | (9512) | **AR** | H *1A* | NC | 9712 | (9534) | **AR** | H *1A* | NC |
| 9705 | (9519) | **AR** | H | NC | 9713 | (9535) | **AR** | H | NC |
| 9707 | (9511) | **AR** | H | NC | 9714 | (9536) | **AR** | H *1A* | NC |
| 9708 | (9530) | **AR** | H *1A* | NC | | | | | |

# AE4E (BUO)          UNCLASSIFIED OPEN BRAKE

Mark 2E. Converted from TSO with new seating for use on Anglo-Scottish overnight services by Railcare, Wolverton. Air conditioned. Stones equipment. B4 bogies. d. –/31 2T. B4 bogies. ETH 4X.

**9800–9803.** Lot No. 30837 Derby 1972. 33.5 t.
**9804–9810.** Lot No. 30844 Derby 1972–73. 33.5 t.

| | | | | | | | | | | |
|---|---|---|---|---|---|---|---|---|---|---|
| 9800 | (5751) | **CS** | H | *SR* | IS | 9806 | (5840) | **CS** | H *SR* | IS |
| 9801 | (5760) | **CS** | H | *SR* | IS | 9807 | (5851) | **CP** | H *SR* | IS |
| 9802 | (5772) | **CS** | H | *SR* | IS | 9808 | (5871) | **CS** | H *SR* | IS |
| 9803 | (5799) | **CS** | H | *SR* | IS | 9809 | (5890) | **CS** | H *SR* | IS |
| 9804 | (5826) | **CS** | H | *SR* | IS | 9810 | (5892) | **CS** | H *SR* | IS |
| 9805 | (5833) | **CS** | H | *SR* | IS | | | | | |

# AJ1G (RFM) RESTAURANT BUFFET FIRST (MODULAR)

Mark 3A. Air conditioned. Converted from HST TRFKs, RFBs and FOs. Refurbished with table lamps and burgundy seat trim (except *). 18/– plus two seats for staff use (*24/–). BT10 bogies. d. ETH 14X.

**10200–10211.** Lot No. 30884 Derby 1977. 39.8 t.
**10212–10229.** Lot No. 30878 Derby 1975–76. 39.8 t.
**10230–10260.** Lot No. 30890 Derby 1979. 39.8 t.

**Non-standard Livery:** 10211 is EWS dark maroon.

| | | | | | | | | | | | | |
|---|---|---|---|---|---|---|---|---|---|---|---|---|
| 10200 | (40519) | * | | P | *1A* | NC | 10229 | (11059) | * 1 | P | *1A* | NC |
| 10201 | (40520) | **V** | | P | | ZB | 10230 | (10021) | 1 | P | | ZB |
| 10202 | (40504) | **V** | | P | | WB | 10231 | (10016) | **V** | P | *CD* | OY |
| 10203 | (40506) | * 1 | | P | *1A* | NC | 10232 | (10027) | **V** | P | | LT |
| 10204 | (40502) | **V** | | P | | WI | 10233 | (10013) | **V** | P | | WI |
| 10205 | (40503) | **V** | | P | | LT | 10235 | (10015) | **CD** | P | *CD* | OY |
| 10206 | (40507) | **V** | | P | *1A* | NC | 10236 | (10018) | **V** | P | | WI |
| 10208 | (40517) | **V** | | P | | WI | 10237 | (10022) | **V** | P | | LM |
| 10211 | (40510) | **0** | | E | *E* | TO | 10240 | (10003) | **V** | P | | LT |
| 10212 | (11049) | **V** | | P | | WB | 10241 | (10009) | * 1 | P | *1A* | NC |
| 10213 | (11050) | **V** | | P | | LT | 10242 | (10002) | **V** | P | | WI |
| 10214 | (11034) | * 1 | | P | *1A* | NC | 10245 | (10019) | **V** | P | | WI |
| 10215 | (11032) | **V** | | P | | WI | 10246 | (10014) | **V** | P | | LT |
| 10216 | (11041) | * **AR** | | P | *1A* | NC | 10247 | (10011) | * 1 | P | *1A* | NC |
| 10217 | (11051) | **V** | | P | | WB | 10249 | (10012) | **V** | P | | WI |
| 10218 | (11053) | **V** | | P | | LT | 10250 | (10020) | **V** | P | | LT |
| 10219 | (11047) | **V** | | P | | WB | 10253 | (10026) | **V** | P | | LT |
| 10223 | (11043) | * **AR** | | P | *1A* | NC | 10255 | (10010) | **V** | P | | WI |
| 10224 | (11062) | **V** | | P | | LT | 10256 | (10028) | **V** | P | | LT |
| 10225 | (11014) | **V** | | P | | LT | 10257 | (10007) | **V** | P | *CD* | OY |
| 10226 | (11015) | **V** | | P | | WI | 10259 | (10025) | **V** | P | | LT |
| 10228 | (11035) | * 1 | | P | *1A* | NC | 10260 | (10001) | **V** | P | | LT |

# AG2J (RSB) MALLARD KITCHEN BUFFET STANDARD

Mark 4. Air conditioned. BT41 bogies. ETH 6X. Rebuilt from first to standard class with bar adjacent to seating area instead of adjacent to end of coach. –/30 1T.

Lot No. 31045 Metro-Cammell 1989–1992. 43.5 t.

| | | | | | | | | | | |
|---|---|---|---|---|---|---|---|---|---|---|
| 10300 | **GN** | H | *GN* | BN | | 10302 | **GN** | H | *GN* | BN |
| 10301 | **GN** | H | *GN* | BN | | 10303 | **GN** | H | *GN* | BN |

| | | | | | | | | |
|---|---|---|---|---|---|---|---|---|
| 10304 | **GN** | H *GN* | BN | | 10319 | **GN** | H *GN* | BN |
| 10305 | **GN** | H *GN* | BN | | 10320 | **GN** | H *GN* | BN |
| 10306 | **GN** | H *GN* | BN | | 10321 | **GN** | H *GN* | BN |
| 10307 | **GN** | H *GN* | BN | | 10323 | **GN** | H *GN* | BN |
| 10308 | **GN** | H *GN* | BN | | 10324 | **GN** | H *GN* | BN |
| 10309 | **GN** | H *GN* | BN | | 10325 | **GN** | H *GN* | BN |
| 10310 | **GN** | H *GN* | BN | | 10326 | **GN** | H *GN* | BN |
| 10311 | **GN** | H *GN* | BN | | 10328 | **GN** | H *GN* | BN |
| 10312 | **GN** | H *GN* | BN | | 10329 | **GN** | H *GN* | BN |
| 10313 | **GN** | H *GN* | BN | | 10330 | **GN** | H *GN* | BN |
| 10315 | **GN** | H *GN* | BN | | 10331 | **GN** | H *GN* | BN |
| 10317 | **GN** | H *GN* | BN | | 10332 | **GN** | H *GN* | BN |
| 10318 | **GN** | H *GN* | BN | | 10333 | **GN** | H *GN* | BN |

## AU4G (SLEP)    SLEEPING CAR WITH PANTRY

Mark 3A. Air conditioned. Retention toilets. 12 compartments with a fixed lower lower berth and a hinged upper berth, plus an attendants compartment. 2T BT10 bogies. ETH 7X.

**Non-standard Livery:** 10546 is EWS dark maroon.

Lot No. 30960 Derby 1981–83. 41 t.

| | | | | | | | | | | |
|---|---|---|---|---|---|---|---|---|---|---|
| 10501 | d | **CS** | P | *SR* | IS | | 10551 | d | **CS** | P | *SR* | IS |
| 10502 | d | **CS** | P | *SR* | IS | | 10553 | d | **CS** | P | *SR* | IS |
| 10504 | d | **CS** | P | *SR* | IS | | 10555 | d | | CD | | KT |
| 10506 | d | **CS** | P | *SR* | IS | | 10559 | d | | CD | | KT |
| 10507 | d | **CS** | P | *SR* | IS | | 10561 | d | **CS** | P | *SR* | IS |
| 10508 | d | **CS** | P | *SR* | IS | | 10562 | d | **CP** | P | *SR* | IS |
| 10510 | d | | P | | ZH | | 10563 | d | **FP** | P | *GW* | PZ |
| 10513 | d | **CS** | P | *SR* | IS | | 10565 | d | **CS** | P | *SR* | IS |
| 10515 | d | | P | | IS | | 10569 | d | **PC** | VS | | CP |
| 10516 | d | **CP** | P | *SR* | IS | | 10580 | d | **CS** | P | *SR* | IS |
| 10519 | d | **CS** | P | *SR* | IS | | 10584 | d | **FP** | P | *GW* | PZ |
| 10520 | d | **CS** | P | *SR* | IS | | 10588 | d | **FP** | P | *GW* | PZ |
| 10522 | d | **CS** | P | *SR* | IS | | 10589 | d | **FP** | P | *GW* | PZ |
| 10523 | d | **CP** | P | *SR* | IS | | 10590 | d | **FP** | P | *GW* | PZ |
| 10526 | d | **CS** | P | *SR* | IS | | 10594 | d | **FP** | P | *GW* | PZ |
| 10527 | d | **CS** | P | *SR* | IS | | 10596 | d | | P | | KT |
| 10529 | d | **CS** | P | *SR* | IS | | 10597 | d | **CS** | P | *SR* | IS |
| 10531 | d | **CS** | P | *SR* | IS | | 10598 | d | **CS** | P | *SR* | IS |
| 10532 | d | **FP** | P | *GW* | PZ | | 10600 | d | **FS** | P | *SR* | IS |
| 10534 | d | **FP** | P | *GW* | PZ | | 10601 | d | **FP** | P | *GW* | PZ |
| 10538 | d | | CD | | KT | | 10605 | d | **CS** | P | *SR* | IS |
| 10539 | d | | CD | | KT | | 10607 | d | **CS** | P | *SR* | IS |
| 10542 | d | **CS** | P | *SR* | IS | | 10610 | d | **CS** | P | *SR* | IS |
| 10543 | d | **CS** | P | *SR* | IS | | 10612 | d | **FP** | P | *GW* | PZ |
| 10544 | d | **CS** | P | *SR* | IS | | 10613 | d | **CS** | P | *SR* | IS |
| 10546 | d | **0** | E | *E* | TO | | 10614 | d | **CS** | P | *SR* | IS |
| 10547 | d | | P | | IS | | 10616 | d | **FP** | P | *GW* | PZ |
| 10548 | d | **CS** | P | *SR* | IS | | 10617 | d | **CS** | P | *SR* | IS |

## AS4G/AQ4G* (SLE/SLED*)                    SLEEPING CAR

Mark 3A. Air conditioned. Retention toilets. 13 compartments with a fixed lower berth and a hinged upper berth (* 11 compartments with a fixed lower berth and a hinged upper berth + one compartment for a disabled person). 2T. BT10 bogies. ETH 6X.

Notes:

10704 has Siemens bogies.
10734 was originally 2914 and used as a Royal Train staff sleeping car. It has 12 berths and a shower room and is ETH11X.

**10647–10732.** Lot No. 30961 Derby 1980–84. 43.5 t.
**10734.** Lot No. 31002 Derby/Wolverton 1985. 42.5 t.

| | | | | | | | | |
|---|---|---|---|---|---|---|---|---|
| 10647 | d |  | P |  | KT | 10699 | d* **CS** | P | *SR* | IS |
| 10648 | d* **CS** | P | *SR* | IS | 10701 | d | P |  | KT |
| 10649 | d |  | CD |  | KT | 10703 | d **CS** | P | *SR* | IS |
| 10650 | d* **CS** | P | *SR* | IS | 10704 | d | AE |  | ZA |
| 10658 | d |  | CD |  | KT | 10706 | d* **CS** | P | *SR* | IS |
| 10663 | d |  | P |  | IS | 10710 | d | CD |  | KT |
| 10666 | d* **CS** | P | *SR* | IS | 10714 | d* **CS** | P | *SR* | IS |
| 10675 | d **CS** | P | *SR* | IS | 10718 | d* **CS** | P | *SR* | IS |
| 10680 | d* **CS** | P | *SR* | IS | 10719 | d* **CS** | P | *SR* | IS |
| 10683 | d **CS** | P | *SR* | IS | 10722 | d* **CS** | P | *SR* | IS |
| 10688 | d **CS** | P | *SR* | IS | 10723 | d* **CS** | P | *SR* | IS |
| 10689 | d* **FG** | P | *SR* | IS | 10729 | **VN** | VS | *VS* | CP |
| 10690 | d **CS** | P | *SR* | IS | 10732 | d | CD |  | KT |
| 10693 | d **CS** | P | *SR* | IS | 10734 | **VN** | VS | *VS* | CP |
| 10697 | d |  | CD |  | OY | | | | | |

## AD1G (FO)                                      OPEN FIRST

Mark 3A. Air conditioned. All now refurbished with table lamps and new seat cushions and trim. 48/– 2T (* 48/– 1T 1TD). BT10 bogies. d. ETH 6X.

11005–7 were open composites 11905–7 for a time.

**Non-standard Livery:** 11039 is EWS dark maroon.

Lot No. 30878 Derby 1975–76. 34.3 t.

| | | | | | | | | | |
|---|---|---|---|---|---|---|---|---|---|
| 11005 |  | **V** | P |  | LT | 11023 | **1** | P |  | LT |
| 11006 |  | **V** | P |  | LT | 11024 | **V** | AM |  | ZH |
| 11007 |  | **V** | P |  | LT | 11026 | **V** | P |  | WI |
| 11011 | * | **V** | P |  | WI | 11027 | **V** | P |  | WB |
| 11013 |  | **V** | P | *CD* | OY | 11028 | **V** | P |  | WB |
| 11016 |  | **V** | P |  | LM | 11029 | **V** | P | *CD* | OY |
| 11017 |  | **V** | P |  | LT | 11030 | **V** | P |  | LM |
| 11018 |  | **V** | P |  | WI | 11031 | **V** | P |  | WI |
| 11019 |  | **V** | P |  | LM | 11033 | **V** | P | *CD* | OY |
| 11020 |  | **V** | P |  | WI | 11036 | **V** | P |  | WB |
| 11021 |  | **V** | P |  | WB | 11037 | **V** | P |  | ZD |

| 11038 | 1 | P |    | LT |
|-------|---|---|----|-----|
| 11039 | 0 | E | E  | TO |
| 11040 | V | P |    | WI |
| 11042 | V | P |    | WI |
| 11044 | V | P | 1A | NC |
| 11045 | V | P |    | LM |
| 11046 | V | P |    | LM |

| 11048 | V | P |    | WB |
|-------|---|---|----|-----|
| 11052 | V | P |    | WI |
| 11054 | V | P |    | LM |
| 11055 | V | P |    | LT |
| 11058 | V | P |    | LT |
| 11060 | V | P |    | WI |

## AD1H (FO)                                              OPEN FIRST

Mark 3B. Air conditioned. Inter-City 80 seats. All now refurbished with table lamps and new seat cushions and trim. 48/– 2T († 37/– 1T 1TD 2W). BT10 bogies. d. ETH 6X.

Lot No. 30982 Derby 1985. 36.5 t.

| 11064 | V | P | CD | WB |
|-------|---|---|----|-----|
| 11065 | V | P | CD | OY |
| 11066 | V | P |    | ZD |
| 11067 | V | P | 1A | NC |
| 11068 | 1 | P | 1A | NC |
| 11069 | 1 | P | 1A | NC |
| 11070 | 1 | P | 1A | NC |
| 11071 | V | P | 1A | NC |
| 11072 | 1 | P | 1A | NC |
| 11073 | 1 | P | 1A | NC |
| 11074 | V | P | 1A | NC |
| 11075 | 1 | P | 1A | NC |
| 11076 | 1 | P | 1A | NC |
| 11077 | V | P | 1A | NC |
| 11078 † | 1 | P | 1A | NC |
| 11079 | V | P |    | WB |
| 11080 | V | P | 1A | NC |
| 11081 | V | P |    | ZD |
| 11082 | 1 | P | 1A | NC |

| 11083 | V | P |    | WB |
|-------|---|---|----|-----|
| 11084 | V | P | 1A | NC |
| 11085 | V | P |    | ZD |
| 11086 | V | P | 1A | NC |
| 11087 | V | P | 1A | NC |
| 11088 † | 1 | P | 1A | NC |
| 11089 | V | P | 1A | NC |
| 11090 | V | P |    | ZD |
| 11091 | V | P | 1A | NC |
| 11092 | V | P |    | ZD |
| 11093 † | 1 | P | 1A | NC |
| 11094 † | 1 | P | 1A | NC |
| 11095 | V | P | 1A | NC |
| 11096 † | 1 | P | 1A | NC |
| 11097 | V | P | 1A | NC |
| 11098 | V | P |    | ZD |
| 11099 | V | P |    | ZD |
| 11100 | V | P |    | ZD |
| 11101 † | 1 | P | 1A | NC |

## AD1J (FO)                      MALLARD            OPEN FIRST

Mark 4. Air conditioned. Rebuilt with new interior by Bombardier Wakefield 2003–05 (some converted from standard class vehicles) 46/– 1T. BT41 bogies. ETH 6X.

Note: 11264–11271 were cancelled and 11296/7 replaced by 11998/9.

**11201–11273.** Lot No. 31046 Metro-Cammell 1989–92. 41.3 t .
**11277–11299.** Lot No. 31049 Metro-Cammell 1989–92. 41.3 t .

| 11201 | (11201) | **GN** H | *GN* | BN |
|-------|---------|----------|------|-----|
| 11219 | (11219) | **GN** H | *GN* | BN |
| 11229 | (11229) | **GN** H | *GN* | BN |
| 11237 | (11237) | **GN** H | *GN* | BN |
| 11241 | (11241) | **GN** H | *GN* | BN |
| 11244 | (11244) | **GN** H | *GN* | BN |

| 11273 | (11273) | **GN** H | *GN* | BN |
|-------|---------|----------|------|-----|
| 11277 | (12408) | **GN** H | *GN* | BN |
| 11278 | (12479) | **GN** H | *GN* | BN |
| 11279 | (12521) | **GN** H | *GN* | BN |
| 11280 | (12523) | **GN** H | *GN* | BN |
| 11281 | (12418) | **GN** H | *GN* | BN |

| 11282 (12524) | **GN** H *GN* BN | 11290 (12530) | **GN** H *GN* BN |
| 11283 (12435) | **GN** H *GN* BN | 11291 (12535) | **GN** H *GN* BN |
| 11284 (12487) | **GN** H *GN* BN | 11292 (12451) | **GN** H *GN* BN |
| 11285 (12537) | **GN** H *GN* BN | 11293 (12536) | **GN** H *GN* BN |
| 11286 (12482) | **GN** H *GN* BN | 11294 (12529) | **GN** H *GN* BN |
| 11287 (12527) | **GN** H *GN* BN | 11295 (12475) | **GN** H *GN* BN |
| 11288 (12517) | **GN** H *GN* BN | 11298 (12416) | **GN** H *GN* BN |
| 11289 (12528) | **GN** H *GN* BN | 11299 (12532) | **GN** H *GN* BN |

## AD1J (FOD) MALLARD OPEN FIRST (DISABLED)

Mark 4. Air conditioned. Rebuilt from FO by Bombardier Wakefield 2003–05. 42/
– 1W 1TD. BT41 bogies. ETH 6X.

Lot No. 31046 Metro-Cammell 1989–92. 40.7 t.

| 11301 (11215) | **GN** H *GN* BN | 11316 (11227) | **GN** H *GN* BN |
| 11302 (11203) | **GN** H *GN* BN | 11317 (11223) | **GN** H *GN* BN |
| 11303 (11211) | **GN** H *GN* BN | 11318 (11251) | **GN** H *GN* BN |
| 11304 (11257) | **GN** H *GN* BN | 11319 (11247) | **GN** H *GN* BN |
| 11305 (11261) | **GN** H *GN* BN | 11320 (11255) | **GN** H *GN* BN |
| 11306 (11276) | **GN** H *GN* BN | 11321 (11245) | **GN** H *GN* BN |
| 11307 (11217) | **GN** H *GN* BN | 11322 (11228) | **GN** H *GN* BN |
| 11308 (11263) | **GN** H *GN* BN | 11323 (11235) | **GN** H *GN* BN |
| 11309 (11259) | **GN** H *GN* BN | 11324 (11253) | **GN** H *GN* BN |
| 11310 (11272) | **GN** H *GN* BN | 11325 (11231) | **GN** H *GN* BN |
| 11311 (11221) | **GN** H *GN* BN | 11326 (11206) | **GN** H *GN* BN |
| 11312 (11225) | **GN** H *GN* BN | 11327 (11236) | **GN** H *GN* BN |
| 11313 (11210) | **GN** H *GN* BN | 11328 (11274) | **GN** H *GN* BN |
| 11314 (11207) | **GN** H *GN* BN | 11329 (11243) | **GN** H *GN* BN |
| 11315 (11238) | **GN** H *GN* BN | 11330 (11249) | **GN** H *GN* BN |

## AD1J (FO)            MALLARD            OPEN FIRST

Mark 4. Air conditioned. Rebuilt from FO by Bombardier Wakefield 2003–05.
Seperate area for 7 smokers, but smoking is no longer allowed. 46/– 1W 1TD.
BT41 bogies. ETH 6X.

Lot Nos. 31046 Metro-Cammell 1989–92. 42.1 t.

| 11401 (11214) | **GN** H *GN* BN | 11414 (11246) | **GN** H *GN* BN |
| 11402 (11216) | **GN** H *GN* BN | 11415 (11208) | **GN** H *GN* BN |
| 11403 (11258) | **GN** H *GN* BN | 11416 (11254) | **GN** H *GN* BN |
| 11404 (11202) | **GN** H *GN* BN | 11417 (11226) | **GN** H *GN* BN |
| 11405 (11204) | **GN** H *GN* BN | 11418 (11222) | **GN** H *GN* BN |
| 11406 (11205) | **GN** H *GN* BN | 11419 (11250) | **GN** H *GN* BN |
| 11407 (11256) | **GN** H *GN* BN | 11420 (11242) | **GN** H *GN* BN |
| 11408 (11218) | **GN** H *GN* BN | 11421 (11220) | **GN** H *GN* BN |
| 11409 (11262) | **GN** H *GN* BN | 11422 (11232) | **GN** H *GN* BN |
| 11410 (11260) | **GN** H *GN* BN | 11423 (11230) | **GN** H *GN* BN |
| 11411 (11240) | **GN** H *GN* BN | 11424 (11239) | **GN** H *GN* BN |
| 11412 (11209) | **GN** H *GN* BN | 11425 (11234) | **GN** H *GN* BN |
| 11413 (11212) | **GN** H *GN* BN | 11426 (11252) | **GN** H *GN* BN |

| 11427 (11200) | **GN** H *GN* BN | 11429 (11275) | **GN** H *GN* BN |
| 11428 (11233) | **GN** H *GN* BN | 11430 (11248) | **GN** H *GN* BN |

## AD1J (FO)  MALLARD  OPEN FIRST

Mark 4. Air conditioned. Converted from TFRB with new interior by Bombardier Wakefield 2005. 46/– 1T. BT41 bogies. ETH 6X.

Lot No. 31046 Metro-Cammell 1989–92. 41.3 t.

| 11998 (10314) | **GN** H *GN* BN | 11999 (10316) | **GN** H *GN* BN |

## AC2G (TSO)  OPEN STANDARD

Mark 3A. Air conditioned. All refurbished with modified seat backs and new layout and further refurbished with new seat trim. –/76 2T (s –/70 2T 2W, z –/70 1TD 1T 2W). BT10 bogies. d. ETH 6X.

t Coaches modified for One Anglia with 8 Compin Pegasus seats at saloon ends for "priority" use and more unidirectional seating. –/80 2T.

Note: 12169–72 were converted from open composites 11908–10/22, formerly FOs 11008–10/22.

**12004–12168.** Lot No. 30877 Derby 1975–77. 34.3 t.
**12169–12172.** Lot No. 30878 Derby 1975–76. 34.3 t.

| 12004 |   | V | P |    | WI | 12033 z |   | V | P |    | LM |
| 12005 |   | V | P | 1A | NC | 12034 |   | V | P |    | ZD |
| 12007 |   | V | P |    | WI | 12035 |   | V | P | 1A | NC |
| 12008 |   | V | P |    | WI | 12036 s |   | V | P |    | WI |
| 12009 t | 1 | P |   | 1A | NC | 12037 t | 1 | P |   | 1A | NC |
| 12010 |   | V | P |    | ZD | 12038 |   | V | P |    | LM |
| 12011 |   | V | P |    | WB | 12040 t | 1 | P |   | 1A | NC |
| 12012 |   | V | P | 1A | NC | 12041 t | 1 | P |   | 1A | NC |
| 12013 |   | V | P |    | ZD | 12042 s |   | V | P |    | ZD |
| 12014 |   | V | P |    | LM | 12043 |   | V | P |    | WB |
| 12015 t | 1 | P |   | 1A | NC | 12044 |   | V | P | 1A | NC |
| 12016 |   | V | P |    | ZD | 12045 |   | V | P |    | WI |
| 12017 |   | V | P |    | WI | 12046 |   | V | P |    | ZD |
| 12019 t | 1 | P |   | 1A | NC | 12047 z |   | V | P |    | WI |
| 12020 |   | V | P |    | ZD | 12048 |   | V | P |    | NC |
| 12021 |   | V | P | 1A | NC | 12049 | 1 | P |   | 1A | NC |
| 12022 |   | V | P |    | WI | 12050 s |   | V | P |    | WI |
| 12023 |   | V | P |    | ZD | 12051 |   | V | P | 1A | NC |
| 12024 t | 1 | P |   | 1A | NC | 12052 |   | V | P | CD | OY |
| 12025 |   | V | P |    | WI | 12053 |   | V | P |    | WB |
| 12026 t | 1 | P |   | 1A | NC | 12054 s |   | V | P |    | WB |
| 12027 |   | V | P |    | ZD | 12055 |   | V | P |    | WI |
| 12028 |   | V | P |    | WI | 12056 |   | V | P |    | ZD |
| 12029 |   | V | P |    | WI | 12057 |   | V | P |    | ZD |
| 12030 t | 1 | P |   | 1A | NC | 12058 |   | V | P | 1A | NC |
| 12031 | 1 | P |   | 1A | NC | 12059 s |   | V | P |    | WI |
| 12032 t | 1 | P |   | 1A | NC | 12060 t | 1 | P | 1A | NC |

| | | | | | | | | | | |
|---|---|---|---|---|---|---|---|---|---|---|
| 12061 | s | **V** | P | *1A* | NC | 12113 | | **V** | P | | WI |
| 12062 | t | **1** | P | *1A* | NC | 12114 | t | **1** | P | *1A* | NC |
| 12063 | | **V** | P | | WB | 12115 | t | **1** | P | *1A* | NC |
| 12064 | | **V** | P | *1A* | NC | 12116 | t | **1** | P | *1A* | NC |
| 12065 | | **V** | P | | LM | 12117 | | **V** | P | | WB |
| 12066 | | **V** | P | | ZD | 12118 | | **1** | P | *1A* | NC |
| 12067 | | **V** | P | | ZD | 12119 | | **V** | P | | WB |
| 12068 | | **V** | P | | ZD | 12120 | t | **1** | P | *1A* | NC |
| 12069 | | **V** | P | | WI | 12121 | | **V** | P | *1A* | NC |
| 12070 | | **V** | P | *1A* | NC | 12122 | z | **V** | P | | WB |
| 12071 | | **V** | P | | WI | 12123 | | **V** | P | | LM |
| 12072 | | **V** | P | | WI | 12124 | | **V** | P | | WI |
| 12073 | | **V** | P | | ZD | 12125 | | **V** | P | *1A* | NC |
| 12075 | | **V** | P | | WI | 12126 | | **V** | P | *1A* | NC |
| 12076 | | **V** | P | | WI | 12127 | | **V** | P | *1A* | NC |
| 12077 | | **V** | P | *CD* | OY | 12128 | s | **V** | P | | LM |
| 12078 | | **V** | P | | WB | 12129 | | **V** | P | *1A* | NC |
| 12079 | | **1** | P | *1A* | NC | 12130 | | **V** | P | *1A* | NC |
| 12080 | | **V** | P | | WI | 12131 | | **V** | P | *1A* | NC |
| 12081 | | **V** | P | | ZD | 12132 | | **V** | P | *1A* | NC |
| 12082 | t | **1** | P | *1A* | NC | 12133 | | **V** | P | | WB |
| 12083 | | **V** | P | | WI | 12134 | | **V** | P | | WI |
| 12084 | | **V** | P | | ZD | 12135 | | **V** | P | | ZD |
| 12085 | s | **V** | P | | WI | 12136 | | **V** | P | *1A* | NC |
| 12086 | s | **V** | P | | WI | 12137 | t | **1** | P | *1A* | NC |
| 12087 | s | **V** | P | | WI | 12138 | | **V** | P | | WB |
| 12088 | z | **1** | P | *CD* | OY | 12139 | | **V** | P | | LM |
| 12089 | | **V** | P | *1A* | NC | 12141 | | **V** | P | *1A* | NC |
| 12090 | t | **1** | P | *1A* | NC | 12142 | z | **V** | P | | WB |
| 12091 | t | **1** | P | *1A* | NC | 12143 | | **1** | P | *1A* | NC |
| 12092 | | **V** | P | | LM | 12144 | s | **V** | P | | WI |
| 12093 | t | **1** | P | *1A* | NC | 12145 | | **V** | P | *1A* | NC |
| 12094 | | **V** | P | *1A* | NC | 12146 | | **1** | P | *1A* | NC |
| 12095 | | **V** | P | | WI | 12147 | | **V** | P | | ZD |
| 12096 | | **V** | AM | | ZH | 12148 | | **1** | P | *1A* | NC |
| 12097 | t | **1** | P | *1A* | NC | 12149 | | **V** | P | *1A* | NC |
| 12098 | | **V** | P | *1A* | NC | 12150 | | **V** | P | *1A* | NC |
| 12099 | | **V** | P | | ZD | 12151 | | **1** | P | *1A* | NC |
| 12100 | z | **V** | P | | LM | 12152 | | **V** | P | *1A* | NC |
| 12101 | s | **V** | P | *1A* | NC | 12153 | | **V** | P | | ZD |
| 12102 | | **V** | P | | WI | 12154 | | **1** | P | | ZD |
| 12103 | | **1** | P | *1A* | NC | 12155 | s | **V** | P | *1A* | NC |
| 12104 | | **V** | P | *1A* | NC | 12156 | | **V** | P | | WI |
| 12105 | t | **1** | P | *1A* | NC | 12157 | | **V** | P | *1A* | NC |
| 12106 | | **V** | P | | WI | 12158 | | **V** | P | *1A* | NC |
| 12107 | | **V** | P | | ZD | 12159 | | **1** | P | *1A* | NC |
| 12108 | s | **V** | P | | ZD | 12160 | s | **V** | P | | WI |
| 12109 | t | **1** | P | *1A* | NC | 12161 | z | **V** | P | | WB |
| 12110 | | **V** | P | | ZD | 12163 | | **V** | P | | WI |
| 12111 | | **V** | P | | ZD | 12164 | | **V** | P | | ZD |
| 12112 | z | **V** | P | *1A* | NC | 12165 | | **V** | P | *1A* | NC |

| 12166 | **1** | P | *1A* | NC |
| 12167 | **V** | P | *1A* | NC |
| 12168 s | **V** | P | | ZD |
| 12169 s | **V** | P | | WI |

| 12170 s | **V** | P | | ZD |
| 12171 s | **1** | P | *1A* | NC |
| 12172 s | **V** | P | | LM |

## AI2J (TSOE) MALLARD OPEN STANDARD (END)

Mark 4. Air conditioned. rebuilt with new interior by Bombardier Wakefield 2003–05. Seperate area for 26 smokers, but smoking is no longer allowed. –/76 1T. BT41 bogies. ETH 6X.

Note: 12232 was converted from the original 12405.

**12200–12231.** Lot No. 31047 Metro-Cammell 1989–91. 41.8 t.
**12232.** Lot No. 31049 Metro-Cammell 1989–92. 41.8 t.

| 12200 | **GN** | H *GN* | BN |
| 12201 | **GN** | H *GN* | BN |
| 12202 | **GN** | H *GN* | BN |
| 12203 | **GN** | H *GN* | BN |
| 12204 | **GN** | H *GN* | BN |
| 12205 | **GN** | H *GN* | BN |
| 12207 | **GN** | H *GN* | BN |
| 12208 | **GN** | H *GN* | BN |
| 12209 | **GN** | H *GN* | BN |
| 12210 | **GN** | H *GN* | BN |
| 12211 | **GN** | H *GN* | BN |
| 12212 | **GN** | H *GN* | BN |
| 12213 | **GN** | H *GN* | BN |
| 12214 | **GN** | H *GN* | BN |
| 12215 | **GN** | H *GN* | BN |
| 12216 | **GN** | H *GN* | BN |
| 12217 | **GN** | H *GN* | BN |
| 12218 | **GN** | H *GN* | BN |
| 12219 | **GN** | H *GN* | BN |
| 12220 | **GN** | H *GN* | BN |
| 12222 | **GN** | H *GN* | BN |
| 12223 | **GN** | H *GN* | BN |
| 12224 | **GN** | H *GN* | BN |
| 12225 | **GN** | H *GN* | BN |
| 12226 | **GN** | H *GN* | BN |
| 12227 | **GN** | H *GN* | BN |
| 12228 | **GN** | H *GN* | BN |
| 12229 | **GN** | H *GN* | BN |
| 12230 | **GN** | H *GN* | BN |
| 12231 | **GN** | H *GN* | BN |
| 12232 | **GN** | H *GN* | BN |

## AL2J (TSOD) MALLARD OPEN STANDARD (DISABLED ACCESS)

Mark 4. Air conditioned. Rebuilt with new interior by Bombardier Wakefield 2003–05. –/68 2W 1TD. BT41 bogies. ETH 6X.

Note: 12331 has been converted from TSO 12531.

**12300–12330.** Lot No. 31048 Metro-Cammell 1989–91. 40.8 t.
**12331.** Lot No. 31049 Metro-Cammell 1989–92. 40.8 t.

| 12300 | **GN** | H *GN* | BN |
| 12301 | **GN** | H *GN* | BN |
| 12302 | **GN** | H *GN* | BN |
| 12303 | **GN** | H *GN* | BN |
| 12304 | **GN** | H *GN* | BN |
| 12305 | **GN** | H *GN* | BN |
| 12307 | **GN** | H *GN* | BN |
| 12308 | **GN** | H *GN* | BN |
| 12309 | **GN** | H *GN* | BN |
| 12310 | **GN** | H *GN* | BN |
| 12311 | **GN** | H *GN* | BN |
| 12312 | **GN** | H *GN* | BN |
| 12313 | **GN** | H *GN* | BN |
| 12315 | **GN** | H *GN* | BN |
| 12316 | **GN** | H *GN* | BN |
| 12317 | **GN** | H *GN* | BN |

| 12318 | **GN** | H *GN* | BN |
|-------|--------|--------|-----|
| 12319 | **GN** | H *GN* | BN |
| 12320 | **GN** | H *GN* | BN |
| 12321 | **GN** | H *GN* | BN |
| 12322 | **GN** | H *GN* | BN |
| 12323 | **GN** | H *GN* | BN |
| 12324 | **GN** | H *GN* | BN |
| 12325 | **GN** | H *GN* | BN |
| 12326 | **GN** | H *GN* | BN |
| 12327 | **GN** | H *GN* | BN |
| 12328 | **GN** | H *GN* | BN |
| 12329 | **GN** | H *GN* | BN |
| 12330 | **GN** | H *GN* | BN |
| 12331 | **GN** | H *GN* | BN |

## AC2J (TSO)    MALLARD    OPEN STANDARD

Mark 4. Air conditioned. Rebuilt with new interior by Bombardier Wakefield 2003–05. –/76 2T. BT41 bogies. ETH 6X.

Lot No. 31049 Metro-Cammell 1989–92. 40.8 t.

Note: 12405 is the second coach to carry that number. It was built from the bodyshell originally intended for 12221. The original 12405 is now 12232. 12490–12512 were cancelled.

| 12400 | **GN** | H *GN* | BN |
|-------|--------|--------|-----|
| 12401 | **GN** | H *GN* | BN |
| 12402 | **GN** | H *GN* | BN |
| 12403 | **GN** | H *GN* | BN |
| 12404 | **GN** | H *GN* | BN |
| 12405 | **GN** | H *GN* | BN |
| 12406 | **GN** | H *GN* | BN |
| 12407 | **GN** | H *GN* | BN |
| 12409 | **GN** | H *GN* | BN |
| 12410 | **GN** | H *GN* | BN |
| 12411 | **GN** | H *GN* | BN |
| 12414 | **GN** | H *GN* | BN |
| 12415 | **GN** | H *GN* | BN |
| 12417 | **GN** | H *GN* | BN |
| 12419 | **GN** | H *GN* | BN |
| 12420 | **GN** | H *GN* | BN |
| 12421 | **GN** | H *GN* | BN |
| 12422 | **GN** | H *GN* | BN |
| 12423 | **GN** | H *GN* | BN |
| 12424 | **GN** | H *GN* | BN |
| 12425 | **GN** | H *GN* | BN |
| 12426 | **GN** | H *GN* | BN |
| 12427 | **GN** | H *GN* | BN |
| 12428 | **GN** | H *GN* | BN |
| 12429 | **GN** | H *GN* | BN |
| 12430 | **GN** | H *GN* | BN |
| 12431 | **GN** | H *GN* | BN |
| 12432 | **GN** | H *GN* | BN |
| 12433 | **GN** | H *GN* | BN |
| 12434 | **GN** | H *GN* | BN |
| 12436 | **GN** | H *GN* | BN |
| 12437 | **GN** | H *GN* | BN |
| 12438 | **GN** | H *GN* | BN |
| 12439 | **GN** | H *GN* | BN |
| 12440 | **GN** | H *GN* | BN |
| 12441 | **GN** | H *GN* | BN |
| 12442 | **GN** | H *GN* | BN |
| 12443 | **GN** | H *GN* | BN |
| 12444 | **GN** | H *GN* | BN |
| 12445 | **GN** | H *GN* | BN |
| 12446 | **GN** | H *GN* | BN |
| 12447 | **GN** | H *GN* | BN |
| 12448 | **GN** | H *GN* | BN |
| 12449 | **GN** | H *GN* | BN |
| 12450 | **GN** | H *GN* | BN |
| 12452 | **GN** | H *GN* | BN |
| 12453 | **GN** | H *GN* | BN |
| 12454 | **GN** | H *GN* | BN |
| 12455 | **GN** | H *GN* | BN |
| 12456 | **GN** | H *GN* | BN |
| 12457 | **GN** | H *GN* | BN |
| 12458 | **GN** | H *GN* | BN |
| 12459 | **GN** | H *GN* | BN |
| 12460 | **GN** | H *GN* | BN |
| 12461 | **GN** | H *GN* | BN |
| 12462 | **GN** | H *GN* | BN |
| 12463 | **GN** | H *GN* | BN |
| 12464 | **GN** | H *GN* | BN |
| 12465 | **GN** | H *GN* | BN |
| 12466 | **GN** | H *GN* | BN |
| 12467 | **GN** | H *GN* | BN |
| 12468 | **GN** | H *GN* | BN |
| 12469 | **GN** | H *GN* | BN |
| 12470 | **GN** | H *GN* | BN |
| 12471 | **GN** | H *GN* | BN |
| 12472 | **GN** | H *GN* | BN |

| 12473 | **GN** | H *GN* | BN | | 12489 | **GN** | H *GN* | BN |
|-------|--------|--------|----|--|-------|--------|--------|----|
| 12474 | **GN** | H *GN* | BN | | 12513 | **GN** | H *GN* | BN |
| 12476 | **GN** | H *GN* | BN | | 12514 | **GN** | H *GN* | BN |
| 12477 | **GN** | H *GN* | BN | | 12515 | **GN** | H *GN* | BN |
| 12478 | **GN** | H *GN* | BN | | 12518 | **GN** | H *GN* | BN |
| 12480 | **GN** | H *GN* | BN | | 12519 | **GN** | H *GN* | BN |
| 12481 | **GN** | H *GN* | BN | | 12520 | **GN** | H *GN* | BN |
| 12483 | **GN** | H *GN* | BN | | 12522 | **GN** | H *GN* | BN |
| 12484 | **GN** | H *GN* | BN | | 12526 | **GN** | H *GN* | BN |
| 12485 | **GN** | H *GN* | BN | | 12533 | **GN** | H *GN* | BN |
| 12486 | **GN** | H *GN* | BN | | 12534 | **GN** | H *GN* | BN |
| 12488 | **GN** | H *GN* | BN | | 12538 | **GN** | H *GN* | BN |

## AA11 (FK)                                          CORRIDOR FIRST

Mark 1. 42/– 2T. ETH 3.

**13229–13230**. Lot No. 30381 Swindon 1959. B4 bogies. 33 t.
**13321**. Lot No. 30667 Swindon 1962. Commonwealth bogies. 36 t.

| 13229 | xk | **M** | BK *BK* | BT | | 13321 | x | **M** | WC | CS |
|-------|----|-------|---------|----|--|-------|---|-------|----|----|
| 13230 | xk | **M** | BK *BK* | BT | | | | | | |

## AA1A (FK)                                          CORRIDOR FIRST

Mark 2A. Pressure ventilated. 42/– 2T. B4 bogies. ETH 4.

**13440**. Lot No. 30774 Derby 1968. 33 t.
**13474**. Lot No. 30785 Derby 1968. 33 t.

| 13440 | v | **G** | FM *FM* | RL | | 13474 | v | **G** | FM *FM* | RL |
|-------|---|-------|---------|----|--|-------|---|-------|---------|----|

## AD1B (FO)                                            OPEN FIRST

Mark 2B. Pressure ventilated. 42/– 2T. B4 bogies. ETH 4.

Lot No. 30789 Derby 1968. 33 t.

These two vehicles were built as FKs, sold to Northern Ireland Railways 1980 and regauged to 5'3". NIR converted them to 56-seater TSOs. Since withdrawn, repatriated to Britain and converted back to standard gauge 2002/3. Under conversion to FO.

| 13498 | (13498, NIR926) | **PC** | RA | CS |
|-------|-----------------|--------|----|----|
| 13508 | (13508, NIR924) | **PC** | RA | CS |

## AB11 (BFK)                                  CORRIDOR BRAKE FIRST

Mark 1. 24/– 1T. Commonwealth bogies. ETH 2.

**14007**. Lot No. 30382 Swindon 1959. 35 t.
**17013–17019**. Lot No. 30668 Swindon 1961. 36 t.
**17023**. Lot No. 30718 Swindon 1963. Metal window frames. 36 t.

Originally numbered in 14xxx series and then renumbered in 17xxx series.

| | | | | | | | | | | |
|---|---|---|---|---|---|---|---|---|---|---|
| 14007 | x | **M** | B1 | *LS* | BH | | 17018 | v | **CH** | VT | *VT* | TM |
| 17013 | | **PC** | JH | *LS* | SO | | 17019 | x | **M** | 92 | *LS* | TM |
| 17015 | x | **G** | E | *E* | OM | | 17023 | x | **G** | E | | SL |

## AB1Z (BFK)                  CORRIDOR BRAKE FIRST

Mark 2. Pressure ventilated. 24/– 1T. B4 bogies. ETH 4.

Lot No. 30756 Derby 1966. 31.5 t.

Originally numbered 14041.

| 17041 | | **M** | DG | *LS* | BQ | |
|---|---|---|---|---|---|---|

## AB1A (BFK)                  CORRIDOR BRAKE FIRST

Mark 2A. Pressure ventilated. 24/– 1T. B4 bogies. ETH 4.

**17056–17077.** Lot No. 30775 Derby 1967–8. 32 t.
**17086–17102.** Lot No. 30786 Derby 1968. 32 t.

Originally numbered 14056–102. 17089 and 17090 were numbered 35502 and 35503 for a time when declassified.

| 17056 | | **CH** | RV | *RV* | CP | | 17090 | v | **CH** | H | | TM |
|---|---|---|---|---|---|---|---|---|---|---|---|---|
| 17077 | | **RV** | RV | *RV* | CP | | 17096 | | **G** | MN | *LS* | SL |
| 17086 | | **RV** | RV | | CD | | 17102 | | **M** | WC | *WC* | CS |
| 17089 | v | **G** | FM | | RL | | | | | | | |

## AX5B                COUCHETTE/GENERATOR COACH

Mark 2B. Formerly part of Royal Train. Converted from a BFK built 1969. Consists of luggage accommodation, guard's compartment, 350 kW diesel generator and staff sleeping accommodation. Pressure ventilated. B5 bogies. ETH 5X.

**Non-standard Livery:** 17105 is Oxford blue.

Lot No. 30888 Wolverton 1977. 46 t.

| 17105 | (14105, 2905) | | **O** | RV | *RV* | CP |
|---|---|---|---|---|---|---|

## AB1D (BFK)                  CORRIDOR BRAKE FIRST

Mark 2D. Air conditioned (Stones equipment). 24/– 1T. B4 Bogies. ETH 5.

Lot No. 30823 Derby 1971–72. 33.5 t.

**Non-Standard Livery:** 17141 is purple.

Originally numbered 14141–72.

| 17141 | **O** | E | | FP | | 17163 | | | VS | | CO |
|---|---|---|---|---|---|---|---|---|---|---|---|
| 17144 | | FM | | BH | | 17165 | | | E | | FP |
| 17153 | **WR** | E | | CS | | 17167 | **VN** | | VS | *VS* | CP |
| 17156 | | MA | | DY | | 17168 | d | **M** | WC | *WC* | CS |
| 17159 | **CH** | RV | | SL | | 17169 | | | E | | CS |
| 17161 | | E | | OM | | 17170 | | | FM | | BH |

17172      E          FP        |

# AE1G (BFO)          OPEN BRAKE FIRST

Mark 3B. Air conditioned. Fitted with hydraulic handbrake. Refurbished with table lamps and burgundy seat trim. 36/– 1T (w 35/– 1T) BT10 bogies. pg. d. ETH 5X.

Lot No. 30990 Derby 1986. 35.81 t.

| 17173 | **V** | P | *CD* | OY | | 17175 w | **V** | P | | LT |
| 17174 | **V** | P | *CD* | OY | | | | | | |

# AA21 (SK)          CORRIDOR STANDARD

Mark 1. Each vehicle has eight compartments. All remaining vehicles have metal window frames and melamine interior panelling. Commonwealth bogies. –/48 2T. ETH 4.

Lot No. 30685 Derby 1961–62. 36 t.

t Rebuilt internally as TSO using components from 4936. –/64 2T.

Originally numbered 25756–25893.

| 18756 | x | **M** | WC | *WC* | CS | | 18808 | x | | **M** | WC | *WC* | CS |
| 18767 | x | **M** | WC | *WC* | CS | | 18862 | x | | **M** | WC | *WC* | CS |
| 18806 | xt | **M** | WC | *WC* | CS | | 18893 | x | | **CH** | WC | | CS |

# AB31 (BCK)      CORRIDOR BRAKE COMPOSITE

Mark 1. There are two variants depending upon whether the standard class compartments have armrests. Each vehicle has two first class and three standard class compartments. 12/18 2T (12/24 2T *). ETH 2.

**21232.** Lot No. 30574 GRCW 1960. B4 bogies. 34 t.
**21241–21246.** Lot No. 30669 Swindon 1961–62. Commonwealth bogies. 36 t.
**21256.** Lot No. 30731 Derby 1963. Commonwealth bogies. 37 t.
**21266–21272.** Lot No. 30732 Derby 1964. Commonwealth bogies. 37 t.

**Non-Standard Livery:** 21232 is in BR Carmine & Cream lined out in black and gold.

| 21232 | x | **0** | 62 | *LS* | SK | | 21266 | x* | **M** | WC | *WC* | CS |
| 21241 | x | **M** | BK | *BK* | BT | | 21268 | * | | BS | | SO |
| 21245 | x | **M** | E | *E* | OM | | 21269 | * | **GC** | E | *E* | OM |
| 21246 | | **BG** | E | *E* | OM | | 21272 | x* | **CH** | RV | *RV* | CP |
| 21256 | x | **M** | WC | *WC* | CS | | | | | | | |

# AB21 (BSK)      CORRIDOR BRAKE STANDARD

Mark 1. There are two variants depending upon whether the compartments have armrests. Each vehicle has four compartments. Lots 30699 and 30721 have metal window frames and melamine interior panelling. –/24 1T. ETH2.

g Fitted with an e.t.s. generator.

**35185.** Lot No. 30427 Wolverton 1959. B4 bogies. 33 t.
**35317–35333.** Lot No. 30699 Wolverton 1962–63. Commonwealth bogies. 37 t.
**35449.** Lot No. 30728 Wolverton 1963. Commonwealth bogies. 37 t.
**35452–35486.** Lot No. 30721 Wolverton 1963. Commonwealth bogies. 37 t.

**Non-Standard Livery:** 35465 is in BR Carmine & Cream lined out in black and gold.

| | | | | | | | | | | |
|---|---|---|---|---|---|---|---|---|---|---|
| 35185 | x | **M** | BK | *BK* | BT | 35463 | v | **M** | WC | *LS* | CS |
| 35317 | x | **G** | IR | *LS* | BQ | 35465 | x | **0** | LW | *LS* | CP |
| 35329 | v | **G** | MH | *LS* | RL | 35468 | v | **M** | NM | *LS* | YK |
| 35333 | x | **CH** | 24 | *LS* | DI | 35469 | xg | **M** | E | *E* | OM |
| 35449 | x | **M** | BE | *LS* | RL | 35470 | v | **CH** | VT | *LS* | TM |
| 35452 | x | **RR** | LW | | CP | 35476 | x | **M** | 62 | *LS* | SK |
| 35453 | x | **CH** | GW | *LS* | DI | 35479 | v | **M** | SV | *LS* | KR |
| 35459 | x | **M** | WC | *WC* | CS | 35486 | x | **M** | SV | *LS* | KR |
| 35461 | x | **CH** | RV | *LS* | OM | | | | | | |

# AB1C (BFK)                  CORRIDOR BRAKE FIRST

Mark 2C. Pressure ventilated. Renumbered when declassified. –/24 1T. B4 bogies. ETH 4.

Lot No. 30796 Derby 1969–70. 32.5 t.

35508   (14128, 17128)      **M**   IR   *LS*   BQ

# AB5C                        BRAKE/POWER KITCHEN

Mark 2C. Pressure ventilated. Converted from BFK (declassified to BSK) built 1970. Converted at West Coast Railway Company 2000–01. Consists of 60 kVA generator, guard's compartment and electric kitchen. B5 bogies. ETH 4.

**Non-Standard Livery:** British Racing Green with gold lining.

Lot No. 30796 Derby 1969–70. 32.5 t.

35511   (14130, 17130)      **0**   RA          CP

# AB1A (BFK)                  CORRIDOR BRAKE FIRST

Mark 2A. Pressure ventilated. Renumbered when declassified. –/24 1T. B4 bogies. Cage removed from brake compartment. ETH 4.

Lot No. 30786 Derby 1968. 32 t.

35517   (14088, 17088)      **M**    IR   *LS*   BQ
35518   (14097, 17097)      **PC**   IR   *LS*   SL

# NAMED COACHES

The following miscellaneous coaches carry names:

| | | | |
|---|---|---|---|
| 1200 | AMBER | 3247 | CHATSWORTH |
| 1659 | CAMELOT | 3267 | BELVOIR |
| 1800 | TINTAGEL | 3273 | ALNWICK |
| 3105 | JULIA | 3275 | HARLECH |
| 3113 | JESSICA | 5193 | CLAN MACLEOD |
| 3117 | CHRISTINA | 5212 | CAPERKAILZIE |
| 3128 | VICTORIA | 5229 | THE GREEN KNIGHT |
| 3130 | PAMELA | 5239 | THE RED KNIGHT |
| 3136 | DIANA | 5278 | MELISANDE |
| 3143 | PATRICIA | 5365 | Deborah |
| 3174 | GLAMIS | 5376 | Michaela |
| 3181 | TOPAZ | 5419 | SIR LAUNCELOT |
| 3182 | WARWICK | 9391 | PENDRAGON |
| 3188 | ONYX | 10569 | LEVIATHAN |
| 3223 | DIAMOND | 10729 | CREWE |
| 3228 | AMETHYST | 10734 | BALMORAL |
| 3229 | JADE | 17013 | ALBANNACH SGIATHACH |
| 3231 | Apollo | 17086 | Georgina |
| 3240 | SAPPHIRE | 35518 | MERLIN |
| 3244 | EMERALD | | |

# 2.2 HIGH SPEED TRAIN TRAILER CARS

HSTs consist of a number of trailer cars (usually seven to nine) with a power car at each end. All trailer cars are classified Mark 3 and have BT10 bogies with disc brakes and central door locking. Heating is by a 415 V three-phase supply and vehicles have air conditioning. Max. Speed is 125 m.p.h.

All vehicles underwent a mid-life refurbishment in the 1980s, and a further refurbishment programme was completed in November 2000, with each train operating company having a different scheme as follows:

**First Great Western.** Green seat covers and extra partitions between seat bays.

**Great North Eastern Railway.** New ceiling lighting panels and brown seat covers. First class vehicles have table lamps and imitation walnut plastic end panels.

**Virgin Cross-Country.** Green seat covers. Standard class vehicles had four seats in the centre of each carriage replaced with a luggage stack. All have now passed to other operators or are in store.

**Midland Mainline.** Grey seat covers, redesigned seat squabs, side carpeting and two seats in the centre of each standard class carriage and one in first class carriages replaced with a luggage stack.

Midland Mainline vehicles underwent a further refurbishment programme during 2003/04. This involved fitting new fluorescent and halogen ceiling lighting and a new design of seat squab with blue upholstery in first class.

In addition, **GNER** buffet cars have been modernised with new corner bars and each set had an extra vehicle added with a disabled persons toilet.

Ten sets ex-Virgin Cross-Country, and some spare vehicles, were temporarily allocated to Midland Mainline for the temporary service to Manchester during 2003/04 and had a facelift. Buffet cars were converted from TRSB to TRFB and renumbered in the 408xx series. These sets are now in use with First Great Western or GNER, or are in store.

## Tops Type Codes

TOPS type codes for HST trailer cars are made up as follows:

(1) Two letters denoting the layout of the vehicle as follows:

| | | | |
|---|---|---|---|
| GH | Open | GL | Kitchen |
| GJ | Open with Guard's compartment. | GN | Buffet |
| GK | Buffet | | |

(2) A digit for the class of passenger accommodation

| | | | |
|---|---|---|---|
| 1 | First | 4 | Unclassified |
| 2 | Standard (formerly second) | | |

(3) A suffix relating to the build of coach.

G    Mark 3

**Operator Codes**

The normal operator codes are given in brackets after the TOPS codes. These are as follows:

| | | | |
|---|---|---|---|
| TF | Trailer First | TGS | Trailer Guard's Standard |
| TRB | Trailer Buffet First | TRSB | Trailer Buffet Standard |
| TRFB | Trailer Buffet First | TS | Trailer Standard |

# GN4G (TRB)  TRAILER BUFFET FIRST

Converted from TRSB by fitting first class seats. Renumbered from 404xx series by subtracting 200. 23/–.

**40204–40228.** Lot No. 30883 Derby 1976–77. 36.12 t.
**40231.** Lot No. 30899 Derby 1978–79. 36.12 t.

| | | | | | | | | |
|---|---|---|---|---|---|---|---|---|
| 40204 | **FG** | A | *GW* | PM | 40210 | **FG** | A | *GW* | PM |
| 40205 | **FG** | A | *GW* | PM | 40221 | **FG** | A | *GW* | PM |
| 40207 | **FG** | A | *GW* | PM | 40228 | **FG** | A | *GW* | PM |
| 40208 | **FG** | A | *GW* | PM | 40231 | **FG** | A | *GW* | PM |
| 40209 | **FG** | A | *GW* | PM | | | | | |

# GK2G (TRSB)  TRAILER BUFFET STANDARD

Renumbered from 400xx series by adding 400. –/33 1W.

**40401–40426.** Lot No. 30883 Derby 1976–77. 36.12 t.
**40433–40437.** Lot No. 30899 Derby 1978–79. 36.12 t.

**Notes:** 40433–40434 were numbered 40233–40234 for a time when fitted with 23 first class seats.

§ Experimentally refurbished First Group vehicle. Converted to TRFB. 23/–.

**Non-standard livery:** 40423 – First Group experimental (indigo, purple and blue with pink, white and blue stripes).

| | | | | | | | |
|---|---|---|---|---|---|---|---|
| 40401 | **V** | FG | BR | 40424 | **V** | P | BR |
| 40402 | **V** | P | LM | 40425 | **V** | P | LM |
| 40403 | **V** | P | BR | 40426 | **V** | P | LM |
| 40416 | **V** | P | BR | 40433 | **V** | P | BR |
| 40417 | **V** | P | BR | 40434 | **V** | P | LM |
| 40419 | **V** | P | LM | 40436 | **GN** | FG | LA |
| 40423 § | **0** | FG | PM | 40437 | **V** | FG | BR |

# GK1G (TRFB)  TRAILER BUFFET FIRST

These vehicles have larger kitchens than the 402xx and 404xx series vehicles, and are used in trains where full meal service is required. They were renumbered from the 403xx series (in which the seats were unclassified) by adding 400 to the previous number. 17/–.

**40700–40721.** Lot No. 30921 Derby 1978–79. 38.16 t.
**40722–40735.** Lot No. 30940 Derby 1979–80. 38.16 t.
**40736–40753.** Lot No. 30948 Derby 1980–81. 38.16 t.

**40754–40757**. Lot No. 30966 Derby 1982. 38.16 t.

r Modified with new corner bar.

| | | | | | | | | | |
|---|---|---|---|---|---|---|---|---|---|
| 40700 | **MN** | P | *MM* | NL | | 40730 | **MN** | P | *MM* | NL |
| 40701 | **MN** | P | *MM* | NL | | 40731 | **FG** | A | *GW* | LA |
| 40702 | **MN** | P | *MM* | NL | | 40732 | **MN** | A | *MM* | NL |
| 40703 | **FG** | A | *GW* | LA | | 40733 | **FG** | A | *GW* | LA |
| 40704 r | **GN** | A | *GN* | EC | | 40734 | **FG** | A | *GW* | LA |
| 40705 r | **GN** | A | *GN* | EC | | 40735 r | **GN** | A | *GN* | EC |
| 40706 r | **GN** | A | *GN* | EC | | 40736 | **FG** | A | *GW* | LA |
| 40707 | **FG** | A | *GW* | LA | | 40737 r | **GN** | A | *GN* | EC |
| 40708 | **MN** | P | *MM* | NL | | 40738 | **FG** | A | *GW* | LA |
| 40709 | **FG** | A | *GW* | LA | | 40739 | **FG** | A | *GW* | LA |
| 40710 | **FG** | A | *GW* | LA | | 40740 r | **GN** | A | *GN* | EC |
| 40711 r | **GN** | A | *GN* | EC | | 40741 | **MN** | P | *MM* | NL |
| 40712 | **FG** | A | *GW* | LA | | 40742 r | **GN** | A | *GN* | EC |
| 40713 | **FG** | A | *GW* | LA | | 40743 | **FG** | A | *GW* | LA |
| 40714 | **FG** | A | *GW* | LA | | 40744 | **FG** | A | *GW* | LA |
| 40715 | **FG** | A | *GW* | LA | | 40745 | **FG** | A | *GW* | LA |
| 40716 | **FG** | A | *GW* | PM | | 40746 | **MN** | P | *MM* | NL |
| 40717 | **FG** | A | *GW* | LA | | 40747 | **FG** | A | *GW* | PM |
| 40718 | **FG** | A | *GW* | LA | | 40748 r | **GN** | A | *GN* | EC |
| 40720 r | **GN** | A | *GN* | EC | | 40749 | **MN** | P | *MM* | NL |
| 40721 | **FG** | A | *GW* | LA | | 40750 r | **GN** | A | *GN* | EC |
| 40722 | **FG** | A | *GW* | LA | | 40751 | **MN** | P | *MM* | NL |
| 40723 | **MN** | A | *MM* | NL | | 40752 | **FG** | A | *GW* | LA |
| 40724 | **FG** | A | *GW* | LA | | 40753 | **MN** | P | *MM* | NL |
| 40725 | **FG** | A | *GW* | LA | | 40754 | **MN** | P | *MM* | NL |
| 40726 | **FG** | A | *GW* | LA | | 40755 | **FG** | A | *GW* | LA |
| 40727 | **FG** | A | *GW* | LA | | 40756 | **MN** | P | *MM* | NL |
| 40728 | **MN** | P | *MM* | NL | | 40757 | **FG** | A | *GW* | LA |
| 40729 | **MN** | P | *MM* | NL | | | | | | |

## GK1G (TRFB)                        TRAILER BUFFET FIRST

These vehicles have been converted from TRSBs in the 404xx series to be similar to the 407xx series vehicles. 17/–.

**40801–40803/40805/40808/40809/40811**. Lot No. 30883 Derby 1976–77. 38.16 t.
**40804/40806/40807/40810**. Lot No. 30899 Derby 1978–79. 38.16 t.

**Note:** 40802/40804/40811 were numbered 40212/40232/40211 for a time when fitted with 23 first class seats.

| | | | | | |
|---|---|---|---|---|---|
| 40801 | (40027, 40427) | **FG** | P | *GW* | LA |
| 40802 | (40012, 40412) | **FG** | P | *GW* | LA |
| 40803 | (40018, 40418) | **FG** | P | *GW* | LA |
| 40804 | (40032, 40432) | **MN** | P | | LM |
| 40805 | (40020, 40420) | **GN** | P | *GN* | EC |
| 40806 | (40029, 40429) | **FG** | P | *GW* | LA |
| 40807 | (40035, 40435) | **CD** | P | | LM |
| 40808 | (40015, 40415) | **FG** | P | *GW* | LA |

| 40809 | (40014, 40414) | **MN** | P |    | LM |
|-------|----------------|--------|---|----|----|
| 40810 | (40030, 40430) | **MN** | P |    | LM |
| 40811 | (40011, 40411) | **GN** | P | *GN* | EC |

## GN4G (TRB)                    TRAILER BUFFET FIRST

Converted from TRSB by First Great Western 23/–.

Lot No. 30883 Derby 1976–77. 36.12 t.

| 40900 | (40022, 40422) | **FG** | FG | *GW* | LA |
|-------|----------------|--------|----|------|----|

## GH1G (TF)                            TRAILER FIRST

**41003–41056**. Lot No. 30881 Derby 1976–77. 33.66 t.
**41057–41120**. Lot No. 30896 Derby 1977–78. 33.66 t.
**41121–41148**. Lot No. 30938 Derby 1979–80. 33.66 t.
**41149–41166**. Lot No. 30947 Derby 1980. 33.66 t.
**41167–41169**. Lot No. 30963 Derby 1982. 33.66 t.
**41170**. Lot No. 30967 Derby 1982. Former prototype vehicle. 33.66 t.
**41179/41180**. Lot No. 30884 Derby 1976–77. 33.66 t.
**41181–41184/41189**. Lot No. 30939 Derby 1979–80. 33.66 t.
**41185–41188**. Lot No. 30969 Derby 1982. 33.66 t.

As built 48/– 2T. (w 47/– 2T 1W).
s Fitted with centre luggage stack. 46/– 1T 1TD 1W.

| 41003 |    | **FG** | A  | *GW* | LA | 41031 |    | **FG** | A  | *GW* | LA |
|-------|----|--------|----|------|----|-------|----|--------|----|------|----|
| 41004 |    | **FG** | A  | *GW* | PM | 41032 |    | **FG** | A  | *GW* | LA |
| 41005 |    | **FG** | A  | *GW* | LA | 41033 |    | **FG** | A  | *GW* | LA |
| 41006 |    | **FG** | A  | *GW* | LA | 41034 |    | **FG** | A  | *GW* | LA |
| 41007 |    | **FG** | A  | *GW* | PM | 41035 |    | **MN** | A  | *MM* | NL |
| 41008 |    | **FG** | A  | *GW* | PM | 41036 | w  | **MN** | A  | *MM* | NL |
| 41009 |    | **FG** | A  | *GW* | PM | 41037 |    | **FG** | A  | *GW* | LA |
| 41010 |    | **FG** | A  | *GW* | PM | 41038 |    | **FG** | A  | *GW* | LA |
| 41011 |    | **FG** | A  | *GW* | PM | 41039 |    | **GN** | A  | *GN* | EC |
| 41012 |    | **FG** | A  | *GW* | PM | 41040 | w  | **GN** | A  | *GN* | EC |
| 41015 |    | **FG** | A  | *GW* | PM | 41041 | s  | **MN** | P  | *MM* | NL |
| 41016 |    | **FG** | A  | *GW* | PM | 41043 |    | **GN** | A  | *GN* | EC |
| 41017 |    | **FG** | A  | *GW* | PM | 41044 | w  | **GN** | A  | *GN* | EC |
| 41018 |    | **FG** | A  | *GW* | PM | 41045 | w  | **V**  | FG |      | BR |
| 41019 |    | **FG** | A  | *GW* | PM | 41046 | s  | **MN** | P  | *MM* | NL |
| 41020 |    | **FG** | A  | *GW* | PM | 41051 |    | **FG** | A  | *GW* | LA |
| 41021 |    | **FG** | A  | *GW* | PM | 41052 |    | **FG** | A  | *GW* | LA |
| 41022 |    | **FG** | A  | *GW* | PM | 41055 |    | **FG** | A  | *GW* | LA |
| 41023 |    | **FG** | A  | *GW* | LA | 41056 |    | **FG** | A  | *GW* | LA |
| 41024 |    | **FG** | A  | *GW* | LA | 41057 |    | **MN** | P  | *MM* | NL |
| 41025 |    | **MN** | A  | *MM* | NL | 41058 | s  | **MN** | P  | *MM* | NL |
| 41026 |    | **MN** | A  | *MM* | NL | 41059 | w  | **V**  | FG |      | BR |
| 41027 |    | **FG** | A  | *GW* | LA | 41061 |    | **MN** | P  | *MM* | NL |
| 41028 |    | **FG** | A  | *GW* | LA | 41062 | rw | **MN** | P  | *MM* | NL |
| 41029 |    | **FG** | A  | *GW* | LA | 41063 |    | **MN** | P  | *MM* | NL |
| 41030 |    | **FG** | A  | *GW* | LA | 41064 | s  | **MN** | P  | *MM* | NL |

| | | | | | | | | | | |
|---|---|---|---|---|---|---|---|---|---|---|
| 41065 | | **FG** | A | *GW* | LA | 41119 w | **MN** | P | | LM |
| 41066 | | **GN** | A | *GN* | EC | 41120 | **GN** | A | *GN* | EC |
| 41067 | s | **MN** | P | *MM* | NL | 41121 | **FG** | A | *GW* | LA |
| 41068 | s | **MN** | P | *MM* | NL | 41122 | **FG** | A | *GW* | LA |
| 41069 | s | **MN** | P | *MM* | NL | 41123 | **FG** | A | *GW* | LA |
| 41070 | s | **MN** | P | *MM* | NL | 41124 | **FG** | A | *GW* | LA |
| 41071 | | **MN** | P | *MM* | NL | 41125 | **FG** | A | *GW* | LA |
| 41072 | s | **MN** | P | *MM* | NL | 41126 | **FG** | A | *GW* | LA |
| 41075 | | **MN** | P | *MM* | NL | 41127 | **FG** | A | *GW* | LA |
| 41076 | s | **MN** | P | *MM* | NL | 41128 | **FG** | A | *GW* | LA |
| 41077 | | **MN** | P | *MM* | NL | 41129 | **FG** | A | *GW* | PM |
| 41078 | | **MN** | P | *MM* | NL | 41130 | **FG** | A | *GW* | PM |
| 41079 | | **MN** | P | *MM* | NL | 41131 | **FG** | A | *GW* | LA |
| 41080 | s | **MN** | P | *MM* | NL | 41132 | **FG** | A | *GW* | LA |
| 41081 | w | **MN** | P | | LM | 41133 | **FG** | A | *GW* | LA |
| 41083 | | **MN** | P | *MM* | NL | 41134 | **FG** | A | *GW* | LA |
| 41084 | s | **MN** | P | *MM* | NL | 41135 | **FG** | A | *GW* | LA |
| 41085 | | **GN** | FG | | LA | 41136 | **FG** | A | *GW* | LA |
| 41086 | w | **V** | FG | | LA | 41137 | **FG** | A | *GW* | PM |
| 41087 | | **GN** | A | *GN* | EC | 41138 | **FG** | A | *GW* | PM |
| 41088 | w | **GN** | A | *GN* | EC | 41139 | **FG** | A | *GW* | LA |
| 41089 | | **FG** | A | *GW* | LA | 41140 | **FG** | A | *GW* | LA |
| 41090 | w | **GN** | A | *GN* | EC | 41141 | **FG** | A | *GW* | LA |
| 41091 | | **GN** | A | *GN* | EC | 41142 | **FG** | A | *GW* | LA |
| 41092 | w | **GN** | A | *GN* | EC | 41143 | **FG** | A | *GW* | LA |
| 41093 | | **FG** | A | *GW* | LA | 41144 | **FG** | A | *GW* | LA |
| 41094 | | **FG** | A | *GW* | LA | 41145 | **FG** | A | *GW* | LA |
| 41095 | w | **GN** | P | *GN* | EC | 41146 | **FG** | A | *GW* | LA |
| 41096 | w | **MN** | P | | LM | 41147 | w | **FG** | P | *GW* | LA |
| 41097 | | **GN** | A | *GN* | EC | 41148 | w | **V** | P | | LM |
| 41098 | w | **GN** | A | *GN* | EC | 41149 | w | **FG** | P | *GW* | LA |
| 41099 | | **GN** | A | *GN* | EC | 41150 | **GN** | A | *GN* | EC |
| 41100 | w | **GN** | A | *GN* | EC | 41151 | **GN** | A | *GN* | EC |
| 41101 | | **FG** | A | *GW* | LA | 41152 | **GN** | A | *GN* | EC |
| 41102 | | **FG** | A | *GW* | LA | 41153 | **MN** | P | *MM* | NL |
| 41103 | | **FG** | A | *GW* | LA | 41154 | s | **MN** | P | *MM* | NL |
| 41104 | | **FG** | A | *GW* | LA | 41155 | **MN** | P | *MM* | NL |
| 41105 | | **FG** | A | *GW* | LA | 41156 | **MN** | P | *MM* | NL |
| 41106 | | **FG** | A | *GW* | LA | 41157 | **FG** | A | *GW* | LA |
| 41107 | w | **FG** | P | *GW* | LA | 41158 | **FG** | A | *GW* | LA |
| 41108 | w | **MN** | P | | LM | 41159 | w | **V** | P | | LM |
| 41109 | w | **FG** | P | *GW* | LA | 41160 | w | **V** | FG | | LA |
| 41110 | | **FG** | A | *GW* | PM | 41161 | w | **MN** | P | | LM |
| 41111 | | **MN** | P | *MM* | NL | 41162 | w | **FG** | FG *GW* | | LA |
| 41112 | | **MN** | P | *MM* | NL | 41163 | w | **V** | FG | | BR |
| 41113 | s | **MN** | P | *MM* | NL | 41164 | w | **GN** | A | *GN* | EC |
| 41114 | | **FG** | FG *GW* | | LA | 41165 | w | **V** | P | | LM |
| 41115 | w | **V** | P | | BR | 41166 | w | **V** | FG | | BR |
| 41116 | | **FG** | A | *GW* | LA | 41167 | w | **GN** | FG | | LA |
| 41117 | | **MN** | P | *MM* | NL | 41168 | w | **FG** | P | *GW* | LA |
| 41118 | w | **GN** | A | *GN* | EC | 41169 | w | **V** | P | | LM |

| 41170 | (41001) | **GN** | A | *GN* | EC | | 41184 | (42270) | **MN** | P | | | LM |
|---|---|---|---|---|---|---|---|---|---|---|---|---|---|
| 41179 | (40505) | **FG** | A | *GW* | PM | | 41185 | (42313) | **GN** | P | *GN* | | EC |
| 41180 | (40511) | **FG** | A | *GW* | LA | | 41186 | (42312) | **FG** | P | *GW* | | LA |
| 41181 | (42282) | **FG** | P | *GW* | LA | | 41187 | (42311) | **MN** | P | | | LM |
| 41182 | (42278) | **FG** | P | *GW* | LA | | 41188 | (42310) | **FG** | P | *GW* | | LA |
| 41183 | (42274) | **FG** | P | *GW* | LA | | 41189 | (42298) | **MN** | P | | | LM |

## GH2G (TS)                                      TRAILER STANDARD

**42003–42090/42362.** Lot No. 30882 Derby 1976–77. 33.60 t.
**42091–42250.** Lot No. 30897 Derby 1977–79. 33.60 t.
**42251–42305.** Lot No. 30939 Derby 1979–80. 33.60 t.
**42306–42322.** Lot No. 30969 Derby 1982. 33.60 t.
**42323–42341.** Lot No. 30983 Derby 1984–85. 33.60 t.
**42342/42360.** Lot No. 30949 Derby 1982. 33.47 t. Converted from TGS.
**42343/42345.** Lot No. 30970 Derby 1982. 33.47 t. Converted from TGS.
**42344/42361.** Lot No. 30964 Derby 1982. 33.47 t. Converted from TGS.
**42346/42347/42350/42351.** Lot No. 30881 Derby 1976–77. 33.66 t. Converted from TF.
**42348/42349/42363.** Lot No. 30896 Derby 1977–78. 33.66 t. Converted from TF.
**42352/42354.** Lot No. 30897 Derby 1977. Were TF from 1983 to 1992. 33.66 t.
**42353/42355–42357.** Lot No. 30967 Derby 1982. Ex-prototype vehicles. 33.66 t.

As built –/76 2T.
s Centre luggage stack –/72 2T.
t Centre luggage stack –/72 2T. Fitted with pt.
u Centre luggage stack –/74 2T.
w Centre luggage stack –/72 2T 1W.
z Seats removed for wheelchair spaces –/70 2T 2W.
* disabled persons toilet and 5 tip-up seats. –/65 1T 1TD.
† disabled persons toilet. –/62 1T 1TD 1W.
e Rebuilt VOLO TV "entertainment" coach with new seats and on-train entertainment systems. 36 seats have monitors fixed to the seatbacks.
§ Experimentally refurbished First Group vehicle.

42158 was also numbered 41177 for a time when fitted with first class seats.

**Non-standard liveries:** 42076 – VOLO TV (all over silver with various images). 42353 – First Group experimental (indigo, purple and blue with pink, white and blue stripes).

| 42003 | | **FG** | A | *GW* | PM | | 42016 | | **FG** | A | *GW* | PM |
|---|---|---|---|---|---|---|---|---|---|---|---|---|
| 42004 | * | **FG** | A | *GW* | LA | | 42019 | | **FG** | A | *GW* | PM |
| 42005 | | **FG** | A | *GW* | PM | | 42021 | * | **FG** | A | *GW* | PM |
| 42006 | | **FG** | A | *GW* | PM | | 42023 | | **FG** | A | *GW* | PM |
| 42007 | * | **FG** | A | *GW* | LA | | 42024 | * | **FG** | A | *GW* | PM |
| 42008 | * | **FG** | A | *GW* | PM | | 42025 | | **FG** | A | *GW* | PM |
| 42009 | | **FG** | A | *GW* | PM | | 42026 | | **FG** | A | *GW* | PM |
| 42010 | | **FG** | A | *GW* | PM | | 42027 | | **FG** | A | *GW* | PM |
| 42012 | * | **FG** | A | *GW* | PM | | 42028 | | **FG** | A | *GW* | PM |
| 42013 | | **FG** | A | *GW* | PM | | 42029 | | **FG** | A | *GW* | PM |
| 42014 | | **FG** | A | *GW* | PM | | 42030 | * | **FG** | A | *GW* | PM |
| 42015 | * | **FG** | A | *GW* | PM | | 42031 | | **FG** | A | *GW* | PM |

| | | | | | | | | | | |
|---|---|---|---|---|---|---|---|---|---|---|
| 42032 | | **FG** | A | *GW* | PM | 42084 s | **MN** | P | | LM |
| 42033 | | **FG** | A | *GW* | LA | 42085 t | **MN** | P | | LM |
| 42034 | | **FG** | A | *GW* | LA | 42086 s | **MN** | P | | LM |
| 42035 | | **FG** | A | *GW* | LA | 42087 s | **MN** | P | | LM |
| 42036 | u | **MN** | A | *MM* | NL | 42088 s | **V** | P | | LM |
| 42037 | u | **MN** | A | *MM* | NL | 42089 | **FG** | A | *GW* | PM |
| 42038 | u | **MN** | A | *MM* | NL | 42090 s | **V** | P | | BR |
| 42039 | | **FG** | A | *GW* | LA | 42091 † | **GN** | A | *GN* | EC |
| 42040 | | **FG** | A | *GW* | LA | 42092 s | **V** | FG | | BR |
| 42041 | | **FG** | A | *GW* | LA | 42093 s | **V** | FG | | BR |
| 42042 | | **FG** | A | *GW* | LA | 42094 s | **V** | FG | | BR |
| 42043 | | **FG** | A | *GW* | LA | 42095 | **FG** | FG | *GW* | LA |
| 42044 | | **FG** | A | *GW* | LA | 42096 | **FG** | A | *GW* | LA |
| 42045 | | **FG** | A | *GW* | LA | 42097 w | **MN** | A | *MM* | NL |
| 42046 | | **FG** | A | *GW* | LA | 42098 | **FG** | A | *GW* | PM |
| 42047 | | **FG** | A | *GW* | LA | 42099 | **FG** | A | *GW* | LA |
| 42048 | | **FG** | A | *GW* | LA | 42100 u | **MN** | P | *MM* | NL |
| 42049 | | **FG** | A | *GW* | LA | 42101 w | **MN** | P | *MM* | NL |
| 42050 | | **FG** | A | *GW* | LA | 42102 u | **MN** | P | *MM* | NL |
| 42051 | u | **MN** | A | *MM* | NL | 42103 z | **GN** | FG | | LA |
| 42052 | u | **MN** | A | *MM* | NL | 42104 | **GN** | A | *GN* | EC |
| 42053 | u | **MN** | A | *MM* | NL | 42105 s | **V** | FG | | BR |
| 42054 | | **FG** | A | *GW* | LA | 42106 | **GN** | A | *GN* | EC |
| 42055 | | **FG** | A | *GW* | LA | 42107 | **FG** | A | *GW* | LA |
| 42056 | | **FG** | A | *GW* | LA | 42108 s | **V** | FG | | BR |
| 42057 | | **GN** | A | *GN* | EC | 42109 s | **V** | P | | BR |
| 42058 | | **GN** | A | *GN* | EC | 42110 s | **V** | P | | BR |
| 42059 | | **GN** | A | *GN* | EC | 42111 u | **MN** | P | *MM* | NL |
| 42060 | | **FG** | A | *GW* | LA | 42112 u | **MN** | P | *MM* | NL |
| 42061 | | **FG** | A | *GW* | PM | 42113 u | **MN** | P | *MM* | NL |
| 42062 | * | **FG** | A | *GW* | LA | 42115 t | **MN** | P | | LM |
| 42063 | | **GN** | A | *GN* | EC | 42116 † | **GN** | A | *GN* | EC |
| 42064 | | **GN** | A | *GN* | EC | 42117 | **GN** | P | *GN* | EC |
| 42065 | | **GN** | A | *GN* | EC | 42118 | **FG** | A | *GW* | LA |
| 42066 | * | **FG** | A | *GW* | LA | 42119 u | **MN** | P | *MM* | NL |
| 42067 | | **FG** | A | *GW* | LA | 42120 u | **MN** | P | *MM* | NL |
| 42068 | | **FG** | A | *GW* | LA | 42121 u | **MN** | P | *MM* | NL |
| 42069 | * | **FG** | A | *GW* | LA | 42122 | **GN** | A | *GN* | EC |
| 42070 | | **FG** | A | *GW* | LA | 42123 u | **MN** | P | *MM* | NL |
| 42071 | | **FG** | A | *GW* | LA | 42124 u | **MN** | P | *MM* | NL |
| 42072 | | **FG** | A | *GW* | PM | 42125 u | **MN** | P | *MM* | NL |
| 42073 | | **FG** | A | *GW* | LA | 42126 | **FG** | A | *GW* | LA |
| 42074 | | **FG** | A | *GW* | LA | 42127 † | **GN** | A | *GN* | EC |
| 42075 | | **FG** | A | *GW* | PM | 42128 † | **GN** | A | *GN* | EC |
| 42076 | e | **0** | A | *GW* | LA | 42129 | **FG** | A | *GW* | LA |
| 42077 | | **FG** | A | *GW* | LA | 42130 t | **V** | P | | LM |
| 42078 | | **FG** | A | *GW* | LA | 42131 u | **MN** | P | *MM* | NL |
| 42079 | | **FG** | A | *GW* | PM | 42132 u | **MN** | P | *MM* | NL |
| 42080 | | **FG** | A | *GW* | PM | 42133 u | **MN** | P | *MM* | NL |
| 42081 | * | **FG** | A | *GW* | LA | 42134 | **GN** | A | *GN* | EC |
| 42083 | | **FG** | A | *GW* | LA | 42135 u | **MN** | P | *MM* | NL |

| Number | | | | | | Number | | | | |
|---|---|---|---|---|---|---|---|---|---|---|
| 42136 | u | **MN** | P | *MM* | NL | 42188 | † | **GN** | A | *GN* | EC |
| 42137 | u | **MN** | P | *MM* | NL | 42189 | † | **GN** | A | *GN* | EC |
| 42138 | * | **FG** | A | *GW* | PM | 42190 | | **GN** | A | *GN* | EC |
| 42139 | u | **MN** | P | *MM* | NL | 42191 | | **GN** | A | *GN* | EC |
| 42140 | u | **MN** | P | *MM* | NL | 42192 | | **GN** | A | *GN* | EC |
| 42141 | u | **MN** | P | *MM* | NL | 42193 | | **GN** | A | *GN* | EC |
| 42143 | | **FG** | A | *GW* | LA | 42194 | w | **MN** | P | *MM* | NL |
| 42144 | | **FG** | A | *GW* | LA | 42195 | | **FG** | P | *GW* | LA |
| 42145 | | **FG** | A | *GW* | LA | 42196 | | **FG** | A | *GW* | LA |
| 42146 | | **GN** | A | *GN* | EC | 42197 | | **FG** | A | *GW* | LA |
| 42147 | u | **MN** | P | *MM* | NL | 42198 | | **GN** | A | *GN* | EC |
| 42148 | u | **MN** | P | *MM* | NL | 42199 | | **GN** | A | *GN* | EC |
| 42149 | u | **MN** | P | *MM* | NL | 42200 | * | **FG** | A | *GW* | LA |
| 42150 | | **GN** | A | *GN* | EC | 42201 | * | **FG** | A | *GW* | LA |
| 42151 | w | **MN** | P | *MM* | NL | 42202 | * | **FG** | A | *GW* | LA |
| 42152 | u | **MN** | P | *MM* | NL | 42203 | | **FG** | A | *GW* | LA |
| 42153 | u | **MN** | P | *MM* | NL | 42204 | | **FG** | A | *GW* | LA |
| 42154 | | **GN** | A | *GN* | EC | 42205 | u | **MN** | P | *MM* | NL |
| 42155 | w | **MN** | P | *MM* | NL | 42206 | * | **FG** | A | *GW* | LA |
| 42156 | u | **MN** | P | *MM* | NL | 42207 | * | **FG** | A | *GW* | LA |
| 42157 | u | **MN** | P | *MM* | NL | 42208 | | **FG** | A | *GW* | LA |
| 42158 | | **GN** | A | *GN* | EC | 42209 | | **FG** | A | *GW* | LA |
| 42159 | s | **V** | P | | BR | 42210 | u | **MN** | P | *MM* | NL |
| 42160 | s | **V** | P | | BR | 42211 | * | **FG** | A | *GW* | LA |
| 42161 | † | **GN** | A | *GN* | EC | 42212 | | **FG** | A | *GW* | LA |
| 42162 | | **FG** | P | *GW* | LA | 42213 | | **FG** | A | *GW* | LA |
| 42163 | w | **MN** | P | *MM* | NL | 42214 | | **FG** | A | *GW* | PM |
| 42164 | u | **MN** | P | *MM* | NL | 42215 | | **GN** | A | *GN* | EC |
| 42165 | u | **MN** | P | *MM* | NL | 42216 | | **FG** | A | *GW* | LA |
| 42166 | | **FG** | P | *GW* | LA | 42217 | | **FG** | P | *GW* | LA |
| 42167 | | **GN** | FG | | LA | 42218 | | **FG** | P | *GW* | LA |
| 42168 | | **GN** | FG | | LA | 42219 | | **GN** | A | *GN* | EC |
| 42169 | | **GN** | FG | | LA | 42220 | w | **MN** | P | *MM* | NL |
| 42170 | | **FG** | P | *GW* | LA | 42221 | | **FG** | A | *GW* | LA |
| 42171 | | **GN** | A | *GN* | EC | 42222 | | **FG** | P | *GW* | LA |
| 42172 | | **GN** | A | *GN* | EC | 42223 | | **FG** | P | *GW* | LA |
| 42173 | | **FG** | P | *GW* | LA | 42224 | | **FG** | P | *GW* | LA |
| 42174 | | **FG** | P | *GW* | LA | 42225 | u | **MN** | P | *MM* | NL |
| 42175 | s | **V** | FG | | BR | 42226 | | **GN** | A | *GN* | EC |
| 42176 | t | **V** | FG | | BR | 42227 | u | **MN** | P | *MM* | NL |
| 42177 | s | **V** | FG | | BR | 42228 | u | **MN** | P | *MM* | NL |
| 42178 | t | **MN** | P | | LM | 42229 | u | **MN** | P | *MM* | NL |
| 42179 | | **GN** | A | *GN* | EC | 42230 | u | **MN** | P | *MM* | NL |
| 42180 | | **GN** | A | *GN* | EC | 42231 | | **FG** | FG | *GW* | LA |
| 42181 | | **GN** | A | *GN* | EC | 42232 | | **FG** | FG | *GW* | LA |
| 42182 | | **GN** | A | *GN* | EC | 42233 | | **FG** | FG | *GW* | LA |
| 42183 | * | **FG** | A | *GW* | LA | 42234 | s | **V** | P | | BR |
| 42184 | | **FG** | A | *GW* | LA | 42235 | | **GN** | A | *GN* | EC |
| 42185 | | **FG** | A | *GW* | LA | 42236 | | **FG** | A | *GW* | PM |
| 42186 | | **GN** | A | *GN* | EC | 42237 | s | **GN** | P | *GN* | EC |
| 42187 | t | **MN** | P | | LM | 42238 | † | **GN** | A | *GN* | EC |

| No. | | Class | A/P | Type | Depot |
|---|---|---|---|---|---|
| 42239 | † | **GN** | A | *GN* | EC |
| 42240 | | **GN** | A | *GN* | EC |
| 42241 | | **GN** | A | *GN* | EC |
| 42242 | | **GN** | A | *GN* | EC |
| 42243 | | **GN** | A | *GN* | EC |
| 42244 | | **GN** | A | *GN* | EC |
| 42245 | | **FG** | A | *GW* | LA |
| 42246 | s | **MN** | P | | LM |
| 42247 | t | **MN** | P | | LM |
| 42248 | s | **MN** | P | | LM |
| 42249 | s | **MN** | P | | LM |
| 42250 | | **FG** | A | *GW* | LA |
| 42251 | * | **FG** | A | *GW* | PM |
| 42252 | | **FG** | A | *GW* | LA |
| 42253 | | **FG** | A | *GW* | LA |
| 42254 | | **FG** | P | *GW* | LA |
| 42255 | * | **FG** | A | *GW* | LA |
| 42256 | | **FG** | A | *GW* | LA |
| 42257 | | **FG** | A | *GW* | LA |
| 42258 | | **FG** | P | *GW* | LA |
| 42259 | * | **FG** | A | *GW* | PM |
| 42260 | | **FG** | A | *GW* | LA |
| 42261 | | **FG** | A | *GW* | LA |
| 42262 | | **FG** | P | *GW* | LA |
| 42263 | | **FG** | A | *GW* | LA |
| 42264 | * | **FG** | A | *GW* | PM |
| 42265 | | **FG** | A | *GW* | LA |
| 42266 | | **FG** | P | *GW* | LA |
| 42267 | * | **FG** | A | *GW* | PM |
| 42268 | * | **FG** | A | *GW* | LA |
| 42269 | | **FG** | A | *GW* | PM |
| 42271 | * | **FG** | A | *GW* | LA |
| 42272 | | **FG** | A | *GW* | LA |
| 42273 | | **FG** | A | *GW* | LA |
| 42275 | * | **FG** | A | *GW* | LA |
| 42276 | | **FG** | A | *GW* | LA |
| 42277 | | **FG** | A | *GW* | LA |
| 42279 | * | **FG** | A | *GW* | LA |
| 42280 | | **FG** | A | *GW* | LA |
| 42281 | | **FG** | A | *GW* | LA |
| 42283 | | **FG** | A | *GW* | LA |
| 42284 | | **FG** | A | *GW* | PM |
| 42285 | | **FG** | A | *GW* | PM |
| 42286 | s | **V** | P | | LM |
| 42287 | * | **FG** | A | *GW* | LA |
| 42288 | | **FG** | A | *GW* | LA |
| 42289 | | **FG** | A | *GW* | LA |
| 42290 | t | **V** | P | | LM |
| 42291 | * | **FG** | A | *GW* | LA |
| 42292 | * | **FG** | A | *GW* | LA |
| 42293 | | **FG** | A | *GW* | LA |
| 42294 | s | **V** | P | | LM |
| 42295 | * | **FG** | A | *GW* | LA |
| 42296 | | **FG** | A | *GW* | LA |
| 42297 | | **FG** | A | *GW* | LA |
| 42299 | * | **FG** | A | *GW* | LA |
| 42300 | | **FG** | A | *GW* | LA |
| 42301 | | **FG** | A | *GW* | LA |
| 42302 | s | **V** | FG | | LA |
| 42303 | t | **V** | FG | | LA |
| 42304 | s | **V** | FG | | LA |
| 42305 | s | **V** | FG | | LA |
| 42306 | s | **GN** | P | *GN* | EC |
| 42307 | s | **GN** | P | *GN* | EC |
| 42308 | s | **MN** | P | | LM |
| 42309 | | **MN** | P | | LM |
| 42314 | | **FG** | P | *GW* | LA |
| 42315 | | **FG** | P | *GW* | LA |
| 42316 | | **FG** | P | *GW* | LA |
| 42317 | | **FG** | P | *GW* | LA |
| 42318 | s | **V** | P | | LM |
| 42319 | t | **V** | P | | LM |
| 42320 | s | **V** | P | | LM |
| 42321 | s | **V** | P | | LM |
| 42322 | s | **V** | P | | BR |
| 42323 | | **GN** | A | *GN* | EC |
| 42324 | w | **MN** | P | *MM* | NL |
| 42325 | | **FG** | A | *GW* | LA |
| 42326 | s | **GN** | P | *GN* | EC |
| 42327 | w | **MN** | P | *MM* | NL |
| 42328 | w | **MN** | P | *MM* | NL |
| 42329 | w | **MN** | P | *MM* | NL |
| 42330 | s | **GN** | P | *GN* | EC |
| 42331 | w | **MN** | P | *MM* | NL |
| 42332 | | **FG** | A | *GW* | PM |
| 42333 | | **FG** | A | *GW* | LA |
| 42334 | | **FG** | P | *GW* | LA |
| 42335 | u | **MN** | P | *MM* | NL |
| 42336 | s | **MN** | P | | LM |
| 42337 | w | **MN** | P | *MM* | NL |
| 42338 | s | **MN** | P | | LM |
| 42339 | w | **MN** | P | *MM* | NL |
| 42340 | | **GN** | A | *GN* | EC |
| 42341 | u | **MN** | P | *MM* | NL |

| No. | | | | Class | A/P | Type | Depot |
|---|---|---|---|---|---|---|---|
| 42342 | (44082) | | u | **MN** | A | *MM* | NL |
| 42343 | (44095) | | | **FG** | A | *GW* | LA |
| 42344 | (44092) | * | | **FG** | A | *GW* | LA |

| 42345 | (44096) | * | FG | A | *GW* | LA |
| 42346 | (41053) | | FG | A | *GW* | PM |
| 42347 | (41054) | * | FG | A | *GW* | LA |
| 42348 | (41073) | * | FG | A | *GW* | LA |
| 42349 | (41074) | | FG | A | *GW* | PM |
| 42350 | (41047) | | FG | A | *GW* | LA |
| 42351 | (41048) | | FG | A | *GW* | LA |
| 42352 | (42142, 41176) | u | MN | P | *MM* | NL |
| 42353 | (42001, 41171) | § | 0 | FG | | PM |
| 42354 | (42114, 41175) | | GN | A | *GN* | EC |
| 42355 | (42000, 41172) | | GN | A | *GN* | EC |
| 42356 | (42002, 41173) | | FG | A | *GW* | PM |
| 42357 | (41002, 41174) | | GN | A | *GN* | EC |
| 42360 | (44084, 45084) | | FG | A | *GW* | PM |
| 42361 | (44099, 42000) | | FG | A | *GW* | LA |
| 42362 | (42011, 41178) | | FG | A | *GW* | LA |
| 42363 | (41082) | † | GN | A | *GN* | EC |

# GJ2G (TGS)          TRAILER GUARD'S STANDARD

**44000.** Lot No. 30953 Derby 1980. 33.47 t.
**44001–44090.** Lot No. 30949 Derby 1980–82. 33.47 t.
**44091–44094.** Lot No. 30964 Derby 1982. 33.47 t.
**44097–44101.** Lot No. 30970 Derby 1982. 33.47 t.

As built –/65 1T (w –/63 1T 1W). pg.
st Fitted with centre luggage stack s –/63 1T, t –/61 1T.

| 44000 | w | FG | P | *GW* | LA | | 44025 | w | FG | A | *GW* | LA |
| 44001 | w | FG | A | *GW* | LA | | 44026 | w | FG | A | *GW* | PM |
| 44002 | w | FG | A | *GW* | PM | | 44027 | s | MN | P | *MM* | NL |
| 44003 | w | FG | A | *GW* | PM | | 44028 | w | FG | A | *GW* | LA |
| 44004 | w | FG | A | *GW* | PM | | 44029 | w | FG | A | *GW* | LA |
| 44005 | w | FG | A | *GW* | PM | | 44030 | w | FG | A | *GW* | LA |
| 44007 | w | FG | A | *GW* | PM | | 44031 | w | GN | A | *GN* | EC |
| 44008 | w | FG | A | *GW* | PM | | 44032 | w | FG | A | *GW* | PM |
| 44009 | w | FG | A | *GW* | PM | | 44033 | w | FG | A | *GW* | LA |
| 44010 | w | FG | A | *GW* | PM | | 44034 | w | FG | A | *GW* | LA |
| 44011 | w | FG | A | *GW* | LA | | 44035 | w | FG | A | *GW* | LA |
| 44012 | s | MN | A | *MM* | NL | | 44036 | w | FG | A | *GW* | PM |
| 44013 | w | FG | A | *GW* | LA | | 44037 | w | FG | A | *GW* | LA |
| 44014 | w | FG | A | *GW* | LA | | 44038 | w | FG | A | *GW* | LA |
| 44015 | w | FG | A | *GW* | LA | | 44039 | w | FG | A | *GW* | LA |
| 44016 | w | FG | A | *GW* | LA | | 44040 | w | FG | A | *GW* | LA |
| 44017 | s | MN | A | *MM* | NL | | 44041 | s | MN | P | *MM* | NL |
| 44018 | w | FG | A | *GW* | LA | | 44042 | t | MN | P | | LM |
| 44019 | w | GN | A | *GN* | EC | | 44043 | w | FG | A | *GW* | LA |
| 44020 | w | FG | A | *GW* | LA | | 44044 | s | MN | P | *MM* | NL |
| 44021 | t | V | P | | LM | | 44045 | w | GN | A | *GN* | EC |
| 44022 | w | FG | A | *GW* | LA | | 44046 | s | MN | P | *MM* | NL |
| 44023 | w | FG | A | *GW* | LA | | 44047 | s | MN | P | *MM* | NL |
| 44024 | w | FG | A | *GW* | LA | | 44048 | s | MN | P | *MM* | NL |

| 44049 | w | **FG** | A | *GW* | LA |
|-------|---|--------|----|------|----|
| 44050 | s | **MN** | P | *MM* | NL |
| 44051 | s | **MN** | P | *MM* | NL |
| 44052 | s | **MN** | P | *MM* | NL |
| 44054 | s | **MN** | P | *MM* | NL |
| 44055 | w | **GN** | FG | | LA |
| 44056 | w | **GN** | A | *GN* | EC |
| 44057 | t | **V** | P | | LM |
| 44058 | w | **GN** | A | *GN* | EC |
| 44059 | w | **FG** | A | *GW* | LA |
| 44060 | t | **MN** | P | | LM |
| 44061 | w | **GN** | A | *GN* | EC |
| 44062 | t | **MN** | P | | LM |
| 44063 | w | **GN** | A | *GN* | EC |
| 44064 | w | **FG** | A | *GW* | LA |
| 44065 | t | **V** | P | | LM |
| 44066 | w | **FG** | A | *GW* | LA |
| 44067 | w | **FG** | A | *GW* | LA |
| 44068 | t | **V** | FG | | LA |
| 44069 | t | **MN** | P | | LM |
| 44070 | s | **MN** | P | *MM* | NL |
| 44071 | s | **MN** | P | *MM* | NL |
| 44072 | t | **V** | P | | LM |
| 44073 | s | **MN** | P | *MM* | NL |
| 44074 | s | **FG** | FG | *GW* | LA |
| 44075 | t | **GN** | P | *GN* | EC |
| 44076 | t | **V** | FG | | BR |
| 44077 | w | **GN** | A | *GN* | EC |
| 44078 | t | **MN** | P | | LM |
| 44079 | w | **FG** | P | *GW* | LA |
| 44080 | w | **GN** | A | *GN* | EC |
| 44081 | t | **V** | FG | | BR |
| 44083 | s | **MN** | P | *MM* | NL |
| 44085 | s | **MN** | P | *MM* | NL |
| 44086 | w | **FG** | A | *GW* | LA |
| 44088 | t | **V** | P | | LM |
| 44089 | t | **V** | P | | LM |
| 44090 | w | **FG** | P | *GW* | LA |
| 44091 | t | **V** | P | | LM |
| 44093 | w | **FG** | A | *GW* | LA |
| 44094 | w | **GN** | A | *GN* | EC |
| 44097 | w | **FG** | P | *GW* | LA |
| 44098 | w | **GN** | A | *GN* | EC |
| 44100 | t | **V** | FG | | OO |
| 44101 | w | **FG** | P | *GW* | LA |

▲ BR SR Green-liveried Mark 1 RBR 1696 at Blaenau Ffestiniog on 23/03/02.
**Ivor Bufton**

▼ BR SR Green-liveried Mark 1 FO 3114 at Blaenau Ffestiniog on 23/03/02.
**Ivor Bufton**

▲ GWR Chocolate & Cream-liveried Mark 1 TSO 4927 passes Gospel Oak on 19/02/05 during a "Buffer Puffer" Pathfinder railtour. **Robert Pritchard**

▼ BR Blue & Grey-liveried Mark 1 BCK 21246 is seen at Milton Keynes on 18/06/05. The coach is displaying a common problem with Mark 1 vehicles – peeling paint on the roof! **Mark Beal**

▲ BR Maroon-liveried Mark 1 BSK 35476 (99041) is used as a Locomotive Support Coach for steam loco 6233 "DUCHESS OF SUTHERLAND". Both are pictured here at Derby on 21/05/05.　　　　**Robert Pritchard**

▼ Riviera Trains Oxford blue & cream-liveried facelifted Mark 2A TSO 5322 at Gospel Oak on 19/02/05, next to the rear train loco 37406.　　　　**Robert Pritchard**

▲ BR Maroon-liveried Mark 2B TSO 5478, owned by West Coast Railway Company, at Bangor on 03/04/05. **Ivor Bufton**

▼ VSOE Northern Belle-liveried Mark 2D FO 3182 "WARWICK" at Chester on 10/09/03. **Ivor Bufton**

▲ First Great Western green-liveried Mark 2D BSO 9490 at Plymouth on 11/07/05, next to 57605 on the 23.50 Paddington–Penzance service.  **Robert Pritchard**

▼ VSOE Northern Belle-liveried Mark 2D BFK 17167 at Worcester Shrub Hill on 10/07/04.  **Stephen Widdowson**

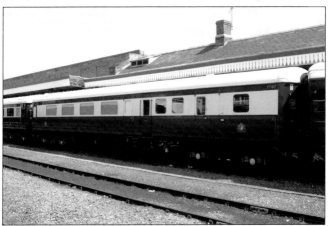

▲ Six Arriva Trains-liveried Mark 2Fs found use on Rhymney line services in summer 2005. TSO 6035 is at Lisvane & Thornhill on 16/07/05.　　**Mark Beal**

▼ Anglia Railways-liveried Mark 2F DBSO 9704 at Ipswich on 21/06/05.
**Rodney Lissenden**

▲ Midland Mainline-liveried HST TF 41117 is in the unusual location, for an HST, of Lincoln Central station on 04/12/04. The MML HST set was on hire to Central Trains for the day for working services between Lincoln and Nottingham in connection with the Lincoln Christmas Market. **Robert Pritchard**

▼ First Great Western-liveried HST TS 42293 at Totnes on 16/07/05.
**Robert Pritchard**

▲ Refurbished GNER-liveried "Mallard" Mark 4 TSO 12405 passes Newark North Gate on 11/12/04.                                                                    **Stephen Widdowson**

▼ VSOE Pullman car-liveried Kitchen First No. 284 "VERA", with B5 (SR) bogies, at Cardiff Central on 29/06/02.                                                   **Ivor Bufton**

▲ Network Rail-liveried Mark 1 Generator Van 6260 and another vehicle in Network Rail yellow livery are seen at Worting Junction on 24/06/05.

**Darren Ford**

▼ BR Blue-liveried Mark 1 Generator Van 6311 at Havant on 27/03/04.

**Darren Ford**

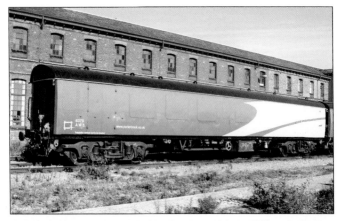

▲ Porterbrook-liveried Mark 1 EMU Translator Vehicle 6379 at Bedford on 04/09/04. **Mark Beal**

▼ Network Rail Yellow-liveried Overhead Line Equipment Test Coach 975091 (also known as "MENTOR" and converted from a Mark 1) at Derby on 03/06/05. **Robert Pritchard**

▲ Serco Railtest-liveried Test Coach 975290, converted from a Mark 2, at RTC Business Park Derby on 26/09/04. **Paul Robertson**

▼ Refurbished Overhead Line Maintenance, stores & roof access coach 975733, converted from a Mark 1, at Rugby Rail Plant depot on 31/12/04. **Mark Beal**

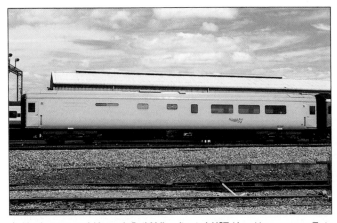

▲ Newly converted Network Rail Yellow-liveried HST New Measurement Train vehicle 977995 (converted from TRFM 40619) at RTC Business Park, Derby on 03/07/05. **Paul Robertson**

▼ BR Maroon-liveried Inspection Coach 999506 "AMANDA", converted from a BR Inspection Saloon, is seen at RTC Business Park, Derby on 03/07/05. **Paul Robertson**

# 2.3. SALOONS

Several specialist passenger carrying vehicles, normally referred to as saloons are permitted to run on the National Rail system. Many of these are to pre-nationalisation designs.

## WCJS FIRST SALOON

Built 1892 by LNWR, Wolverton. Originally dining saloon mounted on six-wheel bogies. Rebuilt with new underframe with four-wheel bogies in 1927. Rebuilt 1960 as observation saloon with DMU end. Gangwayed at other end. The interior has a saloon, kitchen, guards vestibule and observation lounge. Gresley bogies. 19/– 1T. 28.5 t. 75 m.p.h.

**Non-Standard Livery:** London & North Western Railway.

41      (484, 45018)    x   **0**     SH   *SH*     CJ

## LNWR DINING SALOON

Built 1890 by LNWR, Wolverton. Mounted on the underframe of LMS GUV 37908 in the 1980s. Contains kitchen and dining area seating 12 at tables for two. Gresley bogies. 10/–. 75 m.p.h. 25.4 t.

**Non-Standard Livery:** London & North Western Railway.

159     (5159)       x   **0**     SH   *SH*     CJ

## GNR FIRST CLASS SALOON

Built 1912 by GNR, Doncaster. Contains entrance vestibule, lavatory, two seperate saloons, library and luggage space. Gresley bogies. 19/– 1T. 75 m.p.h. 29.4 t.

**Non-Standard Livery:** Teak.

807     (4807)       x   **0**     SH   *SH*     CJ

## LNER GENERAL MANAGERS SALOON

Built 1945 by LNER, York. Gangwayed at one end with a verandah at the other. The interior has a dining saloon seating twelve, kitchen, toilet, office and nine seat lounge. 21/– 1T. B4 bogies. 75 m.p.h. ETH3. 35.7 t.

1999    (902260)        **M**   GS   *GS*    CS           DINING CAR No. 2

## GENERAL MANAGER'S SALOON

Renumbered 1989 from London Midland Region departmental series. Formerly the LMR General Manager's saloon. Rebuilt from LMS period 1 BFK M 5033 M to dia. 1654 and mounted on the underframe of BR suburban BS M 43232. Screw couplings have been removed. B4 bogies. 100 m.p.h. ETH2X.

LMS Lot No. 326 Derby 1927. 27.5 t.

| 6320 | (5033, DM 395707) x | **M** | 62 | *62* | | SK |
|------|---------------------|-------|----|------|--|----|

## GWR FIRST CLASS SALOON

Built 1930 by GWR, Swindon. Contains saloons at either end with body end observation windows, staff compartment, central kitchen and pantry/bar. Numbered DE321011 when in departmental service with British Railways. 20/– 1T. GWR saloon. 75 m.p.h. 34 t.

GWR Lot No. 1431 1930.

| 9004 | | **CH** | RA | *SH* | CJ |
|------|--|--------|----|------|----|

## LMS INSPECTION SALOONS

Built as engineers inspection saloons. Non-gangwayed. Observation windows at each end. The interior layout consists of two saloons interspersed by a central lavatory/kitchen/guards section. BR Mark 1 bogies. 80 m.p.h. 31.5 t.

**45020–45026.** Lot No. LMS 1356 Wolverton 1944.
**45029.** Lot No. LMS 1327 Wolverton 1942.
**999503.** Lot No. BR Wagon Lot. 3093 Wolverton 1957.

| 45020 | | | **E** | E | *E* | ML |
|-------|--|---|-------|----|-----|-----|
| 45026 | | v | **M** | HN | | CS |
| 45029 | | v | **E** | E | | ML |
| 999503 | | v | **M** | E | | OM |

## "QUEEN OF SCOTS" SERVICE CARS

Converted from BR Mark 1 BSKs. Commonwealth bogies. 100 m.p.h. ETH2.

**Non-Standard Livery:** London & North Western Railway.

**99035.** Lot No. 30699 Wolverton 1962–63.
**99886.** Lot No. 30721 Wolverton 1963.

| 99035 | (35322) | x | **0** | SH | *SH* | CJ | SERVICE CAR No. 2 |
|-------|---------|---|-------|----|------|----|-------------------|
| 99886 | (35407) | x | **0** | SH | *SH* | CJ | SERVICE CAR No. 1 |

# VSOE SUPPORT CARS

Converted 1983 (§ 199x) from BR Mark 1 BSK (§Courier vehicle converted from Mark 1 BSK 1986–87). Toilet retained and former compartment area replaced with train manager's office, crew locker room, linen store and dry goods store. The former luggage area has been adapted for use as an engineers' compartment and workshop. Commonwealth bogies. 100 m.p.h. ETH2.

**99538.** Lot No. 30229 Metro-Cammell 1955–57. 36 t.
**99545.** Lot No. 30721 Wolverton 1963. 37 t.

| | | | | | |
|---|---|---|---|---|---|
| 99538 (34991) | **PC** | VS | *VS* | SL | BAGGAGE CAR No. 9 |
| 99545 (35466, 80207) § | **PC** | VS | *VS* | SL | BAGGAGE CAR No. 11 |

# RAILFILMS KITCHEN/SLEEPING SALOON

Converted from BR Mark 1 SK. Contains three sleeping cabins with showers and toilets and a large kitchen/pantry. Commonwealth bogies. 100 m.p.h. ETH 4.

Lot No. 30726 York 1963.

**Non-standard Livery**: London & North Western Railway.

| | | | | |
|---|---|---|---|---|
| 99884 (26208, 19208) **0** | RA | | CS | State Car No. 84 |

# ROYAL SCOTSMAN SALOONS

Built 1960 by Metro-Cammell as Pullman Parlour First (§Pullman Kitchen First) for East Coast Main Line services. Rebuilt 1990 as sleeping cars with four twin sleeping rooms (*§ three twin sleeping rooms and two single sleeping rooms at each end). Commonwealth bogies. 38.5 t.

| | | | | |
|---|---|---|---|---|
| 99961 (324 AMBER) * **M** | GS | *GS* | CS | STATE CAR 1 |
| 99962 (329 PEARL) **M** | GS | *GS* | CS | STATE CAR 2 |
| 99963 (331 TOPAZ) **M** | GS | *GS* | CS | STATE CAR 3 |
| 99964 (313 FINCH) § **M** | GS | *GS* | CS | STATE CAR 4 |

Built 1960 by Metro-Cammell as Pullman Kitchen First for East Coast Main Line services. Rebuilt 1990 as observation car with open verandah seating 32. Commonwealth bogies. 38.5 t.

| | | | | |
|---|---|---|---|---|
| 99965 (319 SNIPE) **M** | GS | *GS* | CS | OBSERVATION CAR |

Built 1960 by Metro-Cammell as Pullman Kitchen First for East Coast Main Line services. Rebuilt 1993 as dining car. Commonwealth bogies. 38.5 t.

| | | | | |
|---|---|---|---|---|
| 99967 (317 RAVEN) **M** | GS | *GS* | CS | DINING CAR |

Mark 3A. Converted from SLEP at Carnforth Railway Restoration and Engineering Services in 1997. BT10 bogies. Attendant's and adjacent two sleeping compartments converted to generator room containing a 160 kW Volvo unit. In 99968 four sleeping compartments remain for staff use with another converted for use as a staff shower and toilet. The remaining five sleeping compartments have been replaced by two passenger cabins. In 99969 seven sleeping compartments remain for staff use. A further sleeping compartment, along with one toilet, have been converted to store rooms. The other two sleeping compartments have been combined to form a crew mess. ETH7X. 41.5 t.

Lot. No. 30960 Derby 1981–3.

| | | | | | |
|---|---|---|---|---|---|
| 99968 (10541) | **M** | GS | *GS* | CS | STATE CAR 5 |
| 99969 (10556) | **M** | GS | *GS* | CS | SERVICE CAR |

## RAILFILMS 'LMS CLUB CAR'

Converted from BR Mark 1 TSO at Carnforth Railway Restoration and Engineering Services in 1994. Contains kitchenette, pantry, coupé, lounge/reception area with two settees and two dining saloons. 24/– 1T. Commonwealth bogies. 100 m.p.h. ETH 4.

Lot. No. 30724 York 1963. 37 t.

| | | | | | |
|---|---|---|---|---|---|
| 99993 (5067) | **M** | RA | *WT* | OM | LMS CLUB CAR |

## BR INSPECTION SALOON

Mark 1. Short frames. Non-gangwayed. Observation windows at each end. The interior layout consists of two saloons interspersed by a central lavatory/kitchen/guards/luggage section. BR Mark 1 bogies. 90 m.p.h.

Lot No. BR Wagon Lot. 3379 Swindon 1960. 30.5 t.

| | | | | |
|---|---|---|---|---|
| 999509 | **E** | E | *E* | ML |

# 2.4. PULLMAN CAR COMPANY SERIES

Pullman cars have never generally been numbered as such, although many
have carried numbers, instead they have carried titles. However, a scheme of
schedule numbers exists which generally lists cars in chronological order. In
this section those numbers are shown followed by the car's title. Cars described
as 'kitchen' contain a kitchen in addition to passenger accommodation and
have gas cooking unless otherwise stated. Cars described as 'parlour' consist
entirely of passenger accomodation. Cars described as 'brake' contain a
compartment for the use of the guard and a luggage compartment in addition
to passenger accommodation.

## PULLMAN PARLOUR FIRST

Built 1927 by Midland Carriage and Wagon Company. Gresley bogies. 26/– 2T.
ETH 2. 41 t.

213  MINERVA              **PC**  VS  *VS*   SL

## PULLMAN PARLOUR FIRST

Built 1928 by Metropolitan Carriage and Wagon Company. Gresley bogies.
24/– 2T. ETH 4. 40 t.

239  AGATHA              **PC**  VS           SL
243  LUCILLE             **PC**  VS   *VS*   SL

## PULLMAN KITCHEN FIRST

Built 1925 by BRCW. Rebuilt by Midland Carriage & Wagon Company in 1928.
Gresley bogies. 20/– 1T. ETH 4. 41 t.

245  IBIS                **PC**  VS   *VS*   SL

## PULLMAN PARLOUR FIRST

Built 1928 by Metropolitan Carriage and Wagon Company. Gresley bogies.
24/– 2T. ETH 4.

254  ZENA                **PC**  VS   *VS*   SL

## PULLMAN KITCHEN FIRST

Built 1928 by Metropolitan Carriage and Wagon Company. Gresley bogies.
20/– 1T. ETH 4. 42 t.

255  IONE                **PC**  VS   *VS*   SL

# PULLMAN KITCHEN COMPOSITE

Built 1932 by Metropolitan Carriage and Wagon Company. Originally included in 6-Pul EMU. Electric cooking. EMU bogies. 12/16 1T.

| 264 | RUTH | **PC** | VS | | SL |
|-----|------|--------|-----|-----|-----|

# PULLMAN KITCHEN FIRST

Built 1932 by Metopolitan Carriage and Wagon Company. Originally included in 'Brighton Belle' EMUs but now used as hauled stock. Electric cooking. B5 (SR) bogies (§ EMU bogies). 20/– 1T. ETH 2. 44 t.

| 280 | AUDREY | | **PC** | VS | *VS* | SL |
|-----|--------|---|--------|-----|------|-----|
| 281 | GWEN | | **PC** | VS | *VS* | SL |
| 283 | MONA | § | **PC** | VS | | SL |
| 284 | VERA | | **PC** | VS | *VS* | SL |

# PULLMAN PARLOUR THIRD

Built 1932 by Metropolitan Carriage and Wagon Company. Originally included in 'Brighton Belle' EMUs. EMU bogies. –/56 2T.

| 285 | CAR No. 85 | **PC** | VS | SL |
|-----|------------|--------|-----|-----|
| 286 | CAR No. 86 | **PC** | VS | SL |

# PULLMAN BRAKE THIRD

Built 1932 by Metropolitan Carriage and Wagon Company. Originally driving motor cars in 'Brighton Belle' EMUs. Traction and control equipment removed for use as hauled stock. EMU bogies. –/48 1T.

| 288 | CAR No. 88 | **PC** | VS | SL |
|-----|------------|--------|-----|-----|
| 292 | CAR No. 92 | **PC** | VS | SL |
| 293 | CAR No. 93 | **PC** | VS | SL |

# PULLMAN PARLOUR FIRST

Built 1951 by Birmingham Railway Carriage and Wagon Company. Gresley bogies. 32/– 2T. ETH 3. 39 t.

| 301 | PERSEUS | **PC** | VS | *VS* | SL |
|-----|---------|--------|-----|------|-----|

Built 1952 by Pullman Car Company, Preston Park using underframe and bogies from 176 RAINBOW, the body of which had been destroyed by fire. Gresley bogies. 26/– 2T. ETH 4. 38 t.

| 302 | PHOENIX | **PC** | VS | *VS* | SL |
|-----|---------|--------|-----|------|-----|

# PULLMAN PARLOUR FIRST

Built 1951 by Birmingham Railway Carriage & Wagon Company. Gresley bogies. 32/– 2T. ETH 3. 39 t.

308  CYGNUS              **PC**   VS   *VS*   SL

# PULLMAN FIRST BAR

Built 1951 by Birmingham Railway Carriage & Wagon Company. Rebuilt 1999 by Blake Fabrications, Edinburgh with original timber-framed body replaced by a new fabricated steel body. Contains kitchen, bar, dining saloon and coupé. Electric cooking. Gresley bogies. 14/– 1T. ETH 3.

310  PEGASUS            **PC**   RA   *WT*   OM

Also carries "THE TRIANON BAR" branding.

# PULLMAN KITCHEN SECOND

Built 1960–1961 by Metro-Cammell for East Coast Main Line services. Commonwealth bogies. –/30 1T. 40 t.

335  CAR No. 335     x  **PC**   VT   *VT*   TM

# PULLMAN PARLOUR SECOND

Built 1960–1961 by Metro-Cammell for East Coast Main Line services. Commonwealth bogies. –/42 2T. 38.5 t.

348  CAR No. 348     x  **PC**   WC        CS
349  CAR No. 349     x  **PC**   VT   *VT*   TM
353  CAR No. 353     x  **PC**   VT   *VT*   TM

# PULLMAN SECOND BAR

Built 1960–1961 by Metro-Cammell for East Coast Main Line services. Commonwealth bogies. –/24 + 17 bar seats. 38.5 t.

354  THE HADRIAN BAR x  **PC**   WC   *WC*   CS

# 2.5. PASSENGER COACHING STOCK AWAITING DISPOSAL

This list contains the last known locations of coaching stock awaiting disposal. The definition of which vehicles are "awaiting disposal" is somewhat vague, but generally speaking these are vehicles of types not now in normal service or vehicles which have been damaged by fire, vandalism or collision.

| | | |
|---|---|---|
| 1644 CS | 5443 KT | 10572 OM |
| 1650 CS | 5446 KT | 10604 OM |
| 1652 CS | 5454 KT | 10653 OM |
| 1653 FP | 5471 KT | 10654 OM |
| 1655 CS | 5475 KT | 10664 ZN |
| 1663 CS | 5480 KT | 10669 OM |
| 1670 CS | 5505 CS | 10682 OM |
| 1674 SL | 5616 FP | 10686 OM |
| 1688 CS | 5781 NC | 10695 ZN |
| 1981 TH | 6178 HM | 10709 ZN |
| 2127 CS | 6335 LA | 10711 OM |
| 3225 KT | 6339 EC | 10712 OM |
| 3226 KT | 6345 EC | 10713 OM |
| 3246 CS | 6356 BH | 10730 OM |
| 3258 KT | 6357 BH | 13306 CS |
| 4849 CD | 6360 NL | 13320 CS |
| 4854 CD | 6361 NL | 13323 CS |
| 4860 CS | 6523 CS | 13582 KT |
| 4932 CS | 6900 Cambridge Station Yard | 13604 FP |
| 4997 CS | 6901 Cambridge Station Yard | 13607 FP |
| 5042 FP | 9385 LT | 17058 KT |
| 5226 LT | 9458 ZB | 18837 CS |
| 5265 KT | 9482 NL | 19013 CS |
| 5267 KT | 10327 ZC | 34525 CS |
| 5354 PY | 10533 MM | 35509 ZH |
| 5389 OM | 10540 OM | 35513 CD |
| 5410 KT | 10554 OM | 35516 KT |
| 5420 OM | | |

# 2.6. 99xxx RANGE NUMBER CONVERSION TABLE

The following table is presented to help readers identify vehicles which may carry numbers in the 99xxx range, the former private owner number series which is no longer in general use.

| 99xxx | BR No. | 99xxx | BR No. | 99xxx | BR No. | 99xxx | BR No. |
|---|---|---|---|---|---|---|---|
| 99040 | 21232 | 99321 | 5299 | 99531 Pullman 302 | | 99676 | 553 |
| 99041 | 35476 | 99322 | 5600 | 99532 Pullman 308 | | 99677 | 586 |
| 99052 Saloon 41 | | 99323 | 5704 | 99534 Pullman 245 | | 99678 | 504 |
| 99121 | 3105 | 99324 | 5714 | 99535 Pullman 213 | | 99679 | 506 |
| 99125 | 3113 | 99325 | 5727 | 99536 Pullman 254 | | 99680 | 17102 |
| 99127 | 3117 | 99326 | 4954 | 99537 Pullman 280 | | 99710 | 18767 |
| 99128 | 3130 | 99327 | 5044 | 99539 Pullman 255 | | 99712 | 18893 |
| 99131 | 1999 | 99328 | 5033 | 99541 Pullman 243 | | 99716 | 18808 |
| 99141 | 17041 | 99329 | 4931 | 99542 | 889202 | 99718 | 18862 |
| 99241 | 35449 | 99348 Pullman 348 | | 99543 Pullman 284 | | 99721 | 18756 |
| 99304 | 21256 | 99349 Pullman 349 | | 99546 Pullman 281 | | 99722 | 18806 |
| 99311 | 1882 | 99353 Pullman 353 | | 99670 | 546 | 99723 | 35459 |
| 99312 | 35463 | 99354 Pullman 354 | | 99671 | 548 | 99792 | 17019 |
| 99316 | 13321 | 99361 Pullman 361 | | 99672 | 549 | 99880 | 159 |
| 99317 | 3766 | 99371 | 3128 | 99673 | 550 | 99881 | 807 |
| 99318 | 4912 | 99405 | 35486 | 99674 | 551 | 99953 | 35468 |
| 99319 | 17168 | 99530 Pullman 301 | | 99675 | 552 | | |

# 2.7. PRESERVED LOCOMOTIVE SUPPORT COACHES TABLE

The following table lists support coaches and the BR numbers of the locomotives which they normally support at present. These coaches can spend considerable periods of time off the National Rail system when the locomotives they support are not being used on that system.

| | | | | | | | |
|---|---|---|---|---|---|---|---|
| 14007 | 61264 | 35329 | RL locos | 35465 | 46035 | 35508 | BQ locos |
| 17013 | 60019 | 35333 | 6024 | 35468 | NM locos | 35517 | BQ locos |
| 17019 | 45305 | 35449 | 45231 | 35470 | TM locos | 35518 | 34067 |
| 17041 | 71000 | 35453 | 5051 | 35476 | 46233 | 80204 | WC locos |
| 17096 | 35028 | 35461 | 5029 | 35479 | SV locos | 80217 | WC locos |
| 21232 | 46233 | 35463 | WC locos | 35486 | SV locos | 80220 | 62005 |
| 35317 | 34067 | | | | | | |

# 3. DIESEL MULTIPLE UNITS

# INTRODUCTION

## DMU CLASSES

DMU Classes are listed in class number order. Principal details and dimensions are quoted for each class in metric and/or imperial units as considered appropriate bearing in mind common usage in the UK.

All dimensions and weights are quoted for vehicles in an "as new" condition with all necessary supplies (e.g. oil, water, sand) on board. Dimensions are quoted in the order Length – Width. All lengths quoted are over buffers or couplers as appropriate. Where two lengths are quoted, the first refers to outer vehicles in a set and the second to inner vehicles. All width dimensions quoted are maxima.

## NUMERICAL LISTINGS

DMUs are listed in numerical order of set – using current numbers as allocated by the RSL. Individual "loose" vehicles are listed in numerical order after vehicles formed into fixed formations. Where numbers carried are different from those officially allocated these are noted in class headings where appropriate. Where sets or vehicles have been renumbered in recent years, former numbering detail is shown in parentheses. Each entry is laid out as in the following example:

| Set No. | Detail | Livery | Owner | Operator | Depot | Formation | Name |
|---------|--------|--------|-------|----------|-------|-----------|------|
| 158 855 | s | **WE** | A | *WX* | CF | 52855 57855 | Exmoor Explorer |

**Detail Differences.** Detail differences which currently affect the areas and types of train which vehicles may work are shown, plus differences in interior layout. Where such differences occur within a class, these are shown either in the heading information or alongside the individual set or vehicle number. The following standard abbreviation is used:

r    Radio Electronic Token Block (RETB) equipment fitted.

In all cases use of the above abbreviation indicates the equipment indicated is normally operable. Meaning of non-standard abbreviations is detailed in individual class headings.

**Set Formations.** Regular set formations are shown where these are normally maintained. Readers should note set formations might be temporarily varied from time to time to suit maintenance and/or operational requirements. Vehicles shown as "spare" are not formed in any regular set formation.

**Codes.** Codes are used to denote the livery, owner, operator and depot of each unit. Details of these will be found in section 7 of this book. Where a unit or spare car is off-lease, the operator column will be left blank.

**Names.** Only names carried with official sanction are listed. As far as possible names are shown in UPPER/lower case characters as actually shown on the name carried on the vehicle(s). Unless otherwise shown, complete units are regarded as named rather than just the individual car(s) which carry the name.

# GENERAL INFORMATION

## CLASSIFICATION AND NUMBERING

First generation ("Heritage") DMUs are classified in the series 100–139.
Second generation DMUs are classified in the series 140–199.
Diesel-electric multiple units are classified in the series 200–249.
Service units are classified in the series 930–999.
First and second generation individual cars are numbered in the series 50000–59999 and 79000–79999.

DEMU individual cars are numbered in the series 60000–60999, except for a few former EMU vehicles which retain their EMU numbers.

Service stock individual cars are numbered in the series 975000–975999 and 977000–977999, although this series is not exclusively used for DMU vehicles.

## OPERATING CODES

These codes are used by train operating company staff to describe the various different types of vehicles and normally appear on data panels on the inner (i.e. non driving) ends of vehicles.

The first part of the code describes whether or not the car has a motor or a driving cab as follows:

DM  Driving motor.
M   Motor
DT  Driving trailer
T   Trailer

The next letter is a "B" for cars with a brake compartment.

This is followed by the saloon details:

F   First
S   Standard
C   Composite

so denotes a semi-open vehicle (part compartments, part open). All other vehicles are assumed to consist solely of open saloons.

L denotes a vehicle with a lavatory compartment.

Finally vehicles with a buffet are suffixed RB or RMB for a miniature buffet.

Where two vehicles of the same type are formed within the same unit, the above codes may be suffixed by (A) and (B) to differentiate between the vehicles.

A composite is a vehicle containing both first and standard class accommodation, whilst a brake vehicle is a vehicle containing separate specific accommodation for the conductor.

**Special Note:** Where vehicles have been declassified, the correct operating code which describes the actual vehicle layout is quoted in this publication.

# BUILD DETAILS

### Lot Numbers
Vehicles ordered under the auspices of BR were allocated a lot (batch) number when ordered and these are quoted in class headings and sub-headings.

### Builders
These are shown in class headings. Abbreviations used are found in section 7.8.

Information on sub-contracting works which built parts of vehicles e.g. the underframes etc. is not shown.

# ACCOMMODATION

The information given in class headings and sub-headings is in the form F/S nT (or TD) nW. For example 12/54 1T 1W denotes 12 first class and 54 standard class seats, one toilet and one space for a wheelchair. A number in brackets denotes tip-up seats. Tip-up seats in vestibules do not count. The seating layout of open saloons is shown as 2+1, 2+2 or 3+2 as the case may be. Where units have first class accommodation as well as standard and the layout is different for each class then these are shown separately prefixed by "1:" and "2:". TD denotes a toilet suitable for use by a disabled person.

# 3.1. DIESEL MECHANICAL & DIESEL HYDRAULIC UNITS

## 3.1.1. FIRST GENERATION UNITS

### CLASS 121                    PRESSED STEEL SUBURBAN

First generation units used by Chiltern Railways on selected Aylesbury–Princes Risborough services (121 020) and by Arriva Trains Wales on Cardiff Queen Street–Cardiff Bay shuttles (121 032, from April 2006).
**Construction:** Steel.
**Engines:** Two Leyland 1595 of 112 kW (150 h.p.) at 1800 r.p.m.
**Transmission:** Mechanical. Cardan shaft and freewheel to a four-speed epicyclic gearbox and final drive.
**Brakes:** Vacuum.
**Gangways:** Non gangwayed single cars with cabs at each end.
**Bogies:** DD10.                          **Couplers:** Screw couplings.
**Dimensions:** 20.45 x 2.82 m.           **Seating Layout:** 3+2 facing.
**Doors:** Manually-operated slam.        **Maximum Speed:** 70 m.p.h.
**Multiple Working:** "Blue Square" coupling code. First Generation vehicles cannot be coupled to Second Generation units.

**55020/55032. DMBS.** Lot No. 30518 1960/1961. –/65. 38.0 t.

**Non-standard livery:** 121 032 All over Chiltern blue with a silver stripe.

**Notes:** Fitted with central door locking.

121 020 formerly in departmental use as unit 960 002 (977722).

121 032 formerly in departmental use as 977842, and more recently in preservation at The Railway Age, Crewe. At the time of writing this unit was undergoing an overhaul for use by Arriva Trains Wales on Cardiff Queen Street–Cardiff Bay services from April 2006.

| 121 020 | **0** | CR | *CR* | AL | 55020 |
| 121 032 |       | AW |      | CP | 55032 |

## 3.1.2. SECOND GENERATION UNITS

All units in this section have air brakes and are equipped with public address, with transmission equipment on driving vehicles and flexible diaphragm gangways. Except where otherwise stated, transmission is Voith 211r hydraulic with a cardan shaft to a Gmeinder GM190 final drive.

# CLASS 142    PACER    BREL DERBY/LEYLAND

DMS–DMSL.

**Construction:** Steel underframe, aluminium alloy body and roof. Built from Leyland National bus parts on four-wheeled underframes.
**Engines:** One Cummins LTA10-R of 172 kW (230 h.p.) at 2100 r.p.m.
**Couplers:** BSI at outer ends, bar within unit.
**Seating Layout:** 3+2 mainly unidirectional bus/bench style unless stated.
**Dimensions:** 15.45 x 2.80 m.
**Gangways:** Within unit only.      **Wheel Arrangement:** 1-A A-1.
**Doors:** Twin-leaf inward pivoting.   **Maximum Speed:** 75 m.p.h.
**Multiple Working:** Within class and with Classes 143, 144, 150, 153, 155, 156, 158 and 159.

**55542–55591. DMS.** Lot No. 31003 1985–1986. –/62 (s –/56, t –/53 or 55 1W, u –/52 or 54 1W, v –/52 1W). 24.5 t.
**55592–55641. DMSL.** Lot No. 31004 1985–1986. –/59 1T (s –/50 1T, u –/60 1T, v –/50 1T). 25.0 t.
**55701–55746. DMS.** Lot No. 31013 1986–1987. –/62 (s –/56, t –/53 or 55 1W, u –/52 or 54 1W, v –/52 1W). 24.5 t.
**55747–55792. DMSL.** Lot No. 31014 1986–1987. –/59 1T (s –/50 1T, u –/60 1T, v–/50 1T). 25.0 t.

**Notes:** s Fitted with 2+2 individual high-back seating.

t Northern (ex-First North Western) facelifted units – DMS fitted with luggage rack and wheelchair space.

u Merseytravel units – Fitted with 3+2 individual low-back seating.

v Refurbished Arriva Trains Wales units. Fitted with 2+2 individual Chapman seating.

| | | | | | | | |
|---|---|---|---|---|---|---|---|
| 142 001 | t | **NW** | A | *NO* | NH | 55542 | 55592 |
| 142 002 | v | **AV** | A | *AW* | CF | 55543 | 55593 |
| 142 003 | | **NW** | A | *NO* | NH | 55544 | 55594 |
| 142 004 | t | **NW** | A | *NO* | NH | 55545 | 55595 |
| 142 005 | t | **NW** | A | *NO* | NH | 55546 | 55596 |
| 142 006 | v | **AV** | A | *AW* | CF | 55547 | 55597 |
| 142 007 | t | **NW** | A | *NO* | NH | 55548 | 55598 |
| 142 009 | t | **NW** | A | *NO* | NH | 55550 | 55600 | Newton Heath 125 1876–2001 |
| 142 010 | v | **AV** | A | *AW* | CF | 55551 | 55601 |
| 142 011 | t | **NW** | A | *NO* | NH | 55552 | 55602 |
| 142 012 | t | **NW** | A | *NO* | NH | 55553 | 55603 |

| | | | | | | |
|---|---|---|---|---|---|---|
| 142 013 | | **NW** | A | *NO* | NH | 55554 | 55604 |
| 142 014 | t | **NW** | A | *NO* | NH | 55555 | 55605 |
| 142 015 | s | **AV** | A | *NO* | HT | 55556 | 55606 |
| 142 016 | s | **AV** | A | *NO* | HT | 55557 | 55607 |
| 142 017 | s | **AV** | A | *NO* | HT | 55558 | 55608 |
| 142 018 | s | **AV** | A | *NO* | HT | 55559 | 55609 |
| 142 019 | s | **AV** | A | *NO* | HT | 55560 | 55610 |
| 142 020 | s | **AV** | A | *NO* | HT | 55561 | 55611 |
| 142 021 | s | **AV** | A | *NO* | HT | 55562 | 55612 |
| 142 022 | s | **AV** | A | *NO* | HT | 55563 | 55613 |
| 142 023 | t | **NW** | A | *NO* | NH | 55564 | 55614 |
| 142 024 | s | **AV** | A | *NO* | HT | 55565 | 55615 |
| 142 025 | s | **NS** | A | *NO* | HT | 55566 | 55616 |
| 142 026 | s | **AV** | A | *NO* | HT | 55567 | 55617 |
| 142 027 | t | **NW** | A | *NO* | NH | 55568 | 55618 |
| 142 028 | t | **NW** | A | *NO* | NH | 55569 | 55619 |
| 142 029 | | **NW** | A | *NO* | NH | 55570 | 55620 |
| 142 030 | | **NW** | A | *NO* | NH | 55571 | 55621 |
| 142 031 | t | **NW** | A | *NO* | NH | 55572 | 55622 |
| 142 032 | t | **NW** | A | *NO* | NH | 55573 | 55623 |
| 142 033 | t | **NW** | A | *NO* | NH | 55574 | 55624 |
| 142 034 | t | **NW** | A | *NO* | NH | 55575 | 55625 |
| 142 035 | t | **NW** | A | *NO* | NH | 55576 | 55626 |
| 142 036 | t | **NW** | A | *NO* | NH | 55577 | 55627 |
| 142 037 | t | **NW** | A | *NO* | NH | 55578 | 55628 |
| 142 038 | t | **NW** | A | *NO* | NH | 55579 | 55629 |
| 142 039 | t | **NW** | A | *NO* | NH | 55580 | 55630 |
| 142 040 | t | **NW** | A | *NO* | NH | 55581 | 55631 |
| 142 041 | u | **MY** | A | *NO* | NH | 55582 | 55632 |
| 142 042 | u | **MY** | A | *NO* | NH | 55583 | 55633 |
| 142 043 | u | **MY** | A | *NO* | NH | 55584 | 55634 |
| 142 044 | u | **MY** | A | *NO* | NH | 55585 | 55635 |
| 142 045 | u | **MY** | A | *NO* | NH | 55586 | 55636 |
| 142 046 | u | **MY** | A | *NO* | NH | 55587 | 55637 |
| 142 047 | u | **MY** | A | *NO* | NH | 55588 | 55638 |
| 142 048 | u | **MY** | A | *NO* | NH | 55589 | 55639 |
| 142 049 | u | **MY** | A | *NO* | NH | 55590 | 55640 |
| 142 050 | s | **NS** | A | *NO* | HT | 55591 | 55641 |
| 142 051 | u | **MY** | A | *NO* | NH | 55701 | 55747 |
| 142 052 | u | **MY** | A | *NO* | NH | 55702 | 55748 |
| 142 053 | u | **MY** | A | *NO* | NH | 55703 | 55749 |
| 142 054 | u | **MY** | A | *NO* | NH | 55704 | 55750 |
| 142 055 | u | **MY** | A | *NO* | NH | 55705 | 55751 |
| 142 056 | u | **MY** | A | *NO* | NH | 55706 | 55752 |
| 142 057 | u | **MY** | A | *NO* | NH | 55707 | 55753 |
| 142 058 | u | **MY** | A | *NO* | NH | 55708 | 55754 |
| 142 060 | t | **NW** | A | *NO* | NH | 55710 | 55756 |
| 142 061 | t | **NW** | A | *NO* | NH | 55711 | 55757 |
| 142 062 | t | **NW** | A | *NO* | NH | 55712 | 55758 |
| 142 063 | t | **NW** | A | *NO* | NH | 55713 | 55759 |
| 142 064 | t | **NW** | A | *NO* | NH | 55714 | 55760 |

| | | | | | | |
|---|---|---|---|---|---|---|
| 142 065 | s | **NS** | A | *NO* | HT | 55715 55761 |
| 142 066 | s | **NS** | A | *NO* | HT | 55716 55762 |
| 142 067 | | **NW** | A | *NO* | NH | 55717 55763 |
| 142 068 | t | **NW** | A | *NO* | NH | 55718 55764 |
| 142 069 | v | **AV** | A | *AW* | CF | 55719 55765 |
| 142 070 | t | **NW** | A | *NO* | NH | 55720 55766 |
| 142 071 | s | **AV** | A | *NO* | HT | 55721 55767 |
| 142 072 | v | **AV** | A | *AW* | CF | 55722 55768 |
| 142 073 | v | **AV** | A | *AW* | CF | 55723 55769 |
| 142 074 | v | **AV** | A | *AW* | CF | 55724 55770 |
| 142 075 | v | **AV** | A | *AW* | CF | 55725 55771 |
| 142 076 | v | **AV** | A | *AW* | CF | 55726 55772 |
| 142 077 | v | **AV** | A | *AW* | CF | 55727 55773 |
| 142 078 | s | **AV** | A | *NO* | HT | 55728 55774 |
| 142 079 | s | **AV** | A | *NO* | HT | 55729 55775 |
| 142 080 | v | **AV** | A | *AW* | CF | 55730 55776 |
| 142 081 | v | **AV** | A | *AW* | CF | 55731 55777 |
| 142 082 | v | **AV** | A | *AW* | CF | 55732 55778 |
| 142 083 | v | **AV** | A | *AW* | CF | 55733 55779 |
| 142 084 | s | **AV** | A | *NO* | HT | 55734 55780 |
| 142 085 | v | **AV** | A | *AW* | CF | 55735 55781 |
| 142 086 | s | **AV** | A | *NO* | HT | 55736 55782 |
| 142 087 | s | **AV** | A | *NO* | HT | 55737 55783 |
| 142 088 | s | **AV** | A | *NO* | HT | 55738 55784 |
| 142 089 | s | **AV** | A | *NO* | HT | 55739 55785 |
| 142 090 | s | **AV** | A | *NO* | HT | 55740 55786 |
| 142 091 | s | **AV** | A | *NO* | HT | 55741 55787 |
| 142 092 | s | **AV** | A | *NO* | HT | 55742 55788 |
| 142 093 | s | **AV** | A | *NO* | HT | 55743 55789 |
| 142 094 | s | **AV** | A | *NO* | HT | 55744 55790 |
| 142 095 | s | **AV** | A | *NO* | HT | 55745 55791 |
| 142 096 | s | **AV** | A | *NO* | HT | 55746 55792 |

# CLASS 143    PACER    ALEXANDER/BARCLAY

DMS–DMSL. Similar design to Class 142, but bodies built by W. Alexander with Barclay underframes.

**Construction:** Steel underframe, aluminium alloy body and roof. Alexander bus bodywork on four-wheeled underframes.
**Engines:** One Cummins LTA10-R of 172 kW (230 h.p.) at 2100 r.p.m.
**Couplers:** BSI at outer ends, bar within unit.
**Seating Layout:** 2+2 high-back Chapman seating, mainly unidirectional.
**Dimensions:** 15.45 x 2.80 m.
**Gangways:** Within unit only.                **Wheel Arrangement:** 1-A A-1.
**Doors:** Twin-leaf inward pivoting.        **Maximum Speed:** 75 m.p.h.
**Multiple Working:** Within class and with Classes 142, 144, 150, 153, 155, 156, 158 and 159.

**DMS**. Lot No. 31005 Andrew Barclay 1985–1986. –/54. 24.0 t.
**DMSL**. Lot No. 31006 Andrew Barclay 1985–1986. –/50 1T. 24.5 t.

**Advertising livery:** 143 601 and 143 609 Arriva Trains Wales "The times are changing" (black with yellow doors).

| | | | | | | | |
|---|---|---|---|---|---|---|---|
| 143 601 | **AL** | BC | *AW* | CF | 55642 | 55667 | |
| 143 602 | **VL** | P | *AW* | CF | 55651 | 55668 | |
| 143 603 | **BI** | P | *WX* | CF | 55658 | 55669 | |
| 143 604 | **VL** | P | *AW* | CF | 55645 | 55670 | |
| 143 605 | **VL** | P | *AW* | CF | 55646 | 55671 | Crimestoppers |
| 143 606 | **VL** | P | *AW* | CF | 55647 | 55672 | |
| 143 607 | **VL** | P | *AW* | CF | 55648 | 55673 | |
| 143 608 | **VL** | P | *AW* | CF | 55649 | 55674 | |
| 143 609 | **AL** | CC | *AW* | CF | 55650 | 55675 | |
| 143 610 | **VL** | BC | *AW* | CF | 55643 | 55676 | |
| 143 611 | **BI** | P | *WX* | CF | 55652 | 55677 | |
| 143 612 | **BI** | P | *WX* | CF | 55653 | 55678 | |
| 143 614 | **VL** | BC | *AW* | CF | 55655 | 55680 | |
| 143 616 | **VL** | P | *AW* | CF | 55657 | 55682 | |
| 143 617 | **BI** | RI | *WX* | CF | 55644 | 55683 | |
| 143 618 | **BI** | RI | *WX* | CF | 55659 | 55684 | |
| 143 619 | **BI** | RI | *WX* | CF | 55660 | 55685 | |
| 143 620 | **BI** | P | *WX* | CF | 55661 | 55686 | |
| 143 621 | **BI** | P | *WX* | CF | 55662 | 55687 | |
| 143 622 | **BI** | P | *AW* | CF | 55663 | 55688 | |
| 143 623 | **BI** | P | *AW* | CF | 55664 | 55689 | |
| 143 624 | **VL** | P | *AW* | CF | 55665 | 55690 | |
| 143 625 | **VL** | P | *AW* | CF | 55666 | 55691 | Valleys Kids |

## CLASS 144 PACER ALEXANDER/BREL DERBY

DMS–DMSL or DMS–MS–DMSL. As Class 143, but underframes built by BREL.

**Construction:** Steel underframe, aluminium alloy body and roof. Alexander bus bodywork on four-wheeled underframes.
**Engines:** One Cummins LTA10-R of 172 kW (230 h.p.) at 2100 r.p.m.
**Couplers:** BSI at outer ends, bar within unit.
**Seating Layout:** 2+2 high-back Richmond seating, mainly unidirectional.
**Dimensions:** 15.45/15.43 x 2.80 m.
**Gangways:** Within unit only.          **Wheel Arrangement:** 1-A A-1.
**Doors:** Twin-leaf inward pivoting.      **Maximum Speed:** 75 m.p.h.
**Multiple Working:** Within class and with Classes 142, 143, 150, 153, 155, 156, 158 and 159.

**DMS.** Lot No. 31015 BREL Derby 1986–1987. –/45(3) 1W. 24.0 t.
**MS.** Lot No. BREL Derby 31037 1987. –/58. 23.5 t.
**DMSL.** Lot No. BREL Derby 31016 1986–1987. –/42(3) 1T. 24.5 t.

**Note:** The centre cars of the 3-car units are owned by West Yorkshire PTE, although managed by Porterbrook Leasing Company.

| | | | | | | |
|---|---|---|---|---|---|---|
| 144 001 | **YP** | P | *NO* | NL | 55801 | 55824 |
| 144 002 | **YP** | P | *NO* | NL | 55802 | 55825 |
| 144 003 | **YP** | P | *NO* | NL | 55803 | 55826 |
| 144 004 | **YP** | P | *NO* | NL | 55804 | 55827 |

| | | | | | | | |
|---|---|---|---|---|---|---|---|
| 144 005 | **YP** | P | *NO* | NL | 55805 | | 55828 |
| 144 006 | **YP** | P | *NO* | NL | 55806 | | 55829 |
| 144 007 | **YP** | P | *NO* | NL | 55807 | | 55830 |
| 144 008 | **YP** | P | *NO* | NL | 55808 | | 55831 |
| 144 009 | **YP** | P | *NO* | NL | 55809 | | 55832 |
| 144 010 | **YP** | P | *NO* | NL | 55810 | | 55833 |
| 144 011 | **YP** | P | *NO* | NL | 55811 | | 55834 |
| 144 012 | **YP** | P | *NO* | NL | 55812 | | 55835 |
| 144 013 | **YP** | P | *NO* | NL | 55813 | | 55836 |
| 144 014 | **YP** | P | *NO* | NL | 55814 | 55850 | 55837 |
| 144 015 | **YP** | P | *NO* | NL | 55815 | 55851 | 55838 |
| 144 016 | **YP** | P | *NO* | NL | 55816 | 55852 | 55839 |
| 144 017 | **YP** | P | *NO* | NL | 55817 | 55853 | 55840 |
| 144 018 | **YP** | P | *NO* | NL | 55818 | 55854 | 55841 |
| 144 019 | **YP** | P | *NO* | NL | 55819 | 55855 | 55842 |
| 144 020 | **YP** | P | *NO* | NL | 55820 | 55856 | 55843 |
| 144 021 | **YP** | P | *NO* | NL | 55821 | 55857 | 55844 |
| 144 022 | **YP** | P | *NO* | NL | 55822 | 55858 | 55845 |
| 144 023 | **YP** | P | *NO* | NL | 55823 | 55859 | 55846 |

**Name (carried on DMSL):**

144 001 THE PENISTONE LINE PARTNERSHIP

---

# CLASS 150/0          SPRINTER          BREL YORK

DMSL–MS–DMS. Prototype Sprinter.

**Construction:** Steel.
**Engines:** One Cummins NT-855-R4 of 213 kW (285 h.p.) at 2100 r.p.m.
**Bogies:** BX8P (powered), BX8T (non-powered).
**Couplers:** BSI at outer end of driving vehicles, bar non-driving ends.
**Seating Layout:** 3+2 (mainly unidirectional).
**Dimensions:** 20.06/20.18 x 2.82 m.
**Gangways:** Within unit only.          **Wheel Arrangement:** 2-B – 2-B – B-2.
**Doors:** Twin-leaf sliding.          **Maximum Speed:** 75 m.p.h.
**Multiple Working:** Within class and with Classes 142, 143, 144, 153, 155, 156, 158, 159 and 170.

**DMSL.** Lot No. 30984 1984. –/72 1T. 35.4 t.
**MS.** Lot No. 30986 1984. –/92. 34.1 t.
**DMS.** Lot No. 30985 1984. –/76. 29.5 t.

| | | | | | | | |
|---|---|---|---|---|---|---|---|
| 150 001 | **CO** | A | *CT* | TS | 55200 | 55400 | 55300 |
| 150 002 | **CO** | A | *CT* | TS | 55201 | 55401 | 55301 |

# CLASS 150/1          SPRINTER          BREL YORK

DMSL–DMS or DMSL–DMSL–DMS or DMSL–DMS–DMS.

**Construction:** Steel.
**Engines:** One Cummins NT855R5 of 213 kW (285 h.p.) at 2100 r.p.m.
**Bogies:** BP38 (powered), BT38 (non-powered).
**Couplers:** BSI.
**Seating Layout:** 3+2 facing as built but Centro units were reseated with mainly unidirectional seating.
**Dimensions:** 20.06 x 2.82 m.
**Gangways:** Within unit only.                    **Wheel Arrangement:** 2-B (– 2-B) – B-2.
**Doors:** Twin-leaf sliding.                       **Maximum Speed:** 75 m.p.h.
**Multiple Working:** Within class and with Classes 142, 143, 144, 153, 155, 156, 158, 159 and 170.

**DMSL.** Lot No. 31011 1985–1986. –/72 1T (s –/59 1TD (except 52144 which is –/62 1TD), t –/71 1W 1T, u –/71 1T). 38.3 t.
**DMS.** Lot No. 31012 1985–1986. –/76 (s –/65, u –/70). 38.1 t.

**Non-standard livery:** 150 134 Plain dark blue.

**Notes:** The centre cars of 3-car units are Class 150/2 vehicles. For details see Class 150/2.

150 133–150 150 have been refurbished with individual Chapman seating.

| | | | | | | | | |
|---|---|---|---|---|---|---|---|---|
| 150 003 | u | **CO** | A | *CT* | TS | 52103 | 57210 | 57103 |
| 150 004 | u | **CO** | A | *CT* | TS | 52104 | 57216 | 57104 |
| 150 005 | u | **CC** | A | *CT* | TS | 52105 | 57210 | 57105 |
| 150 006 | u | **CO** | A | *CT* | TS | 52106 | 57214 | 57106 |
| 150 007 | u | **CO** | A | *CT* | TS | 52107 | 57202 | 57107 |
| 150 008 | u | **CO** | A | *CT* | TS | 52108 | 57216 | 57108 |
| 150 009 | u | **CC** | A | *CT* | TS | 52109 | 57202 | 57109 |
| 150 010 | u | **CO** | A | *CT* | TS | 52110 | 57226 | 57110 |
| 150 011 | u | **CC** | A | *CT* | TS | 52111 | 57204 | 57111 |
| 150 012 | u | **CC** | A | *CT* | TS | 52112 | 57206 | 57112 |
| 150 013 | u | **CO** | A | *CT* | TS | 52113 | 57226 | 57113 |
| 150 014 | u | **CO** | A | *CT* | TS | 52114 | 57204 | 57114 |
| 150 015 | u | **CO** | A | *CT* | TS | 52115 | 57206 | 57115 |
| 150 016 | u | **CO** | A | *CT* | TS | 52116 | 57212 | 57116 |
| 150 017 | u | **CC** | A | *CT* | TS | 52117 | 57209 | 57117 |
| 150 018 | u | **CO** | A | *CT* | TS | 52118 | 57220 | 57118 |
| 150 019 | u | **CC** | A | *CT* | TS | 52119 | 57202 | 57119 |
| 150 022 | u | **CO** | A | *CT* | TS | 52122 | 57214 | 57122 |
| | | | | | | | | |
| 150 101 | u | **CC** | A | *CT* | TS | 52101 | 57101 | |
| 150 102 | u | **CC** | A | *CT* | TS | 52102 | 57102 | |
| 150 120 | t | **SL** | A | *SL* | WN | 52120 | 57120 | Gospel Oak–Barking 2000 |
| 150 121 | u | **SL** | A | *SL* | WN | 52121 | 57121 | Willesden Eight |
| 150 123 | t | **SL** | A | *SL* | WN | 52123 | 57123 | Bletchley Seven |
| 150 124 | u | **CO** | A | *CT* | TS | 52124 | 57124 | |
| 150 125 | u | **CC** | A | *CT* | TS | 52125 | 57125 | |
| 150 126 | u | **CO** | A | *CT* | TS | 52126 | 57126 | |

| 150 127 | t | SL | A | SL | WN | 52127 | 57127 | Bletchley TMD |
| 150 128 | t | SL | A | SL | WN | 52128 | 57128 | Community Forest |
| 150 129 | t | SL | A | SL | WN | 52129 | 57129 | MARSTON VALE |
| 150 130 | t | SL | A | SL | WN | 52130 | 57130 | Bedford–Bletchley 150 |
| 150 131 | t | SL | A | SL | WN | 52131 | 57131 | LESLIE CRABBE |
| 150 132 |   | CO | A | CT | TS | 52132 | 57132 |  |
| 150 133 | s | NW | A | NO | NH | 52133 | 57133 |  |
| 150 134 | s | O  | A | NO | NH | 52134 | 57134 |  |
| 150 135 | s | NW | A | NO | NH | 52135 | 57135 |  |
| 150 136 | s | NW | A | NO | NH | 52136 | 57136 |  |
| 150 137 | s | NW | A | NO | NH | 52137 | 57137 |  |
| 150 138 | s | NW | A | NO | NH | 52138 | 57138 |  |
| 150 139 | s | NW | A | NO | NH | 52139 | 57139 |  |
| 150 140 | s | NW | A | NO | NH | 52140 | 57140 |  |
| 150 141 | s | NW | A | NO | NH | 52141 | 57141 |  |
| 150 142 | s | NW | A | NO | NH | 52142 | 57142 |  |
| 150 143 | s | NW | A | NO | NH | 52143 | 57143 |  |
| 150 144 | s | NW | A | NO | NH | 52144 | 57144 |  |
| 150 145 | s | NO | A | NO | NH | 52145 | 57145 |  |
| 150 146 | s | NW | A | NO | NH | 52146 | 57146 |  |
| 150 147 | s | NW | A | NO | NH | 52147 | 57147 |  |
| 150 148 | s | NW | A | NO | NH | 52148 | 57148 |  |
| 150 149 | s | NW | A | NO | NH | 52149 | 57149 |  |
| 150 150 | s | NW | A | NO | NH | 52150 | 57150 |  |

## CLASS 150/2                 SPRINTER              BREL YORK

DMSL–DMS.

**Construction:** Steel.
**Engines:** One Cummins NT855R5 of 213 kW (285 h.p.) at 2100 r.p.m.
**Bogies:** BP38 (powered), BT38 (non-powered).
**Couplers:** BSI.
**Seating Layout:** 3+2 mainly unidirectional seating as built, but many units have now been refurbished with 2+2 seating.
**Dimensions:** 20.06 x 2.82 m.
**Gangways:** Throughout.              **Wheel Arrangement:** 2-B – B-2.
**Doors:** Twin-leaf sliding.           **Maximum Speed:** 75 m.p.h.
**Multiple Working:** Within class and with Classes 142, 143, 144, 153, 155, 156, 158, 159 and 170.

**DMSL.** Lot No. 31017 1986–1987. –/73 1T (s –/62 1TD, t –/64 1T, v –/68 1T, w –/68 1T). 37.5 t.
**DMS.** Lot No. 31018 1986–1987. –/76 (* –/68, s –/70, t –/66 1W, v –/71, w –/73). 36.5 t.

**Notes:** Units in **NW** livery have been refurbished with 3+2 Chapman seating.

Units in **AR** livery (now in use with Central Trains) have 3+2 Chapman seating and Central decals applied on their Anglia livery.

t Refurbished with 2+2 individual Primarius seating. Programme ongoing at the time of writing.

vw Refurbished units with 2+2 individual Chapman seating.

| 150 201 | s | NW | A | NO | NH | 52201 | 57201 | |
|---------|---|----|---|----|----|-------|-------|---|
| 150 203 | s | NW | A | NO | NH | 52203 | 57203 | |
| 150 205 | s | NW | A | NO | NH | 52205 | 57205 | |
| 150 207 | s | NW | A | NO | NH | 52207 | 57207 | |
| 150 208 | t | AV | P | AW | CF | 52208 | 57208 | |
| 150 211 | s | NW | A | NO | NH | 52211 | 57211 | |
| 150 213 | * | AR | P | CT | TS | 52213 | 57213 | |
| 150 215 | s | NW | A | NO | NH | 52215 | 57215 | |
| 150 217 | * | AR | P | CT | TS | 52217 | 57217 | |
| 150 218 | s | NW | A | NO | NH | 52218 | 57218 | |
| 150 219 | w | WZ | P | WX | CF | 52219 | 57219 | |
| 150 221 | w | WZ | P | WX | CF | 52221 | 57221 | |
| 150 222 | s | NW | A | NO | NH | 52222 | 57222 | |
| 150 223 | s | NW | A | NO | NH | 52223 | 57223 | |
| 150 224 | s | NW | A | NO | NH | 52224 | 57224 | |
| 150 225 | s | NW | A | NO | NH | 52225 | 57225 | |
| 150 227 | * | AR | P | CT | TS | 52227 | 57227 | |
| 150 228 | | RR | P | NO | NH | 52228 | 57228 | |
| 150 229 | * | AR | P | CT | TS | 52229 | 57229 | |
| 150 230 | w | WZ | P | WX | CF | 52230 | 57230 | The Tamar Kingfisher |
| 150 231 | * | AR | P | CT | TS | 52231 | 57231 | |
| 150 232 | w | WZ | P | WX | CF | 52232 | 57232 | The Coastal Connection |
| 150 233 | w | WZ | P | WX | CF | 52233 | 57233 | The Lady Margaret of Looe Valley |
| 150 234 | w | WZ | P | WX | CF | 52234 | 57234 | The National Trust |
| 150 235 | * | AR | P | CT | TS | 52235 | 57235 | |
| 150 236 | w | WZ | P | WX | CF | 52236 | 57236 | |
| 150 237 | * | AR | P | CT | TS | 52237 | 57237 | |
| 150 238 | w | WZ | P | WX | CF | 52238 | 57238 | Exeter Explorer |
| 150 239 | w | WZ | P | WX | CF | 52239 | 57239 | |
| 150 240 | w | WZ | P | WX | CF | 52240 | 57240 | |
| 150 241 | w | WZ | P | WX | CF | 52241 | 57241 | The Tarka Belle |
| 150 242 | w | WZ | P | WX | CF | 52242 | 57242 | |
| 150 243 | w | WZ | P | WX | CF | 52243 | 57243 | |
| 150 244 | w | WZ | P | WX | CF | 52244 | 57244 | The West Cornwall Experience |
| 150 245 | | AV | P | AW | CF | 52245 | 57245 | |
| 150 246 | w | WZ | P | WX | CF | 52246 | 57246 | |
| 150 247 | w | WZ | P | WX | CF | 52247 | 57247 | |
| 150 248 | w | WZ | P | WX | CF | 52248 | 57248 | The Great Gardens of Cornwall |
| 150 249 | w | WZ | P | WX | CF | 52249 | 57249 | |
| 150 250 | | AV | P | AW | CF | 52250 | 57250 | |
| 150 251 | w | WZ | P | WX | CF | 52251 | 57251 | |
| 150 252 | | AV | P | AW | CF | 52252 | 57252 | |
| 150 253 | w | WZ | P | WX | CF | 52253 | 57253 | The Exmouth Avocet |
| 150 254 | w | WZ | P | WX | CF | 52254 | 57254 | |
| 150 255 | * | AR | P | CT | TS | 52255 | 57255 | |
| 150 256 | | AV | P | AW | CF | 52256 | 57256 | |
| 150 257 | * | AR | P | CT | TS | 52257 | 57257 | |
| 150 258 | | AV | P | AW | CF | 52258 | 57258 | |

| 150 259 | t | **AV** | P | *AW* | CF | 52259 | 57259 | |
| 150 260 | | **AV** | P | *AW* | CF | 52260 | 57260 | |
| 150 261 | w | **WZ** | P | *WX* | CF | 52261 | 57261 | The Riviera Flyer |
| 150 262 | | **AV** | P | *AW* | CF | 52262 | 57262 | |
| 150 263 | w | **WZ** | P | *WX* | CF | 52263 | 57263 | The Castles of Cornwall |
| 150 264 | | **AV** | P | *AW* | CF | 52264 | 57264 | |
| 150 265 | w | **WZ** | P | *WX* | CF | 52265 | 57265 | The Falmouth Flyer |
| 150 266 | w | **WZ** | P | *WX* | CF | 52266 | 57266 | The Whitley Wonder |
| 150 267 | v | **VW** | P | *AW* | CF | 52267 | 57267 | |
| 150 268 | | **RR** | P | *NO* | NH | 52268 | 57268 | |
| 150 269 | | **RR** | P | *NO* | NH | 52269 | 57269 | |
| 150 270 | | **RR** | P | *NO* | NH | 52270 | 57270 | |
| 150 271 | | **RR** | P | *NO* | NH | 52271 | 57271 | |
| 150 272 | | **RR** | P | *NO* | NH | 52272 | 57272 | |
| 150 273 | | **RR** | P | *NO* | NH | 52273 | 57273 | |
| 150 274 | | **RR** | P | *NO* | NH | 52274 | 57274 | |
| 150 275 | | **RR** | P | *NO* | NH | 52275 | 57275 | |
| 150 276 | | **RR** | P | *NO* | NH | 52276 | 57276 | |
| 150 277 | | **RR** | P | *NO* | NH | 52277 | 57277 | |
| 150 278 | v | **VW** | P | *AW* | CF | 52278 | 57278 | |
| 150 279 | v | **VW** | P | *AW* | CF | 52279 | 57279 | |
| 150 280 | v | **AV** | P | *AW* | CF | 52280 | 57280 | |
| 150 281 | v | **VW** | P | *AW* | CF | 52281 | 57281 | |
| 150 282 | v | **VW** | P | *AW* | CF | 52282 | 57282 | |
| 150 283 | | **AV** | P | *AW* | CF | 52283 | 57283 | |
| 150 284 | | **AV** | P | *AW* | CF | 52284 | 57284 | |
| 150 285 | t | **AV** | P | *AW* | CF | 52285 | 57285 | |

# CLASS 153   SUPER SPRINTER   LEYLAND BUS

DMSL. Converted by Hunslet-Barclay, Kilmarnock from Class 155 2-car units.

**Construction:** Steel underframe, aluminium alloy body and roof. Built from Leyland National bus parts on bogied underframes.
**Engine:** One Cummins NT855R5 of 213 kW (285 h.p.) at 2100 r.p.m.
**Bogies:** One P3-10 (powered) and one BT38 (non-powered).
**Couplers:** BSI.
**Seating Layout:** 2+2 facing/unidirectional.
**Dimensions:** 23.21 x 2.70 m.
**Gangways:** Throughout.                      **Wheel Arrangement:** 2-B.
**Doors:** Single-leaf sliding plug.          **Maximum Speed:** 75 m.p.h.
**Multiple Working:** Within class and with Classes 142, 143, 144, 150, 155, 156, 158, 159 and 170.

**52301–52335. DMSL.** Lot No. 31026 1987–1988. Converted under Lot No. 31115 1991–1992. –/72(3) 1T 1W (* –/69 1T 1W, s –/72 1T 1W, t –/72(2) 1T 1W). 41.2 t.
**57301–57335. DMSL.** Lot No. 31027 1987–1988. Converted under Lot No. 31115 1991–1992. –/72(3) 1T 1W (* –/69 1T 1W). 41.2 t.

**Advertising liveries:** 153 323 Arriva Trains Wales "The times are changing" (black with yellow doors).
153 329 St. Ives Line promotional livery (light blue with dark blue doors & various images).
153 369 Looe Valley Line promotional livery (light blue with dark blue doors & various images).

**Notes:** Cars numbered in the 573xx series were renumbered by adding 50 to their original number so that the last two digits correspond with the set number.

Central Trains and Northern (**NW** livery) units are fitted with Chapman seating, as have Arriva Trains Wales units in **NW** livery.

Northern (**AV** livery) units are fitted with Richmond seating.

Most Arriva Trains Wales/Wessex Trains units have been reseated with seats removed from the company's Class 158 units.

One Anglia units (and 153 311/326 now in use with ATW) have Chapman seating and a bicycle rack.

| | | | | | | |
|---|---|---|---|---|---|---|
| 153 301 | | **AV** | A | *NO* | NL | 52301 |
| 153 302 | | **DC** | A | *WX* | EX | 52302 |
| 153 303 | | **HW** | A | *AW* | CF | 52303 |
| 153 304 | | **AV** | A | *NO* | NL | 52304 |
| 153 305 | | **WX** | A | *WX* | EX | 52305 |
| 153 306 | r* | **PS** | P | *1A* | NC | 52306 | EDITH CAVELL |
| 153 307 | | **AV** | A | *NO* | NL | 52307 |
| 153 308 | | **DC** | A | *WX* | EX | 52308 |
| 153 309 | r* | **AR** | P | *1A* | NC | 52309 | GERARD FIENNES |
| 153 310 | | **NW** | P | *AW* | CF | 52310 |
| 153 311 | * | **PS** | P | *AW* | CF | 52311 |
| 153 312 | s | **HW** | A | *AW* | CF | 52312 |
| 153 313 | | **NW** | P | *AW* | CF | 52313 |
| 153 314 | r* | **1** | P | *1A* | NC | 52314 | DELIA SMITH |
| 153 315 | | **AV** | A | *NO* | NL | 52315 |
| 153 316 | | **NW** | P | *NO* | NL | 52316 |
| 153 317 | | **AV** | A | *NO* | NL | 52317 |
| 153 318 | | **WX** | A | *WX* | EX | 52318 |
| 153 319 | | **AV** | A | *NO* | NL | 52319 |
| 153 320 | | **HW** | P | *AW* | CF | 52320 |
| 153 321 | | **HW** | P | *AW* | CF | 52321 |
| 153 322 | r* | **AR** | P | *1A* | NC | 52322 | BENJAMIN BRITTEN |
| 153 323 | | **AL** | P | *AW* | CF | 52323 |
| 153 324 | | **NW** | P | *NO* | NL | 52324 |
| 153 325 | | **CT** | P | *CT* | TS | 52325 |
| 153 326 | * | **PS** | P | *AW* | CF | 52326 |
| 153 327 | | **HW** | A | *AW* | CF | 52327 |
| 153 328 | | **AV** | A | *NO* | NL | 52328 |
| 153 329 | | **AL** | P | *WX* | EX | 52329 | The St. Ives Bay Belle |
| 153 330 | | **NW** | P | *NO* | NL | 52330 |
| 153 331 | | **AV** | A | *NO* | NL | 52331 |
| 153 332 | | **NW** | P | *NO* | NL | 52332 |
| 153 333 | s | **CT** | P | *CT* | TS | 52333 |

| 153 334 | t | **CT** | P | *CT* | TS | 52334 | |
| 153 335 | r* | **AR** | P | *1A* | NC | 52335 | MICHAEL PALIN |
| 153 351 | | **AV** | A | *NO* | NL | 57351 | |
| 153 352 | | **AV** | A | *NO* | NL | 57352 | |
| 153 353 | | **HW** | A | *AW* | CF | 57353 | |
| 153 354 | | **CT** | P | *CT* | TS | 57354 | |
| 153 355 | | **WX** | A | *WX* | EX | 57355 | |
| 153 356 | | **CT** | P | *CT* | TS | 57356 | |
| 153 357 | | **AV** | A | *NO* | NL | 57357 | |
| 153 358 | | **NW** | P | *NO* | NL | 57358 | |
| 153 359 | | **NW** | P | *NO* | NL | 57359 | |
| 153 360 | | **NW** | P | *NO* | NL | 57360 | |
| 153 361 | | **NW** | P | *AW* | CF | 57361 | |
| 153 362 | | **HW** | A | *AW* | CF | 57362 | Dylan Thomas 1914–1953 |
| 153 363 | | **NW** | P | *NO* | NL | 57363 | |
| 153 364 | | **CT** | P | *CT* | TS | 57364 | |
| 153 365 | | **CT** | P | *CT* | TS | 57365 | |
| 153 366 | | **CT** | P | *CT* | TS | 57366 | |
| 153 367 | | **NW** | P | *AW* | CF | 57367 | |
| 153 368 | | **WX** | A | *WX* | EX | 57368 | |
| 153 369 | | **AL** | P | *WX* | EX | 57369 | The Looe Valley Explorer |
| 153 370 | | **WX** | A | *WX* | EX | 57370 | |
| 153 371 | | **CT** | P | *CT* | TS | 57371 | |
| 153 372 | | **WX** | A | *WX* | EX | 57372 | |
| 153 373 | | **WX** | A | *WX* | EX | 57373 | |
| 153 374 | | **DC** | A | *WX* | EX | 57374 | |
| 153 375 | | **CT** | P | *CT* | TS | 57375 | |
| 153 376 | | **CT** | P | *CT* | TS | 57376 | |
| 153 377 | | **DC** | A | *WX* | EX | 57377 | |
| 153 378 | | **AV** | A | *NO* | NL | 57378 | |
| 153 379 | | **CT** | P | *CT* | TS | 57379 | |
| 153 380 | | **DC** | A | *WX* | EX | 57380 | |
| 153 381 | | **CT** | P | *CT* | TS | 57381 | |
| 153 382 | | **DC** | A | *WX* | EX | 57382 | |
| 153 383 | | **CT** | P | *CT* | TS | 57383 | |
| 153 384 | | **CT** | P | *CT* | TS | 57384 | |
| 153 385 | | **CT** | P | *CT* | TS | 57385 | |

# CLASS 155   SUPER SPRINTER   LEYLAND BUS

DMSL–DMS.

**Construction:** Steel underframe, aluminium alloy body and roof. Built from Leyland National bus parts on bogied underframes.
**Engines:** One Cummins NT855R5 of 213 kW (285 h.p.) at 2100 r.p.m.
**Bogies:** One P3-10 (powered) and one BT38 (non-powered).
**Couplers:** BSI.
**Seating Layout:** 2+2 facing/unidirectional.
**Dimensions:** 23.21 x 2.70 m.
**Gangways:** Throughout.                    **Wheel Arrangement:** 2-B – B-2.
**Doors:** Single-leaf sliding plug.          **Maximum Speed:** 75 m.p.h.
**Multiple Working:** Within class and with Classes 142, 143, 144, 150, 153, 156, 158, 159 and 170.

**DMSL.** Lot No. 31057 1988. –/80 1TD 1W. 39.4 t.
**DMS.** Lot No. 31058 1988. –/80. 38.6 t.

**Note:** These units are owned by West Yorkshire PTE, although managed by Porterbrook Leasing Company.

| | | | | | |
|---|---|---|---|---|---|
| 155 341 | **WY** | P | *NO* | NL | 52341 | 57341 |
| 155 342 | **WY** | P | *NO* | NL | 52342 | 57342 |
| 155 343 | **WY** | P | *NO* | NL | 52343 | 57343 |
| 155 344 | **WY** | P | *NO* | NL | 52344 | 57344 |
| 155 345 | **WY** | P | *NO* | NL | 52345 | 57345 |
| 155 346 | **WY** | P | *NO* | NL | 52346 | 57346 |
| 155 347 | **WY** | P | *NO* | NL | 52347 | 57347 |

# CLASS 156 SUPER SPRINTER METRO-CAMMELL

DMSL–DMS.

**Construction:** Steel.
**Engines:** One Cummins NT855R5 of 213 kW (285 h.p.) at 2100 r.p.m.
**Bogies:** One P3-10 (powered) and one BT38 (non-powered).
**Couplers:** BSI.
**Seating Layout:** 2+2 facing/unidirectional.
**Dimensions:** 23.03 x 2.73 m.
**Gangways:** Throughout.                     **Wheel Arrangement:** 2-B – B-2.
**Doors:** Single-leaf sliding.               **Maximum Speed:** 75 m.p.h.
**Multiple Working:** Within class and with Classes 142, 143, 144, 150, 153, 155, 158, 159 and 170.

**DMSL.** Lot No. 31028 1988–1989. –/74 (†* –/72, st –/70, u –/68) 1TD 1W. 38.6 t.
**DMS.** Lot No. 31029 1987–1989. –/76 (q –/78, † –/74, tu –/72) 37.9 t.

**Notes:** Central Trains, One Anglia and Northern (Newton Heath-based) units are fitted with Chapman seating.

Northern (Neville Hill/Heaton-based) units are fitted with Richmond seating.

**Non standard liveries:** 156 426, 156 429, 156 455 and 156 459 All over dark blue with white doors.
156 451 Northern experimental(1). Two-tone lilac with a white swoosh.
156 425, 156 460 and 156 464 Northern experimental(2). White with two-tone lilac swooshs.

| | | | | | | | | |
|---|---|---|---|---|---|---|---|---|
| 156 401 | * | CT | P | CT | TS | 52401 | 57401 | |
| 156 402 | r* | P | P | 1A | NC | 52402 | 57402 | |
| 156 403 | * | CT | P | CT | TS | 52403 | 57403 | |
| 156 404 | * | CT | P | CT | TS | 52404 | 57404 | |
| 156 405 | * | CT | P | CT | TS | 52405 | 57405 | |
| 156 406 | * | CT | P | CT | TS | 52406 | 57406 | |
| 156 407 | r* | CT | P | 1A | NC | 52407 | 57407 | |
| 156 408 | * | CT | P | CT | TS | 52408 | 57408 | |
| 156 409 | r* | 1 | P | 1A | NC | 52409 | 57409 | |
| 156 410 | * | CT | P | CT | TS | 52410 | 57410 | |
| 156 411 | * | CT | P | CT | TS | 52411 | 57411 | |
| 156 412 | r* | CT | P | 1A | NC | 52412 | 57412 | |
| 156 413 | * | CT | P | CT | TS | 52413 | 57413 | |
| 156 414 | * | CT | P | CT | TS | 52414 | 57414 | |
| 156 415 | * | CT | P | CT | TS | 52415 | 57415 | |
| 156 416 | r* | 1 | P | 1A | NC | 52416 | 57416 | |
| 156 417 | r* | 1 | P | 1A | NC | 52417 | 57417 | |
| 156 418 | r* | CT | P | 1A | NC | 52418 | 57418 | |
| 156 419 | r* | CT | P | 1A | NC | 52419 | 57419 | |
| 156 420 | s | FS | P | NO | NH | 52420 | 57420 | LA' AL RATTY Ravenglass & Eskdale Railway |
| 156 421 | s | FS | P | NO | NH | 52421 | 57421 | |
| 156 422 | r* | 1 | P | 1A | NC | 52422 | 57422 | |
| 156 423 | s | FS | P | NO | NH | 52423 | 57423 | |
| 156 424 | s | FS | P | NO | NH | 52424 | 57424 | |
| 156 425 | s | 0 | P | NO | NH | 52425 | 57425 | |
| 156 426 | s | 0 | P | NO | NH | 52426 | 57426 | |
| 156 427 | s | FS | P | NO | NH | 52427 | 57427 | |
| 156 428 | s | FS | P | NO | NH | 52428 | 57428 | |
| 156 429 | s | 0 | P | NO | NH | 52429 | 57429 | |
| 156 430 | t | SC | A | SR | CK | 52430 | 57430 | |
| 156 431 | t | SC | A | SR | CK | 52431 | 57431 | |
| 156 432 | t | SC | A | SR | CK | 52432 | 57432 | |
| 156 433 | t | SC | A | SR | CK | 52433 | 57433 | The Kilmarnock Edition |
| 156 434 | t | SC | A | SR | CK | 52434 | 57434 | |
| 156 435 | t | SC | A | SR | CK | 52435 | 57435 | |
| 156 436 | † | SC | A | SR | CK | 52436 | 57436 | |
| 156 437 | t | SC | A | SR | CK | 52437 | 57437 | |
| 156 438 | q | NS | A | NO | HT | 52438 | 57438 | |
| 156 439 | t | SC | A | SR | CK | 52439 | 57439 | |
| 156 440 | s | FS | P | NO | NH | 52440 | 57440 | |
| 156 441 | s | FS | P | NO | NH | 52441 | 57441 | |
| 156 442 | t | SC | A | SR | CK | 52442 | 57442 | |
| 156 443 | q | NS | A | NO | HT | 52443 | 57443 | |
| 156 444 | q | NS | A | NO | HT | 52444 | 57444 | |

| 156 445 | u | SC | A | SR | CK | 52445 | 57445 | |
| 156 446 | rt | FS | A | SR | CK | 52446 | 57446 | |
| 156 447 | ru | SR | A | SR | CK | 52447 | 57447 | |
| 156 448 | q | NS | A | NO | HT | 52448 | 57448 | |
| 156 449 | u | SR | A | SR | CK | 52449 | 57449 | |
| 156 450 | rt | SR | A | SR | CK | 52450 | 57450 | |
| 156 451 | q | 0 | A | NO | HT | 52451 | 57451 | |
| 156 452 | s | FS | P | NO | NH | 52452 | 57452 | |
| 156 453 | ru | SR | A | SR | CK | 52453 | 57453 | |
| 156 454 | q | NS | A | NO | HT | 52454 | 57454 | |
| 156 455 | s | 0 | P | NO | NH | 52455 | 57455 | |
| 156 456 | t | SR | A | SR | CK | 52456 | 57456 | |
| 156 457 | rt | SR | A | SR | CK | 52457 | 57457 | |
| 156 458 | rt | SR | A | SR | CK | 52458 | 57458 | |
| 156 459 | s | 0 | P | NO | NH | 52459 | 57459 | |
| 156 460 | s | 0 | P | NO | NH | 52460 | 57460 | |
| 156 461 | s | NO | P | NO | NH | 52461 | 57461 | |
| 156 462 | | SR | A | SR | CK | 52462 | 57462 | |
| 156 463 | q | NS | A | NO | HT | 52463 | 57463 | |
| 156 464 | s | 0 | P | NO | NH | 52464 | 57464 | |
| 156 465 | ru | SR | A | SR | CK | 52465 | 57465 | |
| 156 466 | s | FS | P | NO | NH | 52466 | 57466 | BUXTON Festival |
| 156 467 | | SR | A | SR | CK | 52467 | 57467 | |
| 156 468 | q | NS | A | NO | NH | 52468 | 57468 | |
| 156 469 | q | NO | A | NO | HT | 52469 | 57469 | |
| 156 470 | q | NS | A | NO | NH | 52470 | 57470 | |
| 156 471 | q | NS | A | NO | NH | 52471 | 57471 | |
| 156 472 | q | NS | A | NO | NH | 52472 | 57472 | |
| 156 473 | q | NS | A | NO | NL | 52473 | 57473 | |
| 156 474 | rt | SR | A | SR | CK | 52474 | 57474 | |
| 156 475 | q | NS | A | NO | NL | 52475 | 57475 | |
| 156 476 | rt | SR | A | SR | CK | 52476 | 57476 | |
| 156 477 | rt | SR | A | SR | CK | 52477 | 57477 | |
| 156 478 | rt | SR | A | SR | CK | 52478 | 57478 | |
| 156 479 | q | NS | A | NO | NL | 52479 | 57479 | |
| 156 480 | q | NS | A | NO | NL | 52480 | 57480 | |
| 156 481 | q | NS | A | NO | NL | 52481 | 57481 | |
| 156 482 | q | NS | A | NO | NL | 52482 | 57482 | |
| 156 483 | q | NS | A | NO | NL | 52483 | 57483 | |
| 156 484 | q | NS | A | NO | NL | 52484 | 57484 | |
| 156 485 | ru | SR | A | SR | CK | 52485 | 57485 | |
| 156 486 | q | NS | A | NO | NL | 52486 | 57486 | |
| 156 487 | q | NS | A | NO | NL | 52487 | 57487 | |
| 156 488 | q | NS | A | NO | NL | 52488 | 57488 | |
| 156 489 | q | NS | A | NO | NL | 52489 | 57489 | |
| 156 490 | q | NS | A | NO | NL | 52490 | 57490 | |
| 156 491 | q | NS | A | NO | NL | 52491 | 57491 | |
| 156 492 | rt | SR | A | SR | CK | 52492 | 57492 | |
| 156 493 | rt | SR | A | SR | CK | 52493 | 57493 | |
| 156 494 | § | SC | A | SR | CK | 52494 | 57494 | |
| 156 495 | u | SC | A | SR | CK | 52495 | 57495 | |

| | | | | | | | |
|---|---|---|---|---|---|---|---|
| 156 496 | ru | **SR** | A | *SR* | CK | 52496 | 57496 |
| 156 497 | q | **NS** | A | *NO* | NL | 52497 | 57497 |
| 156 498 | q | **NS** | A | *NO* | NH | 52498 | 57498 |
| 156 499 | rt | **SR** | A | *SR* | CK | 52499 | 57499 |
| 156 500 | u | **SC** | A | *SR* | CK | 52500 | 57500 |
| 156 501 | | **SC** | A | *SR* | CK | 52501 | 57501 |
| 156 502 | | **SC** | A | *SR* | CK | 52502 | 57502 |
| 156 503 | | **SC** | A | *SR* | CK | 52503 | 57503 |
| 156 504 | | **SC** | A | *SR* | CK | 52504 | 57504 |
| 156 505 | | **SC** | A | *SR* | CK | 52505 | 57505 |
| 156 506 | | **SC** | A | *SR* | CK | 52506 | 57506 |
| 156 507 | | **SC** | A | *SR* | CK | 52507 | 57507 |
| 156 508 | | **SC** | A | *SR* | CK | 52508 | 57508 |
| 156 509 | | **SC** | A | *SR* | CK | 52509 | 57509 |
| 156 510 | | **SC** | A | *SR* | CK | 52510 | 57510 |
| 156 511 | | **SC** | A | *SR* | CK | 52511 | 57511 |
| 156 512 | | **SC** | A | *SR* | CK | 52512 | 57512 |
| 156 513 | | **SC** | A | *SR* | CK | 52513 | 57513 |
| 156 514 | | **SC** | A | *SR* | CK | 52514 | 57514 |

# CLASS 158/0                                    BREL

DMSL(B)–DMSL(A) or DMCL–DMSL or DMCL–MSL–DMSL.

**Construction:** Welded aluminium.
**Engines:** 158 701–158 814, 158 962/158 963 & 158 971–158 976: One Cummins NTA855R of 260 kW (350 h.p.) at 1900 r.p.m.
158 815–158 862, 158 964: One Perkins 2006-TWH of 260 kW (350 h.p.) at 1900 r.p.m.
158 863–158 872 & 158 961, 158 966–158 968: One Cummins NTA855R of 300 kW (400 h.p.) at 2100 r.p.m.
**Bogies:** One BREL P4 (powered) and one BREL T4 (non-powered) per car.
**Couplers:** BSI.
**Seating Layout:** 2+2 facing/unidirectional in all standard and first class except 2+1 in South West Trains first class and 158 750 (TPX).
**Dimensions:** 22.16 x 2.70 m.

| | |
|---|---|
| **Gangways:** Throughout. | **Wheel Arrangement:** 2-B – B-2. |
| **Doors:** Twin-leaf swing plug. | **Maximum Speed:** 90 m.p.h. |

**Multiple Working:** Within class and with Classes 142, 143, 144, 150, 153, 155, 156, 159 and 170.

**DMSL(B).** Lot No. 31051 BREL Derby 1989–1992. –/68 1TD 1W. († –/66 1TD 1W, t –/64 1TD 1W). 38.5 t.
**MSL.** Lot No. 31050 BREL Derby 1991. –/70 2T. 38.5 t.
**DMSL(A).** Lot No. 31052 BREL Derby 1989–1992. –/70 1T († –/68 1T, t –/66 1T). 38.5 t.

The above details refer to the "as built" condition. The following DMSL(B) have now been converted to DMCL as follows:

**52701–52744 (First ScotRail/Trans-Pennine Express).** 15/51 1TD 1W (* 15/53 1TD 1W).
**52747–52751. (Wessex Trains/Trans-Pennine Express).** 9/51 1TD 1W.
**52760–52779/52781. (Trans-Pennine Express 2-car units).** 16/48 1TD 1W.
**52786–52789 (South West Trains).** 13/42 1TD 1W.
**52798–52814 (Trans-Pennine Express 3-car units).** 32/32 1TD 1W.

**Notes:** First ScotRail units 158 701–736/738–741 are fitted with Richmond seating.

s – Trans-Pennine and Central Trains units have been refurbished with new shape seat cushions. Trans-Pennine units are also fitted with table lamps in first class.

t – Arriva Trains Wales and Trans-Pennine Express units with some seats removed for additional luggage space.

u – Refurbished South West Trains units with Class 159-style interiors, including first class seating.

† – Wessex Trains and Arriva Trains Wales units fitted with Chapman seating.

All First ScotRail 158s are "fitted" for RETB. When a unit arrives at Inverness the cab display unit is clipped on and plugged in. Similarly Arriva Trains Wales units have RETB plugged in at Shrewsbury for working the Cambrian Lines.

**Non-standard livery:** 158 750 As **RE** but with a Trans-Pennine Express blue band along the lower bodyside.

**Advertising liveries:** 158 841 Arriva Trains Wales "The times are changing" (black with yellow doors).
158 842 Western Daily Mail (silver, white & red with various images).

| | | | | | | | |
|---|---|---|---|---|---|---|---|
| 158 701 | * | **SR** | P | *SR* | IS | 52701 | 57701 | |
| 158 702 | * | **SR** | P | *SR* | IS | 52702 | 57702 | BBC Scotland – 75 Years |
| 158 703 | * | **SR** | P | *SR* | IS | 52703 | 57703 | |
| 158 704 | * | **SR** | P | *SR* | IS | 52704 | 57704 | |
| 158 705 | * | **SR** | P | *SR* | IS | 52705 | 57705 | |
| 158 706 | * | **SR** | P | *SR* | IS | 52706 | 57706 | |
| 158 707 | * | **SR** | P | *SR* | IS | 52707 | 57707 | Far North Line |
| | | | | | | | | 125th ANNIVERSARY |
| 158 708 | * | **SR** | P | *SR* | IS | 52708 | 57708 | |
| 158 709 | * | **SR** | P | *SR* | IS | 52709 | 57709 | |
| 158 710 | * | **SR** | P | *SR* | IS | 52710 | 57710 | |
| 158 711 | * | **SR** | P | *SR* | IS | 52711 | 57711 | |
| 158 712 | * | **SR** | P | *SR* | IS | 52712 | 57712 | |
| 158 713 | * | **SR** | P | *SR* | IS | 52713 | 57713 | |
| 158 714 | * | **SR** | P | *SR* | IS | 52714 | 57714 | |
| 158 715 | * | **SR** | P | *SR* | IS | 52715 | 57715 | Haymarket |
| 158 716 | * | **SR** | P | *SR* | IS | 52716 | 57716 | |
| 158 717 | * | **SR** | P | *SR* | IS | 52717 | 57717 | |
| 158 718 | * | **SR** | P | *SR* | IS | 52718 | 57718 | |
| 158 719 | * | **SR** | P | *SR* | IS | 52719 | 57719 | |
| 158 720 | * | **FS** | P | *SR* | IS | 52720 | 57720 | Inverness & Nairn |
| | | | | | | | | Railway – 150 years |
| 158 721 | * | **SR** | P | *SR* | IS | 52721 | 57721 | |
| 158 722 | * | **SR** | P | *SR* | IS | 52722 | 57722 | |

| | | | | | | | |
|---|---|---|---|---|---|---|---|
| 158 723 | * | **SR** | P | *SR* | IS | 52723 | 57723 | |
| 158 724 | * | **SR** | P | *SR* | HA | 52724 | 57724 | |
| 158 725 | * | **FS** | P | *SR* | HA | 52725 | 57725 | |
| 158 726 | * | **FS** | P | *SR* | HA | 52726 | 57726 | |
| 158 727 | * | **SR** | P | *SR* | HA | 52727 | 57727 | |
| 158 728 | * | **SR** | P | *SR* | HA | 52728 | 57728 | |
| 158 729 | * | **SR** | P | *SR* | HA | 52729 | 57729 | |
| 158 730 | * | **SR** | P | *SR* | HA | 52730 | 57730 | |
| 158 731 | * | **SR** | P | *SR* | HA | 52731 | 57731 | |
| 158 732 | * | **SR** | P | *SR* | HA | 52732 | 57732 | |
| 158 733 | * | **SR** | P | *SR* | HA | 52733 | 57733 | |
| 158 734 | * | **SR** | P | *SR* | HA | 52734 | 57734 | |
| 158 735 | * | **SR** | P | *SR* | HA | 52735 | 57735 | |
| 158 736 | * | **SR** | P | *SR* | HA | 52736 | 57736 | |
| 158 738 | * | **SR** | P | *SR* | HA | 52738 | 57738 | |
| 158 739 | * | **SR** | P | *SR* | HA | 52739 | 57739 | |
| 158 740 | * | **SR** | P | *SR* | HA | 52740 | 57740 | |
| 158 741 | * | **SR** | P | *SR* | HA | 52741 | 57741 | |
| 158 742 | | **TP** | P | *TP* | NL | 52742 | 57742 | |
| 158 745 | † | **WT** | P | *WX* | CF | 52745 | 57745 | |
| 158 746 | † | **WT** | P | *WX* | CF | 52746 | 57746 | |
| 158 747 | | **WE** | P | *WX* | CF | 52747 | 57747 | Richard Trevithick |
| 158 750 | | **0** | P | *TP* | NL | 52750 | 57750 | |
| 158 752 | | **NW** | P | *NO* | NL | 52752 | 57752 | |
| 158 753 | | **NW** | P | *NO* | NL | 52753 | 57753 | |
| 158 754 | | **NW** | P | *NO* | NL | 52754 | 57754 | |
| 158 755 | | **NW** | P | *NO* | NL | 52755 | 57755 | |
| 158 756 | | **NW** | P | *NO* | NL | 52756 | 57756 | |
| 158 757 | | **NW** | P | *NO* | NL | 52757 | 57757 | |
| 158 758 | | **NW** | P | *NO* | NL | 52758 | 57758 | |
| 158 759 | | **NW** | P | *NO* | NL | 52759 | 57759 | |
| 158 760 | s | **TP** | P | *TP* | NL | 52760 | 57760 | |
| 158 761 | s | **TP** | P | *TP* | NL | 52761 | 57761 | |
| 158 762 | s | **TP** | P | *TP* | NL | 52762 | 57762 | |
| 158 763 | s | **TP** | P | *TP* | NL | 52763 | 57763 | |
| 158 764 | s | **TP** | P | *TP* | NL | 52764 | 57764 | |
| 158 765 | s | **TP** | P | *TP* | NL | 52765 | 57765 | |
| 158 766 | s | **TP** | P | *TP* | NL | 52766 | 57766 | |
| 158 767 | s | **TP** | P | *TP* | NL | 52767 | 57767 | |
| 158 768 | s | **TP** | P | *TP* | NL | 52768 | 57768 | |
| 158 769 | s | **TP** | P | *TP* | NL | 52769 | 57769 | |
| 158 771 | s | **TP** | P | *TP* | NL | 52771 | 57771 | |
| 158 776 | s | **TP** | P | *TP* | NL | 52776 | 57776 | |
| 158 778 | s | **TP** | P | *TP* | NL | 52778 | 57778 | |
| 158 779 | s | **TP** | P | *TP* | NL | 52779 | 57779 | |
| 158 780 | s | **CT** | A | *CT* | TS | 52780 | 57780 | |
| 158 781 | s | **TP** | P | *TP* | NL | 52781 | 57781 | |
| 158 782 | s | **WT** | A | *WX* | CF | 52782 | 57782 | |
| 158 783 | s | **CT** | A | *WX* | CF | 52783 | 57783 | |
| 158 784 | st | **CT** | A | *TP* | NL | 52784 | 57784 | |
| 158 785 | s | **CT** | A | *CT* | TS | 52785 | 57785 | |

| | | | | | | | | |
|---|---|---|---|---|---|---|---|---|
| 158 786 | u | **SW** | A | *SW* | SA | 52786 | 57786 | |
| 158 787 | s | **CT** | A | *NO* | HT | 52787 | 57787 | |
| 158 788 | s | **CT** | A | *CT* | TS | 52788 | 57788 | |
| 158 789 | u | **SW** | A | *SW* | SA | 52789 | 57789 | |
| 158 790 | st | **CT** | A | *TP* | NL | 52790 | 57790 | |
| 158 791 | st | **CT** | A | *TP* | NL | 52791 | 57791 | |
| 158 792 | s | **CT** | A | *CT* | TS | 52792 | 57792 | |
| 158 793 | s | **CT** | A | *CT* | TS | 52793 | 57793 | |
| 158 794 | s | **CT** | A | *WX* | CF | 52794 | 57794 | |
| 158 795 | s | **CT** | A | *CT* | TS | 52795 | 57795 | |
| 158 796 | s | **CT** | A | *CT* | TS | 52796 | 57796 | |
| 158 797 | st | **CT** | A | *TP* | NL | 52797 | 57797 | |
| 158 798 | s | **TP** | P | *TP* | HT | 52798 | 58715 | 57798 |
| 158 799 | s | **TP** | P | *TP* | HT | 52799 | 58716 | 57799 |
| 158 800 | s | **TP** | P | *TP* | HT | 52800 | 58717 | 57800 |
| 158 801 | s | **TP** | P | *TP* | HT | 52801 | 58701 | 57801 |
| 158 802 | s | **TP** | P | *TP* | HT | 52802 | 58702 | 57802 |
| 158 803 | s | **TP** | P | *TP* | HT | 52803 | 58703 | 57803 |
| 158 804 | s | **TP** | P | *TP* | HT | 52804 | 58704 | 57804 |
| 158 805 | s | **TP** | P | *TP* | HT | 52805 | 58705 | 57805 |
| 158 806 | s | **TP** | P | *TP* | HT | 52806 | 58706 | 57806 |
| 158 807 | s | **TP** | P | *TP* | HT | 52807 | 58707 | 57807 |
| 158 808 | s | **TP** | P | *TP* | HT | 52808 | 58708 | 57808 |
| 158 809 | s | **TP** | P | *TP* | HT | 52809 | 58709 | 57809 |
| 158 810 | s | **TP** | P | *TP* | HT | 52810 | 58710 | 57810 |
| 158 811 | s | **TP** | P | *TP* | HT | 52811 | 58711 | 57811 |
| 158 812 | s | **TP** | P | *TP* | HT | 52812 | 58712 | 57812 |
| 158 813 | s | **TP** | P | *TP* | HT | 52813 | 58713 | 57813 |
| 158 814 | s | **TP** | P | *TP* | HT | 52814 | 58714 | 57814 |
| 158 818 | † | **AV** | A | *AW* | CF | 52818 | 57818 | |
| 158 819 | † | **GP** | A | *AW* | CF | 52819 | 57819 | |
| 158 820 | † | **AV** | A | *AW* | CF | 52820 | 57820 | |
| 158 821 | † | **GP** | A | *AW* | CF | 52821 | 57821 | |
| 158 822 | † | **WB** | A | *AW* | CF | 52822 | 57822 | |
| 158 823 | † | **WB** | A | *AW* | CF | 52823 | 57823 | |
| 158 824 | † | **GP** | A | *AW* | CF | 52824 | 57824 | |
| 158 825 | † | **GP** | A | *AW* | CF | 52825 | 57825 | |
| 158 826 | † | **WB** | A | *AW* | CF | 52826 | 57826 | |
| 158 827 | † | **GP** | A | *AW* | CF | 52827 | 57827 | |
| 158 828 | † | **AV** | A | *AW* | CF | 52828 | 57828 | |
| 158 829 | † | **WB** | A | *AW* | CF | 52829 | 57829 | |
| 158 830 | † | **WB** | A | *AW* | CF | 52830 | 57830 | |
| 158 831 | † | **WB** | A | *AW* | CF | 52831 | 57831 | |
| 158 832 | † | **WB** | A | *AW* | CF | 52832 | 57832 | |
| 158 833 | † | **WB** | A | *AW* | CF | 52833 | 57833 | |
| 158 834 | † | **WB** | A | *AW* | CF | 52834 | 57834 | |
| 158 835 | † | **WB** | A | *AW* | CF | 52835 | 57835 | |
| 158 836 | † | **WB** | A | *AW* | CF | 52836 | 57836 | |
| 158 837 | † | **AV** | A | *AW* | CF | 52837 | 57837 | |
| 158 838 | † | **WB** | A | *AW* | CF | 52838 | 57838 | |
| 158 839 | † | **WB** | A | *AW* | CF | 52839 | 57839 | |

| | | | | | | | |
|---|---|---|---|---|---|---|---|
| 158 840 | † | **AV** | A | *AW* | CF | 52840 | 57840 |
| 158 841 | † | **AL** | A | *AW* | CF | 52841 | 57841 |
| 158 842 | † | **AL** | A | *AW* | CF | 52842 | 57842 |
| 158 843 | † | **WB** | A | *AW* | CF | 52843 | 57843 |
| 158 844 | t | **CT** | A | *AW* | CF | 52844 | 57844 |
| 158 845 | t | **CT** | A | *AW* | CF | 52845 | 57845 |
| 158 846 | t | **CT** | A | *AW* | CF | 52846 | 57846 |
| 158 847 | t | **CT** | A | *AW* | CF | 52847 | 57847 |
| 158 848 | t | **CT** | A | *AW* | CF | 52848 | 57848 |
| 158 849 | t | **CT** | A | *AW* | CF | 52849 | 57849 |
| 158 850 | t | **CT** | A | *AW* | CF | 52850 | 57850 |
| 158 851 | t | **CT** | A | *AW* | CF | 52851 | 57851 |
| 158 852 | t | **CT** | A | *AW* | CF | 52852 | 57852 |
| 158 853 | t | **CT** | A | *AW* | CF | 52853 | 57853 |
| 158 854 | t | **CT** | A | *AW* | CF | 52854 | 57854 |
| 158 855 | s | **WE** | A | *WX* | CF | 52855 | 57855 | Exmoor Explorer |
| 158 856 | s | **CT** | A | *CT* | TS | 52856 | 57856 |
| 158 857 | s | **CT** | A | *CT* | TS | 52857 | 57857 |
| 158 858 | s | **CT** | A | *CT* | TS | 52858 | 57858 |
| 158 859 | s | **WT** | A | *WX* | CF | 52859 | 57859 |
| 158 860 | s | **WE** | A | *WX* | CF | 52860 | 57860 | Isambard Kingdom Brunel |
| 158 861 | s | **WT** | A | *WX* | CF | 52861 | 57861 | Spirit of the South West |
| 158 862 | s | **CT** | A | *CT* | TS | 52862 | 57862 |
| 158 863 | † | **WT** | A | *WX* | CF | 52863 | 57863 |
| 158 870 | † | **WT** | A | *WX* | CF | 52870 | 57870 |
| 158 871 | † | **WT** | A | *WX* | CF | 52871 | 57871 |
| 158 872 | † | **WT** | A | *WX* | CF | 52872 | 57872 |

## CLASS 158/9                                              BREL

DMSL–DMS. Units leased by West Yorkshire PTE. Details as for Class 158/0 except for seating layout and toilets.

**DMSL.** Lot No. 31051 BREL Derby 1990–1992. –/70 1TD 1W. 38.5 t.
**DMS.** Lot No. 31052 BREL Derby 1990–1992. –/72 and parcels area. 38.5 t.

**Note:** These units are leased by West Yorkshire PTE and are now managed by HSBC Rail (UK) on behalf of Midland Montague who own the units.

| | | | | | | |
|---|---|---|---|---|---|---|
| 158 901 | **YP** | H | *NO* | NL | 52901 | 57901 |
| 158 902 | **YP** | H | *NO* | NL | 52902 | 57902 |
| 158 903 | **YP** | H | *NO* | NL | 52903 | 57903 |
| 158 904 | **YP** | H | *NO* | NL | 52904 | 57904 |
| 158 905 | **YP** | H | *NO* | NL | 52905 | 57905 |
| 158 906 | **YP** | H | *NO* | NL | 52906 | 57906 |
| 158 907 | **YP** | H | *NO* | NL | 52907 | 57907 |
| 158 908 | **YP** | H | *NO* | NL | 52908 | 57908 |
| 158 909 | **YP** | H | *NO* | NL | 52909 | 57909 |
| 158 910 | **YP** | H | *NO* | NL | 52910 | 57910 |

Chiltern's "Bubble car" 121 020 is seen near Aylesbury whilst working the 18.11 Princes Risborough–Aylesbury on 12/05/05. This unit is dedicated to this short line.

**Kim Fullbrook**

"Pacer" 142 026, in debranded Arriva livery rattles through the Irthing Valley near Denton, Cumbria with the 14.33 Carlisle–Middlesbrough on 30/10/04.
**Dave McAlone**

▲ Cardiff Valley Lines-liveried 143 604 leaves Barry and takes the Barry Island line with the 15.57 Treherbert–Barry Island on 18/05/04. **Andrew Mist**

▼ New West Yorkshire PTE-liveried 144 008 is seen at Knottingley on 27/05/04. **Mervyn Turvey**

Wessex Trains promotional-liveried 150 246 leaves Newton Abbot with the 08.54 Exmouth–Paignton on 11/07/05.
**Robert Pritchard**

▲ Ex-works in Central Trains two tone green livery, 153 354 is seen near Wickenby with the 09.59 Newark North Gate–Grimsby Town service on 19/11/04.
**Robert Pritchard**

▼ Old West Yorkshire PTE-liveried 155 343 and Arriva-liveried 153 328 pass Leeds Midland Road depot with a Leeds–Knottingley service on 19/08/04.
**Gavin Morrison**

▲ Recently repainted in "One" livery following transfer from Central to "One", 156 416 arrives at Norwich with the 13.17 from Great Yarmouth on 02/07/05.
**Mark Beal**

▼ 156 478, in ScotRail livery, leaves Bridge of Orchy with the 18.20 Glasgow Queen Street–Mallaig on 09/06/05. **Robert Pritchard**

First Group (regional/suburban)-liveried 170 413 passes Dalmeny with the 11.23 Aberdeen–Edinburgh on 08/06/05. First took over the ScotRail franchise in October 2004 and the 170s have been the first DMUs to be reliveried, mainly using vinyls.

**Robert Pritchard**

Southern 4-car Class 171 No. 171 802 leaves Hurst Green with the 13.04 Oxted–Uckfield on 30/10/04.

Alex Dasi-Sutton

Class 175s are operated by Arriva Trains Wales, Northern and Trans-Pennine Express. On 21/08/04 175 002 was working for the latter operator as it passes Staveley (Cumbria) with the 12.49 Manchester Airport–Windermere.          **Dave McAlone**

▲ First Great Western's 180 101 is seen at Evesham with the 11.13 Worcester Foregate Street–London Paddington on 19/12/04. **Stephen Widdowson**

▼ The Hastings DEMU still sees occasional use on the "Marshlink" line when Southern are short of Class 171s. Here 1001 arrives at Appledore with the 14.24 Ashford International–Hastings on 02/07/04. **Rodney Lissenden**

▲ Virgin's Voyagers regularly work in pairs at weekends. On 09/07/05 220 010 and 221 140 pass Stoke Works Jn. near Bromsgrove heading north.

**Stephen Widdowson**

▼ The 4-strong fleet of Hull Trains DEMUs entered service in summer 2005. Displaying the striking new Hull Trains livery is 222 104, seen leaving Doncaster on 23/06/05 with the 17.06 Hull–London King's Cross. **Kim Fullbrook**

▲ Network Rail yellow-liveried Ultrasonic Test Unit 901 002 is seen at Redhill on 24/06/05. This unit was converted from a Class 101. **Alex Dasi-Sutton**

▼ Eurailscout GB-liveried Driver Training Unit 977968 is seen at Crewe on 16/07/05. **Cliff Beeton**

## CLASS 158/0 BREL

Units reformed in 2004/2005 for Wessex Trains and Trans-Pennine Express. For vehicle details see above.

**Wessex Trains units. Formation:** DMSL–DMSL–DMSL

| 158 961 | † | **WT** | A | *WX* | CF | 52868 | 57867 | 52867 |
|---------|---|--------|---|------|----|-------|-------|-------|
| 158 962 |   | **WT** | P | *WX* | CF | 57751 | 52751 | 52749 |
| 158 963 |   | **WT** | P | *WX* | CF | 52748 | 57748 | 57749 |
| 158 964 | † | **WT** | A | *WX* | CF | 57815 | 52815 | 57816 |
| 158 965 | † | **WT** | A | *WX* | CF | 52817 | 57817 | 52816 |
| 158 966 | † | **WT** | A | *WX* | CF | 52864 | 57864 | 52865 |
| 158 967 | † | **WT** | A | *WX* | CF | 52866 | 57866 | 57865 |
| 158 968 | † | **WT** | A | *WX* | CF | 52869 | 57869 | 57868 |

**First Trans-Pennine Express units. Formation:** DMCL–DMCL*/DMSL–DMSL. Where 3-car units have a DMCL as the centre vehicle, the first class has been declassified in this vehicle.

**Note:** At the time of writing 158 972 was running as a 2-car unit (minus 52737) which was spare at Heaton.

| 158 971 | s | **TP** | P | *TP* | HT | 52770 | 57737 | 57770 |
|---------|---|--------|---|------|----|-------|-------|-------|
| 158 972 | s | **TP** | P | *TP* | HT | 52772 | 52737 | 57772 |
| 158 973 | s | **TP** | P | *TP* | HT | 52773 | 57743 | 57773 |
| 158 974 | s | **TP** | P | *TP* | HT | 52774 | 52743 | 57774 |
| 158 975 | s | **TP** | P | *TP* | HT | 52775 | 57744 | 57775 |
| 158 976 | s | **TP** | P | *TP* | HT | 52777 | 52744 | 57777 |

## CLASS 159 BREL

DMCL–MSL–DMSL. Built as Class 158. Converted before entering passenger service to Class 159 by Rosyth Dockyard.

**Construction:** Welded aluminium.
**Engines:** One Cummins NTA855R of 300 kW (400 h.p.) at 2100 r.p.m.
**Bogies:** One BREL P4 (powered) and one BREL T4 (non-powered) per car.
**Couplers:** BSI.
**Seating Layout:** 1: 2+1 facing, 2: 2+2 facing/unidirectional.
**Dimensions:** 22.16 x 2.70 m.
**Gangways:** Throughout.                    **Wheel Arrangement:** 2-B – B-2 – B-2.
**Doors:** Twin-leaf swing plug.             **Maximum Speed:** 90 m.p.h.
**Multiple Working:** Within class and with Classes 142, 143, 144, 150, 153, 155, 156, 158 and 170.

**DMCL.** Lot No. 31051 BREL Derby 1992–1993. 24/28 1TD 1W. 38.5 t.
**MSL.** Lot No. 31050 BREL Derby 1992–1993. –/72 1T and parcels area 38.5 t.
**DMSL.** Lot No. 31052 BREL Derby 1992–1993. –/72 1T and parcels area. 38.5 t.

| 159 001 | **SW** P | *SW* | SA | 52873 | 58718 | 57873 | CITY OF EXETER |
|---------|----------|------|----|-------|-------|-------|----------------|
| 159 002 | **SW** P | *SW* | SA | 52874 | 58719 | 57874 | CITY OF SALISBURY |
| 159 003 | **SW** P | *SW* | SA | 52875 | 58720 | 57875 | TEMPLECOMBE |

| 159 004 | **SW** P *SW* | SA | 52876 | 58721 | 57876 | BASINGSTOKE AND DEANE |
| 159 005 | **SW** P *SW* | SA | 52877 | 58722 | 57877 | |
| 159 006 | **SW** P *SW* | SA | 52878 | 58723 | 57878 | |
| 159 007 | **SW** P *SW* | SA | 52879 | 58724 | 57879 | |
| 159 008 | **SW** P *SW* | SA | 52880 | 58725 | 57880 | |
| 159 009 | **SW** P *SW* | SA | 52881 | 58726 | 57881 | |
| 159 010 | **SW** P *SW* | SA | 52882 | 58727 | 57882 | |
| 159 011 | **SW** P *SW* | SA | 52883 | 58728 | 57883 | |
| 159 012 | **SW** P *SW* | SA | 52884 | 58729 | 57884 | |
| 159 013 | **SW** P *SW* | SA | 52885 | 58730 | 57885 | |
| 159 014 | **SW** P *SW* | SA | 52886 | 58731 | 57886 | |
| 159 015 | **SW** P *SW* | SA | 52887 | 58732 | 57887 | |
| 159 016 | **SW** P *SW* | SA | 52888 | 58733 | 57888 | |
| 159 017 | **SW** P *SW* | SA | 52889 | 58734 | 57889 | |
| 159 018 | **SW** P *SW* | SA | 52890 | 58735 | 57890 | |
| 159 019 | **SW** P *SW* | SA | 52891 | 58736 | 57891 | |
| 159 020 | **SW** P *SW* | SA | 52892 | 58737 | 57892 | |
| 159 021 | **SW** P *SW* | SA | 52893 | 58738 | 57893 | |
| 159 022 | **SW** P *SW* | SA | 52894 | 58739 | 57894 | |

## CLASS 165/0      NETWORK TURBO      BREL

DMSL–DMS and DMSL–MS–DMS. All 165/0s now in use with Chiltern. All refurbished 2003–2005 with first class seats removed and air conditioning fitted.

**Construction:** Welded aluminium.
**Engines:** One Perkins 2006-TWH of 260 kW (350 h.p.) at 1900 r.p.m.
**Bogies:** BREL P3-17 (powered), BREL T3-17 (non-powered).
**Couplers:** BSI at outer ends, bar within 3-car units.
**Seating Layout:** 2+2/3+2 facing/unidirectional.
**Dimensions:** 23.50/23.25 x 2.81 m.
**Gangways:** Within unit only.          **Wheel Arrangement:** 2-B (– B-2) – B-2.
**Doors:** Twin-leaf swing plug.          **Maximum Speed:** 75 m.p.h.
**Multiple Working:** Within class and with Classes 166 and 168.

Fitted with tripcocks for working over London Underground tracks between Harrow-on-the-Hill and Amersham.

**58801–58822/58873–58878. DMSL.** Lot No. 31087 BREL York 1990. –/89 1T. 40.1 t.
**58823–58833. DMSL.** Lot No. 31089 BREL York 1991–1992. –/89 1T. 40.1 t.
**MS.** Lot No. 31090 BREL York 1991–1992. –/106. 37.0 t.
**DMS.** Lot No. 31088 BREL York 1991–1992. –/94. 39.4 t.

| 165 001 | **CR** A *CR* | AL | 58801 | 58834 |
| 165 002 | **CR** A *CR* | AL | 58802 | 58835 |
| 165 003 | **CR** A *CR* | AL | 58803 | 58836 |
| 165 004 | **CR** A *CR* | AL | 58804 | 58837 |
| 165 005 | **CR** A *CR* | AL | 58805 | 58838 |
| 165 006 | **CR** A *CR* | AL | 58806 | 58839 |
| 165 007 | **CR** A *CR* | AL | 58807 | 58840 |
| 165 008 | **CR** A *CR* | AL | 58808 | 58841 |

| | | | | | | | |
|---|---|---|---|---|---|---|---|
| 165 009 | **CR** | A | *CR* | AL | 58809 | | 58842 |
| 165 010 | **CR** | A | *CR* | AL | 58810 | | 58843 |
| 165 011 | **CR** | A | *CR* | AL | 58811 | | 58844 |
| 165 012 | **CR** | A | *CR* | AL | 58812 | | 58845 |
| 165 013 | **CR** | A | *CR* | AL | 58813 | | 58846 |
| 165 014 | **CR** | A | *CR* | AL | 58814 | | 58847 |
| 165 015 | **CR** | A | *CR* | AL | 58815 | | 58848 |
| 165 016 | **CR** | A | *CR* | AL | 58816 | | 58849 |
| 165 017 | **CR** | A | *CR* | AL | 58817 | | 58850 |
| 165 018 | **CR** | A | *CR* | AL | 58818 | | 58851 |
| 165 019 | **CR** | A | *CR* | AL | 58819 | | 58852 |
| 165 020 | **CR** | A | *CR* | AL | 58820 | | 58853 |
| 165 021 | **CR** | A | *CR* | AL | 58821 | | 58854 |
| 165 022 | **CR** | A | *CR* | AL | 58822 | | 58855 |
| 165 023 | **CR** | A | *CR* | AL | 58873 | | 58867 |
| 165 024 | **CR** | A | *CR* | AL | 58874 | | 58868 |
| 165 025 | **CR** | A | *CR* | AL | 58875 | | 58869 |
| 165 026 | **CR** | A | *CR* | AL | 58876 | | 58870 |
| 165 027 | **CR** | A | *CR* | AL | 58877 | | 58871 |
| 165 028 | **CR** | A | *CR* | AL | 58878 | | 58872 |
| 165 029 | **CR** | A | *CR* | AL | 58823 | 55404 | 58856 |
| 165 030 | **CR** | A | *CR* | AL | 58824 | 55405 | 58857 |
| 165 031 | **CR** | A | *CR* | AL | 58825 | 55406 | 58858 |
| 165 032 | **CR** | A | *CR* | AL | 58826 | 55407 | 58859 |
| 165 033 | **CR** | A | *CR* | AL | 58827 | 55408 | 58860 |
| 165 034 | **CR** | A | *CR* | AL | 58828 | 55409 | 58861 |
| 165 035 | **CR** | A | *CR* | AL | 58829 | 55410 | 58862 |
| 165 036 | **CR** | A | *CR* | AL | 58830 | 55411 | 58863 |
| 165 037 | **CR** | A | *CR* | AL | 58831 | 55412 | 58864 |
| 165 038 | **CR** | A | *CR* | AL | 58832 | 55413 | 58865 |
| 165 039 | **CR** | A | *CR* | AL | 58833 | 55414 | 58866 |

## CLASS 165/1    NETWORK TURBO    BREL

First Great Western Link units. DMCL–MS–DMS or DMCL–DMS.

**Construction:** Welded aluminium.
**Engines:** One Perkins 2006-TWH of 260 kW (350 h.p.) at 1900 r.p.m.
**Bogies:** BREL P3-17 (powered), BREL T3-17 (non-powered).
**Couplers:** BSI at outer ends, bar within 3-car units.
**Seating Layout:** 1: 2+2 facing, 2: 3+2 facing/unidirectional.
**Dimensions:** 23.50/23.25 x 2.81 m.
**Gangways:** Within unit only.
**Doors:** Twin-leaf swing plug.
**Multiple Working:** Within class and with Classes 166 and 168.

**Wheel Arrangement:** 2-B (– B-2) – B-2.
**Maximum Speed:** 90 m.p.h.

**58953–58969. DMCL.** Lot No. 31098 BREL York 1992. 16/66 1T. 38.0 t.
**58879–58898. DMCL.** Lot No. 31096 BREL York 1992. 16/72 1T. 38.0 t.
**MS.** Lot No. 31099 BREL 1992. –/106. 37.0 t.
**DMS.** Lot No. 31097 BREL 1992. –/98. 37.0 t.

**Advertising livery:** 165 136 – "Back the Bid" (London's Olympic Bid 2012) – blue with various images.

| | | | | | | | | |
|---|---|---|---|---|---|---|---|---|
| 165 101 | TT | A | *FK* | RG | 58953 | 55415 | 58916 |
| 165 102 | TT | A | *FK* | RG | 58954 | 55416 | 58917 |
| 165 103 | TT | A | *FK* | RG | 58955 | 55417 | 58918 |
| 165 104 | TT | A | *FK* | RG | 58956 | 55418 | 58919 |
| 165 105 | TT | A | *FK* | RG | 58957 | 55419 | 58920 |
| 165 106 | TT | A | *FK* | RG | 58958 | 55420 | 58921 |
| 165 107 | TT | A | *FK* | RG | 58959 | 55421 | 58922 |
| 165 108 | TT | A | *FK* | RG | 58960 | 55422 | 58923 |
| 165 109 | TT | A | *FK* | RG | 58961 | 55423 | 58924 |
| 165 110 | TT | A | *FK* | RG | 58962 | 55424 | 58925 |
| 165 111 | TT | A | *FK* | RG | 58963 | 55425 | 58926 |
| 165 112 | TT | A | *FK* | RG | 58964 | 55426 | 58927 |
| 165 113 | TT | A | *FK* | RG | 58965 | 55427 | 58928 |
| 165 114 | TT | A | *FK* | RG | 58966 | 55428 | 58929 |
| 165 116 | TT | A | *FK* | RG | 58968 | 55431 | 58931 |
| 165 117 | TT | A | *FK* | RG | 58969 | | 58932 |
| 165 118 | TT | A | *FK* | RG | 58879 | | 58933 |
| 165 119 | TT | A | *FK* | RG | 58880 | | 58934 |
| 165 120 | TT | A | *FK* | RG | 58881 | | 58935 |
| 165 121 | TT | A | *FK* | RG | 58882 | | 58936 |
| 165 122 | TT | A | *FK* | RG | 58883 | | 58937 |
| 165 123 | TT | A | *FK* | RG | 58884 | | 58938 |
| 165 124 | TT | A | *FK* | RG | 58885 | | 58939 |
| 165 125 | TT | A | *FK* | RG | 58886 | | 58940 |
| 165 126 | TT | A | *FK* | RG | 58887 | | 58941 |
| 165 127 | TT | A | *FK* | RG | 58888 | | 58942 |
| 165 128 | TT | A | *FK* | RG | 58889 | | 58943 |
| 165 129 | TT | A | *FK* | RG | 58890 | | 58944 |
| 165 130 | TT | A | *FK* | RG | 58891 | | 58945 |
| 165 131 | TT | A | *FK* | RG | 58892 | | 58946 |
| 165 132 | TT | A | *FK* | RG | 58893 | | 58947 |
| 165 133 | TT | A | *FK* | RG | 58894 | | 58948 |
| 165 134 | TT | A | *FK* | RG | 58895 | | 58949 |
| 165 135 | TT | A | *FK* | RG | 58896 | | 58950 |
| 165 136 | **AL** | A | *FK* | RG | 58897 | | 58951 |
| 165 137 | TT | A | *FK* | RG | 58898 | | 58952 |

## CLASS 166   NETWORK EXPRESS TURBO   ABB

DMCL(A)–MS–DMCL(B). First Great Western Link units, built for Paddington–Oxford/Newbury services. Air Conditioned.

**Construction:** Welded aluminium.
**Engines:** One Perkins 2006-TWH of 260 kW (350 h.p.) at 1900 r.p.m.
**Bogies:** BREL P3-17 (powered), BREL T3-17 (non-powered).
**Couplers:** BSI.
**Seating Layout:** 1: 2+2 facing, 2: 3+2 facing/unidirectional. 20 standard class seats in 2+2 layout in DMCL(B).
**Dimensions:** 23.50 x 2.81 m.
**Gangways:** Within unit only.          **Wheel Arrangement:** 2-B – B-2 – B-2.
**Doors:** Twin-leaf swing plug.          **Maximum Speed:** 90 m.p.h.
**Multiple Working:** Within class and with Classes 165 and 168.

**DMCL (A).** Lot No. 31116 ABB York 1992–1993. 16/75 1T. 39.6 t.
**MS.** Lot No. 31117 ABB York 1992–1993. –/96. 38.0 t.
**DMCL (B).** Lot No. 31116 ABB York 1992–1993. 16/72 1T. 39.6 t.

| | | | | | | | |
|---|---|---|---|---|---|---|---|
| 166 201 | TT | A | FK | RG | 58101 | 58601 | 58122 |
| 166 202 | TT | A | FK | RG | 58102 | 58602 | 58123 |
| 166 203 | TT | A | FK | RG | 58103 | 58603 | 58124 |
| 166 204 | TT | A | FK | RG | 58104 | 58604 | 58125 |
| 166 205 | TT | A | FK | RG | 58105 | 58605 | 58126 |
| 166 206 | TT | A | FK | RG | 58106 | 58606 | 58127 |
| 166 207 | TT | A | FK | RG | 58107 | 58607 | 58128 |
| 166 208 | TT | A | FK | RG | 58108 | 58608 | 58129 |
| 166 209 | TT | A | FK | RG | 58109 | 58609 | 58130 |
| 166 210 | TT | A | FK | RG | 58110 | 58610 | 58131 |
| 166 211 | TT | A | FK | RG | 58111 | 58611 | 58132 |
| 166 212 | TT | A | FK | RG | 58112 | 58612 | 58133 |
| 166 213 | TT | A | FK | RG | 58113 | 58613 | 58134 |
| 166 214 | TT | A | FK | RG | 58114 | 58614 | 58135 |
| 166 215 | TT | A | FK | RG | 58115 | 58615 | 58136 |
| 166 216 | TT | A | FK | RG | 58116 | 58616 | 58137 |
| 166 217 | TT | A | FK | RG | 58117 | 58617 | 58138 |
| 166 218 | TT | A | FK | RG | 58118 | 58618 | 58139 |
| 166 219 | TT | A | FK | RG | 58119 | 58619 | 58140 |
| 166 220 | TT | A | FK | RG | 58120 | 58620 | 58141 |
| 166 221 | TT | A | FK | RG | 58121 | 58621 | 58142 |

# CLASS 168 CLUBMAN ADTRANZ/BOMBARDIER

These units are shown as they will be formed from Spring 2006. The formations of some units have changed several times in a short space of time! Air conditioned.

**Construction:** Welded aluminium bodies with bolt-on steel ends.
**Engines:** One MTU 6R183TD13H of 315 kW (422 h.p.) at 1900 r.p.m.
**Transmission:** Hydraulic. Voith T211rzze to ZF final drive.
**Bogies:** One Adtranz P3–23 and one BREL T3–23 per car.
**Couplers:** BSI at outer ends, bar within unit.
**Seating Layout:** 2+2 facing/unidirectional.
**Dimensions:** 24.10/23.61 x 2.70 m.
**Gangways:** Within unit only.      **Wheel Arrangement:** 2-B (– B-2 – B-2) – B-2.
**Doors:** Twin-leaf swing plug.      **Maximum Speed:** 100 m.p.h.
**Multiple Working:** Within class and with Classes 165 and 166.

Fitted with tripcocks for working over London Underground tracks between Harrow-on-the-Hill and Amersham.

**Class 168/0.** Original Design. DMSL(A)–MSL–MS–DMSL(B).

**58151–58155. DMSL(A).** Adtranz Derby 1997–1998. –/60 1TD 1W. 43.7 t.
**58651–58655. MSL.** Adtranz Derby 1998. –/73 1T. 41.0 t.
**58451–58455. MS.** Adtranz Derby 1998. –/77. 40.5 t.
**58251–58255. DMSL(B).** Adtranz Derby 1998. –/68 1T. 43.6 t.

**Note:** 58451–58455 were numbered 58656–58660 for a time when used in 168 106–168 110.

| 168 001 | **CR** | P | *CR* | AL | 58151 | 58651 | 58451 | 58251 |
|---------|--------|---|------|----|-------|-------|-------|-------|
| 168 002 | **CR** | P | *CR* | AL | 58152 | 58652 | 58452 | 58252 |
| 168 003 | **CR** | P | *CR* | AL | 58153 | 58653 | 58453 | 58253 |
| 168 004 | **CR** | P | *CR* | AL | 58154 | 58654 | 58454 | 58254 |
| 168 005 | **CR** | P | *CR* | AL | 58155 | 58655 | 58455 | 58255 |

**Class 168/1.** These units are effectively Class 170s. DMSL(A)–MSL–MS–DMSL(B) or DMSL(A)–MS–DMSL(B).

**58156–58163. DMSL(A).** Adtranz Derby 2000. –/59 1TD 2W. 45.2 t.
**58756–58757. MSL.** Bombardier Derby 2002. –/73 1T. 42.9 t.
**58456–58460. MS.** Bombardier Derby 2002. –/76. 41.8 t.
**58461–58463. MS.** Adtranz Derby 2000. –/76. 42.4 t.
**58256–58263. DMSL(B).** Adtranz Derby 2000. –/69 1T. 45.2 t.

**Notes:** 58461–58463 have been renumbered from 58661–58663.

58756 and 58757 have been renumbered from 58656[II] and 58657[II].

| 168 106 | **CR** | P | *CR* | AL | 58156 | 58756 | 58456 | 58256 |
|---------|--------|---|------|----|-------|-------|-------|-------|
| 168 107 | **CR** | P | *CR* | AL | 58157 | 58757 | 58457 | 58257 |
| 168 108 | **CR** | P | *CR* | AL | 58158 |       | 58458 | 58258 |
| 168 109 | **CR** | P | *CR* | AL | 58159 |       | 58459 | 58259 |
| 168 110 | **CR** | P | *CR* | AL | 58160 |       | 58460 | 58260 |
| 168 111 | **CR** | H | *CR* | AL | 58161 |       | 58461 | 58261 |

| 168 112 | **CR** | H | *CR* | AL | 58162 |       | 58462 | 58262 |
| 168 113 | **CR** | H | *CR* | AL | 58163 |       | 58463 | 58263 |

**Class 168/2.** These units are effectively Class 170s. DMSL(A)–MSL–MS–DMSL(B) or DMSL(A)–MS–DMSL(B).

**58164–58169. DMSL(A).** Bombardier Derby 2003–2004. –/59 1TD 2W. 45.4 t.
**58365–58367. MSL.** Bombardier Derby 2006. –/73 1T. 43.3 t.
**58464/58468/58469. MS.** Bombardier Derby 2003–2004. –/76. 44.0 t.
**58465–58467. MS.** Bombardier Derby 2006. –/76. 43.3 t.
**58264–58269. DMSL(B).** Bombardier Derby 2003–2004. –/69 1T. 45.5 t.

**Note:** New vehicles 58365–58367 and 58465–58467 are due to be inserted into 168 215–168 217 in Spring 2006.

| 168 214 | **CR** | P | *CR* | AL | 58164 |       | 58464 | 58264 |
| 168 215 | **CR** | P | *CR* | AL | 58165 | 58365 | 58465 | 58265 |
| 168 216 | **CR** | P | *CR* | AL | 58166 | 58366 | 58466 | 58266 |
| 168 217 | **CR** | P | *CR* | AL | 58167 | 58367 | 58467 | 58267 |
| 168 218 | **CR** | P | *CR* | AL | 58168 |       | 58468 | 58268 |
| 168 219 | **CR** | P | *CR* | AL | 58169 |       | 58469 | 58269 |

# CLASS 170 TURBOSTAR ADTRANZ/BOMBARDIER

Various formations. Air-conditioned.

**Construction:** Welded aluminium bodies with bolt-on steel ends.
**Engines:** One MTU 6R183TD13H of 315 kW (422 h.p.) at 1900 r.p.m.
**Transmission:** Hydraulic. Voith T211rzze to ZF final drive.
**Bogies:** One Adtranz P3–23 and one BREL T3–23 per car.
**Couplers:** BSI at outer ends, bar within later build units.
**Seating Layout:** 1: 2+1 facing/unidirectional (2+2 in first class in Class 170/1 end cars). 2: 2+2 facing/unidirectional.
**Dimensions:** 24.10 x 2.70 m unless stated.
**Gangways:** Within unit only.      **Wheel Arrangement:** 2-B (– B-2) – B-2.
**Doors:** Twin-leaf sliding plug.   **Maximum Speed:** 100 m.p.h.
**Multiple Working:** Within class and with Classes 150, 153, 155, 156, 158 and 159.

**Note:** At the time of writing vehicles 50101 (170 101) and 50207 (170 207) were out of traffic with collision damage. As a result units 170 117, 170 207 and 170 271 are running temporarily misformed.

**Class 170/1. Central Trains units.** Former Midland Mainline units, these now have their first class declassified. DMCL–MCRMB–DMCL or DMCL–DMCL.

**DMCL (A).** Adtranz Derby 1998–1999. 12/45 1TD 2W. 45.0 t.
**MCRMB.** Adtranz Derby 2001. 21/22 and bar. 43.0 t.
**DMCL (B).** Adtranz Derby 1998–1999. 12/52 1T. Catering point. 44.8 t

| 170 102 | **CM** | P | *CT* | TS | 50102 | 55102 | 79102 |
| 170 103 | **CM** | P | *CT* | TS | 50103 | 55103 | 79103 |
| 170 104 | **CM** | P | *CT* | TS | 50104 | 55104 | 79104 |
| 170 105 | **CM** | P | *CT* | TS | 50105 | 55105 | 79105 |
| 170 106 | **CM** | P | *CT* | TS | 50106 | 55106 | 79106 |
| 170 107 | **CM** | P | *CT* | TS | 50107 | 55107 | 79107 |

| 170 108 | **CM** | P | *CT* | TS | 50108 | 55108 | 79108 |
| 170 109 | **CM** | P | *CT* | TS | 50109 | 55109 | 79109 |
| 170 110 | **CM** | P | *CT* | TS | 50110 | 55110 | 79110 |
| 170 111 | **CM** | P | *CT* | TS | 50111 |       | 79111 |
| 170 112 | **CM** | P | *CT* | TS | 50112 |       | 79112 |
| 170 113 | **CM** | P | *CT* | TS | 50113 |       | 79113 |
| 170 114 | **CM** | P | *CT* | TS | 50114 |       | 79114 |
| 170 115 | **CM** | P | *CT* | TS | 50115 |       | 79115 |
| 170 116 | **CM** | P | *CT* | TS | 50116 |       | 79116 |
| 170 117 | **CM** | P | *CT* | TS | 50117 | 55101 | 79117 |
| Spare   | **CM** | P |      | ZC | 50101 |       |       |

**Class 170/2. One Anglia 3-car units.** DMCL–MSLRB–DMSL.

**DMCL.** Adtranz Derby 1999. 29/3 1TD 2W (* 7/39 1TD 2W). 45.0 t.
**MSLRB.** Adtranz Derby 1999. –/58 1T (* –/68 1T). Buffet and guard's office 45.3 t.
**DMSL.** Adtranz Derby 1999. –/66 1T. 43.4 t.

**Note:** * Modified interior. First class seating reduced and buffet removed.

| 170 201 | r  | 1      | P | *1A* | NC | 50201 | 56201 | 79201 |
| 170 202 | r  | 1      | P | *1A* | NC | 50202 | 56202 | 79202 |
| 170 203 | r* | 1      | P | *1A* | NC | 50203 | 56203 | 79203 |
| 170 204 | r  | 1      | P | *1A* | NC | 50204 | 56204 | 79204 |
| 170 205 | r  | 1      | P | *1A* | NC | 50205 | 56205 | 79205 |
| 170 206 | r  | 1      | P | *1A* | NC | 50206 | 56206 | 79206 |
| 170 207 | r  | **CM/1** | P | *1A* | NC | 79101 |       | 79207 |
| 170 208 | r  | 1      | P | *1A* | NC | 50208 | 56208 | 79208 |
| Spare   |    | 1      | P |      | ZC | 50207 |       |       |

**Class 170/2. One Anglia 2-car units.** DMSL–DMCL or DMSL–MSLRB–DMCL.

**DMSL.** Bombardier Derby 2002. –/57 1TD 2W. 45.7 t.
**DMCL.** Bombardier Derby 2002. 9/53 1T. 45.7 t.

| 170 270 | r | 1   | P | *1A* | NC | 50270 |       | 79270 |
| 170 271 | r | **AN** | P | *1A* | NC | 50271 | 56207 | 79271 |
| 170 272 | r | **AN** | P | *1A* | NC | 50272 |       | 79272 |
| 170 273 | r | **AN** | P | *1A* | NC | 50273 |       | 79273 |

**Class 170/3. South West Trains units.** DMCL–DMCL.

**50301–50308. DMCL(A).** Adtranz Derby 2000. 9/43 1TD 2W. 45.8 t.
**50392. DMCL(A).** Bombardier Derby 2003. 9/43 1TD 2W. 46.6 t.
**79301–79308. DMCL(B).** Adtranz Derby 2000. 9/53 1T. 45.8 t.
**79392. DMCL(B).** Bombardier Derby 2003. 9/53 1T. 46.5 t.

**Note:** 170 392 was initially numbered 170 727 in error and painted into Southern livery before being repainted into South West Trains livery.

| 170 301 | **SW** | P | *SW* | SA | 50301 | 79301 |
| 170 302 | **SW** | P | *SW* | SA | 50302 | 79302 |
| 170 303 | **SW** | P | *SW* | SA | 50303 | 79303 |
| 170 304 | **SW** | P | *SW* | SA | 50304 | 79304 |
| 170 305 | **SW** | P | *SW* | SA | 50305 | 79305 |
| 170 306 | **SW** | P | *SW* | SA | 50306 | 79306 |

| 170 307 | **SW** | P | *SW* | SA | 50307 | 79307 |
| 170 308 | **SW** | P | *SW* | SA | 50308 | 79308 |
| 170 392 | **SW** | P | *SW* | SA | 50392 | 79392 |

**Class 170/3. Units built for Hull Trains. Now in use with First ScotRail and dedicated to Edinburgh/Glasgow–Inverness services.** DMCL–MSLRB–DMSL. **Dimensions:** 23.62/23.61 x 2.75 m.

**DMCL.** Bombardier Derby 2004. 29/5 1TD 2W. 46.5 t.
**MSLRB.** Bombardier Derby 2004. –/60 1T. Buffet and guard's office 44.7 t.
**DMSL.** Bombardier Derby 2004. –/71 1T. 46.3 t.

| 170 393 | **FS** | P | *SR* | HA | 50393 | 56393 | 79393 |
| 170 394 | **FS** | P | *SR* | HA | 50394 | 56394 | 79394 |
| 170 395 | **FS** | P | *SR* | HA | 50395 | 56395 | 79395 |
| 170 396 | **FS** | P | *SR* | HA | 50396 | 56396 | 79396 |

**Class 170/3. Porterbrook spot hire units.** DMCL–MC–DMCL.

**DMCL(A).** Bombardier Derby 2002. 9/43 1TD 1W. 45.4 t.
**MC.** Bombardier Derby 2002. 22/36. 43.0 t.
**DMCL(B).** Bombardier Derby 2002. 9/53 1T. 45.8 t.

| 170 397 | **P** | P | *CT* | TS | 50397 | 56397 | 79397 |
| 170 398 | **P** | P | *CT* | TS | 50398 | 56398 | 79398 |

**Class 170/3. Porterbrook spot hire unit.** DMCL–DMCL.

**DMCL(A).** Bombardier Derby 2001. 9/43 1TD 2W. 45.8 t.
**DMCL(B).** Bombardier Derby 2001. 9/53 1T. 45.8 t.

**Advertising livery:** Derwent Valley Mills World Heritage Site (green, grey and blue with various images).

| 170 399 | **AL** | P | *CT* | TS | 50399 | | 79399 |

**Class 170/4. First ScotRail "express" units.** DMCL–MS–DMCL.
**Dimensions:** 23.62/23.61 x 2.75 m unless stated.

**DMCL(A).** Adtranz Derby 1999–2001. 9/43 1TD 2W. 45.2 t.
**MS.** Adtranz Derby 1999–2001. –/76. 42.5 t.
**DMCL(B).** Adtranz Derby 1999–2001. 9/53 1T. 45.2 t.

| 170 401 | **FS** | P | *SR* | HA | 50401 | 56401 | 79401 |
| 170 402 | **FS** | P | *SR* | HA | 50402 | 56402 | 79402 |
| 170 403 | **SR** | P | *SR* | HA | 50403 | 56403 | 79403 |
| 170 404 | **FS** | P | *SR* | HA | 50404 | 56404 | 79404 |
| 170 405 | **FS** | P | *SR* | HA | 50405 | 56405 | 79405 |
| 170 406 | **FS** | P | *SR* | HA | 50406 | 56406 | 79406 |
| 170 407 | **SR** | P | *SR* | HA | 50407 | 56407 | 79407 |
| 170 408 | **FS** | P | *SR* | HA | 50408 | 56408 | 79408 |
| 170 409 | **FS** | P | *SR* | HA | 50409 | 56409 | 79409 |
| 170 410 | **FS** | P | *SR* | HA | 50410 | 56410 | 79410 |
| 170 411 | **FS** | P | *SR* | HA | 50411 | 56411 | 79411 |
| 170 412 | **FS** | P | *SR* | HA | 50412 | 56412 | 79412 |
| 170 413 | **FS** | P | *SR* | HA | 50413 | 56413 | 79413 |
| 170 414 | **FS** | P | *SR* | HA | 50414 | 56414 | 79414 |

| 170 415 | **FS** | P | *SR* | HA | 50415 | 56415 | 79415 |
| 170 416 | **FS** | H | *SR* | HA | 50416 | 56416 | 79416 |
| 170 417 | **FS** | H | *SR* | HA | 50417 | 56417 | 79417 |
| 170 418 | **FS** | H | *SR* | HA | 50418 | 56418 | 79418 |
| 170 419 | **FS** | H | *SR* | HA | 50419 | 56419 | 79419 |
| 170 420 | **SR** | H | *SR* | HA | 50420 | 56420 | 79420 |
| 170 421 | **SR** | H | *SR* | HA | 50421 | 56421 | 79421 |
| 170 422 | **SR** | H | *SR* | HA | 50422 | 56422 | 79422 |
| 170 423 | **SR** | H | *SR* | HA | 50423 | 56423 | 79423 |
| 170 424 | **SR** | H | *SR* | HA | 50424 | 56424 | 79424 |

**Class 170/4. First ScotRail "express" units.** DMCL–MS–DMCL.
**Dimensions:** 23.62/23.61 x 2.75 m.

**DMCL.** Bombardier Derby 2003–2005. 9/43 1TD 2W. 46.8 t.
**MS.** Bombardier Derby 2003–2005. –/76. 43.7 t.
**DMCL.** Bombardier Derby 2003–2005. 9/53 1T. 46.5 t.

| 170 425 | **FS** | P | *SR* | HA | 50425 | 56425 | 79425 |
| 170 426 | **FS** | P | *SR* | HA | 50426 | 56426 | 79426 |
| 170 427 | **FS** | P | *SR* | HA | 50427 | 56427 | 79427 |
| 170 428 | **FS** | P | *SR* | HA | 50428 | 56428 | 79428 |
| 170 429 | **FS** | P | *SR* | HA | 50429 | 56429 | 79429 |
| 170 430 | **FS** | P | *SR* | HA | 50430 | 56430 | 79430 |
| 170 431 | **FS** | P | *SR* | HA | 50431 | 56431 | 79431 |
| 170 432 | **FS** | P | *SR* | HA | 50432 | 56432 | 79432 |
| 170 433 | **FS** | P | *SR* | HA | 50433 | 56433 | 79433 |
| 170 434 | **FS** | P | *SR* | HA | 50434 | 56434 | 79434 |

**Class 170/4. First ScotRail "suburban" units.** DMSL–MS–DMSL.
**Dimensions:** 23.62/23.61 x 2.75 m.

**DMSL.** Bombardier Derby 2004–2005. –/55 1TD 2W. 46.3 t.
**MS.** Bombardier Derby 2004–2005. –/76. 43.4 t.
**DMSL.** Bombardier Derby 2004–2005. –/67 1T. 46.4 t.

| 170 450 | **FS** | P | *SR* | HA | 50450 | 56450 | 79450 |
| 170 451 | **FS** | P | *SR* | HA | 50451 | 56451 | 79451 |
| 170 452 | **FS** | P | *SR* | HA | 50452 | 56452 | 79452 |
| 170 453 | **FS** | P | *SR* | HA | 50453 | 56453 | 79453 |
| 170 454 | **FS** | P | *SR* | HA | 50454 | 56454 | 79454 |
| 170 455 | **FS** | P | *SR* | HA | 50455 | 56455 | 79455 |
| 170 456 | **FS** | P | *SR* | HA | 50456 | 56456 | 79456 |
| 170 457 | **FS** | P | *SR* | HA | 50457 | 56457 | 79457 |
| 170 458 | **FS** | P | *SR* | HA | 50458 | 56458 | 79458 |
| 170 459 | **FS** | P | *SR* | HA | 50459 | 56459 | 79459 |
| 170 460 | **FS** | P | *SR* | HA | 50460 | 56460 | 79460 |
| 170 461 | **FS** | P | *SR* | HA | 50461 | 56461 | 79461 |

**Class 170/4. First ScotRail units.** Standard class only Strathclyde PTE units.
DMSL–MS–DMSL.

**50470–50471. DMSL(A).** Adtranz Derby 2001. –/55 1TD 2W. 45.1 t.
**50472–50478. DMSL(A).** Bombardier Derby 2004–2005. –/57 1TD 2W. 46.3 t.
**56470–56471. MS.** Adtranz Derby 2001. –/76. 42.4 t.

**56472–56478. MS.** Bombardier Derby 2004–2005. –/76. 43.4 t.
**79470–79471. DMSL(B).** Adtranz Derby 2001. –/67 1T. 45.1 t.
**79472–79478. DMSL(B).** Bombardier Derby 2004–2005. –/67 1T. 46.4 t.

| 170 470 | **SC** | P | *SR* | HA | 50470 | 56470 | 79470 |
|---------|--------|---|------|----|-------|-------|-------|
| 170 471 | **SC** | P | *SR* | HA | 50471 | 56471 | 79471 |
| 170 472 | **SP** | P | *SR* | HA | 50472 | 56472 | 79472 |
| 170 473 | **SP** | P | *SR* | HA | 50473 | 56473 | 79473 |
| 170 474 | **SP** | P | *SR* | HA | 50474 | 56474 | 79474 |
| 170 475 | **SP** | P | *SR* | HA | 50475 | 56475 | 79475 |
| 170 476 | **SP** | P | *SR* | HA | 50476 | 56476 | 79476 |
| 170 477 | **SP** | P | *SR* | HA | 50477 | 56477 | 79477 |
| 170 478 | **SP** | P | *SR* | HA | 50478 | 56478 | 79478 |

**Class 170/5. Central Trains 2-car units.** DMSL–DMSL.

**DMSL(A).** Adtranz Derby 1999–2000. –/55 1TD 2W. 45.8 t.
**DMSL(B).** Adtranz Derby 1999–2000. –/67 1T. 45.9 t.

| 170 501 | **CT** | P | *CT* | TS | 50501 | 79501 |
|---------|--------|---|------|----|-------|-------|
| 170 502 | **CT** | P | *CT* | TS | 50502 | 79502 |
| 170 503 | **CT** | P | *CT* | TS | 50503 | 79503 |
| 170 504 | **CT** | P | *CT* | TS | 50504 | 79504 |
| 170 505 | **CT** | P | *CT* | TS | 50505 | 79505 |
| 170 506 | **CT** | P | *CT* | TS | 50506 | 79506 |
| 170 507 | **CT** | P | *CT* | TS | 50507 | 79507 |
| 170 508 | **CT** | P | *CT* | TS | 50508 | 79508 |
| 170 509 | **CT** | P | *CT* | TS | 50509 | 79509 |
| 170 510 | **CT** | P | *CT* | TS | 50510 | 79510 |
| 170 511 | **CT** | P | *CT* | TS | 50511 | 79511 |
| 170 512 | **CT** | P | *CT* | TS | 50512 | 79512 |
| 170 513 | **CT** | P | *CT* | TS | 50513 | 79513 |
| 170 514 | **CT** | P | *CT* | TS | 50514 | 79514 |
| 170 515 | **CT** | P | *CT* | TS | 50515 | 79515 |
| 170 516 | **CT** | P | *CT* | TS | 50516 | 79516 |
| 170 517 | **CT** | P | *CT* | TS | 50517 | 79517 |
| 170 518 | **CT** | P | *CT* | TS | 50518 | 79518 |
| 170 519 | **CT** | P | *CT* | TS | 50519 | 79519 |
| 170 520 | **CT** | P | *CT* | TS | 50520 | 79520 |
| 170 521 | **CT** | P | *CT* | TS | 50521 | 79521 |
| 170 522 | **CT** | P | *CT* | TS | 50522 | 79522 |
| 170 523 | **CT** | P | *CT* | TS | 50523 | 79523 |

**Class 170/6. Central Trains 3-car units.** DMSL–MS–DMSL.

**DMSL(A).** Adtranz Derby 2000. –/55 1TD 2W. 45.8 t.
**MS.** Adtranz Derby 2000. –/74. 42.4 t.
**DMSL(B).** Adtranz Derby 2000. –/67 1T. 45.9 t.

| 170 630 | **CT** | P | *CT* | TS | 50630 | 56630 | 79630 |
|---------|--------|---|------|----|-------|-------|-------|
| 170 631 | **CT** | P | *CT* | TS | 50631 | 56631 | 79631 |
| 170 632 | **CT** | P | *CT* | TS | 50632 | 56632 | 79632 |
| 170 633 | **CT** | P | *CT* | TS | 50633 | 56633 | 79633 |
| 170 634 | **CT** | P | *CT* | TS | 50634 | 56634 | 79634 |

| 170 635 | **CT** | P | *CT* | TS | 50635 | 56635 | 79635 |
| 170 636 | **CT** | P | *CT* | TS | 50636 | 56636 | 79636 |
| 170 637 | **CT** | P | *CT* | TS | 50637 | 56637 | 79637 |
| 170 638 | **CT** | P | *CT* | TS | 50638 | 56638 | 79638 |
| 170 639 | **CT** | P | *CT* | TS | 50639 | 56639 | 79639 |

# CLASS 171        TURBOSTAR        BOMBARDIER

DMCL–DMSL or DMCL–MS–MS–DMCL. Southern units. Air conditioned.

**Construction:** Welded aluminium bodies with bolt-on steel ends.
**Engines:** One MTU 6R183TD13H of 315 kW (422 h.p.) at 1900 r.p.m.
**Transmission:** Hydraulic. Voith T211rzze to ZF final drive.
**Bogies:** One Adtranz P3–23 and one BREL T3–23 per car.
**Couplers:** Dellner 12 at outer ends, bar within unit (Class 171/8s).
**Seating Layout:** 1: 2+1 facing/unidirectional. 2: 2+2 facing/unidirectional.
**Gangways:** Within unit only.         **Wheel Arrangement:** 2-B (– B-2) – B-2.
**Doors:** Twin-leaf swing plug.         **Maximum Speed:** 100 m.p.h.
**Multiple Working:** Within class and with EMU Classes 375 and 377 in an emergency.

**Class 171/7. Southern 2-car units.** DMCL–DMSL.
**Dimensions:** 24.10 x 2.70 m (171 721–171 726). 23.70 x 2.75 m (171 727–171 729).

**Note:** 171 721–171 726 were built as Class 170s (170 721–170726), but renumbered as 171s on fitting with Dellner couplers.

**50721–50726. DMCL.** Bombardier Derby 2003. 9/43 1TD 2W. 47.6 t.
**50727–50729. DMCL.** Bombardier Derby 2005. 9/43 1TD 2W. 46.3 t.
**79721–79726. DMSL.** Bombardier Derby 2003. –/64 1T. 47.8 t.
**79727–79729. DMSL.** Bombardier Derby 2005. –/64 1T. 46.2 t.

| 171 721 | **SN** | P | *SN* | SU | 50721 | 79721 |
| 171 722 | **SN** | P | *SN* | SU | 50722 | 79722 |
| 171 723 | **SN** | P | *SN* | SU | 50723 | 79723 |
| 171 724 | **SN** | P | *SN* | SU | 50724 | 79724 |
| 171 725 | **SN** | P | *SN* | SU | 50725 | 79725 |
| 171 726 | **SN** | P | *SN* | SU | 50726 | 79726 |
| 171 727 | **SN** | P | *SN* | SU | 50727 | 79727 |
| 171 728 | **SN** | P | *SN* | SU | 50728 | 79728 |
| 171 729 | **SN** | P | *SN* | SU | 50729 | 79729 |

**Class 171/8. Southern 4-car units.** DMCL(A)–MS–MS–DMCL(B).
**Dimensions:** 23.70/23.61 x 2.75 m.

**DMCL(A).** Bombardier Derby 2004. 9/43 1TD 2W. 46.5 t.
**MS.** Bombardier Derby 2004. –/74. 43.7 t.
**DMCL(B).** Bombardier Derby 2004. 9/50 1T. 46.5 t.

| 171 801 | **SN** | P | *SN* | SU | 50801 | 54801 | 56801 | 79801 |
| 171 802 | **SN** | P | *SN* | SU | 50802 | 54802 | 56802 | 79802 |
| 171 803 | **SN** | P | *SN* | SU | 50803 | 54803 | 56803 | 79803 |
| 171 804 | **SN** | P | *SN* | SU | 50804 | 54804 | 56804 | 79804 |
| 171 805 | **SN** | P | *SN* | SU | 50805 | 54805 | 56805 | 79805 |
| 171 806 | **SN** | P | *SN* | SU | 50806 | 54806 | 56806 | 79806 |

# CLASS 175          CORADIA 1000          ALSTOM

Air Conditioned.

**Construction:** Steel.
**Engines:** One Cummins N14 of 335 kW (450 h.p.).
**Transmission:** Hydraulic. Voith T211rzze to ZF Voith final drive.
**Bogies:** Alstom FBO–LTB, MBSI, TB and MBI.
**Couplers:** Scharfenberg outer ends and bar within unit (Class 175/1).
**Seating Layout:** 2+2 facing/unidirectional.
**Dimensions:** 23.06/23.93 x 2.80 m.
**Gangways:** Within unit only.          **Wheel Arrangement:** 2-B (– B-2) – B-2.
**Doors:** Single-leaf swing plug.          **Maximum Speed:** 100 m.p.h.
**Multiple Working:** Within class and with Class 180.

**Note:** Although operated by Arriva Trains Wales 11 Class 175s are hired back daily to Trans-Pennine Express and Northern for use on Manchester Airport to Blackpool/Barrow & Millom/Windermere services.

**Class 175/0.** DMSL–DMSL. 2-car units.

**DMSL(A).** Alstom Birmingham 1999–2000. –/54 1TD 2W. 50.7 t.
**DMSL(B).** Alstom Birmingham 1999–2000. –/64 1T. 50.7 t.

| | | | | | | |
|---|---|---|---|---|---|---|
| 175 001 | **FS** | A | *AW* | CH | 50701 | 79701 |
| 175 002 | **FS** | A | *AW* | CH | 50702 | 79702 |
| 175 003 | **FS** | A | *AW* | CH | 50703 | 79703 |
| 175 004 | **FS** | A | *AW* | CH | 50704 | 79704 |
| 175 005 | **FS** | A | *AW* | CH | 50705 | 79705 |
| 175 006 | **FS** | A | *AW* | CH | 50706 | 79706 |
| 175 007 | **FS** | A | *AW* | CH | 50707 | 79707 |
| 175 008 | **AW** | A | *AW* | CH | 50708 | 79708 |
| 175 009 | **FS** | A | *AW* | CH | 50709 | 79709 |
| 175 010 | **FS** | A | *AW* | CH | 50710 | 79710 |
| 175 011 | **FS** | A | *AW* | CH | 50711 | 79711 |

**Names (carried on one side of each DMSL):**

| | |
|---|---|
| 175 003 | Eisteddfod Genadlaethol Cymru |
| 175 004 | MENCAP National Colleges Pengwern College |
| 175 006 | Brondyffryn Trust |

**Class 175/1.** DMSL–MSL–DMSL. 3-car units.

**Note:** Vehicle 50753 of 175 103 is in **AW** livery. This unit was out of service with collision damage at Alstom, Wolverton at the time of writing.

**DMSL(A).** Alstom Birmingham 1999–2001. –/54 1TD 2W. 50.7 t.
**MSL.** Alstom Birmingham 1999–2001. –/68 1T. 47.5 t.
**DMSL(B).** Alstom Birmingham 1999–2001. –/64 1T. 50.7 t.

| | | | | | | | |
|---|---|---|---|---|---|---|---|
| 175 101 | **FS** | A | *AW* | CH | 50751 | 56751 | 79751 |
| 175 102 | **FS** | A | *AW* | CH | 50752 | 56752 | 79752 |
| 175 103 | **FS** | A | *AW* | CH | 50753 | 56753 | 79753 |
| 175 104 | **FS** | A | *AW* | CH | 50754 | 56754 | 79754 |

| 175 105 | **FS** | A | *AW* | CH | 50755 | 56755 | 79755 |
| 175 106 | **FS** | A | *AW* | CH | 50756 | 56756 | 79756 |
| 175 107 | **FS** | A | *AW* | CH | 50757 | 56757 | 79757 |
| 175 108 | **FS** | A | *AW* | CH | 50758 | 56758 | 79758 |
| 175 109 | **FS** | A | *AW* | CH | 50759 | 56759 | 79759 |
| 175 110 | **AW** | A | *AW* | CH | 50760 | 56760 | 79760 |
| 175 111 | **FS** | A | *AW* | CH | 50761 | 56761 | 79761 |
| 175 112 | **FS** | A | *AW* | CH | 50762 | 56762 | 79762 |
| 175 113 | **FS** | A | *AW* | CH | 50763 | 56763 | 79763 |
| 175 114 | **FS** | A | *AW* | CH | 50764 | 56764 | 79764 |
| 175 115 | **FS** | A | *AW* | CH | 50765 | 56765 | 79765 |
| 175 116 | **FS** | A | *AW* | CH | 50766 | 56766 | 79766 |

**Names (carried on one side of each DMSL):**

| 175 107 | CORONATION ST. ROVERS RETURN |
| 175 111 | Brief Encounter |
| 175 112 | South Lakes Wild Animal Park SUMATRAN TIGER |
| 175 114 | Commonwealth Cruiser |
| 175 116 | PETER VL JONES Community Rail Officer – Conwy Valley Line |

# CLASS 180        ADELANTE        ALSTOM

Air Conditioned.

**Construction:** Steel.
**Engines:** One Cummins QSK19 of 560 kW (750 h.p.) at 2100 r.p.m.
**Transmission:** Hydraulic. Voith T312br to Voith final drive.
**Bogies:** Alstom MB2.
**Couplers:** Scharfenberg outer ends, bar within unit.
**Seating Layout:** 1: 2+1 facing/unidirectional, 2: 2+2 facing/unidirectional.
**Dimensions:** 23.71/23.03 x 2.80 m.
**Gangways:** Within unit only.
**Wheel Arrangement:** 2-B – B-2 – B-2 – B-2 – B-2.
**Doors:** Single-leaf swing plug.        **Maximum Speed:** 125 m.p.h.
**Multiple Working:** Within class and with Class 175.

**DMSL(A).** Alstom Birmingham 2000–2001. –/46 2W 1TD. 51.7 t.
**MFL.** Alstom Birmingham 2000–2001. 42/– 1T 1W + catering point. 49.6 t.
**MSL.** Alstom Birmingham 2000–2001. –/68 1T. 49.5 t.
**MSLRB.** Alstom Birmingham 2000–2001. –/56 1T. 50.3 t.
**DMSL(B).** Alstom Birmingham 2000–2001. –/56 1T. 51.4 t.

| 180 101 | **FG** | A | *GW* | OO | 50901 | 54901 | 55901 | 56901 | 59901 |
| 180 102 | **FG** | A | *GW* | OO | 50902 | 54902 | 55902 | 56902 | 59902 |
| 180 103 | **FG** | A | *GW* | OO | 50903 | 54903 | 55903 | 56903 | 59903 |
| 180 104 | **FG** | A | *GW* | OO | 50904 | 54904 | 55904 | 56904 | 59904 |
| 180 105 | **FG** | A | *GW* | OO | 50905 | 54905 | 55905 | 56905 | 59905 |
| 180 106 | **FG** | A | *GW* | OO | 50906 | 54906 | 55906 | 56906 | 59906 |
| 180 107 | **FG** | A | *GW* | OO | 50907 | 54907 | 55907 | 56907 | 59907 |
| 180 108 | **FG** | A | *GW* | OO | 50908 | 54908 | 55908 | 56908 | 59908 |
| 180 109 | **FG** | A | *GW* | OO | 50909 | 54909 | 55909 | 56909 | 59909 |
| 180 110 | **FG** | A | *GW* | OO | 50910 | 54910 | 55910 | 56910 | 59910 |

| | | | | | | | | | |
|---|---|---|---|---|---|---|---|---|---|
| 180 111 | FG | A | GW | OO | 50911 | 54911 | 55911 | 56911 | 59911 |
| 180 112 | FG | A | GW | OO | 50912 | 54912 | 55912 | 56912 | 59912 |
| 180 113 | FG | A | GW | OO | 50913 | 54913 | 55913 | 56913 | 59913 |
| 180 114 | FG | A | GW | OO | 50914 | 54914 | 55914 | 56914 | 59914 |

# CLASS 185          DESIRO UK          SIEMENS

Air Conditioned. New units now being delivered for First Trans-Pennine Express.

**Construction:** Aluminium.
**Engines:** One Cummins QSK19 of 560 kW (750 h.p.) at 2100 r.p.m.
**Transmission:** Voith.
**Bogies:** Siemens.
**Couplers:** Dellner 12.
**Seating Layout:** 1: 2+1 facing/unidirectional, 2: 2+2 facing/unidirectional.
**Dimensions:** 23.76/23.75 x 2.84 m.
**Gangways:** Within unit only.
**Wheel Arrangement:** 2-B – 2-B – B-2.
**Doors:** Double-leaf sliding plug.        **Maximum Speed:** 100 m.p.h.
**Multiple Working:** Within class only.

**DMCL.** Siemens Uerdingen 2004–2006. 15/18(8) 2W 1TD + catering point. 55.6 t.
**MSL.** Siemens Uerdingen 2004–2006. –/72 1T. 52.8 t.
**DMS.** Siemens Uerdingen 2004–2006. –/64(4). 55.0 t.

| | | | | | |
|---|---|---|---|---|---|
| 185 101 | | H | 51101 | 53101 | 54101 |
| 185 102 | FG | H | 51102 | 53102 | 54102 |
| 185 103 | FG | H | 51103 | 53103 | 54103 |
| 185 104 | | H | 51104 | 53104 | 54104 |
| 185 105 | | H | 51105 | 53105 | 54105 |
| 185 106 | FG | H | 51106 | 53106 | 54106 |
| 185 107 | FG | H | 51107 | 53107 | 54107 |
| 185 108 | FG | H | 51108 | 53108 | 54108 |
| 185 109 | FG | H | 51109 | 53109 | 54109 |
| 185 110 | | H | 51110 | 53110 | 54110 |
| 185 111 | | H | 51111 | 53111 | 54111 |
| 185 112 | | H | 51112 | 53112 | 54112 |
| 185 113 | | H | 51113 | 53113 | 54113 |
| 185 114 | | H | 51114 | 53114 | 54114 |
| 185 115 | | H | 51115 | 53115 | 54115 |
| 185 116 | | H | 51116 | 53116 | 54116 |
| 185 117 | | H | 51117 | 53117 | 54117 |
| 185 118 | | H | 51118 | 53118 | 54118 |
| 185 119 | | H | 51119 | 53119 | 54119 |
| 185 120 | | H | 51120 | 53120 | 54120 |
| 185 121 | | H | 51121 | 53121 | 54121 |
| 185 122 | | H | 51122 | 53122 | 54122 |
| 185 123 | | H | 51123 | 53123 | 54123 |
| 185 124 | | H | 51124 | 53124 | 54124 |
| 185 125 | | H | 51125 | 53125 | 54125 |
| 185 126 | | H | 51126 | 53126 | 54126 |

| | | | | |
|---|---|---|---|---|
| 185 127 | H | 51127 | 53127 | 54127 |
| 185 128 | H | 51128 | 53128 | 54128 |
| 185 129 | H | 51129 | 53129 | 54129 |
| 185 130 | H | 51130 | 53130 | 54130 |
| 185 131 | H | 51131 | 53131 | 54131 |
| 185 132 | H | 51132 | 53132 | 54132 |
| 185 133 | H | 51133 | 53133 | 54133 |
| 185 134 | H | 51134 | 53134 | 54134 |
| 185 135 | H | 51135 | 53135 | 54135 |
| 185 136 | H | 51136 | 53136 | 54136 |
| 185 137 | H | 51137 | 53137 | 54137 |
| 185 138 | H | 51138 | 53138 | 54138 |
| 185 139 | H | 51139 | 53139 | 54139 |
| 185 140 | H | 51140 | 53140 | 54140 |
| 185 141 | H | 51141 | 53141 | 54141 |
| 185 142 | H | 51142 | 53142 | 54142 |
| 185 143 | H | 51143 | 53143 | 54143 |
| 185 144 | H | 51144 | 53144 | 54144 |
| 185 145 | H | 51145 | 53145 | 54145 |
| 185 146 | H | 51146 | 53146 | 54146 |
| 185 147 | H | 51147 | 53147 | 54147 |
| 185 148 | H | 51148 | 53148 | 54148 |
| 185 149 | H | 51149 | 53149 | 54149 |
| 185 150 | H | 51150 | 53150 | 54150 |
| 185 151 | H | 51151 | 53151 | 54151 |

# 3.2. DIESEL ELECTRIC UNITS

## CLASS 201/202 PRESERVED "HASTINGS" UNIT BR

DMBS–2TSL–TSRB–TSL–DMBS.

Preserved unit made up from two Class 201 short-frame cars and three Class 202 long-frame cars. The "Hastings" units were made with narrow body-profiles for use on the section between Tonbridge and Battle which had tunnels of restricted loading gauge. These tunnels were converted to single track operation in the 1980s thus allowing standard loading gauge stock to be used. The set also contains a Class 411 EMU trailer (not Hastings line gauge) and a Class 422 EMU buffet car.

**Construction:** Steel.
**Engine:** One English Electric 4SRKT Mk. 2 of 450 kW (600 h.p.) at 850 r.p.m.
**Main Generator:** English Electric EE824.
**Traction Motors:** Two English Electric EE507 mounted on the inner bogie.
**Bogies:** SR Mk. 4. (Former EMU TSL vehicles have Commonwealth bogies).
**Couplers:** Drophead buckeye.
**Dimensions:** 18.40 x 2.70 m (60000), 20.35 x 2.74 m (60116/60118/60529), 18.36 x 2.74 m (60501), 20.35 x 2.82 m (69337), 20.30 x 2.82 (70262).
**Gangways:** Within unit only.
**Doors:** Manually operated slam.
**Brakes:** Electro-pneumatic and automatic air.
**Maximum Speed:** 75 m.p.h.
**Multiple Working:** Other ex-BR Southern Region DEMU vehicles.
**Seating Layout:** 2+2 facing.

**60000. DMBS.** Lot No. 30329 Eastleigh 1957. –/22. 55.0 t.
**60116. DMBS (Spare).** Lot No. 30395 Eastleigh 1957. –/31. 56.0 t.
**60118. DMBS.** Lot No. 30395 Eastleigh 1957. –/30. 56.0 t.
**60501. TSL.** Lot No. 30331 Eastleigh 1957. –/52 2T. 29.5 t.
**60529. TSL.** Lot No. 30397 Eastleigh 1957. –/60 2T. 30.5 t.
**69337. TSRB (ex Class 422 EMU).** Lot No. 30805 York 1970. –/40. 35.0 t.
**70262. TSL (ex Class 411/5 EMU).** Lot No. 30455 Eastleigh 1958. –/64 2T. 31.5 t.

| | | | | | | | | | |
|---|---|---|---|---|---|---|---|---|---|
| 201 001 | **G** | HD *HD* | SE | 60000 | 60529 | 70262 | 69337 | 60501 | 60118 |
| Spare | **G** | HD *HD* | SE | 60116 | | | | | |

**Names:**

60000 Hastings
60116 Mountfield
60118 Tunbridge Wells

# CLASS 220        VOYAGER        BOMBARDIER

DMS–MSRMB–MS–DMF.

**Construction:** Steel.
**Engine:** Cummins QSK19 of 560 kW (750 h.p.) at 1800 r.p.m.
**Transmission:** Two Alstom Onix 800 three-phase traction motors of 275 kW.
**Braking:** Rheostatic and electro-pneumatic.
**Bogies:** Bombardier B5005.
**Couplers:** Dellner 12 at outer ends, bar within unit.
**Seating Layout:** 1: 2+1 facing/unidirectional, 2: 2+2 mainly unidirectional.
**Dimensions:** 23.67/23.00(602xx) x 2.73 m.
**Gangways:** Within unit only.
**Wheel Arrangement:** 1A-A1 – 1A-A1 – 1A-A1 – 1A-A1.
**Doors:** Single-leaf swing plug.
**Maximum Speed:** 125 m.p.h.
**Multiple Working:** Within class and with Classes 221 and 222. Also with Class 57/3 locomotives.

**DMS.** Bombardier Brugge/Wakefield 2000–2001. –/42 1TD 1W. 48.0 t.
**MSRMB.** Bombardier Brugge/Wakefield 2000–2001. –/58. 45.0 t.
**MS.** Bombardier Brugge/Wakefield 2000–2001. –/60 1TD. 44.5 t.
**DMF.** Bombardier Brugge/Wakefield 2000–2001. 26/– 1TD 1W. 48.1 t.

| | | | | | | | |
|---|---|---|---|---|---|---|---|
| 220 001 | **VT** | HX | *VX* | CZ | 60301 | 60701 | 60201 | 60401 |
| 220 002 | **VT** | HX | *VX* | CZ | 60302 | 60702 | 60202 | 60402 |
| 220 003 | **VT** | HX | *VX* | CZ | 60303 | 60703 | 60203 | 60403 |
| 220 004 | **VT** | HX | *VX* | CZ | 60304 | 60704 | 60204 | 60404 |
| 220 005 | **VT** | HX | *VX* | CZ | 60305 | 60705 | 60205 | 60405 |
| 220 006 | **VT** | HX | *VX* | CZ | 60306 | 60706 | 60206 | 60406 |
| 220 007 | **VT** | HX | *VX* | CZ | 60307 | 60707 | 60207 | 60407 |
| 220 008 | **VT** | HX | *VX* | CZ | 60308 | 60708 | 60208 | 60408 |
| 220 009 | **VT** | HX | *VX* | CZ | 60309 | 60709 | 60209 | 60409 |
| 220 010 | **VT** | HX | *VX* | CZ | 60310 | 60710 | 60210 | 60410 |
| 220 011 | **VT** | HX | *VX* | CZ | 60311 | 60711 | 60211 | 60411 |
| 220 012 | **VT** | HX | *VX* | CZ | 60312 | 60712 | 60212 | 60412 |
| 220 013 | **VT** | HX | *VX* | CZ | 60313 | 60713 | 60213 | 60413 |
| 220 014 | **VT** | HX | *VX* | CZ | 60314 | 60714 | 60214 | 60414 |
| 220 015 | **VT** | HX | *VX* | CZ | 60315 | 60715 | 60215 | 60415 |
| 220 016 | **VT** | HX | *VX* | CZ | 60316 | 60716 | 60216 | 60416 |
| 220 017 | **VT** | HX | *VX* | CZ | 60317 | 60717 | 60217 | 60417 |
| 220 018 | **VT** | HX | *VX* | CZ | 60318 | 60718 | 60218 | 60418 |
| 220 019 | **VT** | HX | *VX* | CZ | 60319 | 60719 | 60219 | 60419 |
| 220 020 | **VT** | HX | *VX* | CZ | 60320 | 60720 | 60220 | 60420 |
| 220 021 | **VT** | HX | *VX* | CZ | 60321 | 60721 | 60221 | 60421 |
| 220 022 | **VT** | HX | *VX* | CZ | 60322 | 60722 | 60222 | 60422 |
| 220 023 | **VT** | HX | *VX* | CZ | 60323 | 60723 | 60223 | 60423 |
| 220 024 | **VT** | HX | *VX* | CZ | 60324 | 60724 | 60224 | 60424 |
| 220 025 | **VT** | HX | *VX* | CZ | 60325 | 60725 | 60225 | 60425 |
| 220 026 | **VT** | HX | *VX* | CZ | 60326 | 60726 | 60226 | 60426 |
| 220 027 | **VT** | HX | *VX* | CZ | 60327 | 60727 | 60227 | 60427 |

| 220 028 | **VT** | HX | *VX* | CZ | 60328 | 60728 | 60228 | 60428 |
| 220 029 | **VT** | HX | *VX* | CZ | 60329 | 60729 | 60229 | 60429 |
| 220 030 | **VT** | HX | *VX* | CZ | 60330 | 60730 | 60230 | 60430 |
| 220 031 | **VT** | HX | *VX* | CZ | 60331 | 60731 | 60231 | 60431 |
| 220 032 | **VT** | HX | *VX* | CZ | 60332 | 60732 | 60232 | 60432 |
| 220 033 | **VT** | HX | *VX* | CZ | 60333 | 60733 | 60233 | 60433 |
| 220 034 | **VT** | HX | *VX* | CZ | 60334 | 60734 | 60234 | 60434 |

**Names (carried on MS):**

| 220 001 | Somerset Voyager | 220 019 | Mersey Voyager |
| 220 002 | Forth Voyager | 220 020 | Wessex Voyager |
| 220 003 | Solent Voyager | 220 021 | Staffordshire Voyager |
| 220 004 | Cumbrian Voyager | 220 022 | Brighton Voyager |
| 220 005 | Guildford Voyager | 220 023 | Mancunian Voyager |
| 220 006 | Clyde Voyager | 220 024 | Sheffield Voyager |
| 220 007 | Thames Voyager | 220 025 | Severn Voyager |
| 220 008 | Draig Gymreig/Welsh Dragon | 220 026 | Stagecoach Voyager |
| 220 009 | Gatwick Voyager | 220 027 | Avon Voyager |
| 220 010 | Ribble Voyager | 220 028 | Black Country Voyager |
| 220 011 | Tyne Voyager | 220 029 | Vyajer Kernewek/ |
| 220 012 | Lanarkshire Voyager | | Cornish Voyager |
| 220 013 | Gwibiwr De Cymru/South | 220 030 | Devon Voyager |
| | Wales Voyager | 220 031 | Tay Voyager |
| 220 014 | South Yorkshire Voyager | 220 032 | Grampian Voyager |
| 220 015 | Solway Voyager | 220 033 | Fife Voyager |
| 220 016 | Midland Voyager | 220 034 | Yorkshire Voyager |
| 220 017 | BOMBARDIER Voyager | | |
| 220 018 | Dorset Voyager | | |

# CLASS 221   SUPER VOYAGER   BOMBARDIER

DMS–MSRMB–MS(–MS)–DMF. Tilting units.

**Construction:** Steel.
**Engine:** Cummins QSK19 of 560 kW (750 h.p.) at 1800 r.p.m.
**Transmission:** Two Alstom Onix 800 three-phase traction motors of 275 kW.
**Braking:** Rheostatic and electro-pneumatic.
**Bogies:** Bombardier HVP.
**Couplers:** Dellner 12 at outer ends, bar within unit.
**Seating Layout:** 1: 2+1 facing/unidirectional, 2: 2+2 mainly unidirectional.
**Dimensions:** 23.67 x 2.73 m.
**Gangways:** Within unit only.
**Wheel Arrangement:** 1A-A1 – 1A-A1 – 1A-A1 (– 1A-A1) – 1A-A1.
**Doors:** Single-leaf swing plug.
**Maximum Speed:** 125 m.p.h.
**Multiple Working:** Within class and with Classes 221 and 222. Also with Class 57/3 locomotives.

**DMS.** Bombardier Brugge/Wakefield 2001–2002. –/42 1TD 1W. 56.6 t.
**MSRMB.** Bombardier Brugge/Wakefield 2001–2002. –/58. 53.1 t.
**60951–60994. MS.** Bombardier Brugge/Wakefield 2001–2002. –/60 1TD. 56.6 t.
**60851–60890. MS.** Bombardier Brugge/Wakefield 2001–2002. –/60 1TD. 53.1 t.
**DMF.** Bombardier Brugge/Wakefield 2001–2002. 26/– 1TD 1W. 56.6 t.

| | | | | | | | | |
|---|---|---|---|---|---|---|---|---|
| 221 101 | **VT** | HX | *VX* | CZ | 60351 | 60751 | 60951 | 60851 | 60451 |
| 221 102 | **VT** | HX | *VX* | CZ | 60352 | 60752 | 60952 | 60852 | 60452 |
| 221 103 | **VT** | HX | *VX* | CZ | 60353 | 60753 | 60953 | 60853 | 60453 |
| 221 104 | **VT** | HX | *VX* | CZ | 60354 | 60754 | 60954 | 60854 | 60454 |
| 221 105 | **VT** | HX | *VX* | CZ | 60355 | 60755 | 60955 | 60855 | 60455 |
| 221 106 | **VT** | HX | *VX* | CZ | 60356 | 60756 | 60956 | 60856 | 60456 |
| 221 107 | **VT** | HX | *VX* | CZ | 60357 | 60757 | 60957 | 60857 | 60457 |
| 221 108 | **VT** | HX | *VX* | CZ | 60358 | 60758 | 60958 | 60858 | 60458 |
| 221 109 | **VT** | HX | *VX* | CZ | 60359 | 60759 | 60959 | 60859 | 60459 |
| 221 110 | **VT** | HX | *VX* | CZ | 60360 | 60760 | 60960 | 60860 | 60460 |
| 221 111 | **VT** | HX | *VX* | CZ | 60361 | 60761 | 60961 | 60861 | 60461 |
| 221 112 | **VT** | HX | *VX* | CZ | 60362 | 60762 | 60962 | 60862 | 60462 |
| 221 113 | **VT** | HX | *VX* | CZ | 60363 | 60763 | 60963 | 60863 | 60463 |
| 221 114 | **VT** | HX | *VX* | CZ | 60364 | 60764 | 60964 | 60864 | 60464 |
| 221 115 | **VT** | HX | *VX* | CZ | 60365 | 60765 | 60965 | 60865 | 60465 |
| 221 116 | **VT** | HX | *VX* | CZ | 60366 | 60766 | 60966 | 60866 | 60466 |
| 221 117 | **VT** | HX | *VX* | CZ | 60367 | 60767 | 60967 | 60867 | 60467 |
| 221 118 | **VT** | HX | *VX* | CZ | 60368 | 60768 | 60968 | 60868 | 60468 |
| 221 119 | **VT** | HX | *VX* | CZ | 60369 | 60769 | 60969 | 60869 | 60469 |
| 221 120 | **VT** | HX | *VX* | CZ | 60370 | 60770 | 60970 | 60870 | 60470 |
| 221 121 | **VT** | HX | *VX* | CZ | 60371 | 60771 | 60971 | 60871 | 60471 |
| 221 122 | **VT** | HX | *VX* | CZ | 60372 | 60772 | 60972 | 60872 | 60472 |
| 221 123 | **VT** | HX | *VX* | CZ | 60373 | 60773 | 60973 | 60873 | 60473 |
| 221 124 | **VT** | HX | *VX* | CZ | 60374 | 60774 | 60974 | 60874 | 60474 |
| 221 125 | **VT** | HX | *VX* | CZ | 60375 | 60775 | 60975 | 60875 | 60475 |
| 221 126 | **VT** | HX | *VX* | CZ | 60376 | 60776 | 60976 | 60876 | 60476 |
| 221 127 | **VT** | HX | *VX* | CZ | 60377 | 60777 | 60977 | 60877 | 60477 |
| 221 128 | **VT** | HX | *VX* | CZ | 60378 | 60778 | 60978 | 60878 | 60478 |
| 221 129 | **VT** | HX | *VX* | CZ | 60379 | 60779 | 60979 | 60879 | 60479 |
| 221 130 | **VT** | HX | *VX* | CZ | 60380 | 60780 | 60980 | 60880 | 60480 |
| 221 131 | **VT** | HX | *VX* | CZ | 60381 | 60781 | 60981 | 60881 | 60481 |
| 221 132 | **VT** | HX | *VX* | CZ | 60382 | 60782 | 60982 | 60882 | 60482 |
| 221 133 | **VT** | HX | *VX* | CZ | 60383 | 60783 | 60983 | 60883 | 60483 |
| 221 134 | **VT** | HX | *VX* | CZ | 60384 | 60784 | 60984 | 60884 | 60484 |
| 221 135 | **VT** | HX | *VX* | CZ | 60385 | 60785 | 60985 | 60885 | 60485 |
| 221 136 | **VT** | HX | *VX* | CZ | 60386 | 60786 | 60986 | 60886 | 60486 |
| 221 137 | **VT** | HX | *VX* | CZ | 60387 | 60787 | 60987 | 60887 | 60487 |
| 221 138 | **VT** | HX | *VX* | CZ | 60388 | 60788 | 60988 | 60888 | 60488 |
| 221 139 | **VT** | HX | *VX* | CZ | 60389 | 60789 | 60989 | 60889 | 60489 |
| 221 140 | **VT** | HX | *VX* | CZ | 60390 | 60790 | 60990 | 60890 | 60490 |
| 221 141 | **VT** | HX | *VX* | CZ | 60391 | 60791 | 60991 | | 60491 |
| 221 142 | **VT** | HX | *VX* | CZ | 60392 | 60792 | 60992 | | 60492 |
| 221 143 | **VT** | HX | *VX* | CZ | 60393 | 60793 | 60993 | | 60493 |
| 221 144 | **VT** | HX | *VX* | CZ | 60394 | 60794 | 60994 | | 60494 |

**Names (carried on MS No. 609xx):**

| | |
|---|---|
| 221 101 | Louis Bleriot |
| 221 102 | John Cabot |
| 221 103 | Christopher Columbus |
| 221 104 | Sir John Franklin |
| 221 105 | William Baffin |
| 221 106 | Willem Barents |
| 221 107 | Sir Martin Frobisher |
| 221 108 | Sir Ernest Shackleton |
| 221 109 | Marco Polo |
| 221 110 | James Cook |
| 221 111 | Roald Amundsen |
| 221 112 | Ferdinand Magellan |
| 221 113 | Sir Walter Raleigh |
| 221 114 | Sir Francis Drake |
| 221 115 | Sir Francis Chichester |
| 221 116 | David Livingstone |
| 221 117 | Sir Henry Morton Stanley |
| 221 118 | Mungo Park |
| 221 119 | Amelia Earhart |
| 221 120 | Amy Johnson |
| 221 121 | Charles Darwin |
| 221 122 | Doctor Who |
| 221 123 | Henry Hudson |
| 221 124 | Charles Lindbergh |
| 221 125 | Henry the Navigator |
| 221 126 | Captain Robert Scott |
| 221 127 | Wright Brothers |
| 221 128 | Captain John Smith |
| 221 129 | George Vancouver |
| 221 130 | Michael Palin |
| 221 131 | Edgar Evans |
| 221 132 | William Speirs Bruce |
| 221 133 | Alexander Selkirk |
| 221 134 | Mary Kingsley |
| 221 135 | Donald Campbell |
| 221 136 | Yuri Gagarin |
| 221 137 | Mayflower Pilgrims |
| 221 138 | Thor Heyerdahl |
| 221 139 | Leif Erikson |
| 221 140 | Vasco da Gama |
| 221 141 | Amerigo Vespucci |
| 221 142 | Matthew Flinders |
| 221 143 | Auguste Picard |
| 221 144 | Prince Madoc |

# CLASS 222 MERIDIAN/PIONEER BOMBARDIER

**Construction:** Steel.
**Engine:** Cummins QSK19 of 560 kW (750 h.p.) at 1800 r.p.m.
**Transmission:** Two Alstom Onix 800 three-phase traction motors of 275 kW.
**Braking:** Rheostatic and electro-pneumatic.
**Bogies:** Bombardier B5005.
**Couplers:** Dellner at outer ends, bar within unit.
**Seating Layout:** 1: 2+1, 2: 2+2 facing/unidirectional.
**Dimensions:** 23.85/23.00 x 2.73 m.
**Gangways:** Within unit only.
**Wheel Arrangement:** All cars 1A-A1.
**Doors:** Single-leaf swing plug.
**Maximum Speed:** 125 m.p.h.
**Multiple Working:** Within class and with Classes 220 and 221.

**222 001–222 007. Midland Mainline Meridian.** 9-car units. DMRFO–MFO–MFO–MSORMB–MSO–MSO–MSO–MSO–DMSO.

**DMRFO.** Bombardier Brugge 2004–2005. 22/– 1TD 1W. 52.8 t.
**MFO.** Bombardier Brugge 2004–2005. 42/– 1T. 48.2 t.
**MSO.** Bombardier Brugge 2004–2005. –/68 1T. 48.6 t.
**MSORMB.** Bombardier Brugge 2004–2005. –/62. 49.6 t.
**DMSO.** Bombardier Brugge 2004–2005. –/38 1TD 1W. 51.0 t.

| 222 001 | **MN** | H | *MM* | CZ | 60241 | 60441 | 60341 | 60621 | 60561 |
|---|---|---|---|---|---|---|---|---|---|
| | | | | | 60551 | 60541 | 60531 | 60161 | |

| 222 002 | **MN** | H | *MM* | CZ | 60242 | 60442 | 60342 | 60622 | 60562 |
|         |        |   |      |    | 60552 | 60542 | 60532 | 60162 |       |
| 222 003 | **MN** | H | *MM* | CZ | 60243 | 60443 | 60343 | 60623 | 60563 |
|         |        |   |      |    | 60553 | 60543 | 60533 | 60163 |       |
| 222 004 | **MN** | H | *MM* | CZ | 60244 | 60444 | 60344 | 60624 | 60564 |
|         |        |   |      |    | 60554 | 60544 | 60534 | 60164 |       |
| 222 005 | **MN** | H | *MM* | CZ | 60245 | 60445 | 60345 | 60625 | 60565 |
|         |        |   |      |    | 60555 | 60545 | 60535 | 60165 |       |
| 222 006 | **MN** | H | *MM* | CZ | 60246 | 60446 | 60346 | 60626 | 60566 |
|         |        |   |      |    | 60556 | 60546 | 60536 | 60166 |       |
| 222 007 | **MN** | H | *MM* | CZ | 60247 | 60447 | 60347 | 60627 | 60567 |
|         |        |   |      |    | 60557 | 60547 | 60537 | 60167 |       |

**222 008–222 023. Midland Mainline Meridian.** 4-car units. DMRFO–MCO–MSORMB–DMSO.

**DMRFO.** Bombardier Brugge 2003–2004. 22/– 1TD 1W. 52.8 t.
**MCO.** Bombardier Brugge 2003–2004. 28/22 1T. 48.6 t.
**MSORMB.** Bombardier Brugge 2003–2004. –/62. 49.6 t.
**DMSO.** Bombardier Brugge 2003–2004. –/40 1TD 1W. 51.0 t.

| 222 008 | **MN** | H | *MM* | CZ | 60248 | 60918 | 60628 | 60168 |
| 222 009 | **MN** | H | *MM* | CZ | 60249 | 60919 | 60629 | 60169 |
| 222 010 | **MN** | H | *MM* | CZ | 60250 | 60920 | 60630 | 60170 |
| 222 011 | **MN** | H | *MM* | CZ | 60251 | 60921 | 60631 | 60171 |
| 222 012 | **MN** | H | *MM* | CZ | 60252 | 60922 | 60632 | 60172 |
| 222 013 | **MN** | H | *MM* | CZ | 60253 | 60923 | 60633 | 60173 |
| 222 014 | **MN** | H | *MM* | CZ | 60254 | 60924 | 60634 | 60174 |
| 222 015 | **MN** | H | *MM* | CZ | 60255 | 60925 | 60635 | 60175 |
| 222 016 | **MN** | H | *MM* | CZ | 60256 | 60926 | 60636 | 60176 |
| 222 017 | **MN** | H | *MM* | CZ | 60257 | 60927 | 60637 | 60177 |
| 222 018 | **MN** | H | *MM* | CZ | 60258 | 60928 | 60638 | 60178 |
| 222 019 | **MN** | H | *MM* | CZ | 60259 | 60929 | 60639 | 60179 |
| 222 020 | **MN** | H | *MM* | CZ | 60260 | 60930 | 60640 | 60180 |
| 222 021 | **MN** | H | *MM* | CZ | 60261 | 60931 | 60641 | 60181 |
| 222 022 | **MN** | H | *MM* | CZ | 60262 | 60932 | 60642 | 60182 |
| 222 023 | **MN** | H | *MM* | CZ | 60263 | 60933 | 60643 | 60183 |

**222 101–222 104. Hull Trains Pioneers.** DMRFO–MSO–MSORMB–DMSO.

**DMRFO.** Bombardier Brugge 2005. 22/– 1TD 1W. 52.8 t.
**MSO.** Bombardier Brugge 2005. –/68 1T. 48.6 t.
**MSORMB.** Bombardier Brugge 2005. –/62. 49.6 t.
**DMSO.** Bombardier Brugge 2005. –/40 1TD 1W. 51.0 t.

| 222 101 | **HT** | H | *HT* | XW | 60271 | 60571 | 60681 | 60191 |
| 222 102 | **HT** | H | *HT* | XW | 60272 | 60572 | 60682 | 60192 |
| 222 103 | **HT** | H | *HT* | XW | 60273 | 60573 | 60683 | 60193 |
| 222 104 | **HT** | H | *HT* | XW | 60274 | 60574 | 60684 | 60194 |

**Names (carried on DMRFO and DMSO):**

| | | |
|---|---|---|
| 222 101 | Professor GEORGE GRAY | 222 103 Dr JOHN GODBER |
| 222 102 | Professor STUART PALMER | 222 104 Sir TERRY FARRELL |

# 3.3 PARRY PEOPLE MOVERS PPM 50 LIGHT RAILCAR

## CLASS 999/9                                          PPM-50

Gas/flywheel hybrid drive railcar used on the Stourbridge Junction to Stourbridge Town branch (at the time of writing only on Sundays). The railcar is based at the Pre Metro Operations Ltd. compound at Stourbridge Junction (which is leased from Network Rail).

**Body construction:** Stainless steel framework.
**Chassis construction:** Welded mild steel box section.
**Primary Drive:** Ford MVH420 2.0 litre LPG fuel engine driving through Newage marine gearbox, Tandler bevel box and 4 "V" belt driver to flywheel.
**Flywheel Energy Store:** 500 kg, 1m diameter, normal operational speed range 1000–1500 r.p.m.
**Final transmission:** 4 "V" belt driver from flywheel to Tandler bevel box, Linde hydrostatic transmission and spiral bevel gearbox to No. 2 end axle.
**Braking:** Normal service braking by regeneration to flywheel (1 m/s/s); emergency/parking braking by sprung-on, air-off disc brakes (3 m/s/s).
**Maximum Speed:** 40 m.p.h.
**Dimensions:** 8.7 x 2.4 m.
**Weight:** 9.1 t.
**Doors:** Deans powered doors, double-leaf folding (one per side).
**Multiple Working:** Not applicable.

**999900. DMS.** 2001. –/20 1W. 9.1 t.

999900          **PM**   PM   *PM*    Stourbridge Junction

# 3.4. SERVICE DMUS

This section lists vehicles not used for passenger-carrying purposes. Some vehicles are numbered in the special service stock number series.

## CLASS 901        ULTRASONIC TEST UNIT

DM–DM. Converted 1986 from Class 101. Gangwayed within unit. Often operates with either Overhead Line Equipment Test Coach 975091 (see Page xxx) or 999602 (see below) as a centre car.

**Construction:** Aluminium alloy body on steel underframe.
**Engines:** Two Leyland 680/1 of 112 kW (150 h.p.) at 1800 r.p.m. per power car.
**Transmission:** Mechanical. Cardan shaft and freewheel to a four-speed epicyclic gearbox with a further cardan shaft to the final drive, each engine driving the inner axle of one bogie.
**Brakes:** Air.
**Couplers:** Screw couplings.
**Bogies:** DD15 (motor) and DT11 (trailer).
**Maximum Speed:** 70 m.p.h.
**Dimensions:** 18.50 x 2.82 m.
**Doors:** Manually-operated slam.
**Multiple Working:** "Blue Square" coupling code. First generation vehicles may be coupled together to work in multiple up to a maximum of 6 motor cars or 12 cars in total in a formation. First generation vehicles may not be coupled in multiple with second generation vehicles.

**977391. DM.** Lot No. 30500 Metro-Cammell. 1959. 32.5 t.
**977392. DM.** Lot No. 30254 Metro-Cammell. 1956. 32.5 t.

| 901 001 | **Y** | NR | *SO* | ZA | 977391 | (51433) | 977392 | (53167) |
|---------|-------|----|------|-----|--------|---------|--------|---------|

## CLASS 901 ULTRASONIC TEST UNIT (EXTRA VEHICLE)

T. Converted 1986 from Class 432 EMU. Gangwayed. Operates with 977391/977392 (see above).

**Construction:** Steel.
**Bogies:** SR Mk. 6.
**Brakes:** Twin pipe vacuum.
**Doors:** Manually operated slam.
**Maximum Speed:** 70 m.p.h.
**Couplings:** Screw.
**Multiple Working:** Blue Square.
**Dimensions:** 20.35 x 2.82 m.

**999602. T.** Lot No. 30862 York 1974. 55.5 t.

| - | **Y** | NR | *SO* | ZA | 999602 | (62483) |
|---|-------|----|------|-----|--------|---------|

## CLASS 901        TEST UNIT (Iris 2)

DM–DM. Converted 1991 from Class 101. Gangwayed within unit.

**For details see above.**

**977693. DM.** Lot No. 30261 Metro-Cammell. 1957. 32.5 t.
**977694. DM.** Lot No. 30276 Metro-Cammell. 1958. 32.5 t.

| 901 002 | **Y** | NR | *SO* | ZA | 977693 | (53222) | 977694 | (53338) |
|---------|-------|----|------|-----|--------|---------|--------|---------|

# CLASS 930          SANDITE/DE-ICING UNIT

DMB–T–DMB. Converted 1993 from Class 205. Gangwayed within unit. Sandite Trailer 977870 is replaced by De-icing trailer 977364 (see below) as required.

**Construction:** Steel.
**Engine:** One English Electric 4SRKT Mk. 2 of 450 kW (600 h.p.) at 850 r.p.m.
**Transmission:** Electric. Two English Electric EE507 traction motors mounted on the bogie at the non-driving end of each power car.
**Maximum Speed:** 75 m.p.h.       **Bogies:** SR Mk. 4.
**Brakes:** Electro-pneumatic and automatic air.
**Doors:** Manually operated slam.       **Couplings:** Drophead buckeye.
**Multiple Working:** Classes 201–207.
**Dimensions:** 20.33 x 2.82 m. (DMB); 20.28 x 2.82 m.

**977939–977940. DMB.** Lot No. 30671 Eastleigh 1962. 56.0 t.
**977870. T.** Lot No. 30542 Eastleigh 1959. 30.5 t.

| 930 301 | **RO** | NR | *SN* | SE | 977939 | (60145) | 977870 | (60660) |
|---|---|---|---|---|---|---|---|---|
| | | | | | 977940 | (60149) | | |

# UNCLASSIFIED             DE-ICING UNIT

T. Converted 1960 from 4-Sub EMU vehicle. Non gangwayed. Operates with 977939/977940 (see above) in place of Sandite Trailer 977870.

**Construction:** Steel.
**Maximum Speed:** 70 m.p.h.       **Couplings:** Drophead buckeye.
**Bogies:** Central 43 inch.       **Multiple Working:** SR system.
**Brakes:** Electro-pneumatic and automatic air.
**Doors:** Manually operated slam.       **Dimensions:** 19.99 x 2.74 m.

**977364. T.** Southern Railway Eastleigh 1946. 29.0 t.

| - | **RO** | NR | *SN* | SU | 977364 | (10400) |
|---|---|---|---|---|---|---|

# CLASS 950         TRACK ASSESSMENT UNIT

DM–DM. Purpose built service unit based on the Class 150 design. Gangwayed within unit.

**Construction:** Steel.
**Engine:** One Cummins NT-855-RT5 of 213 kW (285 h.p.) at 2100 r.p.m. per power car.
**Transmission:** Hydraulic. Voith T211r with cardan shafts to Gmeinder GM190 final drive.
**Maximum Speed:** 75 m.p.h.       **Couplers:** BSI automatic.
**Bogies:** BP38 (powered), BT38 (non-powered).
**Brakes:** Electro-pneumatic.       **Dimensions:** 20.06 x 2.82 m.
**Doors:** Manually operated slam & power operated sliding.
**Multiple Working:** Classes 142, 143, 144, 150, 153, 155, 156, 158, 159 and 170.

**999600. DM.** Lot No. 4060 BREL York 1987. 35.0 t.
**999601. DM.** Lot No. 4061 BREL York 1987. 35.0 t.

| 950 001 | **Y** | NR | *SO* | ZA | 999600 | 999601 |
|---|---|---|---|---|---|---|

# CLASS 960       SANDITE & SERVICE UNITS

DMB. Converted from Class 121s. Non gangwayed.

**For details see Page 173.**

960 011 is a Video Survey Unit.
960 012 is a South West Trains Route Learning Unit.
960 014 is a Chiltern Route Learning Unit.

**977723. DMB.** Lot No. 30518 Pressed Steel 1960. 38.0 t.
**977858–60/66/73. DMB.** Lot No. 30518 Pressed Steel 1960. 38.0 t.

| | | | | | | | |
|---|---|---|---|---|---|---|---|
| 960 010 | **M** | NR | *CR* | AL | 977858 | (55024) | |
| 960 011 | **RK** | NR | | ZA | 977859 | (55025) | |
| 960 012 | **SD** | SW | *SW* | SA | 977860 | (55028) | John Cameron |
| 960 013 | **N** | NR | | AL | 977866 | (55030) | |
| 960 014 | **BG** | CR | *CR* | AL | 977873 | (55022) | |
| 960 021 | **RO** | NR | *CR* | AL | 977723 | (55021) | |

# CLASS 960          SANDITE UNIT

DMB. Converted 1991 from Class 122. Non gangwayed.

**Construction:** Steel.
**Engines:** Two Leyland 1595 of 112 kW (150 h.p.) at 1800 r.p.m.
**Transmission:** Mechanical. Cardan shaft and freewheel to a four-speed epicyclic gearbox with a further cardan shaft to the final drive, each engine driving the inner axle of one bogie.
**Maximum Speed:** 70 m.p.h.
**Bogies:** DD10.                 **Couplings:** Screw.
**Brakes:** Twin pipe vacuum.     **Multiple Working:** Blue Square.
**Doors:** Manually operated slam.    **Dimensions:** 20.45 x 2.82 m.

**975042. DMB.** Lot No. 30419 Gloucester 1958. 36.5 t.

| | | | | | | |
|---|---|---|---|---|---|---|
| 960 015 | **Y** | NR | *CR* | AL | 975042 | (55019) |

# CLASS 960      WATER-JETTING UNIT

DMB–IMV–DMB. Converted 2003/04 from Class 117. Non gangwayed.

**Construction:** Steel.
**Engines:** Two Leyland 1595 of 112 kW (150 h.p.) at 1800 r.p.m.
**Transmission:** Mechanical. Cardan shaft and freewheel to a four-speed epicyclic gearbox with a further cardan shaft to the final drive, each engine driving the inner axle of one bogie.
**Maximum Speed:** 70 m.p.h.
**Bogies:** DD10.                 **Couplings:** Screw.
**Brakes:** Twin pipe vacuum.     **Multiple Working:** Blue Square.
**Doors:** Manually operated slam.    **Dimensions:** 20.45 x 2.84 m.

**977987/977988. DMB.** Lot No. 30546/30548 Pressed Steel 1959–1960. 36.5 t.
**977992. IMV (Intermediate Motor Vehicle).** Lot No. 30548 Pressed Steel 1959–1960. 36.5 t.

| 960 301 | **G** | CR | *CR* | AL | 977987 | (51371) | 977992 | (51375) |
|---------|-------|----|------|----|--------|---------|--------|---------|
|         |       |    |      |    | 977988 | (51413) |        |         |

# CLASS 960 EMERGENCY TRAIN UNITS

Converted from Class 121s. Severn Tunnel Emergency Train units.

**For details see Page 173.**

**DMB.** Lot No. 30518 Pressed Steel 1960. 38.5 t.

| 960 302 | **Y** | NR | *E* | SJ | 977975 | (55027) |
|---------|-------|----|-----|----|--------|---------|
| 960 303 | **Y** | NR | *E* | SJ | 977976 | (55031) |

# CLASS 960 DRIVER TRAINING UNIT

Converted from a Class 121.

**For details see Page 173.**

**977968. DMB.**

| - | | ES | CA | *CA* | RU | 977968 | (55029) |
|---|-|----|----|------|----|--------|---------|

# CLASS 960 TRACK ASSESSMENT/RECORDING UNIT

DM–DM. Universal track recording unit for video inspections, for measuring rail profiles etc. Plasser type UFM 160-1. Full details awaited.

| Construction: | Engine: |
|---------------|---------|
| Transmission: | |
| Maximum Speed: 100 m.p.h. | Weight: 68.0 t. |
| Brakes: | Dimensions: 23.86 x 2.57 m. |

**999700. DM.** Austria 2002.
**999701. DM.** Austria 2002.

| - | | ES | ES | *CA* | RU | 999700 999701 |
|---|-|----|----|------|----|---------------|

# CLASS 960 TRACK ASSESSMENT/RECORDING UNIT

DM. Plasser & Theurer EM-SAT 100/RT Survey Cars. Full details awaited.

| Construction: | Engine: |
|---------------|---------|
| Transmission: | |
| Maximum Speed: 55 m.p.h. | Weight: 57 t. |
| Brakes: | Dimensions: 17.70 x 2.75 m. |

**999800/1. DM.** Austria 2003.

| - | **Y** | NR | *CA* | RU | 999800 | Richard Spoors |
|---|-------|----|------|----|--------|----------------|
| - | **Y** | NR | *CA* | RU | 999801 |                |

## UNCLASSIFIED                NR INSPECTION SALOON

T. Converted from Class 202 TRB 60755 at Stewarts Lane in 1969/1970 for use as a BR Southern Region General Manager's Saloon. Overhauled by Fragonset/ FM Rail in 2004/05 for use as a Network Rail New Trains Project Saloon. Can be used in push-pull mode with suitably equipped locomotives such as a Class 33/1.

**Construction:** Steel.
**Maximum Speed:** 90 m.p.h. (restricted when in propelling mode).
**Couplers:** Drophead buckeye.                **Bogies:** SR Mk. 4.
**Brakes:** Electric pneumatic and automatic air.
**Doors:** Manually operated slam.        **Dimensions:** 20.45 x 2.74 m

**975025. DM.** BR Eastleigh. 1958. 34.5 t.

| 975025 | G | | NR | FM | LU | CAROLINE |
|--------|---|---|----|----|----|----------|

# 3.5. DMUS AWAITING DISPOSAL

The list below comprises vehicles awaiting disposal which are stored on the Network Rail network.

**IMPORTANT NOTE:** DMUs already at scrapyards are not included in this list.

**Class 101**

| Spare | **RR** | A | PY | 51496 | 51506 | 54056 | 54061 | 54393 |
|-------|--------|---|----|-------|-------|-------|-------|-------|
| Spare | **S** | A | PY | 51231 | 51435 | 51500 | 53268 | |
| Spare | **RR** | X | PY | 51432 | 51498 | | | |

**Class 117**

| Spare | **N** | A | PY | 51350 | 51366 | 51383 | 51408 |
|-------|-------|---|----|-------|-------|-------|-------|
| Spare | **RR** | CR | AL | 51411 | | | |

**Class 122**

| - | **LH** | X | TE | 977941 (55012) |
|---|--------|---|----|----------------|

**Class 143**

| 143 613 | **BI** | P | ZC | 55654 | 55679* |
|---------|--------|---|----|-------|--------|
| 143 615 | **VL** | P | ZC | 55656 | 55681* |

* Both of these units suffered extensive fire damage. At the time of writing they were due to move to Cardiff for component recovery before being scrapped.

**Class 165**

| Spare | **NT** | A | ZC | 58930 |
|-------|--------|---|----|-------|

**Class 205**

| Spare | **CX** | P | SE | 60811 |
|-------|--------|---|----|-------|

# PLATFORM 5 MAIL ORDER

## SLAM DOORS ON THE SOUTHERN

**Capital Transport Publishing**

A collection of high quality colour photographs illustrating the many types of slam-door electric trains that have operated on the Southern for the past 50 years. Features many different designs, from humble 2-car suburban units to the world famous Brighton Belle Pullman trains. Also contains extended photographic captions. 112 pages. Hardback. **£16.95**.

## SOUTHERN DEMUs

**Capital Transport Publishing**

A pictorial history of the Southern Region DEMU vehicles, that have served Southern England for the past 50 years. Includes high quality colour images throughout, plus historical information relating to each type of unit and the lines on which they have operated. Illustrates many different livery variations and includes much previously unpublished historical and technical information. 96 pages. Hardback. **£16.95**.

### *Also available:*

A Southern Electric Album (1950s-1970s in colour) ........ **£16.95**

Please add postage: 10% UK, 20% Europe, 30% Rest of World.

**Telephone, fax or send your order to the Platform 5 Mail Order Department. See page 384 of this book for details.**

# 4. ELECTRIC MULTIPLE UNITS

# INTRODUCTION

## EMU CLASSES

Principal details and dimensions are quoted for each class in metric and/or imperial units as considered appropriate bearing in mind common UK usage.

All dimensions and weights are quoted for vehicles in an "as new" condition with all necessary supplies on board. Dimensions are quoted in the order length x overall width. All lengths quoted are over buffers or couplers as appropriate. Where two lengths are quoted, the first refers to outer vehicles in a set and the second to inner vehicles.

Bogie Types are quoted in the format motored/non-motored (e.g BP20/BT13 denotes BP20 motored bogies and BT non-motored bogies).

Unless noted to the contrary, all vehicles listed have bar couplings at non-driving ends.

Vehicles ordered under the auspices of BR were allocated a Lot (batch) number when ordered and these are quoted in class headings and sub-headings. Vehicles ordered since 1995 have no Lot Numbers, but the manufacturer and location that they were built in are given.

## NUMERICAL LISTINGS

25 kV AC 50 Hz overhead Electric Multiple Units (EMUs) and dual voltage EMUs are listed in numerical order of set numbers. Individual "loose" vehicles are listed in numerical order after vehicles formed into fixed formations. Where numbers carried were different to those officially allocated, these are noted in class headings where appropriate.

750 V DC third rail EMUs are listed in numerical order of class number, then in numerical order of set number. Some of these use the former Southern Region four-digit set numbers. These are derived from theoretical six digit set numbers which are the four-digit set number prefixed by the first two numbers of the class.

Where sets or vehicles have been renumbered in recent years, former numbering detail is shown alongside current detail. Each entry is laid out as in the following example:

| Set No. | Detail | Livery | Owner | Operator | Allocation | Formation | | | |
|---------|--------|--------|-------|----------|------------|-----------|---|---|---|
| 5736 | s | SS | P | SW | WD | 77797 | 62818 | 71554 | 77798 |

**Detail Differences**. Only detail differences which currently affect the areas and types of train which vehicles may work are shown. All other detail differences are specifically excluded. Where such differences occur within a class or part class, these are shown alongside the individual set or vehicle number. Meaning of abbreviations are detailed in individual class headings.

**Set Formations.** Set formations shown are those normally maintained. Readers should note some set formations might be temporarily varied from time to time to suit maintenance and/or operational requirements. Vehicles shown as "Spare" are not formed in any regular set formation.

**Codes.** Codes are used to denote the livery, owner, operator and depot of each unit. Details of these will be found in section 7 of this book. Where a unit or spare car is off-lease, the operator column will be left blank.

**Names.** Only names carried with official sanction are listed. As far as possible names are shown in UPPER/lower case characters as actually shown on the name carried on the vehicle(s). Unless otherwise shown, complete units are regarded as named rather than just the individual car(s) which carry the name.

# GENERAL INFORMATION

## CLASSIFICATION AND NUMBERING

25 kV AC 50 Hz overhead and "Versatile" EMUs are classified in the series 300–399.

750 V DC third rail EMUs are classified in the series 400–599.
Service units are classified in the series 900–949.

EMU individual cars are numbered in the series 61000–78999, except for vehicles used on the Isle of Wight – which are numbered in a separate series.

Prior to privatisation, Service Stock individual cars were numbered in the series 975000–975999 and 977000–977999, although this series was not used exclusively for EMU vehicles. Since privatisation, use of these series has been sporadic, vehicles often now retaining their former numbers.

Any vehicle constructed or converted to replace another vehicle following accident damage and carrying the same number as the original vehicle is denoted by the suffix[II] in this publication.

## OPERATING CODES

These codes are used by train operating company staff to describe the various different types of vehicles and normally appear on data panels on the inner (i.e. non driving) ends of vehicles.

A "B" prefix indicates a battery vehicle.
A "P" prefix indicates a trailer vehicle on which is mounted the pantograph, instead of the default case where the pantograph is mounted on a motor vehicle.

The first part of the code describes whether or not the car has a motor or a driving cab as follows:

DM Driving motor.
M   Motor

DT  Driving trailer
T   Trailer

The next letter is a "B" for cars with a brake compartment.
This is followed by the saloon details:

F   First
S   Standard
C   Composite

The next letter denotes the style of accommodation as follows:

O   Open
K   Side compartment with lavatory
so  Semi-open (part compartments, part open). All other vehicles are assumed
    to consist solely of open saloons.

Finally vehicles with a buffet are suffixed RB or RMB for a miniture buffet.

Where two vehicles of the same type are formed within the same unit, the
above codes may be suffixed by (A) and (B) to differentiate between the vehicles.

A composite is a vehicle containing both first and standard class
accommodation, whilst a brake vehicle is a vehicle containing separate specific
accommodation for the conductor.

**Special Note:** Where vehicles have been declassified, the correct operating
code which describes the actual vehicle layout is quoted in this publication.

The following codes are used to denote special types of vehicle:

DMLF   Driving Motor Lounge First
DMLV   Driving Motor Luggage Van
MBRBS  Motor buffet standard with luggage space and guard's compartment.
TFH    Trailer First with Handbrake

# BUILD DETAILS

**Lot Numbers**
Vehicles ordered under the auspices of BR were allocated a lot (batch) number
when ordered and these are quoted in class headings and sub-headings.

**Builders**
These are shown in class headings. Abbreviations used are found in section 7.8.

Information on sub-contracting works which built parts of vehicles e.g. the
underframes etc. is not shown.

# ACCOMMODATION

The information given in class headings and sub-headings is in the form F/S
nT (or TD) nW. For example 12/54 1T 1W denotes 12 first class and 54 standard
class seats, 1 toilet and 1 wheelchair space. The seating layout of open saloons
is shown as  2+1, 2+2 or 3+2 as the case may be. Where units have first class
accommodation as well as standard and the layout is different for each class
then these are shown separately prefixed by '1:' and '2:'. Compartments are
three seats a side in first class and mostly four a side in standard class in EMUs.

# 4.1. 25 kV AC 50 Hz OVERHEAD & DUAL VOLTAGE UNITS.

**Note:** Except where otherwise stated, all units in this section operate on 25 kV AC 50 Hz overhead only.

## CLASS 306                 METRO-CAMMELL/BRCW

Museum unit which is currently stored out of use, but may be used on main line work in the future (with One Great Eastern). Originally built as 1500 V DC, but converted to AC in 1960/61.

**Formation:** DMSO–TBSO–DTSO.
**Construction:** Steel.      **Doors:** Power-operated sliding.
**Traction Motors:** Four Crompton-Parkinson 155 kW.
**Gangways:** None.      **Bogies:** LNER ED6/ET6.
**Couplers:** Screw.      **Maximum Speed:** 70 m.p.h.
**Seating Layout:** 2+2 facing.
**Dimensions:** 19.16/17.40/17.63 × 2.80/2.95 m.
**Braking:** Tread brakes.      **Multiple Working:** Within class.

**DMSO.** Lot No. 363 Metro-Cammell 1949. –/62. 52.0 t.
**TBSO.** Lot No. 365 BRCW 1949. –/46. 27.0 t.
**DTSO.** Lot No. 364 Metro-Cammell 1949. –/60. 28.0 t.

| 306 017 | **G** | H | IL | 65217 | 65417 | 65617 |

## CLASS 313                           BREL YORK

WAGN/Silverlink inner suburban units.

**Formation:** DMSO–PTSO–BDMSO.
**Systems:** 25 kV AC overhead/750 V DC third rail.
**Construction:** Steel underframe, aluminium alloy body and roof.
**Traction Motors:** Four GEC G310AZ of 82.125 kW.
**Doors:** Sliding.      **Control System:** Camshaft.
**Gangways:** Within unit + end doors.      **Bogies:** BX1.
**Couplers:** Tightlock.      **Maximum Speed:** 75 m.p.h.
**Seating Layout:** 3+2 low-back facing unless stated.
**Braking:** Disc and rheostatic.      **Dimensions:** 20.33/20.18 × 2.82 m.
**Multiple Working:** Within class.

**DMSO.** Lot No. 30879 1976–1977. –/74. 36.0 t.
**PTSO.** Lot No. 30880 1976–1977. –/83 (313/0), –/80 (313/1). 31.0 t.
**BDMSO.** Lot No. 30885 1976–1977. –/74. 37.5 t.

**Class 313/0. Standard Design.** Refurbished with high back seats.

| 313 018 | **WP** | H | *WN* | HE | 62546 | 71230 | 62610 |
| 313 024 | **WP** | H | *WN* | HE | 62552 | 71236 | 62616 |
| 313 025 | **WP** | H | *WN* | HE | 62553 | 71237 | 62617 |
| 313 026 | **WP** | H | *WN* | HE | 62554 | 71238 | 62618 |

| | | | | | | |
|---|---|---|---|---|---|---|
| 313 027 | **U** | H | *WN* | HE | 62555 | 71239 | 62619 |
| 313 028 | **WP** | H | *WN* | HE | 62556 | 71240 | 62620 |
| 313 029 | **U** | H | *WN* | HE | 62557 | 71241 | 62621 |
| 313 030 | **WP** | H | *WN* | HE | 62558 | 71242 | 62622 |
| 313 031 | **WP** | H | *WN* | HE | 62559 | 71243 | 62623 |
| 313 032 | **U** | H | *WN* | HE | 62560 | 71244 | 62643 |
| 313 033 | **U** | H | *WN* | HE | 62561 | 71245 | 62625 |
| 313 035 | **U** | H | *WN* | HE | 62563 | 71247 | 62627 |
| 313 036 | **U** | H | *WN* | HE | 62564 | 71248 | 62628 |
| 313 037 | **U** | H | *WN* | HE | 62565 | 71249 | 62629 |
| 313 038 | **U** | H | *WN* | HE | 62566 | 71250 | 62630 |
| 313 039 | **U** | H | *WN* | HE | 62567 | 71251 | 62631 |
| 313 040 | **U** | H | *WN* | HE | 62568 | 71252 | 62632 |
| 313 041 | **U** | H | *WN* | HE | 62569 | 71253 | 62633 |
| 313 042 | **WP** | H | *WN* | HE | 62570 | 71254 | 62634 |
| 313 043 | **WP** | H | *WN* | HE | 62571 | 71255 | 62635 |
| 313 044 | **U** | H | *WN* | HE | 62572 | 71256 | 62636 |
| 313 045 | **U** | H | *WN* | HE | 62573 | 71257 | 62637 |
| 313 046 | **U** | H | *WN* | HE | 62574 | 71258 | 62638 |
| 313 047 | **U** | H | *WN* | HE | 62575 | 71259 | 62639 |
| 313 048 | **WP** | H | *WN* | HE | 62576 | 71260 | 62640 |
| 313 049 | **U** | H | *WN* | HE | 62577 | 71261 | 62641 |
| 313 050 | **WP** | H | *WN* | HE | 62578 | 71262 | 62649 |
| 313 051 | **U** | H | *WN* | HE | 62579 | 71263 | 62624 |
| 313 052 | **WP** | H | *WN* | HE | 62580 | 71264 | 62644 |
| 313 053 | **WP** | H | *WN* | HE | 62581 | 71265 | 62645 |
| 313 054 | **WP** | H | *WN* | HE | 62582 | 71266 | 62646 |
| 313 055 | **WP** | H | *WN* | HE | 62583 | 71267 | 62647 |
| 313 056 | **WP** | H | *WN* | HE | 62584 | 71268 | 62648 |
| 313 057 | **WP** | H | *WN* | HE | 62585 | 71269 | 62642 |
| 313 058 | **WP** | H | *WN* | HE | 62586 | 71270 | 62650 |
| 313 059 | **WP** | H | *WN* | HE | 62587 | 71271 | 62651 |
| 313 060 | **WP** | H | *WN* | HE | 62588 | 71272 | 62652 |
| 313 061 | **WP** | H | *WN* | HE | 62589 | 71273 | 62653 |
| 313 062 | **WP** | H | *WN* | HE | 62590 | 71274 | 62654 |
| 313 063 | **WP** | H | *WN* | HE | 62591 | 71275 | 62655 |
| 313 064 | **WP** | H | *WN* | HE | 62592 | 71276 | 62656 |

**Class 313/1. Extra shoegear for Silverlink services.**

| | | | | | | |
|---|---|---|---|---|---|---|
| 313 101 | **SL** | H | *SL* | WN | 62529 | 71213 | 62593 |
| 313 102 | **SL** | H | *SL* | WN | 62530 | 71214 | 62594 |
| 313 103 | **SL** | H | *SL* | WN | 62531 | 71215 | 62595 |
| 313 104 | **SL** | H | *SL* | WN | 62532 | 71216 | 62596 |
| 313 105 | **SL** | H | *SL* | WN | 62533 | 71217 | 62597 |
| 313 106 | **SL** | H | *SL* | WN | 62534 | 71218 | 62598 |
| 313 107 | **SL** | H | *SL* | WN | 62535 | 71219 | 62599 |
| 313 108 | **SL** | H | *SL* | WN | 62536 | 71220 | 62600 |
| 313 109 | **SL** | H | *SL* | WN | 62537 | 71221 | 62601 |
| 313 110 | **SL** | H | *SL* | WN | 62538 | 71222 | 62602 |
| 313 111 | **SL** | H | *SL* | WN | 62539 | 71223 | 62603 |
| 313 112 | **SL** | H | *SL* | WN | 62540 | 71224 | 62604 |

| 313 113 | **SL** | H | *SL* | WN | 62541 | 71225 | 62605 |
| 313 114 | **SL** | H | *SL* | WN | 62542 | 71226 | 62606 |
| 313 115 | **SL** | H | *SL* | WN | 62543 | 71227 | 62607 |
| 313 116 | **SL** | H | *SL* | WN | 62544 | 71228 | 62608 |
| 313 117 | **SL** | H | *SL* | WN | 62545 | 71229 | 62609 |
| 313 119 | **SL** | H | *SL* | WN | 62547 | 71231 | 62611 |
| 313 120 | **SL** | H | *SL* | WN | 62548 | 71232 | 62612 |
| 313 121 | **SL** | H | *SL* | WN | 62549 | 71233 | 62613 |
| 313 122 | **SL** | H | *SL* | WN | 62550 | 71234 | 62614 |
| 313 123 | **SL** | H | *SL* | WN | 62551 | 71235 | 62615 |
| 313 134 | **SL** | H | *SL* | WN | 62562 | 71246 | 62626 |

**Names (carried on PTSO):**

| 313 109 | Arnold Leah | 313 116 | Nikola Tesla |
| 313 120 | PARLIAMENT HILL | | |

# CLASS 314                                          BREL YORK

First ScotRail inner suburban units.

**Formation:** DMSO–PTSO–DMSO.
**Construction:** Steel underframe, aluminium alloy body and roof.
**Traction Motors:** Four GEC G310AZ (* Brush TM61-53) of 82.125 kW.
**Doors:** Sliding.
**Control System:** Thyristor.
**Gangways:** Within unit + end doors.
**Bogies:** BX1.
**Couplers:** Tightlock.
**Maximum Speed:** 70 m.p.h.
**Seating Layout:** 3+2 facing.
**Dimensions:** 20.33/20.18 x 2.82 m.
**Braking:** Disc and rheostatic.
**Multiple Working:** Within class and with Class 315.

**64583–64614. DMSO.** Lot No. 30912 1979. –/68. 34.5 t.
**64588ᴵᴵ. DMSO.** Lot No. 30908 1978–1980. Rebuilt Railcare Glasgow 1996 from Class 507 No. 64426. The original 64588 has been scrapped. This vehicle has an experimental seating layout. –/74. 34.5 t.
**PTSO.** Lot No. 30913 1979. –/76. 33.0 t.

| 314 201 | * | **SC** | A | *SR* | GW | 64583 | 71450 | 64584 | |
| 314 202 | * | **S** | A | *SR* | GW | 64585 | 71451 | 64586 | |
| 314 203 | * | **SC** | A | *SR* | GW | 64587 | 71452 | 64588ᴵᴵ | European Union |
| 314 204 | * | **SC** | A | *SR* | GW | 64589 | 71453 | 64590 | |
| 314 205 | * | **SC** | A | *SR* | GW | 64591 | 71454 | 64592 | |
| 314 206 | * | **SC** | A | *SR* | GW | 64593 | 71455 | 64594 | |
| 314 207 | | **SC** | A | *SR* | GW | 64595 | 71456 | 64596 | |
| 314 208 | | **SC** | A | *SR* | GW | 64597 | 71457 | 64598 | |
| 314 209 | | **SC** | A | *SR* | GW | 64599 | 71458 | 64600 | |
| 314 210 | | **SC** | A | *SR* | GW | 64601 | 71459 | 64602 | |
| 314 211 | | **SC** | A | *SR* | GW | 64603 | 71460 | 64604 | |
| 314 212 | | **SC** | A | *SR* | GW | 64605 | 71461 | 64606 | |
| 314 213 | | **SC** | A | *SR* | GW | 64607 | 71462 | 64608 | |
| 314 214 | | **SC** | A | *SR* | GW | 64609 | 71463 | 64610 | |
| 314 215 | | **SC** | A | *SR* | GW | 64611 | 71464 | 64612 | |
| 314 216 | | **SC** | A | *SR* | GW | 64613 | 71465 | 64614 | |

# CLASS 315                                              BREL YORK

One Great Eastern/West Anglia inner suburban units.

**Formation:** DMSO–TSO–PTSO–DMSO.
**Construction:** Steel underframe, aluminium alloy body and roof.
**Traction Motors:** Four Brush TM61-53 (* GEC G310AZ) of 82.125 kW.
**Doors:** Sliding.                          **Control System:** Thyristor.
**Gangways:** Within unit + end doors.        **Bogies:** BX1.
**Couplers:** Tightlock.                      **Maximum Speed:** 75 m.p.h.
**Seating Layout:** 3+2 facing.               **Dimensions:** 20.33/20.18 x 2.82 m.
**Braking:** Disc and rheostatic.
**Multiple Working:** Within class and with Class 314.

**64461–64582. DMSO.** Lot No. 30902 1980–1981. –/74. 35.0 t.
**71281–71341. TSO.** Lot No. 30904 1980–1981. –/86. 25.5 t.
**71389–71449. PTSO.** Lot No. 30903 1980–1981. –/84. 32.0 t.

**Non-Standard/Advertising liveries:**

315 804, 315 806 and 315 809 All-over First Group blue.
315 812 "Back the bid" (London's Olympic bid 2012) – blue with various images.
315 844 Crime Prevention – White and red with various images.
315 845 WAGN Family Travelcard ("Go to town with WAGN") – White.
315 857 WAGN "Intalink" livery – White with yellow and green bodyside stripes.

| | | | | | | | | |
|---|---|---|---|---|---|---|---|---|
| 315 801 | GE | H | *1E* | IL | 64461 | 71282 | 71389 | 64462 |
| 315 802 | GE | H | *1E* | IL | 64463 | 71282 | 71390 | 64464 |
| 315 803 | 1 | H | *1E* | IL | 64465 | 71283 | 71391 | 64466 |
| 315 804 | O | H | *1E* | IL | 64467 | 71284 | 71392 | 64468 |
| 315 805 | 1 | H | *1E* | IL | 64469 | 71285 | 71393 | 64470 |
| 315 806 | O | H | *1E* | IL | 64471 | 71286 | 71394 | 64472 |
| 315 807 | GE | H | *1E* | IL | 64473 | 71287 | 71395 | 64474 |
| 315 808 | GE | H | *1E* | IL | 64475 | 71288 | 71396 | 64476 |
| 315 809 | O | H | *1E* | IL | 64477 | 71289 | 71397 | 64478 |
| 315 810 | 1 | H | *1E* | IL | 64479 | 71290 | 71398 | 64480 |
| 315 811 | GE | H | *1E* | IL | 64481 | 71291 | 71399 | 64482 |
| 315 812 | AL | H | *1E* | IL | 64483 | 71292 | 71400 | 64484 |
| 315 813 | 1 | H | *1E* | IL | 64485 | 71293 | 71401 | 64486 |
| 315 814 | 1 | H | *1E* | IL | 64487 | 71294 | 71402 | 64488 |
| 315 815 | 1 | H | *1E* | IL | 64489 | 71295 | 71403 | 64490 |
| 315 816 | 1 | H | *1E* | IL | 64491 | 71296 | 71404 | 64492 |
| 315 817 | 1 | H | *1E* | IL | 64493 | 71297 | 71405 | 64494 |
| 315 818 | GE | H | *1E* | IL | 64495 | 71298 | 71406 | 64496 |
| 315 819 | GE | H | *1E* | IL | 64497 | 71299 | 71407 | 64498 |
| 315 820 | GE | H | *1E* | IL | 64499 | 71300 | 71408 | 64500 |
| 315 821 | GE | H | *1E* | IL | 64501 | 71301 | 71409 | 64502 |
| 315 822 | 1 | H | *1E* | IL | 64503 | 71302 | 71410 | 64504 |
| 315 823 | 1 | H | *1E* | IL | 64505 | 71303 | 71411 | 64506 |
| 315 824 | GE | H | *1E* | IL | 64507 | 71304 | 71412 | 64508 |
| 315 825 | GE | H | *1E* | IL | 64509 | 71305 | 71413 | 64510 |
| 315 826 | GE | H | *1E* | IL | 64511 | 71306 | 71414 | 64512 |

| | | | | | | | | |
|---|---|---|---|---|---|---|---|---|
| 315 827 | | **GE** | H | *1E* | IL | 64513 | 71307 | 71415 | 64514 |
| 315 828 | | **GE** | H | *1E* | IL | 64515 | 71308 | 71416 | 64516 |
| 315 829 | | **1** | H | *1E* | IL | 64517 | 71309 | 71417 | 64518 |
| 315 830 | | **GE** | H | *1E* | IL | 64519 | 71310 | 71418 | 64520 |
| 315 831 | | **1** | H | *1E* | IL | 64521 | 71311 | 71419 | 64522 |
| 315 832 | | **GE** | H | *1E* | IL | 64523 | 71312 | 71420 | 64524 |
| 315 833 | | **GE** | H | *1E* | IL | 64525 | 71313 | 71421 | 64526 |
| 315 834 | | **GE** | H | *1E* | IL | 64527 | 71314 | 71422 | 64528 |
| 315 835 | | **GE** | H | *1E* | IL | 64529 | 71315 | 71423 | 64530 |
| 315 836 | | **GE** | H | *1E* | IL | 64531 | 71316 | 71424 | 64532 |
| 315 837 | | **GE** | H | *1E* | IL | 64533 | 71317 | 71425 | 64534 |
| 315 838 | | **GE** | H | *1E* | IL | 64535 | 71318 | 71426 | 64536 |
| 315 839 | | **GE** | H | *1E* | IL | 64537 | 71319 | 71427 | 64538 |
| 315 840 | | **GE** | H | *1E* | IL | 64539 | 71320 | 71428 | 64540 |
| 315 841 | | **GE** | H | *1E* | IL | 64541 | 71321 | 71429 | 64542 |
| 315 842 | * | **GE** | H | *1E* | IL | 64543 | 71322 | 71430 | 64544 |
| 315 843 | * | **GE** | H | *1E* | IL | 64545 | 71323 | 71431 | 64546 |
| 315 844 | * | **AL** | H | *1W* | IL | 64547 | 71324 | 71432 | 64548 |
| 315 845 | * | **AL** | H | *1W* | IL | 64549 | 71325 | 71433 | 64550 |
| 315 846 | * | **U** | H | *1W* | IL | 64551 | 71326 | 71434 | 64552 |
| 315 847 | * | **U** | H | *1W* | IL | 64553 | 71327 | 71435 | 64554 |
| 315 848 | * | **U** | H | *1W* | IL | 64555 | 71328 | 71436 | 64556 |
| 315 849 | * | **U** | H | *1W* | IL | 64557 | 71329 | 71437 | 64558 |
| 315 850 | * | **U** | H | *1W* | IL | 64559 | 71330 | 71438 | 64560 |
| 315 851 | * | **U** | H | *1W* | IL | 64561 | 71331 | 71439 | 64562 |
| 315 852 | * | **U** | H | *1W* | IL | 64563 | 71332 | 71440 | 64564 |
| 315 853 | * | **U** | H | *1W* | IL | 64565 | 71333 | 71441 | 64566 |
| 315 854 | * | **U** | H | *1W* | IL | 64567 | 71334 | 71442 | 64568 |
| 315 855 | * | **U** | H | *1W* | IL | 64569 | 71335 | 71443 | 64570 |
| 315 856 | * | **U** | H | *1W* | IL | 64571 | 71336 | 71444 | 64572 |
| 315 857 | * | **AL** | H | *1W* | IL | 64573 | 71337 | 71445 | 64574 |
| 315 858 | * | **WP** | H | *1W* | IL | 64575 | 71338 | 71446 | 64576 |
| 315 859 | * | **WP** | H | *1W* | IL | 64577 | 71339 | 71447 | 64578 |
| 315 860 | * | **WP** | H | *1W* | IL | 64579 | 71340 | 71448 | 64580 |
| 315 861 | * | **WP** | H | *1W* | IL | 64581 | 71341 | 71449 | 64582 |

**Names (carried on DMSO):**

315 812   London Borough of Newham Host Borough 2012 Olympics Bid
315 817   Transport for London

## CLASS 317                                                      BREL

One West Anglia and WAGN outer suburban units.

**Formation:** Various.
**Traction Motors:** Four GEC G315BZ of 247.5 kW.
**Doors:** Sliding.
**Gangways:** Throughout
**Couplers:** Tightlock.
**Seating Layout:** Various.
**Braking:** Disc.

**Construction:** Steel.
**Control System:** Thyristor.
**Bogies:** BP20 (MSO), BT13 (others).
**Maximum Speed:** 100 m.p.h.
**Dimensions:** 20.13/20.18 x 2.82 m.

**Multiple Working:** Within class and with Classes 318, 319, 320, 321, 322 and 323.

**Class 317/1.** Pressure ventilated.

**Formation:** DTSO–MSO–TCO–DTSO.
**Seating Layout:** 1: 2+2 facing, 2: 3+2 facing.

**DTSO(A)** Lot No. 30955 York 1981–1982. –/74. 29.5 t.
**MSO.** Lot No. 30958 York 1981–1982. –/79. 49.0 t.
**TCO.** Lot No. 30957 Derby 1981–1982. 22/46 2T. 29.0 t.
**DTSO(B)** Lot No. 30956 York 1981–1982. –/70. (* –/71). 29.5 t.

**IMPORTANT NOTE:** The remaining One West Anglia Class 317/1s are to be renumbered during 2006 when they will transfer to Ilford depot. 317 320 is due to become 317 515, with 317 321–317 336 becoming 317 881–317 892 (these will be standard class only units for Stansted Express services).

| | | | | | | | | |
|---|---|---|---|---|---|---|---|---|
| 317 320 | | **WP** | A | *1W* | HE | 77019 | 62680 | 71596 | 77067 |
| 317 321 | | **WP** | A | *1W* | HE | 77020 | 62681 | 71597 | 77068 |
| 317 324 | | **WP** | A | *1W* | HE | 77023 | 62684 | 71600 | 77071 |
| 317 325 | | **WP** | A | *1W* | HE | 77000 | 62685 | 71601 | 77072 |
| 317 326 | | **WP** | A | *1W* | HE | 77025 | 62686 | 71602 | 77073 |
| 317 327 | | **WP** | A | *1W* | HE | 77026 | 62687 | 71603 | 77074 |
| 317 328 | | **WP** | A | *1W* | HE | 77027 | 62688 | 71604 | 77075 |
| 317 330 | | **WP** | A | *1W* | HE | 77043 | 62704 | 71606 | 77077 |
| 317 331 | | **WP** | A | *1W* | HE | 77030 | 62691 | 71607 | 77078 |
| 317 333 | | **WP** | A | *1W* | HE | 77032 | 62693 | 71609 | 77080 |
| 317 334 | | **WP** | A | *1W* | HE | 77033 | 62694 | 71610 | 77081 |
| 317 335 | | **WP** | A | *1W* | HE | 77034 | 62695 | 71611 | 77082 |
| 317 336 | | **WP** | A | *1W* | HE | 77035 | 62696 | 71612 | 77083 |
| 317 337 | * | **WP** | A | *WN* | HE | 77036 | 62671 | 71613 | 77084 |
| 317 338 | * | **WP** | A | *WN* | HE | 77037 | 62698 | 71614 | 77085 |
| 317 339 | * | **WP** | A | *WN* | HE | 77038 | 62699 | 71615 | 77086 |
| 317 340 | * | **WP** | A | *WN* | HE | 77039 | 62700 | 71616 | 77087 |
| 317 341 | * | **WP** | A | *WN* | HE | 77040 | 62701 | 71617 | 77088 |
| 317 342 | * | **WP** | A | *WN* | HE | 77041 | 62702 | 71618 | 77089 |
| 317 343 | * | **WP** | A | *WN* | HE | 77042 | 62703 | 71619 | 77090 |
| 317 344 | * | **WP** | A | *WN* | HE | 77029 | 62690 | 71620 | 77091 |
| 317 345 | * | **WP** | A | *WN* | HE | 77044 | 62705 | 71621 | 77092 |
| 317 346 | * | **WP** | A | *WN* | HE | 77045 | 62706 | 71622 | 77093 |
| 317 347 | * | **WP** | A | *WN* | HE | 77046 | 62707 | 71623 | 77094 |
| 317 348 | * | **WP** | A | *WN* | HE | 77047 | 62708 | 71624 | 77095 |

**Names (carried on TCO):**

317 345    Driver John Webb
317 348    Richard A Jenner

**Class 317/5.** Pressure ventilated. Units renumbered from Class 317/1 in 2005 for One West Anglia Metro services (mainly Liverpool Street–Hertford East). First class declassified. Details as Class 317/1.

**Note:** s – Refurbished with new upholstery and Passenger Information Systems.

| | | | | | | | | | |
|---|---|---|---|---|---|---|---|---|---|
| 317 501 | (317 301) | | **1** | A | *1W* | IL | 77024 | 62661 | 71577 | 77048 |
| 317 502 | (317 302) | | **1** | A | *1W* | IL | 77001 | 62662 | 71578 | 77049 |
| 317 503 | (317 303) | | **1** | A | *1W* | IL | 77002 | 62663 | 71579 | 77050 |
| 317 504 | (317 304) | | **1** | A | *1W* | IL | 77003 | 62664 | 71580 | 77051 |
| 317 505 | (317 305) | | **1** | A | *1W* | IL | 77004 | 62665 | 71581 | 77052 |
| 317 506 | (317 306) | | **1** | A | *1W* | IL | 77005 | 62666 | 71582 | 77053 |
| 317 507 | (317 307) | | **WP** | A | *1W* | IL | 77006 | 62667 | 71583 | 77054 |
| 317 508 | (317 311) | s | **WP** | A | *1W* | IL | 77010 | 62697 | 71587 | 77058 |
| 317 509 | (317 312) | s | **WP** | A | *1W* | IL | 77011 | 62672 | 71588 | 77059 |
| 317 510 | (317 313) | | **WP** | A | *1W* | IL | 77012 | 62673 | 71589 | 77060 |
| 317 511 | (317 315) | | **WP** | A | *1W* | IL | 77014 | 62675 | 71591 | 77062 |
| 317 512 | (317 316) | | **WP** | A | *1W* | IL | 77015 | 62676 | 71592 | 77063 |
| 317 513 | (317 317) | | **WP** | A | *1W* | IL | 77016 | 62677 | 71593 | 77064 |
| 317 514 | (317 318) | | **WP** | A | *1W* | IL | 77017 | 62678 | 71594 | 77065 |

**Class 317/6.** Convection heating. Units converted from Class 317/2 by Railcare Wolverton 1998–99 with new seating layouts.

**Formation:** DTSO–MSO–TSO–DTCO.
**Seating Layout:** 2+2 facing.

**77200–77219. DTSO.** Lot No. 30994 York 1985–1986. –/64. 29.5 t.
**77280–77283. DTSO.** Lot No. 31007 York 1987. –/64. 29.5 t.
**62846–62865. MSO.** Lot No. 30996 York 1985–1986. –/70. 49.0 t.
**62886–62889. MSO.** Lot No. 31009 York 1987. –/70. 49.0 t.
**71734–71753. TSO.** Lot No. 30997 York 1985–1986. –/62 2T. 29.0 t.
**71762–71765. TSO.** Lot No. 31010 York 1987. –/62 2T. 29.0 t.
**77220–77239. DTCO.** Lot No. 30995 York 1985–1986. 24/48. 29.5 t.
**77284–77287. DTCO.** Lot No. 31008 York 1987. 24/48. 29.5 t.

| | | | | | | | | |
|---|---|---|---|---|---|---|---|---|
| 317 649 | **WN** | A | *1W* | HE | 77200 | 62846 | 71734 | 77220 |
| 317 650 | **WN** | A | *1W* | HE | 77201 | 62847 | 71735 | 77221 |
| 317 651 | **WN** | A | *1W* | HE | 77202 | 62848 | 71736 | 77222 |
| 317 652 | **1** | A | *1W* | HE | 77203 | 62849 | 71739 | 77223 |
| 317 653 | **1** | A | *1W* | HE | 77204 | 62850 | 71738 | 77224 |
| 317 654 | **1** | A | *1W* | HE | 77205 | 62851 | 71737 | 77225 |
| 317 655 | **1** | A | *1W* | HE | 77206 | 62852 | 71740 | 77226 |
| 317 656 | **1** | A | *1W* | HE | 77207 | 62853 | 71742 | 77227 |
| 317 657 | **1** | A | *1W* | HE | 77208 | 62854 | 71741 | 77228 |
| 317 658 | **1** | A | *1W* | HE | 77209 | 62855 | 71743 | 77229 |
| 317 659 | **1** | A | *1W* | HE | 77210 | 62856 | 71744 | 77230 |
| 317 660 | **1** | A | *1W* | HE | 77211 | 62857 | 71745 | 77231 |
| 317 661 | **1** | A | *1W* | HE | 77212 | 62858 | 71746 | 77232 |

| | | | | | | | | |
|---|---|---|---|---|---|---|---|---|
| 317 662 | 1 | A | 1W | HE | 77213 | 62859 | 71747 | 77233 |
| 317 663 | 1 | A | 1W | HE | 77214 | 62860 | 71748 | 77234 |
| 317 664 | 1 | A | 1W | HE | 77215 | 62861 | 71749 | 77235 |
| 317 665 | 1 | A | 1W | HE | 77216 | 62862 | 71750 | 77236 |
| 317 666 | 1 | A | 1W | HE | 77217 | 62863 | 71752 | 77237 |
| 317 667 | 1 | A | 1W | HE | 77218 | 62864 | 71751 | 77238 |
| 317 668 | 1 | A | 1W | HE | 77219 | 62865 | 71753 | 77239 |
| 317 669 | 1 | A | 1W | HE | 77280 | 62886 | 71762 | 77284 |
| 317 670 | 1 | A | 1W | HE | 77281 | 62887 | 71763 | 77285 |
| 317 671 | 1 | A | 1W | HE | 77282 | 62888 | 71764 | 77286 |
| 317 672 | 1 | A | 1W | HE | 77283 | 62889 | 71765 | 77287 |

**Name (carried on TCO):**

317 654   Richard Wells

**Class 317/7.** Units converted from Class 317/1 by Railcare Wolverton 2000 for Stansted Express service between London Liverpool Street and Stansted. Air conditioning. Fitted with luggage stacks.

**Formation:** DTSO–MSO–TSO–DTCO.
**Seating Layout:** 1: 2+1 facing, 2: 2+2 facing.

**DTSO.** Lot No. 30955 York 1981–1982. –/52 + catering point. 31.4 t.
**MSO.** Lot No. 30955 York 1981–1982. –/62. 51.3 t.
**TSO.** Lot No. 30957 Derby 1981–1982. –/42 1W 1T 1TD. 30.2 t.
**DTCO.** Lot No. 30956 York 1981–1982. 22/16 + catering point. 31.6 t.

**Advertising livery:** Vehicles 77055 of 317 708, 77066 of 317 719, 77069 of 317 722 and 77079 of 317 732 – Finspreads (white, blue and orange with various images).

| | | | | | | | | |
|---|---|---|---|---|---|---|---|---|
| 317 708 | SX | A | 1S | HE | 77007 | 62668 | 71584 | 77055 |
| 317 709 | SX | A | 1S | HE | 77008 | 62669 | 71585 | 77056 |
| 317 710 | SX | A | 1S | HE | 77009 | 62670 | 71586 | 77057 |
| 317 714 | SX | A | 1S | HE | 77013 | 62674 | 71590 | 77061 |
| 317 719 | SX | A | 1S | HE | 77018 | 62679 | 71595 | 77066 |
| 317 722 | SX | A | 1S | HE | 77021 | 62682 | 71598 | 77069 |
| 317 723 | SX | A | 1S | HE | 77022 | 62683 | 71599 | 77070 |
| 317 729 | 1S | A | 1S | HE | 77028 | 62689 | 71605 | 77076 |
| 317 732 | SX | A | 1S | HE | 77031 | 62692 | 71608 | 77079 |

**Names (carried on DTCO):**

317 709   Len Camp
317 723   The Tottenham Flyer

# CLASS 318                                                    BREL YORK

First ScotRail outer suburban units.

**Formation:** DTSO–MSO–DTSO.
**Construction:** Steel.
**Traction Motors:** Four Brush TM 2141 of 268 kW.
**Doors:** Sliding.                          **Control System:** Thyristor.
**Gangways:** Throughout (not *).           **Bogies:** BP20 (MSO), BT13 (others).
**Couplers:** Tightlock                      **Maximum Speed:** 90 m.p.h.
**Seating Layout:** 3+2 facing.              **Dimensions:** 20.86 x 2.82 m.
**Braking:** Disc.
**Multiple Working:** Within class and with Classes 317, 319, 320, 321, 322 and 323.

**77240–77259. DTSO.** Lot No. 30999 1985–1986. –/66 1T. 30.0 t.
**77288. DTSO.** Lot No. 31020 1987. –/66 1T. 30.0 t.
**62866–62885. MSO.** Lot No. 30998 1985–1986. –/79. 50.9 t.
**62890. MSO.** Lot No. 31019 1987. –/79. 50.9 t.
**77260–77279. DTSO.** Lot No. 31000 1985–1986. –/71. 29.6 t.
**77289. DTSO.** Lot No. 31021 1987. –/71. 29.6 t.

**Note:** * Refurbished – end gangway sealed. Seating layout unchanged.

| | | | | | | | |
|---|---|---|---|---|---|---|---|
| 318 250 | | **SC** | H | *SR* | GW | 77240 | 62866 | 77260 |
| 318 251 | * | **SC** | H | *SR* | GW | 77241 | 62867 | 77261 |
| 318 252 | | **SC** | H | *SR* | GW | 77242 | 62868 | 77262 |
| 318 253 | | **SC** | H | *SR* | GW | 77243 | 62869 | 77263 |
| 318 254 | * | **SC** | H | *SR* | GW | 77244 | 62870 | 77264 |
| 318 255 | | **SC** | H | *SR* | GW | 77245 | 62871 | 77265 |
| 318 256 | | **SC** | H | *SR* | GW | 77246 | 62872 | 77266 |
| 318 257 | * | **SC** | H | *SR* | GW | 77247 | 62873 | 77267 |
| 318 258 | | **SC** | H | *SR* | GW | 77248 | 62874 | 77268 |
| 318 259 | * | **SC** | H | *SR* | GW | 77249 | 62875 | 77269 |
| 318 260 | | **SC** | H | *SR* | GW | 77250 | 62876 | 77270 |
| 318 261 | | **SC** | H | *SR* | GW | 77251 | 62877 | 77271 |
| 318 262 | | **SC** | H | *SR* | GW | 77252 | 62878 | 77272 |
| 318 263 | | **SC** | H | *SR* | GW | 77253 | 62879 | 77273 |
| 318 264 | * | **SC** | H | *SR* | GW | 77254 | 62880 | 77274 |
| 318 265 | | **SC** | H | *SR* | GW | 77255 | 62881 | 77275 |
| 318 266 | | **SC** | H | *SR* | GW | 77256 | 62882 | 77276 |
| 318 267 | | **SC** | H | *SR* | GW | 77257 | 62883 | 77277 |
| 318 268 | | **SC** | H | *SR* | GW | 77258 | 62884 | 77278 |
| 318 269 | | **SC** | H | *SR* | GW | 77259 | 62885 | 77279 |
| 318 270 | | **SC** | H | *SR* | GW | 77288 | 62890 | 77289 |

**Names (carried on MSO):**

318 259    Citizens' Network          | 318 266    STRATHCLYDER

# CLASS 319                                    BREL YORK

Thameslink and Southern express and outer suburban units.

**System:** 25 kV AC overhead/750 V DC third rail.
**Formation:** Various.
**Construction:** Steel.
**Traction Motors:** Four GEC G315BZ of 268 kW.
**Doors:** Sliding.                    **Control System:** GTO chopper.
**Gangways:** Within unit + end doors.  **Bogies:** P7-4 (MSO), T3-7 (others).
**Couplers:** Tightlock                **Maximum Speed:** 100 m.p.h.
**Seating Layout:** Various.            **Dimensions:** 20.17/20.16 x 2.82 m.
**Braking:** Disc.
**Multiple Working:** Within class and with Classes 317, 318, 320, 321, 322 and 323.

**Class 319/0.** These units can be hired to Thameslink. DTSO–MSO–TSO–DTSO.

**Seating Layout:** 3+2 facing.

**DTSO(A).** Lot No. 31022 (odd nos.) 1987–1988. –/82. 28.2 t.
**MSO.** Lot No. 31023 1987–1988. –/82. 49.2 t.
**TSO.** Lot No. 31024 1987–1988. –/77 2T. 31.0 t.
**DTSO(B).** Lot No. 31025 (even nos.) 1987–1988. –/78. 28.1 t.

**Non-standard liveries:** 319 001 White with blue doors.
319 010 Mid blue with yellow doors.

| | | | | | | | |
|---|---|---|---|---|---|---|---|
| 319 001 | **0**  | P | *SN* | SU | 77291 | 62891 | 71772 | 77290 |
| 319 002 | **CX** | P | *SN* | SU | 77293 | 62892 | 71773 | 77292 |
| 319 003 | **CX** | P | *SN* | SU | 77295 | 62893 | 71774 | 77294 |
| 319 004 | **SN** | P | *SN* | SU | 77297 | 62894 | 71775 | 77296 |
| 319 005 | **SN** | P | *SN* | SU | 77299 | 62895 | 71776 | 77298 |
| 319 006 | **CX** | P | *SN* | SU | 77301 | 62896 | 71777 | 77300 |
| 319 007 | **CX** | P | *SN* | SU | 77303 | 62897 | 71778 | 77302 |
| 319 008 | **CX** | P | *SN* | SU | 77305 | 62898 | 71779 | 77304 |
| 319 009 | **CX** | P | *SN* | SU | 77307 | 62899 | 71780 | 77306 |
| 319 010 | **0**  | P | *SN* | SU | 77309 | 62900 | 71781 | 77308 |
| 319 011 | **CX** | P | *SN* | SU | 77311 | 62901 | 71782 | 77310 |
| 319 012 | **CX** | P | *SN* | SU | 77313 | 62902 | 71783 | 77312 |
| 319 013 | **CX** | P | *SN* | SU | 77315 | 62903 | 71784 | 77314 |

**Names (carried on TSO):**

| | | | | |
|---|---|---|---|---|
| 319 008 | Cheriton  | | 319 011 | John Ruskin College |
| 319 009 | Coquelles | | 319 013 | The Surrey Hills |

**Class 319/2.** DTSO–MSO–TSO–DTCO. Units converted from Class 319/0 for
express services from London to Brighton. Pantographs were refitted for use
with Thameslink.

**Seating Layout:** 1: 2+1 facing, 2: 2+2 facing.

**DTSO.** Lot No. 31022 (odd nos.) 1987–1988. –/64. 28.2 t.
**MSO.** Lot No. 31023 1987–1988. –/60 2T. (including 12 seats in a "snug" under
the pantograph area). External sliding doors sealed adjacent to this area. 49.2 t.

**TSO.** Lot No. 31024 1987–1988. –/52 1T 1TD. 31.0 t.
**DTCO.** Lot No. 31025 (even nos.) 1987–1988. 18/36. 28.1 t.

**Advertising liveries:** 319 214 Continental Airlines (mid blue with gold and yellow script).
319 215, 319 218, 319 220 Connex Days out/"Family Zone" (Yellow, green and red with various images).

| | | | | | | | | |
|---|---|---|---|---|---|---|---|---|
| 319 214 | **AL** | P | *SN* | SU | 77317 | 62904 | 71785 | 77316 |
| 319 215 | **AL** | P | *SN* | SU | 77319 | 62905 | 71786 | 77318 |
| 319 216 | **CX** | P | *SN* | SU | 77321 | 62906 | 71787 | 77320 |
| 319 217 | **CX** | P | *SN* | SU | 77323 | 62907 | 71788 | 77322 |
| 319 218 | **AL** | P | *SN* | SU | 77325 | 62908 | 71789 | 77324 |
| 319 219 | **CX** | P | *SN* | SU | 77327 | 62909 | 71790 | 77326 |
| 319 220 | **AL** | P | *SN* | SU | 77329 | 62910 | 71791 | 77328 |

**Names (carried on TSO):**

| | | | | |
|---|---|---|---|---|
| 319 215 | London | | 319 218 | Croydon |
| 319 217 | Brighton | | | |

**Class 319/3.** DTSO–MSO–TSO–DTSO. Converted from Class 319/1 by replacing first class seats with standard class seats. Used mainly on the Luton–Sutton/Wimbledon routes.

**Seating Layout:** 3+2 facing.
**Dimensions:** 19.33 x 2.82 m.

**DTSO(A).** Lot No. 31063 1990. –/70. 29.0 t.
**MSO.** Lot No. 31064 1990. –/78. 50.6 t.
**TSO.** Lot No. 31065 1990. –/74 2T. 31.0 t.
**DTSO(B).** Lot No. 31066 1990. –/78. 29.7 t.

| | | | | | | | | |
|---|---|---|---|---|---|---|---|---|
| 319 361 | **TR** | P | *TR* | SU | 77459 | 63043 | 71929 | 77458 |
| 319 362 | **TR** | P | *TR* | SU | 77461 | 63044 | 71930 | 77460 |
| 319 363 | **TR** | P | *TR* | SU | 77463 | 63045 | 71931 | 77462 |
| 319 364 | **TR** | P | *TR* | SU | 77465 | 63046 | 71932 | 77464 |
| 319 365 | **TR** | P | *TR* | SU | 77467 | 63047 | 71933 | 77466 |
| 319 366 | **TR** | P | *TR* | SU | 77469 | 63048 | 71934 | 77468 |
| 319 367 | **TR** | P | *TR* | SU | 77471 | 63049 | 71935 | 77470 |
| 319 368 | **TR** | P | *TR* | SU | 77473 | 63050 | 71936 | 77472 |
| 319 369 | **TR** | P | *TR* | SU | 77475 | 63051 | 71937 | 77474 |
| 319 370 | **TR** | P | *TR* | SU | 77477 | 63052 | 71938 | 77476 |
| 319 371 | **TR** | P | *TR* | SU | 77479 | 63053 | 71939 | 77478 |
| 319 372 | **TL** | P | *TR* | SU | 77481 | 63054 | 71940 | 77480 |
| 319 373 | **TL** | P | *TR* | SU | 77483 | 63055 | 71941 | 77482 |
| 319 374 | **TR** | P | *TR* | SU | 77485 | 63056 | 71942 | 77484 |
| 319 375 | **TR** | P | *TR* | SU | 77487 | 63057 | 71943 | 77486 |
| 319 376 | **TR** | P | *TR* | SU | 77489 | 63058 | 71944 | 77488 |
| 319 377 | **TR** | P | *TR* | SU | 77491 | 63059 | 71945 | 77490 |
| 319 378 | **TR** | P | *TR* | SU | 77493 | 63060 | 71946 | 77492 |
| 319 379 | **TR** | P | *TR* | SU | 77495 | 63061 | 71947 | 77494 |
| 319 380 | **TR** | P | *TR* | SU | 77497 | 63062 | 71948 | 77496 |
| 319 381 | **TR** | P | *TR* | SU | 77973 | 63093 | 71979 | 77974 |
| 319 382 | **TR** | P | *TR* | SU | 77975 | 63094 | 71980 | 77976 |

| 319 383 | **TR** | P | *TR* | SU | 77977 | 63095 | 71981 | 77978 |
| 319 384 | **TR** | P | *TR* | SU | 77979 | 63096 | 71982 | 77980 |
| 319 385 | **TR** | P | *TR* | SU | 77981 | 63097 | 71983 | 77982 |
| 319 386 | **TR** | P | *TR* | SU | 77983 | 63098 | 71984 | 77984 |

**Class 319/4.** DTCO–MSO–TSO–DTSO. Converted from Class 319/0. Refurbished with carpets. DTSO(A) converted to composite. Used mainly on the Bedford–Gatwick–Brighton route.

**Seating Layout:** 1: 2+1 facing 2: 2+2/3+2 facing.

**77331–77381. DTCO.** Lot No. 31022 (odd nos.) 1987–1988. 12/54. 28.2 t.
**77431–77457. DTCO.** Lot No. 31038 (odd nos.) 1988. 12/54. 28.2 t.
**62911–62936. MSO.** Lot No. 31023 1987–1988. –/77. 49.2 t.
**62961–62974. MSO.** Lot No. 31039 1988. –/77. 49.2 t.
**71792–71817. TSO.** Lot No. 31024 1987–1988. –/72 2T. 31.0 t.
**71866–71879. TSO.** Lot No. 31040 1988. –/72 2T. 31.0 t.
**77330–77380. DTSO.** Lot No. 31025 (even nos.) 1987–1988. –/74. 28.1 t.
**77430–77456. DTSO.** Lot No. 31041 (even nos.) 1988. –/74. 28.1 t.

**Advertising livery:** 319 431, 319 456 Continental Airlines (mid blue with gold and yellow script).

| 319 421 | **TR** | P | *TR* | SU | 77331 | 62911 | 71792 | 77330 |
| 319 422 | **TL** | P | *TR* | SU | 77333 | 62912 | 71793 | 77332 |
| 319 423 | **TR** | P | *TR* | SU | 77335 | 62913 | 71794 | 77334 |
| 319 424 | **TR** | P | *TR* | SU | 77337 | 62914 | 71795 | 77336 |
| 319 425 | **TL** | P | *TR* | SU | 77339 | 62915 | 71796 | 77338 |
| 319 426 | **TR** | P | *TR* | SU | 77341 | 62916 | 71797 | 77340 |
| 319 427 | **TL** | P | *TR* | SU | 77343 | 62917 | 71798 | 77342 |
| 319 428 | **TR** | P | *TR* | SU | 77345 | 62918 | 71799 | 77344 |
| 319 429 | **TR** | P | *TR* | SU | 77347 | 62919 | 71800 | 77346 |
| 319 430 | **TL** | P | *TR* | SU | 77349 | 62920 | 71801 | 77348 |
| 319 431 | **AL** | P | *TR* | SU | 77351 | 62921 | 71802 | 77350 |
| 319 432 | **TR** | P | *TR* | SU | 77353 | 62922 | 71803 | 77352 |
| 319 433 | **TR** | P | *TR* | SU | 77355 | 62923 | 71804 | 77354 |
| 319 434 | **TR** | P | *TR* | SU | 77357 | 62924 | 71805 | 77356 |
| 319 435 | **TL** | P | *TR* | SU | 77359 | 62925 | 71806 | 77358 |
| 319 436 | **TR** | P | *TR* | SU | 77361 | 62926 | 71807 | 77360 |
| 319 437 | **TR** | P | *TR* | SU | 77363 | 62927 | 71808 | 77362 |
| 319 438 | **TL** | P | *TR* | SU | 77365 | 62928 | 71809 | 77364 |
| 319 439 | **TR** | P | *TR* | SU | 77367 | 62929 | 71810 | 77366 |
| 319 440 | **TL** | P | *TR* | SU | 77369 | 62930 | 71811 | 77368 |
| 319 441 | **TR** | P | *TR* | SU | 77371 | 62931 | 71812 | 77370 |
| 319 442 | **TR** | P | *TR* | SU | 77373 | 62932 | 71813 | 77372 |
| 319 443 | **TL** | P | *TR* | SU | 77375 | 62933 | 71814 | 77374 |
| 319 444 | **TL** | P | *TR* | SU | 77377 | 62934 | 71815 | 77376 |
| 319 445 | **TR** | P | *TR* | SU | 77379 | 62935 | 71816 | 77378 |
| 319 446 | **TR** | P | *TR* | SU | 77381 | 62936 | 71817 | 77380 |
| 319 447 | **TR** | P | *TR* | SU | 77431 | 62961 | 71866 | 77430 |
| 319 448 | **TR** | P | *TR* | SU | 77433 | 62962 | 71867 | 77432 |
| 319 449 | **TL** | P | *TR* | SU | 77435 | 62963 | 71868 | 77434 |
| 319 450 | **TR** | P | *TR* | SU | 77437 | 62964 | 71869 | 77436 |

| 319 451 | TR | P | TR | SU | 77439 | 62965 | 71870 | 77438 |
| 319 452 | TR | P | TR | SU | 77441 | 62966 | 71871 | 77440 |
| 319 453 | TR | P | TR | SU | 77443 | 62967 | 71872 | 77442 |
| 319 454 | TR | P | TR | SU | 77445 | 62968 | 71873 | 77444 |
| 319 455 | TL | P | TR | SU | 77447 | 62969 | 71874 | 77446 |
| 319 456 | AL | P | TR | SU | 77449 | 62970 | 71875 | 77448 |
| 319 457 | TR | P | TR | SU | 77451 | 62971 | 71876 | 77450 |
| 319 458 | TL | P | TR | SU | 77453 | 62972 | 71877 | 77452 |
| 319 459 | TR | P | TR | SU | 77455 | 62973 | 71878 | 77454 |
| 319 460 | TL | P | TR | SU | 77457 | 62974 | 71879 | 77456 |

# CLASS 320                                                   BREL YORK

First ScotRail suburban units.

**Formation:** DTSO–MSO–DTSO.
**Construction:** Steel
**Traction Motors:** Four Brush TM2141B of 268 kW.
**Doors:** Sliding.                          **Control System:** Thyristor.
**Gangways:** Within unit.                    **Bogies:** P7-4 (MSO), T3-7 (others).
**Couplers:** Tightlock                       **Maximum Speed:** 75 m.p.h.
**Seating Layout:** 3+2 facing.               **Dimensions:** 19.33 x 2.82 m.
**Braking:** Disc.
**Multiple Working:** Within class and with Classes 317, 318, 319, 321, 322 and 323.

**DTSO (A).** Lot No. 31060 1990. –/76 1W. 30.7 t.
**MSO.** Lot No. 31062 1990. –/76 1W. 52.1 t.
**DTSO (B).** Lot No. 31061 1990. –/75. 31.7 t.

| 320 301 | SC | H | SR | GW | 77899 | 63021 | 77921 |
| 320 302 | SC | H | SR | GW | 77900 | 63022 | 77922 |
| 320 303 | SC | H | SR | GW | 77901 | 63023 | 77923 |
| 320 304 | SC | H | SR | GW | 77902 | 63024 | 77924 |
| 320 305 | SC | H | SR | GW | 77903 | 63025 | 77925 |
| 320 306 | SC | H | SR | GW | 77904 | 63026 | 77926 |
| 320 307 | SC | H | SR | GW | 77905 | 63027 | 77927 |
| 320 308 | SC | H | SR | GW | 77906 | 63028 | 77928 |
| 320 309 | SC | H | SR | GW | 77907 | 63029 | 77929 |
| 320 310 | SC | H | SR | GW | 77908 | 63030 | 77930 |
| 320 311 | SC | H | SR | GW | 77909 | 63031 | 77931 |
| 320 312 | SC | H | SR | GW | 77910 | 63032 | 77932 |
| 320 313 | SC | H | SR | GW | 77911 | 63033 | 77933 |
| 320 314 | SC | H | SR | GW | 77912 | 63034 | 77934 |
| 320 315 | SC | H | SR | GW | 77913 | 63035 | 77935 |
| 320 316 | SC | H | SR | GW | 77914 | 63036 | 77936 |
| 320 317 | SC | H | SR | GW | 77915 | 63037 | 77937 |
| 320 318 | SC | H | SR | GW | 77916 | 63038 | 77938 |
| 320 319 | SC | H | SR | GW | 77917 | 63039 | 77939 |
| 320 320 | SC | H | SR | GW | 77918 | 63040 | 77940 |
| 320 321 | SC | H | SR | GW | 77919 | 63041 | 77941 |
| 320 322 | SC | H | SR | GW | 77920 | 63042 | 77942 |

**Names (carried on MSO):**

| | |
|---|---|
| 320 305 | GLASGOW SCHOOL OF ART 1844–150–1994 |
| 320 306 | Model Rail Scotland |
| 320 308 | High Road 20th Anniversary 2000 |
| 320 309 | Radio Clyde 25th Anniversary |
| 320 311 | Royal College of Physicians and Surgeons of Glasgow |
| 320 312 | Sir William A Smith Founder of the Boys' Brigade |
| 320 321 | The Rt. Hon. John Smith, QC, MP |
| 320 322 | Festive Glasgow Orchid |

# CLASS 321                                              BREL YORK

**Formation:** DTCO (DTSO on Class 321/9)–MSO–TSO–DTSO.
**Construction:** Steel.
**Traction Motors:** Four Brush TM2141C (268 kW).
**Doors:** Sliding.                      **Control System:** Thyristor.
**Gangways:** Within unit.               **Bogies:** P7-4 (MSO), T3-7 (others).
**Couplers:** Tightlock.                 **Maximum Speed:** 100 m.p.h.
**Seating Layout:** 1: 2+2 facing, 2: 3+2 facing.
**Dimensions:** 19.95/19.92 x 2.82 m.   **Braking:** Disc.
**Multiple Working:** Within class and with Classes 317, 318, 319, 320, 322 and 323.

**Class 321/3.** One Great Eastern units.

**DTCO.** Lot No. 31053 1988–1990. 16/57. 29.7 t.
**MSO.** Lot No. 31054 1988–1990. –/82. 51.5 t.
**TSO.** Lot No. 31055 1988–1990. –/75 2T. 29.1 t.
**DTSO.** Lot No. 31056 1988–1990. –/78. 29.7 t.

| | | | | | | | | |
|---|---|---|---|---|---|---|---|---|
| 321 301 | GE | H | 1E | IL | 78049 | 62975 | 71880 | 77853 |
| 321 302 | GE | H | 1E | IL | 78050 | 62976 | 71881 | 77854 |
| 321 303 | GE | H | 1E | IL | 78051 | 62977 | 71882 | 77855 |
| 321 304 | GE | H | 1E | IL | 78052 | 62978 | 71883 | 77856 |
| 321 305 | GE | H | 1E | IL | 78053 | 62979 | 71884 | 77857 |
| 321 306 | GE | H | 1E | IL | 78054 | 62980 | 71885 | 77858 |
| 321 307 | GE | H | 1E | IL | 78055 | 62981 | 71886 | 77859 |
| 321 308 | GE | H | 1E | IL | 78056 | 62982 | 71887 | 77860 |
| 321 309 | GE | H | 1E | IL | 78057 | 62983 | 71888 | 77861 |
| 321 310 | GE | H | 1E | IL | 78058 | 62984 | 71889 | 77862 |
| 321 311 | GE | H | 1E | IL | 78059 | 62985 | 71890 | 77863 |
| 321 312 | GE | H | 1E | IL | 78060 | 62986 | 71891 | 77864 |
| 321 313 | GE | H | 1E | IL | 78061 | 62987 | 71892 | 77865 |
| 321 314 | GE | H | 1E | IL | 78062 | 62988 | 71893 | 77866 |
| 321 315 | GE | H | 1E | IL | 78063 | 62989 | 71894 | 77867 |
| 321 316 | GE | H | 1E | IL | 78064 | 62990 | 71895 | 77868 |
| 321 317 | GE | H | 1E | IL | 78065 | 62991 | 71896 | 77869 |
| 321 318 | GE | H | 1E | IL | 78066 | 62992 | 71897 | 77870 |
| 321 319 | GE | H | 1E | IL | 78067 | 62993 | 71898 | 77871 |
| 321 320 | GE | H | 1E | IL | 78068 | 62994 | 71899 | 77872 |
| 321 321 | GE | H | 1E | IL | 78069 | 62995 | 71900 | 77873 |
| 321 322 | GE | H | 1E | IL | 78070 | 62996 | 71901 | 77874 |
| 321 323 | GE | H | 1E | IL | 78071 | 62997 | 71902 | 77875 |

| | | | | | | | | |
|---|---|---|---|---|---|---|---|---|
| 321 324 | **GE** | H | *1E* | IL | 78072 | 62998 | 71903 | 77876 |
| 321 325 | **GE** | H | *1E* | IL | 78073 | 62999 | 71904 | 77877 |
| 321 326 | **GE** | H | *1E* | IL | 78074 | 63000 | 71905 | 77878 |
| 321 327 | **GE** | H | *1E* | IL | 78075 | 63001 | 71906 | 77879 |
| 321 328 | **GE** | H | *1E* | IL | 78076 | 63002 | 71907 | 77880 |
| 321 329 | **GE** | H | *1E* | IL | 78077 | 63003 | 71908 | 77881 |
| 321 330 | **GE** | H | *1E* | IL | 78078 | 63004 | 71909 | 77882 |
| 321 331 | **GE** | H | *1E* | IL | 78079 | 63005 | 71910 | 77883 |
| 321 332 | **GE** | H | *1E* | IL | 78080 | 63006 | 71911 | 77884 |
| 321 333 | **GE** | H | *1E* | IL | 78081 | 63007 | 71912 | 77885 |
| 321 334 | **GE** | H | *1E* | IL | 78082 | 63008 | 71913 | 77886 |
| 321 335 | **GE** | H | *1E* | IL | 78083 | 63009 | 71914 | 77887 |
| 321 336 | **GE** | H | *1E* | IL | 78084 | 63010 | 71915 | 77888 |
| 321 337 | **GE** | H | *1E* | IL | 78085 | 63011 | 71916 | 77889 |
| 321 338 | **GE** | H | *1E* | IL | 78086 | 63012 | 71917 | 77890 |
| 321 339 | **GE** | H | *1E* | IL | 78087 | 63013 | 71918 | 77891 |
| 321 340 | **GE** | H | *1E* | IL | 78088 | 63014 | 71919 | 77892 |
| 321 341 | **GE** | H | *1E* | IL | 78089 | 63015 | 71920 | 77893 |
| 321 342 | **GE** | H | *1E* | IL | 78090 | 63016 | 71921 | 77894 |
| 321 343 | **GE** | H | *1E* | IL | 78091 | 63017 | 71922 | 77895 |
| 321 344 | **GE** | H | *1E* | IL | 78092 | 63018 | 71923 | 77896 |
| 321 345 | **GE** | H | *1E* | IL | 78093 | 63019 | 71924 | 77897 |
| 321 346 | **GE** | H | *1E* | IL | 78094 | 63020 | 71925 | 77898 |
| 321 347 | **GE** | H | *1E* | IL | 78131 | 63105 | 71991 | 78280 |
| 321 348 | **GE** | H | *1E* | IL | 78132 | 63106 | 71992 | 78281 |
| 321 349 | **GE** | H | *1E* | IL | 78133 | 63107 | 71993 | 78282 |
| 321 350 | **GE** | H | *1E* | IL | 78134 | 63108 | 71994 | 78283 |
| 321 351 | **GE** | H | *1E* | IL | 78135 | 63109 | 71995 | 78284 |
| 321 352 | **GE** | H | *1E* | IL | 78136 | 63110 | 71996 | 78285 |
| 321 353 | **GE** | H | *1E* | IL | 78137 | 63111 | 71997 | 78286 |
| 321 354 | **GE** | H | *1E* | IL | 78138 | 63112 | 71998 | 78287 |
| 321 355 | **GE** | H | *1E* | IL | 78139 | 63113 | 71999 | 78288 |
| 321 356 | **GE** | H | *1E* | IL | 78140 | 63114 | 72000 | 78289 |
| 321 357 | **GE** | H | *1E* | IL | 78141 | 63115 | 72001 | 78290 |
| 321 358 | **GE** | H | *1E* | IL | 78142 | 63116 | 72002 | 78291 |
| 321 359 | **GE** | H | *1E* | IL | 78143 | 63117 | 72003 | 78292 |
| 321 360 | **GE** | H | *1E* | IL | 78144 | 63118 | 72004 | 78293 |
| 321 361 | **GE** | H | *1E* | IL | 78145 | 63119 | 72005 | 78294 |
| 321 362 | **GE** | H | *1E* | IL | 78146 | 63120 | 72006 | 78295 |
| 321 363 | **GE** | H | *1E* | IL | 78147 | 63121 | 72007 | 78296 |
| 321 364 | **GE** | H | *1E* | IL | 78148 | 63122 | 72008 | 78297 |
| 321 365 | **GE** | H | *1E* | IL | 78149 | 63123 | 72009 | 78298 |
| 321 366 | **GE** | H | *1E* | IL | 78150 | 63124 | 72010 | 78299 |

**Names (carried on TSO):**

| | |
|---|---|
| 321 312 | Southend-on-Sea |
| 321 321 | NSPCC ESSEX FULL STOP |
| 321 334 | Amsterdam |
| 321 336 | GEOFFREY FREEMAN ALLEN |
| 321 343 | RSA RAILWAY STUDY ASSOCIATION |
| 321 351 | GURKHA |

**Class 321/4.** Silverlink/One Great Eastern units.

**DTCO.** Lot No. 31067 1989–1990. 28/40. 29.8 t.
**MSO.** Lot No. 31068 1989–1990. –/79. 51.6 t.
**TSO.** Lot No. 31069 1989–1990. –/74 2T. 29.2 t.
**DTSO.** Lot No. 31070 1989–1990. –/78. 29.8 t.

**Note:** The DTCOs of One Great Eastern units have had 12 first class seats declassified.

| | | | | | | | | |
|---|---|---|---|---|---|---|---|---|
| 321 401 | **SL** | H | *SL* | BY | 78095 | 63063 | 71949 | 77943 |
| 321 402 | **SL** | H | *SL* | BY | 78096 | 63064 | 71950 | 77944 |
| 321 403 | **SL** | H | *SL* | BY | 78097 | 63065 | 71951 | 77945 |
| 321 404 | **SL** | H | *SL* | BY | 78098 | 63066 | 71952 | 77946 |
| 321 405 | **SL** | H | *SL* | BY | 78099 | 63067 | 71953 | 77947 |
| 321 406 | **SL** | H | *SL* | BY | 78100 | 63068 | 71954 | 77948 |
| 321 407 | **SL** | H | *NO* | NL | 78101 | 63069 | 71955 | 77949 |
| 321 408 | **SL** | H | *SL* | BY | 78102 | 63070 | 71956 | 77950 |
| 321 409 | **SL** | H | *SL* | BY | 78103 | 63071 | 71957 | 77951 |
| 321 410 | **SL** | H | *SL* | BY | 78104 | 63072 | 71958 | 77952 |
| 321 411 | **SL** | H | *SL* | BY | 78105 | 63073 | 71959 | 77953 |
| 321 412 | **SL** | H | *SL* | BY | 78106 | 63074 | 71960 | 77954 |
| 321 413 | **SL** | H | *SL* | BY | 78107 | 63075 | 71961 | 77955 |
| 321 414 | **SL** | H | *SL* | BY | 78108 | 63076 | 71962 | 77956 |
| 321 415 | **SL** | H | *SL* | BY | 78109 | 63077 | 71963 | 77957 |
| 321 416 | **SL** | H | *SL* | BY | 78110 | 63078 | 71964 | 77958 |
| 321 417 | **SL** | H | *SL* | BY | 78111 | 63079 | 71965 | 77959 |
| 321 418 | **SL** | H | *SL* | BY | 78112 | 63080 | 71968 | 77962 |
| 321 419 | **SL** | H | *SL* | BY | 78113 | 63081 | 71967 | 77961 |
| 321 420 | **SL** | H | *SL* | BY | 78114 | 63082 | 71966 | 77960 |
| 321 421 | **SL** | H | *SL* | BY | 78115 | 63083 | 71969 | 77963 |
| 321 422 | **SL** | H | *SL* | BY | 78116 | 63084 | 71970 | 77964 |
| 321 423 | **SL** | H | *SL* | BY | 78117 | 63085 | 71971 | 77965 |
| 321 424 | **SL** | H | *SL* | BY | 78118 | 63086 | 71972 | 77966 |
| 321 425 | **SL** | H | *SL* | BY | 78119 | 63087 | 71973 | 77967 |
| 321 426 | **SL** | H | *SL* | BY | 78120 | 63088 | 71974 | 77968 |
| 321 427 | **SL** | H | *SL* | BY | 78121 | 63089 | 71975 | 77969 |
| 321 428 | **SL** | H | *SL* | BY | 78122 | 63090 | 71976 | 77970 |
| 321 429 | **SL** | H | *SL* | BY | 78123 | 63091 | 71977 | 77971 |
| 321 430 | **SL** | H | *SL* | BY | 78124 | 63092 | 71978 | 77972 |
| 321 431 | **SL** | H | *SL* | BY | 78151 | 63125 | 72011 | 78300 |
| 321 432 | **SL** | H | *SL* | BY | 78152 | 63126 | 72012 | 78301 |
| 321 433 | **SL** | H | *SL* | BY | 78153 | 63127 | 72013 | 78302 |
| 321 434 | **SL** | H | *SL* | BY | 78154 | 63128 | 72014 | 78303 |
| 321 435 | **SL** | H | *SL* | BY | 78155 | 63129 | 72015 | 78304 |
| 321 436 | **SL** | H | *SL* | BY | 78156 | 63130 | 72016 | 78305 |
| 321 437 | **SL** | H | *SL* | BY | 78157 | 63131 | 72017 | 78306 |
| 321 438 | **GE** | H | *1E* | IL | 78158 | 63132 | 72018 | 78307 |
| 321 439 | **GE** | H | *1E* | IL | 78159 | 63133 | 72019 | 78308 |
| 321 440 | **GE** | H | *1E* | IL | 78160 | 63134 | 72020 | 78309 |
| 321 441 | **GE** | H | *1E* | IL | 78161 | 63135 | 72021 | 78310 |
| 321 442 | **GE** | H | *1E* | IL | 78162 | 63136 | 72022 | 78311 |

| 321 443 | GE | H | *1E* | IL | 78125 | 63099 | 71985 | 78274 |
| 321 444 | GE | H | *1E* | IL | 78126 | 63100 | 71986 | 78275 |
| 321 445 | GE | H | *1E* | IL | 78127 | 63101 | 71987 | 78276 |
| 321 446 | 1  | H | *1E* | IL | 78128 | 63102 | 71988 | 78277 |
| 321 447 | GE | H | *1E* | IL | 78129 | 63103 | 71989 | 78278 |
| 321 448 | GE | H | *1E* | IL | 78130 | 63104 | 71990 | 78279 |

**Names (carried on TSO):**

| 321 407 | HERTFORDSHIRE WRVS |
| 321 413 | Bill Green |
| 321 425 | Silver Service |
| 321 427 | Major Tim Warr |
| 321 444 | Essex Lifeboats |
| 321 446 | George Mullins |

**Class 321/9.** DTSO(A)–MSO–TSO–DTSO(B).
**Dimensions:** 19.33 x 2.82 m.

**DTSO(A).** Lot No. 31108 1991. –/77. 29.0 t.
**MSO.** Lot No. 31109 1991. –/79. 51.0 t.
**TSO.** Lot No. 31110 1991. –/74 2T. 29.0 t.
**DTSO(B).** Dia. EE277. Lot No. 31111 1991. –/77. 29.0 t.

| 321 901 | WY | H | *NO* | NL | 77990 | 63153 | 72128 | 77993 |
| 321 902 | WY | H | *NO* | NL | 77991 | 63154 | 72129 | 77994 |
| 321 903 | WY | H | *NO* | NL | 77992 | 63155 | 72130 | 77995 |

# CLASS 322          BREL YORK

Units built for use on Stansted Airport services, now in use with First ScotRail.

**Formation:** DTCO(declassified)–TSO–MSO–DTSO.
**Construction:** Steel.
**Traction Motors:** Four Brush TM2141C (268 kW).
**Doors:** Sliding.      **Control System:** Thyristor.
**Gangways:** Within unit.      **Bogies:** P7-4 (MSO), T3-7 (others).
**Couplers:** Tightlock      **Maximum Speed:** 100 m.p.h.
**Seating Layout:** 1: 2+1 facing, 2: 2+2 facing.
**Dimensions:** 19.95/19.92 x 2.82 m.
**Braking:** Disc.
**Multiple Working:** Within class and with Classes 317, 318, 319, 320, 321 and 323.

**DTCO.** Lot No. 31094 1990. 35/22. 29.3 t.
**TSO.** Lot No. 31093 1990. –/60 2T. 28.8 t.
**MSO.** Lot No. 31092 1990. –/70. 51.5 t.
**DTSO.** Lot No. 31091 1990. –/65. 29.1 t.

**IMPORTANT NOTE**: These units are due to be renumbered Class 321/5s later in 2006 but the full details of this renumbering programme had not been finalised as this book closed for press.

**Non-standard livery**: Stansted Skytrain livery (light grey with a yellow stripe).

| | | | | | | | | |
|---|---|---|---|---|---|---|---|---|
| 322 481 | 0 | H | *SR* | GW | 78163 | 72023 | 63137 | 77985 |
| 322 482 | 0 | H | *SR* | GW | 78164 | 72024 | 63138 | 77986 |
| 322 483 | 0 | H | *SR* | GW | 78165 | 72025 | 63139 | 77987 |
| 322 484 | NW | H | *SR* | GW | 78166 | 72026 | 63140 | 77988 |
| 322 485 | 0 | H | *SR* | GW | 78167 | 72027 | 63141 | 77989 |

# CLASS 323 HUNSLET TRANSPORTATION PROJECTS

Birmingham and Greater Manchester area suburban units.

**Formation**: DMSO–PTSO–DMSO.
**Construction**: Welded aluminium alloy.
**Doors**: Sliding plug.
**Traction Motors**: Four Holec DMKT 52/24 asynchronous of 146 kW.
**Gangways**: Within unit.
**Bogies**: SRP BP62 (DMSO), BT52 (PTSO).
**Couplers**: Tightlock        **Maximum Speed**: 90 m.p.h.
**Seating Layout**: 3+2 facing/unidirectional.
**Dimensions**: 23.37/23.44 x 2.80 m.
**Braking**: Disc.
**Multiple Working**: Within class and with Classes 317, 318, 319, 320, 321 and 322.

**DMSO(A)**. Lot No. 31112 Hunslet 1992–1993. –/98 (* –/82). 39.1 t.
**TSO**. Lot No. 31113 Hunslet 1992–1993. –/88 1T. (* –/80 1T). 36.5 t.
**DMSO(B)**. Lot No. 31114 Hunslet 1992–1993. –/98 (* –/82). 39.1 t.

| | | | | | | | |
|---|---|---|---|---|---|---|---|
| 323 201 | CO | P | *CT* | SI | 64001 | 72201 | 65001 |
| 323 202 | CO | P | *CT* | SI | 64002 | 72202 | 65002 |
| 323 203 | CO | P | *CT* | SI | 64003 | 72203 | 65003 |
| 323 204 | CO | P | *CT* | SI | 64004 | 72204 | 65004 |
| 323 205 | CO | P | *CT* | SI | 64005 | 72205 | 65005 |
| 323 206 | CO | P | *CT* | SI | 64006 | 72206 | 65006 |
| 323 207 | CO | P | *CT* | SI | 64007 | 72207 | 65007 |
| 323 208 | CO | P | *CT* | SI | 64008 | 72208 | 65008 |
| 323 209 | CO | P | *CT* | SI | 64009 | 72209 | 65009 |
| 323 210 | CO | P | *CT* | SI | 64010 | 72210 | 65010 |
| 323 211 | CO | P | *CT* | SI | 64011 | 72211 | 65011 |
| 323 212 | CO | P | *CT* | SI | 64012 | 72212 | 65012 |
| 323 213 | CO | P | *CT* | SI | 64013 | 72213 | 65013 |
| 323 214 | CO | P | *CT* | SI | 64014 | 72214 | 65014 |
| 323 215 | CO | P | *CT* | SI | 64015 | 72215 | 65015 |
| 323 216 | CO | P | *CT* | SI | 64016 | 72216 | 65016 |
| 323 217 | CO | P | *CT* | SI | 64017 | 72217 | 65017 |
| 323 218 | CO | P | *CT* | SI | 64018 | 72218 | 65018 |
| 323 219 | CO | P | *CT* | SI | 64019 | 72219 | 65019 |
| 323 220 | CO | P | *CT* | SI | 64020 | 72220 | 65020 |
| 323 221 | CO | P | *CT* | SI | 64021 | 72221 | 65021 |

| | | | | | | | |
|---|---|---|---|---|---|---|---|
| 323 222 | **CO** | P | *CT* | SI | 64022 | 72222 | 65022 |
| 323 223 | * **FS** | P | *NO* | LG | 64023 | 72223 | 65023 |
| 323 224 | * **FS** | P | *NO* | LG | 64024 | 72224 | 65024 |
| 323 225 | * **FS** | P | *NO* | LG | 64025 | 72225 | 65025 |
| 323 226 | **FS** | P | *NO* | LG | 64026 | 72226 | 65026 |
| 323 227 | **FS** | P | *NO* | LG | 64027 | 72227 | 65027 |
| 323 228 | **FS** | P | *NO* | LG | 64028 | 72228 | 65028 |
| 323 229 | **FS** | P | *NO* | LG | 64029 | 72229 | 65029 |
| 323 230 | **FS** | P | *NO* | LG | 64030 | 72230 | 65030 |
| 323 231 | **FS** | P | *NO* | LG | 64031 | 72231 | 65031 |
| 323 232 | **FS** | P | *NO* | LG | 64032 | 72232 | 65032 |
| 323 233 | **FS** | P | *NO* | LG | 64033 | 72233 | 65033 |
| 323 234 | **FS** | P | *NO* | LG | 64034 | 72234 | 65034 |
| 323 235 | **FS** | P | *NO* | LG | 64035 | 72235 | 65035 |
| 323 236 | **FS** | P | *NO* | LG | 64036 | 72236 | 65036 |
| 323 237 | **FS** | P | *NO* | LG | 64037 | 72237 | 65037 |
| 323 238 | **FS** | P | *NO* | LG | 64038 | 72238 | 65038 |
| 323 239 | **FS** | P | *NO* | LG | 64039 | 72239 | 65039 |
| 323 240 | **CO** | P | *CT* | SI | 64040 | 72240 | 65040 |
| 323 241 | **CO** | P | *CT* | SI | 64041 | 72241 | 65041 |
| 323 242 | **CO** | P | *CT* | SI | 64042 | 72242 | 65042 |
| 323 243 | **CO** | P | *CT* | SI | 64043 | 72243 | 65043 |

# CLASS 325 — ABB DERBY

Postal units based on Class 319. Compatible with diesel or electric locomotive haulage.

**Formation:** DTPMV–MPMV–TPMV–DTPMV.
**System:** 25 kV AC overhead/750 V DC third rail.
**Construction:** Steel.
**Traction Motors:** Four GEC G315BZ of 268 kW.
**Doors:** Roller shutter.
**Gangways:** None.
**Couplers:** Drop-head buckeye.
**Braking:** Disc.
**Multiple Working:** Within class.

**Control System:** GTO chopper.
**Bogies:** P7-4 (MSO), T3-7 (others).
**Maximum Speed:** 100 m.p.h.
**Dimensions:** 19.33 x 2.82 m.

**DTPMV.** Lot No. 31144 1995. 29.1 t.
**MPMV.** Lot No. 31145 1995. 49.5 t.
**TPMV.** Lot No. 31146 1995. 30.7 t.

**Notes:** Formations of these units are in a state of flux and subject to change.

At the time of writing these units were running effectively as hauled stock in 3-car formations (minus the MPMV vehicle) due to reliability problems.

| | | | | | | | |
|---|---|---|---|---|---|---|---|
| 325 001 | **RM** | RM *GB* | WN | 68300 | 68340 | 68360 | 68301 |
| 325 002 | **RM** | RM *GB* | WN | 68302 | 68341 | 68361 | 68303 |
| 325 003 | **RM** | RM *GB* | WN | 68304 | 68342 | 68362 | 68305 |
| 325 004 | **RM** | RM *GB* | WN | 68306 | 68343 | 68363 | 68307 |
| 325 005 | **RM** | RM *GB* | WN | 68308 | 68344 | 68364 | 68309 |
| 325 006 | **RM** | RM *GB* | WN | 68310 | 68345 | 68365 | 68311 |

| 325 007 | **RM** | RM *GB* | WN | 68312 | 68346 | 68366 | 68313 |
|---|---|---|---|---|---|---|---|
| 325 008 | **RM** | RM *GB* | WN | 68314 | 68347 | 68367 | 68315 |
| 325 009 | **RM** | RM *GB* | WN | 68316 | 68348 | 68368 | 68317 |
| 325 010 | **RM** | RM *GB* | WN | 68318 | 68349 | 68369 | 68319 |
| 325 011 | **RM** | RM *GB* | WN | 68320 | 68350 | 68370 | 68321 |
| 325 012 | **RM** | RM *GB* | WN | 68322 | 68351 | 68371 | 68323 |
| 325 013 | **RM** | RM *GB* | WN | 68324 | 68352 | 68372 | 68325 |
| 325 014 | **RM** | RM *GB* | WN | 68326 | 68353 | 68373 | 68327 |
| 325 015 | **RM** | RM *GB* | WN | 68328 | 68354 | 68374 | 68329 |
| 325 016 | **RM** | RM *GB* | WN | 68330 | 68355 | 68375 | 68331 |

**Names (carried on one side of each DTPMV):**

| 325 002 | Royal Mail North Wales & North West |
|---|---|
| 325 006 | John Grierson |
| 325 008 | Peter Howarth C.B.E. |

# CLASS 332    HEATHROW EXPRESS    SIEMENS

Dedicated Heathrow Express units. Five units were increased from 4-car to 5-car in 2002. Usually operate in coupled pairs.

**Formations:** Various.
**Construction:** Steel.        **Doors:** Sliding plug.
**Traction Motors:** Two Siemens monomotors asynchronous of 350 kW.
**Gangways:** Within unit.        **Bogies:** CAF.
**Couplers:** Scharfenberg      **Maximum Speed:** 100 m.p.h.
**Seating Layout:** 1: 2+1 facing, 2: 2+2 mainly unidirectional.
**Dimensions:** 23.63/23.35 x 2.75 m.    **Braking:** Disc.
**Multiple Working:** Within class and with Class 333.
**Heating & ventilation:** Air conditioning.

**332 001–332 007.** DMFO–TSO–PTSO–(TSO)–DMSO.

**DMFO.** CAF 1997–1998. 26/–. 48.8 t.
**72400–72413. TSO.** CAF 1997–1998. –/56 35.8 t.
**72414–72418. TSO.** CAF 2002. –/56 35.8 t.
**PTSO.** CAF 1997–1998. –/44 1TD 1W. 45.6 t.
**DMSO.** CAF 1997–1998. –/48. 48.8 t.
**DMLFO.** CAF 1997–1998. 14/– 1W. 48.8 t.

**Advertising livery:** Vehicles 78402, 78405, 78406, 78408, 78410, 78412 carry Royal Bank of Scotland advertising livery (deep blue).

| 332 001 | **HE** | HE *HE* | OH | 78400 | 72412 | 63400 | | 78401 |
|---|---|---|---|---|---|---|---|---|
| 332 002 | **HE** | HE *HE* | OH | 78402 | 72409 | 63401 | | 78403 |
| 332 003 | **HE** | HE *HE* | OH | 78404 | 72407 | 63402 | | 78405 |
| 332 004 | **HE** | HE *HE* | OH | 78406 | 72405 | 63403 | | 78407 |
| 332 005 | **HE** | HE *HE* | OH | 78408 | 72411 | 63404 | 72417 | 78409 |
| 332 006 | **HE** | HE *HE* | OH | 78410 | 72410 | 63405 | 72415 | 78411 |
| 332 007 | **HE** | HE *HE* | OH | 78412 | 72401 | 63406 | 72414 | 78413 |

**332 008–332 014.** DMSO–TSO–PTSO–(TSO)–DMLFO.

**Advertising livery:** Vehicles 78414, 78416, 78419, 78421, 78423, 78425, 78427 carry Royal Bank of Scotland advertising livery (deep blue).

| | | | | | | | | |
|---|---|---|---|---|---|---|---|---|
| 332 008 | **HE** | HE *HE* | OH | 78414 | 72413 | 63407 | 72418 | 78415 |
| 332 009 | **HE** | HE *HE* | OH | 78416 | 72400 | 63408 | 72416 | 78417 |
| 332 010 | **HE** | HE *HE* | OH | 78418 | 72402 | 63409 | | 78419 |
| 332 011 | **HE** | HE *HE* | OH | 78420 | 72403 | 63410 | | 78421 |
| 332 012 | **HE** | HE *HE* | OH | 78422 | 72404 | 63411 | | 78423 |
| 332 013 | **HE** | HE *HE* | OH | 78424 | 72408 | 63412 | | 78425 |
| 332 014 | **HE** | HE *HE* | OH | 78426 | 72406 | 63413 | | 78427 |

# CLASS 333            SIEMENS

West Yorkshire area suburban units.

**Formation:** DMSO–PTSO–TSO–DMSO.
**Construction:** Steel.      **Doors:** Sliding plug.
**Traction Motors:** Two Siemens monomotors asynchronous of 350 kW.
**Gangways:** Within unit.      **Bogies:** CAF.
**Couplers:** Scharfenberg      **Maximum Speed:** 100 m.p.h.
**Seating Layout:** 3+2 facing/unidirectional.
**Dimensions:** 22.95 (outer ends)/22.90 (PTSO)/23.35 (TSO) x 2.57 m.
**Braking:** Disc.
**Multiple Working:** Within class and with Class 332.
**Heating & ventilation:** Air conditioning.

**DMSO(A).** (Odd Nos.) CAF 2001. –/90. 50.6 t.
**PTSO.** CAF 2001. –/73 1TD 2W. 46.7 t.
**TSO.** CAF 2002–2003. –/100. 38.5 t.
**DMSO(B).** (Even Nos.) CAF 2001. –/90. 50.6 t.

**Notes:** 333 001–333 008 were made up to 4-car units from 3-car units in 2002.

333 009–333 016 were made up to 4-car units from 3-car units in 2003.

| | | | | | | | |
|---|---|---|---|---|---|---|---|
| 333 001 | **YN** | A | *NO* | NL | 78451 | 74461 | 74477 | 78452 |
| 333 002 | **YN** | A | *NO* | NL | 78453 | 74462 | 74478 | 78454 |
| 333 003 | **YN** | A | *NO* | NL | 78455 | 74463 | 74479 | 78456 |
| 333 004 | **YN** | A | *NO* | NL | 78457 | 74464 | 74480 | 78458 |
| 333 005 | **YN** | A | *NO* | NL | 78459 | 74465 | 74481 | 78460 |
| 333 006 | **YN** | A | *NO* | NL | 78461 | 74466 | 74482 | 78462 |
| 333 007 | **YN** | A | *NO* | NL | 78463 | 74467 | 74483 | 78464 |
| 333 008 | **YN** | A | *NO* | NL | 78465 | 74468 | 74484 | 78466 |
| 333 009 | **YN** | A | *NO* | NL | 78467 | 74469 | 74485 | 78468 |
| 333 010 | **YN** | A | *NO* | NL | 78469 | 74470 | 74486 | 78470 |
| 333 011 | **YN** | A | *NO* | NL | 78471 | 74471 | 74487 | 78472 |
| 333 012 | **YN** | A | *NO* | NL | 78473 | 74472 | 74488 | 78474 |
| 333 013 | **YN** | A | *NO* | NL | 78475 | 74473 | 74489 | 78476 |
| 333 014 | **YN** | A | *NO* | NL | 78477 | 74474 | 74490 | 78478 |
| 333 015 | **YN** | A | *NO* | NL | 78479 | 74475 | 74491 | 78480 |
| 333 016 | **YN** | A | *NO* | NL | 78481 | 74476 | 74492 | 78482 |

# CLASS 334 JUNIPER ALSTOM BIRMINGHAM

First ScotRail outer suburban units.

**Formation:** DMSO–PTSO–DMSO.
**Construction:** Steel.                    **Doors:** Sliding plug.
**Traction Motors:** Two Alstom ONIX 800 asynchronous of 270 kW.
**Gangways:** Within unit.                 **Bogies:** Alstom LTB3/TBP3.
**Couplers:** Tightlock.                    **Maximum Speed:** 90 m.p.h.
**Seating Layout:** 2+2 facing/unidirectional (3+2 in PTSO).
**Dimensions:** 21.01/19.94 x 2.80 m.      **Braking:** Disc.
**Multiple Working:** Within class.
**Heating & ventilation:** Pressure heating and ventilation.

**64101–64140. DMSO.** Alstom Birmingham 1999–2001. –/64. 42.6 t.
**PTSO.** Alstom Birmingham 1999–2001. –/55 1TD 1W. 39.4 t.
**65101–65140. DMSO.** Alstom Birmingham 1999–2001. –/64. 42.6 t.

| | | | | | | | | |
|---|---|---|---|---|---|---|---|---|
| 334 001 | **SP** | H | *SR* | GW | 64101 | 74301 | 65101 | Donald Dewar |
| 334 002 | **SP** | H | *SR* | GW | 64102 | 74302 | 65102 | |
| 334 003 | **SP** | H | *SR* | GW | 64103 | 74303 | 65103 | |
| 334 004 | **SP** | H | *SR* | GW | 64104 | 74304 | 65104 | |
| 334 005 | **SP** | H | *SR* | GW | 64105 | 74305 | 65105 | |
| 334 006 | **SP** | H | *SR* | GW | 64106 | 74306 | 65106 | |
| 334 007 | **SP** | H | *SR* | GW | 64107 | 74307 | 65107 | |
| 334 008 | **SP** | H | *SR* | GW | 64108 | 74308 | 65108 | |
| 334 009 | **SP** | H | *SR* | GW | 64109 | 74309 | 65109 | |
| 334 010 | **SP** | H | *SR* | GW | 64110 | 74310 | 65110 | |
| 334 011 | **SP** | H | *SR* | GW | 64111 | 74311 | 65111 | |
| 334 012 | **SP** | H | *SR* | GW | 64112 | 74312 | 65112 | |
| 334 013 | **SP** | H | *SR* | GW | 64113 | 74313 | 65113 | |
| 334 014 | **SP** | H | *SR* | GW | 64114 | 74314 | 65114 | |
| 334 015 | **SP** | H | *SR* | GW | 64115 | 74315 | 65115 | |
| 334 016 | **SP** | H | *SR* | GW | 64116 | 74316 | 65116 | |
| 334 017 | **SP** | H | *SR* | GW | 64117 | 74317 | 65117 | |
| 334 018 | **SP** | H | *SR* | GW | 64118 | 74318 | 65118 | |
| 334 019 | **SP** | H | *SR* | GW | 64119 | 74319 | 65119 | |
| 334 020 | **SP** | H | *SR* | GW | 64120 | 74320 | 65120 | |
| 334 021 | **SP** | H | *SR* | GW | 64121 | 74321 | 65121 | Larkhall |
| 334 022 | **SP** | H | *SR* | GW | 64122 | 74322 | 65122 | |
| 334 023 | **SP** | H | *SR* | GW | 64123 | 74323 | 65123 | |
| 334 024 | **SP** | H | *SR* | GW | 64124 | 74324 | 65124 | |
| 334 025 | **SP** | H | *SR* | GW | 64125 | 74325 | 65125 | |
| 334 026 | **SP** | H | *SR* | GW | 64126 | 74326 | 65126 | |
| 334 027 | **SP** | H | *SR* | GW | 64127 | 74327 | 65127 | |
| 334 028 | **SP** | H | *SR* | GW | 64128 | 74328 | 65128 | |
| 334 029 | **SP** | H | *SR* | GW | 64129 | 74329 | 65129 | |
| 334 030 | **SP** | H | *SR* | GW | 64130 | 74330 | 65130 | |
| 334 031 | **SP** | H | *SR* | GW | 64131 | 74331 | 65131 | |
| 334 032 | **SP** | H | *SR* | GW | 64132 | 74332 | 65132 | |
| 334 033 | **SP** | H | *SR* | GW | 64133 | 74333 | 65133 | |

| 334 034 | **SP** | H | *SR* | GW | 64134 | 74334 | 65134 |
| 334 035 | **SP** | H | *SR* | GW | 64135 | 74335 | 65135 |
| 334 036 | **SP** | H | *SR* | GW | 64136 | 74336 | 65136 |
| 334 037 | **SP** | H | *SR* | GW | 64137 | 74337 | 65137 |
| 334 038 | **SP** | H | *SR* | GW | 64138 | 74338 | 65138 |
| 334 039 | **SP** | H | *SR* | GW | 64139 | 74339 | 65139 |
| 334 040 | **SP** | H | *SR* | GW | 64140 | 74340 | 65140 |

# CLASS 350      DESIRO UK      SIEMENS

New "West Coast" units for use by Silverlink and Central Trains. Formerly part of
the aborted South West Trains 5-car Class 450/2 order.

**Formation:** DMCO–TCO–PTSO–DMCO.
**Systems:** 25 kV AC overhead.
**Construction:** Welded aluminium.      **Doors:** Sliding plug.
**Traction Motors:** 4 Siemens 1TB2016-0GB02 asynchronous of 250 kW.
**Gangways:** Throughout.      **Bogies:** SGP SF5000.
**Couplers:** Dellner 12.      **Maximum Speed:** 100 m.p.h.
**Seating Layout:** 1: 2+2 facing, 2: 2+2 facing/unidirectional.
**Dimensions:** 20.34 x 2.80 m.      **Multiple Working:** Within class.
**Braking:** Disc & regenerative.
**Heating & ventilation:** Air conditioning.

**DMSO(A).** Siemens Uerdingen 2004–2005. –/60. 48.7 t.
**TCO.** Siemens Wien 2004–2005. 24/32 1T. 36.2 t.
**PTSO.** Siemens Wien 2004–2005. –/57 1TD 2W. 45.2 t.
**DMSO(B).** Siemens Uerdingen 2004–2005. –/60. 49.2 t.

**Note:** 350 103/105/108 were all running mis-formed at the time of writing.

| 350 101 | **WD** | A | *SL/CT* | BY | 63761 | 66811 | 66861 | 63711 |
| 350 102 | **WD** | A | *SL/CT* | BY | 63762 | 66812 | 66862 | 63712 |
| 350 103 | **WD** | A | *SL/CT* | BY | 63765 | 66813 | 66863 | 63713 |
| 350 104 | **WD** | A | *SL/CT* | BY | 63764 | 66814 | 66864 | 63714 |
| 350 105 | **WD** | A | *SL/CT* | BY | 63763 | 66815 | 66868 | 63715 |
| 350 106 | **WD** | A | *SL/CT* | BY | 63766 | 66816 | 66866 | 63716 |
| 350 107 | **WD** | A | *SL/CT* | BY | 63767 | 66817 | 66867 | 63717 |
| 350 108 | **WD** | A | *SL/CT* | BY | 63768 | 66818 | 66865 | 63718 |
| 350 109 | **WD** | A | *SL/CT* | BY | 63769 | 66819 | 66869 | 63719 |
| 350 110 | **WD** | A | *SL/CT* | BY | 63770 | 66820 | 66870 | 63720 |
| 350 111 | **WD** | A | *SL/CT* | BY | 63771 | 66821 | 66871 | 63721 |
| 350 112 | **WD** | A | *SL/CT* | BY | 63772 | 66822 | 66872 | 63722 |
| 350 113 | **WD** | A | *SL/CT* | BY | 63773 | 66823 | 66873 | 63723 |
| 350 114 | **WD** | A | *SL/CT* | BY | 63774 | 66824 | 66874 | 63724 |
| 350 115 | **WD** | A | *SL/CT* | BY | 63775 | 66825 | 66875 | 63725 |
| 350 116 | **WD** | A | *SL/CT* | BY | 63776 | 66826 | 66876 | 63726 |
| 350 117 | **WD** | A | *SL/CT* | BY | 63777 | 66827 | 66877 | 63727 |
| 350 118 | **WD** | A | *SL/CT* | BY | 63778 | 66828 | 66878 | 63728 |
| 350 119 | **WD** | A | *SL/CT* | BY | 63779 | 66829 | 66879 | 63729 |
| 350 120 | **WD** | A | *SL/CT* | BY | 63780 | 66830 | 66880 | 63730 |
| 350 121 | **WD** | A | *SL/CT* | BY | 63781 | 66831 | 66881 | 63731 |
| 350 122 | **WD** | A | *SL/CT* | BY | 63782 | 66832 | 66882 | 63732 |

| 350 123 | **WD** | A | *SL/CT* | BY | 63783 | 66833 | 66883 | 63733 |
| 350 124 | **WD** | A | *SL/CT* | BY | 63784 | 66834 | 66884 | 63734 |
| 350 125 | **WD** | A | *SL/CT* | BY | 63785 | 66835 | 66885 | 63735 |
| 350 126 | **WD** | A | *SL/CT* | BY | 63786 | 66836 | 66886 | 63736 |
| 350 127 | **WD** | A | *SL/CT* | BY | 63787 | 66837 | 66887 | 63737 |
| 350 128 | **WD** | A | *SL/CT* | BY | 63788 | 66838 | 66888 | 63738 |
| 350 129 | **WD** | A | *SL/CT* | BY | 63789 | 66839 | 66889 | 63739 |
| 350 130 | **WD** | A | *SL/CT* | BY | 63790 | 66840 | 66890 | 63740 |

**Names (carried on one side of each TCO):**

| 350 111 | Apollo |
| 350 115 | Archimedes |

# CLASS 357 ELECTROSTAR
## ADTRANZ/BOMBARDIER DERBY

c2c units. Provision for 750 V DC supply if required.

**Formation:** DMSO–MSO–PTSO–DMSO.
**Construction:** Welded aluminium alloy underframe, sides and roof with steel ends. All sections bolted together.
**Traction Motors:** Two Adtranz asynchronous of 250 kW.
**Doors:** Sliding plug.
**Gangways:** Within unit.                    **Bogies:** Adtranz P3-25/T3-25.
**Couplers:** Tightlock.                       **Maximum Speed:** 100 m.p.h.
**Seating Layout:** 3+2 facing/unidirectional.
**Dimensions:** 20.40/19.99 x 2.80 m.
**Braking:** Disc & regenerative.              **Multiple Working:** Within class.
**Heating & ventilation:** Air conditioning.

Class **357/0.** Owned by Porterbrook Leasing.

**DMSO(A).** Adtranz Derby 1999–2001. –/71. 40.7 t.
**MSO.** Adtranz Derby 1999–2001. –/78. 36.7 t.
**PTSO.** Adtranz Derby 1999–2001. –/62 1TD 2W. 39.5 t.
**DMSO(B).** Adtranz Derby 1999–2001. –/71. 40.7 t.

| 357 001 | **C2** | P | *C2* | EM | 67651 | 74151 | 74051 | 67751 |
| 357 002 | **C2** | P | *C2* | EM | 67652 | 74152 | 74052 | 67752 |
| 357 003 | **C2** | P | *C2* | EM | 67653 | 74153 | 74053 | 67753 |
| 357 004 | **C2** | P | *C2* | EM | 67654 | 74154 | 74054 | 67754 |
| 357 005 | **C2** | P | *C2* | EM | 67655 | 74155 | 74055 | 67755 |
| 357 006 | **C2** | P | *C2* | EM | 67656 | 74156 | 74056 | 67756 |
| 357 007 | **C2** | P | *C2* | EM | 67657 | 74157 | 74057 | 67757 |
| 357 008 | **C2** | P | *C2* | EM | 67658 | 74158 | 74058 | 67758 |
| 357 009 | **C2** | P | *C2* | EM | 67659 | 74159 | 74059 | 67759 |
| 357 010 | **C2** | P | *C2* | EM | 67660 | 74160 | 74060 | 67760 |
| 357 011 | **C2** | P | *C2* | EM | 67661 | 74161 | 74061 | 67761 |
| 357 012 | **C2** | P | *C2* | EM | 67662 | 74162 | 74062 | 67762 |
| 357 013 | **C2** | P | *C2* | EM | 67663 | 74163 | 74063 | 67763 |
| 357 014 | **C2** | P | *C2* | EM | 67664 | 74164 | 74064 | 67764 |

| 357 015 | **C2** | P | *C2* | EM | 67665 | 74165 | 74065 | 67765 |
| 357 016 | **C2** | P | *C2* | EM | 67666 | 74166 | 74066 | 67766 |
| 357 017 | **C2** | P | *C2* | EM | 67667 | 74167 | 74067 | 67767 |
| 357 018 | **C2** | P | *C2* | EM | 67668 | 74168 | 74068 | 67768 |
| 357 019 | **C2** | P | *C2* | EM | 67669 | 74169 | 74069 | 67769 |
| 357 020 | **C2** | P | *C2* | EM | 67670 | 74170 | 74070 | 67770 |
| 357 021 | **C2** | P | *C2* | EM | 67671 | 74171 | 74071 | 67771 |
| 357 022 | **C2** | P | *C2* | EM | 67672 | 74172 | 74072 | 67772 |
| 357 023 | **C2** | P | *C2* | EM | 67673 | 74173 | 74073 | 67773 |
| 357 024 | **C2** | P | *C2* | EM | 67674 | 74174 | 74074 | 67774 |
| 357 025 | **C2** | P | *C2* | EM | 67675 | 74175 | 74075 | 67775 |
| 357 026 | **C2** | P | *C2* | EM | 67676 | 74176 | 74076 | 67776 |
| 357 027 | **C2** | P | *C2* | EM | 67677 | 74177 | 74077 | 67777 |
| 357 028 | **C2** | P | *C2* | EM | 67678 | 74178 | 74078 | 67778 |
| 357 029 | **C2** | P | *C2* | EM | 67679 | 74179 | 74079 | 67779 |
| 357 030 | **C2** | P | *C2* | EM | 67680 | 74180 | 74080 | 67780 |
| 357 031 | **C2** | P | *C2* | EM | 67681 | 74181 | 74081 | 67781 |
| 357 032 | **C2** | P | *C2* | EM | 67682 | 74182 | 74082 | 67782 |
| 357 033 | **C2** | P | *C2* | EM | 67683 | 74183 | 74083 | 67783 |
| 357 034 | **C2** | P | *C2* | EM | 67684 | 74184 | 74084 | 67784 |
| 357 035 | **C2** | P | *C2* | EM | 67685 | 74185 | 74085 | 67785 |
| 357 036 | **C2** | P | *C2* | EM | 67686 | 74186 | 74086 | 67786 |
| 357 037 | **C2** | P | *C2* | EM | 67687 | 74187 | 74087 | 67787 |
| 357 038 | **C2** | P | *C2* | EM | 67688 | 74188 | 74088 | 67788 |
| 357 039 | **C2** | P | *C2* | EM | 67689 | 74189 | 74089 | 67789 |
| 357 040 | **C2** | P | *C2* | EM | 67690 | 74190 | 74090 | 67790 |
| 357 041 | **C2** | P | *C2* | EM | 67691 | 74191 | 74091 | 67791 |
| 357 042 | **C2** | P | *C2* | EM | 67692 | 74192 | 74092 | 67792 |
| 357 043 | **C2** | P | *C2* | EM | 67693 | 74193 | 74093 | 67793 |
| 357 044 | **C2** | P | *C2* | EM | 67694 | 74194 | 74094 | 67794 |
| 357 045 | **C2** | P | *C2* | EM | 67695 | 74195 | 74095 | 67795 |
| 357 046 | **C2** | P | *C2* | EM | 67696 | 74196 | 74096 | 67796 |

**Names (carried on DMSO(A) and DMSO(B) (one plate on each)):**

| 357 001 | BARRY FLAXMAN |
| 357 002 | ARTHUR LEWIS STRIDE 1841–1922 |
| 357 003 | JASON LEONARD |
| 357 004 | TONY AMOS |
| 357 011 | JOHN LOWING |
| 357 028 | London, Tilbury & Southend Railway 1854–2004 |
| 357 029 | THOMAS WHITELEGG 1840–1922 |
| 357 030 | ROBERT HARBEN WHITELEGG 1871–1957 |

**Class 357/2.** Owned by Angel Trains.

**Advertising livery:** Vehicle 74716 (357 216). "Cough-free zone" (Benylin). Orange and yellow.

**DMSO(A).** Bombardier Derby 2001–2002. –/71. 40.7 t.
**MSO.** Bombardier Derby 2001–2002. –/78. 36.7 t.
**PTSO.** Bombardier Derby 2001–2002. –/62 1TD 2W. 39.5 t.
**DMSO(B).** Bombardier Derby 2001–2002. –/71. 40.7 t.

| 357 201 | C2 | A | C2 | EM | 68601 | 74701 | 74601 | 68701 |
| 357 202 | C2 | A | C2 | EM | 68602 | 74702 | 74602 | 68702 |
| 357 203 | C2 | A | C2 | EM | 68603 | 74703 | 74603 | 68703 |
| 357 204 | C2 | A | C2 | EM | 68604 | 74704 | 74604 | 68704 |
| 357 205 | C2 | A | C2 | EM | 68605 | 74705 | 74605 | 68705 |
| 357 206 | C2 | A | C2 | EM | 68606 | 74706 | 74606 | 68706 |
| 357 207 | C2 | A | C2 | EM | 68607 | 74707 | 74607 | 68707 |
| 357 208 | C2 | A | C2 | EM | 68608 | 74708 | 74608 | 68708 |
| 357 209 | C2 | A | C2 | EM | 68609 | 74709 | 74609 | 68709 |
| 357 210 | C2 | A | C2 | EM | 68610 | 74710 | 74610 | 68710 |
| 357 211 | C2 | A | C2 | EM | 68611 | 74711 | 74611 | 68711 |
| 357 212 | C2 | A | C2 | EM | 68612 | 74712 | 74612 | 68712 |
| 357 213 | C2 | A | C2 | EM | 68613 | 74713 | 74613 | 68713 |
| 357 214 | C2 | A | C2 | EM | 68614 | 74714 | 74614 | 68714 |
| 357 215 | C2 | A | C2 | EM | 68615 | 74715 | 74615 | 68715 |
| 357 216 | AL | A | C2 | EM | 68616 | 74716 | 74616 | 68716 |
| 357 217 | C2 | A | C2 | EM | 68617 | 74717 | 74617 | 68717 |
| 357 218 | C2 | A | C2 | EM | 68618 | 74718 | 74618 | 68718 |
| 357 219 | C2 | A | C2 | EM | 68619 | 74719 | 74619 | 68719 |
| 357 220 | C2 | A | C2 | EM | 68620 | 74720 | 74620 | 68720 |
| 357 221 | C2 | A | C2 | EM | 68621 | 74721 | 74621 | 68721 |
| 357 222 | C2 | A | C2 | EM | 68622 | 74722 | 74622 | 68722 |
| 357 223 | C2 | A | C2 | EM | 68623 | 74723 | 74623 | 68723 |
| 357 224 | C2 | A | C2 | EM | 68624 | 74724 | 74624 | 68724 |
| 357 225 | C2 | A | C2 | EM | 68625 | 74725 | 74625 | 68725 |
| 357 226 | C2 | A | C2 | EM | 68626 | 74726 | 74626 | 68726 |
| 357 227 | C2 | A | C2 | EM | 68627 | 74727 | 74627 | 68727 |
| 357 228 | C2 | A | C2 | EM | 68628 | 74728 | 74628 | 68728 |

**Names (carried on DMSO(A) and DMSO(B) (one plate on each)):**

| 357 201 | KEN BIRD |
| 357 202 | KENNY MITCHELL |
| 357 203 | HENRY PUMFRETT |
| 357 204 | DEREK FOWERS |
| 357 209 | JAMES SNELLING |

# CLASS 360/0          DESIRO UK          SIEMENS

One Great Eastern units.

**Formation:** DMCO–PTSO–TSO–DMCO.
**Systems:** 25 kV AC overhead.
**Construction:** Welded aluminium.      **Doors:** Sliding plug.
**Traction Motors:** 4 Siemens 1TB2016-0GB02 asynchronous of 250 kW.
**Gangways:** Within unit.               **Bogies:** SGP SF5000.
**Couplers:** Dellner 12.                **Maximum Speed:** 100 m.p.h.
**Seating Layout:** 1: 2+2 facing, 2: 3+2 facing/unidirectional.
**Dimensions:** 20.34 x 2.80 m.          **Multiple Working:** Within class.
**Braking:** Disc & regenerative.
**Heating & ventilation:** Air conditioning.

**DMCO(A).** Siemens Uerdingen 2002–2003. 8/59. 45.0 t.
**PTSO.** Siemens Wien 2002–2003. –/69 1TD 2W. 43.0 t.
**TSO.** Siemens Wien 2002–2003. –/78. 35.0 t.
**DMCO(B).** Siemens Uerdingen 2002–2003. 8/59. 45.0 t.

| | | | | | | | | |
|---|---|---|---|---|---|---|---|---|
| 360 101 | **FS** | A | *1E* | IL | 65551 | 72551 | 74551 | 68551 |
| 360 102 | **FS** | A | *1E* | IL | 65552 | 72552 | 74552 | 68552 |
| 360 103 | **FS** | A | *1E* | IL | 65553 | 72553 | 74553 | 68553 |
| 360 104 | **FS** | A | *1E* | IL | 65554 | 72554 | 74554 | 68554 |
| 360 105 | **FS** | A | *1E* | IL | 65555 | 72555 | 74555 | 68555 |
| 360 106 | **FS** | A | *1E* | IL | 65556 | 72556 | 74556 | 68556 |
| 360 107 | **FS** | A | *1E* | IL | 65557 | 72557 | 74557 | 68557 |
| 360 108 | **FS** | A | *1E* | IL | 65558 | 72558 | 74558 | 68558 |
| 360 109 | **FS** | A | *1E* | IL | 65559 | 72559 | 74559 | 68559 |
| 360 110 | **FS** | A | *1E* | IL | 65560 | 72560 | 74560 | 68560 |
| 360 111 | **FS** | A | *1E* | IL | 65561 | 72561 | 74561 | 68561 |
| 360 112 | **FS** | A | *1E* | IL | 65562 | 72562 | 74562 | 68562 |
| 360 113 | **FS** | A | *1E* | IL | 65563 | 72563 | 74563 | 68563 |
| 360 114 | **FS** | A | *1E* | IL | 65564 | 72564 | 74564 | 68564 |
| 360 115 | **FS** | A | *1E* | IL | 65565 | 72565 | 74565 | 68565 |
| 360 116 | **FS** | A | *1E* | IL | 65566 | 72566 | 74566 | 68566 |
| 360 117 | **FS** | A | *1E* | IL | 65567 | 72567 | 74567 | 68567 |
| 360 118 | **FS** | A | *1E* | IL | 65568 | 72568 | 74568 | 68568 |
| 360 119 | **FS** | A | *1E* | IL | 65569 | 72569 | 74569 | 68569 |
| 360 120 | **FS** | A | *1E* | IL | 65570 | 72570 | 74570 | 68570 |
| 360 121 | **FS** | A | *1E* | IL | 65571 | 72571 | 74571 | 68571 |

# CLASS 360/2      DESIRO UK      SIEMENS

Original 4-car Class 350 testbed units rebuilt for use by Heathrow Express on Paddington–Heathrow Airport stopping services ("Heathrow Connect").

All units to be made up to 5-car sets in 2006 (72431–72434 will be inserted into 360 201–360 204). A fifth unit (360 205) was delivered in late 2005 as a 5-car set.

**Formations:** DMSO–PTSO–TSO–(TSO)–DMSO.
**Systems:** 25 kV AC overhead.
**Construction:** Welded aluminium.     **Doors:** Sliding plug.
**Traction Motors:** 4 Siemens 1TB2016-0GB02 asynchronous of 250 kW.
**Gangways:** Within unit.     **Bogies:** SGP SF5000.
**Couplers:** Dellner 12.     **Maximum Speed:** 100 m.p.h.
**Seating Layout:** 3+2 facing/unidirectional.
**Dimensions:** 20.34 x 2.80 m.     **Multiple Working:** Within class.
**Braking:** Disc & regenerative.
**Heating & ventilation:** Air conditioning.

**DMSO(A).** Siemens Uerdingen 2002–2006. –/63. 44.8 t.
**PTSO.** Siemens Uerdingen 2002–2006. –/66 1TD 2W. 44.2 t.
**TSO.** Siemens Uerdingen 2002–2006. –/74. 34.8 t.
**TSO.** Siemens Uerdingen 2005–2006. –/74. 34.8 t.
**DMSO(B).** Siemens Uerdingen 2002–2006. –/63. 44.4 t.

**IMPORTANT NOTE:** Vehicles 72431–72434 are additional fifth vehicles for 360 201–360 204, due to be inserted in these units in 2006.

| | | | | | | | | |
|---|---|---|---|---|---|---|---|---|
| 360 201 | **HC** | HE *HC* | OH | 78431 | 63421 | 72421 | 72431 | 78441 |
| 360 202 | **HC** | HE *HC* | OH | 78432 | 63422 | 72422 | 72432 | 78442 |
| 360 203 | **HC** | HE *HC* | OH | 78433 | 63423 | 72423 | 72433 | 78443 |
| 360 204 | **HC** | HE *HC* | OH | 78434 | 63424 | 72424 | 72434 | 78444 |
| 360 205 | **HC** | HE *HC* | OH | 78435 | 63425 | 72425 | 72435 | 78445 |

# CLASS 365 NETWORKER EXPRESS ABB YORK

WAGN outer suburban units.

**Formations:** DMCO–TSO–PTSO–DMCO.
**Systems:** 25 kV AC overhead. All units have now had their third rail shoegear removed.
**Construction:** Welded aluminium alloy.
**Traction Motors:** Four GEC-Alsthom G354CX asynchronous of 157 kW.
**Doors:** Sliding plug.
**Gangways:** Within unit.     **Bogies:** ABB P3-16/T3-16.
**Couplers:** Tightlock.     **Maximum Speed:** 100 m.p.h.
**Seating Layout:** 1: 2+2 facing, 2: 3+2 facing.
**Dimensions:** 20.89 x 2.81 m.
**Braking:** Disc, rheostatic & regenerative.
**Multiple Working:** Within class only.

**DMCO(A).** Lot No. 31133 1994–1995. 12/56. 41.7 t.
**TSO.** Lot No. 31134 1994–1995. –/59 1TD. 32.9 t.
**PTSO.** Lot No. 31135 1994–1995. –/68 1T. 34.6 t.
**DMCO(B).** Lot No. 31136 1994–1995. 12/56. 41.7 t.

**Advertising liveries:** 365 510 Cambridge & Ely Cathedral cities (blue and white with various images).
365 519 Peterborough, environment capital (blue and white with various images).
365 531 Nelson's County, Norfolk (blue and white with various images).
365 540 Garden cities of Hertfordshire (blue and white with various images).

| | | | | | | | |
|---|---|---|---|---|---|---|---|
| 365 501 | **NT** | H | *WN* | HE | 65894 | 72241 | 72240 | 65935 |
| 365 502 | **NT** | H | *WN* | HE | 65895 | 72243 | 72242 | 65936 |
| 365 503 | **NT** | H | *WN* | HE | 65896 | 72245 | 72244 | 65937 |
| 365 504 | **NT** | H | *WN* | HE | 65897 | 72247 | 72246 | 65938 |
| 365 505 | **NT** | H | *WN* | HE | 65898 | 72249 | 72248 | 65939 |
| 365 506 | **NT** | H | *WN* | HE | 65899 | 72251 | 72250 | 65940 |
| 365 507 | **NT** | H | *WN* | HE | 65900 | 72253 | 72252 | 65941 |
| 365 508 | **NT** | H | *WN* | HE | 65901 | 72255 | 72254 | 65942 |
| 365 509 | **NT** | H | *WN* | HE | 65902 | 72257 | 72256 | 65943 |
| 365 510 | **AL** | H | *WN* | HE | 65903 | 72259 | 72258 | 65944 |
| 365 511 | **NT** | H | *WN* | HE | 65904 | 72261 | 72260 | 65945 |
| 365 512 | **NT** | H | *WN* | HE | 65905 | 72263 | 72262 | 65946 |
| 365 513 | **NT** | H | *WN* | HE | 65906 | 72265 | 72264 | 65947 |
| 365 514 | **NT** | H | *WN* | HE | 65907 | 72267 | 72266 | 65948 |
| 365 515 | **NT** | H | *WN* | HE | 65908 | 72269 | 72268 | 65949 |

| | | | | | | | |
|---|---|---|---|---|---|---|---|
| 365 516 | **NT** | H | *WN* | HE | 65909 | 72271 | 72270 | 65950 |
| 365 517 | **NT** | H | *WN* | HE | 65910 | 72273 | 72272 | 65951 |
| 365 518 | **NT** | H | *WN* | HE | 65911 | 72275 | 72274 | 65952 |
| 365 519 | **AL** | H | *WN* | HE | 65912 | 72277 | 72276 | 65953 |
| 365 520 | **NT** | H | *WN* | HE | 65913 | 72279 | 72278 | 65954 |
| 365 521 | **NT** | H | *WN* | HE | 65914 | 72281 | 72280 | 65955 |
| 365 522 | **NT** | H | *WN* | HE | 65915 | 72283 | 72282 | 65956 |
| 365 523 | **NT** | H | *WN* | HE | 65916 | 72285 | 72284 | 65957 |
| 365 524 | **NT** | H | *WN* | HE | 65917 | 72287 | 72286 | 65958 |
| 365 525 | **NT** | H | *WN* | HE | 65918 | 72289 | 72288 | 65959 |
| 365 526 | **NT** | H | | ZC | 65919 | 72291 | 72290 | 65960 |
| 365 527 | **NT** | H | *WN* | HE | 65920 | 72293 | 72292 | 65961 |
| 365 528 | **NT** | H | *WN* | HE | 65921 | 72295 | 72294 | 65962 |
| 365 529 | **NT** | H | *WN* | HE | 65922 | 72297 | 72296 | 65963 |
| 365 530 | **NT** | H | *WN* | HE | 65923 | 72299 | 72298 | 65964 |
| 365 531 | **AL** | H | *WN* | HE | 65924 | 72301 | 72300 | 65965 |
| 365 532 | **NT** | H | *WN* | HE | 65925 | 72303 | 72302 | 65966 |
| 365 533 | **NT** | H | *WN* | HE | 65926 | 72305 | 72304 | 65967 |
| 365 534 | **NT** | H | *WN* | HE | 65927 | 72307 | 72306 | 65968 |
| 365 535 | **NT** | H | *WN* | HE | 65928 | 72309 | 72308 | 65969 |
| 365 536 | **NT** | H | *WN* | HE | 65929 | 72311 | 72310 | 65970 |
| 365 537 | **NT** | H | *WN* | HE | 65930 | 72313 | 72312 | 65971 |
| 365 538 | **NT** | H | *WN* | HE | 65931 | 72315 | 72314 | 65972 |
| 365 539 | **NT** | H | *WN* | HE | 65932 | 72317 | 72316 | 65973 |
| 365 540 | **AL** | H | *WN* | HE | 65933 | 72319 | 72318 | 65974 |
| 365 541 | **NT** | H | *WN* | HE | 65934 | 72321 | 72320 | 65975 |

**Name (carried on one DMCO):** 365 518 The Fenman

# CLASS 375 ELECTROSTAR
## ADTRANZ/BOMBARDIER DERBY

South Eastern Trains express and outer suburban units.

**Systems:** 25 kV AC overhead/750 V DC third rail (some third rail only with provision for retro-fitting of AC equipment).
**Formations:** Various.
**Construction:** Welded aluminium alloy underframe, sides and roof with steel ends. All sections bolted together.
**Traction Motors:** Two Adtranz asynchronous of 250 kW.
**Doors:** Sliding plug.                    **Bogies:** Adtranz P3-25/T3-25.
**Gangways:** Throughout.              **Maximum Speed:** 100 m.p.h.
**Couplers:** Dellner 12.                 **Heating & ventilation:** Air conditioning.
**Seating Layout:** 1: 2+2 facing/unidirectional (seats behind drivers cab in each DMCO). 2: 2+2 facing/unidirectional (375/3, 375/6, 375/7 and 375/8), 3+2 facing/unidirectional (375/9).
**Dimensions:** 20.40/19.99 x 2.80 m.      **Braking:** Disc & regenerative.
**Multiple Working:** Within class and with Classes 376 and 377.

**Class 375/3.** Express units. 750 V DC only. DMCO–TSO–DMCO.

**DMCO(A).** Bombardier Derby 2001–2002. 12/48. 43.8 t.
**TSO.** Bombardier Derby 2001–2002. –/56 1TD 2W. 35.5 t.
**DMCO(B).** Bombardier Derby 2001–2002. 12/48. 43.8 t.

| | | | | | | | |
|---|---|---|---|---|---|---|---|
| 375 301 | **CN** | H | *SE* | RM | 67921 | 74351 | 67931 |
| 375 302 | **CN** | H | *SE* | RM | 67922 | 74352 | 67932 |
| 375 303 | **CN** | H | *SE* | RM | 67923 | 74353 | 67933 |
| 375 304 | **CN** | H | *SE* | RM | 67924 | 74354 | 67934 |
| 375 305 | **CN** | H | *SE* | RM | 67925 | 74355 | 67935 |
| 375 306 | **CN** | H | *SE* | RM | 67926 | 74356 | 67936 |
| 375 307 | **CN** | H | *SE* | RM | 67927 | 74357 | 67937 |
| 375 308 | **CN** | H | *SE* | RM | 67928 | 74358 | 67938 |
| 375 309 | **CN** | H | *SE* | RM | 67929 | 74359 | 67939 |
| 375 310 | **CN** | H | *SE* | RM | 67930 | 74360 | 67940 |

**Class 375/6.** Express units. 25 kV AC/750 V DC. DMCO–MSO–PTSO–DMCO.

**DMCO(A).** Adtranz Derby 1999–2001. 12/48. 46.2 t.
**MSO.** Adtranz Derby 1999–2001. –/66 1T. 40.5 t.
**PTSO.** Adtranz Derby 1999–2001. –/56 1TD 2W. 40.7 t.
**DMCO(B).** Adtranz Derby 1999–2001. 12/48. 46.2 t.

**Non-standard livery:** 375 610 is as **CN** but with blue doors instead of yellow and a gold band instead of a grey band on the lower bodyside (a special "Golden Jubilee" livery).

| | | | | | | | | |
|---|---|---|---|---|---|---|---|---|
| 375 601 | **CN** | H | *SE* | RM | 67801 | 74251 | 74201 | 67851 |
| 375 602 | **CN** | H | *SE* | RM | 67802 | 74252 | 74202 | 67852 |
| 375 603 | **CN** | H | *SE* | RM | 67803 | 74253 | 74203 | 67853 |
| 375 604 | **CN** | H | *SE* | RM | 67804 | 74254 | 74204 | 67854 |
| 375 605 | **CN** | H | *SE* | RM | 67805 | 74255 | 74205 | 67855 |
| 375 606 | **CN** | H | *SE* | RM | 67806 | 74256 | 74206 | 67856 |
| 375 607 | **CN** | H | *SE* | RM | 67807 | 74257 | 74207 | 67857 |
| 375 608 | **CN** | H | *SE* | RM | 67808 | 74258 | 74208 | 67858 |
| 375 609 | **CN** | H | *SE* | RM | 67809 | 74259 | 74209 | 67859 |
| 375 610 | **0** | H | *SE* | RM | 67810 | 74260 | 74210 | 67860 |
| 375 611 | **CN** | H | *SE* | RM | 67811 | 74261 | 74211 | 67861 |
| 375 612 | **CN** | H | *SE* | RM | 67812 | 74262 | 74212 | 67862 |
| 375 613 | **CN** | H | *SE* | RM | 67813 | 74263 | 74213 | 67863 |
| 375 614 | **CN** | H | *SE* | RM | 67814 | 74264 | 74214 | 67864 |
| 375 615 | **CN** | H | *SE* | RM | 67815 | 74265 | 74215 | 67865 |
| 375 616 | **CN** | H | *SE* | RM | 67816 | 74266 | 74216 | 67866 |
| 375 617 | **CN** | H | *SE* | RM | 67817 | 74267 | 74217 | 67867 |
| 375 618 | **CN** | H | *SE* | RM | 67818 | 74268 | 74218 | 67868 |
| 375 619 | **CN** | H | *SE* | RM | 67819 | 74269 | 74219 | 67869 |
| 375 620 | **CN** | H | *SE* | RM | 67820 | 74270 | 74220 | 67870 |
| 375 621 | **CN** | H | *SE* | RM | 67821 | 74271 | 74221 | 67871 |
| 375 622 | **CN** | H | *SE* | RM | 67822 | 74272 | 74222 | 67872 |
| 375 623 | **CN** | H | *SE* | RM | 67823 | 74273 | 74223 | 67873 |
| 375 624 | **CN** | H | *SE* | RM | 67824 | 74274 | 74224 | 67874 |
| 375 625 | **CN** | H | *SE* | RM | 67825 | 74275 | 74225 | 67875 |
| 375 626 | **CN** | H | *SE* | RM | 67826 | 74276 | 74226 | 67876 |

| | | | | | | | |
|---|---|---|---|---|---|---|---|
| 375 627 | **CN** | H | *SE* | RM | 67827 | 74277 | 74227 | 67877 |
| 375 628 | **CN** | H | *SE* | RM | 67828 | 74278 | 74228 | 67878 |
| 375 629 | **CN** | H | *SE* | RM | 67829 | 74279 | 74229 | 67879 |
| 375 630 | **CN** | H | *SE* | RM | 67830 | 74280 | 74230 | 67880 |

**Names (carried on one side of each MSO or PTSO):**

| | | | |
|---|---|---|---|
| 375 608 | Bromley Travelwise | 375 610 | Royal Tunbridge Wells |
| 375 611 | Dr. William Harvey | 375 619 | Driver John Neve |
| 375 623 | Hospice in the Weald | 375 624 | White Cliffs Country |

**Class 375/7.** Express units. 750 V DC only. DMCO–MSO–TSO–DMCO.

**DMCO(A).** Bombardier Derby 2001–2002. 12/48. 43.8 t.
**MSO.** Bombardier Derby 2001–2002. –/66 1T. 36.4 t.
**TSO.** Bombardier Derby 2001–2002. –/56 1TD 2W. 34.1 t.
**DMCO(B).** Bombardier Derby 2001–2002. 12/48. 43.8 t.

| | | | | | | | |
|---|---|---|---|---|---|---|---|
| 375 701 | **CN** | H | *SE* | RM | 67831 | 74281 | 74231 | 67881 |
| 375 702 | **CN** | H | *SE* | RM | 67832 | 74282 | 74232 | 67882 |
| 375 703 | **CN** | H | *SE* | RM | 67833 | 74283 | 74233 | 67883 |
| 375 704 | **CN** | H | *SE* | RM | 67834 | 74284 | 74234 | 67884 |
| 375 705 | **CN** | H | *SE* | RM | 67835 | 74285 | 74235 | 67885 |
| 375 706 | **CN** | H | *SE* | RM | 67836 | 74286 | 74236 | 67886 |
| 375 707 | **CN** | H | *SE* | RM | 67837 | 74287 | 74237 | 67887 |
| 375 708 | **CN** | H | *SE* | RM | 67838 | 74288 | 74238 | 67888 |
| 375 709 | **CN** | H | *SE* | RM | 67839 | 74289 | 74239 | 67889 |
| 375 710 | **CN** | H | *SE* | RM | 67840 | 74290 | 74240 | 67890 |
| 375 711 | **CN** | H | *SE* | RM | 67841 | 74291 | 74241 | 67891 |
| 375 712 | **CN** | H | *SE* | RM | 67842 | 74292 | 74242 | 67892 |
| 375 713 | **CN** | H | *SE* | RM | 67843 | 74293 | 74243 | 67893 |
| 375 714 | **CN** | H | *SE* | RM | 67844 | 74294 | 74244 | 67894 |
| 375 715 | **CN** | H | *SE* | RM | 67845 | 74295 | 74245 | 67895 |

**Names (carried on one side of each MSO or TSO):**

| | |
|---|---|
| 375 701 | Kent Air Ambulance Explorer |
| 375 703 | Dickens Traveller |

**Class 375/8.** Express units. 750 V DC only. DMCO–MSO–TSO–DMCO.

**DMCO(A).** Bombardier Derby 2004. 12/48. 43.3 t.
**MSO.** Bombardier Derby 2004. –/66 1T. 39.8 t.
**TSO.** Bombardier Derby 2004. –/52 1TD 2W. 35.9 t.
**DMCO(B).** Bombardier Derby 2004. 12/52. 43.3 t.

| | | | | | | | |
|---|---|---|---|---|---|---|---|
| 375 801 | **CN** | H | *SE* | RM | 73301 | 79001 | 78201 | 73701 |
| 375 802 | **CN** | H | *SE* | RM | 73302 | 79002 | 78202 | 73702 |
| 375 803 | **CN** | H | *SE* | RM | 73303 | 79003 | 78203 | 73703 |
| 375 804 | **CN** | H | *SE* | RM | 73304 | 79004 | 78204 | 73704 |
| 375 805 | **CN** | H | *SE* | RM | 73305 | 79005 | 78205 | 73705 |
| 375 806 | **CN** | H | *SE* | RM | 73306 | 79006 | 78206 | 73706 |
| 375 807 | **CN** | H | *SE* | RM | 73307 | 79007 | 78207 | 73707 |
| 375 808 | **CN** | H | *SE* | RM | 73308 | 79008 | 78208 | 73708 |
| 375 809 | **CN** | H | *SE* | RM | 73309 | 79009 | 78209 | 73709 |

| | | | | | | | | |
|---|---|---|---|---|---|---|---|---|
| 375 810 | **CN** | H | *SE* | RM | 73310 | 79010 | 78210 | 73710 |
| 375 811 | **CN** | H | *SE* | RM | 73311 | 79011 | 78211 | 73711 |
| 375 812 | **CN** | H | *SE* | RM | 73312 | 79012 | 78212 | 73712 |
| 375 813 | **CN** | H | *SE* | RM | 73313 | 79013 | 78213 | 73713 |
| 375 814 | **CN** | H | *SE* | RM | 73314 | 79014 | 78214 | 73714 |
| 375 815 | **CN** | H | *SE* | RM | 73315 | 79015 | 78215 | 73715 |
| 375 816 | **CN** | H | *SE* | RM | 73316 | 79016 | 78216 | 73716 |
| 375 817 | **CN** | H | *SE* | RM | 73317 | 79017 | 78217 | 73717 |
| 375 818 | **CN** | H | *SE* | RM | 73318 | 79018 | 78218 | 73718 |
| 375 819 | **CN** | H | *SE* | RM | 73319 | 79019 | 78219 | 73719 |
| 375 820 | **CN** | H | *SE* | RM | 73320 | 79020 | 78220 | 73720 |
| 375 821 | **CN** | H | *SE* | RM | 73321 | 79021 | 78221 | 73721 |
| 375 822 | **CN** | H | *SE* | RM | 73322 | 79022 | 78222 | 73722 |
| 375 823 | **CN** | H | *SE* | RM | 73323 | 79023 | 78223 | 73723 |
| 375 824 | **CN** | H | *SE* | RM | 73324 | 79024 | 78224 | 73724 |
| 375 825 | **CN** | H | *SE* | RM | 73325 | 79025 | 78225 | 73725 |
| 375 826 | **CN** | H | *SE* | RM | 73326 | 79026 | 78226 | 73726 |
| 375 827 | **CN** | H | *SE* | RM | 73327 | 79027 | 78227 | 73727 |
| 375 828 | **CN** | H | *SE* | RM | 73328 | 79028 | 78228 | 73728 |
| 375 829 | **CN** | H | *SE* | RM | 73329 | 79029 | 78229 | 73729 |
| 375 830 | **CN** | H | *SE* | RM | 73330 | 79030 | 78230 | 73730 |

**Name (carried on one side of each MSO or TSO):**

375 830     City of London

**Class 375/9.** Outer suburban units. 750 V DC only. DMCO–MSO–TSO–DMCO.

**DMCO(A).** Bombardier Derby 2003–2004. 12/59. 43.4 t.
**MSO.** Bombardier Derby 2003–2004. –/73 1T. 39.3 t.
**TSO.** Bombardier Derby 2003–2004. –/59 1TD 2W. 35.6 t.
**DMCO(B).** Bombardier Derby 2003–2004. 12/59. 43.4 t.

| | | | | | | | | |
|---|---|---|---|---|---|---|---|---|
| 375 901 | **CN** | H | *SE* | RM | 73331 | 79031 | 79061 | 73731 |
| 375 902 | **CN** | H | *SE* | RM | 73332 | 79032 | 79062 | 73732 |
| 375 903 | **CN** | H | *SE* | RM | 73333 | 79033 | 79063 | 73733 |
| 375 904 | **CN** | H | *SE* | RM | 73334 | 79034 | 79064 | 73734 |
| 375 905 | **CN** | H | *SE* | RM | 73335 | 79035 | 79065 | 73735 |
| 375 906 | **CN** | H | *SE* | RM | 73336 | 79036 | 79066 | 73736 |
| 375 907 | **CN** | H | *SE* | RM | 73337 | 79037 | 79067 | 73737 |
| 375 908 | **CN** | H | *SE* | RM | 73338 | 79038 | 79068 | 73738 |
| 375 909 | **CN** | H | *SE* | RM | 73339 | 79039 | 79069 | 73739 |
| 375 910 | **CN** | H | *SE* | RM | 73340 | 79040 | 79070 | 73740 |
| 375 911 | **CN** | H | *SE* | RM | 73341 | 79041 | 79071 | 73741 |
| 375 912 | **CN** | H | *SE* | RM | 73342 | 79042 | 79072 | 73742 |
| 375 913 | **CN** | H | *SE* | RM | 73343 | 79043 | 79073 | 73743 |
| 375 914 | **CN** | H | *SE* | RM | 73344 | 79044 | 79074 | 73744 |
| 375 915 | **CN** | H | *SE* | RM | 73345 | 79045 | 79075 | 73745 |
| 375 916 | **CN** | H | *SE* | RM | 73346 | 79046 | 79076 | 73746 |
| 375 917 | **CN** | H | *SE* | RM | 73347 | 79047 | 79077 | 73747 |
| 375 918 | **CN** | H | *SE* | RM | 73348 | 79048 | 79078 | 73748 |
| 375 919 | **CN** | H | *SE* | RM | 73349 | 79049 | 79079 | 73749 |
| 375 920 | **CN** | H | *SE* | RM | 73350 | 79050 | 79080 | 73750 |

| 375 921 | CN | H | *SE* | RM | 73351 | 79051 | 79081 | 73751 |
| 375 922 | CN | H | *SE* | RM | 73352 | 79052 | 79082 | 73752 |
| 375 923 | CN | H | *SE* | RM | 73353 | 79053 | 79083 | 73753 |
| 375 924 | CN | H | *SE* | RM | 73354 | 79054 | 79084 | 73754 |
| 375 925 | CN | H | *SE* | RM | 73355 | 79055 | 79085 | 73755 |
| 375 926 | CN | H | *SE* | RM | 73356 | 79056 | 79086 | 73756 |
| 375 927 | CN | H | *SE* | RM | 73357 | 79057 | 79087 | 73757 |

# CLASS 376 ELECTROSTAR BOMBARDIER DERBY

South Eastern Trains inner suburban units.

**Systems:** 750 V DC third rail.
**Formation:** DMSO–MSO–TSO–MSO–DMSO.
**Construction:** Welded aluminium alloy underframe, sides and roof with steel ends. All sections bolted together. **Doors:** Sliding.
**Traction Motors:** Two Bombardier asynchronous of 250 kW.
**Gangways:** Within unit. **Bogies:** Adtranz P3-25/T3-25.
**Couplers:** Dellner 12. **Maximum Speed:** 75 m.p.h.
**Seating Layout:** 2+2 low density facing (with more standee room and greater use of "perch" seats).
**Dimensions:** 20.40/19.99 x 2.80 m. **Braking:** Disc & regenerative.
**Heating & ventilation:** Pressure heating and ventilation.
**Multiple Working:** Within class and with Classes 375 and 377.

**DMSO(A).** Bombardier Derby 2004–2005. –/42 1W. 42.1 t.
**MSO.** Bombardier Derby 2004–2005. –/48. 36.2 t.
**TSO.** Bombardier Derby 2004–2005. –/48. 36.3 t.
**DMSO(B).** Bombardier Derby 2004–2005. –/42 1W. 42.1 t.

| 376 001 | CN | H | *SE* | SG | 61101 | 63301 | 64301 | 63501 | 61601 |
| 376 002 | CN | H | *SE* | SG | 61102 | 63302 | 64302 | 63502 | 61602 |
| 376 003 | CN | H | *SE* | SG | 61103 | 63303 | 64303 | 63503 | 61603 |
| 376 004 | CN | H | *SE* | SG | 61104 | 63304 | 64304 | 63504 | 61604 |
| 376 005 | CN | H | *SE* | SG | 61105 | 63305 | 64305 | 63505 | 61605 |
| 376 006 | CN | H | *SE* | SG | 61106 | 63306 | 64306 | 63506 | 61606 |
| 376 007 | CN | H | *SE* | SG | 61107 | 63307 | 64307 | 63507 | 61607 |
| 376 008 | CN | H | *SE* | SG | 61108 | 63308 | 64308 | 63508 | 61608 |
| 376 009 | CN | H | *SE* | SG | 61109 | 63309 | 64309 | 63509 | 61609 |
| 376 010 | CN | H | *SE* | SG | 61110 | 63310 | 64310 | 63510 | 61610 |
| 376 011 | CN | H | *SE* | SG | 61111 | 63311 | 64311 | 63511 | 61611 |
| 376 012 | CN | H | *SE* | SG | 61112 | 63312 | 64312 | 63512 | 61612 |
| 376 013 | CN | H | *SE* | SG | 61113 | 63313 | 64313 | 63513 | 61613 |
| 376 014 | CN | H | *SE* | SG | 61114 | 63314 | 64314 | 63514 | 61614 |
| 376 015 | CN | H | *SE* | SG | 61115 | 63315 | 64315 | 63515 | 61615 |
| 376 016 | CN | H | *SE* | SG | 61116 | 63316 | 64316 | 63516 | 61616 |
| 376 017 | CN | H | *SE* | SG | 61117 | 63317 | 64317 | 63517 | 61617 |
| 376 018 | CN | H | *SE* | SG | 61118 | 63318 | 64318 | 63518 | 61618 |
| 376 019 | CN | H | *SE* | SG | 61119 | 63319 | 64319 | 63519 | 61619 |
| 376 020 | CN | H | *SE* | SG | 61120 | 63320 | 64320 | 63520 | 61620 |
| 376 021 | CN | H | *SE* | SG | 61121 | 63321 | 64321 | 63521 | 61621 |
| 376 022 | CN | H | *SE* | SG | 61122 | 63322 | 64322 | 63522 | 61622 |

| 376 023 | **CN** | H | *SE* | SG | 61123 | 63323 | 64323 | 63523 | 61623 |
| 376 024 | **CN** | H | *SE* | SG | 61124 | 63324 | 64324 | 63524 | 61624 |
| 376 025 | **CN** | H | *SE* | SG | 61125 | 63325 | 64325 | 63525 | 61625 |
| 376 026 | **CN** | H | *SE* | SG | 61126 | 63326 | 64326 | 63526 | 61626 |
| 376 027 | **CN** | H | *SE* | SG | 61127 | 63327 | 64327 | 63527 | 61627 |
| 376 028 | **CN** | H | *SE* | SG | 61128 | 63328 | 64328 | 63528 | 61628 |
| 376 029 | **CN** | H | *SE* | SG | 61129 | 63329 | 64329 | 63529 | 61629 |
| 376 030 | **CN** | H | *SE* | SG | 61130 | 63330 | 64330 | 63530 | 61630 |
| 376 031 | **CN** | H | *SE* | SG | 61131 | 63331 | 64331 | 63531 | 61631 |
| 376 032 | **CN** | H | *SE* | SG | 61132 | 63332 | 64332 | 63532 | 61632 |
| 376 033 | **CN** | H | *SE* | SG | 61133 | 63333 | 64333 | 63533 | 61633 |
| 376 034 | **CN** | H | *SE* | SG | 61134 | 63334 | 64334 | 63534 | 61634 |
| 376 035 | **CN** | H | *SE* | SG | 61135 | 63335 | 64335 | 63535 | 61635 |
| 376 036 | **CN** | H | *SE* | SG | 61136 | 63336 | 64336 | 63536 | 61636 |

# CLASS 377   ELECTROSTAR   BOMBARDIER DERBY

Southern express and outer suburban units.

**Systems**: 25 kV AC overhead/750 V DC third rail or third rail only with provision for retro-fitting of AC equipment.
**Formations**: Various.
**Construction**: Welded aluminium alloy underframe, sides and roof with steel ends. All sections bolted together.
**Doors**: Sliding plug.
**Traction Motors**: Two Bombardier asynchronous of 250 kW.
**Gangways**: Throughout.                    **Bogies**: Bombardier P3-25/T3-25.
**Couplers**: Dellner 12.                     **Maximum Speed**: 100 m.p.h.
**Seating Layout**: Various.                  **Dimensions**: 20.40/19.99 x 2.80 m.
**Braking**: Disc & regenerative.
**Heating & ventilation**: Air conditioning.
**Multiple Working**: Within class and with Classes 375 and 376.

**Class 377/1**. 750 V DC only. DMCO–MSO–TSO–DMCO.
**Seating layout**: 1: 2+2 facing/unidirectional, 2: 2+2 facing/unidirectional (377 101–377 119), 3+2 and 2+2 facing/unidirectional (377 120–377 164) (3+2 seating in middle cars only 377 140–377164).

**DMCO(A)**. Bombardier Derby 2002–2003. 12/48 (s 12/56). 43.4 t.
**MSO**. Bombardier Derby 2002–2003. –/62 (s –/70, t –/69). 1T. 39.0 t.
**TSO**. Bombardier Derby 2002–2003. –/52 (s –/60, t –/57). 1TD 2W. 35.4 t.
**DMCO(B)**. Bombardier Derby 2002–2003. 12/48 (s 12/56). 43.4 t.

| 377 101 | **SN** | P | *SN* | BI | 78501 | 77101 | 78901 | 78701 |
| 377 102 | **SN** | P | *SN* | BI | 78502 | 77102 | 78902 | 78702 |
| 377 103 | **SN** | P | *SN* | BI | 78503 | 77103 | 78903 | 78703 |
| 377 104 | **SN** | P | *SN* | BI | 78504 | 77104 | 78904 | 78704 |
| 377 105 | **SN** | P | *SN* | BI | 78505 | 77105 | 78905 | 78705 |
| 377 106 | **SN** | P | *SN* | BI | 78506 | 77106 | 78906 | 78706 |
| 377 107 | **SN** | P | *SN* | BI | 78507 | 77107 | 78907 | 78707 |
| 377 108 | **SN** | P | *SN* | BI | 78508 | 77108 | 78908 | 78708 |
| 377 109 | **SN** | P | *SN* | BI | 78509 | 77109 | 78909 | 78709 |

| | | | | | | | | |
|---|---|---|---|---|---|---|---|---|
| 377 110 | | **SN** | P | *SN* | Bl | 78510 | 77110 | 78910 | 78710 |
| 377 111 | | **SN** | P | *SN* | Bl | 78511 | 77111 | 78911 | 78711 |
| 377 112 | | **SN** | P | *SN* | Bl | 78512 | 77112 | 78912 | 78712 |
| 377 113 | | **SN** | P | *SN* | Bl | 78513 | 77113 | 78913 | 78713 |
| 377 114 | | **SN** | P | *SN* | Bl | 78514 | 77114 | 78914 | 78714 |
| 377 115 | | **SN** | P | *SN* | Bl | 78515 | 77115 | 78915 | 78715 |
| 377 116 | | **SN** | P | *SN* | Bl | 78516 | 77116 | 78916 | 78716 |
| 377 117 | | **SN** | P | *SN* | Bl | 78517 | 77117 | 78917 | 78717 |
| 377 118 | | **SN** | P | *SN* | Bl | 78518 | 77118 | 78918 | 78718 |
| 377 119 | | **SN** | P | *SN* | Bl | 78519 | 77119 | 78919 | 78719 |
| 377 120 | s | **SN** | P | *SN* | SU | 78520 | 77120 | 78920 | 78720 |
| 377 121 | s | **SN** | P | *SN* | SU | 78521 | 77121 | 78921 | 78721 |
| 377 122 | s | **SN** | P | *SN* | SU | 78522 | 77122 | 78922 | 78722 |
| 377 123 | s | **SN** | P | *SN* | SU | 78523 | 77123 | 78923 | 78723 |
| 377 124 | s | **SN** | P | *SN* | SU | 78524 | 77124 | 78924 | 78724 |
| 377 125 | s | **SN** | P | *SN* | SU | 78525 | 77125 | 78925 | 78725 |
| 377 126 | s | **SN** | P | *SN* | SU | 78526 | 77126 | 78926 | 78726 |
| 377 127 | s | **SN** | P | *SN* | SU | 78527 | 77127 | 78927 | 78727 |
| 377 128 | s | **SN** | P | *SN* | SU | 78528 | 77128 | 78928 | 78728 |
| 377 129 | s | **SN** | P | *SN* | SU | 78529 | 77129 | 78929 | 78729 |
| 377 130 | s | **SN** | P | *SN* | SU | 78530 | 77130 | 78930 | 78730 |
| 377 131 | s | **SN** | P | *SN* | SU | 78531 | 77131 | 78931 | 78731 |
| 377 132 | s | **SN** | P | *SN* | SU | 78532 | 77132 | 78932 | 78732 |
| 377 133 | s | **SN** | P | *SN* | SU | 78533 | 77133 | 78933 | 78733 |
| 377 134 | s | **SN** | P | *SN* | SU | 78534 | 77134 | 78934 | 78734 |
| 377 135 | s | **SN** | P | *SN* | SU | 78535 | 77135 | 78935 | 78735 |
| 377 136 | s | **SN** | P | *SN* | SU | 78536 | 77136 | 78936 | 78736 |
| 377 137 | s | **SN** | P | *SN* | SU | 78537 | 77137 | 78937 | 78737 |
| 377 138 | s | **SN** | P | *SN* | SU | 78538 | 77138 | 78938 | 78738 |
| 377 139 | s | **SN** | P | *SN* | SU | 78539 | 77139 | 78939 | 78739 |
| 377 140 | t | **SN** | P | *SN* | SU | 78540 | 77140 | 78940 | 78740 |
| 377 141 | t | **SN** | P | *SN* | SU | 78541 | 77141 | 78941 | 78741 |
| 377 142 | t | **SN** | P | *SN* | SU | 78542 | 77142 | 78942 | 78742 |
| 377 143 | t | **SN** | P | *SN* | SU | 78543 | 77143 | 78943 | 78743 |
| 377 144 | t | **SN** | P | *SN* | SU | 78544 | 77144 | 78944 | 78744 |
| 377 145 | t | **SN** | P | *SN* | SU | 78545 | 77145 | 78945 | 78745 |
| 377 146 | t | **SN** | P | *SN* | SU | 78546 | 77146 | 78946 | 78746 |
| 377 147 | t | **SN** | P | *SN* | SU | 78547 | 77147 | 78947 | 78747 |
| 377 148 | t | **SN** | P | *SN* | SU | 78548 | 77148 | 78948 | 78748 |
| 377 149 | t | **SN** | P | *SN* | SU | 78549 | 77149 | 78949 | 78749 |
| 377 150 | t | **SN** | P | *SN* | SU | 78550 | 77150 | 78950 | 78750 |
| 377 151 | t | **SN** | P | *SN* | SU | 78551 | 77151 | 78951 | 78751 |
| 377 152 | t | **SN** | P | *SN* | Bl | 78552 | 77152 | 78952 | 78752 |
| 377 153 | t | **SN** | P | *SN* | Bl | 78553 | 77153 | 78953 | 78753 |
| 377 154 | t | **SN** | P | *SN* | Bl | 78554 | 77154 | 78954 | 78754 |
| 377 155 | t | **SN** | P | *SN* | Bl | 78555 | 77155 | 78955 | 78755 |
| 377 156 | t | **SN** | P | *SN* | Bl | 78556 | 77156 | 78956 | 78756 |
| 377 157 | t | **SN** | P | *SN* | Bl | 78557 | 77157 | 78957 | 78757 |
| 377 158 | t | **SN** | P | *SN* | Bl | 78558 | 77158 | 78958 | 78758 |
| 377 159 | t | **SN** | P | *SN* | Bl | 78559 | 77159 | 78959 | 78759 |
| 377 160 | t | **SN** | P | *SN* | Bl | 78560 | 77160 | 78960 | 78760 |

| | | | | | | | | |
|---|---|---|---|---|---|---|---|---|
| 377 161 | t | **SN** | P | *SN* | BI | 78561 | 77161 | 78961 | 78761 |
| 377 162 | t | **SN** | P | *SN* | BI | 78562 | 77162 | 78962 | 78762 |
| 377 163 | t | **SN** | P | *SN* | BI | 78563 | 77163 | 78963 | 78763 |
| 377 164 | t | **SN** | P | *SN* | BI | 78564 | 77164 | 78964 | 78764 |

**Class 377/2.** 25 kV AC/750 V DC. DMCO–MSO–PTSO–DMCO. These dual-voltage units are used on the Watford Junction–Gatwick Airport/Brighton services.
**Seating layout:** 1: 2+2 facing/unidirectional, 2: 2+2 and 3+2 facing/unidirectional (3+2 seating in middle cars only).

**DMCO(A).** Bombardier Derby 2003–2004. 12/48. 44.2 t.
**MSO.** Bombardier Derby 2003–2004. –/69 1T. 39.8 t.
**PTSO.** Bombardier Derby 2003–2004. –/57 1TD 2W. 40.1 t.
**DMCO(B).** Bombardier Derby 2003–2004. 12/48. 44.2 t.

| | | | | | | | | |
|---|---|---|---|---|---|---|---|---|
| 377 201 | **SN** | P | *SN* | SU | 78571 | 77171 | 78971 | 78771 |
| 377 202 | **SN** | P | *SN* | SU | 78572 | 77172 | 78972 | 78772 |
| 377 203 | **SN** | P | *SN* | SU | 78573 | 77173 | 78973 | 78773 |
| 377 204 | **SN** | P | *SN* | SU | 78574 | 77174 | 78974 | 78774 |
| 377 205 | **SN** | P | *SN* | SU | 78575 | 77175 | 78975 | 78775 |
| 377 206 | **SN** | P | *SN* | SU | 78576 | 77176 | 78976 | 78776 |
| 377 207 | **SN** | P | *SN* | SU | 78577 | 77177 | 78977 | 78777 |
| 377 208 | **SN** | P | *SN* | SU | 78578 | 77178 | 78978 | 78778 |
| 377 209 | **SN** | P | *SN* | SU | 78579 | 77179 | 78979 | 78779 |
| 377 210 | **SN** | P | *SN* | SU | 78580 | 77180 | 78980 | 78780 |
| 377 211 | **SN** | P | *SN* | SU | 78581 | 77181 | 78981 | 78781 |
| 377 212 | **SN** | P | *SN* | SU | 78582 | 77182 | 78982 | 78782 |
| 377 213 | **SN** | P | *SN* | SU | 78583 | 77183 | 78983 | 78783 |
| 377 214 | **SN** | P | *SN* | SU | 78584 | 77184 | 78984 | 78784 |
| 377 215 | **SN** | P | *SN* | SU | 78585 | 77185 | 78985 | 78785 |

**Class 377/3.** 750 V DC only. DMCO–TSO–DMCO.
**Seating Layout:** 1: 2+2 facing/unidirectional, 2: 2+2 facing/unidirectional.

**Notes:** Units built as Class 375, but renumbered in the Class 377/3 range when fitted with Dellner couplers.

† Wi-fi high-speed internet connection equipment fitted. Units generally used on Victoria–Brighton fast services.

**DMCO(A).** Bombardier Derby 2001–2002. 12/48. 43.5 t.
**TSO.** Bombardier Derby 2001–2002. –/56 1TD 2W. 35.4 t.
**DMCO(B).** Bombardier Derby 2001–2002. 12/48. 43.5 t.

| | | | | | | | | |
|---|---|---|---|---|---|---|---|---|
| 377 301 | (375 311) | | **SN** | P | *SN* | BI | 68201 | 74801 | 68401 |
| 377 302 | (375 312) | | **SN** | P | *SN* | BI | 68202 | 74802 | 68402 |
| 377 303 | (375 313) | | **SN** | P | *SN* | BI | 68203 | 74803 | 68403 |
| 377 304 | (375 314) | † | **SN** | P | *SN* | BI | 68204 | 74804 | 68404 |
| 377 305 | (375 315) | † | **SN** | P | *SN* | BI | 68205 | 74805 | 68405 |
| 377 306 | (375 316) | | **SN** | P | *SN* | BI | 68206 | 74806 | 68406 |
| 377 307 | (375 317) | | **SN** | P | *SN* | BI | 68207 | 74807 | 68407 |
| 377 308 | (375 318) | | **SN** | P | *SN* | BI | 68208 | 74808 | 68408 |
| 377 309 | (375 319) | | **SN** | P | *SN* | BI | 68209 | 74809 | 68409 |
| 377 310 | (375 320) | | **SN** | P | *SN* | BI | 68210 | 74810 | 68410 |
| 377 311 | (375 321) | | **SN** | P | *SN* | BI | 68211 | 74811 | 68411 |

| | | | | | | | | |
|---|---|---|---|---|---|---|---|---|
| 377 312 | (375 322) | | **SN** | P | *SN* | Bl | 68212 | 74812 | 68412 |
| 377 313 | (375 323) | | **SN** | P | *SN* | Bl | 68213 | 74813 | 68413 |
| 377 314 | (375 324) | | **SN** | P | *SN* | Bl | 68214 | 74814 | 68414 |
| 377 315 | (375 325) | † | **SN** | P | *SN* | Bl | 68215 | 74815 | 68415 |
| 377 316 | (375 326) | † | **SN** | P | *SN* | Bl | 68216 | 74816 | 68416 |
| 377 317 | (375 327) | † | **SN** | P | *SN* | Bl | 68217 | 74817 | 68417 |
| 377 318 | (375 328) | | **SN** | P | *SN* | Bl | 68218 | 74818 | 68418 |
| 377 319 | (375 329) | † | **SN** | P | *SN* | Bl | 68219 | 74819 | 68419 |
| 377 320 | (375 330) | † | **SN** | P | *SN* | Bl | 68220 | 74820 | 68420 |
| 377 321 | (375 331) | † | **SN** | P | *SN* | Bl | 68221 | 74821 | 68421 |
| 377 322 | (375 332) | † | **SN** | P | *SN* | Bl | 68222 | 74822 | 68422 |
| 377 323 | (375 333) | † | **SN** | P | *SN* | Bl | 68223 | 74823 | 68423 |
| 377 324 | (375 334) | † | **SN** | P | *SN* | Bl | 68224 | 74824 | 68424 |
| 377 325 | (375 335) | † | **SN** | P | *SN* | Bl | 68225 | 74825 | 68425 |
| 377 326 | (375 336) | † | **SN** | P | *SN* | Bl | 68226 | 74826 | 68426 |
| 377 327 | (375 337) | † | **SN** | P | *SN* | Bl | 68227 | 74827 | 68427 |
| 377 328 | (375 338) | † | **SN** | P | *SN* | Bl | 68228 | 74828 | 68428 |

**Class 377/4.** 750 V DC only. DMCO–MSO–TSO–DMCO.
**Seating Layout:** 1: 2+2 facing/two seats longitudinal, 2: 2+2 and 3+2 facing/ unidirectional (3+2 seating in middle cars only).

**DMCO(A).** Bombardier Derby 2004–2005. 10/48. 43.1 t.
**MSO.** Bombardier Derby 2004–2005. –/69 1T. 39.3 t.
**TSO.** Bombardier Derby 2004–2005. –/56 1TD 2W. 35.3 t.
**DMCO(B).** Bombardier Derby 2004–2005. 10/48. 43.1 t.

| | | | | | | | | |
|---|---|---|---|---|---|---|---|
| 377 401 | **SN** | P | *SN* | Bl | 73401 | 78801 | 78601 | 73801 |
| 377 402 | **SN** | P | *SN* | Bl | 73402 | 78802 | 78602 | 73802 |
| 377 403 | **SN** | P | *SN* | Bl | 73403 | 78803 | 78603 | 73803 |
| 377 404 | **SN** | P | *SN* | Bl | 73404 | 78804 | 78604 | 73804 |
| 377 405 | **SN** | P | *SN* | Bl | 73405 | 78805 | 78605 | 73805 |
| 377 406 | **SN** | P | *SN* | Bl | 73406 | 78806 | 78606 | 73806 |
| 377 407 | **SN** | P | *SN* | Bl | 73407 | 78807 | 78607 | 73807 |
| 377 408 | **SN** | P | *SN* | Bl | 73408 | 78808 | 78608 | 73808 |
| 377 409 | **SN** | P | *SN* | Bl | 73409 | 78809 | 78609 | 73809 |
| 377 410 | **SN** | P | *SN* | Bl | 73410 | 78810 | 78610 | 73810 |
| 377 411 | **SN** | P | *SN* | Bl | 73411 | 78811 | 78611 | 73811 |
| 377 412 | **SN** | P | *SN* | Bl | 73412 | 78812 | 78612 | 73812 |
| 377 413 | **SN** | P | *SN* | Bl | 73413 | 78813 | 78613 | 73813 |
| 377 414 | **SN** | P | *SN* | Bl | 73414 | 78814 | 78614 | 73814 |
| 377 415 | **SN** | P | *SN* | Bl | 73415 | 78815 | 78615 | 73815 |
| 377 416 | **SN** | P | *SN* | Bl | 73416 | 78816 | 78616 | 73816 |
| 377 417 | **SN** | P | *SN* | Bl | 73417 | 78817 | 78617 | 73817 |
| 377 418 | **SN** | P | *SN* | Bl | 73418 | 78818 | 78618 | 73818 |
| 377 419 | **SN** | P | *SN* | Bl | 73419 | 78819 | 78619 | 73819 |
| 377 420 | **SN** | P | *SN* | Bl | 73420 | 78820 | 78620 | 73820 |
| 377 421 | **SN** | P | *SN* | Bl | 73421 | 78821 | 78621 | 73821 |
| 377 422 | **SN** | P | *SN* | Bl | 73422 | 78822 | 78622 | 73822 |
| 377 423 | **SN** | P | *SN* | Bl | 73423 | 78823 | 78623 | 73823 |
| 377 424 | **SN** | P | *SN* | Bl | 73424 | 78824 | 78624 | 73824 |
| 377 425 | **SN** | P | *SN* | Bl | 73425 | 78825 | 78625 | 73825 |

| | | | | | | | | |
|---|---|---|---|---|---|---|---|---|
| 377 426 | **SN** | P | *SN* | BI | 73426 | 78826 | 78626 | 73826 |
| 377 427 | **SN** | P | *SN* | BI | 73427 | 78827 | 78627 | 73827 |
| 377 428 | **SN** | P | *SN* | BI | 73428 | 78828 | 78628 | 73828 |
| 377 429 | **SN** | P | *SN* | BI | 73429 | 78829 | 78629 | 73829 |
| 377 430 | **SN** | P | *SN* | BI | 73430 | 78830 | 78630 | 73830 |
| 377 431 | **SN** | P | *SN* | BI | 73431 | 78831 | 78631 | 73831 |
| 377 432 | **SN** | P | *SN* | BI | 73432 | 78832 | 78632 | 73832 |
| 377 433 | **SN** | P | *SN* | BI | 73433 | 78833 | 78633 | 73833 |
| 377 434 | **SN** | P | *SN* | BI | 73434 | 78834 | 78634 | 73834 |
| 377 435 | **SN** | P | *SN* | BI | 73435 | 78835 | 78635 | 73835 |
| 377 436 | **SN** | P | *SN* | BI | 73436 | 78836 | 78636 | 73836 |
| 377 437 | **SN** | P | *SN* | BI | 73437 | 78837 | 78637 | 73837 |
| 377 438 | **SN** | P | *SN* | BI | 73438 | 78838 | 78638 | 73838 |
| 377 439 | **SN** | P | *SN* | BI | 73439 | 78839 | 78639 | 73839 |
| 377 440 | **SN** | P | *SN* | BI | 73440 | 78840 | 78640 | 73840 |
| 377 441 | **SN** | P | *SN* | BI | 73441 | 78841 | 78641 | 73841 |
| 377 442 | **SN** | P | *SN* | BI | 73442 | 78842 | 78642 | 73842 |
| 377 443 | **SN** | P | *SN* | BI | 73443 | 78843 | 78643 | 73843 |
| 377 444 | **SN** | P | *SN* | BI | 73444 | 78844 | 78644 | 73844 |
| 377 445 | **SN** | P | *SN* | BI | 73445 | 78845 | 78645 | 73845 |
| 377 446 | **SN** | P | *SN* | BI | 73446 | 78846 | 78646 | 73846 |
| 377 447 | **SN** | P | *SN* | BI | 73447 | 78847 | 78647 | 73847 |
| 377 448 | **SN** | P | *SN* | BI | 73448 | 78848 | 78648 | 73848 |
| 377 449 | **SN** | P | *SN* | BI | 73449 | 78849 | 78649 | 73849 |
| 377 450 | **SN** | P | *SN* | BI | 73450 | 78850 | 78650 | 73850 |
| 377 451 | **SN** | P | *SN* | BI | 73451 | 78851 | 78651 | 73851 |
| 377 452 | **SN** | P | *SN* | BI | 73452 | 78852 | 78652 | 73852 |
| 377 453 | **SN** | P | *SN* | BI | 73453 | 78853 | 78653 | 73853 |
| 377 454 | **SN** | P | *SN* | BI | 73454 | 78854 | 78654 | 73854 |
| 377 455 | **SN** | P | *SN* | BI | 73455 | 78855 | 78655 | 73855 |
| 377 456 | **SN** | P | *SN* | BI | 73456 | 78856 | 78656 | 73856 |
| 377 457 | **SN** | P | *SN* | BI | 73457 | 78857 | 78657 | 73857 |
| 377 458 | **SN** | P | *SN* | BI | 73458 | 78858 | 78658 | 73858 |
| 377 459 | **SN** | P | *SN* | BI | 73459 | 78859 | 78659 | 73859 |
| 377 460 | **SN** | P | *SN* | BI | 73460 | 78860 | 78660 | 73860 |
| 377 461 | **SN** | P | *SN* | BI | 73461 | 78861 | 78661 | 73861 |
| 377 462 | **SN** | P | *SN* | BI | 73462 | 78862 | 78662 | 73862 |
| 377 463 | **SN** | P | *SN* | BI | 73463 | 78863 | 78663 | 73863 |
| 377 464 | **SN** | P | *SN* | BI | 73464 | 78864 | 78664 | 73864 |
| 377 465 | **SN** | P | *SN* | BI | 73465 | 78865 | 78665 | 73865 |
| 377 466 | **SN** | P | *SN* | BI | 73466 | 78866 | 78666 | 73866 |
| 377 467 | **SN** | P | *SN* | BI | 73467 | 78867 | 78667 | 73867 |
| 377 468 | **SN** | P | *SN* | BI | 73468 | 78868 | 78668 | 73868 |
| 377 469 | **SN** | P | *SN* | BI | 73469 | 78869 | 78669 | 73869 |
| 377 470 | **SN** | P | *SN* | BI | 73470 | 78870 | 78670 | 73870 |
| 377 471 | **SN** | P | *SN* | BI | 73471 | 78871 | 78671 | 73871 |
| 377 472 | **SN** | P | *SN* | BI | 73472 | 78872 | 78672 | 73872 |
| 377 473 | **SN** | P | *SN* | BI | 73473 | 78873 | 78673 | 73873 |
| 377 474 | **SN** | P | *SN* | BI | 73474 | 78874 | 78674 | 73874 |
| 377 475 | **SN** | P | *SN* | BI | 73475 | 78875 | 78675 | 73875 |

# CLASS 390 PENDOLINO ALSTOM BIRMINGHAM

Tilting Virgin West Coast units.

**Formation:** DMRFO–MFO–PTFO–MFO–TSO–MSO–PTSRMB–MSO–DMSO.
**Construction:** Welded aluminium alloy.
**Traction Motors:** Two Alstom ONIX 800 of 425 kW.
**Doors:** Sliding plug.                          **Bogies:** Fiat-SIG.
**Gangways:** Within unit.                        **Couplers:** Dellner 12.
**Design Speed:** 140 m.p.h.                      **Maximum Speed:** 125 m.p.h.
**Seating Layout:** 1: 2+1 facing, 2: 2+2 facing/unidirectional.
**Dimensions:** 24.80/23.90 x 2.73 m.
**Braking:** Disc, rheostatic & regenerative.
**Heating & ventilation:** Air conditioning.
**Multiple Working:** Within class and with Class 57/3 locomotives.

**DMRFO:** Alstom Birmingham 2001–2005. 18/–. 55.6 t.
**MFO(A):** Alstom Birmingham 2001–2005. 39/– 1TD 1W. 52.0 t.
**PTFO:** Alstom Birmingham 2001–2005. 44/– 1T. 50.1 t.
**MFO(B):** Alstom Birmingham 2001–2005. 46/– 1T. 51.8 t.
**TSO:** Alstom Birmingham 2001–2005. –/76 1T. 45.5 t.
**MSO(A):** Alstom Birmingham 2001–2005. –/66 1TD 1W. 50.0 t.
**PTSRMB:** Alstom Birmingham 2001–2005. –/48. 52.0 t.
**MSO(B):** Alstom Birmingham 2001–2005. –/64 1TD 1W. 51.7 t.
**DMSO:** Alstom Birmingham 2001–2005. –/46 1T. 51.0 t.

**Note:** Units up to 390 034 were delivered as 8-car sets, without the TSO (688xx).
During 2004 and early 2005 these units had their 9th cars added.

| | | | | | | | | | |
|---|---|---|---|---|---|---|---|---|---|
| 390 001 | **VT** | A | *VW* | MA | 69101 | 69401 | 69501 | 69601 | 68801 |
| | | | | | 69701 | 69801 | 69901 | 69201 | |
| 390 002 | **VT** | A | *VW* | MA | 69102 | 69402 | 69502 | 69602 | 68802 |
| | | | | | 69702 | 69802 | 69902 | 69202 | |
| 390 003 | **VT** | A | *VW* | MA | 69103 | 69403 | 69503 | 69603 | 68803 |
| | | | | | 69703 | 69803 | 69903 | 69203 | |
| 390 004 | **VT** | A | *VW* | MA | 69104 | 69404 | 69504 | 69604 | 68804 |
| | | | | | 69704 | 69804 | 69904 | 69204 | |
| 390 005 | **VT** | A | *VW* | MA | 69105 | 69405 | 69505 | 69605 | 68805 |
| | | | | | 69705 | 69805 | 69905 | 69205 | |
| 390 006 | **VT** | A | *VW* | MA | 69106 | 69406 | 69506 | 69606 | 68806 |
| | | | | | 69706 | 69806 | 69906 | 69206 | |
| 390 007 | **VT** | A | *VW* | MA | 69107 | 69407 | 69507 | 69607 | 68807 |
| | | | | | 69707 | 69807 | 69907 | 69207 | |
| 390 008 | **VT** | A | *VW* | MA | 69108 | 69408 | 69508 | 69608 | 68808 |
| | | | | | 69708 | 69808 | 69908 | 69208 | |
| 390 009 | **VT** | A | *VW* | MA | 69109 | 69409 | 69509 | 69609 | 68809 |
| | | | | | 69709 | 69809 | 69909 | 69209 | |
| 390 010 | **VT** | A | *VW* | MA | 69110 | 69410 | 69510 | 69610 | 68810 |
| | | | | | 69710 | 69810 | 69910 | 69210 | |
| 390 011 | **VT** | A | *VW* | MA | 69111 | 69411 | 69511 | 69611 | 68811 |
| | | | | | 69711 | 69811 | 69911 | 69211 | |

| | | | | | | | | |
|---|---|---|---|---|---|---|---|---|
| 390 012 | **VT** | A | *VW* | MA | 69112 | 69412 | 69512 | 69612 | 68812 |
| | | | | | 69712 | 69812 | 69912 | 69212 | |
| 390 013 | **VT** | A | *VW* | MA | 69113 | 69413 | 69513 | 69613 | 68813 |
| | | | | | 69713 | 69813 | 69913 | 69213 | |
| 390 014 | **VT** | A | *VW* | MA | 69114 | 69414 | 69514 | 69614 | 68814 |
| | | | | | 69714 | 69814 | 69914 | 69214 | |
| 390 015 | **VT** | A | *VW* | MA | 69115 | 69415 | 69515 | 69615 | 68815 |
| | | | | | 69715 | 69815 | 69915 | 69215 | |
| 390 016 | **VT** | A | *VW* | MA | 69116 | 69416 | 69516 | 69616 | 68816 |
| | | | | | 69716 | 69816 | 69916 | 69216 | |
| 390 017 | **VT** | A | *VW* | MA | 69117 | 69417 | 69517 | 69617 | 68817 |
| | | | | | 69717 | 69817 | 69917 | 69217 | |
| 390 018 | **VT** | A | *VW* | MA | 69118 | 69418 | 69518 | 69618 | 68818 |
| | | | | | 69718 | 69818 | 69918 | 69218 | |
| 390 019 | **VT** | A | *VW* | MA | 69119 | 69419 | 69519 | 69619 | 68819 |
| | | | | | 69719 | 69819 | 69919 | 69219 | |
| 390 020 | **VT** | A | *VW* | MA | 69120 | 69420 | 69520 | 69620 | 68820 |
| | | | | | 69720 | 69820 | 69920 | 69220 | |
| 390 021 | **VT** | A | *VW* | MA | 69121 | 69421 | 69521 | 69621 | 68821 |
| | | | | | 69721 | 69821 | 69921 | 69221 | |
| 390 022 | **VT** | A | *VW* | MA | 69122 | 69422 | 69522 | 69622 | 68822 |
| | | | | | 69722 | 69822 | 69922 | 69222 | |
| 390 023 | **VT** | A | *VW* | MA | 69123 | 69423 | 69523 | 69623 | 68823 |
| | | | | | 69723 | 69823 | 69923 | 69223 | |
| 390 024 | **VT** | A | *VW* | MA | 69124 | 69424 | 69524 | 69624 | 68824 |
| | | | | | 69724 | 69824 | 69924 | 69224 | |
| 390 025 | **VT** | A | *VW* | MA | 69125 | 69425 | 69525 | 69625 | 68825 |
| | | | | | 69725 | 69825 | 69925 | 69225 | |
| 390 026 | **VT** | A | *VW* | MA | 69126 | 69426 | 69526 | 69626 | 68826 |
| | | | | | 69726 | 69826 | 69926 | 69226 | |
| 390 027 | **VT** | A | *VW* | MA | 69127 | 69427 | 69527 | 69627 | 68827 |
| | | | | | 69727 | 69827 | 69927 | 69227 | |
| 390 028 | **VT** | A | *VW* | MA | 69128 | 69428 | 69528 | 69628 | 68828 |
| | | | | | 69728 | 69828 | 69928 | 69228 | |
| 390 029 | **VT** | A | *VW* | MA | 69129 | 69429 | 69529 | 69629 | 68829 |
| | | | | | 69729 | 69829 | 69929 | 69229 | |
| 390 030 | **VT** | A | *VW* | MA | 69130 | 69430 | 69530 | 69630 | 68830 |
| | | | | | 69730 | 69830 | 69930 | 69230 | |
| 390 031 | **VT** | A | *VW* | MA | 69131 | 69431 | 69531 | 69631 | 68831 |
| | | | | | 69731 | 69831 | 69931 | 69231 | |
| 390 032 | **VT** | A | *VW* | MA | 69132 | 69432 | 69532 | 69632 | 68832 |
| | | | | | 69732 | 69832 | 69932 | 69232 | |
| 390 033 | **VT** | A | *VW* | MA | 69133 | 69433 | 69533 | 69633 | 68833 |
| | | | | | 69733 | 69833 | 69933 | 69233 | |
| 390 034 | **VT** | A | *VW* | MA | 69134 | 69434 | 69534 | 69634 | 68834 |
| | | | | | 69734 | 69834 | 69934 | 69234 | |
| 390 035 | **VT** | A | *VW* | MA | 69135 | 69435 | 69535 | 69635 | 68835 |
| | | | | | 69735 | 69835 | 69935 | 69235 | |
| 390 036 | **VT** | A | *VW* | MA | 69136 | 69436 | 69536 | 69636 | 68836 |
| | | | | | 69736 | 69836 | 69936 | 69236 | |

| | | | | | | | | | |
|---|---|---|---|---|---|---|---|---|---|
| 390 037 | **VT** | A | *VW* | MA | 69137 | 69437 | 69537 | 69637 | 68837 |
| | | | | | 69737 | 69837 | 69937 | 69237 | |
| 390 038 | **VT** | A | *VW* | MA | 69138 | 69438 | 69538 | 69638 | 68838 |
| | | | | | 69738 | 69838 | 69938 | 69238 | |
| 390 039 | **VT** | A | *VW* | MA | 69139 | 69439 | 69539 | 69639 | 68839 |
| | | | | | 69739 | 69839 | 69939 | 69239 | |
| 390 040 | **VT** | A | *VW* | MA | 69140 | 69440 | 69540 | 69640 | 68840 |
| | | | | | 69740 | 69840 | 69940 | 69240 | |
| 390 041 | **VT** | A | *VW* | MA | 69141 | 69441 | 69541 | 69641 | 68841 |
| | | | | | 69741 | 69841 | 69941 | 69241 | |
| 390 042 | **VT** | A | *VW* | MA | 69142 | 69442 | 69542 | 69642 | 68842 |
| | | | | | 69742 | 69842 | 69942 | 69242 | |
| 390 043 | **VT** | A | *VW* | MA | 69143 | 69443 | 69543 | 69643 | 68843 |
| | | | | | 69743 | 69843 | 69943 | 69243 | |
| 390 044 | **VT** | A | *VW* | MA | 69144 | 69444 | 69544 | 69644 | 68844 |
| | | | | | 69744 | 69844 | 69944 | 69244 | |
| 390 045 | **VT** | A | *VW* | MA | 69145 | 69445 | 69545 | 69645 | 68845 |
| | | | | | 69745 | 69845 | 69945 | 69245 | |
| 390 046 | **VT** | A | *VW* | MA | 69146 | 69446 | 69546 | 69646 | 68846 |
| | | | | | 69746 | 69846 | 69946 | 69246 | |
| 390 047 | **VT** | A | *VW* | MA | 69147 | 69447 | 69547 | 69647 | 68847 |
| | | | | | 69747 | 69847 | 69947 | 69247 | |
| 390 048 | **VT** | A | *VW* | MA | 69148 | 69448 | 69548 | 69648 | 68848 |
| | | | | | 69748 | 69848 | 69948 | 69248 | |
| 390 049 | **VT** | A | *VW* | MA | 69149 | 69449 | 69549 | 69649 | 68849 |
| | | | | | 69749 | 69849 | 69949 | 69249 | |
| 390 050 | **VT** | A | *VW* | MA | 69150 | 69450 | 69550 | 69650 | 68850 |
| | | | | | 69750 | 69850 | 69950 | 69250 | |
| 390 051 | **VT** | A | *VW* | MA | 69151 | 69451 | 69551 | 69651 | 68851 |
| | | | | | 69751 | 69851 | 69951 | 69251 | |
| 390 052 | **VT** | A | *VW* | MA | 69152 | 69452 | 69552 | 69652 | 68852 |
| | | | | | 69752 | 69852 | 69952 | 69252 | |
| 390 053 | **VT** | A | *VW* | MA | 69153 | 69453 | 69553 | 69653 | 68853 |
| | | | | | 69753 | 69853 | 69953 | 69253 | |

282

**Names (carried on MFO No. 696xx):**

| | | | |
|---|---|---|---|
| 390 001 | Virgin Pioneer | 390 028 | City of Preston |
| 390 002 | Virgin Angel | 390 029 | City of Stoke-on-Trent |
| 390 003 | Virgin Hero | 390 030 | City of Edinburgh |
| 390 004 | Virgin Scot | 390 031 | City of Liverpool |
| 390 005 | City of Wolverhampton | 390 032 | City of Birmingham |
| 390 006 | Virgin Sun | 390 033 | City of Glasgow |
| 390 007 | Virgin Lady | 390 034 | City of Carlisle |
| 390 008 | Virgin King | 390 035 | City of Lancaster |
| 390 009 | Virgin Queen | 390 036 | City of Coventry |
| 390 010 | Chris Green | 390 037 | Virgin Difference |
| 390 011 | City of Lichfield | 390 038 | City of London |
| 390 012 | Virgin Star | 390 039 | Virgin Quest |
| 390 013 | Virgin Spirit | 390 040 | Virgin Pathfinder |
| 390 014 | City of Manchester | 390 041 | City of Chester |
| 390 015 | Virgin Crusader | 390 042 | City of Bangor/Dinas Bangor |
| 390 016 | Virgin Champion | 390 043 | Virgin Explorer |
| 390 017 | Virgin Prince | 390 044 | Virgin Lionheart |
| 390 018 | Virgin Princess | 390 045 | Virgin Valiant |
| 390 019 | Virgin Warrior | 390 046 | Virgin Soldiers |
| 390 020 | Virgin Cavalier | 390 047 | Virgin Atlantic |
| 390 021 | Virgin Dream | 390 048 | Virgin Harrier |
| 390 022 | Virgin Hope | 390 049 | Virgin Express |
| 390 023 | Virgin Glory | 390 050 | Virgin Invader |
| 390 024 | Virgin Venturer | 390 051 | Virgin Ambassador |
| 390 025 | Virgin Stagecoach | 390 052 | Virgin Knight |
| 390 026 | Virgin Enterprise | 390 053 | Mission Accomplished |
| 390 027 | Virgin Buccaneer | | |

# 4.2. 750 V DC THIRD RAIL EMUs

These classes use the third rail system at 750–850 V DC. Outer couplings are buckeyes on units built before 1982 with bar couplings within the units. Newer units generally have Dellner outer couplers.

## CLASS 421                                              BR YORK

Mark 1 "slam-door" units built for Portsmouth and Brighton lines. Facelifted with new trim and fluorescent lighting in saloons.

**SR designation:** 3 Cig.
**Formation:** DTCso–MBSO–DTCso.
**Construction:** Steel.
**Gangways:** Throughout.
**Traction Motors:** Four EE507 of 185 kW.
**Bogies:** Mark 6 motor bogies (MBSO). B5 (SR) bogies (trailer cars).
**Maximum Speed:** 90 m.p.h.
**Seating Layout:** 1: Compartments, 2: 2+2 facing (plus one four-a-side compartment per DTC).
**Braking:** Tread brakes.
**Multiple Working:** Not required.

**Doors:** Slam.
**Electrical Equipment:** 1963-type.
**Couplers:** Buckeye.

**Dimensions:** 20.18 x 2.82 m.

**Class 421/7. Phase 2 sets.** Specially converted 3-car units for use on the Lymington branch line. Central Door Locking system fitted and wheelchair space created. Toilets removed.

**76764/76773. DTCso(A).** Lot No. 30814 1971. 18/36. 35.5 t.
**62402/62411. MBSO.** Lot No. 30816 1971. –/56 1W + 3 tip-up seats. 49 t.
**76835/76844. DTCso(B).** Lot No. 30815 1971. 18/36. 35 t.

| | | | | | | | |
|---|---|---|---|---|---|---|---|
| 1497 | (1883) | **BG** | SW | *SW* | BM | 76764 | 62402 | 76835 |
| 1498 | (1888) | **G** | SW | *SW* | BM | 76773 | 62411 | 76844 |

**Names (carried on MBSO):**

| 1497 | Freshwater | | 1498 | Farringford |
|---|---|---|---|---|

# CLASS 442    WESSEX EXPRESS BREL DERBY

Stock built for Waterloo–Bournemouth–Weymouth services. Can be hauled and heated by any ETH-fitted locomotive.

**SR designation:** 5 Wes.
**Formation:** DTFso–TSO–MBRSM–TSO–DTSO.
**Construction:** Steel.                    **Doors:** Sliding plug.
**Gangways:** Throughout.              **Electrical Equipment:** 1986-type.
**Traction Motors:** Four EE546 of 300 kW recovered from Class 432s.
**Bogies:** Two BREL P7 motor bogies (MBSO). T4 bogies (trailer cars).
**Maximum Speed:** 100 m.p.h.          **Couplers:** Buckeye.
**Seating Layout:** 1: 2+2 facing/compartments, 2: 2+2 facing/unidirectional.
**Dimensions:** 22.15 x 2.74 m.        **Braking:** Tread brakes.
**Heating & Ventilation:** Air conditioning.
**Multiple Working:** Within class and with Classes 411, 421, 423 and locos of Classes 33/1 and 73 in emergency.

**DTFso.** Lot No. 31030 Derby 1988–1989. 50/– 1T. (36 in six compartments and 14 in one saloon). 34.0 t.
**TSO (A).** Lot No. 31032 Derby 1988–1989. –/82 2T. 34.0 t.
**MBRSM.** Lot No. 31034 Derby 1988–1989. Modified Adtranz Crewe 1998. –/52 1W. 55.4 t.
**TSO (B).** Lot No. 31033 Derby 1988–1989. –/78 2T 1W. 34.0 t.
**DTSO.** Lot No. 31031 Derby 1988–1989. –/78 1T. 34.0 t.

| | | | | | | | | |
|---|---|---|---|---|---|---|---|---|
| 2401 | **SW** | A | *SW* | BM | 77382 | 71818 | 62937 | 71842 | 77406 |
| 2402 | **SW** | A | *SW* | BM | 77383 | 71819 | 62938 | 71843 | 77407 |
| 2403 | **SW** | A | *SW* | BM | 77384 | 71820 | 62941 | 71844 | 77408 |
| 2404 | **SW** | A | *SW* | BM | 77385 | 71821 | 62939 | 71845 | 77409 |
| 2405 | **SW** | A | *SW* | BM | 77386 | 71822 | 62944 | 71846 | 77410 |
| 2406 | **SW** | A | *SW* | BM | 77389 | 71823 | 62942 | 71847 | 77411 |
| 2407 | **SW** | A | *SW* | BM | 77388 | 71824 | 62943 | 71848 | 77412 |
| 2408 | **SW** | A | *SW* | BM | 77387 | 71825 | 62945 | 71849 | 77413 |
| 2409 | **SW** | A | *SW* | BM | 77390 | 71826 | 62946 | 71850 | 77414 |
| 2410 | **SW** | A | *SW* | BM | 77391 | 71827 | 62948 | 71851 | 77415 |
| 2411 | **SW** | A | *SW* | BM | 77392 | 71828 | 62940 | 71858 | 77422 |
| 2412 | **SW** | A | *SW* | BM | 77393 | 71829 | 62947 | 71853 | 77417 |
| 2413 | **SW** | A | *SW* | BM | 77394 | 71830 | 62949 | 71854 | 77418 |
| 2414 | **SW** | A | *SW* | BM | 77395 | 71831 | 62950 | 71855 | 77419 |
| 2415 | **SW** | A | *SW* | BM | 77396 | 71832 | 62951 | 71856 | 77420 |
| 2416 | **SW** | A | *SW* | BM | 77397 | 71833 | 62952 | 71857 | 77421 |
| 2417 | **SW** | A | *SW* | BM | 77398 | 71834 | 62953 | 71852 | 77416 |
| 2418 | **SW** | A | *SW* | BM | 77399 | 71835 | 62954 | 71859 | 77423 |
| 2419 | **SW** | A | *SW* | BM | 77400 | 71836 | 62955 | 71860 | 77424 |
| 2420 | **SW** | A | *SW* | BM | 77401 | 71837 | 62956 | 71861 | 77425 |
| 2421 | **SW** | A | *SW* | BM | 77402 | 71838 | 62957 | 71862 | 77426 |
| 2422 | **SW** | A | *SW* | BM | 77403 | 71839 | 62958 | 71863 | 77427 |
| 2423 | **SW** | A | *SW* | BM | 77404 | 71840 | 62959 | 71864 | 77428 |
| 2424 | **SW** | A | *SW* | BM | 77405 | 71841 | 62960 | 71865 | 77429 |

**Names (carried on MBRSM):**

| | |
|---|---|
| 2401 | BEAULIEU |
| 2402 | COUNTY OF HAMPSHIRE |
| 2403 | THE NEW FOREST |
| 2404 | BOROUGH OF WOKING |
| 2405 | CITY OF PORTSMOUTH |
| 2406 | VICTORY |
| 2407 | THOMAS HARDY |
| 2408 | COUNTY OF DORSET |
| 2409 | BOURNEMOUTH ORCHESTRAS |
| 2410 | MERIDIAN TONIGHT |
| 2411 | THE RAILWAY CHILDREN |
| 2412 | SPECIAL OLYMPICS |
| 2415 | MARY ROSE |
| 2416 | MUM IN A MILLION 1997 DOREEN SCANLON |
| 2417 | WOKING HOMES |
| 2418 | WESSEX CANCER TRUST |
| 2419 | BBC SOUTH TODAY |
| 2420 | CITY OF SOUTHAMPTON |
| 2422 | OPERATION OVERLORD |
| 2423 | COUNTY OF SURREY |
| 2424 | GERRY NEWSON |

# CLASS 444       DESIRO UK       SIEMENS

South West Trains express units.

**Formation:** DMCO–TSO–TSO–TSORMB–DMSO.
**Construction:** Aluminium.       **Doors:** Single-leaf sliding plug.
**Traction Motors:** 4 Siemens 1TB2016-0GB02 asynchronous of 250 kW.
**Gangways:** Throughout.       **Bogies:** SGP SF5000.
**Couplers:** Dellner 12.       **Maximum Speed:** 100 m.p.h.
**Seating Layout:** 1: 2+1 facing/unidirectional, 2: 2+2 facing/unidirectional.
**Dimensions:** 23.57 m x 2.80 m.
**Braking:** Disc and rheostatic.
**Heating & Ventilation:** Air conditioning.
**Multiple Working:** Within class and with Class 450.

**DMSO.** Siemens Wien/Uerdingen 2003–2004. –/76. 52.0 t.
**TSO 67101–67145.** Siemens Wien/Uerdingen 2003–2004. –/76 1T. 41.0 t.
**TSO 67151–67195.** Siemens Wien/Uerdingen 2003–2004. –/76 1T. 37.0 t.
**TSORMB.** Siemens Wien/Uerdingen 2003–2004. –/47 1T 1TD 2W. 42.0 t.
**DMCO.** Siemens Wien/Uerdingen 2003–2004. 35/24. 52.0 t.

| | | | | | | | | | |
|---|---|---|---|---|---|---|---|---|---|
| 444 001 | **SW** | A | _SW_ | NT | 63801 | 67101 | 67151 | 67201 | 63851 |
| 444 002 | **SW** | A | _SW_ | NT | 63802 | 67102 | 67152 | 67202 | 63852 |
| 444 003 | **SW** | A | _SW_ | NT | 63803 | 67103 | 67153 | 67203 | 63853 |
| 444 004 | **SW** | A | _SW_ | NT | 63804 | 67104 | 67154 | 67204 | 63854 |
| 444 005 | **SW** | A | _SW_ | NT | 63805 | 67105 | 67155 | 67205 | 63855 |
| 444 006 | **SW** | A | _SW_ | NT | 63806 | 67106 | 67156 | 67206 | 63856 |
| 444 007 | **SW** | A | _SW_ | NT | 63807 | 67107 | 67157 | 67207 | 63857 |

| | | | | | | | | |
|---|---|---|---|---|---|---|---|---|
| 444 008 | **SW** | A | *SW* | NT | 63808 | 67108 | 67158 | 67208 | 63858 |
| 444 009 | **SW** | A | *SW* | NT | 63809 | 67109 | 67159 | 67209 | 63859 |
| 444 010 | **SW** | A | *SW* | NT | 63810 | 67110 | 67160 | 67210 | 63860 |
| 444 011 | **SW** | A | *SW* | NT | 63811 | 67111 | 67161 | 67211 | 63861 |
| 444 012 | **SW** | A | *SW* | NT | 63812 | 67112 | 67162 | 67212 | 63862 |
| 444 013 | **SW** | A | *SW* | NT | 63813 | 67113 | 67163 | 67213 | 63863 |
| 444 014 | **SW** | A | *SW* | NT | 63814 | 67114 | 67164 | 67214 | 63864 |
| 444 015 | **SW** | A | *SW* | NT | 63815 | 67115 | 67165 | 67215 | 63865 |
| 444 016 | **SW** | A | *SW* | NT | 63816 | 67116 | 67166 | 67216 | 63866 |
| 444 017 | **SW** | A | *SW* | NT | 63817 | 67117 | 67167 | 67217 | 63867 |
| 444 018 | **SW** | A | *SW* | NT | 63818 | 67118 | 67168 | 67218 | 63868 |
| 444 019 | **SW** | A | *SW* | NT | 63819 | 67119 | 67169 | 67219 | 63869 |
| 444 020 | **SW** | A | *SW* | NT | 63820 | 67120 | 67170 | 67220 | 63870 |
| 444 021 | **SW** | A | *SW* | NT | 63821 | 67121 | 67171 | 67221 | 63871 |
| 444 022 | **SW** | A | *SW* | NT | 63822 | 67122 | 67172 | 67222 | 63872 |
| 444 023 | **SW** | A | *SW* | NT | 63823 | 67123 | 67173 | 67223 | 63873 |
| 444 024 | **SW** | A | *SW* | NT | 63824 | 67124 | 67174 | 67224 | 63874 |
| 444 025 | **SW** | A | *SW* | NT | 63825 | 67125 | 67175 | 67225 | 63875 |
| 444 026 | **SW** | A | *SW* | NT | 63826 | 67126 | 67176 | 67226 | 63876 |
| 444 027 | **SW** | A | *SW* | NT | 63827 | 67127 | 67177 | 67227 | 63877 |
| 444 028 | **SW** | A | *SW* | NT | 63828 | 67128 | 67178 | 67228 | 63878 |
| 444 029 | **SW** | A | *SW* | NT | 63829 | 67129 | 67179 | 67229 | 63879 |
| 444 030 | **SW** | A | *SW* | NT | 63830 | 67130 | 67180 | 67230 | 63880 |
| 444 031 | **SW** | A | *SW* | NT | 63831 | 67131 | 67181 | 67231 | 63881 |
| 444 032 | **SW** | A | *SW* | NT | 63832 | 67132 | 67182 | 67232 | 63882 |
| 444 033 | **SW** | A | *SW* | NT | 63833 | 67133 | 67183 | 67233 | 63883 |
| 444 034 | **SW** | A | *SW* | NT | 63834 | 67134 | 67184 | 67234 | 63884 |
| 444 035 | **SW** | A | *SW* | NT | 63835 | 67135 | 67185 | 67235 | 63885 |
| 444 036 | **SW** | A | *SW* | NT | 63836 | 67136 | 67186 | 67236 | 63886 |
| 444 037 | **SW** | A | *SW* | NT | 63837 | 67137 | 67187 | 67237 | 63887 |
| 444 038 | **SW** | A | *SW* | NT | 63838 | 67138 | 67188 | 67238 | 63888 |
| 444 039 | **SW** | A | *SW* | NT | 63839 | 67139 | 67189 | 67239 | 63889 |
| 444 040 | **SW** | A | *SW* | NT | 63840 | 67140 | 67190 | 67240 | 63890 |
| 444 041 | **SW** | A | *SW* | NT | 63841 | 67141 | 67191 | 67241 | 63891 |
| 444 042 | **SW** | A | *SW* | NT | 63842 | 67142 | 67192 | 67242 | 63892 |
| 444 043 | **SW** | A | *SW* | NT | 63843 | 67143 | 67193 | 67243 | 63893 |
| 444 044 | **SW** | A | *SW* | NT | 63844 | 67144 | 67194 | 67244 | 63894 |
| 444 045 | **SW** | A | *SW* | NT | 63845 | 67145 | 67195 | 67245 | 63895 |

**Name (carried on TSORMB):**

444 018   THE FAB 444

# CLASS 450          DESIRO UK          SIEMENS

South West Trains outer suburban units.

**Formation:** DMSO–TCO–TSO–DMSO.
**Construction:** Aluminium.                    **Doors:** Sliding plug.
**Traction Motors:** 4 Siemens 1TB2016-0GB02 asynchronous of 250 kW.
**Gangways:** Throughout.                        **Bogies:** SGP SF5000.
**Couplers:** Dellner 12.                         **Maximum Speed:** 100 m.p.h.
**Seating Layout:** 1: 2+2 facing/unidirectional, 2: 3+2 facing/unidirectional.
**Dimensions:** 20.34 x 2.80 m.
**Braking:** Disc and rheostatic.
**Heating & Ventilation:** Air conditioning.
**Multiple Working:** Within class and with Class 444.

**DMSO(A).** Siemens Uerdingen/Wien 2002–2004. –/70. 46.0 t.
**TCO.** Siemens Uerdingen/Wien 2002–2004. 24/36 1T. 35.0 t.
**TSO.** Siemens Uerdingen/Wien 2002–2004. –/70 1TD 2W. 35.0 t.
**DMSO(B).** Siemens Uerdingen/Wien 2002–2004. –/70. 46.0 t.

| | | | | | | | | |
|---|---|---|---|---|---|---|---|---|
| 450 001 | **SD** | A | *SW* | NT | 63201 | 64201 | 68101 | 63601 |
| 450 002 | **SD** | A | *SW* | NT | 63202 | 64202 | 68102 | 63602 |
| 450 003 | **SD** | A | *SW* | NT | 63203 | 64203 | 68103 | 63603 |
| 450 004 | **SD** | A | *SW* | NT | 63204 | 64204 | 68104 | 63604 |
| 450 005 | **SD** | A | *SW* | NT | 63205 | 64205 | 68105 | 63605 |
| 450 006 | **SD** | A | *SW* | NT | 63206 | 64206 | 68106 | 63606 |
| 450 007 | **SD** | A | *SW* | NT | 63207 | 64207 | 68107 | 63607 |
| 450 008 | **SD** | A | *SW* | NT | 63208 | 64208 | 68108 | 63608 |
| 450 009 | **SD** | A | *SW* | NT | 63209 | 64209 | 68109 | 63609 |
| 450 010 | **SD** | A | *SW* | NT | 63210 | 64210 | 68110 | 63610 |
| 450 011 | **SD** | A | *SW* | NT | 63211 | 64211 | 68111 | 63611 |
| 450 012 | **SD** | A | *SW* | NT | 63212 | 64212 | 68112 | 63612 |
| 450 013 | **SD** | A | *SW* | NT | 63213 | 64213 | 68113 | 63613 |
| 450 014 | **SD** | A | *SW* | NT | 63214 | 64214 | 68114 | 63614 |
| 450 015 | **SD** | A | *SW* | NT | 63215 | 64215 | 68115 | 63615 |
| 450 016 | **SD** | A | *SW* | NT | 63216 | 64216 | 68116 | 63616 |
| 450 017 | **SD** | A | *SW* | NT | 63217 | 64217 | 68117 | 63617 |
| 450 018 | **SD** | A | *SW* | NT | 63218 | 64218 | 68118 | 63618 |
| 450 019 | **SD** | A | *SW* | NT | 63219 | 64219 | 68119 | 63619 |
| 450 020 | **SD** | A | *SW* | NT | 63220 | 64220 | 68120 | 63620 |
| 450 021 | **SD** | A | *SW* | NT | 63221 | 64221 | 68121 | 63621 |
| 450 022 | **SD** | A | *SW* | NT | 63222 | 64222 | 68122 | 63622 |
| 450 023 | **SD** | A | *SW* | NT | 63223 | 64223 | 68123 | 63623 |
| 450 024 | **SD** | A | *SW* | NT | 63224 | 64224 | 68124 | 63624 |
| 450 025 | **SD** | A | *SW* | NT | 63225 | 64225 | 68125 | 63625 |
| 450 026 | **SD** | A | *SW* | NT | 63226 | 64226 | 68126 | 63626 |
| 450 027 | **SD** | A | *SW* | NT | 63227 | 64227 | 68127 | 63627 |
| 450 028 | **SD** | A | *SW* | NT | 63228 | 64228 | 68128 | 63628 |
| 450 029 | **SD** | A | *SW* | NT | 63229 | 64229 | 68129 | 63629 |
| 450 030 | **SD** | A | *SW* | NT | 63230 | 64230 | 68130 | 63630 |
| 450 031 | **SD** | A | *SW* | NT | 63231 | 64231 | 68131 | 63631 |

| | | | | | | | | |
|---|---|---|---|---|---|---|---|---|
| 450 032 | **SD** | A | *SW* | NT | 63232 | 64232 | 68132 | 63632 |
| 450 033 | **SD** | A | *SW* | NT | 63233 | 64233 | 68133 | 63633 |
| 450 034 | **SD** | A | *SW* | NT | 63234 | 64234 | 68134 | 63634 |
| 450 035 | **SD** | A | *SW* | NT | 63235 | 64235 | 68135 | 63635 |
| 450 036 | **SD** | A | *SW* | NT | 63236 | 64236 | 68136 | 63636 |
| 450 037 | **SD** | A | *SW* | NT | 63237 | 64237 | 68137 | 63637 |
| 450 038 | **SD** | A | *SW* | NT | 63238 | 64238 | 68138 | 63638 |
| 450 039 | **SD** | A | *SW* | NT | 63239 | 64239 | 68139 | 63639 |
| 450 040 | **SD** | A | *SW* | NT | 63240 | 64240 | 68140 | 63640 |
| 450 041 | **SD** | A | *SW* | NT | 63241 | 64241 | 68141 | 63641 |
| 450 042 | **SD** | A | *SW* | NT | 63242 | 64242 | 68142 | 63642 |
| 450 043 | **SD** | A | *SW* | NT | 63243 | 64243 | 68143 | 63643 |
| 450 044 | **SD** | A | *SW* | NT | 63244 | 64244 | 68144 | 63644 |
| 450 045 | **SD** | A | *SW* | NT | 63245 | 64245 | 68145 | 63645 |
| 450 046 | **SD** | A | *SW* | NT | 63246 | 64246 | 68146 | 63646 |
| 450 047 | **SD** | A | *SW* | NT | 63247 | 64247 | 68147 | 63647 |
| 450 048 | **SD** | A | *SW* | NT | 63248 | 64248 | 68148 | 63648 |
| 450 049 | **SD** | A | *SW* | NT | 63249 | 64249 | 68149 | 63649 |
| 450 050 | **SD** | A | *SW* | NT | 63250 | 64250 | 68150 | 63650 |
| 450 051 | **SD** | A | *SW* | NT | 63251 | 64251 | 68151 | 63651 |
| 450 052 | **SD** | A | *SW* | NT | 63252 | 64252 | 68152 | 63652 |
| 450 053 | **SD** | A | *SW* | NT | 63253 | 64253 | 68153 | 63653 |
| 450 054 | **SD** | A | *SW* | NT | 63254 | 64254 | 68154 | 63654 |
| 450 055 | **SD** | A | *SW* | NT | 63255 | 64255 | 68155 | 63655 |
| 450 056 | **SD** | A | *SW* | NT | 63256 | 64256 | 68156 | 63656 |
| 450 057 | **SD** | A | *SW* | NT | 63257 | 64257 | 68157 | 63657 |
| 450 058 | **SD** | A | *SW* | NT | 63258 | 64258 | 68158 | 63658 |
| 450 059 | **SD** | A | *SW* | NT | 63259 | 64259 | 68159 | 63659 |
| 450 060 | **SD** | A | *SW* | NT | 63260 | 64260 | 68160 | 63660 |
| 450 061 | **SD** | A | *SW* | NT | 63261 | 64261 | 68161 | 63661 |
| 450 062 | **SD** | A | *SW* | NT | 63262 | 64262 | 68162 | 63662 |
| 450 063 | **SD** | A | *SW* | NT | 63263 | 64263 | 68163 | 63663 |
| 450 064 | **SD** | A | *SW* | NT | 63264 | 64264 | 68164 | 63664 |
| 450 065 | **SD** | A | *SW* | NT | 63265 | 64265 | 68165 | 63665 |
| 450 066 | **SD** | A | *SW* | NT | 63266 | 64266 | 68166 | 63666 |
| 450 067 | **SD** | A | *SW* | NT | 63267 | 64267 | 68167 | 63667 |
| 450 068 | **SD** | A | *SW* | NT | 63268 | 64268 | 68168 | 63668 |
| 450 069 | **SD** | A | *SW* | NT | 63269 | 64269 | 68169 | 63669 |
| 450 070 | **SD** | A | *SW* | NT | 63270 | 64270 | 68170 | 63670 |
| 450 071 | **SD** | A | *SW* | NT | 63271 | 64271 | 68171 | 63671 |
| 450 072 | **SD** | A | *SW* | NT | 63272 | 64272 | 68172 | 63672 |
| 450 073 | **SD** | A | *SW* | NT | 63273 | 64273 | 68173 | 63673 |
| 450 074 | **SD** | A | *SW* | NT | 63274 | 64274 | 68174 | 63674 |
| 450 075 | **SD** | A | *SW* | NT | 63275 | 64275 | 68175 | 63675 |
| 450 076 | **SD** | A | *SW* | NT | 63276 | 64276 | 68176 | 63676 |
| 450 077 | **SD** | A | *SW* | NT | 63277 | 64277 | 68177 | 63677 |
| 450 078 | **SD** | A | *SW* | NT | 63278 | 64278 | 68178 | 63678 |
| 450 079 | **SD** | A | *SW* | NT | 63279 | 64279 | 68179 | 63679 |
| 450 080 | **SD** | A | *SW* | NT | 63280 | 64280 | 68180 | 63680 |
| 450 081 | **SD** | A | *SW* | NT | 63281 | 64281 | 68181 | 63681 |
| 450 082 | **SD** | A | *SW* | NT | 63282 | 64282 | 68182 | 63682 |

| | | | | | | | | |
|---|---|---|---|---|---|---|---|---|
| 450 083 | **SD** | A | *SW* | NT | 63283 | 64283 | 68183 | 63683 |
| 450 084 | **SD** | A | *SW* | NT | 63284 | 64284 | 68184 | 63684 |
| 450 085 | **SD** | A | *SW* | NT | 63285 | 64285 | 68185 | 63685 |
| 450 086 | **SD** | A | *SW* | NT | 63286 | 64286 | 68186 | 63686 |
| 450 087 | **SD** | A | *SW* | NT | 63287 | 64287 | 68187 | 63687 |
| 450 088 | **SD** | A | *SW* | NT | 63288 | 64288 | 68188 | 63688 |
| 450 089 | **SD** | A | *SW* | NT | 63289 | 64289 | 68189 | 63689 |
| 450 090 | **SD** | A | *SW* | NT | 63290 | 64290 | 68190 | 63690 |
| 450 091 | **SD** | A | *SW* | NT | 63291 | 64291 | 68191 | 63691 |
| 450 092 | **SD** | A | *SW* | NT | 63292 | 64292 | 68192 | 63692 |
| 450 093 | **SD** | A | *SW* | NT | 63293 | 64293 | 68193 | 63693 |
| 450 094 | **SD** | A | *SW* | NT | 63294 | 64294 | 68194 | 63694 |
| 450 095 | **SD** | A | *SW* | NT | 63295 | 64295 | 68195 | 63695 |
| 450 096 | **SD** | A | *SW* | NT | 63296 | 64296 | 68196 | 63696 |
| 450 097 | **SD** | A | *SW* | NT | 63297 | 64297 | 68197 | 63697 |
| 450 098 | **SD** | A | *SW* | NT | 63298 | 64298 | 68198 | 63698 |
| 450 099 | **SD** | A | *SW* | NT | 63299 | 64299 | 68199 | 63699 |
| 450 100 | **SD** | A | *SW* | NT | 63300 | 64300 | 68200 | 63700 |
| 450 101 | **SD** | A | *SW* | NT | 63701 | 66851 | 66801 | 63751 |
| 450 102 | **SD** | A | *SW* | NT | 63702 | 66852 | 66802 | 63752 |
| 450 103 | **SD** | A | *SW* | NT | 63703 | 66853 | 66803 | 63753 |
| 450 104 | **SD** | A | *SW* | NT | 63704 | 66854 | 66804 | 63754 |
| 450 105 | **SD** | A | *SW* | NT | 63705 | 66855 | 66805 | 63755 |
| 450 106 | **SD** | A | *SW* | NT | 63706 | 66856 | 66806 | 63756 |
| 450 107 | **SD** | A | *SW* | NT | 63707 | 66857 | 66807 | 63757 |
| 450 108 | **SD** | A | *SW* | NT | 63708 | 66858 | 66808 | 63758 |
| 450 109 | **SD** | A | *SW* | NT | 63709 | 66859 | 66809 | 63759 |
| 450 110 | **SD** | A | *SW* | NT | 63710 | 66860 | 66810 | 63760 |

**Names (carried on DMSO(B)):**

450 015   DESIRO
450 042   TRELOAR COLLEGE

# CLASS 455                                    BR YORK

South West Trains/Southern inner suburban units.

**Formation:** DTSO–MSO–TSO–DTSO.
**Construction:** Steel. Class 455/7 TSO have a steel underframe and an aluminium alloy body & roof.
**Doors:** Sliding.
**Gangways:** Within unit + end doors (sealed on Southern units).
**Electrical Equipment:** 1982-type, camshaft and chopper.
**Traction Motors:** Four GEC507-20J of 185 kW, some recovered from Class 405s.
**Bogies:** P7 (motor) and T3 (455/8 & 455/9) BX1 (455/7) trailer.
**Couplers:** Tightlock.                      **Braking:** Disc brakes.
**Maximum Speed:** 75 m.p.h.
**Seating Layout:** 3+2 low-back facing unless shown.
**Dimensions:** 20.28/20.18 x 2.82 m.
**Heating & Ventilation:** Various.
**Multiple Working:** Within class and with Class 456.

South West Trains refurbished units (shown as "s") have been fitted with new 2+2 facing/unidirectional high-back seating, with some tip-up and "perch" seating.

**Class 455/7.** Second series with TSOs originally in Class 508s. Pressure heating and ventilation.

**DTSO.** Lot No. 30976 1984–1985. –/74 (s –/54 1W). 29.5 t.
**MSO.** Lot No. 30975 1984–1985. –/84 (s –/68). 45.5 t.
**TSO.** Lot No. 30944 1979–1980. –/86 (s –/68). 25.5 t.

| | | | | | | | | |
|---|---|---|---|---|---|---|---|---|
| 5701 | | **ST** | P | *SW* | WD | 77727 | 62783 | 71545 | 77728 |
| 5702 | | **ST** | P | *SW* | WD | 77729 | 62784 | 71547 | 77730 |
| 5703 | | **ST** | P | *SW* | WD | 77731 | 62785 | 71540 | 77732 |
| 5704 | | **ST** | P | *SW* | WD | 77733 | 62786 | 71548 | 77734 |
| 5705 | s | **SS** | P | *SW* | WD | 77735 | 62787 | 71565 | 77736 |
| 5706 | | **ST** | P | *SW* | WD | 77737 | 62788 | 71534 | 77738 |
| 5707 | s | **SS** | P | *SW* | WD | 77739 | 62789 | 71536 | 77740 |
| 5708 | | **ST** | P | *SW* | WD | 77741 | 62790 | 71560 | 77742 |
| 5709 | s | **SS** | P | *SW* | WD | 77743 | 62791 | 71532 | 77744 |
| 5710 | | **ST** | P | *SW* | WD | 77745 | 62792 | 71566 | 77746 |
| 5711 | s | **SS** | P | *SW* | WD | 77747 | 62793 | 71542 | 77748 |
| 5712 | | **ST** | P | *SW* | WD | 77749 | 62794 | 71546 | 77750 |
| 5713 | s | **SS** | P | *SW* | WD | 77751 | 62795 | 71567 | 77752 |
| 5714 | s | **SS** | P | *SW* | WD | 77753 | 62796 | 71539 | 77754 |
| 5715 | s | **SS** | P | *SW* | WD | 77755 | 62797 | 71535 | 77756 |
| 5716 | s | **SS** | P | *SW* | WD | 77757 | 62798 | 71564 | 77758 |
| 5717 | | **ST** | P | *SW* | WD | 77759 | 62799 | 71528 | 77760 |
| 5718 | | **ST** | P | *SW* | WD | 77761 | 62800 | 71557 | 77762 |
| 5719 | s | **SS** | P | *SW* | WD | 77763 | 62801 | 71558 | 77764 |
| 5720 | s | **SS** | P | *SW* | WD | 77765 | 62802 | 71568 | 77766 |
| 5721 | s | **SS** | P | *SW* | WD | 77767 | 62803 | 71553 | 77768 |
| 5722 | s | **SS** | P | *SW* | WD | 77769 | 62804 | 71533 | 77770 |

| 5723 | s | **SS** | P | *SW* | WD | 77771 | 62805 | 71526 | 77772 |
|------|---|--------|---|------|----|-------|-------|-------|-------|
| 5724 |   | **ST** | P | *SW* | WD | 77773 | 62806 | 71561 | 77774 |
| 5725 | s | **SS** | P | *SW* | WD | 77775 | 62807 | 71541 | 77776 |
| 5726 | s | **SS** | P | *SW* | WD | 77777 | 62808 | 71556 | 77778 |
| 5727 |   | **ST** | P | *SW* | WD | 77779 | 62809 | 71562 | 77780 |
| 5728 | s | **SS** | P | *SW* | WD | 77781 | 62810 | 71527 | 77782 |
| 5729 |   | **ST** | P | *SW* | WD | 77783 | 62811 | 71550 | 77784 |
| 5730 | s | **SS** | P | *SW* | WD | 77785 | 62812 | 71551 | 77786 |
| 5731 | s | **SS** | P | *SW* | WD | 77787 | 62813 | 71555 | 77788 |
| 5732 | s | **SS** | P | *SW* | WD | 77789 | 62814 | 71552 | 77790 |
| 5733 | s | **SS** | P | *SW* | WD | 77791 | 62815 | 71549 | 77792 |
| 5734 | s | **SS** | P | *SW* | WD | 77793 | 62816 | 71531 | 77794 |
| 5735 | s | **SS** | P | *SW* | WD | 77795 | 62817 | 71563 | 77796 |
| 5736 | s | **SS** | P | *SW* | WD | 77797 | 62818 | 71554 | 77798 |
| 5737 |   | **ST** | P | *SW* | WD | 77799 | 62819 | 71544 | 77800 |
| 5738 | s | **SS** | P | *SW* | WD | 77801 | 62820 | 71535 | 77802 |
| 5739 |   | **ST** | P | *SW* | WD | 77803 | 62821 | 71537 | 77804 |
| 5740 | s | **SS** | P | *SW* | WD | 77805 | 62822 | 71530 | 77806 |
| 5741 | s | **SS** | P | *SW* | WD | 77807 | 62823 | 71559 | 77808 |
| 5742 | s | **SS** | P | *SW* | WD | 77809 | 62824 | 71543 | 77810 |
| 5750 |   | **ST** | P | *SW* | WD | 77811 | 62825 | 71538 | 77812 |

**Name (carried on TSO):**

5750    Wimbledon Train Care

**Class 455/8. Southern units.** First series. Pressure heating and ventilation.

All units refurbished with new 3+2 high-back seating. Also fitted with in-cab air-conditioning systems meaning that the end door has been sealed.

**DTSO.** Lot No. 30972 York 1982–1984. –/74. 29.5 t.
**MSO.** Lot No. 30973 York 1982–1984. –/78 2W. 50.0 t.
**TSO.** Lot No. 30974 York 1982–1984. –/84. 28.0 t.

**Note:** Several units were reformed during refurbishment at Alstom, Eastleigh in 2005.

| 455 801 | **SN** | H | *SN* | SU | 77627 | 62709 | 71657 | 77580 |
|---------|--------|---|------|----|-------|-------|-------|-------|
| 455 802 | **SN** | H | *SN* | SU | 77581 | 62710 | 71664 | 77582 |
| 455 803 | **SN** | H | *SN* | SU | 77583 | 62711 | 71639 | 77584 |
| 455 804 | **SN** | H | *SN* | SU | 77585 | 62712 | 71640 | 77586 |
| 455 805 | **SN** | H | *SN* | SU | 77587 | 62713 | 71641 | 77588 |
| 455 806 | **SN** | H | *SN* | SU | 77589 | 62714 | 71642 | 77590 |
| 455 807 | **SN** | H | *SN* | SU | 77591 | 62715 | 71643 | 77592 |
| 455 808 | **SN** | H | *SN* | SU | 77637 | 62716 | 71644 | 77594 |
| 455 809 | **SN** | H | *SN* | SU | 77623 | 62717 | 71648 | 77602 |
| 455 810 | **SN** | H | *SN* | SU | 77597 | 62718 | 71646 | 77598 |
| 455 811 | **SN** | H | *SN* | SU | 77599 | 62719 | 71647 | 77600 |
| 455 812 | **SN** | H | *SN* | SU | 77595 | 62720 | 71645 | 77626 |
| 455 813 | **SN** | H | *SN* | SU | 77603 | 62721 | 71649 | 77604 |
| 455 814 | **SN** | H | *SN* | SU | 77605 | 62722 | 71650 | 77606 |
| 455 815 | **SN** | H | *SN* | SU | 77607 | 62723 | 71651 | 77608 |
| 455 816 | **SN** | H | *SN* | SU | 77609 | 62724 | 71652 | 77633 |

| 455 817 | **SN** | H | *SN* | SU | 77611 | 62725 | 71653 | 77612 |
| 455 818 | **SN** | H | *SN* | SU | 77613 | 62726 | 71654 | 77632 |
| 455 819 | **SN** | H | *SN* | SU | 77615 | 62727 | 71637 | 77616 |
| 455 820 | **SN** | H | *SN* | SU | 77617 | 62728 | 71656 | 77618 |
| 455 821 | **SN** | H | *SN* | SU | 77619 | 62729 | 71655 | 77620 |
| 455 822 | **SN** | H | *SN* | SU | 77621 | 62730 | 71658 | 77622 |
| 455 823 | **SN** | H | *SN* | SU | 77601 | 62731 | 71659 | 77596 |
| 455 824 | **SN** | H | *SN* | SU | 77593 | 62732 | 71660 | 77624 |
| 455 825 | **SN** | H | *SN* | SU | 77579 | 62733 | 71661 | 77628 |
| 455 826 | **SN** | H | *SN* | SU | 77630 | 62734 | 71662 | 77629 |
| 455 827 | **SN** | H | *SN* | SU | 77610 | 62735 | 71663 | 77614 |
| 455 828 | **SN** | H | *SN* | SU | 77631 | 62736 | 71638 | 77634 |
| 455 829 | **SN** | H | *SN* | SU | 77635 | 62737 | 71665 | 77636 |
| 455 830 | **SN** | H | *SN* | SU | 77625 | 62743 | 71666 | 77638 |
| 455 831 | **SN** | H | *SN* | SU | 77639 | 62739 | 71667 | 77640 |
| 455 832 | **SN** | H | *SN* | SU | 77641 | 62740 | 71668 | 77642 |
| 455 833 | **SN** | H | *SN* | SU | 77643 | 62741 | 71669 | 77644 |
| 455 834 | **SN** | H | *SN* | SU | 77645 | 62742 | 71670 | 77646 |
| 455 835 | **SN** | H | *SN* | SU | 77647 | 62738 | 71671 | 77648 |
| 455 836 | **SN** | H | *SN* | SU | 77649 | 62744 | 71672 | 77650 |
| 455 837 | **SN** | H | *SN* | SU | 77651 | 62745 | 71673 | 77652 |
| 455 838 | **SN** | H | *SN* | SU | 77653 | 62746 | 71674 | 77654 |
| 455 839 | **SN** | H | *SN* | SU | 77655 | 62747 | 71675 | 77656 |
| 455 840 | **SN** | H | *SN* | SU | 77657 | 62748 | 71676 | 77658 |
| 455 841 | **SN** | H | *SN* | SU | 77659 | 62749 | 71677 | 77660 |
| 455 842 | **SN** | H | *SN* | SU | 77661 | 62750 | 71678 | 77662 |
| 455 843 | **SN** | H | *SN* | SU | 77663 | 62751 | 71679 | 77664 |
| 455 844 | **SN** | H | *SN* | SU | 77665 | 62752 | 71680 | 77666 |
| 455 845 | **SN** | H | *SN* | SU | 77667 | 62753 | 71681 | 77668 |
| 455 846 | **SN** | H | *SN* | SU | 77669 | 62754 | 71682 | 77670 |

**Class 455/8. South West Trains units**. First series. Pressure heating and ventilation.

**DTSO**. Lot No. 30972 York 1982–1984. –/74. 29.5 t.
**MSO**. Lot No. 30973 York 1982–1984. –/84. 50.0 t.
**TSO**. Lot No. 30974 York 1982–1984. –/84. 28.0 t.

**Advertising liveries**: 5853 Cotes du Rhone wine (All over deep red with various images).
5856 Legoland Windsor (Yellow, blue and red with various images).
5868 Golden Jubilee/Hampton Court Palace (Gold with various images).
5869 Royal British Legion poppy appeal (white with poppy images).

| 5847 | **ST** | P | *SW* | WD | 77671 | 62755 | 71683 | 77672 |
| 5848 | **ST** | P | *SW* | WD | 77673 | 62756 | 71684 | 77674 |
| 5849 | **ST** | P | *SW* | WD | 77675 | 62757 | 71685 | 77676 |
| 5850 | **ST** | P | *SW* | WD | 77677 | 62758 | 71686 | 77678 |
| 5851 | **ST** | P | *SW* | WD | 77679 | 62759 | 71687 | 77680 |
| 5852 | **ST** | P | *SW* | WD | 77681 | 62760 | 71688 | 77682 |
| 5853 | **AL** | P | *SW* | WD | 77683 | 62761 | 71689 | 77684 |
| 5854 | **ST** | P | *SW* | WD | 77685 | 62762 | 71690 | 77686 |
| 5855 | **ST** | P | *SW* | WD | 77687 | 62763 | 71691 | 77688 |

| 5856 | **AL** | P | *SW* | WD | 77689 | 62764 | 71692 | 77690 |
|------|--------|---|------|----|-------|-------|-------|-------|
| 5857 | **ST** | P | *SW* | WD | 77691 | 62765 | 71693 | 77692 |
| 5858 | **ST** | P | *SW* | WD | 77693 | 62766 | 71694 | 77694 |
| 5859 | **ST** | P | *SW* | WD | 77695 | 62767 | 71695 | 77696 |
| 5860 | **ST** | P | *SW* | WD | 77697 | 62768 | 71696 | 77698 |
| 5861 | **ST** | P | *SW* | WD | 77699 | 62769 | 71697 | 77700 |
| 5862 | **ST** | P | *SW* | WD | 77701 | 62770 | 71698 | 77702 |
| 5863 | **ST** | P | *SW* | WD | 77703 | 62771 | 71699 | 77704 |
| 5864 | **ST** | P | *SW* | WD | 77705 | 62772 | 71700 | 77706 |
| 5865 | **ST** | P | *SW* | WD | 77707 | 62773 | 71701 | 77708 |
| 5866 | **ST** | P | *SW* | WD | 77709 | 62774 | 71702 | 77710 |
| 5867 | **ST** | P | *SW* | WD | 77711 | 62775 | 71703 | 77712 |
| 5868 | **AL** | P | *SW* | WD | 77713 | 62776 | 71704 | 77714 |
| 5869 | **AL** | P | *SW* | WD | 77715 | 62777 | 71705 | 77716 |
| 5870 | **ST** | P | *SW* | WD | 77717 | 62778 | 71706 | 77718 |
| 5871 | **ST** | P | *SW* | WD | 77719 | 62779 | 71707 | 77720 |
| 5872 | **ST** | P | *SW* | WD | 77721 | 62780 | 71708 | 77722 |
| 5873 | **ST** | P | *SW* | WD | 77723 | 62781 | 71709 | 77724 |
| 5874 | **ST** | P | *SW* | WD | 77725 | 62782 | 71710 | 77726 |

**Class 455/9**. Third series. Convection heating.
**Dimensions**: 19.96/20.18 x 2.82 m.

**DTSO**. Lot No. 30991 York 1985. –/74 (s –/54 1W). 29.0 t.
**MSO**. Lot No. 30992 York 1985. –/84 (s –/68). 45.5 t.
**TSO**. Lot No. 30993 York 1985. –/84 (s –/68). 27.1 t.
**TSO†**. Lot No. 30932 Derby 1981. –/84. 26.5 t.

**Note**: † Prototype vehicle 67400 converted from a Class 210 DEMU.

| 5901 |   | **ST** | P | *SW* | WD | 77813 | 62826 | 71714 | 77814 |
|------|---|--------|---|------|----|-------|-------|-------|-------|
| 5902 |   | **ST** | P | *SW* | WD | 77815 | 62827 | 71715 | 77816 |
| 5903 |   | **ST** | P | *SW* | WD | 77817 | 62828 | 71716 | 77818 |
| 5904 | s | **SS** | P | *SW* | WD | 77819 | 62829 | 71717 | 77820 |
| 5905 |   | **ST** | P | *SW* | WD | 77821 | 62830 | 71725 | 77822 |
| 5906 |   | **ST** | P | *SW* | WD | 77823 | 62831 | 71719 | 77824 |
| 5907 |   | **ST** | P | *SW* | WD | 77825 | 62832 | 71720 | 77826 |
| 5908 |   | **ST** | P | *SW* | WD | 77827 | 62833 | 71721 | 77828 |
| 5909 |   | **ST** | P | *SW* | WD | 77829 | 62834 | 71722 | 77830 |
| 5910 |   | **ST** | P | *SW* | WD | 77831 | 62835 | 71723 | 77832 |
| 5911 |   | **ST** | P | *SW* | WD | 77833 | 62836 | 71724 | 77834 |
| 5912 | † | **ST** | P | *SW* | WD | 77835 | 62837 | 67400 | 77836 |
| 5913 |   | **ST** | P | *SW* | WD | 77837 | 62838 | 71726 | 77838 |
| 5914 |   | **ST** | P | *SW* | WD | 77839 | 62839 | 71727 | 77840 |
| 5915 |   | **ST** | P | *SW* | WD | 77841 | 62840 | 71728 | 77842 |
| 5916 |   | **ST** | P | *SW* | WD | 77843 | 62841 | 71729 | 77844 |
| 5917 |   | **ST** | P | *SW* | WD | 77845 | 62842 | 71730 | 77846 |
| 5918 |   | **ST** | P | *SW* | WD | 77847 | 62843 | 71732 | 77848 |
| 5919 |   | **ST** | P | *SW* | WD | 77849 | 62844 | 71718 | 77850 |
| 5920 |   | **ST** | P | *SW* | WD | 77851 | 62845 | 71733 | 77852 |

# CLASS 456                                    BREL YORK

Southern inner suburban units.

**Formation:** DMSO–DTSO.
**Construction:** Steel underframe, aluminium alloy body & roof.
**Doors:** Sliding.
**Gangways:** Within unit.                    **Electrical Equipment:** 1982-type.
**Traction Motors:** Two GEC507-20J of 185 kW, some recovered from Class 405s.
**Bogies:** P7 (motor) and T3 (trailer).    **Couplers:** Tightlock.
**Maximum Speed:** 75 m.p.h.                 **Seating Layout:** 3+2 facing.
**Dimensions:** 20.61 x 2.82 m.              **Braking:** Disc brakes.
**Heating & Ventilation:** Convection heating.
**Multiple Working:** Within class and with Class 455.

**DMSO.** Lot No. 31073 1990–1991. –/79. 41.1 t.
**DTSO.** Lot No. 31074 1990–1991. –/73 1T. 31.4 t.

| | | | | | |
|---|---|---|---|---|---|
| 456 001 | N | P | *SN* | SU | 64735 78250 |
| 456 002 | N | P | *SN* | SU | 64736 78251 |
| 456 003 | N | P | *SN* | SU | 64737 78252 |
| 456 004 | N | P | *SN* | SU | 64738 78253 |
| 456 005 | N | P | *SN* | SU | 64739 78254 |
| 456 006 | N | P | *SN* | SU | 64740 78255 |
| 456 007 | N | P | *SN* | SU | 64741 78256 |
| 456 008 | N | P | *SN* | SU | 64742 78257 |
| 456 009 | N | P | *SN* | SU | 64743 78258 |
| 456 010 | N | P | *SN* | SU | 64744 78259 |
| 456 011 | N | P | *SN* | SU | 64745 78260 |
| 456 012 | N | P | *SN* | SU | 64746 78261 |
| 456 013 | N | P | *SN* | SU | 64747 78262 |
| 456 014 | N | P | *SN* | SU | 64748 78263 |
| 456 015 | N | P | *SN* | SU | 64749 78264 |
| 456 016 | N | P | *SN* | SU | 64750 78265 |
| 456 017 | N | P | *SN* | SU | 64751 78266 |
| 456 018 | N | P | *SN* | SU | 64752 78267 |
| 456 019 | N | P | *SN* | SU | 64753 78268 |
| 456 020 | N | P | *SN* | SU | 64754 78269 |
| 456 021 | N | P | *SN* | SU | 64755 78270 |
| 456 022 | N | P | *SN* | SU | 64756 78271 |
| 456 023 | N | P | *SN* | SU | 64757 78272 |
| 456 024 | CX | P | *SN* | SU | 64758 78273 |

**Name (carried on DTSO):** 456 024 Sir Cosmo Bonsor.

# CLASS 458 JUNIPER ALSTOM BIRMINGHAM

South West Trains outer suburban units. These units now only see very limited use.

**Formation:** DMCO–PTSO–MSO–DMCO.
**SR designation:** 4 Jop.
**Construction:** Steel.
**Gangways:** Throughout.
**Doors:** Sliding plug.
**Electrical Equipment:** IGBT control.
**Traction Motors:** Two Alstom ONIX 800 asynchronous of 270 kW.
**Couplers:** Scharfenberg.
**Bogies:** ACR.
**Maximum Speed:** 100 m.p.h.
**Dimensions:** 21.16/19.94 x 2.80 m.
**Seating Layout:** 1: 2+2 facing, 2: 3+2 facing/unidirectional.
**Braking:** Disc and regenerative brakes.
**Multiple Working:** Within class.
**Heating & Ventilation:** Air conditioning.

**DMCO(A).** Alstom 1998–2000. 12/63. 45.2 t.
**PTSO.** Alstom 1998–2000. –/49 1TD 2W. 33.3 t.
**MSO.** Alstom 1998–2000. –/75 1T. 40.6 t.
**DMCO(B).** Alstom 1998–2000. 12/63. 45.2 t.

| | | | | | | | |
|---|---|---|---|---|---|---|---|
| 8001 | **SW** | P | | SL | 67601 | 74001 | 74101 | 67701 |
| 8002 | **SW** | P | | SL | 67602 | 74002 | 74102 | 67702 |
| 8003 | **SW** | P | *SW* | WD | 67603 | 74003 | 74103 | 67703 |
| 8004 | **SW** | P | *SW* | WD | 67604 | 74004 | 74104 | 67704 |
| 8005 | **SW** | P | *SW* | WD | 67605 | 74005 | 74105 | 67705 |
| 8006 | **SW** | P | *SW* | WD | 67606 | 74006 | 74106 | 67706 |
| 8007 | **SW** | P | *SW* | WD | 67607 | 74007 | 74107 | 67707 |
| 8008 | **SW** | P | *SW* | WD | 67608 | 74008 | 74108 | 67708 |
| 8009 | **SW** | P | *SW* | WD | 67609 | 74009 | 74109 | 67709 |
| 8010 | **SW** | P | *SW* | WD | 67610 | 74010 | 74110 | 67710 |
| 8011 | **SW** | P | *SW* | WD | 67611 | 74011 | 74111 | 67711 |
| 8012 | **SW** | P | *SW* | WD | 67612 | 74012 | 74112 | 67712 |
| 8013 | **SW** | P | *SW* | WD | 67613 | 74013 | 74113 | 67713 |
| 8014 | **SW** | P | *SW* | WD | 67614 | 74014 | 74114 | 67714 |
| 8015 | **SW** | P | *SW* | WD | 67615 | 74015 | 74115 | 67715 |
| 8016 | **SW** | P | *SW* | WD | 67616 | 74016 | 74116 | 67716 |
| 8017 | **SW** | P | *SW* | WD | 67617 | 74017 | 74117 | 67717 |
| 8018 | **SW** | P | *SW* | WD | 67618 | 74018 | 74118 | 67718 |
| 8019 | **SW** | P | *SW* | WD | 67619 | 74019 | 74119 | 67719 |
| 8020 | **SW** | P | *SW* | WD | 67620 | 74020 | 74120 | 67720 |
| 8021 | **SW** | P | *SW* | WD | 67621 | 74021 | 74121 | 67721 |
| 8022 | **SW** | P | *SW* | WD | 67622 | 74022 | 74122 | 67722 |
| 8023 | **SW** | P | *SW* | WD | 67623 | 74023 | 74123 | 67723 |
| 8024 | **SW** | P | *SW* | WD | 67624 | 74024 | 74124 | 67724 |
| 8025 | **SW** | P | *SW* | WD | 67625 | 74025 | 74125 | 67725 |
| 8026 | **SW** | P | *SW* | WD | 67626 | 74026 | 74126 | 67726 |
| 8027 | **SW** | P | *SW* | WD | 67627 | 74027 | 74127 | 67727 |
| 8028 | **SW** | P | *SW* | WD | 67628 | 74028 | 74128 | 67728 |
| 8029 | **SW** | P | *SW* | WD | 67629 | 74029 | 74129 | 67729 |
| 8030 | **SW** | P | *SW* | WD | 67630 | 74030 | 74130 | 67730 |

# CLASS 460                          GEC-ALSTHOM JUNIPER

Gatwick Express units. Only the last two digits of the unit number are carried on the front ends of these units.

**Formation:** DMLFO–TFO–TCO–2MSO–TSO–MSO–DMSO.
**SR designation:** 8 Gat.
**Construction:** Steel.          **Doors:** Sliding plug.
**Gangways:** Within unit.    **Electrical Equipment:** IGBT control.
**Traction Motors:** Two Alstom ONIX 800 asynchronous of 270 kW.
**Couplers:** Scharfenberg.
**Maximum Speed:** 100 m.p.h.          **Bogies:** ACR.
**Seating Layout:** 1: 2+1 facing, 2: 2+2 facing/unidirectional.
**Dimensions:** 21.01/19.94 x 2.80 m. **Braking:** Disc and regenerative brakes.
**Heating & Ventilation:** Air conditioning.
**Multiple Working:** Within class.

**DMLFO.** Alstom 1998–1999. 10/– 42.6 t.
**TFO.** Alstom 1998–1999. 28/– 1TD 1W. 33.5 t.
**TCO.** Alstom 1998–1999. 9/42 1T. 34.9 t.
**MSO(A).** Alstom 1998–1999. –/60. 42.5 t.
**MSO(B).** Alstom 1998–1999. –/60. 42.5 t.
**TSO.** Alstom 1998–1999. –/38 1TD 1W. 35.2 t.
**MSO(C).** Alstom 1998–1999. –/60. 40.5 t.
**DMSO.** Alstom 1998–1999. –/56. 45.3 t.

**Advertising livery:** 460 003 and 460 005 Continental Airlines (mid blue with gold and yellow script).

| | | | | | | | |
|---|---|---|---|---|---|---|---|
| 460 001 | **GV** | P | *GX* | SL | 67901 | 74401 | 74411 | 74421 |
| | | | | | 74431 | 74441 | 74451 | 67911 |
| 460 002 | **GV** | P | *GX* | SL | 67902 | 74402 | 74412 | 74422 |
| | | | | | 74432 | 74442 | 74452 | 67912 |
| 460 003 | **AL** | P | *GX* | SL | 67903 | 74403 | 74413 | 74423 |
| | | | | | 74433 | 74443 | 74453 | 67913 |
| 460 004 | **GV** | P | *GX* | SL | 67904 | 74404 | 74414 | 74424 |
| | | | | | 74434 | 74444 | 74454 | 67914 |
| 460 005 | **AL** | P | *GX* | SL | 67905 | 74405 | 74415 | 74425 |
| | | | | | 74435 | 74445 | 74455 | 67915 |
| 460 006 | **GV** | P | *GX* | SL | 67906 | 74406 | 74416 | 74426 |
| | | | | | 74436 | 74446 | 74456 | 67916 |
| 460 007 | **GV** | P | *GX* | SL | 67907 | 74407 | 74417 | 74427 |
| | | | | | 74437 | 74447 | 74457 | 67917 |
| 460 008 | **GV** | P | *GX* | SL | 67908 | 74408 | 74418 | 74428 |
| | | | | | 74438 | 74448 | 74458 | 67918 |

# CLASS 465                 NETWORKER

South Eastern Trains suburban units.

**Formation:** DMSO–TSO–TSO–DMSO.
**Construction:** Welded aluminium alloy.
**Doors:** Sliding plug.         **Gangways:** Within unit.
**Electrical Equipment:** 1992-type GTO inverters.
**Traction Motors:** Four Brush TIM970 (Classes 465/0 and 465/1) or GEC-Alsthom G352AY (Class 465/2) asynchronous of 280 kW.
**Couplers:** Tightlock.
**Bogies:** BREL P3/T3 (Classes 465/0 and 465/1) SRP BP62/BT52 (Classes 465/2 and 465/9).
**Maximum Speed:** 75 m.p.h.     **Dimensions:** 20.89/20.06 x 2.81 m.
**Seating Layout:** 3+2 (* 2+2) facing/unidirectional.
**Braking:** Disc, rheostatic and regenerative.
**Multiple Working:** Within class and with Class 466.

**64759–64808. DMSO(A).** Lot No. 31100 BREL York 1991–1993. –/86 (* –/74). 39.2 t.
**64809–64858. DMSO(B).** Lot No. 31100 BREL York 1991–1993. –/86 (* –/74). 39.2 t.
**65734–65749. DMSO(A).** Lot No. 31103 Metro-Cammell 1991–1993. –/86. 39.2 t.
**65784–65799. DMSO(B).** Lot No. 31103 Metro-Cammell 1991–1993. –/86. 39.2 t.
**65800–65846. DMSO(A).** Lot No. 31130 ABB York 1993–1994. –/86. 39.2 t.
**65847–65893. DMSO(B).** Lot No. 31130 ABB York 1993–1994. –/86. 39.2 t.
**72028–72126 (even nos.) TSO.** Lot No. 31102 BREL York 1991–1993. –/90 (* –/80). 27.2 t.
**72029–72127 (odd nos.) TSO.** Lot No. 31101 BREL York 1991–1993. –/86 1T (* –/76 1T). 28.0 t.
**72787–72817 (odd nos.) TSO.** Lot No. 31104 Metro-Cammell 1991–1992. –/86 1T. 28.0 t.
**72788–72818 (even nos.) TSO.** Lot No. 31105 Metro-Cammell 1991–1992. –/90. 27.2 t.
**72900–72992 (even nos.) TSO.** Lot No. 31102 ABB York 1993–1994. –/90. 27.2 t.
**72901–72993 (odd nos.) TSO.** Lot No. 31101 ABB York 1993–1994. –/86 1T. 28.0 t.

**Class 465/0.** Built by BREL/ABB.

| | | | | | | | | |
|---|---|---|---|---|---|---|---|---|
| 465 001 | | CN | H | *SE* | SG | 64759 | 72028 | 72029 | 64809 |
| 465 002 | | CN | H | *SE* | SG | 64760 | 72030 | 72031 | 64810 |
| 465 003 | | CB | H | *SE* | SG | 64761 | 72032 | 72033 | 64811 |
| 465 004 | | NT | H | *SE* | SG | 64762 | 72034 | 72035 | 64812 |
| 465 005 | | CN | H | *SE* | SG | 64763 | 72036 | 72037 | 64813 |
| 465 006 | | CN | H | *SE* | SG | 64764 | 72038 | 72039 | 64814 |
| 465 007 | | CB | H | *SE* | SG | 64765 | 72040 | 72041 | 64815 |
| 465 008 | | CB | H | *SE* | SG | 64766 | 72042 | 72043 | 64816 |
| 465 009 | | CB | H | *SE* | SG | 64767 | 72044 | 72045 | 64817 |
| 465 010 | | CB | H | *SE* | SG | 64768 | 72046 | 72047 | 64818 |
| 465 011 | | CN | H | *SE* | SG | 64769 | 72048 | 72049 | 64819 |
| 465 012 | | CN | H | *SE* | SG | 64770 | 72050 | 72051 | 64820 |
| 465 013 | | CB | H | *SE* | SG | 64771 | 72052 | 72053 | 64821 |
| 465 014 | * | CB | H | *SE* | SG | 64772 | 72054 | 72055 | 64822 |
| 465 015 | | CB | H | *SE* | SG | 64773 | 72056 | 72057 | 64823 |

| 465 016 | **CB** | H | *SE* | SG | 64774 | 72058 | 72059 | 64824 |
| 465 017 | **CB** | H | *SE* | SG | 64775 | 72060 | 72061 | 64825 |
| 465 018 | **CB** | H | *SE* | SG | 64776 | 72062 | 72063 | 64826 |
| 465 019 | **CB** | H | *SE* | SG | 64777 | 72064 | 72065 | 64827 |
| 465 020 | **CB** | H | *SE* | SG | 64778 | 72066 | 72067 | 64828 |
| 465 021 | **CN** | H | *SE* | SG | 64779 | 72068 | 72069 | 64829 |
| 465 022 | **NT** | H | *SE* | SG | 64780 | 72070 | 72071 | 64830 |
| 465 023 | **NT** | H | *SE* | SG | 64781 | 72072 | 72073 | 64831 |
| 465 024 | **NT** | H | *SE* | SG | 64782 | 72074 | 72075 | 64832 |
| 465 025 | **NT** | H | *SE* | SG | 64783 | 72076 | 72077 | 64833 |
| 465 026 | **NT** | H | *SE* | SG | 64784 | 72078 | 72079 | 64834 |
| 465 027 | **NT** | H | *SE* | SG | 64785 | 72080 | 72081 | 64835 |
| 465 028 | **NT** | H | *SE* | SG | 64786 | 72082 | 72083 | 64836 |
| 465 029 | **CN** | H | *SE* | SG | 64787 | 72084 | 72085 | 64837 |
| 465 030 | **NT** | H | *SE* | SG | 64788 | 72086 | 72087 | 64838 |
| 465 031 | **NT** | H | *SE* | SG | 64789 | 72088 | 72089 | 64839 |
| 465 032 | **NT** | H | *SE* | SG | 64790 | 72090 | 72091 | 64840 |
| 465 033 | **NT** | H | *SE* | SG | 64791 | 72092 | 72093 | 64841 |
| 465 034 | **NT** | H | *SE* | SG | 64792 | 72094 | 72095 | 64842 |
| 465 035 | **CN** | H | *SE* | SG | 64793 | 72096 | 72097 | 64843 |
| 465 036 | **NT** | H | *SE* | SG | 64794 | 72098 | 72099 | 64844 |
| 465 037 | **CN** | H | *SE* | SG | 64795 | 72100 | 72101 | 64845 |
| 465 038 | **CN** | H | *SE* | SG | 64796 | 72102 | 72103 | 64846 |
| 465 039 | **NT** | H | *SE* | SG | 64797 | 72104 | 72105 | 64847 |
| 465 040 | **NT** | H | *SE* | SG | 64798 | 72106 | 72107 | 64848 |
| 465 041 | **NT** | H | *SE* | SG | 64799 | 72108 | 72109 | 64849 |
| 465 042 | **NT** | H | *SE* | SG | 64800 | 72110 | 72111 | 64850 |
| 465 043 | **NT** | H | *SE* | SG | 64801 | 72112 | 72113 | 64851 |
| 465 044 | **CN** | H | *SE* | SG | 64802 | 72114 | 72115 | 64852 |
| 465 045 | **NT** | H | *SE* | SG | 64803 | 72116 | 72117 | 64853 |
| 465 046 | **CN** | H | *SE* | SG | 64804 | 72118 | 72119 | 64854 |
| 465 047 | **NT** | H | *SE* | SG | 64805 | 72120 | 72121 | 64855 |
| 465 048 | **NT** | H | *SE* | SG | 64806 | 72122 | 72123 | 64856 |
| 465 049 | **NT** | H | *SE* | SG | 64807 | 72124 | 72125 | 64857 |
| 465 050 | **CN** | H | *SE* | SG | 64808 | 72126 | 72127 | 64858 |

**Class 465/1.** Built by BREL/ABB. Similar to Class 465/0 but with detail differences.

| 465 151 | **NT** | H | *SE* | SG | 65800 | 72900 | 72901 | 65847 |
| 465 152 | **NT** | H | *SE* | SG | 65801 | 72902 | 72903 | 65848 |
| 465 153 | **NT** | H | *SE* | SG | 65802 | 72904 | 72905 | 65849 |
| 465 154 | **NT** | H | *SE* | SG | 65803 | 72906 | 72907 | 65850 |
| 465 155 | **NT** | H | *SE* | SG | 65804 | 72908 | 72909 | 65851 |
| 465 156 | **NT** | H | *SE* | SG | 65805 | 72910 | 72911 | 65852 |
| 465 157 | **NT** | H | *SE* | SG | 65806 | 72912 | 72913 | 65853 |
| 465 158 | **NT** | H | *SE* | SG | 65807 | 72914 | 72915 | 65854 |
| 465 159 | **NT** | H | *SE* | SG | 65808 | 72916 | 72917 | 65855 |
| 465 160 | **NT** | H | *SE* | SG | 65809 | 72918 | 72919 | 65856 |
| 465 161 | **NT** | H | *SE* | SG | 65810 | 72920 | 72921 | 65857 |
| 465 162 | **NT** | H | *SE* | SG | 65811 | 72922 | 72923 | 65858 |
| 465 163 | **NT** | H | *SE* | SG | 65812 | 72924 | 72925 | 65859 |

| | | | | | | | | |
|---|---|---|---|---|---|---|---|---|
| 465 164 | **CN** | H | *SE* | SG | 65813 | 72926 | 72927 | 65860 |
| 465 165 | **NT** | H | *SE* | SG | 65814 | 72928 | 72929 | 65861 |
| 465 166 | **NT** | H | *SE* | SG | 65815 | 72930 | 72931 | 65862 |
| 465 167 | **NT** | H | *SE* | SG | 65816 | 72932 | 72933 | 65863 |
| 465 168 | **NT** | H | *SE* | SG | 65817 | 72934 | 72935 | 65864 |
| 465 169 | **NT** | H | *SE* | SG | 65818 | 72936 | 72937 | 65865 |
| 465 170 | **NT** | H | *SE* | SG | 65819 | 72938 | 72939 | 65866 |
| 465 171 | **NT** | H | *SE* | SG | 65820 | 72940 | 72941 | 65867 |
| 465 172 | **NT** | H | *SE* | SG | 65821 | 72942 | 72943 | 65868 |
| 465 173 | **NT** | H | *SE* | SG | 65822 | 72944 | 72945 | 65869 |
| 465 174 | **NT** | H | *SE* | SG | 65823 | 72946 | 72947 | 65870 |
| 465 175 | **NT** | H | *SE* | SG | 65824 | 72948 | 72949 | 65871 |
| 465 176 | **NT** | H | *SE* | SG | 65825 | 72950 | 72951 | 65872 |
| 465 177 | **NT** | H | *SE* | SG | 65826 | 72952 | 72953 | 65873 |
| 465 178 | **NT** | H | *SE* | SG | 65827 | 72954 | 72955 | 65874 |
| 465 179 | **NT** | H | *SE* | SG | 65828 | 72956 | 72957 | 65875 |
| 465 180 | **NT** | H | *SE* | SG | 65829 | 72958 | 72959 | 65876 |
| 465 181 | **NT** | H | *SE* | SG | 65830 | 72960 | 72961 | 65877 |
| 465 182 | **NT** | H | *SE* | SG | 65831 | 72962 | 72963 | 65878 |
| 465 183 | **NT** | H | *SE* | SG | 65832 | 72964 | 72965 | 65879 |
| 465 184 | **NT** | H | *SE* | SG | 65833 | 72966 | 72967 | 65880 |
| 465 185 | **NT** | H | *SE* | SG | 65834 | 72968 | 72969 | 65881 |
| 465 186 | **NT** | H | *SE* | SG | 65835 | 72970 | 72971 | 65882 |
| 465 187 | **NT** | H | *SE* | SG | 65836 | 72972 | 72973 | 65883 |
| 465 188 | **NT** | H | *SE* | SG | 65837 | 72974 | 72975 | 65884 |
| 465 189 | **CN** | H | *SE* | SG | 65838 | 72976 | 72977 | 65885 |
| 465 190 | **NT** | H | *SE* | SG | 65839 | 72978 | 72979 | 65886 |
| 465 191 | **NT** | H | *SE* | SG | 65840 | 72980 | 72981 | 65887 |
| 465 192 | **NT** | H | *SE* | SG | 65841 | 72982 | 72983 | 65888 |
| 465 193 | **NT** | H | *SE* | SG | 65842 | 72984 | 72985 | 65889 |
| 465 194 | **NT** | H | *SE* | SG | 65843 | 72986 | 72987 | 65890 |
| 465 195 | **NT** | H | *SE* | SG | 65844 | 72988 | 72989 | 65891 |
| 465 196 | **NT** | H | *SE* | SG | 65845 | 72990 | 72991 | 65892 |
| 465 197 | **NT** | H | *SE* | SG | 65846 | 72992 | 72993 | 65893 |

**Class 465/2.** Built by Metro-Cammell. **Dimensions:** 20.80/20.15 x 2.81 m.
**Advertising livery:** 465 237 Continental Airlines (mid blue with gold & yellow script).

| | | | | | | | | |
|---|---|---|---|---|---|---|---|---|
| 465 235 | **CN** | A | *SE* | SG | 65734 | 72787 | 72788 | 65784 |
| 465 236 | **CN** | A | *SE* | SG | 65735 | 72789 | 72790 | 65785 |
| 465 237 | **AL** | A | *SE* | SG | 65736 | 72791 | 72792 | 65786 |
| 465 238 | **CN** | A | *SE* | SG | 65737 | 72793 | 72794 | 65787 |
| 465 239 | **CN** | A | *SE* | SG | 65738 | 72795 | 72796 | 65788 |
| 465 240 | **CN** | A | *SE* | SG | 65739 | 72797 | 72798 | 65789 |
| 465 241 | **CN** | A | *SE* | SG | 65740 | 72799 | 72800 | 65790 |
| 465 242 | **CN** | A | *SE* | SG | 65741 | 72801 | 72802 | 65791 |
| 465 243 | **CN** | A | *SE* | SG | 65742 | 72803 | 72804 | 65792 |
| 465 244 | **CN** | A | *SE* | SG | 65743 | 72805 | 72806 | 65793 |
| 465 245 | **CN** | A | *SE* | SG | 65744 | 72807 | 72808 | 65794 |
| 465 246 | **CN** | A | *SE* | SG | 65745 | 72809 | 72810 | 65795 |
| 465 247 | **CN** | A | *SE* | SG | 65746 | 72811 | 72812 | 65796 |
| 465 248 | **CN** | A | *SE* | SG | 65747 | 72813 | 72814 | 65797 |

| 465 249 | **CN** | A | *SE* | SG | 65748 | 72815 | 72816 | 65798 |
| 465 250 | **CN** | A | *SE* | SG | 65749 | 72817 | 72818 | 65799 |

**Class 465/9.** Built by Metro-Cammell. Refurbished at Wabtec, Doncaster in 2005 for longer distance services, with the addition of first class seating areas and wheelchair spaces. Details as Class 465/2 unless stated.

**Formation:** DMCO–TSO(A)–TSO(B)–DMCO.
**Seating Layout:** 1: 2+2 facing/unidirectional, 2: 3+2 facing/unidirectional.

**65700–65733. DMCO(A).** Lot No. 31103 Metro-Cammell 1991–1993. 12/68. 39.2 t.
**72719–72785 (odd nos.) TSO(A).** Lot No. 31104 Metro-Cammell 1991–1992. –/76 1T 2W. 30.3 t.
**72720–72786 (even nos.) TSO(B).** Lot No. 31105 Metro-Cammell 1991–1992. –/90. 29.5 t.
**65750–65783. DMCO(B).** Lot No. 31103 Metro-Cammell 1991–1993. 12/68. 39.2 t.

| 465 901 | (465 201) | **CN** | A | *SE* | GI | 65700 | 72719 | 72720 | 65750 |
| 465 902 | (465 202) | **CN** | A | *SE* | GI | 65701 | 72721 | 72722 | 65751 |
| 465 903 | (465 203) | **CN** | A | *SE* | GI | 65702 | 72723 | 72724 | 65752 |
| 465 904 | (465 204) | **CN** | A | *SE* | GI | 65703 | 72725 | 72726 | 65753 |
| 465 905 | (465 205) | **CN** | A | *SE* | GI | 65704 | 72727 | 72728 | 65754 |
| 465 906 | (465 206) | **CN** | A | *SE* | GI | 65705 | 72729 | 72730 | 65755 |
| 465 907 | (465 207) | **CN** | A | *SE* | GI | 65706 | 72731 | 72732 | 65756 |
| 465 908 | (465 208) | **CN** | A | *SE* | GI | 65707 | 72733 | 72734 | 65757 |
| 465 909 | (465 209) | **CN** | A | *SE* | GI | 65708 | 72735 | 72736 | 65758 |
| 465 910 | (465 210) | **CN** | A | *SE* | GI | 65709 | 72737 | 72738 | 65759 |
| 465 911 | (465 211) | **CN** | A | *SE* | GI | 65710 | 72739 | 72740 | 65760 |
| 465 912 | (465 212) | **CN** | A | *SE* | GI | 65711 | 72741 | 72742 | 65761 |
| 465 913 | (465 213) | **CN** | A | *SE* | GI | 65712 | 72743 | 72744 | 65762 |
| 465 914 | (465 214) | **CN** | A | *SE* | GI | 65713 | 72745 | 72746 | 65763 |
| 465 915 | (465 215) | **CN** | A | *SE* | GI | 65714 | 72747 | 72748 | 65764 |
| 465 916 | (465 216) | **CN** | A | *SE* | GI | 65715 | 72749 | 72750 | 65765 |
| 465 917 | (465 217) | **CN** | A | *SE* | GI | 65716 | 72751 | 72752 | 65766 |
| 465 918 | (465 218) | **CN** | A | *SE* | GI | 65717 | 72753 | 72754 | 65767 |
| 465 919 | (465 219) | **CN** | A | *SE* | GI | 65718 | 72755 | 72756 | 65768 |
| 465 920 | (465 220) | **CN** | A | *SE* | GI | 65719 | 72757 | 72758 | 65769 |
| 465 921 | (465 221) | **CN** | A | *SE* | GI | 65720 | 72759 | 72760 | 65770 |
| 465 922 | (465 222) | **CN** | A | *SE* | GI | 65721 | 72761 | 72762 | 65771 |
| 465 923 | (465 223) | **CN** | A | *SE* | GI | 65722 | 72763 | 72764 | 65772 |
| 465 924 | (465 224) | **CN** | A | *SE* | GI | 65723 | 72765 | 72766 | 65773 |
| 465 925 | (465 225) | **CN** | A | *SE* | GI | 65724 | 72767 | 72768 | 65774 |
| 465 926 | (465 226) | **CN** | A | *SE* | GI | 65725 | 72769 | 72770 | 65775 |
| 465 927 | (465 227) | **CN** | A | *SE* | GI | 65726 | 72771 | 72772 | 65776 |
| 465 928 | (465 228) | **CN** | A | *SE* | GI | 65727 | 72773 | 72774 | 65777 |
| 465 929 | (465 229) | **CN** | A | *SE* | GI | 65728 | 72775 | 72776 | 65778 |
| 465 930 | (465 230) | **CN** | A | *SE* | GI | 65729 | 72777 | 72778 | 65779 |
| 465 931 | (465 231) | **CN** | A | *SE* | GI | 65730 | 72779 | 72780 | 65780 |
| 465 932 | (465 232) | **CN** | A | *SE* | GI | 65731 | 72781 | 72782 | 65781 |
| 465 933 | (465 233) | **CN** | A | *SE* | GI | 65732 | 72783 | 72784 | 65782 |
| 465 934 | (465 234) | **CN** | A | *SE* | GI | 65733 | 72785 | 72786 | 65783 |

**Name:** 465 903    Remembrance

# CLASS 466     NETWORKER     GEC-ALSTHOM

South Eastern Trains suburban units.

**Formation:** DMSO–DTSO.
**Construction:** Welded aluminium alloy.
**Doors:** Sliding plug.
**Gangways:** Within unit.
**Electrical Equipment:** 1992-type GTO inverters.
**Traction Motors:** Four GEC-Alsthom G352AY asynchronous of 280 kW.
**Couplers:** Tightlock.                    **Bogies:** BREL P3/T3.
**Maximum Speed:** 75 m.p.h.               **Dimensions:** 20.80 x 2.80 m.
**Seating Layout:** 3+2 (* 2+2) facing/unidirectional.
**Braking:** Disc, rheostatic and regenerative.
**Multiple Working:** Within class and with Class 465.

**DMSO.** Lot No. 31128 Birmingham 1993–1994. –/86 (* –/72). 40.6 t.
**DTSO.** Lot No. 31129 Birmingham 1993–1994. –/82 1T (* –/68 1T). 31.4 t.

| | | | | | | |
|---|---|---|---|---|---|---|
| 466 001 | | **CN** | A | *SE* | SG | 64860 78312 |
| 466 002 | | **CN** | A | *SE* | SG | 64861 78313 |
| 466 003 | | **CN** | A | *SE* | SG | 64862 78314 |
| 466 004 | | **CN** | A | *SE* | SG | 64863 78315 |
| 466 005 | | **CN** | A | *SE* | SG | 64864 78316 |
| 466 006 | | **CN** | A | *SE* | SG | 64865 78317 |
| 466 007 | | **CN** | A | *SE* | SG | 64866 78318 |
| 466 008 | | **CN** | A | *SE* | SG | 64867 78319 |
| 466 009 | | **CN** | A | *SE* | SG | 64868 78320 |
| 466 010 | | **CN** | A | *SE* | SG | 64869 78321 |
| 466 011 | | **CN** | A | *SE* | SG | 64870 78322 |
| 466 012 | | **CN** | A | *SE* | SG | 64871 78323 |
| 466 013 | | **CN** | A | *SE* | SG | 64872 78324 |
| 466 014 | | **CN** | A | *SE* | SG | 64873 78325 |
| 466 015 | | **CN** | A | *SE* | SG | 64874 78326 |
| 466 016 | | **CN** | A | *SE* | SG | 64875 78327 |
| 466 017 | * | **CN** | A | *SE* | SG | 64876 78328 |
| 466 018 | | **CN** | A | *SE* | SG | 64877 78329 |
| 466 019 | | **CN** | A | *SE* | SG | 64878 78330 |
| 466 020 | | **CN** | A | *SE* | SG | 64879 78331 |
| 466 021 | | **CN** | A | *SE* | SG | 64880 78332 |
| 466 022 | | **CN** | A | *SE* | SG | 64881 78333 |
| 466 023 | | **CN** | A | *SE* | SG | 64882 78334 |
| 466 024 | | **CN** | A | *SE* | SG | 64883 78335 |
| 466 025 | | **CN** | A | *SE* | SG | 64884 78336 |
| 466 026 | | **CN** | A | *SE* | SG | 64885 78337 |
| 466 027 | | **CN** | A | *SE* | SG | 64886 78338 |
| 466 028 | | **CN** | A | *SE* | SG | 64887 78339 |
| 466 029 | | **CN** | A | *SE* | SG | 64888 78340 |
| 466 030 | | **CN** | A | *SE* | SG | 64889 78341 |
| 466 031 | | **CN** | A | *SE* | SG | 64890 78342 |
| 466 032 | | **CN** | A | *SE* | SG | 64891 78343 |

| 466 033 | **CN** | A | *SE* | SG | 64892 | 78344 |
| 466 034 | **CN** | A | *SE* | SG | 64893 | 78345 |
| 466 035 | **CN** | A | *SE* | SG | 64894 | 78346 |
| 466 036 | **CN** | A | *SE* | SG | 64895 | 78347 |
| 466 037 | **CN** | A | *SE* | SG | 64896 | 78348 |
| 466 038 | **CN** | A | *SE* | SG | 64897 | 78349 |
| 466 039 | **CN** | A | *SE* | SG | 64898 | 78350 |
| 466 040 | **CN** | A | *SE* | SG | 64899 | 78351 |
| 466 041 | **CN** | A | *SE* | SG | 64900 | 78352 |
| 466 042 | **CN** | A | *SE* | SG | 64901 | 78353 |
| 466 043 | **CN** | A | *SE* | SG | 64902 | 78354 |

# CLASS 483                                        METRO-CAMMELL

Built 1938 onwards for LTE. Converted 1989–1990 for Isle of Wight Line.

**Formation:** DMSO–DMSO.
**System:** 660 V DC third rail.
**Construction:** Steel.                        **Doors:** Sliding.
**Gangways:** None. End doors.                  **Electrical Equipment:** IGBT control.
**Traction Motors:** Two Crompton Parkinson/GEC/BTH LT100 of 125 kW.
**Couplers:** Wedglock.                         **Bogies:** LT design.
**Maximum Speed:** 45 m.p.h.                    **Multiple Working:** Within class.
**Seating Layout:** Longitudinal or 2+2 facing/unidirectional.
**Dimensions:** 16.15 x 2.69 m.                 **Braking:** Tread brakes.

**Notes:** The last three numbers of the unit number only are carried.

Former London Underground numbers are shown in parentheses.

**DMSO (A).** Lot No. 31071. –/40. 27.4 t.
**DMSO (B).** Lot No. 31072. –/42. 27.4 t.

**Non-standard livery:** 483 007 and 483 009 Original London Transport Maroon
and cream.

| 483 002 | **IL** | H | *IL* | RY | 122 | (10221) | 225 | (11142) |
| 483 003 | **N** | H | | RY | 123 | (10116) | 221 | (11184) |
| 483 004 | **IL** | H | *IL* | RY | 124 | (10205) | 224 | (11205) |
| 483 006 | **IL** | H | *IL* | RY | 126 | (10297) | 226 | (11297) |
| 483 007 | **0** | H | *IL* | RY | 127 | (10291) | 227 | (11291) |
| 483 008 | **IL** | H | *IL* | RY | 128 | (10255) | 228 | (11255) |
| 483 009 | **0** | H | *IL* | RY | 129 | (10289) | 229 | (11229) |

# CLASS 488 | BR DERBY

Converted 1983–1984 from Mk. 2F FOs and TSOs for Victoria–Gatwick services. The seating layout was modified with and the removal of one toilet to provide additional luggage space.

**Formation:** TFOH–TSO (Class 488/3 only)–TSOH.
**Construction:** Steel.     **Doors:** Slam.
**Gangways:** Throughout.     **Couplers:** Buckeye.
**Bogies:** B4.     **Maximum Speed:** 90 m.p.h.
**Seating Layout:** 1: 2+1 facing, 2: 2+2 facing.
**Dimensions:** 20.60 x 2.84 m.     **Braking:** Tread brakes.
**Heating & Ventilation:** Air conditioning.
**Multiple Working:** SR.

**72505/72507. TFOH.** Lot No. 30859 Derby 1973–1974. 41/– 1T. 35.0 t.
**72603–72614/72620–72643. TSOH.** Lot No. 30860 Derby 1973–1974. –/48 1T. 33.5 t.
**72615/72645. TSOH.** Lot No. 30846 Derby 1973. –/48 1T. 33.5 t.
**72702–72714. TSO.** Lot No. 30860 Derby 1973–1974. –/48 1T. 33.5 t.

**Advertising livery:** As **GX** but with a deep blue instead of a white lower bodyside, advertising Continental Airlines.

**Class 488/2.** TFOH–TSOH.

| | | | | | | |
|---|---|---|---|---|---|---|
| 8208 | **AL** | GB | PB | 72507 (3412) | 72643 (6040) | |
| Spare | **AL** | NR | DY | | 72640 (6097) | |
| Spare | **AL** | NR | DY | | 72641 (6079) | |

**Class 488/3.** TSOH–TSO–TSOH.

| | | | | | | |
|---|---|---|---|---|---|---|
| 8303 | **GX** | NR | DY | 72603 (6093) | | 72608 (6077) |
| 8308 | **GX** | NR | DY | 72614 (6090) | 72707 (6127) | 72615 (5938) |
| 8312 | **GX** | GB | PY | 72622 (6004) | 72711 (6109) | 72623 (6118) |
| 8315 | **GX** | GB | PY | 72636 (6071) | 72714 (6092) | 72645 (5942) |
| Spare | **GX** | NR | AS | | 72702 (6099) | |

## CLASS 489                                    BR EASTLEIGH

Converted 1983–1984 from Class 414/3 (2 Hap) DMBSOs to work with Class 488.

**Formation:** DMLV.
**Construction:** Steel.                        **Doors:** Slam.
**Gangways:** Gangwayed at inner end only.
**Electrical Equipment:** 1957-type.
**Traction Motors:** Two EE507 of 185 kW.      **Couplers:** Buckeye.
**Bogies:** Mark 4.                             **Maximum Speed:** 90 m.p.h.
**Dimensions:** 20.00 x 2.82 m.                 **Braking:** Tread brakes.
**Multiple Working:** SR.

DMLV. Lot No. 30452 1959. 42.0 t.

**Note.** s – Converted for use as de-icing vehicles on the Southern Region.

| | | | | | | |
|---|---|---|---|---|---|---|
| 9102 | s | **GX** | NR | TN | 68501 | (61281) |
| 9105 | | **GX** | GB | PB | 68504 | (61286) |
| 9106 | | **GX** | GB | PB | 68505 | (61299) |
| 9109 | s | **GX** | NR | TN | 68508 | (61272) |
| 9110 | | **GX** | P | SL | 68509 | (61280) |

# PLATFORM 5 MAIL ORDER

## BRITISH RAILWAY PICTORIAL: FIRST GENERATION SOUTHERN EMUs

### Ian Allan

An illustrated review of British Railways Southern Region EMU vehicles from nationalisation to the early 1970s. Includes elderly units of pre-grouping design, standard suburban, semi-fast and express stock designed by the Southern Railway and later BR designs including those derived from the Mark 1 coaching stock vehicle. Also includes tabulated details of EMU vehicle classification codes and the Southern Region EMU numbering scheme. 80 pages. £12.99.

**Please add postage:** 10% UK, 20% Europe, 30% Rest of World

**Telephone, fax or send your order to the Platform 5 Mail Order Department. See page 384 of this book for details.**

◀ WAGN purple-liveried 313 063 arrives at Potters Bar with the 16.28 (SuO) Welwyn Garden City–London King's Cross stopping service on 20/03/05.

**Robert Pritchard**

▼ New Strathclyde PTE-liveried 314 205 arrives at Newton with the 14.10 from Glasgow Central on 22/07/05.

**Ian Lothian**

"One"-liveried 317 660+317 652 pass Shepreth Branch Junction shortly after departure with the 11.34 Cambridge–London Liverpool Street on 23/01/05.
**Anthony Kay**

▲ Recently repainted into the new Thameslink livery, 319 427 leads 319 433 (in the old livery), near Norwood Junction with an e.c.s. for Selhurst on 21/06/05.
**Alex Dasi-Sutton**

▼ 320 303 pauses at Westerton with the 12.14 Dalmuir–Motherwell on 12/07/05.
**Adrian Sumner**

▲ Still in old West Yorkshire PTE livery (at the time of writing) 321 901 passes Skellow near Adwick on 03/09/04 with the 14.14 Doncaster–Leeds stopping service.                                                                    **Chris Booth**

▼ Centro-liveried 323 202 at Birmingham International with the 13.22 Wolverhampton–Coventry service on 07/08/04.                                              **Stephen Widdowson**

▲ Royal Mail-liveried 325 016 leads a 12-car formation at Headstone Lane with 1S96 16.26 Willesden Railnet–Shieldmuir loaded mail train on 08/06/05. This service is operated by GBRf. **Gavin Morrison**

▼ One of the dedicated West Yorkshire suburban EMUs, 333 013, pauses at Shipley with the 10.18 Skipton–Leeds on 09/07/05. **Dave McAlone**

▲ 334 020 stands at Motherwell prior to forming the 14.50 to Dalmuir on 15/05/04. **Adrian Sumner**

▼ The first of the 30-strong Class 350 "West Coast Desiro" fleet entered service in summer 2005. On 08/06/05 350 114+350 115 pass Ledburn Junction with a test run. **Gavin Morrison**

▲ The 45-strong Class 444 fleet entered service with South West Trains in 2004/05, mainly on Portsmouth line services, but also on some other routes. Here 444 038 arrives at Southampton Central on 16/07/05 with the 13.39 from London Waterloo.                                    **John Chalcraft**

▼ The outer suburban Class 450s are also now all in traffic with SWT, wearing the outer suburban blue livery. On 04/11/04 450 006 passes Northam an e.c.s. movement to Northam depot.                                    **John Chalcraft**

▲ Refurbished Southern Class 455 No. 455 846 leaves East Croydon with the 07.16 Caterham–London Bridge on a sunny 14/07/05. These refurbished Southern units are recognisable from the unrefurbished sets as they have a revised end to incorporate the in-cab air conditioning system.　　　　**Robert Pritchard**

▼ Still in NSE livery, Southern 456 005 arrives at South Croydon with the 12.42 London Charing Cross–Tattenham Corner. All Southern Class 456s were due to be refurbished during late 2005/2006.　　　　**Rodney Lissenden**

▲ Class 458s 8018 and 8005 are seen near Twickenham with the 07.12 Reading–London Waterloo on 29/04/05.  **Alex Dasi-Sutton**

▼ The eight Class 460s now cover all Gatwick Express services. On 14/07/05 460 002 (only displaying the number "02" on the front end) is seen at Stoats Nest Junction with the 08.20 Gatwick Airport–London Victoria.  **Robert Pritchard**

▲ Refurbished Networker 465 918, with first class added, pauses at Otford with the 16.56 London Victoria–Ashford International on 23/05/05. **Rodney Lissenden**

▼ Island Line 009, in maroon livery, is the rear unit of the 09.13 Shanklin–Ryde Pier Head at Ryde Esplanade on 10/07/04. An Island Line "Dinosaur"-liveried set leads the train. **Martyn Hilbert**

GNER-liveried Eurostar 3303+3304 passes Eaton Lane, near Retford with the 14.05 London King's Cross–Leeds on 14/05/04.

**Chris Booth**

▲ All Merseyrail Class 507s and 508s have now been refurbished and are in the attractive new silver and yellow livery. On 08/06/05 507 025 leaves Southport with a train for Hunts Cross. **Rodney Lissenden**

▼ Three Class 508s are operated by Silverlink. On 14/07/05 508 301 rests at Watford Junction prior to forming the 10.22 stopping service to London Euston. **Mark Beal**

# CLASS 507                                                              BREL YORK

Merseyrail suburban units.

**Formation:** BDMSO–TSO–DMSO.
**System:** 750 V DC third rail.
**Traction Motors:** Four GEC G310AZ of 82.125 kW.
**Construction:** Steel underframe, aluminium alloy body and roof.
**Doors:** Sliding.
**Gangways:** Within unit + end doors.   **Bogies:** BX1.
**Couplers:** Tightlock.                  **Maximum Speed:** 75 m.p.h.
**Seating Layout:** All refurbished with 2+2 high-back facing seating.
**Braking:** Disc and rheostatic.         **Dimensions:** 20.33/20.18 x 2.82 m.
**Multiple Working:** Within class and with Class 508.

**BDMSO.** Lot No. 30906 1978–1980. –/59 1W. 37.0 t.
**TSO.** Lot No. 30907 1978–1980. –/74. 25.5 t.
**DMSO.** Lot No. 30908 1978–1980. –/59 1W. 35.5 t.

| | | | | | | | |
|---|---|---|---|---|---|---|---|
| 507 001 | **ME** | A | *ME* | BD | 64367 | 71342 | 64405 |
| 507 002 | **ME** | A | *ME* | BD | 64368 | 71343 | 64406 |
| 507 003 | **ME** | A | *ME* | BD | 64369 | 71344 | 64407 |
| 507 004 | **ME** | A | *ME* | BD | 64388 | 71345 | 64408 |
| 507 005 | **ME** | A | *ME* | BD | 64371 | 71346 | 64409 |
| 507 006 | **ME** | A | *ME* | BD | 64372 | 71347 | 64410 |
| 507 007 | **ME** | A | *ME* | BD | 64373 | 71348 | 64411 |
| 507 008 | **ME** | A | *ME* | BD | 64374 | 71349 | 64412 |
| 507 009 | **ME** | A | *ME* | BD | 64375 | 71350 | 64413 |
| 507 010 | **ME** | A | *ME* | BD | 64376 | 71351 | 64414 |
| 507 011 | **ME** | A | *ME* | BD | 64377 | 71352 | 64415 |
| 507 012 | **ME** | A | *ME* | BD | 64378 | 71353 | 64416 |
| 507 013 | **ME** | A | *ME* | BD | 64379 | 71354 | 64417 |
| 507 014 | **ME** | A | *ME* | BD | 64380 | 71355 | 64418 |
| 507 015 | **ME** | A | *ME* | BD | 64381 | 71356 | 64419 |
| 507 016 | **ME** | A | *ME* | BD | 64382 | 71357 | 64420 |
| 507 017 | **ME** | A | *ME* | BD | 64383 | 71358 | 64421 |
| 507 018 | **ME** | A | *ME* | BD | 64384 | 71359 | 64422 |
| 507 019 | **ME** | A | *ME* | BD | 64385 | 71360 | 64423 |
| 507 020 | **ME** | A | *ME* | BD | 64386 | 71361 | 64424 |
| 507 021 | **ME** | A | *ME* | BD | 64387 | 71362 | 64425 |
| 507 023 | **ME** | A | *ME* | BD | 64389 | 71364 | 64427 |
| 507 024 | **ME** | A | *ME* | BD | 64390 | 71365 | 64428 |
| 507 025 | **ME** | A | *ME* | BD | 64391 | 71366 | 64429 |
| 507 026 | **ME** | A | *ME* | BD | 64392 | 71367 | 64430 |
| 507 027 | **ME** | A | *ME* | BD | 64393 | 71368 | 64431 |
| 507 028 | **ME** | A | *ME* | BD | 64394 | 71369 | 64432 |
| 507 029 | **ME** | A | *ME* | BD | 64395 | 71370 | 64433 |
| 507 030 | **ME** | A | *ME* | BD | 64396 | 71371 | 64434 |
| 507 031 | **ME** | A | *ME* | BD | 64397 | 71372 | 64435 |
| 507 032 | **ME** | A | *ME* | BD | 64398 | 71373 | 64436 |
| 507 033 | **ME** | A | *ME* | BD | 64399 | 71374 | 64437 | Cllr GEORGE HOWARD |

# CLASS 508                           BREL YORK

Merseyrail/South Eastern Trains/Silverlink suburban units.

**Formation:** DMSO–TSO–BDMSO.
**System:** 750 V DC third rail.
**Traction Motors:** Four GEC G310AZ of 82.125 kW.
**Construction:** Steel underframe, aluminium alloy body and roof.
**Doors:** Sliding.
**Gangways:** Within unit + end doors.    **Bogies:** BX1.
**Couplers:** Tightlock.    **Maximum Speed:** 75 m.p.h.
**Seating Layout:** All Merseyrail units refurbished with 2+2 high-back facing seating. SET and Silverlink units have 3+2 low-back facing seating.
**Braking:** Disc and rheostatic.    **Dimensions:** 20.33/20.18 x 2.82 m.
**Multiple Working:** Within class and with Class 507.

**DMSO.** Lot No. 30979 1979–1980. –/59 1W. 36.0 t.
**TSO.** Lot No. 30980 1979–1980. –/74. 26.5 t.
**BDMSO.** Lot No. 30981 1979–1980. –/59 1W. 36.5 t.

**Class 508/1.** Merseyrail units.

| | | | | | | | | |
|---|---|---|---|---|---|---|---|---|
| 508 103 | **ME** | A | *ME* | BD | 64651 | 71485 | 64694 | |
| 508 104 | **ME** | A | *ME* | BD | 64652 | 71486 | 64695 | |
| 508 108 | **ME** | A | *ME* | BD | 64656 | 71490 | 64699 | |
| 508 110 | **ME** | A | *ME* | BD | 64658 | 71492 | 64701 | |
| 508 111 | **ME** | A | *ME* | BD | 64659 | 71493 | 64702 | |
| 508 112 | **ME** | A | *ME* | BD | 64660 | 71494 | 64703 | |
| 508 114 | **ME** | A | *ME* | BD | 64662 | 71496 | 64705 | |
| 508 115 | **ME** | A | *ME* | BD | 64663 | 71497 | 64706 | |
| 508 117 | **ME** | A | *ME* | BD | 64665 | 71499 | 64708 | |
| 508 120 | **ME** | A | *ME* | BD | 64668 | 71502 | 64711 | |
| 508 122 | **ME** | A | *ME* | BD | 64670 | 71504 | 64713 | |
| 508 123 | **ME** | A | *ME* | BD | 64671 | 71505 | 64714 | |
| 508 124 | **ME** | A | *ME* | BD | 64672 | 71506 | 64715 | |
| 508 125 | **ME** | A | *ME* | BD | 64673 | 71507 | 64716 | |
| 508 126 | **ME** | A | *ME* | BD | 64674 | 71508 | 64717 | |
| 508 127 | **ME** | A | *ME* | BD | 64675 | 71509 | 64718 | |
| 508 128 | **ME** | A | *ME* | BD | 64676 | 71510 | 64719 | |
| 508 130 | **ME** | A | *ME* | BD | 64678 | 71512 | 64721 | |
| 508 131 | **ME** | A | *ME* | BD | 64679 | 71513 | 64722 | |
| 508 134 | **ME** | A | *ME* | BD | 64682 | 71516 | 64725 | |
| 508 136 | **ME** | A | *ME* | BD | 64684 | 71518 | 64727 | Capital of Culture |
| 508 137 | **ME** | A | *ME* | BD | 64685 | 71519 | 64728 | |
| 508 138 | **ME** | A | *ME* | BD | 64686 | 71520 | 64729 | |
| 508 139 | **ME** | A | *ME* | BD | 64687 | 71521 | 64730 | |
| 508 140 | **ME** | A | *ME* | BD | 64688 | 71522 | 64731 | |
| 508 141 | **ME** | A | *ME* | BD | 64689 | 71523 | 64732 | |
| 508 143 | **ME** | A | *ME* | BD | 64691 | 71525 | 64734 | |

**Class 508/2.** Facelifted South Eastern Trains units. Refurbished 1998–1999 by Wessex Traincare/Alstom, Eastleigh.

**DMSO.** Lot No. 30979 1979–1980. –/66. 36.0 t.
**TSO.** Lot No. 30980 1979–1980. –/79 1W. 26.5 t.
**BDMSO.** Lot No. 30981 1979–1980. –/74. 36.5 t.

| | | | | | | | |
|---|---|---|---|---|---|---|---|
| 508 201 | (508 101) | **CX** | A | *SE* | Gl | 64649 | 71483 | 64692 |
| 508 202 | (508 105) | **CX** | A | *SE* | Gl | 64653 | 71487 | 64696 |
| 508 203 | (508 106) | **CX** | A | *SE* | Gl | 64654 | 71488 | 64697 |
| 508 204 | (508 107) | **CX** | A | *SE* | Gl | 64655 | 71489 | 64698 |
| 508 205 | (508 109) | **CX** | A | *SE* | Gl | 64657 | 71491 | 64700 |
| 508 206 | (508 113) | **CX** | A | *SE* | Gl | 64661 | 71495 | 64704 |
| 508 207 | (508 116) | **CX** | A | *SE* | Gl | 64664 | 71498 | 64707 |
| 508 208 | (508 119) | **CN** | A | *SE* | Gl | 64667 | 71501 | 64710 |
| 508 209 | (508 121) | **CX** | A | *SE* | Gl | 64669 | 71503 | 64712 |
| 508 210 | (508 129) | **CX** | A | *SE* | Gl | 64677 | 71511 | 64720 |
| 508 211 | (508 132) | **CX** | A | *SE* | Gl | 64680 | 71514 | 64723 |
| 508 212 | (508 133) | **CX** | A | *SE* | Gl | 64681 | 71515 | 64724 |

**Class 508/3.** Facelifted units for Silverlink for use on Euston–Watford Junction services. Refurbished 2002–2003 by Alstom, Eastleigh.

**DMSO.** Lot No. 30979 1979–1980. –/68 1W. 36.0 t.
**TSO.** Lot No. 30980 1979–1980. –/86. 26.5 t.
**BDMSO.** Lot No. 30981 1979–1980. –/68 1W. 36.5 t.

| | | | | | | | |
|---|---|---|---|---|---|---|---|
| 508 301 | (508 102) | **SL** | A | *SL* | WN | 64650 | 71484 | 64693 |
| 508 302 | (508 135) | **SL** | A | *SL* | WN | 64683 | 71517 | 64726 |
| 508 303 | (508 142) | **SL** | A | *SL* | WN | 64690 | 71524 | 64733 |

# 4.3. EUROSTAR UNITS (CLASS 373)

Eurostar units were built for and are normally used on services between Britain and Continental Europe via the Channel Tunnel. Apart from such workings units may be used as follows:

- SNCF-owned units 3203/04, 3225/26 and 3227/28 have been removed from the Eurostar pool, and only operate SNCF-internal services between Paris and Lille.
- Three 8-car sets are used daily by GNER for its "White Rose" services.

Each train consists of two Eurostar units coupled, with a motor car at each driving end. Services starting from/terminating at London Waterloo International are formed of two 10-car units coupled, whilst GNER services are formed of two 8-car units coupled. All units are articulated with an extra motor bogie on the coach adjacent to the motor car.

Sets marked "r" have been refurbished. This now includes all sets used by Eurostar, but not 3101/02 (in store) and the sets used by SNCF.

DM–MSO–4TSO–RB–2TFO–TBFO or DM–MSO–3TSO–RB–TFO–TBFO.
Gangwayed within pair of units. Air conditioned.
**Construction:** Steel.
**Supply Systems:** 25 kV AC 50 Hz overhead or 3000 V DC overhead or 750 V DC third rail (* also equipped for 1500 V DC overhead operation).
**Wheel Arrangement:** Bo–Bo + Bo–2–2–2–2–2–2–2–2–Bo.
**Length:** 22.15 m (DM), 21.85 m (MS & TBF), 18.70 m (other cars).
**Maximum Speed:** 300 km/h.
**Built:** 1992–1993 by GEC-Alsthom/Brush/ANF/De Dietrich/BN Construction/ACEC.
**Note:** DM vehicles carry the set numbers indicated below.

**Class 373/0. 10-Car Sets.** Built for services starting from/terminating at London Waterloo. Individual vehicles in each set are allocated numbers 373xxx0 + 373xxx1 + 373xxx2 + 373xxx3 + 373xxx4 + 373xxx5 + 373xxx6 + 373xxx7 + 373xxx8 + 373xxx9, where 3xxx denotes the set number.

**Non-standard Livery: 0** – grey with silver ends, TGV symbol and green or blue doors.

**373xxx0 series. DM.** Lot No. 31118 1992–1995. 68.5 t.
**373xxx1 series. MSO.** Lot No. 31119 1992–1995. –/48 2T. 44.6 t.
**373xxx2 series. TSO.** Lot No. 31120 1992–1995. –/58 1T (r –/56 1T). 28.1 t.
**373xxx3 series. TSO.** Lot No. 31121 1992–1995. –/58 2T (r –/56 2T). 29.7 t.
**373xxx4 series. TSO.** Lot No. 31122 1992–1995. –/58 1T (r –/56 1T). 28.3 t.
**373xxx5 series. TSO.** Lot No. 31123 1992–1995. –/58 2T (r –/56 2T). 29.2 t.
**373xxx6 series. RB.** Lot No.31124 1992–1995. 31.1 t.
**373xxx7 series. TFO.** Lot No. 31125 1992–1995. 39/– 1T. 29.6 t.
**373xxx8 series. TFO.** Lot No. 31126 1992–1995. 39/– 1T. 32.2 t.
**373xxx9 series. TBFO.** Lot No. 31127 1992–1995. 25/– 1TD. 39.4 t.

| | | | | | | | | |
|---|---|---|---|---|---|---|---|---|
| 3001 | r **EU** | EU | *EU* | NP | 3006 | r **EU** | EU | *EU* | NP |
| 3002 | r **EU** | EU | *EU* | NP | 3007 | r **EU** | EU | *EU* | NP |
| 3003 | r **EU** | EU | *EU* | NP | 3008 | r **EU** | EU | *EU* | NP |
| 3004 | r **EU** | EU | *EU* | NP | 3009 | r **EU** | EU | *EU* | NP |
| 3005 | r **EU** | EU | *EU* | NP | 3010 | r **EU** | EU | *EU* | NP |

| | | | | | |
|---|---|---|---|---|---|
| 3011 | r **EU** | EU | *EU* | NP | |
| 3012 | r **EU** | EU | *EU* | NP | |
| 3013 | r **EU** | EU | *EU* | NP LONDON 2012 | |
| 3014 | r **EU** | EU | *EU* | NP LONDON 2012 | |
| 3015 | r **EU** | EU | *EU* | NP | |
| 3016 | r **EU** | EU | *EU* | NP | |
| 3017 | r **EU** | EU | *EU* | NP | |
| 3018 | r **EU** | EU | *EU* | NP | |
| 3019 | r **EU** | EU | *EU* | NP | |
| 3020 | r **EU** | EU | *EU* | NP | |
| 3021 | r **EU** | EU | *EU* | NP | |
| 3022 | r **EU** | EU | *EU* | NP | |
| 3101 | **EU** | SB | | FF | |
| 3102 | **EU** | SB | | FF | |
| 3103 | r **EU** | SB | *EU* | FF | |
| 3104 | r **EU** | SB | *EU* | FF | |
| 3105 | r **EU** | SB | *EU* | FF | |
| 3106 | r **EU** | SB | *EU* | FF | |
| 3107 | r **EU** | SB | *EU* | FF | |
| 3108 | r **EU** | SB | *EU* | FF | |
| 3201 | r\***EU** | SF | *EU* | LY | |
| 3202 | r\***EU** | SF | *EU* | LY | |
| 3203 | \* **0** | SF | *SF* | LY | |
| 3204 | \* **0** | SF | *SF* | LY | |
| 3205 | r **EU** | SF | *EU* | LY | |
| 3206 | r **EU** | SF | *EU* | LY | |
| 3207 | r\* **EU** | SF | *EU* | LY | MICHEL HOLLARD |
| 3208 | r\* **EU** | SF | *EU* | LY | MICHEL HOLLARD |
| 3209 | r\* **EU** | SF | *EU* | LY | |
| 3210 | r\* **EU** | SF | *EU* | LY | |
| 3211 | r **EU** | SF | *EU* | LY | |
| 3212 | r **EU** | SF | *EU* | LY | |
| 3213 | r\* **EU** | SF | *EU* | LY | |
| 3214 | r\* **EU** | SF | *EU* | LY | |
| 3215 | r\* **EU** | SF | *EU* | LY | |
| 3216 | r\* **EU** | SF | *EU* | LY | |
| 3217 | r\* **EU** | SF | *EU* | LY | |
| 3218 | r\* **EU** | SF | *EU* | LY | |
| 3219 | r **EU** | SF | *EU* | LY | |
| 3220 | r **EU** | SF | *EU* | LY | |
| 3221 | r\* **EU** | SF | *EU* | LY | |
| 3222 | r\* **EU** | SF | *EU* | LY | |
| 3223 | r\* **EU** | SF | *EU* | LY | |
| 3224 | r\* **EU** | SF | *EU* | LY | |
| 3225 | \* **0** | SF | *SF* | LY | |
| 3226 | \* **0** | SF | *SF* | LY | |
| 3227 | \* **0** | SF | *SF* | LY | |
| 3228 | \* **0** | SF | *SF* | LY | |
| 3229 | r\* **EU** | SF | *EU* | LY | |
| 3230 | r\* **EU** | SF | *EU* | LY | |
| 3231 | r **EU** | SF | *EU* | LY | |
| 3232 | r **EU** | SF | *EU* | LY | |

**Class 373/2. 8-Car Sets. Built for Regional Eurostar services.** Individual vehicles in each set are allocated numbers 373xxx0 + 373xxx1 + 373xxx2 + 373xxx3 + 373xxx5 + 373xxx6 + 373xxx7 + 373xxx9, where 3xxx denotes the set number. Set 3313/14 is used by Eurostar for special workings.

**3733xx0 series. DM.** 68.5 t.
**3733xx1 series. MSO.** –/48 1T. 44.6 t.
**3733xx2 series. TSO.** –/58 2T. 28.1 t.
**3733xx3 series. TSO.** –/58 1T. 29.7 t.
**3733xx5 series. TSO.** –/58 1T. 29.2 t.
**3733xx6 series. RB.** 31.1 t.
**3733xx7 series. TFO.** 39/– 1T. 29.6 t.
**3733xx9 series. TBFO.** 18/– 1TD. 39.4 t.

| | | | | | | | | | |
|---|---|---|---|---|---|---|---|---|---|
| 3301 | **EU** | EU | | NP | | 3308 | **EU** | EU | NP |
| 3302 | **EU** | EU | | NP | | 3309 | **EU** | EU | NP |
| 3303 | **EU** | EU | | NP | | 3310 | **EU** | EU | NP |
| 3304 | **EU** | EU | | NP | | 3311 | **EU** | EU | NP |
| 3305 | **EU** | EU | | NP | | 3312 | **EU** | EU | NP |
| 3306 | **EU** | EU | | NP | | 3313 | **EU** | EU | *EU* NP |
| 3307 | **EU** | EU | | NP | | 3314 | **EU** | EU | *EU* NP |

**Spare DM:**

3999   **EU**   EU   *EU*   NP

**Other names:** 3313 and 3314   ENTENTE CORDIALE

# 4.4. SERVICE EMUS

## CLASS 910/0                    BRAKE FORCE RUNNER SETS

Converted from Class 488/3 ex-Gatwick Express hauled stock (formerly Mark 2 coaches). Used as part of Network Rail's Radio Survey locomotive-hauled trains. Radio Survey Train 1 usually operates with 910 001, Radio Equipment Survey Coach 977868 (see Page 348) and Overhead Line Equipment Test Coach 975091 (see Page 347). Radio Survey Train 2 usually operates with 910 002, Radio Survey Coach 977869 (see Page 348) and Track Recording Coach 999508 (see Page 349). Vehicles 72630 and 72631 are used in the locomotive-hauled Network Rail Ultrasonic Test Train with 999606 (see below), 62482 (see below) or Ultrasonic Test Coach 99666 (see Page 343).

**Formation:** TSOH–TSO–TSOH or TSOH–TSOH.
**Construction:** Steel.                          **Doors:** Slam.
**Gangways:** Throughout.                         **Bogies:** B4.
**Couplers:** Buckeye (ends). Bar-coupled within sets
**Maximum Speed:** 90 m.p.h.
**Braking:** Tread brakes.                        **Dimensions:** 20.18 x 2.82 m.
**Multiple Working:** SR type.

**72612–72616/72630/72631/72639. TFOH.** Lot No. 30860 Derby 1973–1974. 33.5 t.
**72706/72708. TSO.** Lot No. 30860 Derby 1973–1974. 33.5 t.

| | | | | | | | |
|---|---|---|---|---|---|---|---|
| 910 001 | **RK** | NR | *SO* | ZA | 72616 (6007) | 72708 (6095) | 72639 (6070) |
| 910 002 | **RK** | NR | *SO* | ZA | 72612 (6156) | 72706 (6143) | 72613 (6126) |
| - | **Y** | NR | *SO* | ZA | 72630 (6094) | | 72631 (6096) |

# ULTRASONIC TEST TRAIN (ADDITIONAL VEHICLE)

T. Converted 2003 from Class 432 EMU. Gangwayed. Used as part of a locomotive-hauled Ultrasonic Test Train.

**Construction:** Steel.                          **Maximum Speed:** 75 m.p.h.
**Bogies:** SR Mk. 6.                             **Couplings:** Buckeye.
**Brakes:** Twin pipe vacuum.                     **Multiple Working:** Blue Square.
**Doors:** Manually operated slam.               **Dimensions:** 19.66 x 2.82  m.

**62482. T.** Lot No. 30862 York 1974. 50.7 t.

| | | | | | |
|---|---|---|---|---|---|
| - | **RK** | NR | *SO* | ZA | 62482 |

# ULTRASONIC TEST VEHICLE

T. Converted 2004/05 from Class 421 MBSO 62356. Used as part of a locomotive-hauled Ultrasonic Test Train.

**Construction:** Steel.
**Bogies:**
**Braking:** Tread brakes.
**Doors:** Manually operated slam.

**Maximum Speed:** 90 m.p.h.
**Couplers:** Buckeye.
**Dimensions:** 20.18 x 2.82 m.

**999606**. **T.** Lot No. 30816 York 1970.　.　t.

999606　　**Y**　　NR *SO*　ZA

---

# CLASS 930/2　SANDITE/DE-ICING/TRACTOR UNITS

Converted from Class 416/2. Currently used only within the confines of Selhurst depot.

**Formation:** DMB–DMB.
**Supply System:** 750 V DC third rail.
**Traction Motors:** Two English Electric 507 of 185 kW.
**Construction:** Steel.
**Gangways:** Within unit.
**Couplers:** Buckeye.
**Braking:** Tread brakes.
**Multiple Working:** SR type.
**Doors:** Slam.
**Bogies:** Mk. 3B.
**Maximum Speed:** 75 m.p.h.
**Dimensions:** 20.44 x 2.82 m.

**977566/977567. DMB.** Lot No. 30116 Eastleigh 1954–1955. 40.5 t.
**977804/977864. DMB.** Lot No. 30119 Eastleigh 1954. 40.5 t.
**977805/977865/977871. DMB.** Lot No. 30167 Eastleigh 1955. 40.5 t.
**977872/977924/977925. DMB.** Lot. No. 30314. Eastleigh 1956–1958. 40.5 t.
**977874/977875. DMB.** Lot No. 30114 Eastleigh 1954. 40.5 t.

| | | | | | | | |
|---|---|---|---|---|---|---|---|
| 930 204 | **RK** | SN | *SN* | SU | 977874 | (65302) | 977875 | (65304) |
| 930 206 | **RK** | SN | *SN* | SU | 977924 | (65382) | 977925 | (65379) |

# CLASS 960/2                          HITACHI "V" TRAIN

Hitachi Traction System Verification Train ("V" Train). Converted 2003 from vehicles from Class 310 units 310 109 and 310 113 and Class 423 MBSO 62138. Train was for testing on AC or DC lines but it is now stored out of use.

**Formation:** BDTS–MBS–MBS (AC/DC)–DTC
**Supply System:** 25 kV AC 50 Hz overhead or 750 V DC third rail.
**Traction Motors:** Four English Electric 546 of 201.5 kW each or four English Electric 507 of 185 kW each (977979).

| | |
|---|---|
| **Construction:** Steel. | **Doors:** Slam. |
| **Gangways:** Within unit. | **Bogies:** B4/Mark 4/B5 (SR) |
| **Couplers:** Buckeye. | **Maximum Speed:** 75 m.p.h. |
| **Dimensions:** 20.29 x 2.82 m. | |

**Non-standard Livery**: Deep green & black.

**977977. BDTS.** Lot No. 30745 Derby 1965–1967. 37.5 t.
**977978. MBS.** Lot No. 30746 Derby 1965–1967. 57.0 t.
**977979. MBS.** Lot No. 30746 Derby 1965–1967. 57.0 t.
**977980. DTC.** Lot No. 30748 Derby 1965–1967. 34.5 t.
**977981. MBS.** Lot No. 30760 Derby 1967. 49.0 t.

| | | | | | | | |
|---|---|---|---|---|---|---|---|
| 960 201 | **0** | H | PY | 977977 | (76137) | 977978 | (62090) |
| | | | | 977981 | (62138) | 977980 | (76187) |
| Spare | **0** | H | PY | 977979 | (62078) | | |

# PLATFORM 5 MAIL ORDER

## LONDON RAILWAY ATLAS
### Ian Allan

With historically more than a dozen main line termini, as well as both surface and underground lines, the railway network in London is one of the most complicated in the world. London Railway Atlas provides the reader with a comprehensive study of the railways in Greater London, showing all lines, open and closed, as well as all stations, changes of station name, opening and closing dates. Also includes additional notation and a full index to stations. Printed in colour throughout. 96 pages. Hardback. **£14.99**.

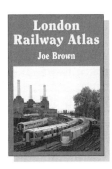

## THE GREAT INDIAN RAILWAY ATLAS
### Samit Roychoudhury

An excellent series of maps showing the railway network of India in 1:1,500,000 scale. Includes 55 map pages showing all open lines and stations, most closed lines and stations, gauge, single/double track, electrification, loco sheds, freight yards and other important features. Also includes 7 enlargement maps, Metro maps of Delhi and Kolkata and a complete station index. Key is in English, French and German. 84 pages. **£15.99**.

**Please add postage: 10% UK, 20% Europe, 30% Rest of World.**

**Telephone, fax or send your order to the Platform 5 Mail Order Department. See page 384 of this book for details.**

# 5. EMUS AWAITING DISPOSAL

The list below comprises vehicles awaiting disposal which are stored on Network Rail, together with those stored at other locations which, although awaiting disposal, remain Network Rail registered.

Generally, units that are stored but where others in that class are still in service are listed in the main part of this book. This list mainly comprises classes of units of which there are none of that particular class still in revenue earning service. However all slam-door rolling stock now not in use is listed here because of its short future life. Spare cars which are unlikely to run on Network Rail again are also listed here.

**IMPORTANT NOTE:** EMUs still intact but already at scrapyards are not included in this list.

## 25 kV AC 50 Hz OVERHEAD UNITS:

**Non-standard livery**: 960 101 and 960 102 – Light blue & white.

| | | | | | | |
|---|---|---|---|---|---|---|
| 310 046 | **N** | H | PY | 76130 | 62071 | 70731 | 76180 |
| 310 047 | **N** | H | PY | 76131 | 62072 | 70732 | 76181 |
| 310 049 | **N** | H | KT | 76133 | 62074 | 70734 | 76183 |
| 310 050 | **N** | H | KT | 76134 | 62075 | 70735 | 76184 |
| 310 051 | **N** | H | KT | 76135 | 62076 | 70736 | 76185 |
| 310 052 | **N** | H | PY | 76136 | 62077 | 70737 | 76186 |
| 310 057 | **N** | H | PY | 76141 | 62082 | 70742 | 76191 |
| 310 058 | **N** | H | PY | 76142 | 62083 | 70743 | 76192 |
| 310 059 | **N** | H | KT | 76143 | 62084 | 70744 | 76205 |
| 310 060 | **N** | H | PY | 76144 | 62085 | 70745 | 76194 |
| 310 064 | **N** | H | PY | 76148 | 62089 | 70749 | 76198 |
| 310 067 | **N** | H | PY | 76151 | 62092 | 70752 | 76201 |
| 310 068 | **N** | H | PY | 76152 | 62093 | 70753 | 76202 |
| 310 069 | **N** | H | PY | 76153 | 62094 | 70754 | 76203 |
| 310 070 | **N** | H | PY | 76154 | 62095 | 70755 | 76204 |
| 310 101 | **RR** | H | PY | 76157 | 62098 | | 76207 |
| 310 102 | **RR** | H | PY | 76139 | 62080 | | 76189 |
| 310 107 | **RR** | H | PY | 76146 | 62087 | | 76196 |
| 310 108 | **RR** | H | PY | 76132 | 62073 | | 76182 |
| 310 110 | **RR** | H | PY | 76138 | 62079 | | 76188 |
| 310 111 | **RR** | H | PY | 76147 | 62088 | | 76197 |

| | | | | |
|---|---|---|---|---|
| 960 101 | **O** | A | PY | 977962 (75642) 977963 (61937) 977964 (75981) |
| 960 102 | **O** | A | PY | 977965 (75965) 977966 (61928) 977967 (75972) |

**Spare cars:**

| | | | | | | | | |
|---|---|---|---|---|---|---|---|---|
| Cl. 307 | **BG** | MD | KT | 75023 | | | | |
| Cl. 309 | **RN** | A | PY | 71758 | | | | |
| Cl. 310 | **RR** | H | PY | 62086 | 76140 | 76156 | 76190 | 76193 |
| | **N** | H | PY | 62091 | 70751 | 76145 | 76200 | 76206 |
| Cl. 312 | **N** | A | PY | 71205 | 78037 | | | |

# 750 V DC THIRD RAIL UNITS:

| | | | | | | | | |
|---|---|---|---|---|---|---|---|---|
| 1304 | **ST** | H | PY | 76583 | 62289 | 70969 | 76613 | |
| 1705 | **CX** | SN | PY | 76076 | 62017 | 70695 | 76022 | |
| 1711 | **CX** | A | PY | 76114 | 62055 | 71766 | 76060 | |
| 1805 | **CX** | A | PY | 76782 | 62420 | 71100 | 76853 | |
| 1850 | **CX** | NR | TH | 76629 | | 71036 | 76789 | |
| 1866 | **CX** | A | PY | 76743 | 62381 | 71061 | 76814 | |
| 1881 | **ST** | H | PY | 76762 | 62400 | 71080 | 76833 | |
| 1884 | **ST** | H | PY | 76767 | 62405 | 71085 | 76838 | |
| 1903 | **CX** | A | PY | 76081 | 62022 | 70700 | 76027 | |
| 1904 | **CX** | A | PY | 76107 | 62048 | 70726 | 76053 | |
| 3417 | **B** | H | BM | 76262 | 62236 | 70797 | 76263 | Gordon Pettitt |
| 3536 | **ST** | H | PY | 76384 | 62207 | 70897 | 76383 | |
| 3568 | **CX** | A | PY | 76887 | 62440 | 71128 | 76888 | |
| 3905 | **CX** | P | AF | 76398 | 62266 | 70904 | 76397 | |
| 3918 | **CX** | P | AF | 76528 | 62321 | 70950 | 76527 | |
| | | | | | | | | |
| 4308 | **N** | H | PY | 61275 | 75395 | | | |
| 6213 | **BG** | NR | PY | 65327 | 77512 | | | |
| 6308 | **N** | NR | PY | 14564 | 16108 | | | |
| 6309 | **N** | NR | PY | 14562 | 16106 | | | |
| 930 010 | **RK** | MA | DY | 975600 | (10988) | 975601 | (10843) | |
| 930 101 | **N** | NR | AF | 977207 | (61658) | 977609 | (65414) | |

**Spare cars:**

**Non-standard livery**: 76112 – Silver (prototype Class 424 "Networker Classic" conversion).

| | | | | | | | | |
|---|---|---|---|---|---|---|---|---|
| Cl. 411 | **N** | H | ZI | 61390 | 70293 | | | |
| Cl. 421 | **CX** | A | PY | 76031 | 76049 | 76066 | 76073 | 76085 |
| | | | | 76103 | 76120 | 76127 | | |
| | **ST** | H | PY | 76765 | 76774 | 76775 | 76836 | 76845 |
| | | | | 76846 | | | | |
| | **GA** | A | PY | 76051 | 76069 | 76072 | 76117 | 76129 |
| | **U** | A | PY | 76061 | 76067 | 76115 | 76121 | |
| Cl. 423 | **CX** | A | PY | 76875 | 76877 | 76878 | 76891 | |
| | **CX** | H | PY | 76508 | 76666 | | | |
| Cl. 424 | **O** | BT | ZD | 76112 | | | | |
| Cl. 930 | **RO** | NR | AF | 975598 | (10989) | | 975605 | (10940) |

# 5. NON-PASSENGER-CARRYING COACHING STOCK

The notes shown for locomotive-hauled passenger stock generally apply also to non-passenger-carrying coaching stock (often abbreviated to NPCCS).

## TOPS TYPE CODES

TOPS type codes for NPCCS are made up as follows:

(1) Two letters denoting the type of the vehicle:

| | |
|---|---|
| AX | Nightstar generator van |
| AY | Eurostar barrier vehicle |
| NA | Propelling control vehicle. |
| NB | High security brake van (100 m.p.h.). |
| ND | Gangwayed brake van (90 m.p.h.). |
| NE | Gangwayed brake van (100 m.p.h.). |
| NH | Gangwayed brake van (110 m.p.h.). |
| NI | High security brake van (110 m.p.h.). |
| NJ | General utility van (90 m.p.h.). |
| NK | High security general utility van (100 m.p.h.). |
| NL | Newspaper van. |
| NN | Courier vehicle. |
| NO | General utility van (100 m.p.h. e.t.h. wired). |
| NP | Motorail van (110 m.p.h.). |
| NQ | High security brake van (110 m.p.h.). |
| NR | BAA container van (100 m.p.h.). |
| NV | Motorail van (side loading). |
| NX | Motorail van (100 m.p.h.). |
| NY | Exhibition van. |
| NZ | Driving brake van (also known as driving van trailer). |
| YR | Ferry van (special Southern Region version of NJ with two pairs of side doors instead of three). |

(2) A third letter denoting the brake type:

| | |
|---|---|
| A | Air braked |
| V | Vacuum braked |
| X | Dual braked |

## OPERATING CODES

The normal operating codes are given in parentheses after the TOPS type codes. These are as follows:

| | |
|---|---|
| BG | Gangwayed brake van. |
| BV | Barrier vehicle. |
| DLV | Driving brake van (also known as driving van trailer – DVT). |
| GUV | General utility van. |
| PCV | Propelling control van. |

# AK51 (RK)                                         KITCHEN CAR

Mark 1. Converted 1989 from RBR. Fluorescent lighting. Commonwealth bogies. x. ETH 2X.

Lot No. 30628 Pressed Steel 1960–61. 39 t.

Note: Kitchen cars have traditionally been numbered in the NPCCS series, but have passenger coach diagram numbers!

| | | | | | |
|---|---|---|---|---|---|
| 80041 | (1690) | M | E | *E* | OM |

# NN                                              COURIER VEHICLE

Mark 1. Converted 1986–7 from BSKs. One compartment and toilet retained for courier use. One set of roller shutter doors inserted on each side. x. ETH 2.

**80204/17/23.** Lot No. 30699 Wolverton 1962. Commonwealth bogies. 37 t.
**80220.** Lot No. 30573 Gloucester 1960. B4 bogies. 33 t.

Note: 80223 has been converted to a bar car with the former stowage area becoming an open saloon with a bar.

| | | | | | |
|---|---|---|---|---|---|
| 80204 | (35297) | M | WC | *LS* | CS |
| 80217 | (35299) | M | WC | *LS* | CS |
| 80220 | (35276) | M | NE | *LS* | NY |
| 80223 | (35331) | G | MH | *MH* | RL |

# ND (BG)  GANGWAYED BRAKE VAN (90 m.p.h.)

Mark 1. Short frames (57'). Load 10t. All vehicles were built with BR Mark 1 bogies. ETH 1. Vehicles numbered 81xxx had 3000 added to the original numbers to avoid confusion with Class 81 locomotives. The full lot number list is listed here for reference purposes with renumbered vehicles. No unmodified vehicles remain in service.

**80621.** Lot No. 30046 York 1954. 31.5 t.
**80826.** Lot No. 30144 Cravens 1955. 31.5 t.
**80855–80959.** Lot No. 30162 Pressed Steel 1956–57. 32 t.
**80980–81001.** Lot No. 30173 York 1956. 31.5 t.
**81025–81026.** Lot No. 30224 Cravens 1956. 31.5 t.
**81077–81173.** Lot No. 30228 Metro-Cammell 1957–58. 31.5 t.
**81205–81265.** Lot No. 30163 Pressed Steel 1957. 31.5 t.
**81266–81289.** Lot No. 30323 Pressed Steel 1957. 32 t.
**81325–81497.** Lot No. 30400 Pressed Steel 1957–58. 32 t.
**81500–81568.** Lot No. 30484 Pressed Steel 1958. 32 t.
**81606.** Lot No. 30716 Gloucester 1962. 31 t.

**Non-standard Livery:** 81025 is British racing green with gold lining.

The following vehicle is an ND rebogied with Commonwealth bogies and adapted for use as exhibition van 1998 at Lancastrian Carriage & Wagon Co. Ltd. 33 t.

| | | | | | | |
|---|---|---|---|---|---|---|
| 81025 | (81025, 84025) | **O** | RA | *RA* | CP | VALIANT |

# NZ (DLV)    DRIVING BRAKE VAN (110 m.p.h.)

Mark 3B. Air conditioned. T4 bogies. dg. ETH 5X.

Lot No. 31042 Derby 1988. 45.18 t.

**Non-standard Livery:** 82146 is EWS silver.

| | | | | | | | | | |
|---|---|---|---|---|---|---|---|---|---|
| 82101 | V | P | | WB | 82128 | V | P | E | OM |
| 82102 | 1 | P | 1A | NC | 82129 | V | P | | LT |
| 82103 | V | P | 1A | NC | 82130 | V | P | | LT |
| 82104 | V | P | 1A | NC | 82131 | V | P | E | OM |
| 82105 | V | P | 1A | NC | 82132 | V | P | 1A | NC |
| 82106 | V | P | | LM | 82133 | V | P | 1A | NC |
| 82107 | V | P | 1A | NC | 82134 | V | P | | LM |
| 82108 | V | P | | LM | 82135 | V | P | | LT |
| 82109 | V | P | | LM | 82136 | V | P | 1A | NC |
| 82110 | V | P | | LT | 82137 | V | P | | LT |
| 82111 | V | P | | LM | 82138 | V | P | | LM |
| 82112 | V | P | 1A | NC | 82139 | V | P | 1A | NC |
| 82113 | V | P | | LM | 82140 | V | P | | LT |
| 82114 | V | P | 1A | NC | 82141 | V | P | | LT |
| 82115 | V | P | | LM | 82142 | V | P | | LT |
| 82116 | V | P | | LM | 82143 | V | P | 1A | NC |
| 82117 | V | P | | LT | 82144 | V | P | | LM |
| 82118 | V | P | 1A | NC | 82145 | V | P | E | OM |
| 82120 | V | P | | LM | 82146 | 0 | E | E | TO |
| 82121 | V | P | 1A | NC | 82147 | V | P | | LT |
| 82122 | V | P | | LT | 82148 | V | P | | WB |
| 82123 | V | P | | LT | 82149 | V | P | | LT |
| 82124 | V | P | | LT | 82150 | V | P | | LT |
| 82125 | V | P | | WB | 82151 | V | P | E | OM |
| 82126 | V | P | | WB | 82152 | V | P | 1A | NC |
| 82127 | 1 | P | 1A | NC | | | | | |

Names:

| 82101 | 101 Squadron |
|---|---|
| 82118 | Britannia |
| 82126 | Wembley Traincare Centre |

# NZ (DLV)    DRIVING BRAKE VAN (140 m.p.h.)

Mark 4. Air conditioned. Swiss-built (SIG) bogies. dg. ETH 6X.

† Fitted with transceiver for wi-fi.

Lot No. 31043 Metro-Cammell 1988. 45.18 t.

| | | | | | | | | | |
|---|---|---|---|---|---|---|---|---|---|
| 82200 | | GN | H | GN | BN | 82205 | † | GN | H | GN | BN |
| 82201 | | GN | H | GN | BN | 82206 | | GN | H | GN | BN |
| 82202 | | GN | H | GN | BN | 82207 | | GN | H | GN | BN |
| 82203 | | GN | H | GN | BN | 82208 | † | GN | H | GN | BN |
| 82204 | † | GN | H | GN | BN | 82209 | † | GN | H | GN | BN |

| 82210 |   | **GN** | H | *GN* | BN | | 82222 |   | **GN** | H | *GN* | BN |
|-------|---|--------|---|------|----|-|-------|---|--------|---|------|----|
| 82211 | † | **GN** | H | *GN* | BN | | 82223 |   | **GN** | H | *GN* | BN |
| 82212 | † | **GN** | H | *GN* | BN | | 82224 |   | **GN** | H | *GN* | BN |
| 82213 | † | **GN** | H | *GN* | BN | | 82225 |   | **GN** | H | *GN* | BN |
| 82214 | † | **GN** | H | *GN* | BN | | 82226 |   | **GN** | H | *GN* | BN |
| 82215 | † | **GN** | H | *GN* | BN | | 82227 |   | **GN** | H | *GN* | BN |
| 82216 |   | **GN** | H | *GN* | BN | | 82228 |   | **GN** | H | *GN* | BN |
| 82217 |   | **GN** | H | *GN* | BN | | 82229 |   | **GN** | H | *GN* | BN |
| 82218 | † | **GN** | H | *GN* | BN | | 82230 |   | **GN** | H | *GN* | BN |
| 82219 | † | **GN** | H | *GN* | BN | | 82231 |   | **GN** | H | *GN* | BN |
| 82220 |   | **GN** | H | *GN* | BN | |       |   |        |   |      |    |

Name: 82219    Duke of Edinburgh

# NJ (GUV)                                   GENERAL UTILITY VAN

Mark 1. Short frames. Load 14 t. Screw couplings. These vehicles had 7000
added to the original numbers to avoid confusion with Class 86 locomotives.
The full lot number list is listed here for reference purposes with renumbered
vehicles. No unmodified vehicles remain in service. All vehicles were built with
BR Mark 2 bogies. ETH 0 or 0X*.

**86081–86499.** Lot No. 30417 Pressed Steel 1958–59. 30 t.
**86508–86518.** Lot No. 30343 York 1957. 30 t.
**86521–86648.** Lot No. 30403 York/Glasgow 1958–60. 30 t.
**86656–86820.** Lot No. 30565 Pressed Steel 1959. 30 t.
**86849–86956.** Lot No. 30616 Pressed Steel 1959–60. 30 t.

# NE/NH (BG)
# GANGWAYED BRAKE VAN (100/110 m.p.h.)

NE are ND but rebogied with B4 bogies suitable for 100 m.p.h. NH are identical
but are allowed to run at 110 m.p.h. with special maintenance of the bogies. For
lot numbers refer to original number series. Deduct 1.5t from weights. 92901–
92938 were renumbered from 920xx series by adding 900 to number to avoid
conflict with Class 92 locos. All NHA are *pg. ETH 1 (1X*).

| 92100 | (81391)        | to   |    | RV | | CP |
|-------|----------------|------|----|----|-|----|
| 92111 | (81432)        | NHA  |    | LW | | CP |
| 92159 | (81534)        | NHA  | H  |    | | KT |
| 92174 | (81567)        | NHA  | H  |    | | PY |
| 92175 | (81568)        | pg   | H  |    | | CD |
| 92194 | (81606)        | to   | H  |    | | PY |
| 92901 | (80855, 92001) | NHA  | H  | *VW* | WB |
| 92904 | (80867, 92004) | *pg  | **G** | VS | | SL |
| 92908 | (80895, 92008) | NHA  |    | WC | | CS |
| 92929 | (81077, 92029) | NHA  |    | LW | | CP |
| 92931 | (81102, 92031) | NHA  | H  |    | | PY |
| 92935 | (81150, 92035) | *pg  | H  |    | | PY |
| 92936 | (81158, 92036) | NHA  | H  |    | | CD |
| 92938 | (81173, 92038) | NHA  | H  |    | | PY |

# NL                                          NEWSPAPER VAN

Mark 1. Short frames (57'). Converted from NJ (GUV). Fluorescent lighting, toilets and gangways fitted. Load 14 t. Now used for materials storage. B5 Bogies. ETH 3X.

Lot No. 30922 Wolverton 1977–78. 31 t.

| | | | | | |
|---|---|---|---|---|---|
| 94003 | (86281, 93999) | x | **RX** FG *GW* | OO |
| 94006 | (86202, 85506) | | **RX** FG *GW* | OO |

# NKA    HIGH SECURITY GENERAL UTILITY VAN

Mark 1. These vehicles are GUVs further modified with new floors, three roller shutter doors per side and the end doors removed. For lot Nos. see original number series. Commonwealth bogies. Add 2 t to weight. ETH0X.

**Non-Standard Livery:** 94121 is grey.

| | | | | |
|---|---|---|---|---|
| 94100 | (86668, 95100) | **RX** | E | ML |
| 94101 | (86142, 95101) | **RX** | E | TE |
| 94102 | (86762, 95102) | **RX** | E | OM |
| 94103 | (86956, 95103) | **RX** | E | SD |
| 94104 | (86942, 95104) | **RX** | E | OM |
| 94106 | (86353, 95106) | **RX** | E | *E* | ML |
| 94107 | (86576, 95107) | **RX** | E | OM |
| 94108 | (86600, 95108) | **RX** | E | OM |
| 94110 | (86393, 95110) | **RX** | E | ER |
| 94111 | (86578, 95111) | **RX** | E | ML |
| 94112 | (86673, 95112) | **RX** | E | OM |
| 94113 | (86235, 95113) | **RX** | E | OM |
| 94114 | (86081, 95114) | **RX** | E | WE |
| 94116 | (86426, 95116) | **RX** | E | TY |
| 94117 | (86534, 95117) | **RX** | E | TE |
| 94118 | (86675, 95118) | **RX** | E | EN |
| 94119 | (86167, 95119) | **RX** | E | TY |
| 94121 | (86518, 95121) | **0** | E | TO |
| 94123 | (86376, 95123) | **RX** | E | ML |
| 94126 | (86692, 95126) | **RX** | E | ER |
| 94132 | (86607, 95132) | **RX** | E | ML |
| 94133 | (86604, 95133) | **RX** | E | ML |
| 94137 | (86610, 95137) | **RX** | E | *E* | ML |
| 94140 | (86571, 95140) | **RX** | E | TY |
| 94146 | (86648, 95146) | **RX** | E | OM |
| 94147 | (86091, 95147) | **RX** | E | *E* | ML |
| 94150 | (86560, 95150) | **RX** | E | *E* | ML |
| 94153 | (86798, 95153) | **RX** | E | WE |
| 94155 | (86820, 95155) | **RX** | E | *E* | ML |
| 94157 | (86523, 95157) | **RX** | E | OM |
| 94160 | (86581, 95160) | **RX** | E | ML |
| 94164 | (86104, 95164) | **RX** | E | ML |

| | | | | | |
|---|---|---|---|---|---|
| 94166 | (86112, 95166) | **RX** | E | *E* | ML |
| 94168 | (86914, 95168) | **RX** | E | | TY |
| 94170 | (86395, 95170) | **RX** | E | *E* | ML |
| 94172 | (86429, 95172) | **RX** | E | | ML |
| 94174 | (86852, 95174) | **RX** | E | | WE |
| 94175 | (86521, 95175) | **RX** | E | | ML |
| 94176 | (86210, 95176) | **RX** | E | *E* | ML |
| 94177 | (86411, 95177) | **RX** | E | | SM |
| 94180 | (86362, 95141) | **RX** | E | | ML |
| 94182 | (86710, 95182) | **RX** | E | | TE |
| 94190 | (86624, 95350) | **RX** | E | | BK |
| 94191 | (86596, 95351) | **RX** | E | | TE |
| 94192 | (86727, 95352) | **RX** | E | *E* | ML |
| 94193 | (86514, 95353) | **RX** | E | | WE |
| 94195 | (86375, 95355) | **RX** | E | *E* | ML |
| 94196 | (86478, 95356) | **RX** | E | *E* | ML |
| 94197 | (86508, 95357) | **RX** | E | *E* | ML |
| 94198 | (86195, 95358) | **RX** | E | | ML |
| 94199 | (86854, 95359) | **RX** | E | | TE |
| 94200 | (86207, 95360) | **RX** | E | | ML |
| 94202 | (86563, 95362) | **RX** | E | | ML |
| 94203 | (86345, 95363) | **RX** | E | *E* | ML |
| 94204 | (86715, 95364) | **RX** | E | | ER |
| 94205 | (86857, 95365) | **RX** | E | | TE |
| 94207 | (86529, 95367) | **RX** | E | | OM |
| 94208 | (86656, 95368) | **RX** | E | | SM |
| 94209 | (86390, 95369) | **RX** | E | | SD |
| 94212 | (86728, 95372) | **RX** | E | | TY |
| 94213 | (86258, 95373) | **RX** | E | *E* | ML |
| 94214 | (86367, 95374) | **RX** | E | | TY |
| 94215 | (86862, 94077) | **RX** | E | | TY |
| 94217 | (86131, 93131) | **RX** | E | | ML |
| 94218 | (86541, 93541) | **RX** | E | | TE |
| 94221 | (86905, 93905) | **RX** | E | | ML |
| 94222 | (86474, 93474) | **RX** | E | | ML |
| 94223 | (86660, 93660) | **RX** | E | | TY |
| 94224 | (86273, 93273) | **RX** | E | | CD |
| 94225 | (86849, 93849) | **RX** | E | | ML |
| 94226 | (86525, 93525) | **RX** | E | | ML |
| 94227 | (86585, 93585) | **RX** | E | | TE |
| 94228 | (86511, 93511) | **RX** | E | | TE |
| 94229 | (86720, 93720) | **RX** | E | *E* | ML |

# NAA          PROPELLING CONTROL VEHICLE

Mark 1. Class 307 driving trailers converted for use in propelling mail trains out of termini. Fitted with roller shutter doors. Equipment fitted for communication between cab of PCV and locomotive. B5 bogies. ETH 2X.

Lot No. 30206 Eastleigh 1954–56. Converted at Hunslet-Barclay, Kilmarnock 1994–6.

| | | | | | | | | | | | |
|---|---|---|---|---|---|---|---|---|---|---|---|
| 94302 | (75124) | **RX** | E | | TY | | 94303 | (75131) | **RX** | E | TY |
| 94304 | (75107) | **RX** | E | | ML | | 94324 | (75103) | **RX** | E | MG |
| 94305 | (75104) | **RX** | E | | EN | | 94325 | (75113) | **RX** | E | EN |
| 94306 | (75112) | **RX** | E | | TY | | 94326 | (75123) | **RX** | E | TY |
| 94307 | (75127) | **RX** | E | | SD | | 94327 | (75116) | **RX** | E | EN |
| 94308 | (75125) | **RX** | E | *E* | ML | | 94331 | (75022) | **RX** | E | SD |
| 94309 | (75130) | **RX** | E | | EN | | 94332 | (75011) | **RX** | E | TY |
| 94310 | (75119) | **RX** | E | | WE | | 94333 | (75016) | **RX** | E | TY |
| 94311 | (75105) | **RX** | E | | WE | | 94334 | (75017) | **RX** | E | CD |
| 94312 | (75126) | **RX** | E | | MG | | 94335 | (75032) | **RX** | E | TY |
| 94313 | (75129) | **RX** | E | | WE | | 94336 | (75031) | **RX** | E | TY |
| 94314 | (75109) | **RX** | E | | MG | | 94337 | (75029) | **RX** | E | WE |
| 94315 | (75132) | **RX** | E | | Rugby | | 94338 | (75028) | **RX** | E | WE |
| 94316 | (75108) | **RX** | E | | SM | | 94339 | (75024) | **RX** | E | TD |
| 94317 | (75117) | **RX** | E | | OM | | 94340 | (75012) | **RX** | E | CD |
| 94318 | (75115) | **RX** | E | | SD | | 94341 | (75007) | **RX** | E | EN |
| 94319 | (75128) | **RX** | E | | EN | | 94342 | (75005) | **RX** | E | EN |
| 94320 | (75120) | **RX** | E | | Norwich | | 94343 | (75027) | **RX** | E | ML |
| 94321 | (75122) | **RX** | E | | EN | | 94344 | (75014) | **RX** | E | SM |
| 94322 | (75111) | **RX** | E | | ML | | 94345 | (75004) | **RX** | E | EN |
| 94323 | (75110) | **RX** | E | *E* | ML | | | | | | |

# NBA   HIGH SECURITY BRAKE VAN (100 m.p.h.)

Mark 1. These vehicles are NEs further modified with sealed gangways, new floors, built-in tail lights and roller shutter doors. For lot Nos. see original number series. B4 bogies. 31.4 t. ETH 1X.

| | | | | | |
|---|---|---|---|---|---|
| 94400 | (81224, 92954) | **RX** | E | | SD |
| 94401 | (81277, 92224) | **RX** | E | *E* | ML |
| 94403 | (81479, 92629) | **RX** | E | | ML |
| 94404 | (81486, 92135) | **RX** | E | | MG |
| 94405 | (80890, 92233) | **RX** | E | | EN |
| 94406 | (81226, 92956) | **RX** | E | *E* | ML |
| 94407 | (81223, 92553) | **RX** | E | | MG |
| 94408 | (81264, 92981) | **RX** | E | | TY |
| 94410 | (81205, 92941) | **RX** | E | | WE |
| 94411 | (81378, 92997) | **RX** | E | | SD |
| 94412 | (81210, 92945) | **RX** | E | | ML |
| 94413 | (80909, 92236) | **RX** | E | *E* | ML |
| 94414 | (81377, 92996) | **RX** | E | | EN |
| 94416 | (80929, 92746) | **RX** | E | | TY |

| | | | | | |
|---|---|---|---|---|---|
| 94418 | (81248, 92244) | **RX** | E | | EN |
| 94420 | (81325, 92263) | **RX** | E | | ML |
| 94422 | (81516, 92651) | **RX** | E | | OM |
| 94423 | (80923, 92914) | **RX** | E | E | ML |
| 94424 | (81400, 92103) | **RX** | E | | ML |
| 94427 | (80894, 92754) | **RX** | E | | WE |
| 94428 | (81550, 92166) | **RX** | E | | ML |
| 94429 | (80870, 92232) | **RX** | E | | TE |
| 94431 | (81401, 92604) | **RX** | E | | MO |
| 94432 | (81383, 92999) | **RX** | E | | TY |
| 94433 | (81495, 92643) | **RX** | E | | AC |
| 94434 | (81268, 92584) | **RX** | E | | TY |
| 94435 | (81485, 92134) | **RX** | E | | WE |
| 94436 | (81237, 92565) | **RX** | E | | EN |
| 94437 | (81403, 92208) | **RX** | E | | EN |
| 94438 | (81425, 92251) | **RX** | E | | TO |
| 94439 | (81480, 92130) | **RX** | E | | ER |
| 94440 | (81497, 92645) | **RX** | E | | TY |
| 94441 | (81492, 92140) | **RX** | E | | ML |
| 94443 | (81473, 92127) | **RX** | E | | ML |
| 94444 | (81484, 92133) | **RX** | E | | ML |
| 94445 | (81444, 92615) | **RX** | E | | WE |
| 94446 | (80857, 92242) | **RX** | E | | ER |
| 94447 | (81515, 92266) | **RX** | E | | EN |
| 94448 | (81541, 92664) | **RX** | E | | TY |
| 94449 | (81536, 92747) | **RX** | E | | SD |
| 94450 | (80927, 92915) | **RX** | E | | WE |
| 94451 | (80955, 92257) | **RX** | E | | WE |
| 94453 | (81170, 92239) | **RX** | E | | ML |
| 94454 | (81465, 92124) | **RX** | E | | WE |
| 94455 | (81239, 92264) | **RX** | E | | SD |
| 94458 | (81255, 92974) | **RX** | E | | SD |
| 94459 | (81490, 92138) | **RX** | E | | ML |
| 94460 | (81266, 92983) | **RX** | E | | ML |
| 94461 | (81487, 92136) | **RX** | E | | TY |
| 94462 | (81289, 92270) | **RX** | E | | CD |
| 94463 | (81375, 92995) | **RX** | E | | TY |
| 94464 | (81240, 92262) | **RX** | E | | TY |
| 94465 | (81481, 92131) | **RX** | E | | TY |
| 94466 | (81236, 92964) | **RX** | E | | WE |
| 94467 | (81245, 92969) | **RX** | E | | EN |
| 94468 | (81259, 92978) | **RX** | E | | ML |
| 94469 | (81260, 92979) | **RX** | E | | TY |
| 94470 | (81442, 92113) | **RX** | E | | OM |
| 94471 | (81518, 92152) | **RX** | E | | ER |
| 94472 | (81256, 92975) | **RX** | E | | ML |
| 94473 | (81262, 92272) | **RX** | E | | TY |
| 94474 | (81452, 92618) | **RX** | E | | ML |
| 94475 | (81208, 92943) | **RX** | E | | TY |
| 94476 | (81209, 92944) | **RX** | E | | CD |
| 94477 | (81494, 92642) | **RX** | E | | TY |

| | | | | | |
|---|---|---|---|---|---|
| 94478 | (81488, 92637) | **RX** | E | | TY |
| 94479 | (81482, 92132) | **RX** | E | | OM |
| 94480 | (81411, 92608) | **RX** | E | | ML |
| 94481 | (81493, 92641) | **RX** | E | | SD |
| 94482 | (81491, 92639) | **RX** | E | | ML |
| 94483 | (81500, 92647) | **RX** | E | | SD |
| 94484 | (81426, 92110) | **RX** | E | | EN |
| 94485 | (81496, 92644) | **RX** | E | | SD |
| 94486 | (81254, 92973) | **RX** | E | | ML |
| 94487 | (81413, 92609) | **RX** | E | | ML |
| 94488 | (81405, 92105) | **RX** | E | | CD |
| 94490 | (81409, 92606) | **RX** | E | | MO |
| 94492 | (80888, 92721) | **RX** | E | | WE |
| 94494 | (81451, 92617) | **RX** | E | | EN |
| 94495 | (80871, 92755) | **RX** | E | *E* | ML |
| 94496 | (81514, 92650) | **RX** | E | | EN |
| 94497 | (80877, 92717) | **RX** | E | *E* | ML |
| 94498 | (81225, 92555) | **RX** | E | *E* | ML |
| 94499 | (81258, 92577) | **RX** | E | | CD |

# NBA/NIA/NQA
## HIGH SECURITY BRAKE VAN (100/110 m.p.h.)

Mark 1. These vehicles are NEs further modified with sealed gangways, new floors, built-in tail lights and roller shutter doors. For lot Nos. see original number series. B4 bogies. 31.4 t. ETH 1X.

These vehicles are identical to the 94400–94499 series. Certain vehicles are being given a special maintenance regime whereby tyres are reprofiled more frequently than normal and are then allowed to run at 110 m.p.h. Vehicles from the 94400 series upgraded to 110 m.p.h. are being renumbered in this series. Vehicles are NBA (100 m.p.h.) unless marked NIA or NQA (110 m.p.h.). NQA are vehicles which were modified for haulage by Class 90/2 locomotives which were fitted with composition brake blocks.

| | | | | | | |
|---|---|---|---|---|---|---|
| 94500 | (81457, 92121) | NIA | **RX** | E | | OM |
| 94501 | (80891, 92725) | | **RX** | E | | OM |
| 94502 | (80924, 92720) | NQA | **RX** | E | | ML |
| 94503 | (80873, 92709) | NIA | **RX** | E | | SD |
| 94504 | (80935, 92748) | NQA | **RX** | E | *E* | ML |
| 94506 | (80958, 92922) | NIA | **RX** | E | | ML |
| 94508 | (80887, 92722) | NQA | **RX** | E | | ML |
| 94509 | (80897, 92509) | NQA | **RX** | E | | OM |
| 94510 | (80945, 92265) | | **RX** | E | | WE |
| 94511 | (81504, 92714) | NIA | **RX** | E | | OM |
| 94512 | (81265, 92582) | | **RX** | E | | TY |
| 94514 | (81459, 92122) | NIA | **RX** | E | *E* | ML |
| 94515 | (80916, 92513) | NQA | **RX** | E | | ML |
| 94516 | (81267, 92211) | NQA | **RX** | E | | TY |
| 94517 | (81489, 92243) | NIA | **RX** | E | | CD |

| 94518 | (81346, 92258) |     | **RX** | E |   | ML |
|-------|----------------|-----|--------|---|---|----|
| 94519 | (80930, 92916) | NQA | **RX** | E | *E* | ML |
| 94520 | (80940, 92917) | NQA | **RX** | E |   | TY |
| 94521 | (80900, 92510) | NIA | **RX** | E |   | CD |
| 94522 | (80880, 92907) | NIA | **RX** | E | *E* | ML |
| 94523 | (81509, 92649) | NIA | **RX** | E |   | EN |
| 94524 | (81454, 94457) | NQA | **RX** | E |   | SD |
| 94525 | (80902, 92229) | NIA | **RX** | E | *E* | ML |
| 94526 | (80941, 92518) | NIA | **RX** | E |   | TY |
| 94527 | (80921, 92728) | NQA | **RX** | E |   | TY |
| 94528 | (81404, 92267) |     | **RX** | E | *E* | ML |
| 94529 | (80959, 92252) | NQA | **RX** | E |   | CD |
| 94530 | (81511, 94409) | NIA | **RX** | E | *E* | ML |
| 94531 | (80879, 94456) | NQA | **RX** | E |   | TY |
| 94532 | (81423, 94489) | NQA | **RX** | E |   | OM |
| 94534 | (80908, 94430) | NIA | **RX** | E | *E* | ML |
| 94535 | (80858, 94419) | NIA | **RX** | E |   | EN |
| 94536 | (80936, 94491) | NIA | **RX** | E | *E* | ML |
| 94537 | (81230, 94421) | NIA | **RX** | E |   | MG |
| 94538 | (81283, 94426) | NQA | **RX** | E |   | ML |

## NBA  HIGH SECURITY BRAKE VAN (100 m.p.h.)

Mark 1. Details as for 94400–99 but fitted with Commonwealth bogies. 34.4 t.
ETH 1X.

| 94539 | (81501, 92302) | **RX** | E | *E* | ML |
|-------|----------------|--------|---|---|----|
| 94540 | (81431, 92860) | **RX** | E |   | TJ |
| 94541 | (80980, 92316) | **RX** | E | *E* | ML |
| 94542 | (80995, 92330) | **RX** | E |   | TY |
| 94543 | (81026, 92389) | **RX** | E |   | ML |
| 94544 | (81083, 92345) | **RX** | E |   | MO |
| 94545 | (81001, 92329) | **RX** | E |   | TE |
| 94546 | (81339, 92804) | **RX** | E |   | TY |
| 94547 | (80861, 92392) | **RX** | E |   | MO |
| 94548 | (81154, 92344) | **RX** | E |   | TY |

## NRA          BAA CONTAINER VAN (100 m.p.h.)

Mark 1. Modified for carriage of British Airports Authority containers with roller
shutter doors and roller floors and gangways removed. Now used for general
parcels traffic. For lot Nos. see original number series. Commonwealth bogies.
Add 2 t to weight. ETH3.

| 95400 | (80621, 95203) | **E** | E |   | ML |
|-------|----------------|-------|---|---|----|
| 95410 | (80826, 95213) | **E** | E | *E* | ML |

# NOA    HIGH SECURITY GENERAL UTILITY VAN

Mark 1. These vehicles are GUVs further modified with new floors, two roller shutter doors per side, middle doors sealed and end doors removed. For lot Nos. see original number series. Commonwealth bogies. Add 2 t to weight. ETH 0X.

| | | | | | |
|---|---|---|---|---|---|
| 95715 | (86174, 95115) | **R** | E | | TY |
| 95727 | (86323, 95127) | **R** | E | | WE |
| 95734 | (86462, 95134) | **R** | E | | EN |
| 95739 | (86172, 95139) | **R** | E | | WE |
| 95743 | (86485, 95143) | **R** | E | | EN |
| 95749 | (86265, 95149) | **R** | E | | TY |
| 95754 | (86897, 95154) | **R** | E | | TY |
| 95758 | (86499, 95158) | **R** | E | *E* | ML |
| 95759 | (86084, 95159) | **R** | E | | EN |
| 95761 | (86205, 95161) | **R** | E | | WE |
| 95762 | (86122, 95162) | **R** | E | | WE |
| 95763 | (86407, 95163) | **R** | E | *E* | ML |

# NP/NX/NV (GUV)    MOTORAIL VAN (100 m.p.h.)

Mark 1. For details and lot numbers see original number series. ETH 0 (0X*).

Notes:

96100 was authorised for 110 m.p.h. and is classified NP.
96101 has a new prototype body built 1998 by Marcroft Engineering with side loading and one end sealed and is classified NV.

| | | | | | | |
|---|---|---|---|---|---|---|
| 96100 | (86734, 93734) | *B5 | | H | | TM |
| 96101 | (86741, 93741) | *B5 | **HB** | H | | PY |
| 96132 | (86754, 93754) | *C | | WC | | CS |
| 96139 | (86751, 93751) | C | | H | *VW* | MA |
| 96164 | (86880, 93880) | *C | | WC | | CS |
| 96181 | (86875, 93875) | *C | | H | | KT |

# AX5G    NIGHTSTAR GENERATOR VAN

Mark 3A. Generator vans converted from sleeping cars for use on 'Nightstar' services. Designed to operate between two Class 37/6 locomotives. Gangways removed. Two Cummins diesel generator groups providing a 1500 V train supply. Hydraulic parking brake. 61-way ENS interface jumpers. BT10 bogies.

Lot No. 30960 Derby 1981–83. 46.01 t.

| | | | | | |
|---|---|---|---|---|---|
| 96371 | (10545, 6371) | **EP** | EU | | NP |
| 96372 | (10564, 6372) | **EP** | EU | | NP |
| 96373 | (10568, 6373) | **EP** | EU | | NP |
| 96374 | (10585, 6374) | **EP** | EU | | NP |
| 96375 | (10587, 6375) | **EP** | EU | | NP |

## AY5 (BV)                    EUROSTAR BARRIER VEHICLE

Mark 1. Converted from GUVs. Bodies removed. B4 bogies.

**96380–96382**. Lot No. 30417 Pressed Steel 1958–59. 40 t.
**96383**. Lot No. 30565 Pressed Steel 1959. 40 t.
**96384**. Lot No. 30616 Pressed Steel 1959–60. 40 t.

| | | | | | |
|---|---|---|---|---|---|
| 96380 | (86386, 6380) | **B** | EU | *EU* | NP |
| 96381 | (86187, 6381) | **B** | EU | *EU* | NP |
| 96382 | (86295, 6382) | **B** | EU | *EU* | NP |
| 96383 | (86664, 6383) | **B** | EU | *EU* | NP |
| 96384 | (86955, 6384) | **B** | EU | *EU* | NP |

## NVA                      MOTORAIL VAN (100 m.p.h.)

Mark 1. Built 1998–9 by Marcroft Engineering using underframe and running gear from Motorail GUVs. Side loading with one end sealed. The vehicles run in pairs and access is available to the adjacent vehicle. For details and lot numbers see original number series. B5 bogies. ETH 0X.

| | | | | | |
|---|---|---|---|---|---|
| 96602 | (86097, 96150) | **GL** | H | *GW* | PZ |
| 96603 | (86334, 96155) | **GL** | H | *GW* | PZ |
| 96604 | (86337, 96156) | **GL** | H | *GW* | PZ |
| 96605 | (86344, 96157) | **GL** | H | *GW* | PZ |
| 96606 | (86324, 96213) | **GL** | H | *GW* | PZ |
| 96607 | (86351, 96215) | **GL** | H | *GW* | PZ |
| 96608 | (86385, 96216) | **GL** | H | *GW* | PZ |
| 96609 | (86327, 96217) | **GL** | H | *GW* | PZ |

## NY                          ULTRASONIC TEST COACH

Converted Railway Age, Crewe 1996 from FO to Exhibition Van. Further converted at Alstom, Wolverton Works 2002 to Ultrasonic Test Coach. B4 bogies.

Lot No. 30843 Derby 1972–73.

| | | | | | |
|---|---|---|---|---|---|
| 99666 | (3250) | **RK** | NR | *SO* | ZA |

## YR                                        FERRY VAN

This vehicle was built to a wagon lot although the design closely resembles that of NJ except it only has two sets of doors per side. Short Frames (57'). Load 14 t. Commonwealth bogies.

Built Eastleigh 1958. Wagon Lot. No. 2849. 30 t.

**Non-Standard Livery**: 889202 is Pullman Car umber with gold lining and lettering.

| | | | |
|---|---|---|---|
| 889202 | **0** | VS | CP |

**Name**: 889202 is branded 'BAGGAGE CAR No.8'.

# PLATFORM 5 MAIL ORDER

## EISENBAHNATLAS ÖSTERREICH

### Schweers & Wall

The definitive colour atlas of Austria's railways in 1:150000 scale. Shows all lines with identification of double track, single track, narrow gauge, freight only, former line now removed, rack lines and lines under construction. Colours are used to show different electrification voltages and Austrian timetable numbers are shown beside passenger lines. Also shows all stations, halts, junctions, yards, freight facilities, preservation centres, museum lines, tramways and funiculars, plus many general geographical features including rivers and motorways. Includes enlargements of Wien, Linz, Salzburg, Innsbruck, Graz and Villach at 1:50000 scale. Text is in German with key in English, German, French and Italian. **£21.95.**

*Also available:*
**Eisenbahnatlas Deutschland** ............................................................. **£27.95**
**Eisenbahnatlas Schweiz** .................................................................... **£21.95**

## STRASSENBAHNATLAS DEUTSCHLAND 2005

### Blickpunkt Strassenbahn

Maps and fleet lists for all German tramway networks, museum tramways, trolleybus systems, U-Bahn and S-Bahn networks. Lists all passenger vehicles, museum and works cars with details of build date, manufacturer, vehicle type and other information. Route numbers are indicated on the maps and contact details are provided for every undertaking, including web addresses. Also includes a full list of builders and a list of commonly used abbreviations. German text, but includes two pages of 'How to use this Atlas' in English. Illustrated. 296 pages. **£10.95.**

*Also available:*
**Strassenbahnatlas Rumanien 2004** ................................................ **£7.95**
**Tramway Atlas of the Former Soviet Union 2003** .......................... **£19.95**

**Please add postage: 10% UK, 20% Europe, 30% Rest of World**

### Telephone, fax or send your order to the Platform 5 Mail Order Department. See page 384 of this book for details.

# NPCCS AWAITING DISPOSAL

| | | |
|---|---|---|
| 80211 DY | 80373 EN | 80434 TO |
| 80319 ER | 80374 WE | 80435 EN |
| 80320 EN | 80375 EN | 80436 ER |
| 80321 EN | 80376 WE | 80437 EN |
| 80322 SD | 80377 EN | 80438 EN |
| 80323 EN | 80378 EN | 80439 MG |
| 80324 WE | 80379 EN | 80456 EN |
| 80325 WE | 80380 EN | 80457 EN |
| 80326 EN | 80381 WE | 80458 EN |
| 80327 EN | 80382 EN | 80865 Hornsey Sand Terminal |
| 80331 EN | 80383 WE | 84364 DW |
| 80332 WE | 80384 TJ | 84519 CD |
| 80333 TJ | 80385 EN | 92114 DY |
| 80334 WE | 80386 SD | 92146 DY |
| 80337 EN | 80392 ER | 92193 Preston Carriage Sidings |
| 80339 EN | 80393 WE | 92198 ZB |
| 80340 TJ | 80394 EN | 92303 OM |
| 80341 ER | 80395 EN | 92314 CD |
| 80342 ER | 80400 MG | 92321 FP |
| 80343 WE | 80401 TO | 92350 OM |
| 80344 EN | 80402 EN | 92400 CD |
| 80345 EN | 80403 WE | 92530 OM |
| 80346 EN | 80404 WE | 92939 DY |
| 80347 EN | 80405 WE | 93180 Derby South Dock Siding |
| 80348 WE | 80406 TJ | 93723 BY |
| 80349 EN | 80411 ER | 93930 CD |
| 80350 EN | 80412 ER | 94027 FP |
| 80351 EN | 80413 WE | 95228 NC |
| 80352 EN | 80414 EN | 95300 ML |
| 80353 ER | 80415 ER | 95301 ML |
| 80354 EN | 80416 TJ | 96110 CS |
| 80355 ER | 80417 EN | 96135 CS |
| 80356 EN | 80419 EN | 96165 CS |
| 80357 SD | 80420 ER | 96170 CS |
| 80358 EN | 80421 WE | 96175 CS |
| 80359 EN | 80422 SD | 96177 CP |
| 80360 EN | 80423 EN | 96178 CS |
| 80361 EN | 80424 SD | 96182 CS |
| 80362 ER | 80425 TJ | 96191 CS |
| 80363 EN | 80426 EN | 96192 CS |
| 80364 SD | 80427 EN | 96210 AS |
| 80365 EN | 80428 EN | 96212 AS |
| 80366 WE | 80429 EN | 96218 AS |
| 80367 EN | 80430 EN | 96452 BR |
| 80368 EN | 80431 EN | 96453 BR |
| 80369 SD | 80432 TO | 99645 FP |
| 80371 MG | 80433 EN | 99646 FP |
| 80372 TJ | | |

# PLATFORM 5 MAIL ORDER

## BRITISH MULTIPLE UNITS VOLUME 2:
## EPBs, Haps, Saps and Caps
### Coorlea Publishing

A complete listing of all multiple units of classes EPB, Hap, Sap and Cap. For each vehicle details of build date, withdrawal date, disposal date and disposal location are given. Also includes details of use conversions, renumberings and vehicles in preservation. 48 pages. **£6.95**.

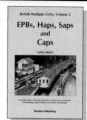

## BRITISH MULTIPLE UNITS VOLUME 3:
## Classes 302-390
### Coorlea Publishing

Complete listing of all AC Electric Multiple Units of classes 302-390. Shows introduction to service dates for every vehicle, unit formations, subsequent reformations, renumberings, withdrawal dates and disposal information. Includes a listing in set number order, plus a full index in vehicle number order. Also covers departmental vehicles. 84 pages. **£9.95**.

## BRITISH MULTIPLE UNITS VOLUME 4:
## Classes 410-490 & 508
### Coorlea Publishing

A detailed listing of all Southern Region DC EMU vehicles, plus class 508 (originally delivered to SR) but excluding EPBs, Haps, Caps & Saps (covered in volume 2). Contains build date, withdrawal date, disposal date and disposal location for every vehicle, plus unit formations, reformations, use conversions and renumberings. Also includes a separate listing of departmental vehicles and units in preservation. 96 pages. **£13.95**.

**Please add postage: 10% UK, 20% Europe, 30% Rest of World.**

Telephone, fax or send your order to the Platform 5 Mail Order Department. See page 384 for details.

# 6. SERVICE STOCK

Vehicles in this section are numbered in the former BR departmental number series. They are used for internal purposes within the railway industry, i.e. they do not generate revenue from outside the industry.

## EMU TRANSLATOR VEHICLES

These vehicles are used to move EMU vehicles around the National Rail system in the same way as other vehicles included in this book. Similar vehicles numbered in the BR capital stock series are included elsewhere in this book. Converted from Mark 1 TSO, RSOs, RUOs, BSKs and GUVs (NP/NL).

**975864.** Lot No. 30054 Eastleigh 1951–54. Commonwealth bogies.
**975867.** Lot No. 30014 York 1950–51. Commonwealth bogies.
**975875.** Lot No. 30143 Charles Roberts 1954–55. Commonwealth bogies.
**975974–975978.** Lot No. 30647 Wolverton 1959–61. Commonwealth bogies.
**977087.** Lot No. 30229 Metro–Cammell 1955–57. Commonwealth bogies.
**977942/948.** Lot No. 30417 Pressed Steel 1958–59. B5 bogies.
**977943/949.** Lot No. 30565 Pressed Steel 1959. B5 bogies.

**Non-standard livery:** 975974 and 975978 are in plain grey.

| | | | | | |
|---|---|---|---|---|---|
| 975864 | (3849) | **HB** | H | *FL* | ZJ |
| 975867 | (1006) | **HB** | H | *FL* | ZJ |
| 975875 | (34643) | **HB** | H | *FL* | ZJ |
| 975974 | (1030) | **0** | A | *ME* | BD |
| 975976 | (1033) | **N** | A | | KT |
| 975977 | (1023) | **N** | A | | KT |
| 975978 | (1025) | **0** | A | *ME* | BD |
| 977087 | (34971) | **HB** | H | *FL* | ZJ |
| 977942 | (86467, 80251) | **E** | E | *E* | TO |
| 977943 | (86718, 80252) | **E** | E | *E* | TO |
| 977948 | (86733, 94028) | **E** | E | *E* | TO |
| 977949 | (86377, 94025) | **E** | E | *E* | TO |

## LABORATORY, TESTING & INSTRUCTION COACHES

These coaches are used for research, development, instruction, testing and inspection on the National Rail system. Many are fitted with sophisticated technical equipment.

**Structure Gauging Driving Trailer Coach.** Converted from BR Mark 1 BSK. Lot No. 30699 Wolverton 1961–63. B4 bogies.

| | | | | | |
|---|---|---|---|---|---|
| 975081 | (35313) | **Y** | NR | *SO* | ZA |

**Overhead Line Equipment Test Coach.** Can either be locomotive hauled or included between DMU vehicles 977391/2. Converted from BR Mark 1 BSK. Lot No. 30142 Gloucester 1954–5. B4 bogies.

| | | | | | |
|---|---|---|---|---|---|
| 975091 | (34615) | **Y** | NR | *SO* | ZA |

**Structure Gauging Train Dormitory and Generator Coach.** Converted from BR Mark 1 BCK Lot No. 30732 Derby 1962–4. B4 bogies.

975280  (21263)              **Y**      NR     *SO*     ZA

**Test Coach.** Converted from BR Mark 2 FK Lot No. 30734 Derby 1962–64. B4 bogies.

975290  (13396)              **SO**     SO     *SO*     ZA

**Test Coach.** Converted from BR Mark 1 BSK Lot No. 30699 Wolverton 1961–63. Commonwealth bogies.

975397  (35386)              **SO**     SO     *SO*     ZA

**Cinema Coach.** Converted from BR Mark 1 TSO Lot No. 30243 York 1955–57. BR Mark 1 bogies.

975403  (4598)               **FG**     FG     *GW*     PM

**Test Coach.** Converted from BR Mark 1 BSK Lot No. 30223 Charles Roberts 1955–56. BT5 bogies.

975422  (34875)              **SO**     SO     *SO*     ZA

**New Measurement Train Conference Coach.** Converted from prototype HST TF Lot No. 30848 Derby 1972. BT10 bogies.

975814  (11000,41000)        **Y**      NR     *SO*     EC

**New Measurement Train Lecture Coach.**  Converted from prototype HST TRUB Lot No. 30849 Derby 1972–3. BT10 bogies.

975984  (10000, 40000)       **Y**      NR     *SO*     EC

**Track Recording Train Dormitory Coach.** Converted from BR Mark 2 BSO. Lot No 30757 Derby 1965–66. B4 bogies.

977337  (9395)               **Y**      NR     *SO*     ZA

**Track Recording Train Brake & Stores Coach.** Converted from Mark 2 BSO. Lot No. 30757 Derby 1965–66. B4 bogies.

977338  (9387)               **SO**     SO     *SO*     ZA

**Radio Equipment Survey Coaches.** Converted from BR Mark 2E TSO. Lot No. 30844 Derby 1972–73. B4 bogies.

977868  (5846)               **RK**     NR     *SO*     ZA
977869  (5858)               **RK**     NR     *SO*     ZA

**Ultrasonic Test Train Staff Coach.** Converted from Royal Household couchette Lot No. 30889, which in turn had been converted from BR Mark 2B BFK Lot No. 30790 Derby 1969. B5 bogies.

977969  (14112, 2906)        **Y**      NR     *SO*     ZA

**New Measurement Train Laboratory Coach.** Converted from BR Mark 2E TSO. Lot No. 30844 Derby 1972–73.  B4 bogies.

977974  (5854)               **Y**      AE     *SO*     ZA

**Hot Box Detection Coach.** Converted from BR Mark 2F FO converted to Class 488/2 EMU TFOH. Lot No. 30859 Derby 1973–74. B4 bogies.

Note: Still carries 72503.

977983 (3407, 72503)   **RK**   NR        ZA

**New Measurement Train Staff Coach.** Converted from HST TRFK. Lot No. 30884 Derby 1976–77. BT10 bogies.

977984 (40501)   **Y**   P   *SO*   EC

**Structure Gauging Train Coach.** Converted from BR Mark 2F TSO converted to Class 488/3 EMU TSO. Lot No. 30860 Derby 1973–74. B4 bogies.

977985 (6019, 72715)   **Y**   NR   *SO*   ZA

**Structure Gauging Train Coach.** Converted from BR Mark 2D FO subsequently declassified to SO and then converted to exhibition van. Lot No. 30821 Derby 1971.

977986 (3189, 99664)   **Y**   NR   *SO*   ZA

**New Measurement Train Overhead Line Equipment Test Coach.** Converted from HST TGS. Lot No. 30949 Derby 1982. BT10 bogies.

977993 (44053)   **Y**   P   *SO*   EC

**New Measurement Train Laboratory Coach.** Converted from HST TGS. Lot No. 30949 Derby 1982. BT10 bogies.

977994 (44087)   **Y**   P   *SO*   EC

**New Measurement Train Coach.** Converted from HST TRFM. Lot No. 30921 Derby 1978–79. BT10 bogies.

977995 (40719, 40619)   **Y**   P        ZA

**Inspection Coach.** Converted from BR Inspection Saloon. BR Wagon Lot No. 3095. Swindon 1957. B4 bogies.

999506 AMANDA   **M**   NR   *SO*   ZA

**Track Recording Coach.** Converted from BR Inspection Saloon. BR Wagon Lot No. 3379. Swindon 1960. B4 bogies.

999508   **SO**   SO   *SO*   ZA

**New Measurement Train Track Recording Coach.** Purpose built Mark 2. B4 bogies.

999550   **Y**   NR   *SO*   EC

# TEST TRAIN BRAKE FORCE RUNNERS

These vehicles are included in test trains to provide brake force and are not used for any other purposes. Other vehicles included in this book may also be similarly used on a temporary basis if required. Converted from BR Mark 2 TSOs and BFKs.

**977468/470/801/2.** Lot No. 30751 Derby 1964–7. B4 bogies.
**977789.** Lot No. 30837 Derby 1971–72. B4 bogies.
**977790/1.** Lot No. 30844 Derby 1972–73. B4 bogies.
**977793.** Lot No. 30795 Derby 1969–70. B4 bogies.

**977794.** Lot No. 30823 Derby 1969–72. B4 bogies.

**Non-Standard Liveries:** 977789–94 are Adtranz White with yellow stripe.

| | | | | | |
|---|---|---|---|---|---|
| 977468 | (5169) | **SO** | SO | *SO* | ZA |
| 977470 | (5134) | **SO** | SO | *SO* | ZA |
| 977789 | (5765) | **0** | FM | | LU |
| 977790 | (5830) | **0** | FM | | LU |
| 977791 | (5855) | **0** | FM | | LU |
| 977793 | (5596) | **0** | FM | | LU |
| 977794 | (14139, 17139) | **0** | FM | | LU |
| 977801 | (5153) | **SO** | SO | *SO* | ZA |
| 977802 | (5176) | **SO** | SO | *SO* | ZA |

# BREAKDOWN TRAIN COACHES

These coaches are formed in trains used for the recovery of derailed railway vehicles and were converted from BR Mark 1 BCK, BG, BSK and SK. The current use of each vehicle is given. 975611–613 were previously converted to trailer luggage vans in 1968. BR Mark 1 bogies.

**975080.** Lot No. 30155 Wolverton 1955–56.
**975087.** Lot No. 30032 Wolverton 1951–52.
**975463/573.** Lot No. 30156 Wolverton 1954–55.
**975465/477/494.** Lot No. 30233 GRCW 1955–57.
**975471.** Lot No. 30095 Wolverton 1953–55.
**975481/482/574.** Lot No. 30141 GRCW 1954–55.
**975498.** Lot No. 30074 Wolverton 1953–54.
**975611–613.** Lot No. 30162 Pressed Steel 1954–57.
**977088/235.** Lot No. 30229 Metro-Cammell 1955–57.
**977107.** Lot No. 30425 Metro-Cammell 1956–58.

r refurbished

| | | | | | | | |
|---|---|---|---|---|---|---|---|
| 975080 | (25079) | r | **Y** | NR | *E* | TO | Tool Van |
| 975087 | (34289) | r | **NR** | NR | *E* | LU | Generator Van |
| 975463 | (34721) | r | **Y** | NR | *E* | TE | Staff Coach |
| 975465 | (35109) | r | **Y** | NR | *E* | TO | Staff Coach |
| 975471 | (34543) | r | **NR** | NR | *E* | LU | Staff & Tool Coach |
| 975477 | (35108) | r | **NR** | NR | *E* | LU | Staff Coach |
| 975481 | (34606) | r | **Y** | NR | *E* | TO | Generator Van |
| 975482 | (34602) | r | **Y** | NR | *E* | TE | Generator Van |
| 975494 | (35082) | r | **Y** | NR | *E* | MG | Generator Van |
| 975498 | (34367) | r | **Y** | NR | *E* | TE | Tool Van |
| 975573 | (34729) | r | **Y** | NR | *E* | MG | Staff Coach |
| 975574 | (34599) | r | **Y** | NR | *E* | OM | Staff Coach |
| 975611 | (80915, 68201) | r | **Y** | NR | *E* | OM | Generator Van |
| 975612 | (80922, 68203) | r | **Y** | NR | *E* | MG | Tool Van |
| 975613 | (80918, 68202) | r | **Y** | NR | *E* | OM | Tool Van |
| 977088 | (34990) | | **Y** | NR | *E* | CE | Generator Van |
| 977107 | (21202) | | **Y** | NR | *E* | CE | Staff Coach |
| 977235 | (34989, 083172) | | **Y** | NR | *E* | CE | Tool Van |

**Note:** 975087/471/477 are currently in use on the Southern Power upgrade Project.

# INFRASTRUCTURE MAINTENANCE COACHES

### Overhead Line Maintenance Coaches

These coaches are formed in trains used for the maintenance, repair and renewal of overhead lines and were converted from BR Mark 1 BSK, CK and SK. The current use of each vehicle is given. All have been refurbished.

**Non-standard livery:** 975697/698/713/723/733/743 are light grey with red stripe, 975699/700/714/724/734/744 are light grey with blue stripe.

**975697/698, 975700.** Lot No. 30025 Wolverton 1950–52. BR Mark 1 bogies.
**975699.** Lot No. 30233 GRCW 1955–57. BR Mark 1 bogies.
**975713/744.** Lot No. 30350 Wolverton 1956–57. BR Mark 1 bogies.
**975714.** Lot No. 30374. York 1958. Commonwealth bogies.
**975723/743.** Lot No. 30349 Wolverton 1956–57. BR Mark 1 bogies.
**975724.** Lot No. 30471 Metro-Cammell 1957–59. Commonwealth bogies.
**975733.** Lot No. 30351 Wolverton 1956–57. BR Mark 1 bogies.
**975734.** Lot No. 30426 Wolverton 1956–58. BR Mark 1 Bogies.

| | | | | | |
|---|---|---|---|---|---|
| 975697 | (34147) | **0** | NR | *CA* | RU | Pantograph coach |
| 975698 | (34148) | **0** | NR | *CA* | RU | Pantograph coach |
| 975699 | (35105) | **0** | NR | *CA* | Preston | Pantograph coach |
| 975700 | (34138) | **0** | NR | *CA* | Preston | Pantograph coach |
| 975713 | (25402) | **0** | NR | *CA* | RU | Stores van |
| 975714 | (25466) | **0** | NR | *CA* | Preston | Stores van |
| 975723 | (25388) | **0** | NR | *CA* | RU | Stores & generator van |
| 975724 | (16079) | **0** | NR | *CA* | Preston | Stores & generator van |
| 975733 | (16001) | **0** | NR | *CA* | RU | Stores & roof access coach |
| 975734 | (25695) | **0** | NR | *CA* | Preston | Stores & roof access coach |
| 975743 | (25358) | **0** | NR | *CA* | RU | Staff & office coach |
| 975744 | (25440) | **0** | NR | *CA* | Preston | Staff & office coach |

### Snowblower Train Coaches

These coaches work with Snowblower ADB 968501. They were converted from BR Mark 1 BSK. The current use of each vehicle is given. Commonwealth bogies.

**975464.** Lot No. 30386 Charles Roberts 1956–58.
**975486.** Lot No. 30025 Wolverton 1950–52.

| | | | | | |
|---|---|---|---|---|---|
| 975464 | (35171) | **Y** | NR | *E* | ZK | Staff & dormitory coach |
| 975486 | (34100) | **Y** | NR | *E* | ZK | Tool van |

### Snowblower Train Tool Vans

These vans work with Snowblower ADB 968500.

**200715.** Wagon Lot No. 3855 Ashford 1976. 4-wheeled.
**787395.** Wagon Lot No. 3567 Eastleigh 1966. 4-wheeled.

| | | | | |
|---|---|---|---|---|
| 200715 | **Y** | NR | *E* | IS |
| 787395 | **Y** | NR | *E* | IS |

**Severn Tunnel Emergency Train Coaches**

These coaches were formed in a train used in the event of incidents in the Severn Tunnel. They were converted from BR Mark 1 BSK & BG. The use of each vehicle is given. 975615 was previously converted to a trailer luggage van in 1968.

**975497.** Lot No. 30427 Wolverton 1956–59. BR Mark 1 bogies.
**975615.** Lot No. 30162 Pressed Steel 1954–57. BR Mark 1 bogies.
**977526.** Lot No. 30229 Metro-Cammell 1955–57. Commonwealth bogies.

| | | | | | |
|---|---|---|---|---|---|
| 975497 | (35218) | **Y** | NR | Sudbrook | Tool & generator van |
| 975615 | (80951, 68206) | **Y** | NR | SJ | Tool van |
| 977526 | (35010) | **BG** | NR | SJ | Emergency casualty coach |

**Spray Coaches**

These coaches are used to spray various concoctions onto the rails or trackbed. In addition to spraying equipment they contain storage tanks. They were converted from BR Mark 1 RMB & GUV.

**99019.** Lot No. 30702 Wolverton 1961–62. Commonwealth bogies.
**99025/26.** Lot No. 30565 Pressed Steel 1959. B5 bogies.
**99027.** Lot No. 30417 Pressed Steel 1958–59. B5 bogies.

| | | | | | |
|---|---|---|---|---|---|
| 99019 | (1870) | **NR** | NR | *E* | ZA |
| 99025 | (86744, 96103) | **RK** | NR | | KT |
| 99026 | (86745, 96211) | **RK** | NR | | KT |
| 99027 | (86331, 96214) | **RK** | NR | | KT |

**Miscellaneous Infrastructure Coaches**

These coaches are used for various infrastructure projects on National Rail. They were converted from BR Mark 1 BSK & BG, BR Mark 2 BFK and BR Mark 3 SLEP. The current use of each vehicle is given.

**977163/165/166.** Lot No. 30721 Wolverton 1961–63. Commonwealth bogies.
**977167.** Lot No. 30699 Wolverton 1961–63. Commonwealth bogies.
**977168.** Lot No. 30573 GRCW 1959–60. B4 bogies.
**977591.** Lot No. 30756 Derby 1965–66. B4 bogies.
**977989.** Lot No. 30960 Derby 1981–83. BT 10 bogies.
**977990.** Lot No. 30228 Metro-Cammell 1957-58. B4 bogies.
**977991.** Lot No. 30323 Pressed steel 1957. B4 bogies.

**Non-standard liveries:**

977163 and167 are white with a blue stripe.
977165, 975166 and 975168 are all over white.
977591 is red and yellow.

| | | | | | | |
|---|---|---|---|---|---|---|
| 977163 | (35487) | **O** | BB | *BB* | AP | Staff & generator coach |
| 977165 | (35408) | **O** | BB | *BB* | AP | Staff & generator coach |
| 977166 | (35419) | **O** | BB | *BB* | AP | Staff & generator coach |
| 977167 | (35400) | **O** | BB | *BB* | AP | Staff & generator coach |
| 977168 | (35289) | **O** | BB | *BB* | AP | Staff & generator coach |
| 977591 | (14033, 17033) | **O** | E | *E* | Newport | Staff & tool coach |
| 977989 | (10536) | **M** | J | *J* | Washwood Heath | Staff & Dormitory Coach |
| 977990 | (81165, 92937) | **NR** | NR | *E* | LU | Tool Van |
| 977991 | (81308, 92991) | **NR** | NR | *E* | LU | Tool Van |

# PLATFORM 5 MAIL ORDER

# BRITISH RAILWAYS POCKET BOOKS 2006

The Platform 5 British Railways Pocket Books contain a full list of all vehicles in service with owner, operation, livery and depot information for every vehicle, plus pool codes for locomotives. Each book also includes an overview of Britain's railway network today and detailed lists of all train operating companies, depot and maintenance facilities, leasing companies and other useful information.

BRPB No. 1: Locomotives ............................ £3.75
BRPB No. 2: Coaching Stock ...................... £3.75
BRPB No. 3: Diesel Multiple Units .............. £3.75
BRPB No. 4: Electric Multiple Units ........... £3.75

A complete source of reference used throughout the railway industry.

# HOW TO ORDER

Telephone your order and credit/debit card details to our 24-hour sales orderline:

## 0114 255 8000 or Fax: 0114 255 2471.

An answerphone is attached for calls made outside of normal UK office hours.
Or send your credit/debit card details, sterling cheque or British Postal order payable to 'Platform 5 Publishing Ltd.' to:

## Mail Order Department (LCS), Platform 5 Publishing Ltd, 3 Wyvern House, Sark Road, SHEFFIELD, S2 4HG, ENGLAND

Please add postage & packing: 10% UK; 20% Europe; 30% Rest of World.
Please allow 28 days for delivery in the UK.

# INTERNAL USER VEHICLES

These vehicles are confined to yards and depots or do not normally move at all.
Details are given of the internal user number, type and former identity, current
use and location. Many of these listed no longer see regular use.

| | | | |
|---|---|---|---|
| 024709 | BR fish van 87122 | Stores van | Wembley heavy repair shop |
| 024710 | BR fish van 87146 | Stores van | Wembley heavy repair shop |
| 024711 | BR fish van 87227 | Stores van | Wembley heavy repair shop |
| 024877 | BR CCT 94698 | Stores van | Wavertree Yard,Edge Hill |
| 024909 | BR BSOT 9106 | Staff accommodation | Preston Station |
| 024953 | BR GUV 93682 | Stores van | DY |
| 025000 | BR BSO 9423 | Staff accommodation | Preston Station |
| 025026 | BR TSO 5259 | Staff accommodation | Wavertree Yard,Edge Hill |
| 025027 | LMS CCT 37210 | Stores van | ZA |
| 041379 | LMS CCT 35527 | Stores van | Leeman Road EY, York |
| 041898 | BR BG 84608 | Stores van | Leeman Road EY, York |
| 041947 | BR GUV 93425 | Stores van | IL |
| 041963 | LMS milk tank 44047 | Storage tank | DR |
| 042154 | BR GUV 93975 | Stores van | Ipswich Upper Yard |
| 061034 | BR CCT 94798 | Stores van | Marsh Junction, Bristol |
| 061061 | BR CCT 94135 | Stores van | Oxford station |
| 061171 | BR GUV 93480 | Stores van | RG |
| 061223 | BR GUV 93714 | Stores van | Oxford station |
| 083264 | BR TSO 4047 | Staff accommodation | Ashford station down sidings |
| 083439 | BR CCT 94752 | Stores van | WD |
| 083602 | BR CCT 94494 | Stores van | Three Bridges station |
| 083633 | BR GUV 93724 | Stores van | BI |
| 083644 | BR Ferry Van 889201 | Stores van | EH |
| 083650 | BR GUV 93100 | Stores van | Ashford station down sidings |
| 083664 | BR Ferry Van 889203 | Stores van | EH |
| 095020 | LNER BG 70170 | Stores van | Inverness Yard |
| 095030 | BR GUV 96140 | Stores van | EC |

Note: CCT = Covered Carriage Truck (a 4-wheeled van similar to a GUV)

# SERVICE STOCK AWAITING DISPOSAL

This list contains the last known locations of service vehicles awaiting disposal. The definition of which vehicles are "awaiting disposal" is somewhat vague, but generally speaking these are vehicles of types not now in normal service or vehicles which have been damaged by fire, vandalism or collision.

| | |
|---|---|
| 70220 | Western Trading Estate Siding, North Acton |
| 99014 | Horsham Yard |
| 99015 | Horsham Yard |
| 320645 | Leeman Road EY, York |
| 975000 | ZA |
| 975051 | CD |
| 975379 | Leeman Road EY, York |
| 975454 | TO |
| 975484 | CS |
| 975491 | TH |
| 975535 | Carnforth Bottom End Sidings |
| 975554 | DW |
| 975555 | DW |
| 975639 | CS |
| 975658 | York South Sidings |
| 975681 | Portobello |
| 975682 | Portobello |
| 975685 | Portobello |
| 975686 | Portobello |
| 975687 | Portobello |
| 975688 | Portobello |
| 975706 | Oxford Hinksey Yard* |
| 975717 | Oxford Hinksey Yard* |
| 975721 | DW |
| 975727 | Oxford Hinksey Yard* |

| | |
|---|---|
| 975737 | Oxford Hinksey Yard* |
| 975747 | Oxford Hinksey Yard* |
| 975991 | CD |
| 975995 | Wolverhampton Low Level Stn |
| 977077 | Ripple Lane Yard |
| 977085 | BH |
| 977095 | CS |
| 977111 | Ripple Lane Yard |
| 977112 | Ripple Lane Yard |
| 977193 | BH |
| 977331 | BR |
| 977359 | ZN |
| 977390 | CD |
| 977399 | NL |
| 977449 | CD |
| 977510 | FP |
| 977595 | CD |
| 977618 | BY |
| 977695 | Eastleigh Down CS |
| 977787 | TH |
| 977855 | ZA |
| 977905 | EH |
| 977944 | TO |
| 977945 | TO |
| 977946 | TO |
| 977947 | TO |

* In use as environmental sound protection barrier.

# Keep right up to date with....

# Today's Railways UK

## The UK railway magazine from Platform 5 Publishing.

Read all the very latest news from Britain and Ireland and unrivalled coverage of UK rolling stock news, every month.

**On sale 2nd Monday of EVERY MONTH**

Subscribe to Today's Railways UK TODAY!

---

### Never miss an issue!
- Your copy delivered to your door at no extra cost.
- Recieve every issue hot off the press.
- No price increase for the duration of your subscription.
- Exclusive reduced prices on selected books and videos from the Platform 5 Mail Order Department

---

Today's Railways UK subscriptions:
☎: (+44) 0114 255 8000    Fax: (+44) 0114 255 2471

# Subscription order form

To subscribe, please complete the form below (or a copy) and return it with your remittance to:

**Today's Railways UK (Dept. LCS), 3 Wyvern House, Sark Road, SHEFFIELD, S2 4HG, ENGLAND.**

**BLOCK CAPITALS PLEASE**

(All prices include postage and packing.)

---

**Today's Railways UK: Subscription (12 issues)**

☐ UK £42.00 (post free);  ☐ Overseas Airmail £51.60.

**JAN  FEB  MAR  APR  MAY  JUN  JUL  AUG  SEP  OCT  NOV  DEC**

Please circle start issue required

---

Name: ..................................................................................

Address: ..............................................................................

.............................................................................................

............................................. **Postcode:** ...........................

Daytime Tel. No: ................................................................

E-mail: .................................................................................

---

I enclose my cheque/UK postal order for £ ..................................

made payable to **'PLATFORM 5 PUBLISHING LTD.'**

**Please debit my Visa/Mastercard/Maestro**

Card No: ................................. **Expiry Date:** ......................

Card Issue No./Date (Maestro only): ...................................

for £ ..................................... **Date:** .................................

Signature: ...........................................................................

---

or if ordering by debit/credit card, telephone our subscription department on the numbers opposite.

**Special note:** Subscriptions may begin with the current issue or the next to be published. Subscriptions cannot be backdated.

# 7. CODES

## 7.1. LIVERY CODES

Livery codes are used to denote the various liveries carried. It is impossible to list every livery variation which currently exists. In particular items ignored for this publication include:

- Minor colour variations.
- Omission of logos.
- All numbering, lettering and brandings.

Descriptions quoted are thus a general guide only. Logos as appropriate for each livery are normally deemed to be carried.

The colour of the lower half of the bodyside is stated first. Minor variations to these liveries are ignored.

*Code  Description*

| | |
|---|---|
| **1** | "One" (metallic grey with a broad black bodyside stripe. Pink, yellow, grey, pale green and light blue stripes at the unit/vehicle ends). |
| **1S** | One Stansted Express (metallic grey with a broad black bodyside stripe. Orange stripes at unit ends). |
| **ACT** | ACTS (Netherlands) (Deep blue with a broad yellow stripe). |
| **AL** | Advertising/promotional livery (see class heading for details). |
| **AN** | Anglia Railways Class 170s (white & turquoise with blue vignette). |
| **AR** | Anglia Railways (turquoise blue with a white stripe). |
| **AV** | Arriva Trains (turquoise blue with white doors & a cream "swish"). |
| **AW** | Revised Arriva Trains {Class 175} (turquoise blue with white vignette & two yellow stripes). |
| **B** | BR blue. |
| **BG** | BR blue & grey lined out in white. |
| **BI** | "Visit Bristol" promotional livery (deep blue with various images). |
| **BL** | BR Revised blue with yellow cabs, grey roof, large numbers & logo. |
| **BP** | Blue Pullman ("Nanking" blue & white (all over blue for locos)). |
| **BR** | BR blue with a red solebar stripe. |
| **C2** | c2c Rail (blue with metallic grey doors & pink c2c branding). |
| **CB** | Old Connex South Eastern (NSE blue with a yellow lower bodyside). |
| **CC** | New Central Trains {Class 150} (light green with a broad blue lower bodyside band & blue cab end sections). |
| **CD** | Cotswold Rail (silver with blue & red logo). |
| **CE** | BR Civil Engineers (yellow & grey with black cab doors & window surrounds). |
| **CH** | BR Western Region/GWR (chocolate & cream lined out in gold). |
| **CO** | Centro (grey & green with light blue, white & yellow stripes). |
| **CM** | Revised old Midland Mainline (Midland Mainline teal green with white Central logos). |
| **CN** | Revised Connex South Eastern/South Eastern Trains (white with yellow doors, black window surrounds & grey lower band). |
| **CP** | First ScotRail Caledonian Sleepers {interim} (all over purple). |
| **CR** | Chiltern Railways (blue & white with a thin red stripe). |
| **CS** | ScotRail Caledonian Sleepers (two-tone purple with a silver stripe). |

**CT**  Central Trains (two-tone green with yellow doors. Blue flash & red stripe at vehicle ends).
**CU**  Corus (silver with red logos).
**CX**  Connex (white with yellow lower body & blue solebar).
**DC**  Scenic lines of Devon & Cornwall promotional livery (black with gold cantrail stripe).
**DG**  BR Departmental (dark grey with black cab doors & window surrounds).
**DR**  Direct Rail Services (dark blue with light blue or dark grey roof).
**DS**  Revised Direct Rail Services (dark blue, light blue & green).
**E**   English Welsh & Scottish Railway (maroon bodyside & roof with a broad gold bodyside band).
**EB**  Eurotunnel (two-tone grey with a broad blue stripe).
**EG**  "EWS grey" (As **F** but with large yellow & red EWS logo).
**EN**  Enron Teesside Operations (Trafalgar blue with red solebar stripe).
**EP**  European Passenger Services (two-tone grey with dark blue roof).
**ES**  Eurailscout GB (Light orange with a blue and purple logo).
**EU**  Eurostar (white with dark blue & yellow stripes).
**F**   BR Trainload Freight (two-tone grey with black cab doors & window surrounds. Various logos).
**FB**  Revised Fragonset {freight locos} (Black with large bodyside FRAGONSET lettering).
**FE**  Railfreight Distribution International (two tone-grey with black cab doors & dark blue roof).
**FER** Fertis (light grey with a dark grey roof & solebar).
**FF**  Freightliner grey (two-tone grey with black cab doors & window surrounds. Freightliner logo).
**FG**  First Group corporate Inter-City (indigo blue with a white roof & gold, pink & white stripes).
**FL**  Freightliner (dark green with yellow cabs).
**FM**  FM Rail (all over black with FM Rail logo).
**FO**  BR Railfreight (grey bodysides, yellow cabs & large BR double arrow).
**FP**  Old First Great Western (green & ivory with thin green & broad gold stripes).
**FR**  Fragonset Railways (black with silver roof & a red bodyside band lined out in white).
**FS**  First Group corporate regional/suburban (indigo blue with pink & white stripes).
**FY**  Foster Yeoman (blue & silver. Cast numberplates).
**G¹**  BR Green (plain green, with white stripe on main line locomotives).
**G²**  BR Southern Region/SR or BR DMU green.
**GA**  Southern "Heritage" EMUs (white & dark green with light green semi-circular patches at cab ends. Light green stripe along length of unit).
**GB**  GB Railfreight (blue with orange cantrail & solebar stripes, orange cabs).
**GC**  British racing green & cream lined out in gold.
**GE**  First Great Eastern (grey, green, blue & white).
**GG**  BR green (two-tone green).
**GIF** GIF (Spain) light blue with dark blue band.
**GL**  First Great Western locos/Motorail vans (green with a gold stripe).
**GN**  Great North Eastern Railway (dark blue with a red stripe).
**GP**  Ginsters Cornish Pasties promotional livery (Black & red with various images & cartoons etc.)

| | |
|---|---|
| **GS** | Royal Scotsman/Great Scottish & Western Railway (maroon). |
| **GV** | Gatwick Express EMU (red, white & indigo blue with mauve & blue doors). |
| **GW** | Great Western Railway (green, lined out in black & orange. Cast nameplates). |
| **GX** | Gatwick Express InterCity (dark grey/white/burgundy/white). |
| **GY** | Eurotunnel (grey & yellow). |
| **HA** | Hanson Quarry Products (dark blue & silver). |
| **HB** | HSBC Rail (Oxford blue & white). |
| **HC** | Heathrow Connect (grey with a broad deep blue bodyside band & orange doors). |
| **HE** | Heathrow Express (grey & indigo blue with black window surrounds). |
| **HN** | Harry Needle Railroad Company (orange & grey, lined out in black). |
| **HW** | Heart of Wales Line promotional livery (orange with yellow stripes). |
| **HT** | Hull Trains (dark green & silver with two gold stripes). |
| **IC** | BR InterCity (dark grey/white/red/white). |
| **IL** | Island Line (light blue, with illustrations featuring dinosaurs etc). |
| **IM** | BR InterCity Mainline (dark grey/white/red/light grey & yellow lower cabsides except shunters). |
| **K** | Black. |
| **LA** | Lafarge (white, orange & blue). |
| **LH** | BR Loadhaul (black with orange cabsides). |
| **LN** | LNER Tourist (green & cream). |
| **LW** | LNWR black with grey & red lining. |
| **M** | BR maroon (maroon lined out in straw & black). |
| **MA** | Maintrain (blue). |
| **ME** | Merseyrail Electrics (metallic silver with yellow doors). |
| **ML** | BR Mainline Freight (Aircraft blue with a silver stripe). |
| **MM** | Old Midland Mainline (Teal green with grey lower body sides & three tangerine stripes). |
| **MN** | New Midland Mainline (Thin tangerine stripe on the lower bodyside, ocean blue, grey & white). |
| **MR** | Mendip Rail (Green, red & silver). |
| **MY** | Merseytravel (yellow & white with a grey stripe). |
| **N** | BR Network South East (white & blue with red lower bodyside stripe, grey solebar & cab ends). |
| **NO** | Northern (deep blue, lilac & white). |
| **NR** | Network Rail (blue with a red stripe). |
| **NS** | Northern Spirit (turquoise blue with a lime green "N"). |
| **NT** | BR Network SouthEast (white & blue with red lower bodyside & cantrail stripes). |
| **NW** | North Western Trains (blue with gold cantrail stripe & star). |
| **O** | Non standard livery (see class heading for details). |
| **P** | Porterbrook Leasing Company (white or grey & purple). |
| **PC** | Pullman Car Company (umber & cream with gold lettering lined out in gold). |
| **PM** | Pre Metro Operations (green & white). |
| **PS** | Provincial Services (dark blue & grey with light blue & white stripes). |
| **R** | Plain red. |
| **RE** | Provincial Services/Regional Railways Express (light grey/buff/dark grey with white, dark blue & light blue stripes). |
| **RG** | BR Parcels (dark grey & red). |

**RK**  New Railtrack (green & blue).
**RL**  RMS Locotech (light grey).
**RM**  Royal Mail (red with yellow stripes above solebar).
**RN**  North West Regional Railways (dark blue & grey with green & white stripes).
**RO**  Old Railtrack (orange with white & grey stripes).
**RP**  Royal Train (claret, lined out in red & black).
**RR**  Regional Railways (dark blue & grey with light blue & white stripes, three narrow dark blue stripes at vehicle ends).
**RT**  RT Rail (black, lined out in red).
**RV**  Riviera Trains (Oxford blue & cream lined out in gold {blue only for locos}).
**RX**  Rail Express Systems (dark grey & red with or without blue markings).
**RZ**  Royal Train revised (plain claret, no lining).
**S**  Old Strathclyde PTE (orange & black lined out in white).
**SB**  Serco Railtest blue (deep blue with white Serco brandings).
**SC**  New Strathclyde PTE (carmine & cream lined out in black & gold).
**SD**  South West Trains outer suburban livery {Class 450 style} (deep blue with red doors & orange & red cab sides).
**SCO**  Seco-Rail (orange with a broad yellow bodyside band).
**SL**  Silverlink (indigo blue with white stripe, green lower body & yellow doors).
**SP**  New Strathclyde PTE {Class 334 style} (carmine & cream, with a turquoise stripe).
**SN**  Southern (white & dark green with light green semi-circles at one end of each vehicle. Light grey band at solebar level).
**SO**  Serco Railtest (red & grey).
**SR**  ScotRail (white, terracotta, purple & aquamarine).
**SS**  South West Trains inner suburban {Class 455 style} (red with blue & orange flashes at unit ends).
**ST**  Stagecoach (white & blue with orange & red stripes).
**SW**  South West Trains {long-distance stock} (white & dark blue with black window surrounds, red doors & red panel with orange stripe at unit ends).
**SX**  Stansted Express (two-tone metallic blue with grey doors).
**TL**  New Thameslink (silver with blue window surrounds & ends).
**TP**  First Trans-Pennine Express (Plum with a yellow "N" and First Group indigo blue lower bodyside band).
**TR**  Thameslink Rail (dark blue with a broad orange stripe & two narrower white bodyside stripes plus white cantrail stripe).
**TSO**  TSO (all over yellow with a blue solebar).
**TT**  Thames Trains (blue & white with lime green doors).
**U**  Plain white or grey undercoat.
**V**  Virgin Trains (red with black doors extending into bodysides, three white lower bodysides stripes).
**VL**  Valley Lines (dark green & red with white & light green stripes. Light green doors).
**VP**  Virgin Trains shunters (black with a large black & white chequered flag on the bodyside).
**VN**  Venice Simplon Orient Express "Northern Belle" (crimson lake & cream).
**VT**  New Virgin Trains (silver, with black window surrounds, white cantrail stripe & red roof. Red swept down at unit ends. Black & white striped doors on units).

| | |
|---|---|
| **VW** | Visit Wales promotional livery (green & red with various images). |
| **WA** | Wabtec Rail (black). |
| **WB** | Wales & Borders Alphaline (metallic silver with blue doors). |
| **WC** | Old West Coast Railway Company (all over maroon with a black bodyside stripe). |
| **WD** | West Coast Main Line Desiro (grey with a broad blue bodyside band). |
| **WE** | Wessex Trains Alphaline promotional livery (metallic silver with various images, pink doors). |
| **WN** | Old West Anglia Great Northern (white with blue, grey & orange stripes). |
| **WP** | New West Anglia Great Northern (deep purple with white or light purple doors). |
| **WR** | Waterman Railways (maroon with cream stripes). |
| **WS** | West Coast Railway Company maroon. |
| **WT** | Wessex Trains Alphaline (metallic silver with maroon or pink doors). |
| **WX** | Heart of Wessex Line promotional livery (cerise pink with various images.) |
| **WY** | Old West Yorkshire PTE (red/cream with thin yellow stripe). |
| **WZ** | Wessex Trains claret promotional livery with various images. |
| **Y** | Network Rail or Eurotunnel plain yellow. |
| **YN** | West Yorkshire PTE {Class 333 style} (red with light grey "N"). |
| **YP** | New West Yorkshire PTE (red with grey semi-circles). |

# PLATFORM 5 MAIL ORDER

**Don't miss your copies of the PLATFORM 5 BRITISH RAILWAYS POCKET BOOKS or BRITISH RAILWAYS LOCOMOTIVES & COACHING STOCK.**

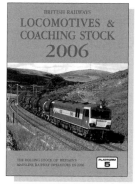

Our annual guides to the rolling stock operating on Britain's mainline railways are published every year in November and March/April respectively. You can make sure you never miss your copy by joining our free mailing list.

Customers on our mailing list receive advance notice of these books a few weeks before they are published, plus a full catalogue of new titles from other transport publishers. To subscribe to this free service, simply register your name and address with our Mail Order Department and we'll send details of the 2007 editions to you shortly before they are published. We do not pass customer details on to any other organisations and we do not conduct any telesales activity.

Please be aware that by subscribing to our mailing lists you are NOT obliged to order any books at any time.

**Note:** Customers ordering books from the Platform 5 Mail Order Department are automatically added to our mailing list unless specifically requested otherwise. Any customers already on our mailing list who would rather not receive information from us, please contact our Mail Order Department. We will be happy to remove your details from our mailing list.

Details of new publications from Platform 5 and a range of other publishers can also be found in the latest issues of **Today's Railways UK** and **Today's Railways Europe** magazines.

# RAILWAY TIMETABLES ON CD-ROM

The **ELECTRONIC TIMETABLE CD-ROM** contains full railway timetable information* for most European countries, including Great Britain, France, Germany, Belgium, Netherlands, Luxembourg, Italy, Switzerland, Austria etc.

## Simply specify the following:

- Date of travel
- Destination station
- Departure station
- Preferred time of travel (arrival or departure)

## The journey planner facility will calculate your rail travel options.

- Specify a particular route or routes for your journey.
- Print a full itinerary for each journey option.
- Print full arrival/departure listings for any station.
- Print a diagrammatic map of your route for each journey option.
- Simple reverse facility for calculating your return journey.

\* In some countries where a timetable change occurs during the period of validity, information is included only up to the date of timetable change. Regular updates can be downloaded over the internet, by choosing 'file', 'update' and following the instructions given. You MUST have the CD-ROM in your CD-ROM drive to successfully download updates.

# RAILWAY TIMETABLES ON CD-ROM

The system is not restricted to international travel and also works for entirely domestic journeys within any country selected.

Also includes a useful German hotel guide. Capable of running in English, French, German or Italian languages. Minimum system requirements: Windows 98 or later, 486/33 MHz, 8MB RAM.

**PRICE: £9.95 (post free to UK and Europe, please add £1.00 postage to rest of World).**

**Note:** The electronic timetable is released twice a year in June and December. Our mail order department will be able to take advance orders from the beginning of May and November for each forthcoming timetable. To register on our CD-ROM timetable mailing list, please contact our Mail Order Department.

## HOW TO ORDER:

Telephone your order and credit card details to our 24 hour sales hotline:
**0114-255-8000 (UK), +44-114-255-8000 (from overseas), or fax: +44(0)114-255-2471.**

Or send your credit/debit card details, sterling cheque, or British postal order payable to 'Platform 5 Publishing Limited' to:
**Mail Order Department (LCS), Platform 5 Publishing Ltd., 3 Wyvern House, Sark Road, SHEFFIELD, S2 4HG, ENGLAND.**

## 7.2. OWNER CODES

Locomotives and rolling stock are owned by various companies and are allotted codes as follows:

*Code* *Owner*

| | |
|---|---|
| 24 | 6024 Preservation Society |
| 40 | The Class 40 Preservation Society |
| 50 | The Fifty Fund |
| 62 | The Princess Royal Locomotive Trust |
| 73 | The Class 73 Locomotive Preservation Society |
| 92 | City of Wells Supporters Association |
| A | Angel Trains |
| AE | AEA Technology Rail |
| AM | Alstom |
| AW | Arriva Trains Wales |
| B1 | Thompson B1 Locomotive Society |
| BB | Balfour Beatty Rail Plant |
| BC | Bridgend County Borough Council/Rhondda Cynon Taff District Council |
| BE | Bert Hitchins |
| BK | The Scottish Railway Preservation Society |
| BS | Bressingham Steam Museum |
| BT | Bombardier Transportation |
| CA | Carillion Rail Plant |
| CC | Cardiff City Council |
| CD | Cotswold Rail Engineering |
| CM | Cambrian Trains |
| CR | Chiltern Railways |
| DG | Duke of Gloucester Steam Locomotive Trust |
| DP | The Deltic Preservation Society |
| DM | Dartmoor Railways |
| DR | Direct Rail Services |
| DT | The Diesel Traction Group |
| E | English Welsh & Scottish Railway |
| EN | Enron Teesside Operations |
| ES | Eurailscout GB |
| ET | Eurotunnel |
| EU | Eurostar (UK) |
| FG | First Group |
| FL | Freightliner |
| FM | FM Rail (Fragonset Merlin Railways) |
| FY | Foster Yeoman |
| GB | GB Railfreight (owned by First Group) |
| GD | Garsdale Railtours |
| GS | The Great Scottish & Western Railway Company |
| GW | The Great Western Society |
| H | HSBC Rail (UK) |
| HA | The Hanson Group |
| HD | Hastings Diesels |
| HE | British Airports Authority |

| | |
|---|---|
| HJ | Howard Johnston Engineering |
| HN | Harry Needle Railroad Company |
| HS | Harry Schneider |
| HU | Hunslet Engine Company |
| HX | Halifax Asset Finance/Halifax Bank of Scotland |
| IR | Ian Riley Engineering |
| J | Fastline (Jarvis Rail) |
| JB | John Ball |
| JH | Jeremy Hosking |
| JK | Dr. John Kennedy |
| LW | London & North Western Railway Company |
| MA | Maintrain |
| MD | Ministry of Defence |
| MH | Mid-Hants Railway |
| MN | Merchant Navy Locomotive Preservation Society |
| MW | Martin Walker (Beaver Sports) |
| NE | North Eastern Locomotive Preservation Group |
| NM | National Railway Museum |
| NR | Network Rail |
| P | Porterbrook Leasing Company |
| PD | Project Defiance |
| PM | Parry People Movers |
| PO | Other owner |
| RA | Railfilms |
| RI | Rail Assets Investments |
| RL | RMS Locotec |
| RM | Royal Mail |
| RP | Rampart Carriage & Wagon Services |
| RT | RT Rail Tours |
| RV | Riviera Trains |
| SA | Sea Containers Rail Services |
| SB | SNCB/NMBS (Société Nationale des Chemins de fer Belges/ Nationale Maatschappij der Belgische Spoorwegen) |
| SF | SNCF (Société Nationale des Chemins de fer Français) |
| SH | Scottish Highland Railway Company |
| SM | Siemens Transportation |
| SN | Southern |
| SO | Serco Railtest |
| SV | Severn Valley Railway |
| SW | South West Trains |
| TT | Type Three Traction Group |
| VS | Venice-Simplon Orient Express |
| VT | Vintage Trains |
| VW | Virgin West Coast |
| WA | Wabtec Rail |
| WC | West Coast Railway Company |
| WF | Western Falcon Rail (Alan and Tracy Lear) |
| WH | Waterman Heritage Trust |
| WN | West Anglia Great Northern Railway |
| WT | Wessex Trains |
| X | Sold for scrap/further use and awaiting collection or owner unknown |

# Keep right up to date with....

# Today's Railways

**EUROPE**

**The only UK railway magazine exclusively devoted to events on Mainland Europe's railways.**

Every issue is packed with the latest news, informative articles and comprehensive features, plus useful travel information, heritage news, light rail news, diary of events, readers letters and much much more!

**On sale 4th Monday of EVERY MONTH**

## Subscribe to Today's Railways Europe TODAY!

### Never miss an issue!
- Your copy delivered to your door at no extra cost.
- Recieve every issue hot off the press.
- No price increase for the duration of your subscription.
- Exclusive reduced prices on selected books and videos from the Platform 5 Mail Order Department

Today's Railways Europe subscriptions:
☎: (+44) 0114 255 8000    Fax: (+44) 0114 255 2471

# Subscription order form

To subscribe, please complete the form below (or a copy) and return it with your remittance to:

**Today's Railways Europe (Dept. LCS), 3 Wyvern House, Sark Road, SHEFFIELD, S2 4HG, ENGLAND.**

**BLOCK CAPITALS PLEASE**

(All prices include postage and packing.)

---

**Today's Railways Europe: Subscription (12 issues)**

☐ UK £42.00 (post free);　　　　☐ Overseas Airmail £51.60.

JAN　FEB　MAR　APR　MAY　JUN　JUL　AUG　SEP　OCT　NOV　DEC

Please circle start issue required

---

Name: .......................................................................................................

Address: ...................................................................................................

.................................................................................................................

........................................................... Postcode: ...................................

Daytime Tel. No: .....................................................................................

E-mail: ....................................................................................................

---

I enclose my cheque/UK postal order for £ .............................................

made payable to **'PLATFORM 5 PUBLISHING LTD.'**

**Please debit my Visa/Mastercard/Maestro**

Card No: ............................................ Expiry Date: .............................

Card Issue No./Date (Maestro only): ....................................................

for £ ........................................................ Date: ...................................

Signature: ...............................................................................................

---

or if ordering by debit/credit card, telephone our subscription department on the numbers opposite.

**Special note:** Subscriptions may begin with the current issue or the next to be published. Subscriptions cannot be backdated.

## 7.3. LOCOMOTIVE POOL CODES

Locomotives are split into operational groups ("pools") for diagramming and maintenance purposes. The official codes used to denote these pools are shown in this publication.

| Code | Pool |
|------|------|
| ACXX | AC Locomotive Group stored locomotive. |
| ARZG | Alstom Class 08 (Eastleigh). |
| ARZH | Alstom Class 08 (Glasgow Springburn). |
| ARZN | Alstom Class 08 (Wolverton). |
| ATLO | Alstom Class 08. |
| ATTB | Alstom Class 57. |
| ATXX | Alstom locos for long-term repair. |
| CDJD | Serco Railtest Class 08. |
| CREL | Cotswold Rail operational locomotives – contract hire. |
| CROL | Cotswold Rail stored locomotives. |
| CRRH | Cotswold Rail operational locomotives – spot-hire contracts. |
| CRUR | Cotswold Rail stored locomotives – undergoing restoration. |
| DFGC | Freightliner Intermodal Class 86/5. |
| DFGM | Freightliner Intermodal Class 66. |
| DFHG | Freightliner Heavy Haul modified Class 66 (general). |
| DFHH | Freightliner Heavy Haul Class 66. |
| DFIM | Freightliner Intermodal modified Class 66. |
| DFLC | Freightliner Intermodal Class 90. |
| DFLH | Freightliner Heavy Haul Class 47. |
| DFLS | Freightliner Class 08. |
| DFNC | Freightliner Intermodal Class 86/6. |
| DFNR | Freightliner Heavy Haul modified Class 66. Infrastructure services. |
| DFRT | Freightliner Heavy Haul Class 66. Infrastructure services. |
| DFTZ | Freightliner Intermodal Class 57. |
| DHLT | Freightliner locomotives awaiting maintenance/repair/disposal. |
| FGXP | First Group Class 43 (stored). |
| GBAC | GB Railfreight Class 87. |
| GBCM | GB Railfreight Class 66. Railfreight contracts. |
| GBED | GB Railfreight Class 73. |
| GBRT | GB Railfreight Class 66. Network Rail contracts. |
| GBZZ | GB Railfreight. Stored pool. |
| GPSN | Eurostar (UK) Class 73. |
| GPSS | Eurostar (UK) Class 08. |
| GPSV | Eurostar (UK) Class 37. |
| HBSH | Wabtec hire shunting locomotives. |
| HGSS | Maintrain Class 08 (Tyseley/Soho). |
| HISE | Maintrain Class 08 (Derby). |
| HISL | Maintrain Class 08 (Neville Hill). |
| HJSE | First Great Western Class 08 (Landore). |
| HJSL | First Great Western Class 08 (Laira). |
| HJXX | First Great Western Class 08 (Old Oak HST & St. Philip's Marsh). |
| HLSV | Arriva Trains Wales Class 08 (spot-hire). |
| HNRL | Harry Needle Railroad Company hire locomotives. |

| | |
|---|---|
| HNRS | Harry Needle Railroad Company stored locomotives. |
| HQXX | West Anglia Great Northern Railway Class 03. |
| HWSU | Southern Class 09. |
| HYWD | South West Trains Class 73 (standby locomotives). |
| IANA | One Anglia Class 90. |
| IECA | Great North Eastern Railway Class 91. |
| IECP | Great North Eastern Railway Class 43. |
| IMLP | Midland Mainline Class 43. |
| IVGA | Gatwick Express Class 73 (standby locomotive). |
| IWCA | Virgin West Coast Class 87. |
| IWLA | First Great Western Class 57. |
| IWRP | First Great Western Class 43. |
| KCSI | Bombardier Class 08 (Ilford). |
| KDSD | Bombardier Class 08 (Doncaster). |
| MBDL | Non TOC-owned diesel locomotives. |
| MBEL | Non TOC-owned electric locomotives. |
| MOLO | RT Rail Tours locomotives. |
| MOLS | RT Rail Tours stored locomotives. |
| QACL | Network Rail Class 86. |
| QADD | Network Rail Class 31. |
| QAED | Network Rail Class 73. |
| QCAR | Network Rail New Measurement Train Class 43. |
| QETS | Network Rail stored locomotives. |
| RCJA | Fastline (Jarvis Rail) locomotives. |
| RFSH | Wabtec hire fleet. |
| RTLO | Riviera Trains operational fleet. |
| RTLS | Riviera Trains stored locomotives. |
| SAXL | HSBC Rail (UK) off-lease locomotives. |
| SBXL | Porterbrook Leasing Company off-lease locomotives. |
| SDED | FM Rail Class 73. |
| SDFL | FM Rail locomotives (freight traffic). |
| SDFR | FM Rail locomotives (general). |
| SDPP | FM Rail operational locomotives (push-pull capability). |
| SDMS | FM Rail museum locomotive. |
| SDXL | FM Rail stored locomotives. |
| TTTC | Type Three Traction Group Class 37. |
| WAAK | EWS Class 67. |
| WABK | EWS Class 67 RETB fitted. |
| WBAN | EWS Class 66 General. |
| WBBM | EWS Class 66 RETB fitted. |
| WBEN | EWS Class 66 for Euro Cargo Rail, France. |
| WBLN | EWS Class 66 dedicated locos for Lickey Incline banking duties. Fitted with additional lights and drawgear. |
| WCAN | EWS Class 60 (standard fuel tanks). |
| WCBN | EWS Class 60 (extended-range fuel tanks). |
| WDAG | EWS Class 59/2. |
| WEFE | EWS Class 90. |
| WKBM | EWS Class 37 Scotland. |
| WKCK | EWS Class 37 South Wales. |
| WMOC | EWS stored "heritage" locomotives. |
| WNSO | EWS main line locomotives – sold awaiting collection. |

| | |
|---|---|
| WNSS | EWS main line locomotives – stored serviceable. |
| WNTA | EWS locomotives – stored Sandite locos. |
| WNTR | EWS locomotives – tactical reserve. |
| WNTS | EWS locomotives – tactical stored serviceable. |
| WNWX | EWS main line locomotives – for major repairs. |
| WNXX | EWS locomotives – stored unserviceable. |
| WNYX | EWS locomotives – authorised for component recovery. |
| WNZX | EWS locomotives – awaiting disposal. |
| WREM | EWS Shunting locomotives (Eastern and East Midlands – contract hire). |
| WRGW | EWS Shunting locomotives (Great Western and South Wales – contract hire). |
| WRLN | EWS shunting locomotives (North London – contract hire). |
| WRLS | EWS Shunting locomotives (South London – contract hire). |
| WRSC | EWS Shunting locomotives (Scotland and Carlisle area – contract hire). |
| WRWM | EWS Shunting locomotives (West Midlands and North West – contract hire). |
| WRWR | EWS Shunting locomotives (Western Region – contract hire). |
| WSAW | EWS Shunting locomotives (South Wales, on hire to Celsa (formerly Allied Steel & Wire)). |
| WSEM | EWS Shunting locomotives (Eastern and East Midlands). |
| WSGW | EWS Shunting locomotives (Great Western and South Wales). |
| WSLN | EWS Shunting locomotives (North London). |
| WSLS | EWS Shunting locomotives (South London). |
| WSNE | EWS Shunting locomotives (North East). |
| WSSC | EWS Shunting locomotives (Scotland and Carlisle area). |
| WSWM | EWS Shunting locomotives (West Midlands and North West). |
| WSWR | EWS Shunting locomotives (Western Region). |
| WSXX | EWS Shunting locomotives – internal/depot use. |
| WTAE | EWS Class 92. |
| WZFF | EWS Class 58 – hire locomotives France. |
| WZFH | EWS Class 58 – hire locomotives The Netherlands. |
| WZFS | EWS Class 58 – hire locomotives Spain. |
| WZGF | EWS Class 56 – hire locomotives France. |
| WZKF | EWS Class 37 – possible hire locomotives France. |
| WZKS | EWS Class 37 – hire locomotives Spain. |
| WZTS | EWS locomotives – tactical stored. |
| XHBS | Direct Rail Services locomotives – Blue Star multiple working fitted. |
| XHIM | Direct Rail Services locomotives – Intermodal traffic. |
| XHKM | Direct Rail Services locomotives – Class 47s. |
| XHMW | Direct Rail Services locomotives undergoing long-term repairs. |
| XHNC | Direct Rail Services locomotives – Nuclear Flask traffic. |
| XHNR | Direct Rail Services locomotives – Network Rail traffic. |
| XHSS | Direct Rail Services stored locomotives. |
| XYPA | Mendip Rail Class 59/1. |
| XYPO | Mendip Rail Class 59/0. |

# 7.4. OPERATOR CODES

Operator codes are used to denote the organisation that facilitates the use of that vehicle, and may not be the actual Train Operating Company which runs the train. Where no operator code is shown, vehicles are currently not in use.

| Code | Operator |
|------|----------|
| 62 | The Princess Royal Locomotive Trust |
| 1A | One Anglia |
| 1E | One Great Eastern |
| 1S | One Stansted Express |
| 1W | One West Anglia |
| AW | Arriva Trains Wales |
| BB | Balfour Beatty Rail Plant |
| BK | The Scottish Railway Preservation Society |
| C2 | c2c Rail |
| CA | Carillion Rail Plant |
| CD | Cotswold Rail Engineering |
| CR | Chiltern Railways |
| CT | Central Trains |
| DR | Direct Rail Services |
| E | English Welsh & Scottish Railway |
| EU | Eurostar (UK) |
| FL | Freightliner |
| FK | First Great Western Link |
| FM | FM Rail (Fragonset Merlin Railways) |
| GB | GB Railfreight (owned by First Group) |
| GN | Great North Eastern Raiway |
| GS | The Great Scottish & Western Railway Company |
| GW | First Great Western |
| GX | Gatwick Express |
| HC | Heathrow Connect (joint Heathrow Express/FGW Link operation) |
| HD | Hastings Diesels |
| HE | Heathrow Express |
| HT | Hull Trains |
| IL | Island Line |
| J | Fastline (Jarvis Rail). |
| LS | Locomotive support coach |
| ME | Merseyrail Electrics |
| MH | Mid-Hants Railway |
| MM | Midland Mainline |
| NO | Northern |
| PM | Pre Metro Operations |
| RA | Railfilms |
| RP | Royal Train |
| RV | Riviera Trains |
| SE | South Eastern Trains |
| SF | SNCF (French Railways) |
| SH | Scottish Highland Railway Company |
| SL | Silverlink |

| | |
|---|---|
| *SN* | Southern |
| *SO* | Serco Railtest |
| *SR* | First ScotRail |
| *SW* | South West Trains |
| *TP* | First Trans-Pennine Express |
| *TR* | Thameslink Rail |
| *VS* | Venice-Simplon Orient Express |
| *VT* | Vintage Trains |
| *VW* | Virgin West Coast |
| *VX* | Virgin Cross-Country |
| *WC* | West Coast Railway Company |
| *WN* | (West Anglia) Great Northern |
| *WT* | Wessex Trains |
| *WX* | Wessex Trains (TOC) |

# PLATFORM 5 MAIL ORDER

## SWISS RAILWAYS ON DVD

### Eisenbahn Kurier

German publisher Eisenbahn Kurier has produced a series of high quality DVDs featuring mountain railways in Switzerland that are now available with English commentary. Each DVD follows the route of the featured railway through spectacular alpine scenery in all weathers. Also looks at trains on the route, old and new, and places of interest along the way. All the DVDs include a mixture of archive and present-day material, including a range of vintage and modern locomotives & rolling stock. The following are currently available:

**Glacier Express** (68 minutes) .......................................... £17.50
**Dampfbahn Furka-Bergstrecke** (55 minutes) ................. £14.95
**Gotthardbahn** (110 minutes) ...................................... £17.50
**Die Centovallibahn** (40 minutes) ............................... £17.50
**Lago Maggiore Express** (45 minutes) .......................... £17.50
**Simplon** (Due SUMMER 2006) (75 minutes) ................. £19.50

**Please add postage and packing £1.00 (UK), £2.00 (overseas) per DVD.**

**Telephone, fax or send your order to the Platform 5 Mail Order Department. See page 384 of this book for details.**

# PLATFORM 5 MAIL ORDER

The Platform 5 European Railway Handbooks are the most comprehensive guides to the rolling stock of selected European railway administrations available. Each book lists all locomotives

and railcars of the country concerned, giving details of number carried and depot allocation, together with a wealth of technical data for each class of vehicle. Each book is A5 size, thread sewn and includes 32 pages of colour illustrations. The Benelux book also contain details of hauled coaching stock.

Dates of publication are shown.

| No. 1 | Benelux Railways (2000) | £14.50 |
|---|---|---|
| No. 2A | German Railways Part 1: DB Locomotives & Multiple Units (2004) | £16.95 |
| No. 2B | German Railways Part 2: Private Operators, Preserved & Museums (2004) | £16.95 |
| No. 3 | Austrian Railways (2005) | £17.50 |
| No. 4 | French Railways (1999) | £14.50 |
| No. 6 | Italian Railways (1996) | £13.50 |

**Please add postage: 10% UK, 20% Europe, 30% Rest of World.**

**Telephone, fax or send your order to the Platform 5 Mail Order Department. See page 384 of this book for details.**

# 7.5. ALLOCATION & LOCATION CODES

Allocation codes are used in this publication to denote the normal maintenance base ("depots") of each operational locomotive, multiple unit or coach. However, maintenance may be carried out at other locations and may also be carried out by mobile maintenance teams.

Location codes are used to denote common storage locations whilst the full place name is used for other locations. The designation (S) denotes stored. However, when a locomotive pool code denotes that a loco is stored anyway then the (S) is not shown.

| Code | Depot | Operator |
|------|-------|----------|
| AC | Aberdeen Clayhills | *Storage location only* |
| AF | Ashford Chart Leacon (Kent) | Bombardier Transportation |
| AK† | Ardwick (Manchester) | Siemens/Trans-Pennine Express |
| AL | Aylesbury | Chiltern Railways |
| AN | Allerton (Liverpool) | EWS |
| AP* | Ashford Rail Plant | Balfour Beatty Rail Plant |
| AS* | Allely's, Studley (Warwickshire) | *Storage location only* |
| AY | Ayr | EWS |
| BA | Basford Hall Yard (Crewe) | *Storage location only* |
| BD | Birkenhead North | Merseyrail Electrics |
| BH | Barrow Hill (Chesterfield) | Barrow Hill Engine Shed Society |
| BI | Brighton Lovers Walk | Southern |
| BK | Bristol Barton Hill | EWS |
| BM | Bournemouth | South West Trains |
| BN | Bounds Green (London) | GNER |
| BR* | MoD DSDC Bicester | Ministry of Defence |
| BQ | Bury (Greater Manchester) | East Lancashire Railway |
| BS | Bescot (Walsall) | EWS |
| BT | Bo'ness (West Lothian) | Bo'ness & Kinneil Railway |
| BY | Bletchley | Silverlink |
| BZ | St. Blazey (Par) | EWS |
| CD | Crewe Diesel | EWS |
| CE | Crewe International Electric | EWS |
| CF | Cardiff Canton | Arriva Trains Wales/Pullman Rail |
| CH | Chester | Alstom/Arriva Trains Wales |
| CJ | Clapham Yard (London) | South West Trains |
| CK | Corkerhill (Glasgow) | First ScotRail |
| CO | Cranmore (Somerset) | East Somerset Railway |
| CP | Crewe Carriage | London & North Western Railway Co. |
| CQ | Crewe (The Railway Age) | London & North Western Railway Co. |
| CS | Carnforth | West Coast Railway Company |
| CT* | MoD Caerwent AFD (Caldicot) | Ministry of Defence |
| CU | Carlisle Currock | *Storage location only* |
| CZ | Central Rivers (Burton) | Bombardier Transportation |
| DC* | Didcot Yard | EWS |
| DF | Derby FM Rail | FM Rail |
| DI | Didcot Railway Centre | Great Western Society |
| DR | Doncaster | EWS |

| DY | Derby Etches Park | Maintrain |
| DW* | Doncaster West Yard | *Storage location only* |
| EA* | Earles Sidings (Hope) | Lafarge |
| EC | Edinburgh Craigentinny | GNER |
| EH | Eastleigh | EWS |
| EM | East Ham (London) | c2c |
| EN | Euston Downside (London) | *Storage location only* |
| ER* | Exeter Riverside Yard | *Storage location only* |
| ES* | On hire to GIF, Spain | GIF |
| EU* | Coquelles Eurotunnel (France) | Eurotunnel |
| EX | Exeter | Wessex Trains |
| FB | Ferrybridge | EWS |
| FD | Freightliner diesels nationwide | Freightliner |
| FE | Freightliner electrics nationwide | Freightliner |
| FF* | Forest (Brussels) | SNCB/NMBS |
| FN* | On hire to Fertis/TSO/Seco, France | Fertis/TSO/Seco-Rail |
| FP | Ferme Park sidings | *Storage location only* |
| GI | Gillingham (Kent) | South Eastern Trains |
| GL | Gloucester Horton Road | Cotswold Rail |
| GW | Shields Road (Glasgow) | First ScotRail |
| HA | Haymarket (Edinburgh) | First ScotRail |
| HE | Hornsey (London) | WAGN |
| HG | Hither Green (London) | EWS |
| HM | Healey Mills (Wakefield) | EWS |
| HT | Heaton (Newcastle) | Northern |
| IM | Immingham | EWS |
| IL | Ilford (London) | "One" |
| IP | Ipswich stabling point | Freightliner |
| IR* | Immingham Railfreight Terminal | *Storage location only* |
| IS | Inverness | First ScotRail |
| KE* | Ketton Cement Works | Castle Cement |
| KM | Carlisle Kingmoor | Direct Rail Services |
| KR | Kidderminster | Severn Valley Railway |
| KT | MoD Kineton (Warwickshire) | Ministry of Defence |
| LA | Laira (Plymouth) | First Great Western |
| LB | Loughborough | Brush Traction |
| LD | Leeds Midland Road | LNWR/Freightliner |
| LE | Landore (Swansea) | First Great Western |
| LG | Longsight (Manchester) | Northern |
| LL | Edge Hill (Liverpool) | West Coast Traincare |
| LM | MoD Long Marston (Warwickshire) | Ministry of Defence |
| LR | Leicester | EWS |
| LT | MoD Longtown/Smalmstown (Cumbria) | Ministry of Defence |
| LU* | MoD Ludgershall | Ministry of Defence |
| LY* | Le Landy (Paris) | SNCF |
| MA | Manchester Longsight | West Coast Traincare |
| MD | Merehead | Mendip Rail |
| MG | Margam (Port Talbot) | EWS |
| MH | Millerhill Yard | EWS |
| ML | Motherwell (Glasgow) | EWS |
| MM | Fire Service College, Moreton-in-Marsh | Cotswold Rail |

| Code | Location | Operator |
|---|---|---|
| MO* | Mossend Yard | EWS |
| MQ* | Meldon Quarry (Okehampton) | Dartmoor Railways |
| MY* | Whitemoor Yard (March) | GBRf |
| NC | Norwich Crown Point | "One" |
| NH | Newton Heath (Manchester) | Northern |
| NL | Neville Hill (Leeds) | Maintrain/Northern |
| NN† | Northampton | Siemens/Silverlink |
| NP | North Pole International (London) | Eurostar (UK) |
| NT | Northam (Southampton) | Siemens/South West Trains |
| NW* | Brunner Mond Works, Northwich (Cheshire) | Brunner Mond |
| NY | Grosmont (North Yorkshire) | North Yorkshire Moors Railway |
| OC | Old Oak Common locomotive (London) | EWS |
| OH | Old Oak Common Heathrow | Heathrow Express |
| OO | Old Oak Common HST | First Great Western |
| OM | Old Oak Common carriage | Riviera Trains/EWS |
| OY | Oxley (Wolverhampton) | West Coast Traincare |
| PB | Peterborough Yards | EWS/GBRf |
| PC | Polmadie (Glasgow) | West Coast Traincare |
| PM | St. Philip's Marsh (Bristol) | First Great Western |
| PY* | MoD DERA Pig's Bay (Shoeburyness) | Ministry of Defence |
| PZ | Penzance | First Great Western |
| RG | Reading | First Great Western Link |
| RL | Ropley (Hampshire) | Mid-Hants Railway |
| RM | Ramsgate | South Eastern Trains |
| RU | Rugby Rail Plant | Carillion Rail Plant |
| RY | Ryde (Isle of Wight) | Island Line |
| SA | Salisbury | South West Trains |
| SB* | Sandbach Works | Albion Chemicals |
| SD* | Stoke Gifford Yard (Bristol Parkway) | Storage location only |
| SE | St. Leonards (Hastings) | St. Leonards Railway Engineering |
| SG | Slade Green (London) | South Eastern Trains |
| SI | Soho (Birmingham) | Maintrain/Central Trains |
| SJ* | Severn Tunnel Junction | EWS |
| SK | Swanwick Junction (Derbyshire) | Midland Railway-Butterley |
| SL | Stewarts Lane (London) | Gatwick Express/VSOE |
| SM* | Swansea Maliphant Sidings | Storage location only |
| SO* | Southall (Greater London) | Flying Scotsman Railways |
| SP | Springs Branch CRDC (Wigan) | EWS |
| SU | Selhurst (Croydon) | Southern |
| SY | Saltley (Birmingham) | EWS |
| SZ | Southampton Maritime | Freightliner |
| TB* | Tilburg (Netherlands) | NedTrain |
| TD | Temple Mills (Stratford, London) | EWS |
| TE | Thornaby (Middlesbrough) | EWS |
| TH* | Pershore Airfield, Throckmorton, Worcs. | Storage location only |
| TJ* | Tavistock Junction Yard (Plymouth) | Storage location only |
| TM | Tyseley Locomotive Works | Birmingham Railway Mueseum |
| TN* | Tonbridge West Yard | GBRf |
| TO | Toton (Nottinghamshire) | EWS |
| TP | Trafford Park FLT | Manchester Ship Canal |
| TS | Tyseley (Birmingham) | Maintrain/Central Trains |

| TT* | Toton Training School Compound (Notts.) | *Storage location only* |
| TV* | Teesport, Middlesbrough | AV Dawson |
| TY | Tyne Yard (Newcastle) | EWS |
| WB | Wembley (London) | EWS |
| WD | Wimbledon (London) | South West Trains |
| WE | Willesden Brent sidings | *Storage location only* |
| WI | Wilton, Teesside | SembCorp Utilities |
| WN | Willesden (London) | West Coast Traincare |
| WY | Westbury Yard | EWS |
| XW | Crofton (Wakefield) | Bombardier Transportation |
| YJ* | Yeovil Junction Railway Centre | Somerset & Dorset Loco Company |
| YK | National Railway Museum (York) | Science Museum |
| | | |
| ZA | RTC Business Park (Derby) | Serco Railtest/AEA Technology |
| ZB | Doncaster Works | Wabtec |
| ZC | Crewe Works | Bombardier Transportation |
| ZD | Derby, Litchurch Lane Works | Bombardier Transportation |
| ZF | Doncaster Works | Bombardier Transportation |
| ZG | Eastleigh Works | Alstom |
| ZH | Springburn Works, Glasgow | Alstom |
| ZI | Ilford Works | Bombardier Transportation |
| ZJ | Marcroft, Stoke | Turners |
| ZK | Kilmarnock Works | Hunslet-Barclay |
| ZN | Wolverton Works | Alstom |
| ZP | Horbury Works (Wakefield) | Bombardier Transportation |

\* unofficial code
† Due to open in 2006

## 7.6. ABBREVIATIONS

**The following general abbreviations are used in this book:**

| | |
|---|---|
| AC | Alternating Current (i.e. Overhead supply). |
| AFD | Air Force Department |
| BR | British Railways. |
| BSI | Bergische Stahl Industrie. |
| CRDC | Component Recovery & Disposal Centre |
| C&W | Carriage & Wagon |
| DC | Direct Current (i.e. Third Rail). |
| DEMU | Diesel Electric Multiple Unit. |
| DERA | Defence Evaluation & Research Agency |
| Dia. | Diagram number. |
| DMU | Diesel Multiple Unit (general term). |
| DSDC | Defence Storage & Distribution CentreEMU Electric Multiple Unit. |
| GNER | Great North Eastern Railway |
| GWR | Great Western Railway. |
| H-B | Hunslet-Barclay. |
| h.p. | horse power. |
| HNRC | Harry Needle Railroad Company |
| Hz | Hertz. |
| kN | kilonewtons. |
| km/h | kilometres per hour. |
| kW | kilowatts. |
| lbf | pounds force. |
| LT | London Transport. |
| LUL | London Underground Limited. |
| m. | metres. |
| mm. | millimetres. |
| m.p.h. | miles per hour. |
| RCH | Railway Clearing House. |
| r.p.m. | revolutions per minute. |
| RR | Rolls Royce. |
| RSL | Rolling Stock Library. |
| SR | BR Southern Region. |
| t. | tonnes. |
| T | Toilets. |
| TD | Toilets suitable for disabled passengers. |
| TDM | Time Division Multiplex. |
| V | volts. |
| w | wheelchair spaces. |

# 7.7 BUILDERS

These are shown in class headings. The workshops of British Railways and the pre-nationalisation and pre-grouping companies were first transferred to a wholly-owned subsidiary called "British Rail Engineering Ltd.", abbreviated to BREL. These workshops were later privatised, BREL then becoming "BREL Ltd.". Some of the works were then taken over by ABB, which was later merged with Daimler-Benz Transportation to become "Adtranz". This company has now been taken over by Bombardier Transportation, which had taken over Procor at Horbury previously. Bombardier also builds vehicles for the British market in Brugge, Belgium.

Other workshops were the subject of separate sales, Springburn, Glasgow and Wolverton becoming "Railcare" and Eastleigh becoming "Wessex Traincare". These are now owned by Alstom (previously GEC-Alsthom), as was the former Metro-Cammell Works in Birmingham. Eastleigh Works was due to close in Spring 2006.

**Note:** Part of Doncaster works was sold to RFS Engineering, which became insolvent and was bought out and renamed RFS Industries. This has now been taken over by Wabtec.

The builder details in the class headings show the owner at the time of vehicle construction followed by the works as follows:

| | |
|---|---|
| Ashford | Ashford Works (Note that this is not the same as the current Bombardier Ashford depot which is at Chart Leacon). |
| Birmingham | The former Metro-Cammel works at Saltley, Birmingham. |
| Cowlairs | Cowlairs Works, Glasgow. |
| Derby | Derby Carriage Works (also known as Litchurch Lane). |
| Doncaster | Doncaster Works. |
| Eastleigh | Eastleigh Works |
| Swindon | Swindon Works. |
| Wolverton | Wolverton Works. |
| York | York Carriage Works. |

Other builders are:

| | |
|---|---|
| Alexander | Walter Alexander, Falkirk. |
| Barclay | Andrew Barclay, Caledonia Works, Kilmarnock (now Hunslet-Barclay). |
| BRCW | Birmingham Railway Carriage & Wagon, Smethwick. |
| CAF | Construcciones y Auxiliar de Ferrocarriles, Zaragosa, Spain. |
| Cravens | Cravens, Sheffield. |
| Gloucester | Gloucester Railway Carriage & Wagon, Gloucester. |
| Hunslet-Barclay | Hunslet-Barclay, Caledonia Works, Kilmarnock. |
| Hunslet TPL | Hunslet Transportation Projects, Leeds. |
| Lancing | SR, Lancing Works. |
| Leyland Bus | Leyland Bus, Workington. |
| Metro-Cammell | Metropolitan-Cammell, Saltley, Birmingham |
| Pressed Steel | Pressed Steel, Linwood. |
| Charles Roberts | Charles Roberts, Horbury Junction, Wakefield. |
| SGP | Simmering-Graz-Pauker, Austria (now owned by Siemens). |
| Siemens | Siemens Transportation Systems (various works in Germany and Austria). |
| SRP | Specialist Rail Products Ltd (A subsidiary of RFS). |

NOTES

NOTES

# PLATFORM 5 MAIL ORDER

The Platform 5 Publishing Mail Order Catalogue contains a wide range of high quality transport books from many leading and smaller publishers. Topics covered include:

- **British Railways.**
- **Overseas Railways.**
- **Light Rail Transit & Metros.**
- **Preservation.**
- **Nostalgia.**
- **Maps & Track Diagrams.**
- **CD-ROMs.**
- **Road Transport.**
- **Clearance Titles.**

64 pages in full colour throughout plus regular updates including the very latest publications.

For your **FREE** copy, please phone, fax or write to:

**Mail Order Department (LCS),
Platform 5 Publishing Ltd.,
3 Wyvern House, Sark Road,
SHEFFIELD, S2 4HG, ENGLAND.**

☎: (+44) 0114 255 8000  Fax: (+44) 0114 255 2471

# A NATURALI... ...O THE

# Birds ... a

## and Singapore

## G.W.H. Davison & Yeap Chin Aik

BEAUFOY BOOKS

First published in the United Kingdom in 2010 by Beaufoy Books
11 Blenheim Court, 316 Woodstock Road, Oxford OX2 7NS, England
www.johnbeaufoy.com

10 9 8 7 6 5 4 3 2 1

Copyright © 2010 John Beaufoy Publishing Limited
Copyright in text © 2010 G.W.H. Davison & Yeap Chin Aik
Copyright in photographs © 2010 David Bakewell, David Lai, Ooi Beng Yean, Cede Prudente and John Corder
as specified below
Copyright in maps © 2010 John Beaufoy Publishing Limited

**Photo Credits**
**Front cover:** *top left* Blue-tailed Bee-eater (David Bakewell); *top right* Olive-backed Sunbird (Cede Prudente); *bottom left* Cinnamon Bittern (David Bakewell); *bottom middle* Blue-winged Pitta (Robert Teo); *bottom right* Long-tailed Parakeet (Lin Yangchen). **Back cover:** Collared Kingfisher (David Bakewell). **Title page:** Little Spiderhunter (Cede Prudente). **Contents page:** Black-and-yellow Broadbill (Cede Prudente).
**Main descriptions:** photos are denoted by a page number followed by t (top), b (bottom), l (left) or r (right).
**David Bakewell:** 12b, 15t, 16tr, 18t, 18b, 20t, 20m, 20b, 21t, 21b, 22t, 22b, 26tl, 27t, 28t, 28b, 29b, 31t, 32b, 34t, 35t, 35b, 36tl, 36tr, 36b, 37t, 37b, 38t, 39t, 39b, 40t, 41t, 41b, 42b, 43b, 47t, 48bl, 49t, 53t, 53b, 55t, 56t, 57t, 57b, 58t, 58b, 59t, 62t, 63t, 64b, 65t, 68t, 71t, 72t, 78b, 81t, 81b, 83t, 83b, 85t, 87t, 87b, 89t, 89br, 90b, 93t, 93b, 94b, 96t, 97t, 97b, 100tl, 100tr, 100b, 103t, 103b, 104t, 104bl, 104br, 105tr, 106br, 107b, 109b, 110b, 111b, 113t, 113b, 116t, 116b, 117t, 117b, 118t, 120tl, 120tr, 121bl, 122t, 123t, 124t, 128b, 131t, 132t, 133t, 133b, 134t, 134b, 135t, 135b, 136t, 136b, 137t, 137b, 138t, 138b, 139t, 141t, 141b, 142t, 142b, 143t, 144t, 144b, 145t, 145b, 146t, 147t, 147b, 148b. **David Lai:** 14t. **John Corder:** 13m, 14b, 17b, 32t, 33t, 33b, 40b, 42t, 43t, 44b, 45t, 45b, 50t, 67b, 70b, 74b, 84t, 91t, 92tl, 99t, 107tl, 126b, 127t, 127b, 149t. **J. Cede Prudente:** 13b, 16b, 17t, 24t, 30b, 44t, 48t, 55b, 62b, 66t, 73t, 82t, 82b, 92tr, 95t, 95b, 99b, 102b, 106tr, 108b, 112t, 114b, 115t, 119b, 139b, 146b. **Ooi Beng Yean:** 12t, 13t, 15b, 16tl, 19t, 19b, 23t, 23b, 24b, 25t, 25b, 26tr, 26b, 27b, 29t, 30t, 31b, 34b, 38b, 46t, 46b, 47t, 48br, 49b, 50b, 51t, 51b, 52t, 52b, 54t, 54b, 56b, 59bl, 59br, 60t, 60b, 61t, 61b, 63b, 64t, 65b, 66b, 67t, 68b, 69t, 69b, 70t, 71b, 72b, 73b, 74t, 75t, 75b, 76t, 76b, 77t, 77b, 78t, 79t, 79b, 80t, 80b, 84b, 85b, 86tl, 86tr, 86b, 88t, 88b, 89bl, 90t, 91b, 92b, 94t, 96b, 98t, 98b, 101t, 101b, 102t, 105tl, 105b, 106tl, 106bl, 107tr, 108t, 109t, 110t, 111t, 112b, 114t, 115bl, 115br, 118b, 119t, 120b, 121t, 121br, 122b, 123b, 124b, 125t, 125b, 126t, 128t, 129t, 129b, 130t, 130b, 131b, 132b, 140t, 140b, 143b, 148t, 149b, 150t, 150b, 151t, 151b.

All rights reserved. No part of this publication may be reproduced, stored in a retrieval system or transmitted in any form or by any means, electronic, mechanical, photocopying, recording or otherwise, without the prior written permission of the publishers.

ISBN 978-1-906780-21-0

Edited, designed and typeset by D & N Publishing, Baydon, Wiltshire, UK

Printed and bound in Malaysia by Times Offset (M) Sdn. Bhd.

# ·CONTENTS·

## Acknowledgements

Thanks go to Ken Scriven, the generosity of the photographers, David Bakewell, David Lai, Ooi Beng Yean, Cede Prudente and John Corder, and to colleagues at the National Parks Board, Singapore, and the Malaysian Nature Society, including Jessie Ong.

## Introduction

Five important land masses – the Malay Peninsula, Sumatra, Borneo, Palawan, and Java and Bali combined – make up the biogeographical area known as Sundaland, in Southeast Asia. This area is characterised by its humid equatorial climate, maritime climatic influence, limited seasonality and climax vegetation of tropical evergreen rainforest. Five countries are covered by Sundaland: Malaysia, Singapore, Indonesia, Brunei and the Philippines. This book introduces the birds of Malaysia and Singapore, many of which are shared with the other three countries in this diverse and fascinating area. Peninsular Malaysia is the southernmost part of mainland Asia, while the two big Malaysian states of Sabah and Sarawak lie on the island of Borneo.

## Climate

Sundaland lies within the Intertropical Convergence Zone, where the prevailing directions of the northeast monsoon (November–April) and southwest monsoon (May–October) are modified by the region's proximity to the Equator. Strictly, this is not a monsoon zone but an inter-monsoon zone. Peak rainfall tends to be at the changeover from one monsoon direction to the other, and may occur once or twice a year depending on site. Annual rainfall totals vary from around 1,500mm in drier localities within the lowlands, to over 3,000mm in wetter localities and some montane areas. The wettest weather typically occurs between October and January, when there are more gloomy days and consistent rain; if there is a secondary rainfall peak around April–May, it tends to consist of fewer, shorter, more intense storms. Late-afternoon rainfall is typical year-round, but heavy storms can roll in from the sea in the early morning. Although this is the general picture, many local variations occur, and as elsewhere in the world the weather can do virtually anything at any time.

Daily maximum temperatures in the lowlands are around 32–35°C; night minima are around 24°C in urban areas, but inside undisturbed lowland forest they can be as low as 17°C. Mountains are correspondingly cooler, with a fall in night-time temperatures of about 1°C per 250m altitude. Hail is a rarity, provoking newspaper comment, and short-lived, thin ice has been recorded near the summit of Mount Kinabalu. The drought in 1982–83 changed perceptions of weather patterns for ever: several major El Niño years have occurred since then, with consequent fires and 'haze'.

*El Niño*
In weather terms, no two years are alike, and weather patterns and seasons are based on statistical averages. There are daily, seasonal and superannual statistical changes, of which

the El Niño Southern Oscillation (ENSO) is one of the most notorious. This phenomenon is caused by atmospheric pressure differences between the eastern and western Pacific, resulting from alterations every few years in sea currents and hence sea temperature, air temperature and rainfall. The changes in the eastern Pacific during severe El Niño years (cooler temperatures and usually wetter weather) are quite different from those in the western Pacific, including Southeast Asia, where several months of drought can occur. An El Niño 'year' can span parts of more than one calendar year, and is typically followed by a wetter-than-usual La Niña year in the western Pacific. The effects of the ENSO on the forest, the birds and other wildlife of Sundaland are profound.

## VEGETATION

The climatic climax vegetation throughout the region is tropical evergreen rainforest. Semi-evergreen (or semi-deciduous) forest occurs only further north in Thailand, and in drier, more seasonal parts of Java and lands to the east. Rainforest is a general term, covering various forest types growing in areas where rainfall typically exceeds evapotranspiration for at least nine months of the year. (There are many other definitions in the literature.) The classical progression from the coast to inland is from mangroves to peat-swamp forest, freshwater swamp forest, dryland lowland dipterocarp forest, hill dipterocarp forest, lower montane forest and upper montane forest. Above this, only one mountain in Malaysia, Mount Kinabalu (4,095m), reaches beyond the tree-line, although there are others nearby in Sumatra and Java.

Only about 30–35 plant species constitute 'true' mangroves (plants not able to survive in other forest types). Low species diversity, fairly simple vegetation structure with a uniform canopy, lack of understorey and daily inundation by tides create a demanding environment. Woodpeckers such as the Sunda Pygmy (p. 75) and Common Flameback (p. 77) cope well here. The Mangrove Pitta, like the Blue-winged (p. 81) but with a heftier bill, is a ground feeder in mangroves, and must retreat with the tide and find a secure mound above water level for its leaf-bundle nest. The dried mounds created by mud-lobsters – home also to a species of trapdoor spider and other exotic creatures – provide possible sites. Herons and egrets, foraging on adjacent mudflats at low tide, retreat to mangroves at high tide and at night: Little Herons (p. 20) and Little Egrets (p. 22) tend to roost on the stilt roots and lower branches, while Great Egrets (p. 22) and Grey and Purple herons (p. 23) favour the tree crowns. The region's two species of night-heron, including the Black-crowned (p. 19), are both specialist mangrove nesters.

Lesser Adjutants (p. 17) and many shoreline waders (pp. 34–40) feed at pools in clearings in mangroves. Sites such as Bako-Buntal Bay (Sarawak) and the Kuala Selangor and Matang mangroves (Peninsular Malaysia) are famed for the large numbers of waders that can be seen on their huge exposed mudflats. Various wader species forage on sandy or muddy areas of differing wetness and consistency. They specialise in different species of burrowing worms, small molluscs or crustaceans, excavated at different depths below the surface according to the species' preference and bill length, which determines how deeply the birds can probe for food.

Lowland rainforest (from the extreme lowlands up to about 900m altitude) is the premier birding habitat, with high species diversity and classic Southeast Asian groups such as leafbirds, barbets and hornbills. Undisturbed forest has a complex three-dimensional structure, the layers often recognised as understorey, lower storey, middle storey and canopy, with scattered emergent trees overtopping the rest at heights of up to 60–70m. The forest is usually dominated by large timber trees of the family Dipterocarpaceae (dipterocarps), but these provide little food for wildlife. Important fruiting trees are laurels, mangoes and mangosteens, among many others, and for birds especially the vast array of figs (more than 100 species), of which at least some species are in fruit at any one time. Statistically identifiable fruiting seasons, and the great distances between individual trees of any given species, mean that large frugivores (fruit-eaters) such as Great and Rhinoceros hornbills (p. 70) must often travel long distances over the forest canopy. By contrast, small understorey insectivores (insect-eaters) such as the Scaly-crowned Babbler (p. 143) and Short-tailed Babbler (p. 144) have small home ranges. The forest is very heterogeneous, with, for example, White-chested Babblers (p. 144) near riverbanks, Velvet-fronted Nuthatches (p. 112) on the main trunk and larger boughs of trees in the upper storey, Abbott's Babblers (p. 143) in swampy forest and forest edges, and Little Spiderhunters (p. 101) in old treefall areas with banana regrowth. Many more notes are needed from naturalists on the detailed habitat preferences of each species.

Zones of altitudinal change from lowlands to lower (roughly 900–1500m) and upper montane forest (roughly 1,500m upwards) are of great interest. The character of these zones varies from place to place depending on topography and rainfall, tree species composition and also the species of birds present. The Velvet-fronted Nuthatch (p. 112), for example, ranges higher in Sabah and Sarawak (where the montane Blue Nuthatch, p. 112, is absent) than it does in Peninsular Malaysia.

## Biogeography

Repeatedly in the following pages are described species that are found 'from the Himalayas though southern China and Southeast Asia' to Peninsular Malaysia, Sumatra, Borneo and Java. This area represents the eastern half of the Oriental region, otherwise known as the Indo-Malayan region, whereas its western half is made up primarily of Pakistan, India, Sri Lanka and Bangladesh. The Indo-Malayan region is one of the world's great geographical zones and is crucial to biological diversity. Largely covered in tropical rainforest, its total flora and fauna are vast, and include some of the world's most charismatic large land mammal species, such as the Asian Elephant *Elephas maximus*, the Bornean and Sumatran orang-utans *Pongo pygmaeus* and *P. abelii*, and the Javan Rhinoceros *Rhinoceros sondaicus* and Sumatran Rhinoceros *Dicerorhinus sumatrensis*. Also included are pheasants (pp. 13–14), raptors (pp. 24–30), doves and pigeons (pp. 43–46), hornbills (pp. 69–71) and barbets (pp. 72–74) in great array. Many species are confined to Peninsular Malaysia, Sumatra and Borneo, the ever-humid core of Sundaland, and are particularly vulnerable to forest loss. The forest here contains more than 300 species of dipterocarp trees, many of them endemic, and the total flora comprises well over 15,000 plant species for the whole region.

Some birds of mainly Himalayan or at least continental Asian distribution reach no further than Peninsular Malaysia, such as the Blue-winged Siva (p. 147). Others may reach as far as Sumatra, such as the Silver-eared Mesia and Long-tailed Sibia (p. 148). Although these species can be regarded as lowland or foothill birds in the northern part of their range, they are confined to montane forest further south.

Forest specialisation is especially true of the species found in the more restricted region of Sundaland. Here, species are characteristically confined to the undisturbed forest. Thus, for example, the Coppersmith Barbet (p. 74), found from the Himalayas through southern China and Southeast Asia to the Philippines, but missing from forest-rich Borneo, is a bird of semi-open country and park-like woodlands with spacing between the main trees. In contrast, the Yellow-crowned Barbet (p. 74) is confined to the Sunda Shelf, and is exclusively found in the canopy of deep forest.

Most of the endemic birds of Sundaland are forest birds, and most are confined to mountains. Examples are the Chestnut-crested Yuhina (p. 139) of Borneo, and the Sunda Laughingthrush (p. 146) of Borneo and Sumatra. The Dusky Munia (p. 108) is one of the few open-country lowland Sunda endemics, in this case confined to Borneo.

Where birds are found extensively both in mainland Asia and Sundaland, some large genetic differences have been detected between populations north and south of Peninsular Thailand. It is risky to be too precise about the transition point, which is often pinpointed as the Isthmus of Kra; reality is often more complex and fuzzy. The Little Spiderhunter (p. 101) is such a bird, showing large genetic differences but almost no plumage distinctions between northern and southern Asian populations.

The notes on distribution in this book are generalisations. They are not meant to define the past or present distribution of the species very precisely, so they often miss out details of the smaller islands, and in particular omit places where the birds once occurred but no longer do so. All records of birds on islands are of potential scientific value, and need to be recorded meticulously. On the mainland, birdwatchers tend to visit just a handful of well-known, accessible places repeatedly, so new locality records from a wider spread of visits will be very valuable.

Climate, vegetation and biogeographical conditions conspire every two to seven years to produce mass fruiting events, during which most dipterocarps and many other trees in the lowland forest fruit, or fruit more heavily. This provides much more food than usual for many animals, and bird activity and breeding tend to be more obvious at such times. Mass fruiting may be triggered by a succession of cool nights during dry weather, and may also be linked to El Niño climatic events, although this is still unclear. The droughts associated with powerful El Niños can be times of food shortage and stress among many birds, displacing them to unusual localities, altitudes and habitats, and sometimes forcing them to take food items they would not normally touch.

## Nests

Many forest birds make tiny nests, designed to be inconspicuous to predators, such as those of the White-throated Fantail (p. 91) and Black-winged Flycatcher-shrike (p. 84). Nests may be incredibly well camouflaged: the nest of Gould's Frogmouth (p. 56), for example, is particularly hard to spot and the plumage of the incubating bird makes it harder still. Hanging the nest in an inaccessible position is typical of the Black-naped Monarch and Asian Paradise-Flycatcher (p. 93), and also of the Black-and-red Broadbill (p. 80), whose nest is hung over water and looks like a tangle of litter left behind by a flood.

In forest, the abundance of trees makes cavity nesting an obvious strategy. Barbets (pp. 72–74) and woodpeckers (pp. 75–77) make their own cavities in rotten or slightly rotting wood, whereas Blue-eared Kingfisher (p. 66) makes a burrow in a forested riverbank, and Collared Kingfisher (p. 65) may nest in a mangrove bank, roadside cutting or hollow tree cavity, and perhaps even in an arboreal termites' nest. Trogons (pp. 60–62) use natural cavities in rotten stumps in the forest, whereas hornbills (pp. 69–71) need to seek out cavities that are roomy, safe and high enough inside large living trees. It is sometimes possible to observe nests of large raptors, such as White-bellied Sea-eagle (p. 28), or Blyth's Hawk-eagle (p. 29) from a distance, and this gives plenty of scope for naturalists to study nest-building and incubation, care of the young, and the amount and type of food brought to the nest.

In spite of much birdwatching in the region, there are still dozens of species whose nests are known from only a handful of examples, and others whose nests have never been found. All observations of nests, including the date, position, construction materials and other details, should be recorded.

## TIDES, SEASHORES AND WADERS

Most of the 60 or so waders that occur in Southeast Asia are widespread, and are well known through much of Europe and Asia: Whimbrel (p. 37), Common Greenshank (p. 38) and Common Redshank (p. 39) are familiar examples. A few, such as Nordmann's Greenshank *Tringa guttifer* and Spoon-billed Sandpiper *Eurynorhynchus pygmeus* (not included here), are special and rare, with very restricted breeding grounds and small numbers occurring unpredictably at a few wintering sites in Peninsular Malaysia and Singapore.

The west coast of Peninsular Malaysia (around Matang, Pulau Kelang and Kuala Selangor), and some spots in western Sarawak (Bako-Buntal Bay and Pulau Bruit), have extensive mudflats that attract huge numbers of passage and winter migrants. Low tides occur once or twice a day, depending on locality, often leaving the mud exposed mainly at night and in the early morning. Ringing has shown the importance of a continuous chain of feeding sites at which migrants can refuel en route from the Siberian tundra and Korea southwards, including to Australasia. Coastal reclamation, bunds, industrial and residential development, and pollution are all potential pressures on most such sites.

Wader concentrations are less well known in Sabah, where the extensive mudflats of the east coast (Labuk, Darvel Bay and Tawau) are less accessible to birdwatchers. Investigation of these areas could reveal important bird sites, not only for waders but also for herons and egrets. Only one wader breeds locally, the Malaysian Plover *Charadrius peronii*, which is confined to sandy beaches and hence is being impacted by seafront development and tourism.

## SEABIRDS

There's no doubt that seabirds in Southeast Asia are severely underwatched. Not many birdwatchers go out to sea for long periods, and while scuba-diving is increasingly popular most divers are not birdwatchers. There are few seabird nesting islands in the region. Pulau Perak (between the Malay Peninsula and Sumatra) and Pulau Layang-Layang north of Sabah are the best known, but only Layang-Layang is easily accessible. There are other very important seabird nesting islands in the Spratly Group, at Tubbataha Reef in the Philippines and elsewhere, but these are also remote. Birdwatchers tend to see single birds or small flocks foraging far from their nesting and roosting sites, and notes about these sightings are worryingly scarce. The distribution and seasonality of seabirds in the region (mostly terns, but also gulls, skuas and jaegers, petrels and shearwaters) are all poorly understood. Sea and weather conditions, foraging habits and movements all require investigation. New records of many species are possible.

## OPPORTUNITIES FOR NATURALISTS

Local and foreign birdwatchers tend to visit a few well-known sites in the region. However, there is a lot of scope for visiting new places and expanding the bare list of localities from which many birds have been recorded. Upper and lower altitude limits have become a significant concern in detecting the impacts of climate change, but much caution needs to be exercised in recording altitudes (roadsigns can be highly misleading and maps unreliable). Due recognition also needs to be given to the point that the sport of finding the highest or lowest individual tends to emphasise the exceptional bird, not the population norm. Not too much should be read into single records.

The spread of recent invaders is sometimes poorly recorded, because these can be common birds of little interest to birdwatchers, such as the Javan Myna (p. 113) or Eurasian Tree-sparrow (p. 110). The Collared Kingfisher (p. 65) and Oriental Magpie-robin (p. 123) have both expanded their ranges inland from mangrove coastal habitat into woodland, agricultural estates and open country, and similar changes leading to spread through new habitats could be expected in other species.

Records from islands can give clues about colonisation ability, and if repeated they may show species turnover rates. Records from many mountains, still with poor coverage, may indicate distance from other known populations, faunal composition, and ability to survive in small habitat patches.

Group size, height in the vegetation at which a species occurs and normal foraging behaviour are not well described for many birds. How the different tailorbirds (pp. 149–150), flycatchers (pp. 118–122) or forest babblers (pp. 140–145) partition their habitat could be very interesting. Sometimes, species-specific habitat differences (such as between mangrove, riverine and inland habitats) seem clear, but in places the distinctions appear to break down; there could be many subtleties in avoidance of competition.

Migration dates, numbers and directions should be recorded. Very few observations have been published on migrant landfall on the Sarawak and Sabah coasts, where the arrival of waders, flycatchers, warblers and raptors should be of great interest.

In short, there is a lot for naturalists to do besides seeking out rarities or compiling checklists, and almost every day out should result in small facts that will add to the overall knowledge of the bird species found in this fascinating area.

## Where to Go

Rather than describing a few places, with their attendant birds and details of how to get there, a list of place-names is provided below that can be researched on websites or in previous site guides. For more detailed descriptions and lists, but rather outdated information, read Bransbury (1993); and for online site reports, visit www.travellingbirder. com or www.eurobirding.com.

*Peninsular Malaysia*
Matang; Taman Negara National Park; Krau Wildlife Reserve; Kuala Selangor Nature Park; Tanjung Karang coast and rice fields; Kuala Gula; Tasik Bera and Tasik Chini; Fraser's Hill; Cameron Highlands; Genting Highlands, Gunung Bunga Buah and Old Gombak Road; Pekan and Nenasi peat-swamp forest; Belum-Temengor forest; Panti forest.

*Singapore*
Sungei Buloh Wetland Reserve; Pulau Ubin; Bukit Timah Nature Reserve; Central Catchment Nature Reserve; Pulau Semakau; Changi Village and Changi coast; Kranji Reservoir and Neo Tiew.

*Sarawak*
Bako-Buntal Bay; Semengoh; Borneo Highlands Resort; Bako National Park; Gunung Mulu National Park; Bario and the Kelabit Highlands.

*Sabah*
Tunku Abdul Rahman Park; Long Pasia (Ulu Padas); Kampung Benoni; Likas Lagoon (Kota Kinabalu Wetlands Centre); Tempasuk Plain and lagoon; Kinabalu Park; Sukau and Kinabatangan River; Danum Valley; Tabin Wildlife Reserve; Semporna and its offshore islands; Pulau Layang-Layang; Sepilok forest.

## Where to Submit Records

Bird records are an important source of information in helping to understand more fully the avifauna of this region. For Malaysia, birdwatchers are encouraged to submit their sightings to the MNS-Bird Conservation Council electronically via the bird-i-witness database at www.worldbirds.org/malaysia or email mnsrc.rc@gmail.com. For Singapore, record submissions can be made to the Nature Society (Singapore) Bird Group website at http://wildbirdsingapore.nss.org.sg.

## WHERE TO PUBLISH INFORMATION

*Suara Enggang* is the bi-monthly birding magazine of the Malaysian Nature Society, which accepts short articles on sightings and birdwatching. The society also publishes the quarterly magazine *Malaysian Naturalist* and the scientific publication *Malayan Nature Journal*. The society has branches in most Malaysian states, including Sabah and Sarawak.

In Singapore, the Bird Group of the Nature Society (Singapore) solicits and reviews sightings, and the Bird Ecology Study Group has an online blog. The society publishes the quarterly *Nature Watch*.

The Oriental Bird Club, based in Sandy, Bedfordshire, publishes *Birding Asia* twice yearly, with summaries of records from many Asian countries, including Malaysia and Singapore; it also published the annual scientific journal *Forktail*.

For contact details of these organisations, see p. 172.

## BIRD TOPOGRAPHY

crown · iris · forehead · hind-crown · bill · upper mandible · lower mandible · nape · chin · wing coverts · throat · scapulars · back · breast · flanks · belly · secondaries · toes · primaries · vent · under-tail coverts · tail · tail streamers

The scientific and English names of birds included here, and the sequence of families and species, are based on the second edition (2008) of *A Field Guide to the Birds of South-East Asia*, by Craig Robson (New Holland, London). Malay names are given in parentheses. The photographs that follow should be assumed to be of adult male birds, where there is a difference between the sexes, in breeding plumage, unless otherwise labelled.

## Barred Buttonquail ▪ *Turnix suscitator* (Burung Puyuh Tanah) 16cm

DESCRIPTION Placed here for ease of comparison, but not related to quails and partridges. Stocky ground-bird whose breast and flanks are strongly marked with black lozenge-shaped bars, upperparts scaled and mottled, belly and under-tail coverts a rich cinnamon. Female

(shown here) has black throat and upper breast, absent in duller male. Strong bill and staring yellow eye.

DISTRIBUTION India through S China to Taiwan and Japan, southwards through Southeast Asia to the Philippines, Sulawesi and Lesser Sundas. Resident in Peninsular Malaysia and Singapore, but absent from Borneo, including Sabah and Sarawak.

HABITS AND HABITAT Increasingly scarce, but always hard to see even where present, in old agricultural land, thick grass and roadside scrub. Reversed sexual dimorphism, the dull male incubating eggs and tending chicks. Female's call is a series of soft booms, increasing in volume towards the end.

## Red-breasted Partridge
▪ *Arborophila hyperythra* (Kangkerang) 27cm

DESCRIPTION Chubby, secretive brown ground-bird whose flanks are strongly marked with white discs on a black surround; brow and face bright chestnut (with much grey on eyebrow in some populations), crown and eye-line dark brown. Grey bill, red legs and red skin around eye. Sexes are alike.

DISTRIBUTION Endemic to Borneo, in mountains at 650–3,050m (usually 900–2,200m). Resident from Mount Kinabalu in Sabah to Mount Mulu and the Kelabit Highlands in Sarawak, and southwards into Kalimantan.

HABITS AND HABITAT Often heard once the call is known, but seldom seen; appears to be thin on the ground, in montane forest where vegetation is undisturbed, and in dense old regrowth several years after shifting cultivation has ceased. Long, straight claws are used for raking in the leaf litter for food. Pairs duet, 1 bird giving a long series of single piping whistles *too, too, too*, while the other gives 2-note whistles, *kee-too, kee-too….*

# Red Junglefowl ■ *Gallus gallus*
(Ayam Hutan) 45–75cm

DESCRIPTION Unmistakably chicken-like, male with bright golden-brown neck hackles, black underparts and glossy greenish sickle-shaped tail; female oatmeal-brown or darker, with paler face and darker tail. Breeding males have bright red comb and face, and white earlobes, but in dull eclipse the neck hackles and tail sickles are shed.
DISTRIBUTION Resident from India to Nepal and S China, through most of Southeast Asia; natural E limit is Java, but now occurs through to the Philippines and Lesser Sundas owing to ancient human intervention. Wild or semi-wild birds are found through much of Peninsular Malaysia and Singapore, and feral birds are now spreading in Sabah.
HABITS AND HABITAT Typically, single males, or 1 male with a few females, or mated pairs, sometimes with young, forage among low vegetation beneath the trees. Old, poorly maintained rubber estates and oil-palm estates are the favoured habitat, with nests made at tree bases or among dense undergrowth. Male's crow is like that of a domestic cockerel but with a sharp cut-off.

# Crested Fireback ■ *Lophura ignita*
(Ayam Pegar) 65–70cm

DESCRIPTION Very attractive pheasant with diagnostic bushy crest, blue facial skin and pale feet. Adult males from Peninsula have iridescent blue-black plumage with white flank-streaks, maroon and orange rump, and black-and-white vaulted tail; males from Borneo have buff and black tail and chestnut-red belly. Females are mainly brown with white streaks on chest and scales on underparts.
DISTRIBUTION Resident in southernmost Myanmar, Malay Peninsula, Sumatra and Borneo, including both Sabah and Sarawak. Not in Singapore.
HABITS AND HABITAT Restricted to primary lowland forests, and just into montane forest to 1,200m in places. Like other pheasants, is quite gregarious and travels in small parties in search of fallen fruits, ants and termites. Voice is a range of whirrs and gurgles, and a loud cluck, but no powerful advertising call; males stand and whirr their wings briefly to produce a throbbing sound as advertisement.

ABOVE RIGHT: *Peninsular Malaysia.* RIGHT: *Borneo*

## Malaysian Peacock-pheasant ▪

*Polyplectron malacense* (Kuang Bongsu)
Male 50–55cm; female 40–45cm

DESCRIPTION A handsome medium-sized pheasant. Plumage in both sexes is generally dark cinnamon-brown, intricately spotted and vermiculated, the male with many iridescent green ocelli on the mantle, wings and tail. Bare facial skin bright orange in male, dull orange to grey in female. Adult males sport a short brush-like crest hanging forward over the bill.

DISTRIBUTION Resident in southernmost Myanmar through the Malay Peninsula; now possibly extinct in both Myanmar and Thailand. Not found in Singapore, or in Borneo where a different species occurs. Resident at low elevations up to 300m.

HABITS AND HABITAT Resident of lowland forests, often heard but rarely seen, usually alone or in pairs. Males can be very vocal during the breeding season with haunting two-note whistle, incessant harsh clucking, and angry chicken-like squawks. Males maintain short-term dancing grounds for their displays.

## Great Argus ▪ *Argusianus argus* (Kuang Raya) Male 160–200cm; female 70–75cm

DESCRIPTION Largest pheasant in the forest, with a bare blue head, red feet and generally brownish plumage in both sexes. Adult males have extraordinarily long central tail feathers and greatly expanded wing feathers with ocelli that are usually hidden from view. Females have shorter tail and wings, and no ocelli.

DISTRIBUTION Resident in S Myanmar, Malay Peninsula, Sumatra and Borneo, including Sabah and Sarawak. Not in Singapore, though conceivably once present.

HABITS AND HABITAT Encounters are confined to pairs or singles in lowland and hilly primary and old secondary forests. Males are territorial and construct dancing grounds that are kept free from leaves, sticks and stones. These grounds are each used by 1 male to stage spectacular displays to attract females. Highly vocal, giving an explosive, repeated *kuau* that echoes through the forests.

## Lesser Whistling-duck
▪ *Dendrocygna javanica* (Itik Belibis) 40cm

DESCRIPTION Lightly built duck with a slim neck, the plumage overall buffy brown with brighter chestnut on wing coverts and rump. In flight, wings are black beneath and black with chestnut coverts above. Similar to **Wandering Whistling-duck** *D. arcuata*, but lacks white on rump and long, pale flank plumes of that species.
DISTRIBUTION Resident in India, Indochina and S China, and throughout Southeast Asia to the Lesser Sundas. Formerly common, but now may be hunted, displaced by removal of habitat and disturbed by human activity.
HABITS AND HABITAT Usually found in small flocks, although there are old reports of much greater numbers. Within the flock, mated pairs stay together, sometimes performing display rushes across the water, each bird with 1 wing raised. Dives are brief. A tree nester, choosing sites in cavities or clefts between large boughs; ducklings jump to ground after hatching.

## Cotton Pygmy-goose ▪ *Nettapus coromandelianus* (Itik Kapas) 36cm

DESCRIPTION Small silky white duck, male with green-glossed black cap, breast-band and wings, and broad white wing bar visible in flight. Female is similar but with smoky-grey underparts, less glossy above, and lacking breast-band.
DISTRIBUTION India and Sri Lanka through S China to Taiwan, southwards through Southeast Asia and the Lesser Sundas to New Guinea and N Australia. Perhaps resident in parts of Peninsular Malaysia, Sabah and Sarawak, but seldom seen and apparently mobile over short or long distances; appears irregularly and patchily in Singapore.
HABITS AND HABITAT Freshwater ponds and marshes, old mining pools, rarely in brackish ponds; probably more characteristic of the seasonal tropics N and S of region, and not well adapted to ever-humid forested habitats. Large flocks can be seen occasionally in northernmost Peninsular Malaysia; gangs of males pursue females in display flights, giving high-pitched gaggling calls.

LEFT: *Male*. RIGHT: *Female*

# Little Grebe ■ *Tachybaptus ruficollis* (Burung Gerib Kecil) 27cm

LEFT: *Adult*. ABOVE: *Juvenile*

DESCRIPTION Small, dark waterbird with short bill and dark cap. Plumage generally brown with slight greyish tone, darker on upperparts. Neck and sides of head in breeding birds are bright reddish brown but turn buffy when non-breeding. A prominent light yellowish spot at base of gape and pale iris are useful identification features.
DISTRIBUTION Widely distributed throughout Africa, Europe, temperate Asia, India, China, and Southeast Asia to New Guinea. Resident and migrant in Peninsular Malaysia and Singapore; vagrant in Sabah but not yet recorded from Sarawak.
HABITS AND HABITAT Generally adaptable; can be found singly or in small groups in inland freshwater and man-made wetlands such as oxidation ponds and former tin-mining lakes/pools. Spends much time in water swimming, diving to feed or when alarmed. Can be quite aggressive during breeding season, chasing other individual males over the water's surface to protect its territory.

# Oriental Darter ■ *Anhinga melanogaster* (Burung Kosa) 85–95cm

DESCRIPTION Large, slim black bird with small head, snake-like neck and pointed yellowish bill. Plumage is generally black, with conspicuous pale streaks on wings, especially when sunning in the open. Head and neck are brown with a narrow white stripe running from gape down side of neck. Flies with neck outstretched.
DISTRIBUTION India and Southeast Asia to the Sundas. Scattered throughout lowland

Sabah and Sarawak; the Kinabatangan wetlands in Sabah are a major stronghold for the resident population. No longer found in Peninsular Malaysia, and no records from Singapore.
HABITS AND HABITAT Mainly restricted to remote inland freshwater swamps, lakes and rivers, and coastal forest. When swimming, its body is slightly submerged, leaving only head protruding. Often seen sunning for long periods on exposed branches with outstretched wings and tail to dry its waterlogged plumage. Roosts communally on bare trees near the riverbank.

## Storm's Stork ■ *Ciconia stormi*
(Burung Botak Hutan) 85cm

DESCRIPTION Medium-sized stork. Mainly
black on crown, upperparts and underparts,
but throat, hind-neck and tail (usually
visible only in flight) are white. Bill and
legs red. Very large, bright yellow eye-ring is
diagnostic.
DISTRIBUTION Malay Peninsula, Sumatra
and Borneo, including Sabah and Sarawak;
not in Singapore. Rare resident in lowlands,
reduced everywhere but with a stronghold in the Kinabatangan wetlands, Sabah, and
remnant populations in Taman Negara National Park, Panti Forest Reserve, Baram River
and a few other sites.
HABITS AND HABITAT Confined to streams, rivers and pools in dense lowland forests
and peat-swamp forests. Encounters are with solitary birds or small groups feeding at edge
of water or soaring on thermals. At times, can be seen perched on emergent forest trees or
exposed bare branches.

## Lesser Adjutant ■ *Leptoptilos*
*javanicus* (Burung Botak Babi) 110cm

DESCRIPTION Largest stork in Malaysia.
Slate-grey to black upperparts and wings, and
white underparts; head and neck are largely
bare with scattered tufts, showing yellowish
skin and pouch, this turning brighter orange
when breeding. Iris white; bill massive and
greyish white or ivory coloured, as are legs.
DISTRIBUTION India, S China and
Southeast Asia to the Greater Sundas.
Resident in small numbers in Peninsular
Malaysia, Sabah and Sarawak; increasingly
often as a vagrant in Singapore.
HABITS AND HABITAT Generally found in
coastal wetlands but can occur further inland
in rice fields or grassland. Often seen on
mudflats, slowly pacing in search of prey and
offal, in loose groups or solitary, or soaring
on thermals; in flight, is as large as a vulture
but with a heavy, straight bill and projecting
legs. Known to nest on tall, isolated or
emergent trees.

*Female*

# Yellow Bittern

▪ *Ixobrychus sinensis* (Burung Pucong Merah) 37cm

DESCRIPTION Plumage generally yellowish brown with lighter tones on wings. Throat and underparts white with brown streaks. Black crown and primaries (sometimes not visible when standing); in flight, distinctly 3-coloured cream, brown and black appearance. Iris orange-yellow. Bill yellow with some black on upper mandible. Immatures heavily streaked.

DISTRIBUTION India, China and Southeast Asia through to New Guinea. Resident in Peninsular Malaysia and Singapore, Sabah and Sarawak, the population boosted by migrants outside the breeding season.

HABITS AND HABITAT Solitary individuals usually seen hiding or stalking prey in midst of thick vegetation and reedbeds at edge of wetlands such as rivers and canals. Very cautious, will take flight easily if approached too close. If among reeds or tall grasses, will freeze and point bill upwards to blend in when alarmed.

# Cinnamon Bittern ▪ *Ixobrychus cinnamomeus* (Burung Pucong Bendang) 37cm

DESCRIPTION Like Yellow Bittern (above) but overall adult plumage mainly rich cinnamon on head, nape, upperparts and flanks, with a lighter tone on throat and

underparts. Bill yellow with some black on upper mandible. Iris and feet yellow. Immatures more mottled and streaked.

DISTRIBUTION India to China and through Southeast Asia to the Greater Sundas, Philippines and Sulawesi. Resident in Peninsular Malaysia and Singapore, Sabah and Sarawak, boosted by migratory individuals outside the breeding season.

HABITS AND HABITAT Individuals generally seen at inland wetlands such as rice fields and former tin-mining pools. Like the Yellow Bittern, is very shy and secretive, and will always seek to hide in vegetation cover.

# Black Bittern ■ *Dupetor flavicollis* (Burung Pucong Hitam) 58cm

DESCRIPTION Dark bronzy black, browner in female (shown here), with dark bill and legs; rich buff on neck and upper breast, heavily streaked. In flight, very dark with slow, steady wingbeats, and almost as big as a night-heron.

DISTRIBUTION India and Sri Lanka through S China to Taiwan, southwards through Southeast Asia to New Guinea, Australia and the Solomon Islands; apparently a non-breeding migrant in Peninsular Malaysia, Singapore, Sabah and Sarawak.

HABITS AND HABITAT Mainly nocturnal, with peak activity at dawn and dusk, and seldom seen by day. Perches among tall, thick reeds and grasses at edges of ponds and rivers, where it can occasionally be spotted in torchlight from a boat. Migrants can occur in any habitat, from lowland forest to towns, but do not linger. Little information exists on behaviour and diet, because the birds are so difficult to observe.

# Black-crowned Night-heron ■ *Nycticorax nycticorax*
(Burung Pucong Kuak) 60cm

DESCRIPTION Handsome, small but stocky heron. Mainly ashy-grey plumage with black short bill, cap and mantle in adult, and creamy-white underside. 2 white head plumes are sometimes visible. Iris red and legs yellow, brighter when breeding. Immatures mainly scruffy-looking, streaked and mottled brown, similar to immature Little Heron (p. 20) but with pale spots rather than streaks.

DISTRIBUTION Widespread in both New and Old worlds except Australia. Resident in Peninsular Malaysia and Singapore, Sabah and Sarawak, but localised and patchy.

HABITS AND HABITAT The only nocturnal heron through most of the region, feeding mainly at night in shallow water. Forms large, noisy roosts and breeding colonies at man-made or natural wetlands, mostly in coastal mangroves; numbers fluctuate and colonies are displaced by habitat loss and direct persecution.

## Little Heron ■ *Butorides striata*
(Burung Pucong Keladi) 45cm

DESCRIPTION Commonest small heron in region. Slaty grey with a dark crown, pale face markings and pale fringes to wing feathers. Juveniles are brownish, spotted above and heavily streaked below. Bill dark, and legs varying from greenish to yellow or bright orange depending on age and breeding status. There is much plumage variation between individuals depending on sex and geographical origins.
DISTRIBUTION Through much of the tropics and subtropics in South America, Africa and Australasia, and in Asia extending as far N as Japan and Ussuriland. Common throughout Southeast Asia as a resident and migrant.
HABITS AND HABITAT Generally seen singly, quite often in flight but usually stalking or standing on mud at the edge of rivers, mangroves or the sea, or even along small forest streams. Small fish, crabs and other invertebrates are the main foods.

## Chinese Pond-heron ■ *Ardeola bacchus*
(Burung Pucong Cina) 45–52cm

DESCRIPTION Non-breeding birds have light brown upperparts and wing coverts; brown streaks from head to chest, and white underparts and wings; bill blackish with some yellow on lower mandible; legs yellow. When breeding, head, throat, nape and breast turn a rich chestnut; mantle black; underparts remain white; feet orange.
DISTRIBUTION Resident from India to China and Southeast Asia. Common non-breeding visitor to Peninsular Malaysia and Singapore, less common in Sabah and Sarawak.
HABITS AND HABITAT Non-breeding birds are encountered in small numbers in a variety of wetlands, from coastal mangroves to former tin-mining pools, often solitary or in loose associations. Prior to spring migration, some individuals will assume full or partial breeding plumage. At times, birds form large communal roosts, as recorded in the Teluk Air Tawar–Kuala Muda rice scheme area on mainland Penang.

ABOVE LEFT: *Adult breeding.* LEFT: *Non-breeding*

# Eastern Cattle Egret ■ *Bubulcus coromandus* (Bangau Kendi) 50–55cm

DESCRIPTION Small, stocky egret with a comparatively short neck and bill, and bunchy feathers beneath chin. Non-breeding birds have a yellow bill and black legs, but bill and legs turn red when breeding and cinnamon-orange patches develop on plumage of head, neck, chest and back.

DISTRIBUTION Nearly global distribution, having aggressively expanded range over past decades. Mostly a migrant to Peninsular Malaysia, Singapore, Sabah and Sarawak, but breeding recorded at 1 site in Peninsular Malaysia; feral birds occur year-round in Singapore. Wild migrants begin to assume breeding plumage in Feb, before departure, but feral birds do so from Dec onwards.

HABITS AND HABITAT Unlike other white egrets, prefers grasslands and pastures as well as nearby wetlands such as rice fields and former tin-mining pools. Seeks the company of cows or Water Buffalo, feeding off insects disturbed by their grazing movements.

# Intermediate Egret
■ *Mesophoyx intermedia* (Bangau Kerbau) 65–72cm

DESCRIPTION Like Great Egret (p. 22) when not breeding, and hard to distinguish except by direct comparison, but smaller in size and has a smooth, S-shaped neck without kink. During breeding, long head and breast plumes form; bill black and lores yellow.

DISTRIBUTION Africa, S and E Asia down to Southeast Asia and Australia. Non-breeding migrant in Peninsular Malaysia and Singapore, Sabah and Sarawak.

HABITS AND HABITAT Shares similar wetland habitats and habits with Great Egret, including both freshwater and coastal areas, mangroves, mudflats and paddy fields. Found in loose flocks or singly, and will congregate with other white egrets to feed or breed.

# Little Egret ■ *Egretta garzetta* (Bangau Kecil) 55–65cm

DESCRIPTION Slim, graceful, very active egret, slightly larger but markedly thinner-necked than stocky Eastern Cattle Egret (p. 21). Non-breeding birds sport slender black bill, legs and

feet, and yellowish lores. Breeding birds develop head, back and breast plumes. At all seasons, look for contrast between dark legs and yellow toes.
DISTRIBUTION Africa, Europe, Asia and Australia. Mainly passage migrants and winter visitors to Malaysia and Singapore, but scattered records of breeding in Peninsular Malaysia and Sabah.
HABITS AND HABITAT Mixes with other white egrets, mainly Great Egret and Intermediate (p. 21), in both natural and man-made wetlands. Habits are similar to those of other white egrets, but more actively chases food items, and stirs shallow water with 1 foot to disturb prey into movement.

# Great Egret ■ *Ardea alba* (Bangau Besar) 85–100cm

DESCRIPTION Largest of all white egrets in region, with an unmistakable angular kink in neck. Non-breeding adults (as shown) show bright yellow bill and lores, and black legs. When breeding, lores turn blue, bill black and long head plumes emerge; leg colour remains unchanged, or may develop red 'knees'.
DISTRIBUTION Global distribution. Mostly migrants in Peninsular Malaysia, Singapore, Sabah and Sarawak, but small breeding populations in Sabah and Peninsular Malaysia.
HABITS AND HABITAT Found in a wide variety of natural and man-made wetlands. Seen singly or in same-species flocks, or in the company of Little and/or Intermediate Egrets (p. 21). Mostly a stand-and-wait hunter, but follows behind tractors with other white egrets in rice fields to take advantage of ploughed-up invertebrates and frogs, and can 'helicopter' to pick prey from surface of sea. A graceful flyer with slow wingbeats and neck held in 'S' position.

## Grey Heron ■ *Ardea cinerea*
(Burung Pucong Seriap) 90–98cm

DESCRIPTION One of the large herons in region. Plumage is generally grey, white on head, neck and underparts, and darker on mantle and wings. Broad black eye-stripe, primaries and head plume (may not be visible at times). White central stripe down front of neck is bordered by irregular black streaks; black patch on sides of body near bend of wing. Bill and legs yellow, brighter when breeding.
DISTRIBUTION Widely distributed across Africa, Europe, continental Asia and the Sundas. Common in Southeast Asia as a resident and migrant. Both resident and migrant in Peninsular Malaysia and Singapore, but so far recorded only as a migrant in Sabah and Sarawak.
HABITS AND HABITAT Found along coastal and inland wetlands, usually stalking fish in shallow waters. Makes deep, guttural calls when alarmed. Forms large nesting colonies in trees, building untidy stick nests.

## Purple Heron ■ *Ardea purpurea*
(Burung Pucong Serandau) 80–90cm

DESCRIPTION Almost same size as Grey Heron (above) but slimmer. Plumage ashy grey at base of neck, upper body and wings. Head and neck rufous with a black stripe from base of gape down to belly. Cap black. Bill yellow with some black on upper mandible; feet light yellow. In flight, separated from Grey Heron by dark plumage, chestnut underwings and skinny appearance.
DISTRIBUTION Africa, Europe and Asia to the Sundas. Resident and migrant in Peninsular Malaysia and Singapore; so far, known only as a resident in Sabah and Sarawak.
HABITS AND HABITAT Associated with brackish and freshwater wetlands. Mainly solitary, often hunting quietly for fish in the shallow waters by stalking and stabbing. Like the Grey Heron, forms large breeding colonies, sometimes with other herons such as Black-crowned Night-herons (p. 19), but often nests in thick vegetation on the ground.

## White-fronted Falconet
■ *Microhierax latifrons* (Rajawali Dahi Putih) 16cm

DESCRIPTION One of the world's smallest raptors, mainly black above and white below, the white continuing in a broad patch across cheek and on forehead. Female has rufous forehead.

DISTRIBUTION Endemic to Borneo, and there found only in Sabah. Elsewhere in Southeast Asia, Singapore and the rest of Borneo, is replaced by the similar **Black-thighed Falconet** M. *fringillarius*, which has a narrow white line behind eye curling around a black cheek patch; narrow white forehead, throat, breast and marks on tail; rufous belly and vent; juveniles have rufous tinge to pale band from cheek to brow.

HABITS AND HABITAT Sociable, forming loose family associations in the canopy of lowland rainforest, where individuals sit separately on bare, exposed perches, visible to each other up to several hundred metres apart, sometimes exchanging perches and sharing prey. Feeds on large insects (katydids, locusts, cicadas) and small birds.

## Peregrine Falcon ■ *Falco peregrinus*
(Burung Falko Peregrin) 40–48cm

DESCRIPTION Large, dark falcon. Resident race *F. p. ernesti* is shown here, in which the black hood is distinctive; upperparts and tail dark grey; throat and underparts cream with dark streaks and heavy barring. Juveniles of resident race rich rufous below, but told from Oriental Hobby *F. severus* by large size, and by barring rather than streaks below. Migrants are paler, and hood is broken by pale cheeks separating dark moustache from rear of head and neck. Narrow orbital ring and legs yellow; bill yellow at base and dark towards tip.

DISTRIBUTION Global distribution. Resident mainly near limestone cliffs in Peninsular Malaysia, Singapore, Sabah and Sarawak; migrants more widespread throughout region.

HABITS AND HABITAT Peregrines are usually solitary or in pairs, seen at limestone outcrops in forest, and in open country where residents are much outnumbered by migrants. Both residents and migrants have been recorded using city buildings in lieu of natural cliffs. They use high vantage points to look out for prey – mainly smaller birds such as pigeons and waders, sometimes bats – and hunt by diving and knocking them over in flight.

## Osprey ▪ *Pandion haliaetus* (Lang Tiram) 54cm

DESCRIPTION Medium-sized raptor with brown upperparts and tail. Head white with prominent brown/black eye-stripe. Short crest, but not always visible. Underparts and legs white with brown patches on chest. Iris yellow.

DISTRIBUTION Globally distributed, breeding in temperate and subtropical regions, and wintering in tropical areas. Non-breeding visitor at low elevations in Peninsular Malaysia, Singapore, Sabah and Sarawak.

HABITS AND HABITAT Seen along sea coasts, and on inland natural and man-made wetlands such as former tin-mining areas and dams, usually in flight. Feeds primarily on fishes, which it catches by diving spectacularly into water from the air before emerging and taking off from surface with prey in talons. Recorded in all months, and migrants may arrive from both N and S hemispheres.

## Black Baza ▪ *Aviceda leuphotes* (Lang Baza Hitam) 32cm

DESCRIPTION Beautiful black and white raptor, typically seen in flight with rounded, butterfly-like wings. Black, with large white wing-patches; white below with broad black breast-band, and belly often strongly and widely barred blackish chestnut and white.

DISTRIBUTION From India, the Himalayas and Nepal through S China to Hainan and continental Southeast Asia as far as 14°N. Migrant to Southeast Asia at least to Sumatra and Java, including Peninsular Malaysia and Singapore; not recorded from Sabah or Sarawak.

HABITS AND HABITAT Small parties soar on broad, rounded wings, showing typical pied appearance. They occur over wooded habitats of all kinds in lowland plains, including rubber and oil-palm plantations, secondary woodland and forest, flying down to take insects from foliage and also resting in canopy. In the S part of Peninsular Malaysia migrants arrive in last week of Oct, and heaviest northward passage is in late Mar.

# Oriental Honey-buzzard ■ *Pernis ptilorhyncus* (Lang Lebah) 55–65cm

DESCRIPTION Medium-large raptor with variable individual plumages. In flight, shows a longish, proportionately small, chicken-like head, a long, square-cut tail with 2–3 dark bands, and long wings with numerous dark bands on undersurface. Upperparts brown to chocolate or blackish; underparts from cinnamon to white, with highly variable amount of streaks and barring.

DISTRIBUTION Temperate NE Asia, from Siberia to Japan and N China, and from India, S China and Southeast Asia to the Greater Sundas. Passage migrant and winter visitor to Peninsular Malaysia, Singapore, Sabah and Sarawak (*P. p. orientalis*); also resident in Peninsular Malaysia, Sabah and Sarawak (*P. p. torquatus*), with a few dispersants of this race reaching Singapore.

*Resident* orientalis *(left); migrant* torquatus *(right)*

HABITS AND HABITAT Seen in large numbers at key migration points such as Tanjung Tuan (Port Dickson) and Taiping. Prefers forests (the resident race) as well as plantations and other wooded areas, and feeds on honey-bee and wasp larvae by raiding their nests. However, also said to take small vertebrate prey and chickens in villages opportunistically.

# Bat Hawk ■ *Macheiramphus alcinus* (Lang Malam) 45cm

DESCRIPTION Mainly black, with small crest, light yellow eye, and variable amount of white on throat and upper breast, this marred by some black streaks. Notable for rapid flight, with powerful, deliberate strokes of its long, narrow-tipped wings.
DISTRIBUTION Tropical Africa and Madagascar; and Malay Peninsula to Sumatra, Borneo, Sulawesi and New Guinea. Resident in Peninsular Malaysia, Sabah and Sarawak; scarce non-breeding dispersant to Singapore.
HABITS AND HABITAT Typically seen in the late afternoon and evening, in forest especially near limestone cliffs with caves, where bats emerge and are hunted; also over secondary woodland and open country. Bat Hawks can overhaul most bats in direct flight, or grab one from the edge of a flock, using the foot to catch the bat and then swallowing it in flight. Its big stick nests have been found a number of times, pairs using the same nest site repeatedly.

## Black-shouldered Kite ■ *Elanus caeruleus* (Lang Tikus) 32cm

DESCRIPTION Elegant, fairly small raptor with light grey crown, darker grey upperparts and black primaries. Face and underparts white to cream or pearly grey. Bill black, iris red, eyebrows black and legs yellow.

DISTRIBUTION Africa, S Eurasia, India and S China through Southeast Asia to New Guinea. Resident at low elevations in Peninsular Malaysia, Singapore, Sabah and Sarawak.
HABITS AND HABITAT A raptor of open country and agricultural areas, such as rice fields, oil-palm plantations and grassland. Often seen hovering in search of rodents during daytime, but also uses utility poles as a hunting perch.

## Brahminy Kite ■ *Haliastur indus* (Lang Merah) 45cm

DESCRIPTION Medium-sized raptor. Adults sport a dark-streaked white head, nape and chest, and a chestnut-brown body; legs yellow; bill light yellow. Immatures are mostly brown with streaked breast.

DISTRIBUTION India, S China and throughout Southeast Asia to Australia. Common resident at low elevations in Malaysia and Singapore.
HABITS AND HABITAT One of the common raptors along coastal areas, but can also be found further inland, above rice fields, former tin-mining wetlands and cities/towns with urban wetlands. Usually seen soaring most of the time over its preferred habitats looking for live prey or scavenging. Encounters range from solitary birds to large groups.

## White-bellied Sea-eagle ◾
*Haliaeetus leucogaster* (Lang Siput) 70cm

DESCRIPTION Large raptor with white head, underparts and tail; upperparts and wings black; bill grey, iris brown/black, legs light yellow. Tail wedged, visible in flight. Immatures in various stages of mottled brown.
DISTRIBUTION India and Southeast Asia to Australia. Resident in Malaysia and Singapore.
HABITS AND HABITAT Common raptor frequenting coastal wetlands and even large inland wetlands such as former tin-mining areas and dams. Feeds mainly on fish. Hunts by soaring and circling over water bodies before swooping down swiftly to catch fishes near the water surface. Builds a large nest on tall canopy trees or man-made structures, e.g. telecommunication towers. Pairs are very vocal.

## Crested Serpent-eagle
◾ *Spilornis cheela* (Lang Kuik) 54cm

DESCRIPTION Medium-sized, generally brownish raptor. Upperparts greyish brown; underparts lighter brown with small white spots on breast, belly and top of shoulder. Head darker brown (almost black in some individuals). Cere, iris and feet yellow. Bill grey. Short crest (not always visible when perched). Immatures mottled brown.
DISTRIBUTION India, S China and Southeast Asia to Greater Sundas. Resident in Malaysia and Singapore.
HABITS AND HABITAT Usually solitary, often heard or seen in various habitat types, e.g. mangroves, forests, residential areas (with nearby forested areas) and oil-palm plantations. At times, seen perched on vantage points. Diet consists mainly of snakes.

# Grey-faced Buzzard

■ *Butastur indicus*
(Lang Belalang) 45cm

DESCRIPTION Fairly small raptor when perched, with distinctive face pattern, black streak down centre of throat and dark bars on tail; chocolate breast with bars on flanks and belly; staring yellow eye. In flight, shows a chequered cinnamon panel on inner primaries and secondaries, and wings appear fairly long and narrow when soaring.
DISTRIBUTION Cool temperate NE Asia, from Amurland to Japan and N China, migrating S to Java, Bali and the Lesser Sundas. Migrant in Peninsular Malaysia, Singapore and, more often, Sabah and Sarawak.
HABITS AND HABITAT Most often seen on migration, predominantly in Oct and Mar, in open country with scattered trees and in agricultural land. Feeds on lizards, insects and, perhaps, rats.

# Blyth's Hawk-eagle ■ *Nisaetus alboniger* (Lang Hantu) 52–58cm

DESCRIPTION Medium-sized raptor with black upperparts and prominent crest visible when perched; underparts white, marked with black vertical streaks on chest and horizontal barring on belly; tail black with broad white band; feet yellow. Sub-adult light sandy buff on head and breast, darker brown on back and wings, with 3 or 4 dark bars across tail.

DISTRIBUTION From *c.* 10°N through the Malay Peninsula, Sumatra and Borneo. Resident in hills up to 1,900m in Peninsular Malaysia, Sabah and Sarawak; recorded from Singapore.
HABITS AND HABITAT Usually seen soaring over the forest canopy, in lowlands and montane forest, or waiting on a high branch in search of prey, which includes lizards, bats and other small mammals. Builds large nest in a tall tree, at the point where several main boughs diverge to form tree crown and where flight access is easy.

# Changeable Hawk-eagle

■ *Nisaetus limnaeetus* (Lang Hindik) 60–75cm

DESCRIPTION Medium-sized raptor with 2 morphs. Dark-morph individuals are blackish brown in plumage with yellow feet; dark terminal band on tail visible in flight. Pale-morph birds are generally dark brown on upperparts with whitish underparts and head, marked with streaks on chest and belly; in flight, shows 4 or 5 dark bands across tail (up to 7 in juveniles). At times, small crest is visible in both when perched.
DISTRIBUTION India, through Southeast Asia to the Sundas. Resident at low elevations in Peninsular Malaysia, Singapore, Sabah and Sarawak.
HABITS AND HABITAT Pale morph is more commonly encountered than dark morph. A raptor of wooded country and forest (ranging from disturbed to primary forest), or of forest patches in a matrix of agriculture and settlements. Usually seen soaring over canopy, or heard calling a 2- or 3-note *whe Wheet!*

# Wallace's Hawk-eagle

■ *Nisaetus nanus* (Lang Hantu Kasturi) 45cm

DESCRIPTION Like a sub-adult Blyth's Hawk-eagle (p. 29), but slightly smaller, with more uniform dark upperparts and 3 (not 2) dark bands across tail. Adult Blyth's is more black and white in appearance, whereas Wallace's has brown and rufous plumage.
DISTRIBUTION From *c.* 12°N in Thailand through Malay Peninsula, Sumatra and Borneo; resident in Peninsular Malaysia, Sabah and Sarawak, but not recorded from Singapore.
HABITS AND HABITAT Tall forest in level lowlands, including forest edges alongside rivers and disturbed areas, where birds perch in the lower part of the tree crown and keep a lookout for prey. Known food includes lizards, but there are few records. Builds a nest of sticks in a main fork of a tall canopy or emergent tree, and produces a single chick.

# Slaty-breasted Rail

■ *Gallirallus striatus*
(Burung Sintar Biasa) 25cm

DESCRIPTION Slaty-grey face, throat, chest and underparts; chestnut crown; light brown upperparts and wings; white barring on belly and upperparts; feet greyish; bill red.

DISTRIBUTION India, S China and through Southeast Asia to the Sundas and the Philippines. Resident at low elevations in Peninsular Malaysia, Sabah, Sarawak aand Singapore.

HABITS AND HABITAT Found in inland freshwater swamps, flooded rice fields, reedbeds and grasslands. Generally shy and keeps to thick vegetation, affording brief glimpses of itself as it appears at edges or small openings; remains solitary except when accompanied by chicks.

# White-breasted Waterhen ■ *Amaurornis phoenicurus*

(Burung Ruak-ruak) 33cm

DESCRIPTION White face and breast, merging to rufous beneath tail, and dark back and wings make species unmistakable. Sexes are alike.

DISTRIBUTION India, S China and Southeast Asia. Resident throughout Malaysia and Singapore, the populations there being augmented by migrants and winter visitors from the temperate zone.

HABITS AND HABITAT Commonly seen in rank vegetation, overgrown drains and along roadsides in rural areas, sometimes flying up when disturbed.

Adults may be accompanied by several half-grown fluffy black chicks, the pale breast plumage gradually appearing as they grow. Monotonous single piping note endlessly repeated, or a chorus of grating and gurgling notes in which both the male and female participate, competing with neighbouring pairs.

*Female*

# Watercock ▪ *Gallicrex cinerea* (Burung Ayam-ayam) 42cm

DESCRIPTION A bulky rail; the female and non-breeding male predominantly mottled brown, buff and black, with light yellow legs and bill. Breeding males are more attractive, with prominent red frontal shield adjoining bill; black head, neck and chest; red legs.
DISTRIBUTION India, China, Southeast Asia and the Philippines. Predominantly non-breeding winter visitor and passage migrant in Peninsular Malaysia and Singapore, Sabah and Sarawak, with scarce breeding records.
HABITS AND HABITAT Prefers natural and man-made freshwater wetlands. Usually solitary and moves about under thick vegetation, affording observers brief glimpses at small clearings. Possesses nocturnal habits.

# Grey-headed Swamphen
▪ *Porphyrio poliocephalus* (Burung Pangling) 42cm

DESCRIPTION Big, gaudy rail with deep purplish-blue plumage; red bill, forehead and legs; white below tail. In poor light it can look merely blackish at a distance. Sexes are alike, juveniles darker and duller.
DISTRIBUTION Resident across much of Africa, the Mediterranean and Middle East, through S Asia to Australasia and Oceania, including Peninsular Malaysia, Singapore and Borneo; has recently spread and become commoner in Sabah and Sarawak.
HABITS AND HABITAT Occasionally seen in 1s or 2s in swampy habitat, where it feeds on succulent water plants, holding material in 1 foot and slicing it with the scissor-like bill. Nest is a bowl of piled-up weeds in dense vegetation in the marsh. A variety of loud braying, chuckling and clattering notes may be heard in the morning and evening, but birds are secretive, falling silent and retreating into vegetation when approached.

## Common Moorhen
■ *Gallinula chloropus* (Tiong Air)
32cm

DESCRIPTION Dusky-black
waterbird with a narrow
white band along flanks and
white beneath cocked-up tail.
Prominent red frontal shield and
bill with yellow tip.
DISTRIBUTION Almost
worldwide distribution in
temperate and tropical zones,
except Australia and New
Zealand. Resident in Peninsular
Malaysia and Singapore, Sabah
and Sarawak, the population
having expanded during the past
3 decades; also supplemented
everywhere by migrants from *c.* Oct–Mar.
HABITS AND HABITAT Favours former tin-mining wetlands, flooded rice fields and
canals. Often seen in small, loose groups, family parties or individually. Spends much time
around water, feeding on surface vegetation and insects.

## Masked Finfoot
■ *Heliopais personata* (Burung
Pedendang) 54cm

DESCRIPTION Both sexes
are generally olive-brown but
slightly darker on upperparts;
iris yellow; bill large and yellow;
feet greenish yellow and webbed.
Adult male has a black throat
and face with a white line from
back of eye. Female has a white
throat.

*Female*

DISTRIBUTION India, Bangladesh and Southeast Asia. Non-breeding winter visitor at
low elevations in Peninsular Malaysia. Vagrant in Singapore and Sabah, and recently also
recorded in Sarawak in a protected area.
HABITS AND HABITAT Encounters are limited to individuals in the species' preferred
habitats of forested waterways, former tin-mining wetlands and coastal mangroves. Very
shy and secretive. Swims with head bobbing and usually keeps close to water's edge and
vegetation.

## Pacific Golden Plover ▪ *Pluvialis fulva*
(Burung Rapang Keriyut) 25cm

DESCRIPTION Non-breeding plumage is brown, spangled with gold above and with paler buffy face, neck and underparts. After arrival and before departure, many are in part breeding plumage (as shown), with brighter upperparts and patchy black face and underparts separated by a white line from brow to neck and flanks.
DISTRIBUTION Resident in NE Siberia and W Alaska, migrating to E Africa, and S and Southeast Asia as far as New Guinea, Australia and New Zealand. Migrant throughout coastal lowlands of Peninsular Malaysia, Sabah, Sarawak and Singapore.
HABITS AND HABITAT Loose flocks settle on open mud or short grass, standing motionless and well camouflaged, or foraging for small bivalves, snails and worms. Takes off with a piping *kieu-wik*, especially vocal at night.

## Black-winged Stilt ▪ *Himantopus himantopus* (Burung Stilt) 38cm

DESCRIPTION Slim and elegant, with long pink legs and a slender bill. Head, neck and underparts are white with variable dusky markings on crown, face and neck; wings

are black in adults, dusky in juveniles. Migrants from Australasia, sometimes separated as White-headed Stilt *H. leucocephalus*, have a whiter face and crown, and a black patch on hind-neck.
DISTRIBUTION Resident through most of the temperate Old and New worlds, migrating to the tropics; migrant to coastal lowlands and fresh waters of Peninsular Malaysia (where there are increasing numbers of nestings), Singapore, Sabah and Sarawak.
HABITS AND HABITAT Small flocks occur in wet rice fields, open marshes and, occasionally, near the sea. The few nests found have been on muddy banks of lakes or on wet vegetation.

*Adult (left) and juveniles (right)*

# Little Ringed Plover ■ *Charadrius dubius*
(Burung Rapang Biji Nangka) 17cm

DESCRIPTION Small plover with a pale forehead, throat and collar, a complete dark breast-band and white underparts. Small bill is all dark, ring of skin around eye is pale, and legs are pale olive to pink. Coming into breeding plumage, contrasts are heightened, black face mask is distinct, and eye-ring is a clear yellow.
DISTRIBUTION Resident through sub-Arctic and temperate Eurasia to the Middle East, Sri Lanka, the Philippines and New Guinea; migrates S to N Africa, China, Southeast Asia and Australia. Migrant in Peninsular Malaysia, Singapore, Sarawak and Sabah.
HABITS AND HABITAT Primarily in freshwater habitats near temporary pools, on short grass and open ground, mud, ploughed farmland and rice fields; occasionally on intertidal mud. Birds often wander separately over the feeding habitat, flying up to form a flock when disturbed.

*Winter*

# Lesser Sand-plover ■ *Charadrius mongolus* (Burung Rapang Mongolia) 20cm

DESCRIPTION Moderate-sized plover. Non-breeding plumage is grey-brown and white; forehead, brow, throat and narrow collar white, separated from white underparts by an incomplete grey-brown breast-band. Legs and bill dark. Similar **Greater Sand-plover** *C. leschenaultii* is larger, with a heavier bill, more complete breast-band and paler legs. Many birds show fragmentary breeding plumage with a chestnut breast-band.
DISTRIBUTION Resident in sub-Arctic Russia and Siberia S to China; migrates S to coasts of Indian Ocean, Southeast Asia and Australasia, including all of Malaysia and Singapore, where it is a passage migrant and non-breeding visitor.
HABITS AND HABITAT An abundant migrant in small flocks, foraging on intertidal mudflats, where it seeks worms and small bivalves in the soft mud.

*Winter*

# Greater Painted-snipe ■ *Rostratula benghalensis* (Burung Meragi) 24cm

DESCRIPTION Female deep chestnut on head, neck and breast, this sharply set off from white around eye and on underparts; buff central crown-stripe, and brown back and wings beautifully mottled and spotted. Male is duller, with grey-brown on breast and buff around eye. Legs greenish and slightly downcurved bill orange in both sexes.
DISTRIBUTION Africa, Madagascar and Indian sub-continent through S China to Japan, and Southeast Asia through the Lesser Sundas to Australia. Resident in Peninsular Malaysia, Singapore, Sabah and Sarawak.

HABITS AND HABITAT This species has reversed sexual dimorphism, the duller male incubating the eggs and tending the chicks. Greater Painted-snipe are very secretive and hard to see, creeping among dense foliage such as water hyacinths and reeds in swamps and rice fields. They tend to be more active at dusk, and may be commoner than they seem.

*Male (left) and female (right)*

# Black-tailed Godwit ■ *Limosa limosa* (Burung Kedidi Ekor Hitam) 40cm

DESCRIPTION Tall wader, here with 3 Common Redshank. Non-breeding plumage is plain grey above and off-white below; blackish legs and black tip to pink bill. In flight, shows a white band across rump and base of tail, and white wing bar. In breeding plumage, is largely rufous on head, upperparts and breast, with a barred black and whitish belly and flanks.
DISTRIBUTION Sub-Arctic and temperate Eurasia from Iceland to Siberia, migrating S to N Africa and SW, S and Southeast Asia as far as New Guinea and Australasia. Non-breeding migrant in coastal lowlands throughout Malaysia and Singapore.
HABITS AND HABITAT Found on intertidal mudflats and around pools in open mangroves, roosting in the lower branches of mangrove trees at high tide; small to very large flocks forage for bivalves and worms in the mud.

# Whimbrel ■ *Numenius phaeopus*
(Burung Kedidi Pisau Raut) 44cm

DESCRIPTION Large wader, mottled, spotted and barred with brown and buff; best recognised by dark lateral stripes on crown with central pale line, and long, curved bill. Most show white rump in flight, but some are from dark-rumped population. The scarcer Eurasian Curlew *N. arquata* is also white-rumped but bigger, and has no bold crown-stripes and a much longer bill.
DISTRIBUTION Resident in Arctic and sub-Arctic Eurasia and parts of North America; migrant to South America, Africa, and S and Southeast Asia as far as Australasia, including Peninsular Malaysia, Sabah, Sarawak and Singapore.
HABITS AND HABITAT Typically on coastal mudflats fronting mangroves, sometimes in big flocks, probing mud or wet sand for worms. Call is a clear musical trill, often uttered when taking flight.

# Terek Sandpiper ■ *Xenus cinereus* (Burung Kedidi Sereng) 25cm

DESCRIPTION Small wader with pale grey-brown upperparts, slightly darker carpal-patch on wing, and pale brow. Orange-yellow legs and orange base to upturned bill. In flight, rump and tail are same colour as back, but secondaries show a white trailing edge to wing.

DISTRIBUTION Resident in Arctic and cool temperate Eurasia, from Scandinavia to the Amur; migrates to South Africa and the borders of the Indian Ocean as far as S and Southeast Asia, Australia and New Zealand. Migrant in moderate numbers to Peninsular Malaysia, Singapore, Sabah and Sarawak.
HABITS AND HABITAT On sandy beaches and mudflats, foraging for invertebrates in soft intertidal mud. Call is a ringing *kleet-kleet* when flushed, with emphasis on the 1st note.

## Common Sandpiper ▪ *Actitis hypoleucos* (Burung Kedidi Biasa) 20cm

DESCRIPTION Small wader with pale grey-brown upperparts; white below, with distinctive brown patch on each side of upper breast; pale brow and eye-ring. Dark bill and olive legs. In flight, shows a white wing bar and white sides to narrow brown rump.

DISTRIBUTION Resident across N Eurasia from W Europe to Japan and S to Iran, the Himalayas and China; migrates S to Africa, and S and Southeast Asia as far as the Philippines and Australia, rarely to W Pacific islands and New Zealand. Migrant in Peninsular Malaysia, Singapore, Sabah and Sarawak, but with sightings in all months. HABITS AND HABITAT Abundant but thinly distributed in many habitats, including coasts, wet rice fields, rivers, ditches and even concrete-lined drains in towns. Usually alone or in pairs, seen teetering along with a bobbing tail. Makes a shrill, piping call when flushed, as it flies low over water on bowed wings.

## Common Greenshank ▪ *Tringa nebularia* (Burung Kedidi Kaki Hijau) 35cm

DESCRIPTION Fairly large, slim wader, light grey above and whitish below, with a long, dark bill and greenish legs. In flight, shows a wedge of white from rump to back, but no white wing bar. In breeding plumage, face, upper breast and back are more spotted and mottled.

DISTRIBUTION Resident across N temperate Eurasia from Europe to the Amur; migrates S to tropical Africa, and SW, S and Southeast Asia as far as the Philippines, Australia and New Zealand. Migrant throughout Peninsular Malaysia, Singapore, Sabah and Sarawak.
HABITS AND HABITAT A common migrant on mudflats; also occurs in small numbers inland on wet rice fields or marshes. Numbers increase through Oct and decline markedly in Mar, but like many wader species 1 or 2 birds can be found in almost any month.

*Non-breeding*

## Little Tern ■ *Sternula albifrons*
(Burung Camar Kecil) 22cm

DESCRIPTION Small-sized, pale tern. Breeding birds have black crown, nape and eye-stripe, with white forehead; feet and bill yellow with black tip. Non-breeding birds sport black eye-stripe, white crown and lores, black bill and feet. Tail slightly forked.
DISTRIBUTION Found in coastal temperate and tropical waters. Malaysia and Singapore have both resident and migrant populations.
HABITS AND HABITAT Normally encountered in pairs or small, loose groups along coastal areas and estuaries, but also occasionally recorded from inland reservoirs and large rivers. Hunts for small fishes by hovering and diving.

## White-winged Tern ■ *Chlidonias leucopterus* (Burung Camar Bahu Putih) 25cm

DESCRIPTION Breeding birds have a black head, chest, underparts and upperparts, with a red bill. Wings grey and tail white. Non-breeding birds are similar to Whiskered Tern (p. 42), white crown and black dot behind ear coverts.
DISTRIBUTION Breeds in Europe and temperate regions of Asia, wintering S to Africa, Southeast Asia and Australia. Passage migrant and winter visitor to Malaysia and Singapore.
HABITS AND HABITAT Probably the most common migratory tern to the region's shores, frequenting coastal areas, rivers and inland wetlands such as rice fields, former tin-mining lakes/pools and reservoirs. Usually found in small groups, skimming over the water's surface to feed. At times, seen following ploughing tractors in rice fields in the company of white egrets. Perches on wooden poles and utility wires along the coast.

*Winter*

# Whiskered Tern ■ *Chlidonias hybrida* (Burung Camar Tasik) 27cm

DESCRIPTION Breeding birds sport a red bill and legs, black crown and nape, and grey underparts and mantle. Non-breeding birds are generally greyish, with white forehead and

sides of head, and black bill and streak behind eye. DISTRIBUTION Breeds in S Africa, S Europe, temperate Asia, Southeast Asia and Australia. Passage migrant and winter visitor to Malaysia and Singapore. HABITS AND HABITAT Similar to White-winged Tern (p. 41), and also commonly encountered on the region's coasts and inland wetlands. Congregates in small to large groups. Hunts for food by making shallow plunges or skimming low over water.

*Winter*

# Black-naped Tern
■ *Sterna sumatrana* (Burung Camar Sumatera) 30cm

DESCRIPTION Elegant tern with predominantly white plumage except for black nape; deeply forked tail. Narrow black bill.
DISTRIBUTION Found in tropical waters of the Indian and Pacific oceans. Breeds on small rocky outcrops and islets in the Melaka Straits and South China Sea. More commonly encountered along the E coast of Peninsular Malaysia.
HABITS AND HABITAT Congregates in small groups and, at times, with other terns. Does not move inland, unlike some other terns.

# Little Green-pigeon
■ *Treron olax* (Punai Daun) 20cm

DESCRIPTION The smallest of the *Treron* pigeons. Both sexes have green plumage, yellow wing bars, black terminal band on tail, yellow eye-ring and red legs. Adult males have a greyish head and nape, prominent orange patch on chest, and maroon mantle and wing coverts. Females have a light greyish cap and green wing coverts.
DISTRIBUTION Malay Peninsula to the Greater Sundas. Resident in Malaysia and Singapore.
HABITS AND HABITAT Favours the canopy and/or middle storey of forests and forest edges. Can be seen at times feeding on fruiting fig trees and shrubs with other *Treron* pigeons.

# Pink-necked Green-pigeon ■ *Treron vernans* (Punai Kericau) 27cm

DESCRIPTION Adult males have a grey head and throat, subtle pink on neck and breast, orange chest and light green belly; mantle and upperparts green. Females are mainly green. Both have yellow wing bars and red legs, and a pinkish/reddish eye-ring.
DISTRIBUTION Malay Peninsula, Borneo, the Philippines and the Indonesian islands of Sumatra, Java, Bali and Lesser Sundas. Resident in Malaysia and Singapore.
HABITS AND HABITAT Possibly the most common of the green-pigeons, found at low elevations from coastal mangroves and open country to forest edges and secondary forests. At times, will visit wooded urban gardens like the Lake Gardens in Kuala Lumpur. Usually in pairs but will congregate in large numbers to feed in fruiting trees and shrubs. Tends to stay in tree crowns.

## Thick-billed Green-pigeon ■ *Treron curvirostra* (Punai Lengguak) 27cm

DESCRIPTION Both sexes have overall olive-green plumage, with yellow wing bars, light green eye-ring, thick bill with maroon at base, and red legs. Adult males have maroon

mantle and wing coverts; vent cinnamon. Females have darker olive-green wing coverts.
DISTRIBUTION India, Nepal and Southeast Asia. Resident in Malaysia and Singapore.
HABITS AND HABITAT Frequents mangroves, well-wooded gardens, forest edges and forests; usually seen in the canopy or middle storey. Often feeds in large parties (sometimes 50 birds) in fruiting fig trees, and at times with other frugivorous birds.

*Male (left) and female (right)*

## Mountain Imperial-pigeon ■ *Ducula badia* (Pergam Gunung) 46cm

DESCRIPTION Large, sombre pigeon with light grey plumage and whitish or light grey throat; mantle, wings and tail dark brown with bronze iridescence; legs pink.

DISTRIBUTION India, S China, Southeast Asia, Sumatra, Java and Borneo. Resident in Peninsular Malaysia, Sabah and Sarawak, but absent in Singapore.
HABITS AND HABITAT One of the pigeons commonly encountered in montane forests above 900m, where it remains in tree crowns and can be inconspicuous until it moves or calls. 1 or 2 are often seen feeding together with other frugivores at fruiting fig trees. Call is a deep, resonating *whoo-Whoomp*.

# Long-tailed Parakeet ■ *Psittacula longicauda* (Bayan Nuri) Male 42cm; female 30cm

DESCRIPTION Moderately sized, bright green parrot, with a dark crown, reddish face and black throat, the wings and tail bluer than the back. All the markings and colours are brighter and more distinct in the male, which has a red rather than black bill, and a longer tail.

DISTRIBUTION Resident in Peninsular Malaysia, Sumatra and Borneo, including Sabah and Sarawak, and extending to the Andamans and S Thailand and Myanmar.

HABITS AND HABITAT Rocketing flocks pass across the canopy of lowland forest, or even parks and gardens where they are not persecuted, seeking trees that bear small, hard fruits. Evening flocks gathering to roost can contain hundreds of birds, all screeching as they fly. Pairs nest in tree-holes in dead standing timber, or enlarge crevices in live trees.

# Blue-crowned Hanging-parrot ■ *Loriculus galgulus* (Burung Serindit) 14cm

DESCRIPTION Smallest parrot in the region, generally green in both sexes. Adult males have red breast and rump, yellow/orange patch on mantle, and small blue crown. Females lack the blue crown and red breast-patch.

DISTRIBUTION Malay Peninsula, Sumatra and Borneo. Resident in Malaysia and Singapore.

HABITS AND HABITAT Typically confined to the tree canopy in forests, forest edges and wooded gardens. Seldom descends low except to feed on small fruit and flower buds. Interestingly, will hang upside down like a bat when roosting. Often calls in flight, a high-pitched single note, soft but carrying.

# Bornean Ground-cuckoo
■ *Carpococcyx radiatus* (Burung Butbut Tanah) 60cm

DESCRIPTION Large, lanky ground bird, with a black head, back, wings and tail glossed with green and purple; neck and breast grey, shading to lightly barred flanks and belly. Heavy bill, bare facial skin and legs are light green. Juveniles are browner and less glossy, with the breast light rufous.
DISTRIBUTION Endemic to Borneo, where it is found in both Sabah and Sarawak.
HABITS AND HABITAT Difficult to detect as it moves quietly among the litter or on low branches, either alone or in pairs, seeking beetles and other invertebrates. Reputed to follow migrating Bearded Pigs *Sus barbatus*, presumably to catch animals disturbed by them or to pick up scattered fragments of fruit. Call is a soft moan, repeated at intervals of 4 or 5 seconds, as well as a cough of alarm.

# Asian Koel ■ *Eudynamys scolopaceus*
(Burung Sewah Tahu) 42cm

DESCRIPTION Large bird with a red iris. Males generally glossy black. Females mainly dark brown with spots on head, upperparts and barred upper tail; light brown underparts with dark brown streaks and bars.
DISTRIBUTION Found across India, China and Southeast Asia to Australia. In Malaysia and Singapore, residents are boosted by

passage migrants and winter visitors.
HABITS AND HABITAT Seen in coastal areas, plantations, and wooded gardens in towns and cities. Generally shy and confined to the security of dense foliage, but loud calls, *Ko-el, Ko-el*, betray its presence. More vocal during the breeding period, much to the annoyance of city-dwellers. Known brood parasite of the House Crow (p. 94) in Malaysia.

FAR LEFT: *Male*. LEFT: *Female*

# Dark Hawk-cuckoo

▪ *Hierococcyx bocki* (Burung Sewah Tekukur Besar) 33cm

DESCRIPTION Medium-sized cuckoo with grey-brown head and back, wings and banded tail. Underparts white, with rich orange breast, variably streaked; the white flanks with well-spaced bars. Yellow eye-ring and legs.
DISTRIBUTION Resident in mountains of Peninsular Malaysia, Sumatra and Borneo. This species recently split off from **Large Hawk-cuckoo** *H. sparverioides* from Himalayas to S China (bigger, duller, with black chin and streaked throat), an uncommon migrant to highlands and lowlands of Southeast Asia including Peninsular Malaysia, Singapore, Sabah and Sarawak.
HABITS AND HABITAT Fairly common but secretive resident in montane forest, 900–1,800m, usually solitary, and best detected by its advertising call, a series of disyllables *pi-pi*; *pi-pi*; … that gradually rise to become frantic.

# Malaysian Hawk-cuckoo ▪ *Hierococcyx fugax*
(Burung Sewah Hantu) 29cm

DESCRIPTION Dark grey-brown head with a little white on lores; traces of a white hind-collar; dull, dark brown upperparts; and 3 or 4 black bars (the last the widest) across ashy-grey tail. Underparts creamy white with bold black streaks. The migrant form, with grey upperparts and lighter streaking below, is now separated as the species Hodgson's Hawk-cuckoo *H. nisicolor*.
DISTRIBUTION Resident in Peninsular Malaysia, Borneo (including Sabah and Sarawak) and Sumatra, with several records but no proven breeding in Singapore.
HABITS AND HABITAT Found in lowland forest, both pristine and partly disturbed, on coastal plains up to c. 250m, keeping to the middle and lower storeys. A parasitic species, possibly laying in nests of shamas, but more details of host species are needed. Calls include a succession of 2 notes on the same pitch, with emphasis on each 1st note; and a succession of 2 notes that gradually rise and accelerate, with emphasis on each 2nd note, before breaking up into bubbling sounds.

## Chestnut-bellied Malkoha ■ *Rhopodytes sumatranus*
(Burung Cenuk Kecil) 40cm

DESCRIPTION Large, elongated bird with a light grey head, throat and chest. Prominent red orbital skin; light green bill; glossy, dark green upperparts and wings; inconspicuous dark cinnamon belly and vent. Long tail has white tips.

DISTRIBUTION From *c.* 12°N in Myanmar, through the Malay Peninsula to Borneo and Sumatra. Resident in Peninsular Malaysia, Sabah, Sarawak and Singapore.

HABITS AND HABITAT Generally unobtrusive in lowland habitats such as mangroves, primary forests and forest edges, secondary forests and plantations. Forages in the middle storey of the vegetation in search of insect prey, peering around to locate large insects, caterpillars, small lizards, and some seeds or fruits. The only malkoha species now remaining in Singapore.

## Green-billed Malkoha
■ *Rhopodytes tristis* (Burung Cenuk Kera) 55cm

DESCRIPTION Large and grey, with a very long, white-tipped tail. Similar to the Chestnut-bellied Malkoha (above), but with a paler breast and grey (not brown) belly and vent. Green bill and red skin around eye.
DISTRIBUTION From the Himalayas and NE India through S China and S to Peninsular Malaysia, Sumatra and Kangean. Resident in the N half of Peninsular Malaysia, above *c.* 3°N. Not known from Singapore, Sabah or Sarawak.
HABITS AND HABITAT Similar in habits to other malkohas, foraging for large insect prey in dense foliage around tree trunks. In Peninsular Malaysia it prefers montane forest above *c.* 850m, although in Thailand and further northwards it occurs in a wider range of habitats down to coastal mangroves, bamboo groves, orchards and plantations.

# Red-billed Malkoha

■ *Zanclostomus javanicus*
(Burung Cenuk Api) 45cm

DESCRIPTION Ashy grey above and rich cinnamon-fawn from chin to vent, with grey flanks; long, dark grey tail with white tips. The only malkoha with an entirely red bill; small area of blue skin around eye.
DISTRIBUTION From *c.* 14°N in Myanmar through the Malay Peninsula to Sumatra, Borneo and Java. Resident in Peninsular Malaysia, Sabah and Sarawak, but now locally extinct in Singapore.
HABITS AND HABITAT Similar to other malkohas, occurring in forests and forest edges from the lowlands up to *c.* 1,200m in lower montane forest. There is little information about its diet, and the means of ecological separation between different malkohas would be a useful study topic.

# Chestnut-breasted Malkoha ■ *Zanclostomus curvirostris*

(Burung Cenuk Birah) 45cm

DESCRIPTION Large malkoha with greyish head, and rufous-brown throat and underparts all the way to vent; glossy, dark green upperparts, wings and slightly more than half of long tail (distal part is rufous). Prominent red eye-patch, the red colour continuing across lower mandible; yellow iris.
DISTRIBUTION From *c.* 15°N in Myanmar and Thailand through the Malay Peninsula to the Greater Sundas. Resident in Peninsular Malaysia, Sabah and Sarawak, but now locally extinct in Singapore.
HABITS AND HABITAT Prefers forests, forest edges, plantations and wooded gardens. Usually in pairs and generally unobtrusive.

## Greater Coucal

■ *Centropus sinensis* (Burung Butbut Cari Anak) 52cm

DESCRIPTION Large, crow-like bird with heavy, clumsy flight. Plumage glossy black overall, wings chestnut, eyes red.
DISTRIBUTION From India through S China to Southeast Asia. Resident in Peninsular Malaysia, Sabah, Sarawak and Singapore.
HABITS AND HABITAT Often encountered at forest edges, scrub, riverine vegetation and plantations, singly or, rarely, in pairs. Very shy and confined to thick vegetation, showing itself while sunning or scrambling among the foliage. Call is a prolonged series of deep booms.

## Lesser Coucal ■ *Centropus bengalensis*
(Burung Butbut Kecil) 37cm

DESCRIPTION Generally black with chestnut wings; similar to Greater Coucal (above), but smaller and with a variable amount of pale streaks on head, throat, chest and wings (Greater Coucal never streaked).
DISTRIBUTION From India through S China to Southeast Asia. Resident in Peninsular Malaysia, Singapore, Sabah and Sarawak.
HABITS AND HABITAT Common resident in the lowlands up to *c*. 1,500m. Often encountered in grasslands and scrub, foraging in dense shrubs or on the ground, or sunning with wings drooping or outstretched. Makes occasional low, short flights over vegetation. Typical call (one of several) is a guttural *ko-kok, ko-kok….*

# Common Barn-owl ■ *Tyto alba* (Burung Pungguk Jelapang) 35cm

DESCRIPTION One of the most easily recognisable owls, with a white heart-shaped face and buffy rim. Throat and underparts white; head, upperparts and tail buffy with small whitish spots; legs long.

DISTRIBUTION Virtually global distribution. Common resident in Peninsular Malaysia and Singapore since the 1960s, but recorded in Sabah and Sarawak only as a result of deliberate human introductions.

HABITS AND HABITAT Usually seen solitary in low flight, or perched in open country, rice fields, oil-palm plantations and cultivation. Used as a biological agent in rice fields and plantations to control rodent populations. Roosts in trees and uninhabited buildings, or in nestboxes provided by landowners to boost numbers of the species.

# Collared Scops-owl ■ *Otus bakkamoena* (Burung Hantu Reban) 21cm

DESCRIPTION Small rufous-brown owl with short ear tufts; back speckled, mottled and spotted darker; underparts faintly vermiculated, each feather with a dark spot near tip. Fronts of ear tufts and a variable broad collar around neck cream to deep warm buff. Eyes dark brown.

DISTRIBUTION Resident from India and Sri Lanka to Siberia and Japan, S through Southeast Asia to Java and Bali. Resident in Peninsular Malaysia, Singapore, Sabah and Sarawak.

HABITS AND HABITAT Keeps to tall secondary woodland, tree plantations, well-wooded gardens and, less commonly, undisturbed forest, hunting for beetles, cockroaches, crickets, small lizards and other small vertebrates at night. Call is a soft *po-up*, on 1 pitch or deflected downwards on the 2nd note, and repeated at regular intervals of *c*. 12 seconds; from a distance, it sounds like a single note.

## Barred Eagle-owl ■ *Bubo sumatranus* (Burung Hantu Bubu) 45cm

DESCRIPTION Large bird, but not reaching size of European and American eagle-owls. Mottled and barred buff on dark brown upperparts, and broadly, closely barred below on white underparts. Big, dark eyes; long ear tufts give it a rather flat-crowned appearance. Juvenile plumage contains a lot of white.

DISTRIBUTION From *c.* 13°N in Thailand, through the Malay Peninsula to Sumatra, Borneo, Java and Bali. Resident in Peninsular Malaysia, Sabah and Sarawak; former resident, now locally extinct, in Singapore.

HABITS AND HABITAT Typically solitary, in the middle and upper storeys of undisturbed forest in lowlands, from plains level to *c.* 900m, rarely higher. Typical call is a deep, 2-note *huh huh*, repeated at intervals.

## Buffy Fish-owl ■ *Ketupa ketupu* (Burung Hantu Kuning) 45cm

DESCRIPTION Large, bright buffy-cinnamon owl; dark streaks on underparts; darker brown above with buff streaks and bars. Conspicuous angular ear tufts; pale patch above bill, and staring yellow eyes.

DISTRIBUTION From NW India and Myanmar through Indochina to Laos and Vietnam, southwards through the Malay Peninsula to Sumatra, Borneo, Java and Bali. Resident in Peninsular Malaysia, Singapore, Sabah and Sarawak.

HABITS AND HABITAT Usually forest edges close to rivers or lakes, including both natural and artificial ponds; perches on a low branch at water's edge, waiting for prey, such as fish, frogs and other small animals. Also found in lowlands in mangroves, orchards and plantations. Calls include harsh, hair-raising wails.

# Spotted Wood-owl

■ *Strix seloputo* (Burung Hantu Carik Kafan)
46cm

DESCRIPTION Distinctive orange-brown
facial disc, topped by dark brown crown
with whitish spots; dark brown upperparts
with white spots, and pale underparts with
regular bars. Eyes contrasting dark brown
against facial disc.
DISTRIBUTION SE of a line from N
Thailand to southernmost Vietnam, through
the Malay Peninsula to Sumatra, Java and
the Philippines, including Palawan, but
absent from Borneo. Resident in Peninsular
Malaysia and, since 1985, in Singapore.
HABITS AND HABITAT Forest edges,
plantations, tall secondary woodland and
thickly tree-dominated gardens, avoiding
the interior of undisturbed forest. Rats and
other small vertebrates are the usual food.
Typical call is a single powerful note, *huh*,
repeated at intervals of 10–20 seconds, at
night and often just before dawn.

# Brown Wood-owl ■ *Strix leptogrammica*
(Burung Hantu Punggur) 45cm

DESCRIPTION Similar to the Barred Eagle-owl
(p. 54), but with a rounded head lacking ear tufts, and
a distinct rufous mask outlined with a dark surround
and darkening to smudges around dark eyes. Finely
barred below, and lacking spots on crown.
DISTRIBUTION From India S of the Himalayas,
through S China to Taiwan, and through Southeast
Asia to Sumatra, Borneo and Java. Resident in
Peninsular Malaysia, Sabah and Sarawak; not
recorded from Singapore.
HABITS AND HABITAT Occurs in forest interiors,
from the extreme lowlands up through lower montane
forest to *c.* 1,700m. Will sometimes come to the forest
edge, but usually waits on a branch in the middle
storey, looking and listening for prey. Call, around
dusk and at night, is a wavering, deep *huhuhooo*.

## Brown Boobook ■ *Ninox scutulata* (Burung Hantu Betemak) 30cm

DESCRIPTION Larger than a scops-owl, with a rounded head, no ear tufts and round, staring yellow eyes. Plumage dark brown, including face, with some pale spotting on upperparts, and the brown increasingly broken up by white on lower breast and belly; tail barred.

DISTRIBUTION From India and Sri Lanka across E Asia to Korea and Japan, and through Southeast Asia to Sumatra, Borneo, Java, Bali and the Philippines. Of these, N continental Asian birds are now split as the separate species Northern Boobook *N. japonica*. Resident in Peninsular Malaysia, Singapore, Sabah and Sarawak, and also occurs as a migrant throughout the region.

HABITS AND HABITAT Resident in lowland forest, forest edges and tall secondary woodland at low altitudes. Hunts primarily for insects, and can sometimes be seen by day. Most often detected by frequent calling, *ke-wick*. The migrant form occurs at a wider range of altitudes up to 2,000m.

## Gould's Frogmouth ■ *Batrachostomus stellatus* (Burung Segan Bintik Mas) 22cm

DESCRIPTION Immensely wide gape, big eyes and mottled brown plumage are typical of frogmouths. Underparts buffy white, with darker edges forming regular scallops; several lines of small, black-edged white spots on wing coverts and a larger series close to scapulars; large yellow eyes. Dark brown, rufous-brown and, rarely, greyish-brown phases occur.

DISTRIBUTION From *c*. 10°N in the Malay Peninsula through Sumatra, Borneo and the larger intervening islands. Resident in Peninsular Malaysia, Sabah and Sarawak; former resident in Singapore, now locally extinct.

HABITS AND HABITAT Within tall forest in the extreme lowlands, up to 200m. Roosts on a branch in the middle storey by day, well camouflaged, and flies at night to catch insects on the wing. Male's call is a soft, 3-part *ooo-tuiloo-kuk*, with the last part either rising or falling.

# Large-tailed Nightjar ■ *Caprimulgus macrurus* (Burung Tukang Kubur) 32cm

DESCRIPTION Beautifully camouflaged, mainly brown bird, mottled with black and grey, and with wide greyish sides to crown. Male has white throat, white patches on primaries and white corners to tail, all of which are present but more buff-coloured in female.

DISTRIBUTION From NE India through S China to Hainan, and southwards through Southeast Asia to the Philippines, Greater Sundas and N Australia; there is some disagreement in defining species limits through part of this range. Resident in Peninsular Malaysia, Singapore, Sabah and Sarawak.
HABITS AND HABITAT Very common in lowland habitats, in areas with tall secondary woodland, gardens, and open ground with mixed scrub. Perches on fences, lamp-posts, etc., or even on the ground, and hawks for prey over open stretches. Often detected by its call, a repetitive *klok, klok, klok…*, like someone knocking on wood, continued in bursts for long periods of the night.

# Savanna Nightjar ■ *Caprimulgus affinis* (Burung Tukang Padang) 25cm

DESCRIPTION Small nightjar, with a shorter tail and finer mottling than Large-tailed Nightjar (above), and without bold black markings. Male has white wing-patches and mostly white outer tail feathers. Female has buff wing-patches, and outer tail feathers do not differ from rest of tail.
DISTRIBUTION From the Himalayas through southernmost China to Taiwan, and Southeast Asia to Sumatra, Java, Bali, parts of Borneo, Sulawesi and the Lesser Sundas.

Resident and spreading in Peninsular Malaysia and Singapore since the 1980s, now extending in Borneo and perhaps reaching Sabah.
HABITS AND HABITAT Typical of more open grassland than the Large-tailed, including grassy dunes near coasts and reclaimed land. Call is an explosive *chewee*, given in flight, usually for a fairly short period around and just after dusk.

## Glossy Swiftlet ■ *Collocalia esculenta*
(Burung Layang-layang Licin) 10cm

DESCRIPTION Smaller than House Swift (p. 59), and glossy blue-black overall; greyish chin and dirty whitish belly without clearly defined margins; tail slightly notched. Separated from other swiftlets in flight by its small size and habit of flying very close to the surface of vegetation such as tree crowns.
DISTRIBUTION From Myanmar through Southeast Asia to the SW Pacific. Resident from extreme lowlands to highlands in Peninsular Malaysia, Sabah and Sarawak; formerly resident in Singapore but now apparently only a visitor.
HABITS AND HABITAT Often seen in flight in small flocks over forests, forest edges, open country, towns and cities. Occasionally, will skim over rivers or pools to drink. Nests in cave mouths, under eaves, and in tunnels and similar structures where light penetrates.

## Himalayan Swiftlet ■ *Aerodramus brevirostris* (Burung Layang-layang Himalaya) 14cm

DESCRIPTION Field identification of swiftlets is extremely difficult. Himalayan has a moderate tail notch and pale rump, and is said to have a stiff-winged, flicking flight. In comparison, **Edible-nest Swiftlet** *A. fuciphagus* is smaller with a moderate tail notch and pale rump; and **Black-nest Swiftlet** *A. maximus* is slightly larger and heavier-looking with broader wings and less of a tail notch.
DISTRIBUTION Himalayan is resident from the Himalayas through to Hubei in central China, and southwards to N Thailand; also in Java. Passage migrant and non-breeding visitor in Peninsular Malaysia, and likely in Singapore (with some disagreement over identification criteria); not known from Sabah or Sarawak. Edible-nest is resident from the Andamans and S Myanmar through Peninsular Malaysia, Sumatra, Borneo and Java to parts of the Lesser Sundas. Black-nest is resident from S Myanmar through Peninsular Malaysia to Sumatra, Borneo and Java.
HABITS AND HABITAT All 3 of these swiftlet species spend most of their time flying, from low to very high in the sky and at all altitudes, from the extreme lowlands to mountain tops, over forest, and in disturbed and open habitats.

# House Swift ■ *Apus affinis*
(Burung Layang-layang Rumah) 15cm

DESCRIPTION Generally medium-sized bird with glossy black plumage and prominent white rump; throat white; tail slightly notched.
DISTRIBUTION Africa, Middle East, India and S China to Southeast Asia and the Greater Sundas. Resident in Peninsular Malaysia, Singapore, Sabah and Sarawak.
HABITS AND HABITAT Prefers open country, forest edges, towns and cities. Gregarious by nature, often forming large breeding colonies under eaves of man-made structures such as buildings or bridges, and on cliffs or cave mouths. Harsh, trilling screams are given around roosting and nesting sites.

# Whiskered Treeswift ■ *Hemiprocne comata*
(Layang-layang Berjambul Kecil) 16cm

DESCRIPTION Small, slim brown bird, with long wings and deeply forked tail. Dark brown body with 2 white lines on side of head (brow and moustache), and white on innermost wing feathers. Ear coverts between the 2 white lines are maroon in male, blackish in female.
DISTRIBUTION From *c.* 12°N in southernmost Myanmar through the Malay Peninsula to Sumatra, Borneo and the Philippines. Resident in Peninsular Malaysia, Sabah and Sarawak; considered formerly resident in Singapore but now only a rare visitor.
HABITS AND HABITAT Often seen perched on the end twigs of tree crowns, with wing-tips crossed over rump, or in flight over lowland forest and just into montane forest to *c.* 1,100m. Makes short flights after insects, typically returning to the same perch.

RIGHT: *Female*.
FAR RIGHT:
*Male*

# Red-naped Trogon
■ *Harpactes kasumba* (Burung Kesumba Batang) 32cm

DESCRIPTION Male has a narrow white line separating scarlet breast from black upper breast and throat, and a broad scarlet patch behind neck, this meeting the blue facial skin that is contiguous with the blue bill. Female has a brownish-buff lower breast, sharply defined from dark brown upper breast. In both sexes, tail feathers are tipped by unmarked white. DISTRIBUTION From *c.* 8°N in Peninsular Thailand through to Borneo and Sumatra. Resident in Peninsular Malaysia, Sabah and Sarawak; former resident in Singapore, now locally extinct.

HABITS AND HABITAT In the middle and upper storeys of tall lowland forest, to *c.* 600m on hill slopes, occasionally higher. Insects are snatched from the foliage. Call is a mellow *taup taup taup taup*, usually only 3 or 4 notes; generally lower in pitch and delivered more slowly by male than female.

# Diard's Trogon ■ *Harpactes diardii* (Burung Kesumba Diard) 33cm

DESCRIPTION Male has a pink band separating scarlet breast from black upper breast and throat; and a broad pink patch behind neck, not meeting the violet facial skin that is itself separated from the blue bill. Female has a uniform brown head and upper breast, distinct

from reddish-pink lower breast and belly. In both sexes, white tips of tail feathers are vermiculated with black. DISTRIBUTION From *c.* 9°N in Peninsular Thailand through to Borneo and Sumatra. Resident in Peninsular Malaysia, Sabah and Sarawak; former resident in Singapore, now locally extinct. HABITS AND HABITAT In the middle and lower storeys of tall lowland forest, to *c.* 900m on hill slopes. Insects are snatched from the foliage. Call is a resonant series of 10–12 notes, delivered fast, on a falling pitch after the 2nd note, and accelerating.

# Scarlet-rumped Trogon
■ *Harpactes duvaucelii* (Burung Kesumba Puteri)
25cm

DESCRIPTION Smaller trogon. Male has a black throat, bright scarlet upper and lower breast, and extensive bright scarlet rump. Female has brown head and throat, buff breast merging into pinkish belly, and rufous rump with traces of pink. In both sexes, blue skin on head is limited to a projecting line on brow, and at base of bill is a bright blue gape.
DISTRIBUTION From *c.* 14°N in Myanmar through the Malay Peninsula to Borneo and Sumatra. Resident in Peninsular Malaysia, Sabah and Sarawak; never reliably recorded from Singapore.
HABITS AND HABITAT In the middle and lower storeys of tall lowland forest, to above 1,000m on hill slopes. Insects are snatched from the foliage and, occasionally, in flight. Call is a rapid series of 10–12 notes, delivered so fast that they run together as they accelerate.

# Orange-breasted Trogon
■ *Harpactes oreskios* (Burung Kesumba Harimau)
29cm

DESCRIPTION Medium-small trogon. Olive head and upper breast, greener in male and browner in female; brown upperparts, more chestnut in male; orange-yellow lower breast. Around eye is a small circle of blue skin.
DISTRIBUTION From SW China through Myanmar, mainland Southeast Asia and the Malay Peninsula to Sumatra, Borneo and Java. Resident in Peninsular Malaysia, Sabah and Sarawak; not recorded from Singapore.
HABITS AND HABITAT In the middle and lower storeys of tall lowland and lower montane forest, from sea-level to *c.* 1,300m on mountain slopes. Like other trogons, it builds its nest in rotten stumps. Call is introduced by 1 or 2 slow, separate notes, followed by a series of 3 or 4 quick notes on 1 pitch. Insects are snatched from the foliage.

## Red-headed Trogon ■ *Harpactes erythrocephalus* (Burung Kesumba Gunung) 33cm

DESCRIPTION Large trogon with diagnostic red head in males and cinnamon head in females. Both sexes have reddish underparts with a white 'crescent' on chest (sometimes hidden between feathers), cinnamon back and upper tail, and black wings with whitish stripes on wing coverts.
DISTRIBUTION Resident from the Himalaya to S China, Southeast Asia and Sumatra. Resident in the Main Range, Larut Range and Mount Benom in Peninsular Malaysia; not in Singapore, Sabah and Sarawak.
HABITS AND HABITAT Prefers hill forests at 700m, and usually seen in the middle storey. Generally unobtrusive. Has been recorded participating in mixed-species feeding flocks.

## Whitehead's Trogon
■ *Harpactes whiteheadi* (Burung Kesumba Kinabalu) 33cm

DESCRIPTION Male has a brilliant scarlet crown, dark blue facial skin and black throat, scarlet lower breast and belly. Female has cinnamon head and belly. In both sexes, black throat shades gradually into light grey and almost white on upper breast; cinnamon upperparts and black wings; wing coverts with narrow whitish stripes.
DISTRIBUTION Endemic to N Borneo, in high mountains from Mount Kinabalu in Sabah westwards to Mount Mulu, Mount Dulit and Usun Apau in Sarawak.
HABITS AND HABITAT Montane forest, usually above 1,000m. Often seen perched in the lower storey, from where it sallies out to snatch insects from nearby foliage. Generally silent.

# Rufous-collared Kingfisher

■ *Actenoides concretus* (Burung Pekaka Rimba)
24cm

DESCRIPTION Forest kingfisher with greenish crown, bold black stripe through eye, blue-black moustache, and entirely rufous-buff underparts. Male is brighter overall, with glossy blue back and wings; in female, upperparts are dull green with buff speckles on wings.
DISTRIBUTION From *c.* 11°30'N in Myanmar and Thailand, through the Malay Peninsula to Borneo and Sumatra. Resident in Peninsular Malaysia, Sabah and Sarawak; formerly resident in Singapore, now locally extinct.
HABITS AND HABITAT Found in the middle and, especially, lower storeys of lowland forest from sea-level up into lower montane forest at *c.* 1,200m. Perches motionless until it spots an insect or small lizard or snake. Usual call is a wavering upward whistle, delivered in a long series.

# Stork-billed Kingfisher ■ *Pelargopsis capensis* (Burung Pekaka Buaya) 37cm

DESCRIPTION Large kingfisher with a massive red bill. Brown head with light orange/rufous nape, throat, underparts and vent; dull bluish-green wings and tail; red feet.
DISTRIBUTION Resident from India to Southeast Asia, usually at low elevations.
HABITS AND HABITAT Solitary and rather silent kingfisher, often spotted perched in mangroves, former tin-mining wetlands and forested river courses. Diet consists mainly of fish, but will not hesitate to take insects and amphibians.

# White-throated Kingfisher
■ *Halcyon smyrnensis* (Burung Pekaka Dusun)
28cm

DESCRIPTION Brown head and belly; white throat and breast, resembling a bib; iridescent blue back and tail; red bill and feet; black upperwing coverts.
DISTRIBUTION Widespread from Middle East through India to China and Southeast Asia. The most common resident kingfisher in Peninsular Malaysia and Singapore.
HABITS AND HABITAT Found in a wide range of habitats near human habitation, such as mangroves, agricultural areas, plantations, gardens and urban areas. Diet is varied, ranging from insects to amphibians. Often solitary on exposed perches, its calls announcing its presence, a loud but mellow trill, *kikikiki….*

# Black-capped Kingfisher ■ *Halcyon pileata*
(Burung Pekaka Kopiah Hitam) 30cm

DESCRIPTION Medium-sized kingfisher with a black head and upperwing coverts; bright bluish mantle, upperparts and upper tail. White collar, throat (sometimes with slight scaling) and breast grading into a rufous belly and vent; bright red bill and feet.
DISTRIBUTION Found mainly in India, Myanmar, China and Korea. Populations in Southeast Asia, including Malaysia, are either passage migrants or winter visitors.
HABITS AND HABITAT Usually seen individually at coastal wetlands such as mangroves, estuaries and large rivers in lowlands up to 1,200m. Not as vocal as Collared Kingfisher (p. 65).

# Collared Kingfisher

■ *Todiramphus chloris* (Burung Pekaka Bakau)
25cm

DESCRIPTION Unmistakable bird with bluish-green head, upperparts and wings, and a white collar adjoining white underparts. Black eye-stripe not prominent at times. Bill grey and flesh-coloured. Might be confused with the Sacred Kingfisher *T. sanctus*, which occurs in the same habitats but is quite rare.
DISTRIBUTION Recorded from S and Southeast Asia through New Guinea and Australia. Resident populations in Malaysia are augmented by seasonal migrants.
HABITS AND HABITAT Usually encountered in mangroves, beach scrub and plantations. Has a varied diet, ranging from small crustaceans to reptiles and amphibians inland. Probably the most vocal of all kingfishers in Malaysia, with harsh, loud territorial calls typically consisting of repeated clusters of 2–4 shrieks.

# Rufous-backed Kingfisher ■ *Ceyx rufidorsa* (Burung Pekaka Sepah) 13cm

DESCRIPTION Tiny forest kingfisher with brilliant orange-red bill and feet; rufous head, back and wings; yellow breast; white patch behind ear coverts. Belongs to a complex whose members range to the Black-backed Kingfisher *C. erithaca*, with a black mantle, deep blue wing coverts, and deep blue patches on the forehead and ear coverts; many intermediates occur.

DISTRIBUTION Rufous-backed birds occur from the Malay Peninsula to Sumatra, Borneo, Java, the Philippines and Lesser Sundas. Black-backed birds range from India and Indochina as far S as Java. Rufous-backed birds are resident in Peninsular Malaysia, with visitors to Singapore; Black-backed birds are migrants. In Sabah and Sarawak, all resident populations are much more mixed.
HABITS AND HABITAT In the lower storey of lowland forest, forest edges and mangroves, feeding at and near forest streams on insects and worms.

# Blue-eared Kingfisher ■ *Alcedo meninting*
(Burung Pekaka Bintik-bintik) 16cm

DESCRIPTION Small kingfisher with deep iridescent blue head and wings, metallic light blue on back and tail, white ear-patch, white chin, rufous underparts, red legs; bill may be

red or black with red near base. DISTRIBUTION Found across India and Southeast Asia. Uncommon resident in Malaysia and Singapore. HABITS AND HABITAT Frequents forested streams, rivers, lakes and mangroves. Often seen perched low down, overlooking water to hunt small fishes, which it secures with lightning dives before returning to the same perch. Generally shy but can be seen flying low over the water's surface.

# Common Kingfisher
■ *Alcedo atthis* (Burung Pekaka Citcit) 18cm

DESCRIPTION One of the smallest kingfishers in the region. Head, mantle and wings bluish; back iridescent blue; ear coverts and underparts rufous; white behind ear coverts and chin; bill black with tinges of orange; legs red.
DISTRIBUTION Found across N Africa, Europe and temperate Asia to Southeast Asia. Resident and winter visitor to Peninsular Malaysia and Singapore. In Borneo, it is a rare winter visitor.
HABITS AND HABITAT Owing to its size and habits, often hard to detect in its preferred habitats of forested streams, mangroves and former tin-mining wetlands. Occasionally seen flitting across the water, giving a high-pitched *peep*, or perched silently low down overlooking water in pursuit of prey.

## Dollarbird

■ *Eurystomus orientalis*
(Tiong Batu) 30cm

DESCRIPTION Dark brown head
with prominent red bill and feet;
dark bluish-green body with some
bluish-purple streaks at neck. In
flight, shows white patches on
wings.
DISTRIBUTION Resident
from India to Southeast Asia
and Australia; populations are
augmented by migrants from the N.
HABITS AND HABITAT Solitary
birds are commonly encountered
in mangroves, beach scrub,
plantations and open country,
usually on prominent vantage
points. Often sallies forth from
these perches to hunt for prey of
winged insects such as ants and
termites.

## Red-bearded Bee-eater

■ *Nyctyornis amictus* (Burung Berek-
berek Janggut Merah) 33cm

DESCRIPTION Generally, plumpish
green bird with red throat and breast
resembling a 'beard'; lilac crown,
orangey-red iris and grey feet. Bill
thin, almost sickle-like.
DISTRIBUTION Resident
from Myanmar to Sumatra and
Borneo, from the lowlands up to
approximately 1,100m.
HABITS AND HABITAT Typically
found in forests or forest edges on a
perch, from which it sallies forth in
pursuit of insects such as bees, wasps,
termites and butterflies. Usually
solitary. Excavates burrows in the
banks of streams to nest.

## Blue-tailed Bee-eater

■ *Merops philippinus* (Burung Berek-berek Sawah) 24cm plus tail spikes

DESCRIPTION Generally light green on upperparts, wings and underparts (grading into light blue at vent); white patch below bill; throat brownish yellow; black eye-stripe with red iris; conspicuous bright blue tail with central streamer.

DISTRIBUTION Found from India and S China through Southeast Asia and New Guinea. Populations in Malaysia and Singapore are mainly passage migrants and winter visitors.

HABITS AND HABITAT Usually seen in open areas, including beach scrub, former tin-mining areas and rice fields. Individuals or groups often seen perched on utility lines, using these to sally forth in pursuit of winged insects. Also uses the same perch to disarm prey such as bees of their sting. Roosts in groups.

## Blue-throated Bee-eater

■ *Merops viridis* (Burung Berek-berek Pirus) 23cm plus tail spikes

DESCRIPTION Similar in size to Blue-tailed Bee-eater (above). Brown cap, nape and mantle; black eye-stripe with red iris; bluish throat, blending into light green chest and underparts; darker green wing coverts, bluish-green primaries and tail.

DISTRIBUTION Found from S China to Southeast Asia. Common breeding visitor in Malaysia.

HABITS AND HABITAT Frequents open habitats, such as beach scrub, former tin-mining areas and rice fields, perched on utility lines. Forms communal roosts and nests underground, usually in areas with little grassy vegetation.

# Oriental Pied Hornbill ■ *Anthracoceros albirostris*
(Burung Enggang Kelingking) 68–70cm

DESCRIPTION This small hornbill is one of the commoner species. Black head, neck and wings; white lower breast and outer tail feathers. Bare, pale skin patches around eye and

gape. Bill and casque are ivory-coloured, with obscure dark patches in female, and fewer but more defined, intense black marks in male.
DISTRIBUTION Resident from India to SW China and throughout Southeast Asia to Sumatra, Borneo and Java.
HABITS AND HABITAT In lowland forest edges, mangroves and along rivers, seldom above 500m. Like other hornbills, it nests in tree cavities, the female being sealed in with mud except for a narrow slit through which the male passes food to mother and offspring. Exciting recent work with cameras and satellite tracking has revealed many details of the species' breeding cycle, including its astonishing range of animal prey.

# Black Hornbill ■ *Anthracoceros malayanus* (Burung Enggang Gatalbirah) 75cm

DESCRIPTION Entirely black except for white outer corners to tail and, in some individuals, a grey or white eyebrow stripe. Male has ivory bill and black facial skin; female has black bill and dull pink skin around eye.
DISTRIBUTION Resident in Borneo (Sabah, Sarawak, Brunei, Kalimantan), Sumatra, Bangka, Belitung, Singkep and Peninsular Malaysia northwards to *c*. 8°N in Thailand.
HABITS AND HABITAT In the middle and upper storeys of lowland evergreen rainforest, typically in extreme lowlands over level ground, rarely to 600m. Territorial and accompanied by previous young, searching for many kinds of fruits and, occasionally, small animals. Breeds monogamously, usually without helpers (see Bushy-crested Hornbill, p. 71). Pairs give a harsh rasping or vomiting call.

*Female*

# Great Hornbill ■ *Buceros bicornis* (Burung Enggang Papan) 110–120cm

DESCRIPTION One of the bulkiest hornbills, easily recognised by its pied appearance, with head and white parts of plumage often stained yellow by oils from preen gland. Male and female are alike, except for eye colour (red in males, white in females). Casque tends to be larger in males, with black trimmings.
DISTRIBUTION Resident in parts of India, Bangladesh and Myanmar to SW China and southwards through Peninsular Malaysia to *c.* 3°N. Absent from the S part of the Malay Peninsula and Singapore, and from Borneo, but reappears in Sumatra.
HABITS AND HABITAT In lowland and hill forest from sea-level to *c.* 1,300m. Typically occurs in pairs, but sometimes gathers in larger groups at good food sources, such as heavily fruiting fig trees. Call is a loud barking, the male and female alternating, either when perched or in flight.

# Rhinoceros Hornbill ■ *Buceros rhinoceros* (Burung Enggang Badak) 90–120cm

DESCRIPTION Enormous black hornbill with white belly, white tail crossed by a black bar, and brilliant yellow and red bill and casque. Male has larger casque with black line, and a red eye; female has white eye surrounded by red skin.
DISTRIBUTION Resident in suitable habitats throughout Borneo, Java, Sumatra and Peninsular Malaysia, to *c.* 7°N in Thailand; historically resident in Singapore.
HABITS AND HABITAT Canopy of lowland evergreen rainforest, to 1,400m. Typically occurs in pairs and, sometimes, with previous young. Flocks of up to 25 occur rarely at good fruiting trees. Monogamous pair breeds without helpers (see Bushy-crested Hornbill, p. 71), in natural tree cavities. Members of the pair advertise their territory and keep in touch with a loud, nasal, barking duet, *eng – gang*, often in flight.

# Bushy-crested Hornbill ■ *Anorrhinus*
*galeritus* (Burung Enggang Mengilai) 90cm

DESCRIPTION Dark grey-brown all over; darkest on
head, becoming paler down to wings and basal half
of tail, with distal half of tail forming blackish band.
Male has blue face and black bill; female has pink face
and particoloured bill.
DISTRIBUTION Resident in Borneo (Sabah,
Sarawak, Brunei, Kalimantan), Natuna Besar,
Sumatra and the Malay Peninsula, northwards
through Peninsular Thailand and Myanmar to
*c.* 14°N.
HABITS AND HABITAT In lowland and,
occasionally, lower montane forest, from sea-level to
*c.* 1,400m or more, but commonest in foothills. Noisy
groups of adults and their young, giving raucous,
puppy-like yelping choruses, seek a variety of fruits,
including some figs, and small invertebrates. Nesting
takes place in a tree cavity, helped by group members
– often a previous batch of young, which assist by
bringing food to the nest.

# White-crowned Hornbill
■ *Berenicornis comatus* (Burung Enggang Jambul
Putih) 90–100cm

DESCRIPTION Perhaps the hornbill that is least often
seen. Distinctive shaggy white head (crown only in
female) and tail, and entirely black wings except for
white trailing edge; males also have a white breast.
Juveniles dark all over with white-speckled head, and
only distal half of tail is white.
DISTRIBUTION Resident patchily throughout Borneo
(Sabah, Sarawak, Brunei, Kalimantan), Sumatra
and the Malay Peninsula, northwards in Peninsular
Thailand to *c.* 15°N and in Myanmar to 14°N.
HABITS AND HABITAT In lowland evergreen
rainforest to 900m. Typically in the lower to middle
storeys in small territorial groups usually including an
adult pair with helpers (see Bushy-crested Hornbill,
above) and juveniles. Feeds on lizards, snakes, small
birds, bats and large insects, as well as fruits but rather
few figs. Call is a soft ventriloqual cooing.

## Fire-tufted Barbet ■ *Psilopogon pyrolophus* (Burung Takur Jambang Api) 28cm

DESCRIPTION Large barbet, grass-green on body and wings; dark collar, above which throat is yellow and ear coverts are greyish white; crown dark, with fiery chestnut tuft above pale greenish bill, this crossed by a black band. Sexes are alike.
DISTRIBUTION Resident in mountains of Sumatra and Peninsular Malaysia.
HABITS AND HABITAT Found in the canopy and middle storey of montane evergreen rainforest at *c.* 900–2,000m, and sometimes down into the understorey along disturbed forest edges. Feeds on many kinds of figs and other soft fruits, plus a few insects. Often located by its weird rasping call, the notes accelerating to a whirr like a buzzing insect.

## Lineated Barbet ■ *Megalaima lineata* (Burung Takur Kukup) 28cm

DESCRIPTION Has the typical barbet pattern of green back, wings and tail, but head and forequarters are distinctively oatmeal with brown streaking. Bill and skin around eye bright yellow. Sexes are alike.
DISTRIBUTION Resident from the basal E Himalayas through Myanmar, Thailand and Indochina to N Peninsular Malaysia; also in Java and Bali. Now spreading southwards to fill in parts of coastal Peninsular Malaysia, and introduced to Singapore.
HABITS AND HABITAT Open and disturbed forest and forest edges, especially near the coast. Like other barbets, it excavates holes in small trees or branches to nest; this species usually chooses living trees or may reuse old cavities. Eats mainly fruits, but fewer figs than most barbets. Call is a distinctive *ku-kruk*, repeated about once a second in a long series.

# Golden-naped Barbet

■ *Megalaima pulcherrima* (Burung Takur Bintarang) 21cm

DESCRIPTION Green with light blue forehead, crown and throat, black lores, and blur of golden yellow on hind-neck in adults (lacking in juveniles). Sexes are alike.

DISTRIBUTION Endemic to Borneo, where it is resident in mountains of Sabah and Sarawak as well as adjacent East Kalimantan.

HABITS AND HABITAT Montane forest at *c.* 1,100–2,500m, where it seeks fruits such as figs and may also take some insects; it is a fig specialist but takes other fruits such as *Medinilla* from the middle and lower storeys. Nest is a cavity excavated in mouthfuls of rotten wood from a dead tree, often a very slim one at the forest edge. Most commonly recorded from its call, *tuk tuk tukrrrk*, given regularly every few seconds from a perch among dense foliage in smaller trees and the middle canopy. Like most other barbets, also has a serial trilling call, each trill shorter than the last.

# Golden-throated Barbet

■ *Megalaima franklinii* (Burung Takur Gunung) 22cm

DESCRIPTION Green with yellow upper throat, greyish lower throat, red forehead and yellow hind-crown. Red spot on nape; sides of head mostly grey.

DISTRIBUTION From Nepal and NE India to S China, and patchily southwards in mountains to Peninsular Malaysia; resident there, but not recorded in Singapore, Sabah or Sarawak.

HABITS AND HABITAT A barbet of montane forest on the Malay Peninsula, in the Larut Range, the S part of the Main Range and scattered mountains further E. Occurs in the upper montane forest above 1,400m, feeding on figs and other fruits, although its diet is not well documented. Call is a rapid, repeated *ke-triuk, ke-triuk….*

# Yellow-crowned Barbet

■ *Megalaima henricii* (Burung Takur Mahkota Kuning) 22cm

DESCRIPTION Green with a yellow forecrown and eyebrow, and blue hind-crown and throat; black lores and narrow eye-ring. As in most other barbets, sexes are alike.
DISTRIBUTION From *c.* 8°30'N in the Malay Peninsula, through Borneo and most of Sumatra. Resident in Peninsular Malaysia, Sabah and Sarawak, but never reliably recorded from Singapore.
HABITS AND HABITAT The upper storey of lowland forest, from sea-level to *c.* 900m at the transition to lower montane forest, where it meets but does not overlap with Black-browed Barbet M. *oorti*. Birds gather in the canopy at fruiting figs with other barbets and frugivorous birds, but are otherwise fairly solitary. Call is a repeated *tuk tuk tuk tuk trrrk*, with 4 short notes and 1 long.

# Coppersmith Barbet

■ *Megalaima haemacephala* (Burung Takur Tukang Besi) 17cm

DESCRIPTION The smallest barbet locally, green above and streaky buff and green below. Yellow above and below eye and on throat; red forehead and breast-band. Sexes are alike, juveniles somewhat duller.
DISTRIBUTION Resident from the Indian sub-continent through Southeast Asia to Peninsular Malaysia, Sumatra, Java and the Philippines, but absent from the whole of Borneo.
HABITS AND HABITAT The only barbet typical of open country with scattered trees, parkland and even urban gardens; also found in plantations and the landward side of mangroves. Single birds, or occasionally loose aggregations at fruiting figs, are often seen perched on bare, protruding canopy twigs. Calls attention to itself by a monotonous, repeated *toink, toink, toink…*, which gives the species its common name.

## Sunda Pygmy Woodpecker

▪ *Dendrocopos moluccensis* (Burung Belatuk Belacan) 13cm

DESCRIPTION Small woodpecker with dark brown cap (with a red flash in males); broad, dark brown stripe through and behind eye, and another dark moustachial stripe. Upperparts dark brown, striped with white; underparts whitish with streaks. Wide, pale eyebrow is usually a striking feature in the field.
DISTRIBUTION Resident in India and Sri Lanka, Peninsular Malaysia, Sumatra, Borneo, Java and the Lesser Sundas.
HABITS AND HABITAT Found in mangroves, coastal woodlands, secondary growth and, in places, the trees in parks and on roadsides, always at low altitudes fairly near the coast. Sometimes comes down to the understorey, even foraging on wooden fenceposts. Usually seen singly or in pairs.

*Female*

## Rufous Woodpecker

▪ *Micropternus brachyurus* (Burung Belatuk Biji Nangka) 25cm

DESCRIPTION Overall rufous brown, slightly darker on head and tail, with black bars on back, wings and tail. No significant crest. Males have a patch of red below eye (absent in female), but this is not very conspicuous against the generally brown colour.
DISTRIBUTION From the Himalayan foothills, E India and Sri Lanka through S China to Hainan, and southwards through Indochina to the Malay Peninsula, Sumatra, Borneo and Java. Resident in Peninsular Malaysia, Singapore, Sabah and Sarawak.
HABITS AND HABITAT Found in lowland forest, from sea-level to *c.* 1,000m, where it may just enter lower montane forest; also in mangroves and tall secondary forest. Usually in tree crowns, coming lower at forest edges and in clearings.

## Banded Woodpecker ■

*Chrysophlegma mineaceus*
(Burung Belatuk Merah) 26cm

DESCRIPTION One of several yellow-crested woodpeckers. Rufous head and throat are diagnostic, merging into barred green back and irregularly buff- and brown-banded breast and belly. Rump yellow, wings crimson. In females, sides of face are duller with more white speckles.
DISTRIBUTION Resident in Java, Sumatra, Nias, Borneo, Bangka, Belitung, Singapore and northwards through Peninsular Malaysia to *c.* 13°N in Peninsular Thailand.
HABITS AND HABITAT Inhabits the middle storey of tall secondary forest, parks, gardens and forest edges, up to *c.* 1,200m. May be located by its loud, repeated scream, *kwee, kwee.*

## Chequer-throated Woodpecker ■ *Chrysophlegma mentalis*

(Burung Belatuk Ranting) 28cm

DESCRIPTION Another yellow-crested woodpecker, but set apart by greenish crown and broad zone of light chestnut running from behind eye, down neck and around underside

of throat, the throat being chequered black and white. In female, the chestnut continues as a malar stripe.
DISTRIBUTION Resident in southernmost Myanmar and Peninsular Thailand, Peninsular Malaysia, Sumatra, Bangka, Java and Borneo; now lost from Singapore.
HABITS AND HABITAT Found foraging on trunks and larger boughs in the middle storey of lowland and hill evergreen rainforest to *c.* 1,200 m, but scarcer than either the Crimson-winged (p. 77) or Banded (above) woodpeckers. Calls have an upward inflection, *kiyee*, compared with all those of Crimson-winged, which have a downward inflection.

## Crimson-winged Woodpecker

▪ *Picus puniceus* (Burung Belatuk Mas) 26cm

DESCRIPTION Similar to the Banded Woodpecker
(p. 76), but sides of head and throat green (males
with a red moustache streak), breast plain green with
barring lower on belly, back plain green. Rump yellow
and wings bright crimson. Contrast between red crown
and green face is a useful feature for identification.
DISTRIBUTION Resident in Java, Sumatra, Nias,
Borneo and Peninsular Malaysia, northwards to
c. 13°N in Peninsular Thailand. Now lost from
Singapore.
HABITS AND HABITAT More characteristic of
primary lowland evergreen rainforest than the Banded
Woodpecker, but also occurs in rubber and oil-palm
plantations and secondary woodland. Characteristic
call is a 2-note wail, *kee-bee*, the 2nd note lower; also
has several other types of call, each presumably with a
differing function.

*Female*

## Common Flameback

▪ *Dinopium javanense* (Burung Belatuk Pinang
Muda) 30cm

DESCRIPTION Golden-brown back and
wings, and bright orange-red rump (hence its
common name); white underside with black
scallops and bold black and white face stripes
make it conspicuous. Crown and crest red in
male, black in female.
DISTRIBUTION Resident in parts of India
through to S China and the whole Indo-
Malayan region as far as Sumatra, Borneo,
Java, Bali and parts of the Philippines. Found
throughout Peninsular Malaysia, Singapore,
Sabah and Sarawak.
HABITS AND HABITAT Probes and gleans for
ants, termites and other insects on the bark
of big trees in lowland parkland, gardens, and
timber, oil-palm and rubber plantations, and
especially in mangroves. Usually seen in pairs,
often calling with loud, short rattles in flight.

# Green Broadbill ■ *Calyptomena viridis* (Burung Seluwit) 16cm

DESCRIPTION Entirely brilliant, glowing green. Male more emerald, with a yellow spot before eye, black spot behind ear, 3 black wing bars, and more bluish under-tail coverts

*Female*

and tail. Female more grass-green, lacking markings but with same blue beneath tail. DISTRIBUTION Resident from *c.* 16°N in Myanmar through Peninsular Thailand and Peninsular Malaysia (though now lost from Singapore) to Sumatra, Bunguran and Borneo.
HABITS AND HABITAT Lowland evergreen rainforest from sea-level to *c.* 760m, with occasional long-distance dispersal possible at other altitudes. In pairs, singly or in small groups whose significance is unknown (and worth detailed study), snatching fruits and some insects in flight. Nest is a neat hanging bag suspended from an understorey twig, sometimes at human head height. Call is an accelerating, descending series of taps; also short cat-like moans and frog-like croaks.

# Whitehead's Broadbill
■ *Calyptomena whiteheadi* (Burung Seluwit Kinabalu) 25cm

DESCRIPTION Hefty emerald-green broadbill. Male iridescent with a scatter of black marks over breast, black patches on throat and in front of and behind eye, and black bars on wings. Female duller green but still with black throat-patch and obscure mark behind eye.
DISTRIBUTION Resident only in Borneo, where it is endemic in the mountains.
HABITS AND HABITAT Occurs rather unpredictably in middle storey of tall lower montane forest and fringes of upper montane forest, at *c.* 1,000–1500m; rare records of dispersal into lowlands. Fruits are swallowed whole, with regurgitation of astonishingly large, indigestible seeds. Can sit quietly for long periods, but gives characteristic whirring; also gulps and croaks in a social context.

# Long-tailed Broadbill
■ *Psarisomus dalhousiae* (Takau Bayan) 26cm

DESCRIPTION Like a parakeet, with a brilliant grass-green back and wings, paler lime-green on breast, and bluer on primaries and long tail. Narrow white collar (perhaps better defined in female) joins yellow throat, with yellow patch over ear; sides and top of head black, with a little blue skullcap.
DISTRIBUTION Resident from central Himalayan foothills, through S China and Indochina to Peninsular Malaysia, Sumatra and Borneo. Not in Singapore.
HABITS AND HABITAT Montane forest at *c.* 850–1,500m defines this bird's distribution, with scattered records as low as 250m in foothills. Occurs in small (family?) parties, seeking insects on foliage and twigs of trees in the middle and upper storeys, occasionally in small trees along quiet forest roads. Flock members bob, flaunt tails and call to each other in a descending series of trills.

# Silver-breasted Broadbill
■ *Serilophus lunatus* (Takau Hujan) 16cm

DESCRIPTION Most elegant bird, with a silvery-grey head and breast (crossed in female by a silver-white line), shading to an ashy-brown back and rich chestnut rump. Conspicuous black eyebrow; wings black with flashes of blue and white. Bill silvery blue and yellow.
DISTRIBUTION Resident from E Himalayas through S China and the Indo-Malayan region as far as Peninsular Malaysia and Sumatra (not Singapore or Borneo).
HABITS AND HABITAT In Peninsular Malaysia occurs only along the Main Range, up to *c.* 1,200m and down to a variable altitude, sometimes as low as 230m, in the middle and lower storeys. Could be considered a hill-slope, rather than strictly montane, bird. Nests are hung from small trees over hillside gullies, the lining replenished with fresh green leaves throughout incubation, as in other broadbills. Thought to feed on insects.

# Black-and-red Broadbill
■ *Cymbirhynchus macrorhynchos* (Takau Rakit)
22–24cm

DESCRIPTION Black crown, breast-band, wings and tail; longitudinal white flash on coverts overlying secondaries; large bib above breast-band, breast, belly and rump a rich, deep, gorgeous red. Bill dramatic turquoise and yellow. Sexes are alike.
DISTRIBUTION Resident in Indochina, Myanmar and Thailand, through Peninsular Malaysia (now only sporadic in Singapore) to Sumatra, Borneo and some intervening islands.
HABITS AND HABITAT Best viewing opportunities are along forest-fringed rivers, as the untidy dead-leaf nests hang above water from overhead branches or protruding snags. Also seen in mangroves and in forest edge far from water, with some invasion of tall plantations in lowlands, to *c.* 300m. Calls include a rasping, rising trill.

# Black-and-yellow Broadbill
■ *Eurylaimus ochromalus* (Takau Kasturi) 15cm

DESCRIPTION Small broadbill with black head, white collar, conspicuous black breast-band (broken medially in female) and pale pink underparts; wings and tail largely black with multiple flashes of yellow on back, coverts, secondaries and rump. Comical yellow eye and blue bill.
DISTRIBUTION Resident from central Thailand and Myanmar through Peninsular Malaysia (not, or perhaps no longer, in Singapore), Sumatra, Belitung and Borneo.
HABITS AND HABITAT In the canopy and middle storey of lowland forest, peat-swamp forest and, sometimes, rubber plantations, although it may be hard to see. Bag-like dead-leaf nest is hung from a branch or twig, usually above a space. Advertises its presence by a long series of notes, accelerating and rising, before ending sharply.

# Blue-winged Pitta ■ *Pitta moluccensis* (Burung Pacat Sayap Biru) 20cm

DESCRIPTION Brilliantly particoloured bird with black mask, buff underparts that are red beneath tail, green upperparts and bright blue wings. In flight, wings are bold blue and black with white panels, like those of many pittas and some kingfishers. 2 similar species are the large-billed **Mangrove Pitta** *P. megarhyncha* in Peninsular Malaysia and the chestnut-crowned hillside **Fairy Pitta** *P. nympha* migrant in Borneo. DISTRIBUTION Resident in China and Indochina southwards to N Peninsular Malaysia; migrant to rest of Malay Peninsula, Singapore, Sabah and Sarawak, occasionally reaching as far as Java. HABITS AND HABITAT Usually alone, in lowland forest or dense vegetation in plantations or even

large gardens, where it hops on the ground, turning leaf litter to seek insects and grubs. Migrates at night; many records are of birds stunned by hitting buildings when disoriented by lights. Call is a 4-note *chew-chew, chew-chew*.

# Garnet Pitta ■ *Pitta granatina* (Burung Pacat Merah) 15cm

DESCRIPTION Deep, shining blue-black, with scarlet crown, lower breast and belly, and bright blue iridescence on bend of wing; narrow brow light blue. Juvenile is dark brown all over, without any spots or streaks. DISTRIBUTION From *c*. 6°N in Peninsular Malaysia, through Sumatra and Borneo. N Sumatran birds are sometimes separated as **Graceful Pitta** *P. venusta*, and Sabah birds sometimes as **Black-crowned Pitta** *P. ussheri*. Formerly resident in Singapore, now locally extinct. HABITS AND HABITAT The floor of tall lowland forest to *c*. 200m. Nest is a dome of dead leaves on the ground next to a tree root. Call is a low, pure whistle, 1.5 seconds long except in Sabah, where it is 2 or 3 seconds long.

## Blue-headed Pitta ▪ *Pitta baudii*
(Burung Pacat Kepala Biru) 18cm

DESCRIPTION In male, black sides of face separate brilliant blue cap and brilliant white throat; chestnut brown above; deep, dark blue below; long white wing bar. Female brown above and fawn below, with pale throat, long white wing bar on dark wing, and bluish tail.
DISTRIBUTION Resident only in Borneo, where it is endemic in the lowlands of Sabah and Sarawak, as well as Brunei and Kalimantan.
HABITS AND HABITAT Solitary individuals are seen foraging for insects among ground litter in lowland evergreen rainforest, usually below 300m but once reported up to 1,200m. Nest is a ball of leaves lodged by roots on the ground. Usual call is a soft *pwi-wi-wi*, with emphasis on the 1st note.

## White-bellied Erpornis
▪ *Erpornis zantholeuca* (Burung Rimba Berjambul Hijau) 13cm

DESCRIPTION Pale grey face, breast and (nearly white) belly; crown with short, erectile crest; back, wings and tail light green; yellow touch to fringes of primaries and yellow beneath tail. Sexes are alike.
DISTRIBUTION Resident from the western Himalayan foothills through southern China to Taiwan, and through Southeast Asia to Peninsular Malaysia (not Singapore), Sumatra and Borneo.
HABITS AND HABITAT Formerly considered to be a yuhina, but now not even included among the babblers. Seen singly or in pairs in the canopy and middle storey of lowland evergreen rainforest, from the extreme lowlands to c. 900m, and occasionally into lower montane forest to a maximum 1,200m. This foliage-gleaning insectivore is a persistent but still scarce participant of mixed foraging flocks.

## White-browed Shrike-babbler
▪ *Pteruthius flaviscapis* (Burung Rimba Kening Putih)
17cm

DESCRIPTION Both sexes with entirely pearl-white undersides. Crown and mask of male black with white eyebrow; back grey; wings and tail black, inner secondaries ochre and chestnut, tips of primaries white. Female with subdued grey head and back, light olive-green wings and tail.

DISTRIBUTION Resident from W Himalayan foothills through S China discontinuously to Peninsular Malaysia (not Singapore), Sumatra, Borneo and Java. In Peninsular Malaysia it is confined to the Larut and Main ranges, and various outlying mountains.

HABITS AND HABITAT From 900m in tall lower montane forest to 2,000m in elfin upper montane vegetation, mainly in the canopy but also at forest edges. Territorial pairs call loudly, nesting early Feb–Jun on a branch in the canopy or middle storey. Insectivorous, known to take caterpillars and other invertebrates.

*Female*

## Black-eared Shrike-babbler ▪ *Pteruthius melanotis*
(Burung Rimba Telinga Hitam) 12cm

DESCRIPTION All ages and both sexes have a black line before, around and behind eye, curling down around ear coverts and emphasising white eye-ring; crown and back green; wings blacker, with 2 pale bars. Male has orange throat and yellow underparts; female and young have faintly yellow ear coverts and pearly breast.

DISTRIBUTION Resident from central Himalayan foothills through S China discontinuously to Peninsular Malaysia (not Singapore).

HABITS AND HABITAT Confined to tall montane forest of the Main Range and various outlying mountains at *c.* 1,000–1,800m, where it forages in the canopy and middle storey. Insectivorous, taking caterpillars and, presumably, other insects by searching the foliage, lichen-covered branches and trunks. Call is a scolding trill.

# Javan Cuckooshrike ■ *Coracina javensis* (Burung Kelabu Gunung) 28cm

DESCRIPTION Previously called *C. novaehollandiae*. Subtly shaded ash-grey all over, darkest on face and around base of bill, palest on belly and beneath tail; robust bill and legs black.

DISTRIBUTION Resident from W Himalayas through S China to Taiwan, and Southeast Asia to Peninsular Malaysia (not Singapore, Sabah or Sarawak), Java and Bali. Other cuckooshrike species occur in lowland forest of Peninsular Malaysia, and lowland and montane forest of Sabah and Sarawak.
HABITS AND HABITAT Singly or in pairs in the canopy of montane forest at 1,000–2,050m, foraging for small, round fruits and arthropods among the foliage, and taking some insects in flight. Nest is a deep cup of twigs and lichen in the horizontal fork of a branch. Has an amusing habit of alternately lifting each folded wing.

# Black-winged Flycatcher-shrike ■ *Hemipus hirundinaceus* (Rembah Sayap Hitam) 15cm

DESCRIPTION Male has black face and crown, neck, back, wings and tail; pure white rump; pearly-grey to white underparts from chin to vent. Female is like male but duller and browner.
DISTRIBUTION From *c.* 7°N southwards through the Malay Peninsula, Sumatra, Borneo and intervening islands to Java and Bali. Resident in Peninsular Malaysia, Sabah and Sarawak; never reliably recorded from Singapore.
HABITS AND HABITAT Lowland forest, swamp forest and the landward side of mangroves, from sea-level up to *c.* 300m, rarely to 800m. Lives in the upper storey, or lower at the forest edge. Usually seen as a pair or alone, flycatching and gleaning the foliage for insects. Call is a short, fairly harsh trill.

## Pied Triller ■ *Lalage nigra* (Rembah Kening Putih) 17cm

DESCRIPTION Small birds, black above and white below, with a white brow and extensive white wing panel, and pale grey rump. Female has similar pattern but all markings are more subdued; also slightly scaly on breast.
DISTRIBUTION Resident in Andaman and Nicobar islands through Peninsular Thailand, Peninsular Malaysia and Singapore to Sumatra, Belitung, Borneo, the Philippines and Java.
HABITS AND HABITAT In coastal lowlands, from pandan scrub and the landward side of mangroves on the coast, to secondary woodland, parks and large gardens inland,

*Female*

including suburban fringes and isolated trees in e.g. buffalo grazing grounds. Likes to forage in the crowns of tall trees, but also comes down low, seeking insects among the foliage. Nest is a cup of dead fibres and casuarina needles, decorated with lichen, in the horizontal fork of a small branch. Harsh buzzing and complaining sounds, none very loud.

## Ashy Minivet ■ *Pericrocotus divaricatus* (Burung Matahir Kelabu) 19cm

DESCRIPTION Small black and white bird, longer and slimmer than Pied Triller (above), and with short, narrow white brow and long, narrow white wing bar (not a broad panel). Sexes are alike.
DISTRIBUTION Breeds from Siberia through N China to Korea and Japan; winters southwards to India and Southeast Asia, including Peninsular Malaysia, Singapore, Sabah, Sarawak and the Philippines.
HABITS AND HABITAT Non-breeding birds are characteristic of coastal forest, but also occur in the canopy of lowland and peat-swamp forest, and occasionally up into lower montane forest. Flocks of 20 or more trickle from tree to tree, follow-my-leader fashion, calling soft, tinkling notes and foraging for insects before moving on.

# Grey-chinned Minivet ■ *Pericrocotus solaris* (Burung Matahari Gunung) 18cm

DESCRIPTION Adult male black and red, chin only slightly greyer than head; single long red wing bar (male Scarlet Minivet, below, has a 2nd red wing spot). Female has similar pattern, but is dark grey and yellow, with dark grey forehead. Similar **Fiery Minivet** *P. igneus* is slightly smaller with a different flight call (an upward, slurred *swee-eet*).
DISTRIBUTION Resident from central Himalayan foothills through S China to Taiwan, and in highlands southwards to Peninsular Malaysia (not Singapore), Sumatra and Borneo, including Sabah and Sarawak.

*Male*    *Female*

HABITS AND HABITAT In the crowns of tall trees in lower and upper montane forest, 975–2,075m, into stunted elfin forest. Searches for insects in foliage while perched, and hovers at shoot tips; in pairs and, outside the Feb–Apr breeding season, in flocks of up to 30. Flight call is a twittering *sri-sisi*, repeatedly.

# Scarlet Minivet ■ *Pericrocotus flammeus* (Burung Matahari Besar) 19cm

DESCRIPTION Male black and red, very like Grey-chinned Minivet (above) but with a 2nd small, rounded patch of red on secondaries. Female grey and yellow, paler than female Grey-chinned, with 2nd (yellow) wing-patch and yellowish forehead.
DISTRIBUTION Resident from the W Himalayas and Indian sub-continent through S China and Southeast Asia to Peninsular Malaysia, Singapore, Sumatra, Belitung, Borneo, the Philippines, Java, Bali and Lombok.
HABITS AND HABITAT Like other minivets, it prefers the crowns of tall trees, in this case in lowland evergreen rainforest from the extreme lowlands to c. 1,000m (just into lower montane forest, where it overlaps with Grey-chinned), and in peat-swamp forest. All sorts of small invertebrates are taken; pairs after breeding (Jan–Jun) group into flocks.

# Bornean Whistler
■ *Pachycephala hypoxantha* (Murai Mas)
16cm

DESCRIPTION Sides of face and entire underparts from chin to vent bright yellow; lores dark, upperparts olive-green without wing bars. Females duller than males on face and underparts.
DISTRIBUTION Resident and endemic in montane Borneo, including Sabah, Sarawak and Kalimantan.
HABITS AND HABITAT Middle storey of tall montane forest, at 830–2,400m, but commonest at *c.* 1,300–1,800m. Will come to quiet forest edges, sometimes near streams and in montane valleys, flycatching and taking insects from twigs and foliage. Usually seen singly or in mixed-species flocks, with breeding known or suspected Nov–Mar.

# Mangrove Whistler
■ *Pachycephala cinerea* (Murai Bakau)
16cm

DESCRIPTION Entirely ashy brown, palest on the belly, without any wing bars or eye-ring. Eye and the robust bill black; legs are grey.
DISTRIBUTION Resident from E India to Indochina and Southeast Asia, as far as Peninsular Malaysia, Singapore, Sumatra, Borneo, Java and Lombok.
HABITS AND HABITAT Intrudes from mangroves into peat-swamp and freshwater-swamp forest, and recorded occasionally inland in forest over impoverished soils in Sabah and Sarawak. An insectivore, with breeding noted in Mar–Jun. Though plain, it is a common and easily located bird in mangroves because of its song: 4 or 5 staccato whistles on 1 pitch, followed by a couple of higher-pitched notes and a whistled whip-crack ending.

# Black-naped Oriole ■ *Oriolus chinensis* (Burung Kunyit Besar) 26cm

DESCRIPTION Males brilliant yellow over most of plumage – even black wings and tail have yellow bars and flashes. Black band runs from bill through eye, joining at back of

head. Bill rosy pink, feet grey. Females slightly duller, more olive above. Juveniles olive-green, streaky below, with only faint indications of future adult pattern. DISTRIBUTION Naturally resident from Mongolia discontinuously through E and Southeast Asia to the Lesser Sundas. Also migrant to much of Southeast Asia, including Peninsular Malaysia, Singapore and, rarely, Borneo; natural and human-assisted spread of residents has occurred through Singapore and Peninsular Malaysia since 1925. HABITS AND HABITAT Gardens, parkland, orchards and secondary woodland in lowlands are its preferred habitat, where it forages for all sorts of fruits and insects; also mangroves. There is much interaction between individuals, with loud, fluting calls *ku-eyou-ou*, instantly recognisable but tremendously variable, and chasing, following and displacement from food sources.

# Black-hooded Oriole ■ *Oriolus xanthornus* (Burung Kunyit Topeng Hitam) 23cm

DESCRIPTION Adult brilliant yellow with black head and upper breast, and black tail and wings with yellow markings. Young birds are duller, with less intense black on wings, tail, crown and ear coverts, and streaked with whitish on throat. DISTRIBUTION From the Himalayan foothills to Sri Lanka and SW China, through Indochina, discontinuously in Thailand, and to N Sumatra and NE Borneo. Resident in Peninsular Malaysia perhaps only in Langkawi, and in a very limited area in E Sabah. Scarce migrant in Peninsular Malaysia southwards to Fraser's Hill. HABITS AND HABITAT In mangroves, the landward side of mangroves and adjacent wooded landscapes; an apparently relict distribution is confined to the drier seasonal corners of the Sunda region. Records of migrants up to *c.* 1,300m. Little local information is available.

# Black-and-crimson Oriole
■ *Oriolus cruentus* (Murai Hitam Merah) 22cm

DESCRIPTION Entirely black, except male has a brilliant crimson breast-patch and crimson primary wing coverts; bill silvery grey, feet grey. In females, breast-patch may be faintly indicated by grey tone, but Borneo females are said to develop red patch as brilliant as that of males – this confusion now being resolved.
DISTRIBUTION Resident in the mountains of Peninsular Malaysia, Sumatra, Borneo and Java.
HABITS AND HABITAT Singly or in pairs in tall forest from 600m on hill slopes to 1,500m in montane forest in the Malay Peninsula, and to 2,300m in Borneo. Keeps largely to the canopy, but sometimes in the middle storey and edge along quiet forested roadsides or tracks, taking foliage-eating caterpillars as well as other insects and some fruits. A cat-like mewing and harsh nasal notes have been described throughout its range; a melodious call is mentioned only from Borneo.

# White-breasted Woodswallow ■ *Artamus leucorynchus*
(Tirjup Layang-layang Dada Putih) 17cm

DESCRIPTION Smooth grey above and white below and on rump; head and bib darker grey. Tail slightly forked. In flight, wings appear triangular and starling-shaped, but birds glide for great distances between bouts of flapping. Juveniles have buff fringes to wing feathers.
DISTRIBUTION Resident in the Andamans, Sumatra, Borneo, the Philippines, Java and Bali eastwards to Pacific, including Fiji and the New Hebrides. Abundant in Sabah and Sarawak; first colonised the W coast of Peninsular Malaysia in 1977, and still scarce and restricted there.
HABITS AND HABITAT The flight behaviour makes even distant birds easy to identify, and the bill can be heard snapping as they catch flying insects. Perched birds are sociable but boisterous to aggressive, performing mutual preening and huddling in social roosts.

# ▪ Ioras ▪

*Female*

## Common Iora ▪ *Aegithina tiphia*
(Burung Kunyit Kecil) 13cm

DESCRIPTION Green above with black tail and, in male, black on crown; yellow below, fading to white on under-tail coverts, which curl sideways and up over rump to make rump seem white; wings black with 2 white bars and pale fringes.
DISTRIBUTION Resident from foothills of the W Himalayas to India, Sri Lanka, S China, Peninsular Malaysia, Singapore, Sumatra and its outlying islands, Borneo, Java, Bali and the Philippines.
HABITS AND HABITAT In display flight from tree to tree, male sings and shows off his false white rump. Takes insects from foliage in mangroves and the landward side of mangroves, plantations, trees in parks and roadsides, and at the edge of lowland evergreen forest. Often forages high in the canopy, for example in tall *Albizia* trees, but also comes down to the understorey. Breeds Jan–Jun. Has a huge range of calls and song types.

## Green Iora ▪ *Aegithina viridissima*
(Burung Kunyit Hijau) 13cm

DESCRIPTION Deep sage-green, with a cream mark above and below eye, and wings blackish with 2 pale bars and pale fringes. The pale under-tail coverts curl up over rump to make it appear at least partly white. Female duller than male with lighter tail and paler head.
DISTRIBUTION Resident from *c.* 13°N in Thailand and 12°N in Myanmar through Peninsular Malaysia, Singapore, Sumatra, the Natunas and Borneo.
HABITS AND HABITAT An attractive, small bird of the canopy of lowland evergreen rainforest from sea-level to *c.* 820m, peat-swamp forest and tree plantations; also within mangroves in Sabah and Sarawak, and on some islands off Peninsular Malaysia. In pairs or small groups, seeking all kinds of soft-bodied insects among foliage, and also taking some small soft fruits such as figs; often a participant in mixed foraging flocks in the canopy.

# White-throated Fantail ■ *Rhipidura albicollis* (Murai Gila Gunung) 19cm

DESCRIPTION Blackish above and below, except for the white throat triangle, white brow and white tips to tail feathers. Juveniles duller and browner, with less well defined brow and throat mark.

DISTRIBUTION Resident from the W Himalayas to S China and Southeast Asia as far as Peninsular Malaysia (not Singapore), Sumatra and Borneo.
HABITS AND HABITAT Confined to lower montane forest, usually from *c.* 850m upwards into upper montane forest as high as 2,070m. Seeks insects in the middle and lower storeys, where it is one of the commoner birds and a common participant in mixed foraging flocks. Nest is a cup slung in the fork of a small lateral branch in the middle storey, hardly big enough to contain 2 growing young. Has a repeated tuneful song of 7 or 8 notes

# Pied Fantail ■ *Rhipidura javanica* (Murai Gila Biasa) 18cm

DESCRIPTION Black above and white below (throat, lower breast and belly) with a broad black breast-band; flaunted tail is black with white tips. Adults have a short, narrow white brow, this obscure in the browner juveniles.

DISTRIBUTION Resident from S Indochina through Peninsular Thailand and Peninsular Malaysia to Singapore, Sumatra, Belitung, Borneo, the Philippines, Java and Bali.
HABITS AND HABITAT Common in most tall mangroves, extending into peat-swamp and other wet forested habitats, forest edges, plantations, gardens and secondary growth on abandoned land. This and other fantails skip and flirt through the vegetation, swinging their body this way and that, and fanning the tail repeatedly, to disturb insects that are then snapped up.

## Ashy Drongo ■ *Dicrurus leucophaeus* (Cecawi Kelabu) 28cm

DESCRIPTION Several subspecies occur. Those resident on Borneo mountains are always pale grey with whitish sides to face and red eye; in Malay Peninsula and Singapore, similar-looking migrants occur, but also nearly black glossy residents. All have ruby eye and deeply forked, faintly upswept tail. Migrant **Black Drongo** *D. macrocercus* is elegant with a dark eye and more upswept tail tips; migrant **Crow-billed Drongo** *D. annectans* is stocky with a heavier bill and spangled plumage.

DISTRIBUTION Resident from Afghanistan eastwards through S China and Southeast Asia to Palawan, Borneo, Java, Bali and Lombok. Migrant to Southeast Asia, including Peninsular Malaysia and Singapore. HABITS AND HABITAT Predominantly in mangroves, and open ground with fairly closely spaced trees that provide sites for foraging on insects. Migrants tend to occur more in parkland and gardens, but in Sabah and Sarawak they live in the forest canopy at 500–2,200m in hill and montane forest. Mimics other bird calls, but less well than the Greater Racket-tailed Drongo (below).

*Malay Peninsula and Singapore (left); Borneo (right)*

# Greater Racket-tailed Drongo
■ *Dicrurus paradiseus* (Cecawi Kera) 32–57cm

DESCRIPTION Noisy, conspicuous, glossy black bird with red eye; the 2 outer-tail feathers project as wires, with 1 rounded and twisted racket on each side, 1 or both of which may be missing owing to moult or damage.
DISTRIBUTION Resident from the Indian sub-continent eastwards to Hainan and through Peninsular Malaysia, Singapore, Sumatra, Borneo, Java and Bali.
HABITS AND HABITAT The canopy and middle storey of lowland evergreen rainforest from the extreme lowlands to *c.* 850m, and in mangroves, tree plantations (rubber and oil palm), parkland with abundant trees, and secondary woodland. Typically seen in pairs, and flies out from a high perch to catch passing insects. Gives a wide range of calls, including good imitations of many other birds.

## Black-naped Monarch
■ *Hypothymis azurea* (Kelicap Ranting) 16cm

DESCRIPTION Bright blue forequarters, shading down to ashy-brown wings and tail, and whitish belly. Male has black throat bar, crown spot and dab over bill. Female has greyer breast and black dab over bill. DISTRIBUTION Resident from India through S China and Southeast Asia to Peninsular Malaysia (and formerly Singapore), Borneo, the Philippines and the Lesser Sundas. HABITS AND HABITAT In the lower and middle storeys of lowland evergreen rainforest, from the extreme lowlands to *c*. 915m in the Malay Peninsula, or 1,100–1,200m in Sabah and Sarawak. Usually alone or in pairs, or in mixed foraging flocks. One of the commoner birds glimpsed during journeys along forested rivers, aerial flycatching within the forest and occasionally bathing by diving into the water.

## Asian Paradise-flycatcher
■ *Terpsiphone paradisi* (Murai Ekor Gading) 22–40cm

DESCRIPTION Female has black cowl shading down to grey neck and breast, and whitish belly; rufous-chestnut wings and tail. Male either similar and with an extremely long tail (nearly triple its body length), or else body, wings and tail are pure white with fine black edgings to some feathers. Significance of the male colour types is unclear, but it may not be age related. DISTRIBUTION Resident through central Asia to Korea and southwards to Peninsular Malaysia, Singapore, Sumatra, Borneo, Java and the Lesser Sundas; non-breeding migrants also reach much of Southeast Asia. HABITS AND HABITAT The white-phase male is spectacular, and is not rare as a resident in the middle and upper storeys of tall lowland forest. Migrants also occur in tall secondary woodland. It is usually solitary and insectivorous, taking fairly big insects, and lives from the extreme lowlands to *c*. 880m in the Malay Peninsula, and up to 1,200m in Sabah and Sarawak.

## House Crow ■ *Corvus splendens*
(Gagak Rumah) 42cm

DESCRIPTION Typical crow, glossy black all over, except that the black face and forehead are defined rearwards by a paler zone of grey over the hind-face and neck, down to sides of breast. This colour develops with age, juveniles looking entirely black.
DISTRIBUTION Naturally resident from Afghanistan eastwards through Indian sub-continent and S China to SW Thailand. Widely introduced by man as far as S Africa, Europe, North America and Australia. Present in Peninsular Malaysia and Singapore since *c.* 1904, and a few birds in Kota Kinabalu, Sabah, since 1998.
HABITS AND HABITAT The abundant crow of Singapore and Peninsular Malaysian towns (at least, the larger towns on the W coast), forming noisy communal roosts and mainly dependent on man-made refuse.

## Short-tailed Green Magpie
■ *Cissa thalassina* (Gagak Hijau Ekor Pendek) 35cm

DESCRIPTION Brilliant lime-green bird the size of a small crow, with a black face mask, chestnut wings, and white tips to tail and innerwing feathers. The **Common Green Magpie** *C. chinensis*, found lower down in the mountains of Borneo and Peninsular Malaysia, is very similar but has a longer tail, black and white (not just white) tips to innerwing feathers, broader black subterminal bars on tail, and sometimes traces of yellow on crown. Both species have red bill, legs and skin around eye, but this is dark red lake in Short-tailed and brilliant red in Common Green.
DISTRIBUTION Resident in the mountains of Borneo and Java; now considered distinct from continental Indochinese **Green Magpie** *C. hypoleuca*.
HABITS AND HABITAT In Sabah and Sarawak this bird replaces the Common Green at *c.* 900m, and in lower and upper montane forest reaches 2,440m. Although the 2 species' altitudinal ranges overlap, they never seem to occur together. A range of whistles and buzzing notes may reveal a solitary bird or small group in dense vegetation of the middle or lower storey, seeking beetles, caterpillars, snails and other invertebrates.

# Bornean Treepie

■ *Dendrocitta cinerascens* (Burung Tontihak) 45–50cm

DESCRIPTION Ashy brown from forehead and over face to breast, shading more rufous towards belly; crown and back grey, wings black with basal white patch, and very long tail grey with black tip. Sexes are similar, juveniles only a little duller.
DISTRIBUTION Resident in the mountains and hill slopes of Borneo. Now considered distinct from the closely related **Sumatran Treepie** (*D. occipitalis*).
HABITS AND HABITAT In the canopy and middle storey of montane forest, to a maximum 2,900m; usually not below 800m, but occasional records on hill slopes down to 100m. Attractive bell-like calls are interspersed with buzzes, made when perched and in flight, and answered between individuals, pairs and, occasionally, small flocks. Frugivore and insectivore, taking most food from the canopy but even coming to the ground in forest clearings. Breeding has been reported in Jan–Mar.

# Black Magpie ■ *Platysmurus leucopterus* (Burung Kambing) 40cm

DESCRIPTION Heavy, active black bird, tail almost as long as head and body, with a slight crest and red iris. In Peninsular Malaysian populations a white wing bar extends from greater coverts down secondaries, but wings of birds in Sabah and Sarawak (shown) are entirely black.
DISTRIBUTION Resident from *c.* 14°N in Myanmar and Peninsular Thailand through Peninsular Malaysia, Singapore, Bintan, Sumatra, Bangka and Borneo, including Sabah and Sarawak.
HABITS AND HABITAT Typically in the upper and middle storeys of lowland evergreen rainforest, occasionally peat-swamp forest, from the extreme lowlands to *c.* 300m, and in scraps of gallery forest and adjacent tree plantations. Usual food includes insects and small vertebrates, but some fruit too. Bell-like hoots or a sheep-like bleat, separately or interspersed, are made between individuals, which forage in pairs or small social groups.

## Crested Jay ▪ *Platylophus galericulatus* (Burung Menjerit) 32cm

DESCRIPTION Blackish or, in the Borneo race photographed, chocolate-brown with a fine vertical or forward-tilting crest; white marks around eye and white patch on side of neck.

DISTRIBUTION Resident from *c.* 13°N in Peninsular Thailand through Peninsular Malaysia (but not Singapore) to Sumatra, Borneo and Java.

HABITS AND HABITAT Not easy to see, but can be curious, raising a shrike-like rattling chatter when it sees people. Keeps to the middle and lower storeys of lowland evergreen rainforest, rarely in montane forest to 1,200m in Peninsular Malaysia and a record 1,525m in Sarawak. Usually solitary or in pairs, seeking invertebrates such as beetles, grasshoppers, wasps and cicadas. Nest is a sturdy cup made of twigs on a lower branch, and has only been described recently, from a single observation in Java.

## Tiger Shrike ▪ *Lanius tigrinus* (Tirjup Harimau) 18cm

DESCRIPTION Back, wings and tail rich brown; back and lesser wing coverts always finely barred black. Strong contrast between brown back and grey cap; black mask and relatively thick bill. Females may show some barring on flanks.

DISTRIBUTION Resident in far E Russia, Japan and Korea through central China; non-breeding migrant to S China and Southeast Asia as far as Java and Bali.

HABITS AND HABITAT In forest edges, bamboo groves, dense roadside vegetation and abandoned cultivation, extending into heavily logged forest. Noted singly throughout Peninsular Malaysia, Singapore, Sabah and Sarawak to *c.* 850m, but most Borneo records are only from the N. Beetles and grasshoppers are the chief prey.

## Brown Shrike ■ *Lanius cristatus* (Tirjup Padang) 19cm

DESCRIPTION Several subspecies occur, these differing in tone but always with a plain back, never finely barred. Black mask, pale supercilium and either brown or grey crown; back and tail brown, undersides off-white; bill relatively small. Sexes are alike.
DISTRIBUTION Resident through vast areas of temperate E Asia, from 70°E to Sakhalin

and southwards through China; migrates to China, India and Southeast Asia as far as Sumatra, Borneo, the Philippines, Java and the Lesser Sundas.
HABITS AND HABITAT In our non-breeding range, arriving birds set up territories in cultivation, gardens, and open ground with bushes, scattered trees and grassland, advertising their presence with a chattering call around their Sep arrival and Mar departure. They occur singly, on fences, trees and bush-tops, descending to catch invertebrates (mostly beetles and grasshoppers) on the ground, but occasionally lizards and small birds.

## Long-tailed Shrike ■ *Lanius schach* (Tirjup Ekor Panjang) 26cm

DESCRIPTION Black mask extending over forehead; underparts white with peach-buff flanks; crown and back grey, merging to buff on scapulars. Long tail and blackish wings showing strong contrast with body; white wing-spot, most visible in flight.
DISTRIBUTION Resident from Kyrgyzstan through central Asia and the Indian sub-continent to all but N China, and patchily through Southeast Asia to Java, Bali, the Lesser Sundas and New Guinea. N populations migrate, a few as far as Borneo.
HABITS AND HABITAT Spread of cultivation suggests possible arrival of this species in Peninsular Malaysia in the 2nd half of the 19th century. Still found only W of the Main Range but commonly in Singapore; in Sabah and Sarawak perhaps just a scarce migrant. In open rice fields and grassland with shrubs, taking mainly insects.

# Brown-throated Sunbird

■ *Anthreptes malacensis* (Kelicap Mayang Kelapa) 13cm

DESCRIPTION Male has brilliant yellow breast and belly; throat glossy purplish brown; crown purple, shading to blue wings and tail; sides of face and wings olive-green. Female olive-green, fairly bright yellow on breast and belly, and with yellow throat contrasting with sides of face. DISTRIBUTION Resident from Myanmar and central Thailand through Indochina, Peninsular Malaysia, Singapore, Sumatra, Borneo and the Philippines to Sulawesi, Java, the Lesser Sundas and most intervening small island groups. HABITS AND HABITAT 1 of the 2 most common sunbirds. Seen singly or in pairs in parks and gardens, coconut and other tree plantations, secondary woodland and mangroves. Feeds on much nectar (e.g. from coconut palms, and hibiscus and tubular flowers), small colourful fruits, and invertebrates such as spiders. Usually in the lowlands but recorded up to 900m, with breeding mostly Jan–Aug.

# Red-throated Sunbird ■ *Anthreptes rhodolaema* (Kelicap Pinang) 13cm

DESCRIPTION Care is needed to distinguish it from Brown-throated Sunbird (above). Male has maroon-red sides of face and upperwing coverts, with only a small blue carpal

wing-patch; crown and upperparts iridescent greenish. Female like female Brown-throated but with duller greenish sides to breast. DISTRIBUTION Patchily from *c.* 12°N in the Malay Peninsula, southwards through Sumatra and Borneo. Resident in Peninsular Malaysia, Sabah and Sarawak; presumed former resident in Singapore, now locally extinct. HABITS AND HABITAT The upper storey of tall lowland forest, including lightly disturbed forest and peat-swamp forest, up to *c.* 400m or, rarely, 900m. Insects, nectar and fruit are taken. It may be less territorial, or at least less aggressive, than Brown-throated.

# Olive-backed Sunbird

■ *Cinnyris jugularis* (Kelicap Pantai)
12cm

DESCRIPTION Olive-green from crown to rump, with lower breast and belly bright, deep yellow. In male, forehead, throat and upper breast are iridescent blue-black; female is paler and duller overall with whitish chin, and lacks any blue-black markings.
DISTRIBUTION Resident from S China through most of Southeast Asia to New Guinea, the Solomon Islands and N Australia.
HABITS AND HABITAT Locally the most common and conspicuous sunbird throughout the region, in parks and gardens, scrub, mangroves and plantations. Takes nectar from a wide range of flower species and shapes, including mangrove trees as well as garden flowers, plus many invertebrates, especially spiders. Tiny but very active, often in pairs, with territorial males pursuing each other from treetop to treetop.

# Crimson Sunbird

■ *Aethopyga siparaja* (Kelicap Sepah Raja) 11–13.5cm

DESCRIPTION Deep scarlet red with a yellow rump and dark purple tail. Lower breast and belly grey, and sides of face dark with violet moustache stripe; iridescent green forehead and forecrown (often looking black). Wings, including wing coverts, black. Female olive-grey, darker olive on breast than female Temminck's Sunbird (p. 100) and without any rufous in tail.
DISTRIBUTION Resident from the central Himalayan foothills through S China and throughout all Southeast Asia to the Philippines and Sulawesi.
HABITS AND HABITAT Nectar and small invertebrates are the main foods, *Heliconia* flowers being favourites. Similar to, and the open-edge equivalent of, Temminck's Sunbird in the lowlands, occurring in forest edges, gardens, mangroves and peat-swamp forest. There are both habitat and altitudinal trade-offs between Temminck's and Crimson in Borneo, and between these and Black-throated Sunbird (p. 100) in the Malay Peninsula.

## Temminck's Sunbird ■ *Aethopyga temminckii* (Kelicap Merah) 10–12.5cm

DESCRIPTION Brilliant scarlet overall with yellow rump and scarlet tail. Lower breast and belly off-white; on face, 2 violet moustache stripes and 2 crown stripes join over nape. Black wings with red coverts. Female olive-grey with rufous sides to base of tail, and faintly rufous fringes to wing feathers; rump plain.
DISTRIBUTION Resident from *c.* 8°30'N in Peninsular Thailand and Malaysia (but not Singapore) through to Sumatra and Borneo.
HABITS AND HABITAT The middle and lower storeys of lowland evergreen rainforest, from the extreme lowlands to 300m, and exceptionally to 1,200m in the Malay Peninsula

and 1,650m in Sarawak and Sabah. Usually solitary or in pairs, taking nectar from a variety of forest epiphytes, rhododendrons and introduced flowers, plus various small insects. Formerly called the Scarlet Sunbird, but that name is now reserved for *A. mystacalis* in Java.

LEFT: *Male.* ABOVE: *Female*

## Black-throated Sunbird ■ *Aethopyga saturata* (Kelicap Gunung)
Male 15cm; female 11cm

DESCRIPTION Male overall very dark with a yellow rump and long central tail feathers; head iridescent blue-black, breast and back maroon, belly grey. Female olive-grey with a

pale yellow rump and grey throat.
DISTRIBUTION Resident from the central Himalayas through S China and discontinuously in Southeast Asian highlands to Peninsular Malaysia.
HABITS AND HABITAT Found at 820–2,000m, from the canopy to the lower storey and edges of lower and upper montane forest, including stunted forest on ridgetops. Seen singly or in pairs, often in mixed foraging flocks, taking tiny invertebrates, and nectar from the tubular flowers of forest epiphytes as well as from garden flowers and weeds. Breeding is inferred over a wide range of months.

# Streaked Spiderhunter ■ *Arachnothera*
*magna* (Kelicap Jantung Gunung) 18cm

DESCRIPTION Olive-green above from forehead to
tail, and buffy white below from chin to vent, entire
plumage finely streaked blackish. Bright orange-yellow
feet often clearly visible.
DISTRIBUTION Resident from central Himalayan
foothills through S China and the highlands of
Southeast Asia to Peninsular Malaysia.
HABITS AND HABITAT A characteristic bird of lower
and upper montane forest in the Malay Peninsula at
c. 800–1,800m, in the middle and upper storeys, and
in roadside vegetation at the hill stations. Takes nectar
from banana flowers at the forest edge, and insects
from the tangles of epiphytes and lichen on branches.
Nesting is remarkably under-recorded considering the
species is fairly common. Quick, single alarm notes
and a 2-note flight call can often be heard.

# Little Spiderhunter ■ *Arachnothera longirostra* (Kelicap Jantung Kecil) 16cm

DESCRIPTION Face and upper breast grey, shading to yellow belly; narrow, dark moustache
borders pale sides of face; crown is scaly dark grey, leading to olive wings and tail. Orange
tuft may be revealed at bend of
wing.
DISTRIBUTION Resident in the
Himalayas and India, through
S China and Southeast Asia to
Peninsular Malaysia, Singapore,
Sumatra, Borneo, Java, and central
and S Philippines.
HABITS AND HABITAT Among
the commonest birds of the
understorey in logged and unlogged
lowland evergreen rainforest,
from the extreme lowlands into
montane forest at 1,680m. Typically
associated with wild bananas,
whose flowers are a major source
of nectar; also eats invertebrates.
Lively and often noisy, with an
endlessly repeated *chip* when
perched, or singly when in flight.

# Yellow-eared Spiderhunter

■ *Arachnothera chrysogenys* (Kelicap Jantung Telinga Kuning) 18cm

DESCRIPTION Dark olive-green spiderhunter, with breast and belly faintly streaked, reaching to yellow thighs; bright yellow but often incomplete eye-ring, which typically touches large yellow cheek-patch. Juveniles are duller, especially eye-ring and cheek-patch. Very similar **Spectacled Spiderhunter** A. *flavigaster* is slightly larger and has a complete yellow eye-ring separated from yellow on ears.

DISTRIBUTION Resident from *c.* 13°N in Thailand through Peninsular Malaysia and Singapore to Sumatra, Riau, Borneo and Java.

HABITS AND HABITAT In lowland evergreen rainforest, from sea-level upwards, and at least visiting montane forest to a maximum record of 2,010m. Also in logged forest and tree plantations, and visits roadside trees such as *Erythrina*. Flowers of epiphytes and canopy trees provide most of its food. Call is a single loud *chak!*

# Whitehead's Spiderhunter

■ *Arachnothera juliae* (Kelicap Jantung Tasam) 18cm

DESCRIPTION Blackish brown all over, except that all feathers of head and body have white streaks, these becoming larger and more conspicuous on breast and flanks; wings and tail plain blackish, and rump and under-tail coverts brilliant yellow.

DISTRIBUTION Endemic to the mountains of Borneo, where it occurs in limited parts of Sabah, E Sarawak and East Kalimantan.

HABITS AND HABITAT Lower and upper montane forest at *c.* 950–2,100m, where it is found singly or in pairs in the canopy of primary and tall secondary forest. The diet, behaviour and nesting are hardly described. Not very conspicuous, but has a wide range of calls, including a 2-note buzzing *wee-chit*, and an array of chattering and trilling sounds.

# Yellow-breasted Flowerpecker
■ *Dicaeum maculatus* (Sepah Puteri Raja) 9cm

DESCRIPTION Dark olive-green above. White moustache and white chin separated by dark malar stripe; rest of underparts bright yellow with strong olive-green streaks, leaving a central band of unmarked yellow down breast. Inconspicuous crown spot is fiery orange in male, dull ochre in female. DISTRIBUTION Resident from *c.* 13°N in Peninsular Thailand through Malaysia to Singapore (where it is a past resident and possible dispersant), Sumatra, Bunguran and Borneo. HABITS AND HABITAT Common in the middle and lower storeys of lowland evergreen rainforest from the extreme lowlands to *c.* 900m, and sparsely in lower montane forest to 1,250m in Sabah and Sarawak, and up to 1,500m in Peninsular Malaysia. An arboreal foliage-gleaning insectivore and partial frugivore, usually seen alone.

# Orange-bellied Flowerpecker ■ *Dicaeum trigonostigma*
(Sepah Puteri Dada Biru) 8cm

DESCRIPTION Male with slaty-blue head, upper breast, back, wings and tail; grey throat; brilliant orange from lower breast to vent, and orange-yellow lower back and rump. Female olive-grey, unstreaked, with creamy-yellow rump and centre to belly. DISTRIBUTION Resident from Bangladesh through Peninsular Thailand and Malaysia to Singapore, Sumatra, Borneo, the Philippines, Java and Bali. HABITS AND HABITAT Edges of lowland evergreen rainforest from sea-level upwards into montane habitats, with a typical maximum of 1,200m (exceptionally 1,650m in Sarawak). Also enters tall plantations, well-wooded parkland, logged forest and, occasionally, mangroves and peat-swamp forest. Feeds on varied small fruits, including mistletoes, plus insects and nectar. Nest is a hanging pouch in the understorey, with records over a wide scatter of months.

## Black-sided Flowerpecker ▪ *Dicaeum monticolum* (Sepah Puteri Kerongkong Merah) 8cm

DESCRIPTION Male has a dark grey head, shading to dark blue on wings and tail, more buff on belly; throat and upper breast with a brilliant carmine patch. Female similar, olive-grey with less blue on wings and lacking red patch.

DISTRIBUTION Resident and endemic in mountains of Borneo (Sabah, the E part of Sarawak, and Kalimantan), though some books include this within the species **Grey-sided Flowerpecker** *D. celebicum* of Sulawesi.

HABITS AND HABITAT Recorded down to 500m, but typically in the middle and upper storeys of montane forest at *c.* 1,000–2,100m. Single birds or occasionally pairs seek food among the lichens and epiphytes on branches and trunks, taking small, soft fruits and various insects. Nest is a hanging pouch of plant fibres and moss, decorated outside with lichens, and has been found Nov–Feb.

## Scarlet-backed Flowerpecker ▪ *Dicaeum cruentatum* (Sepah Puteri Merah) 8cm

DESCRIPTION Male has a broad scarlet line all the way from forehead over crown and down back to rump; white band extends from throat down centre of breast to vent; black sides of face, wings and tail; grey flanks. Female olive-grey, with a broader creamy band from throat to vent, and red rump.

DISTRIBUTION Resident from the E Himalayas through S China and Southeast Asia to Peninsular Malaysia, Singapore, Sumatra, Riau and Borneo.

HABITS AND HABITAT One of the most often seen flowerpeckers, in tall secondary growth, orchards, tree plantations and parkland, usually singly; also along the edges of lowland evergreen and peat-swamp forests to a maximum 870m. Eats soft fruits (nibbled to pieces if too big to swallow), mistletoes and soft-bodied invertebrates. Breeding noted from Nov–Aug.

*Male*

*Female*

# Greater Green Leafbird ■ *Chloropsis sonnerati* (Burung Daun Besar) 21cm

DESCRIPTION Male bright grass-green all over, with a black throat-patch reaching eye, where eyelid forms entirely black surround; superimposed blue moustache. Female has yellow throat, light blue moustache, and yellow ring around eye. Juvenile has yellow throat and separate yellow moustache.
DISTRIBUTION Resident from *c.* 15°N in Myanmar through Peninsular Thailand and Malaysia to Singapore, Sumatra, the Natunas, Borneo and Java.
HABITS AND HABITAT In lowland evergreen rainforest, peat-swamp

*Male*

*Female*

forest and forest edges, spilling out to adjacent parkland. Feeds on soft fruits of secondary growth at the forest edge, figs and, possibly, also nectar from flowers. Usually solitary or in pairs, sometimes joining mixed foraging flocks seeking insects. Song loud and quite attractive, imitating other species.

# Lesser Green Leafbird

■ *Chloropsis cyanopogon* (Burung Daun Kecil) 18cm

DESCRIPTION Tough to distinguish. Male's throat-patch tends to be outlined faintly yellow, its bill is proportionately smaller than that of Greater Green Leafbird (above), and black does not completely surround eye. Female has a green throat, blue moustache and no blue on wing.
DISTRIBUTION Resident from nearly 12°N in Myanmar through Peninsular Thailand and Malaysia to Singapore, Sumatra and Borneo.
HABITS AND HABITAT Very like that of Greater Green Leafbird, being found in the crowns of trees in lowland evergreen rainforest, secondary forest and forest edges. Also about as common as that species, ranging from the extreme lowlands just into montane forest at *c.* 1,100m. Takes various fruits and figs, possibly nectar, and invertebrates while in mixed foraging flocks. Little is known of its nesting. Has an attractive warbling song.

## Blue-winged Leafbird ■ *Chloropsis cochinchinensis*
(Burung Daun Sayap Biru) 18cm

DESCRIPTION Bright grass-green, the male with a black throat-patch, yellow flush over most of head, blue flash on carpel and down edge of wing, and bluish tail. Female has a green throat and blue moustache like female Lesser Green Leafbird (p. 105), but distinct blue flash and edge of wing.

*Male*          *Female*

DISTRIBUTION Resident from NE India to S China and Southeast Asia, as far as Peninsular Malaysia, Singapore (at least some introduced), Sumatra, the Natunas, Borneo and Java.
HABITS AND HABITAT Edges of lowland evergreen rainforest, and sometimes also the canopy, as well as peat-swamp forest and secondary woodland, from extreme lowlands to c. 1,250m. In Borneo mountains and at all elevations in Sabah, it is replaced by the Bornean Leafbird C. *kinabaluensis*, which in both sexes closely resembles male Blue-winged. A very wide range of fruits and invertebrates is eaten. There is little information on its breeding or song.

## Orange-bellied Leafbird ■ *Chloropsis hardwickii* (Burung Daun Bukit) 19cm

DESCRIPTION Bright sage-green above and subtle orange below, with black sides to face and throat, and a long purplish-black panel along wing. Female grass-green with an orange flush on lower belly and under-tail coverts; limited blue on wing coverts and inner secondaries.

DISTRIBUTION Resident from W Himalayan foothills through S China to Hainan, and in Southeast Asia to the mountains of Peninsular Malaysia.
HABITS AND HABITAT Found in the region only in montane forest at c. 900–1,900m, in the canopy and mid-levels of upper and lower montane forest and along forested roadsides; occasionally down to 820m in hill forest. Surprisingly, considering that the hill stations are so well visited by birdwatchers, its nesting behaviour is unknown. The male and female both sing a wide range of beautiful notes, including imitations of other species.

*Male*          *Female*

## Asian Fairy-bluebird ▪ *Irena puella* (Murai Gajah) 25cm

DESCRIPTION In male, most of face, throat and underparts are black; largely black wings; crown, back, innerwing coverts, rump, vent and tail coverts brilliant, glossy sky-blue. Female a deep, dark powder-blue all over. Both sexes have reddish eyes and are quite bulky. DISTRIBUTION Resident from the central Himalayas through much of India and Sri Lanka, S China and Southeast Asia to Peninsular Malaysia, Singapore, Sumatra, Borneo, Java and Palawan. HABITS AND HABITAT In the canopy and middle storey of lowland evergreen rainforest, peat-swamp forest and secondary woodland, less often at high altitudes into lower and even stunted upper montane forest to 1,900m. Takes many species of fruits and invertebrates, often snatching food while in flight, and seen singly or in pairs except at

major fig and fruit trees, where numbers can gather. Nesting c. Feb–Jun. Its song is much less varied and prolonged than leafbird songs.

LEFT: *Female*. ABOVE: *Male*

## Baya Weaver ▪ *Ploceus philippinus* (Tempua) 15cm

DESCRIPTION Chequered brown and blackish back and wings, plain rump and russet-brown breast. In male, entire cap is deep yellow; ear coverts and throat blackish. Female has faintly striped brown crown, and buffy-brown throat, face and eyebrow. DISTRIBUTION Resident from India and Sri Lanka to S China and parts of Southeast Asia as far as Peninsular Malaysia, Singapore, Sumatra, Java and Bali. HABITS AND HABITAT Among tall coconut palms, grassland and the edges of secondary woodland or oil-palm estates, where tall grass is adjacent to suitable nesting trees. These trees are typically acacias, or sometimes coconut palms or bamboo, with several to many males building 1 to several nests each (a flask of drying grass, cunningly woven, suspended from a slender branch), some of which will be chosen by females for laying. In decline, through poaching of nests for sale and loss of habitat.

## Java Sparrow ▪ *Padda oryzivora* (Ciak Jawa) 16cm

DESCRIPTION Black crown, throat, primaries and tail; large, rounded white patch on ear coverts. Breast, back and wings light grey, sharply delineated from pink lower breast and

belly. Bill and eye-ring rose-red. DISTRIBUTION Naturally resident only in Java and Bali, but widely introduced by man in tropical Asia and the Americas. Feral in scattered localities in Peninsular Malaysia, Singapore, Sabah and Sarawak. HABITS AND HABITAT Introduced populations tend to boom for a few years after their arrival, then gradually decline, sometimes persisting for decades in very low numbers. They are able to survive only where low-intensity agriculture or careless handling of grain provides food, and old or crannied buildings provide nest sites. These conditions are now rare throughout the region, and survival is supplemented by the release of birds at religious festivals.

## Dusky Munia ▪ *Lonchura fuscans* (Pipit Hitam) 10cm

DESCRIPTION Small bird, dark chocolate-brown all over; blue-grey feet; dark upper and silvery-grey lower mandibles.
DISTRIBUTION Resident and endemic to Borneo, including 1 Philippine island (Cagayan

de Sulu) that lies within Borneo coastal waters. HABITS AND HABITAT Singly, in pairs or small groups, never large flocks, from the coast to 1,600m, in old cultivation and forest edges. Requires more heavily vegetated habitats than other munias, and is less of a rice-eater, instead taking various grass seeds and fragments from the ground, including some apparently from animal dung. Nests of grass are built in dense vegetation or in crannies in earth banks.

# Scaly-breasted Munia

■ *Lonchura punctulata* (Pipit Pinang) 10cm

DESCRIPTION Head, throat, back and wings chestnut, darkest around face; breast and belly white, strongly scalloped with black, the scallops extending to the rump. Juveniles sandy brown all over like most munias, best identified by association with adults.

DISTRIBUTION Resident from the Himalayas through S China and Southeast Asia as far as the Lesser Sundas; introduced to various tropical areas. In Peninsular Malaysia, Singapore and, since 1993, Sabah, where it is spreading.

HABITS AND HABITAT Associated with human cultivation, especially paddy fields, grassland, old mining land and suburban areas. Many types of grass seed are eaten, as well as ripening rice, and large flocks can build up. Nest is a grassy oval in dense vegetation; nesting has been recorded nearly throughout the year, with fewest records in the rainy season.

# Chestnut Munia ■ *Lonchura atricapilla* (Pipit Rawa) 11cm

DESCRIPTION Entire head and throat black; entire body, wings and tail bright rufous chestnut. Bill grey, flushing bright turquoise during breeding.

DISTRIBUTION Resident from India through S China to Taiwan, and throughout Southeast Asia to the Philippines, Java, Bali and the Malukus.

HABITS AND HABITAT Probably now the commonest munia, found in damp grassland, tall, scrubby grass over abandoned land, paddy fields and suburban areas, to a maximum 1,650m. Large flocks can occur in ripe rice, but pairs split off to breed at any time of year, the nest being a ball of grass among shrubby plants, or in tall grass, or even in the crown of a palm tree. At a resort hotel in Kota Kinabalu, Sabah, in 2006, every bougainvillea on the balcony of every room at each storey had 2 or 3 nests of this and the Dusky Munia (p. 108) interspersed, totalling hundreds of current or past nests.

# Eurasian Tree-sparrow
■ *Passer montanus* (Ciak Rumah) 14cm

DESCRIPTION Chestnut cap and small black bib, separated by grey-white cheeks with a black spot on ear coverts. Back and wing coverts streaky brown with black streaks, and black and white wing bar; underside buffy grey. Sexes are alike, juveniles similar but duller

DISTRIBUTION Occurs discontinuously from Europe through central Asia to Japan, southwards to the Philippines and Indonesia, and throughout the region.

HABITS AND HABITAT Commonly associated with towns and villages, factories and ports, often in large flocks, feeding on short grass and pavements, and in roadside bushes; also in rural habitats to a maximum of 1,400m within the region. After their initial colonisation, populations tend to decline again if the habitat is too well managed, especially where nesting opportunities are lost in crevices and roofs of old buildings. Eats grass seeds, spilt food and any tiny fragments picked from the ground, feeding both by day and night in brightly lit places.

# Paddyfield Pipit ■ *Anthus rufulus* (Ciak Padang) 16cm

DESCRIPTION Fairly slim, upright pipit present year-round in the region, with a well-spotted breast. Very similar **Richard's Pipit** *A. richardi* is bigger and less heavily spotted,

typically has a single-note *shreep* flight call, and is present only as a winter visitor.

DISTRIBUTION India and S China through Indo-Malaya to Peninsular Malaysia, Singapore, Sumatra, Borneo, Java, the Philippines and Lesser Sundas.

HABITS AND HABITAT On short grass such as airfields and golf courses, often with wagtails, foraging for small insects, flies, grasshoppers and spiders. Runs forward and draws itself upright on halting, often on a tussock or soil clod. Nests are well hidden among grass. Typically gives a 3-note *tchep tchep tchep* flight call when disturbed.

# Grey Wagtail
■ *Motacilla cinerea* (Kedidi Batu) 19cm

DESCRIPTION Slim, with long tail that bobs up and down; grey back, darker grey crown and sides of face, white brow; pale yellowish beneath, leading to yellow vent; white sides of tail. In flight, shows a white wing bar and yellow rump.

DISTRIBUTION From N Africa through Europe and Asia to Japan, migrating southwards to Africa, India and Southeast Asia as far as N Australia. Migrant in Peninsular Malaysia, Singapore, Sabah and Sarawak.

HABITS AND HABITAT Typically seen singly on the ground, on unfrequented roads, logging tracks and, especially, near streams, at any altitude from sea-level to mountains. Runs after small insects and other invertebrates on the surface of rocks, at the water's edge or even on wet tarmac, with tail wagging intermittently. A sharp 2-syllable call, *chit-chit*, is given when taking flight, unlike Eastern Yellow Wagtail (below), which usually utters a single syllable.

# Eastern Yellow Wagtail ■ *Motacilla tschutschensis* (Kedidi Kuning) 18cm

DESCRIPTION Adults at all seasons show olive-green back and rump, yellow underparts, and dark crown and face mask, but vary greatly in tone (especially head, and extent and colour of supercilium). Female duller than male, and non-breeding birds duller than breeding. Juvenile can be virtually grey and white, always with face mask meeting nape, not defined by pale rim behind.

DISTRIBUTION Resident virtually throughout N Africa, Europe and Asia; migrates to all Africa, and Southeast Asia as far as New Guinea and Australia. Migrant in Peninsular Malaysia, Singapore and Borneo.

HABITS AND HABITAT Often seen on short grass, including coastal grassland, lawns and golf courses; forms communal roosts in wet reedbeds and at sewage farms, and by day forages singly or in small, loose groups spaced out over habitat. The 1st migrants arrive in Sep; last departures in early May. Typically makes single-note calls when taking flight.

# Velvet-fronted Nuthatch
▪ *Sitta frontalis* (Burung Patuk Dahi Hitam) 13cm

DESCRIPTION Bright purplish blue above and pearly grey below, with bright red bill and feet. Black velvety stubble on forehead at base of bill, continuing backwards through eye to nape in male only; red eye-ring.
DISTRIBUTION Resident from E Himalayan foothills, discontinuously through parts of India and Sri Lanka, to S China and Southeast Asia as far as Peninsular Malaysia, Singapore, Sumatra, Borneo, Palawan and Java.
HABITS AND HABITAT Seen in pairs or, often, small groups, including within mixed foraging flocks. Favours the upper storey of tall evergreen rainforest, from the extreme lowlands to 1,150m in lower montane forest in the Malay Peninsula, and even to 2,200m on Mount Kinabalu, Borneo (where the Blue Nuthatch, below, is absent). Forages on the larger boughs. Nesting is reported in Feb–Jun.

# Blue Nuthatch ▪ *Sitta azurea*
(Burung Patuk Gunung) 13cm

DESCRIPTION White chin, throat and upper breast are sharply demarcated from rest of blackish head and belly; back, wings and tail increasingly blue towards rear, with bright blue edges to wing feathers. White iris and eye-ring.
DISTRIBUTION Resident in the mountains of the far S of Peninsular Thailand, Peninsular Malaysia, Sumatra and Java.
HABITS AND HABITAT Found in the middle and upper storeys of lower and upper montane forest at *c.* 900–1,960m, presumably displacing the Velvet-fronted Nuthatch (above) from such altitudes in the Malay Peninsula. In pairs or small parties, foraging on trunks and boughs for a variety of invertebrates. Very little is recorded about its breeding.

## Javan Myna ■ *Acridotheres javanicus* (Tiong Jawa) 25cm

DESCRIPTION Ashy grey, the head darker, with yellow bill and cream iris but no bare skin around eye. White vent, wing-patch and tips to tail. DISTRIBUTION Formerly endemic to Java and Bali, but spread or deliberately introduced to Sumatra, Singapore and Peninsular Malaysia, scattered points in Sarawak, Sabah and Kalimantan, and the Lesser Sundas. HABITS AND HABITAT The bulk of Peninsular Malaysia was colonised from the 1970s onwards, by northward spread through agricultural land and along highways from Singapore. Now it is the commonest myna in the S half of the Malay Peninsula, but still struggling for footholds around Kuching and Sandakan. Forages in pairs or in gatherings of pairs, and roosts communally.

## Common Myna

■ *Acridotheres tristis* (Tiong Rumah) 25cm

DESCRIPTION Smooth, plummy cinnamon-brown, the head nearly black, with yellow bill and bare yellow skin around dark eye. White vent, large white wing-patch, and white tips to tail. In moult, some birds have an entirely bare, scrawny yellow head. DISTRIBUTION Resident from the Middle East through India and S China to Southeast Asia. Invaded Peninsular Malaysia and Singapore over the past century, then Sumatra, and recently in small numbers in Sarawak. HABITS AND HABITAT At one time the commonest myna in Peninsular Malaysia and Singapore. Associated with human agriculture and settlements, foraging on the ground (especially on short turf) for grubs; also takes fruits and rubbish from dumps. Forms communal roosts, often with crows and other starlings and mynas; numbers have been severely reduced by invasion of Javan Myna (above).

# Asian Glossy Starling

■ *Aplonis panayensis* (Perling Mata Merah) 20cm

DESCRIPTION Adults black with an oily green gloss all over, and bright red eye. Juveniles mostly blackish olive above, and heavily streaked white and blackish below, the whole plumage streaky overall and the iris dark.
DISTRIBUTION Resident from the Bay of Bengal through Myanmar and Thailand to Peninsular Malaysia and Singapore, Sumatra, Borneo, Java, Bali, the Philippines and N Sulawesi.
HABITS AND HABITAT From mangroves and coasts, it has spread inland with human intrusion into all habitats except dryland forest, and is especially abundant in towns and villages, parkland and secondary woodland. It feeds on fruits such as overripe papayas and palm fruits, insects and nectar of the African Tulip Tree *Spathodea campanulata* (a common invasive species in the region), and forms large communal roosts, often with mynas and crows.

# Common Hill-myna

■ *Gracula religiosa* (Tiong Besar) 29cm

DESCRIPTION Entirely glossy blue-black, relieved by a small white patch at base of primaries; yellow legs; rosy-yellow bill; bare yellow skin lappets on head, 1 hanging below and behind eye, another from behind eye and joining around nape. In some subspecies the lower and hind lappets join, and the situation is further confused by the release of imported cagebirds.
DISTRIBUTION Resident from the central Himalayan foothills through S China and Southeast Asia to Peninsular Malaysia, Singapore, Sumatra, Borneo, Java, Bali to the Lesser Sundas.
HABITS AND HABITAT In the canopy of evergreen rainforest in the extreme lowlands, extending up hill slopes only on some of the offshore islands. Even parkland is acceptable habitat if tall trees are sufficiently dense and poaching is controlled. Tremendous whistles and gurgles are made by interacting pairs, especially at fruiting fig trees.

# Bornean Bristlehead

■ *Pityriasis gymnocephala* (Tiong Batu Kepala Merah) 25cm

DESCRIPTION Smoky-black body, wings and tail, with a scalloped effect; crown with short orange stubble; rounded black patch on ear coverts; rest of head and neck brilliant carmine-red, including bare skin around eye; red thighs. Females have some red blotching on flanks. Juveniles have red ear coverts, but most of head dull blackish, and thighs black. DISTRIBUTION Resident and endemic in Borneo. HABITS AND HABITAT The chunky black bill with its fierce hooked tip enables feeding on hard, massive insects such as beetles and cicadas. Small parties overfly the canopy of peat-swamp and lowland evergreen rainforest to a maximum 1,200m; hard to detect by ground-based observers, but the whirring, croaking and nasal whines are distinctive once learned. Occasionally enters the middle and even lower storeys, peering and craning around to spot food.

# Blue Rock-thrush ■ *Monticola solitarius* (Murai Tarum) 22cm

DESCRIPTION Male plain, dark blue-grey; during breeding season, variable light and dark scale-like markings develop on body plumage. Migrant race has chestnut belly from lower breast to vent. Resident and migrant females both light uniform scaly brown all over. DISTRIBUTION From the Mediterranean across temperate Europe and Asia to Korea and Japan, southwards to Peninsular Malaysia and the Philippines; migrates to Africa, and S and Southeast Asia as far as the Malukus. Local resident in parts of Peninsular Malaysia; chestnut-bellied race is a scarce migrant in Peninsular Malaysia, Singapore, Sabah and Sarawak. HABITS AND HABITAT Residents are most often seen near limestone and other cliffs; migrants occur anywhere, but often near buildings, roadside cuttings, dams and other exposed faces, or near the seashore.

*Female*

*Male*

# Chestnut-naped Forktail

■ *Enicurus ruficapillus* (Cegar Tengkuk Merah) 20cm

DESCRIPTION White forehead and rich chestnut crown; black back (brown in female), wings and throat; long, forked tail with white edges and bars; white wing bar; scaly white breast. Females duller than males, juveniles duller still. DISTRIBUTION Resident from 15°N in Thailand southwards through Peninsular Malaysia, Sumatra and Borneo. HABITS AND HABITAT In lowland evergreen rainforest, mainly on hill slopes to *c.* 900m. An observor's 1st view is usually of a pied bird with a flash of chestnut, speeding away low over a rocky stream in the forest. Settles on rocks, especially near swirls around timber snags in the water, and often cocks, fans and lowers tail. Build nest in a rock cleft or bank, in most months of year. Call is a piercing whistle.

# Slaty-backed Forktail ■ *Enicurus schistaceus* (Cegar Tengkuk Kelabu) 23cm

DESCRIPTION Adult has a black face below eye to throat, grey crown and mantle, and white rump; wings and tail black with white bars and tips to tail feathers; underside white.

Juvenile light brown above and paler, scaly brown below, with same wing and tail pattern. DISTRIBUTION From N India through S China and Indochina to the Malay Peninsula. Resident in Peninsular Malaysia; absent from Singapore, Sabah and Sarawak. HABITS AND HABITAT In hilly and montane forest and forest edges, along small rocky streams or wet roadsides in secluded areas, at *c.* 600–1,300m in our region.

*Juvenile*

# Northern White-crowned Forktail ■ *Enicurus sinensis*
(Cegar Dahi Putih Borneo) 28cm

DESCRIPTION Coal-black on face, crown, back and upper breast, with a white rump
and white lower breast to vent; wings black with a single broad white cross-bar; tail long
and black with white tips. On head, white is confined to a small, erect, mobile patch
on forehead. The lowland **Southern
White-crowned Forktail** *E. leschenaulti*
of Peninsular Malaysia and Borneo has a
proportionately shorter tail, and a larger
patch of white on forehead and forecrown.
DISTRIBUTION Resident in mainland
Asia and mountains of Borneo; absent
from Peninsular Malaysia and Singapore.
HABITS AND HABITAT In Sarawak
occurs only in the higher mountains, but
in Sabah is found from 2,000m down
to *c.* 900m, and in parts of E Sabah
possibly as low as 200m. Along streams in
forest and sometimes at wet roadsides or
culverts.

# Bornean Whistling-thrush ■ *Myophonus borneensis*
(Tiong Biru Borneo) 23cm

DESCRIPTION Male very dark slaty blue,
gradually shading to brownish on wing-
tips and tail; bill and legs black. Female
similar but more chocolate-brown in
tone.
DISTRIBUTION Endemic resident in
Borneo mountains, including Sabah and
Sarawak. The **Sumatran Whistling-
thrush** M. *castaneus* is closely related.
HABITS AND HABITAT Solitary, in the
middle and lower storeys of montane
forest, mainly at 1,000–2,800m but
extending down hill slopes to the extreme
lowlands, especially where limestone caves
provide nesting sites. Forages for litter-
surface invertebrates and on lower parts
of tree trunks, trotting forwards and then
fanning the lowered tail. Call is a long-
sustained monotone whistle.

# Blue Whistling-thrush
■ *Myophonus caeruleus* (Tiong Belacan)
32cm

DESCRIPTION Very large thrush, black all over with a strong blue gloss; brighter blue spangles on wing coverts, and (depending on race) on back and breast. Bill bright yellow, feet grey. The Malaysian Whistling-thrush M. *robinsoni* is a montane species and lacks any speckling.
DISTRIBUTION From central Asia southwards through S China to Southeast Asia and Peninsular Malaysia (not S of 3°N and not in Singapore), as far as Sumatra and Java but not in Borneo.
HABITS AND HABITAT Resident around forested limestone outcrops, where it feeds on large common snails, leaving conspicuous middens of broken shells. Nests in rock crevices, even within cave mouths. Dispersal away from limestone is limited, with records into nearby mangroves (e.g. Langkawi), along forested streams, and locally at the lowland–montane transition. Call is an intense 1–3-note whistle.

# Pale Blue Flycatcher
■ *Cyornis unicolor* (Sambar Biru Muda)
17cm

DESCRIPTION Male powder-blue, paler and greyer on belly and vent. Female with rufous tail and upper-tail coverts, otherwise largely ashy grey, whiter on belly. The similar **Verditer Flycatcher** *Eumyias thalassinus* is more turquoise (both sexes), with brighter wings and distinct black lores.
DISTRIBUTION From NE India through S China to the Malay Peninsula, Sumatra, Borneo and Java. Resident in Peninsular Malaysia, Sabah and Sarawak; absent from Singapore.
HABITS AND HABITAT Favours forests and the edges of forest clearings, in the middle and upper storeys, often on lower hill slopes at *c.* 200–900m, but recorded at extremes of nearly sea-level up to 1,400m. Rather inconspicuous, but shows typical flycatching behaviour from an exposed perch.

# Hill Blue Flycatcher

■ *Cyornis banyumas* (Sambar Biru Bukit)
15cm

DESCRIPTION Male deep blue above and orange-rufous below, shading gradually to pale belly and vent; no black on chin. Female brown above, slightly more rufous on wings and tail, and orange-rufous below, also shading steadily paler downwards like the male. DISTRIBUTION From SW China through Indochina and the Malay Peninsula to Borneo and Java. Resident in Peninsular Malaysia, Sabah and Sarawak; absent from Singapore. HABITS AND HABITAT A bird of hill forest from *c.* 400m upwards, extending to *c.* 1,200m in lower montane forest. Flycatches in the middle and lower-middle storeys of the forest, and is usually seen singly. Its distribution seems rather patchy, and it is thought to be scarce in parts of Sabah but common in other forested areas at suitable altitudes.

# Malaysian Blue Flycatcher ■ *Cyornis turcosus*

(Sambar Biru Malaysia) 14cm

DESCRIPTION Deep blue above, with a shining forehead and brow; light rufous below, shading steadily to white lower breast, belly and vent. Female is rufous all the way up to the bill; male has a black chin and throat. DISTRIBUTION Resident in southernmost Peninsular Thailand and Peninsular Malaysia (not Singapore), and in Sumatra and Borneo (including Sabah and Sarawak). HABITS AND HABITAT Found in evergreen rainforest in the extreme lowlands, in the understorey near streams and in peat-swamp forest. Claims of higher altitudes may be due to confusion with very similar species. Seen singly or in pairs, sallying out to catch passing insects. Nesting recorded *c.* Apr–Jun, with fledglings still tended by parents in Sabah until early Sep.

*Female*

## Large Niltava ▪ *Niltava grandis* (Sambar Raya) 21cm

DESCRIPTION Large flycatcher, the male very deep, dark violet, virtually black below, with brighter blue highlights on crown and sides of neck. Female rich dark brown, faintly

streaked on face and upper breast, with bluish crown and blue patch on sides of neck. DISTRIBUTION Resident from the central Himalayas to Yunnan, and in uplands of Southeast Asia to Peninsular Malaysia and Sumatra. HABITS AND HABITAT Seen singly or in pairs in lower and, less often, upper montane forest at 1,200–2,050m, often in mixed foraging flocks with other birds. Perches in the middle storey and at forest edges, sallying out to catch flying insects. Nesting is estimated to occur Feb–Jul.

*Female*                    *Male*

## Yellow-rumped Flycatcher ▪ *Ficedula zanthopygia*
(Sambar Belakang Kuning) 13.5cm

DESCRIPTION Male brilliant black and yellow with yellow rump; separated from male Narcissus Flycatcher *F. narcissina* by white (not yellow) brow and white wing bar extending down secondaries. Female is grey above and scaled buffy white below, with white wing bar

and yellow rump. DISTRIBUTION Resident in Siberia, Mongolia and China, migrating to Peninsular Malaysia, Singapore, Sumatra, Borneo and Java. HABITS AND HABITAT Edges of lowland evergreen forest and plantations, gardens and roadside trees, where it forages for insects on the foliage by perching, snatching or hovering. The bulk of migrants arrive from mid-Sep onwards, and most departures are in Mar–May, overflying the forest habitat. Usually solitary, foraging in the evenings.

# Mugimaki Flycatcher

■ *Ficedula mugimaki* (Sambar Mugimaki) 13cm

DESCRIPTION Male blackish grey with a short white brow behind eye, and white wing-patch; rufous orange below, shading gradually paler to belly and vent. Female greyish brown above, with 2 narrow, pale wing bars; light rufous orange below, shading paler.
DISTRIBUTION Cool temperate E Palaearctic, in Siberia and NE China, migrating southwards to Sundaland, the Philippines and Sulawesi. Migrant in Peninsular Malaysia, Singapore, Sabah and Sarawak.
HABITS AND HABITAT Migrants have been seen from mangroves at sea-level up to more than 1,500m, in the forest and forest edges, tall secondary woodland, parks and gardens. Perches in the middle and upper storeys of forest, and flycatches for insects.

# Little Pied Flycatcher ■ *Ficedula westermanni* (Sambar Hitam-putih) 11cm

DESCRIPTION Dumpy little flycatcher. Male black and grey, with very wide white eyebrow and long white wing bar. Female grey-brown above and grey-white below, with dull rufous tail and narrow wing bar.
DISTRIBUTION Resident from the W Himalayas through S China to Peninsular Malaysia (not Singapore), Sumatra, Java, Borneo, the Philippines, Sulawesi and the Lesser Sundas.
HABITS AND HABITAT Occurs alone or in pairs, in the crown of lower and upper montane forests and forest edges, at *c.* 1,050–2,030m and reaching a maximum of 3,100m on Mount Kinabalu. Gleans insects from the foliage and also sallies out to catch passing insects in flight. Nests mostly Mar–early Jun, building a cup among epiphytes or against an embankment.

*Female*

*Male*

# Indigo Flycatcher

■ *Eumyias indigo* (Sambar Sindidara) 14cm

DESCRIPTION Bright, light blue all over, nearly black around base of bill and eye, and with blue-white forehead, shading to whitish belly. Juveniles duller, with some blue colour but warm grey-brown on breast.
DISTRIBUTION Resident in Sumatra, Java and Borneo.
HABITS AND HABITAT Usually found perched in an upright stance along forested roadsides, in the trees or on dense vegetation along embankments, sallying out for insects as well as foliage-gleaning, and taking some berries. In lower and upper montane forest at 900–2,650m, but commonest at *c.* 1,600–1,700m. Nest is a deep cup close to the ground, beside a bank or rock face.

# Asian Brown Flycatcher ■ *Muscicapa dauurica* (Sambar Dusun) 13.5cm

DESCRIPTION Ashy grey or grey-brown, with pale lores between bill and eye, and a pale eye-ring; throat is pale with no trace of backwards extension forming a collar (unlike in Dark-sided Flycatcher M. *sibirica*); breast pale grey-brown, sometimes with faint streaks. Black feet, and yellow base to lower mandible. Several races occur as migrants from different parts of Asia, hence there is plenty of plumage variation, but the foot and bill colour, and the pale eye-ring, are good distinguishing features.

DISTRIBUTION Resident throughout the whole of NE Asia, and from the Himalayas through S China and Southeast Asia to Peninsular Thailand; perhaps also resident into Peninsular Malaysia, Borneo, the Philippines and the Lesser Sundas. Migrants occur throughout the region. A breeding population has been discovered in Sabah within the past 2 decades, and others may be revealed.
HABITS AND HABITAT Found in gardens and parkland with tall scattered trees, and forest edges. Single migrants perch on bare twigs of treetops, sallying out to snap up flies, mosquitoes, moths and other insects.

# Oriental Magpie-robin
■ *Copsychus saularis* (Murai Kampung) 20cm

DESCRIPTION Male has a glossy black head, breast, back, wings and white-sided tail; those in the Malay Peninsula, Singapore and Sarawak have a brilliant white belly, while Sabah males have an entirely black belly. All have a strong white wing bar. Females are more subdued grey and cream with a wing bar. DISTRIBUTION Resident through the Indian sub-continent, the S 3rd of China and Southeast Asia to Peninsular Malaysia, Singapore, Sumatra, Borneo, Java, Bali and most of the Philippines. HABITS AND HABITAT Garden bird par excellence, with a fine and varied song given by the male or both sexes from orchard trees; also occurs in plantations, secondary woodland and mangroves. Can invade edges of heavily logged forest adjacent to cultivation, and forested riverbanks. Drops to the ground for insects, worms and small vertebrates. Breeds *c.* Jan–Jun.

# White-rumped Shama ■ *Copsychus malabaricus* (Murai Rimba)
Male 28cm; female 22cm

DESCRIPTION Male has a blue-glossed black head, breast, back, wings and tail; rufous belly; white rump and white edges to long tail. Female has same pattern but is duller and shorter-tailed. Juvenile similar with buff wing spots. DISTRIBUTION Resident from the central Himalayan foothills patchily through the Indian sub-continent and S China to Hainan, and through Peninsular Malaysia to Singapore, Sumatra, Borneo and Java. HABITS AND HABITAT Favours the understorey of lowland forest from sea-level upwards, rarely to 1,200m in the lower montane zone, including overgrown plantations and secondary woodland. Nesting occurs from at least Feb to Aug, the nest a cup placed in any recess. Like magpie-robins, has been persecuted by trapping for sale as a cagebird owing to its fine, varied, sustained song. The White-crowned Shama *C. stricklandii* of Sabah, an endemic species or race, produces distinctive powerful bursts of disyllables.

# Grey-headed Canary-flycatcher ■ *Culicicapa ceylonensis*
(Sambar Kepala Kelabu) 12cm

DESCRIPTION Grey head, throat and upper breast; remainder of underparts rather bright greeny yellow; back and wings olive-green. Sexes are alike.

DISTRIBUTION Resident from the Himalayas through S and central China, southwards to Peninsular Malaysia (not Singapore), Sumatra, Borneo, Java, the Lesser Sundas and Flores.
HABITS AND HABITAT Likely to be found in territorial pairs, in the middle storey from lowland evergreen rainforest in the plains to at least 1,700m in tall upper montane forest. Usually not shy, flycatching from regular perches. In Borneo, it is a brood host of the parasitic Hodgson's Hawk-cuckoo (p. 49). Call consists of 4 notes in 2 couplets, usually followed by a 5th note.

# Straw-headed Bulbul
■ *Pycnonotus zeylanicus* (Barau-barau) 29cm

DESCRIPTION Largest bulbul in the region. Grey-brown above and dusky on breast, streaked whitish; white throat separated by dark moustache from straw-coloured crown and sides of face; under-tail coverts buffy yellow. Sexes are alike.
DISTRIBUTION Resident from 12°30'N in Peninsular Thailand, through Peninsular Malaysia and Singapore to Sumatra, Nias, Borneo and Java.
HABITS AND HABITAT Prefers forest edges along watercourses, including forest trees and bamboo, but also occurs in disturbed vegetation at any forest edge and in dense tree clumps in rural areas. Nest is a shallow cup of small twigs and fibres, in branches of small trees at forest edges or in plantations. Decimated in most places by bird trappers, because of its wonderful song, a loud, liquid duet, but experience shows it can recover well when fully protected.

# Black-headed Bulbul

▪ *Pycnonotus atriceps* (Merbah Siam) 18cm

DESCRIPTION Both sexes are bright olive-green, yellower on wings and tail, and with black flight feathers, including black band on tail; tip of tail bright yellow; head glossy blue-black, with contrasting pale eye. Tail pattern is easy to see in flight. Juveniles duller, with non-contrasting brown head; usually easily identified by association with adults.
DISTRIBUTION From NE India through SW China to the Malay Peninsula, Sumatra, Java, Borneo and Palawan. Resident in Peninsular Malaysia, Singapore, Sabah and Sarawak.
HABITS AND HABITAT Forests and forest edges, flying in small flocks from tree to tree and over low scrub in disturbed areas such as old cultivation. Takes a wide variety of small fruits, and some insects.

# Black-crested Bulbul

▪ *Pycnonotus flaviventris* (Merbah Jambul Hitam) 19cm

DESCRIPTION Dull olive-green above and olive-yellow below, with entire head and throat black; iris cream, and vertical crest black. The endemic Bornean Bulbul *P. montis* is almost the same but has a yellow throat.
DISTRIBUTION Resident from the central Himalayan foothills and Indian sub-continent through Southeast Asia, including Peninsular Malaysia (not Singapore, except for a few escapees) and Sumatra.
HABITS AND HABITAT Although it is a lowland bird in the N part of its range, the species is largely confined to foothills and slopes in Peninsular Malaysia, in lowland evergreen forest largely at 200–1,970m, and well into upper montane forest. Occurs singly or in pairs, flying out to snap at passing insects, and taking varied small fruits and figs. Breeds roughly Jan–Jul, building a nest in dense forest-edge creepers, climbers and ferns.

# Scaly-breasted Bulbul

■ *Pycnonotus squamatus* (Merbah Dada Bersisik) 15cm

DESCRIPTION Small bulbul with a scaly, dusky breast, black and white head, and olive-yellow wings; under-tail coverts yellow. Sexes are alike.

DISTRIBUTION Resident in Peninsular Thailand and Malaysia from *c.* 8°N (not Singapore), and Sumatra, Borneo (including Sabah and Sarawak) and W Java.

HABITS AND HABITAT Lowland evergreen rainforest on hill slopes to *c.* 890m is the typical habitat of this delicate-looking bulbul, which feeds on small forest fruits, soft figs and, possibly, insects. It moves about in the tree crowns, rarely low down. The bird is poorly known and its breeding has never been described. Reputed to have a cheerful whistling song, a repeated pretty trill.

# Stripe-throated Bulbul ■ *Pycnonotus finlaysoni* (Merbah Kunyit) 19cm

DESCRIPTION At 1st glance this is a rather an ordinary brown bulbul, but the bright yellow under-tail coverts and, in particular, heavy yellow flecking on forehead, crown, ear coverts, throat and upper breast are very

attractive. Sexes are alike.

DISTRIBUTION Resident from Yunnan in S China through Myanmar, Thailand and Indochina to Peninsular Malaysia; not in Singapore, Sabah or Sarawak.

HABITS AND HABITAT In the N of its range it comes down into the lowlands, but in Peninsular Malaysia it is largely confined to hill and montane forests; hence, it is found from sea-level upwards in Thailand, but mostly between 400m and 1,750m towards the centre and S of the Malay Peninsula. Feeds on fruits and insects. Nests in small bushes Feb–Aug.

# Pale-faced Bulbul

■ *Pycnonotus leucops* (Merbah Meperek) 19cm

DESCRIPTION Superficially rather like the ubiquitous Yellow-vented Bulbul (below), pale below and brown above, and with yellow under-tail coverts, but the face pattern is different: it has an extensively white face without a black eye-line, and its crown has a broader brown patch rather than a narrow black top.

DISTRIBUTION Resident from NE India discontinuously across S China to Hainan, and in Borneo including both Sabah and Sarawak.

HABITS AND HABITAT Only in montane forest, at *c.* 1,000–3,000m, and in forest edges; seen overflying open patches, hill rice cultivation and landslides. Its food includes various small, soft fruits such as figs and wild raspberries, and possibly insects.

# Yellow-vented Bulbul

■ *Pycnonotus goiavier* (Merbah Kapur) 20cm

DESCRIPTION Pale below (breast whiter than in Pale-faced Bulbul *P. leucops*) and brown above, with yellow under-tail coverts; black line from bill to eye, and narrow blackish strip along crown, including short erectile crest. Sexes are alike.

DISTRIBUTION Resident from *c.* 12°30'N in Myanmar, Indochina, Peninsular Thailand and Malaysia, Singapore, Sumatra, Java, Bali, Borneo and the Philippines.

HABITS AND HABITAT One of the commonest garden birds throughout the region, feeding on fruits of plants around cultivation, e.g. figs, *Lantana*, *Melastoma*, overripe papayas and many others. Also occurs in cultivation and invading forest edges along roads into the highlands. Often seen to lift both wings when landing on overhead wires. Has a cheerful, simple song.

# Olive-winged Bulbul

■ *Pycnonotus plumosus* (Merbah Belukar)
20cm

DESCRIPTION Slightly larger than Yellow-vented Bulbul (p. 127) and rather plain brown above and below; wings brown but with a more olive-yellow obscure panel when folded; ear coverts faintly streaked. Sexes are alike.
DISTRIBUTION Resident from *c*. 12°30'N in Myanmar, Peninsular Thailand and Malaysia, Singapore (including many offshore islands), Sumatra, Borneo, Java and Palawan.
HABITS AND HABITAT Throughout the lowlands to *c*. 500m, in forest edges and along logging tracks, but not in undisturbed forest; also in scrub, coastal vegetation and tree plantations. Seen singly, in pairs or with young, never in big flocks, feeding on small fruits such as figs in dense, tangled vegetation. Nesting occurs Jan–Jun.

# Cream-vented Bulbul

■ *Pycnonotus simplex* (Merbah Mata Putih)
18cm

DESCRIPTION Slim, small-headed bulbul, brown above and paler below, lightening to cream beneath tail; eyes white in Peninsular Malaysia, red in Sabah and Sarawak (where it is distinguished from similar Red-eyed Bulbul, p. 129, by paler underside and vent). Sexes are alike.
DISTRIBUTION Resident from nearly 12°N in Myanmar and Peninsular Thailand to Malaysia, Singapore, Sumatra, Bunguran, Borneo and Java.
HABITS AND HABITAT Favours the interior understorey of lowland evergreen rainforest and peat-swamp forest; commoner in disturbed areas than in totally primary vegetation. Feeds on many kinds of small, rounded fruits, and usually occurs in pairs or, sometimes, follows mixed foraging flocks. Nesting occurs mainly Feb–Apr.

# Red-eyed Bulbul

■ *Pycnonotus brunneus*
(Merbah Mata Merah) 19cm

DESCRIPTION Brown above and below, warmer on breast, paler on throat and under-tail coverts; iris red. Sexes are alike.

DISTRIBUTION Resident from *c.* 12°30'N in Myanmar and Peninsular Thailand to Malaysia, Singapore (where it is scarce), Sumatra and its offshore islands, and Borneo.

HABITS AND HABITAT One of many common bulbul species that come together to feed on abundant figs in the middle storey and canopy of forests; otherwise, it often occurs down to lower levels in forests and forest edges, from sea-level to 900m. Single birds and pairs are the normal unit, and nesting has been reported or suspected from Feb through to Aug.

# Spectacled Bulbul ■ *Pycnonotus erythropthalmos* (Merbah Mata Merah Kecil) 17cm

DESCRIPTION Yet another brown bulbul, smaller and more delicate-looking than the Red-eyed (above), and slightly paler below with buff under-tail; eye is red, circled by a ring of clear yellow skin.

DISTRIBUTION Resident from *c.* 10°N in Peninsular Thailand through Peninsular Malaysia (and formerly in Singapore), to Sumatra, Belitung and Borneo.

HABITS AND HABITAT Somewhat less common than other brown bulbuls such as the Red-eyed and Cream-vented (p. 128), this is also a bird of the middle and lower storeys of lowland evergreen rainforest from sea-level to *c.* 800m. Like the others, it is less common within deep forest than along edges and abandoned forest roads, taking fruits of *Macaranga*, figs and other edge plants. Nesting is thought to occur *c.* Feb–May.

# Red-whiskered Bulbul

■ *Pycnonotus jocosus* (Merbah Pipi Merah) 19cm

DESCRIPTION Vertical black crest, white cheeks with a red flash behind eye and red under-tail coverts are distinctive; largely white below and brown above, with a narrow moustache stripe. Sexes are alike.
DISTRIBUTION Naturally resident in the Indian sub-continent through S China to Hainan and N Peninsular Malaysia, but heavily traded, and introduced to Penang, Ipoh, Kuala Lumpur, Singapore and, evidently, other towns. Not in Borneo.
HABITS AND HABITAT Where successful (and not endangered by trapping) it can reach high densities, feeding on fruits from a range of garden and forest-edge plant species as well as insects, occasionally coming to the ground. Nest is a large cup of grass and creepers, hidden in dense-foliage conifers or other trees.

# Buff-vented Bulbul

■ *Iole olivacea* (Merbah Riang) 20cm

DESCRIPTION Though fairly uniform grey-brown all over, is a little greyer below, with buff beneath tail. Pale iris, and slightly elongated crest feathers that often give the crown a faintly striped appearance. Sexes are alike.
DISTRIBUTION Resident from possibly 15°N in Thailand, then discontinuously through Peninsular Thailand and Malaysia, Sumatra, the Natunas and Borneo.
HABITS AND HABITAT Occurs in the canopy and middle levels of lowland evergreen rainforest, occasionally into the lower storey, where it sometimes participates in mixed foraging flocks, flushing insects from the foliage and pursuing them. It also takes a variety of fruits, and there is one report of a bird eating an enormous worm longer than its own body. Nesting occurs from at least May to Jul, but probably begins considerably earlier.

# Hairy-backed Bulbul ■ *Tricholestes criniger* (Merbah Bulu Tengkuk) 17cm

DESCRIPTION Look for the yellowish sides of face and around eye, contrasting with more rufous crown, brown back and slightly mottled breast, shading to yellowish buff on belly and under-tail coverts. Sexes are alike.

'Hairs' on upper back are, in fact, fine, elongated feather shafts, invisible in the field.

DISTRIBUTION Resident from *c.* 13°N in Peninsular Thailand and 11°30'N in Myanmar, Peninsular Malaysia (with dispersants to Singapore), Sumatra, the Natunas and Borneo.

HABITS AND HABITAT Favours the middle and lower storeys of lowland evergreen rainforest, from the extreme lowlands to *c.* 900m, and peat-swamp forest, freshwater swamp forest during dry periods, and disturbed vegetation, including logged forest and regrowth. Pairs are typically seen taking insects and small fruits, but nesting is poorly described.

# Yellow-bellied Bulbul ■ *Alophoixus phaeocephalus* (Merbah Kepala Kelabu) 20cm

DESCRIPTION Quite a large bulbul, with a puffed-out white throat, blue-grey face and short, dark grey crest; olive-brown above and bright, uniform yellow below. Sexes are alike.

DISTRIBUTION Resident in S Indochina and from *c.* 10°N in Peninsular Thailand to Peninsular Malaysia, Sumatra, the

Natunas and Borneo.

HABITS AND HABITAT Typically found in pairs, which can be noisy and are sometimes seen flying at high speed through the understorey. Prefers primary forest, from the extreme lowlands to *c.* 760m; tolerates some forest disturbance, but then occurs at lower densities. Participates in mixed foraging flocks, taking mainly insects and some fruits, and is thought to breed *c.* Feb–Jul.

## Ochraceous Bulbul ■ *Alophoixus ochraceus* (Merbah Berjanggut) 20cm

DESCRIPTION One of the larger bulbuls, with a strong bill; grey-brown above and below, slightly greyer on sides of head, with throat white and often puffed out; short, erectile crest rufous or ochre-brown. Sexes are alike.
DISTRIBUTION Resident in S Indochina and from *c.* 14°N in Peninsular Thailand, Peninsular Malaysia, Sumatra and Borneo.
HABITS AND HABITAT In continental Asia this is a lowland bird, but in Peninsular Malaysia, Sabah and Sarawak it is confined to slopes and mountains, from *c.* 700m upwards. It occurs in pairs, often in association with mixed foraging flocks in the middle storey of montane forest. Breeding occurs in *c.* Feb–Jul. It has a range of hoarse and sweet notes, delivered in a rather random series.

## Streaked Bulbul ■ *Ixos malaccensis* (Merbah Dada Berjalur) 23cm

DESCRIPTION Gives the appearance of a cool grey bird, becoming almost white on belly and under-tail coverts; sides of head, throat and upper breast with pale streaks on centre of each feather. Sexes are alike.
DISTRIBUTION Resident from *c.* 12°30'N in Myanmar, Peninsular Malaysia (and 1 doubtful record from Singapore), Sumatra, Lingga, Bangka and Borneo.
HABITS AND HABITAT Occurs in the forest canopy of lowland evergreen rainforest, up slopes and just reaching into montane forest at *c.* 1,100m. Figs of various species are commonly eaten, as are flying insects such as termite swarms. Because of its preference for canopy-level perches, it is often overlooked, and its nesting behaviour is virtually unknown.

# Cinereous Bulbul ■ *Hemixos cinereus* (Merbah Kelabu) 21cm

DESCRIPTION Largely grey, with a puffy white throat that is often highly visible, and a contrasting darker moustache that merges upwards into grey sides of face; crown feathers erectile. Sexes are alike.
DISTRIBUTION Resident discontinuously to Peninsular Thailand and Malaysia, Singapore, Sumatra and Borneo. Birds from the central Himalayan foothills through S China and Indochina are now separated as **Ashy Bulbul**, *H. flavala*.

HABITS AND HABITAT Small flocks are often seen, churring to each other as they puff out their throat feathers. Lives in forests on slopes from *c.* 400m through lower and upper montane forest to *c.* 2,000m, occasionally making long-distance dispersal movements into lowlands, even as far as Singapore. Feeds on flying insects taken while perched or snatched in flight, and on fruits. Nesting may occur Feb–Jul.

# Mountain Bulbul ■ *Hypsipetes mcclellandii* (Merbah Gunung) 22cm

DESCRIPTION Sturdy bulbul, common though not very well studied. Olive-green back, wings and tail; pale grey breast and bushy head, the crown feathers brown with pale central streaks. Sexes are alike.
DISTRIBUTION Resident from the central Himalayas through S China to Hainan, and parts of Indochina and Thailand to central Peninsular Malaysia.

HABITS AND HABITAT In Peninsular Malaysia, it is confined to montane forest of the Main and Larut ranges, Mount Tahan and a few outliers. It is a fairly common bulbul at *c.* 100–2,100m, in the forest canopy and forest edges, often among mixed foraging flocks. Various small fruits comprise the bulk of its food, along with some insects. In pairs or small groups, nesting *c.* Mar–May.

# Barn Swallow ■ *Hirundo rustica* (Layang-layang Pekan) 15–20cm

DESCRIPTION Larger swallow with a black band between reddish upper breast and clean white, buff or pinkish underparts; upperparts and tail (with whitish spots) dark blue-black, the tail deeply forked with long streamers (often missing during moult).

DISTRIBUTION Resident almost throughout the N hemisphere, in Asia southwards to N Thailand and Vietnam; non-breeding migrant to all the S continents and throughout our region.

HABITS AND HABITAT Found almost everywhere, from lowlands to mountains, over

towns, villages, agricultural land and forest. A few individuals are present in almost every month, but predominantly in Aug–Apr. Sometimes gathers in huge flocks, especially when roosting on overhead wires in well-lit, busy small towns. Numbers have declined over the decades, but the species is still considered common. Not hard to identify by its size, clean appearance and tail shape. Feeding birds may displace smaller House Swallows (below).

# House Swallow ■ *Hirundo tahitica* (Layang-layang Pasifik) 14cm

DESCRIPTION Small swallow previously named Pacific Swallow with reddish forehead, throat and upper breast, this transiting directly to sullied greyish-white underparts; crown, back, wings and tail (with whitish spots) dark blue-black. Juveniles are duller, browner, and less rufous on forehead and throat.

DISTRIBUTION Resident from India, S China and Taiwan throughout Southeast Asia to New Guinea and the W Pacific.

HABITS AND HABITAT Abundant throughout our region at all times of year. On the wing, appears smaller, dirtier-looking and with a short-forked tail compared with Barn Swallow (above). Often perches on wires and twigs, though not in large flocks (cf. Barn Swallow), and spends most time on the wing, flying energetically over coasts and islands, open country, mangroves and forest edges. Mud nests are built under bridges, and sometimes in roof overhangs and other buildings, mostly Feb–Jun.

# Striated Swallow

■ *Cecropis striolata* (Layang-layang
Ekor Hitam) 16–20cm

DESCRIPTION Dark blue crown, wings
and deeply forked tail; sides of face
and underparts mealy white, narrowly
streaked blackish. Behind face to nape,
and a distinct square patch on rump,
are orange-rufous in adults, buff in
juveniles.

DISTRIBUTION Resident from
tropical Africa through Eurasia to the
Himalayas, Japan and Korea; Asian
birds migrate to Peninsular Malaysia,
Singapore and Sumatra, perhaps
further.

HABITS AND HABITAT Occasional
birds can be picked out from wintering Barn Swallows (p. 134) by their more deliberate
flight and obvious rump colour. Has become commoner over the past 30–40 years, in
habitats ranging from the landward side of mangroves at sea-level to 1,250m over forested
mountains, but mostly in open coastal plains, cultivation, grassland and scrub.

# Rufous-bellied Swallow

■ *Cecropis badia* (Layang-layang Batu)
18–20cm

DESCRIPTION Notably large swallow.
The subspecies found in Peninsular
Malaysia, *C. b. badia*, is a gorgeous
brick-red colour evenly over face,
breast and broad, square rump; crown,
nape, back, wings and tail blackish with
rich blue gloss. Juveniles are slightly
duller.

DISTRIBUTION Resident from
S China through Southeast Asia
to Peninsular Malaysia (not yet
Singapore); also recorded once from
Sumatra. Other subspecies much
resembling the Striated Swallow
(above), with pale, streaky breasts, occur as scarce migrants in Borneo and beyond.

HABITS AND HABITAT The brick-red Malay Peninsula birds frequent limestone outcrops
but forage to many kilometres beyond these breeding sites, over forest and cultivation.

## Mountain Tailorbird ■ *Phyllergates cucullatus* (Perenjak Gunung) 12cm

DESCRIPTION Green nape, back, wings and tail; white eyebrow, throat and breast, merging to yellow belly. Tiny, with a black line through eye and a long, slim bill. Forehead and forecrown chestnut in adults, green in juveniles.
DISTRIBUTION Resident from E Himalayan foothills through S China to Peninsular Malaysia, Sumatra, Borneo, Java, and all the way to the Philippines and Lesser Sundas.
HABITS AND HABITAT The only tailorbird that does not stitch leaves together to make its nest, a grassy pouch of dead leaves in tangled vegetation at the forest edge. Found in lower and upper montane forest at 1,050–2,000m in the understorey and, more typically, at disturbed edges. Song is a roughly ascending series of 5 high notes, accompanied by buzzing from the partner.

## Sunda Bush-warbler ■ *Cettia vulcania* (Cekup Keter-keter) 13cm

DESCRIPTION Entirely dull grey-brown with a faint eyebrow, the breast greyer with impressions of speckling. Legs pinkish brown, base of lower mandible yellow. Similar

**Friendly Bush-warbler** *Bradypterus accentor* is darker, with a blotched throat and upper breast, rufous brow and dark grey legs.
DISTRIBUTION Resident in mountains from Sumatra to Borneo, Java and Timor.
HABITS AND HABITAT In middle- to high-altitude montane forest, 1,450–3,700m, from Mount Kinabalu, Sabah, to Mount Mulu and Murud, Sarawak. Mouse-like, skulking among dense, low ferns and weeds along forested roadsides and landslips. Members of a pair have a long, rising and then falling whistle; also a 5-note song, *witch-a-wee-cheee-wee*.

# Chestnut-crowned Warbler

■ *Seicercus castaniceps* (Cekup Mata Putih)
10cm

DESCRIPTION Chestnut central crown-stripe
and eyebrows separated by a black line, but
sides of face, back and underparts light grey,
shading to pale yellowish on flanks and rump;
2 pale yellowish wing bars. Sexes are alike,
juveniles duller.

DISTRIBUTION Resident from central
Himalayan foothills through S China and
Southeast Asia to Vietnam, and in the
mountains of Peninsular Malaysia and
Sumatra.

HABITS AND HABITAT In lower montane
forest at *c.* 900–1,380m. On mountains where
the Yellow-breasted Warbler (below) is absent

(N part of the Main Range), it extends up to 1,800m; apparently the 2 species partially
exclude one another. Nest is built under an overhanging bank, predominantly in Jan–Jun.

# Yellow-breasted Warbler ■ *Seicercus montis* (Cekup Lumut) 10cm

DESCRIPTION Bright chestnut crown and sides of face, and black lateral crown-stripes,
are easy identification features; entirely bright yellow below and on rump, with green wings
and tail, and 2 yellow wing bars. Sexes are alike, juveniles duller.

DISTRIBUTION Resident in
mountains from Peninsular
Malaysia to Sumatra,
Borneo, Palawan, Flores and
Timor.

HABITS AND HABITAT
Small, colourful, active
warbler of upper montane
forest, at 1,250–2,070m in
the Malay Peninsula, and
reported up to 2,450m on
Mount Kinabalu. Hovers
to pick insects from foliage
within the forest, in the
canopy down to near the
understorey. Nest is purse-
shaped, built in a recess on a
bank in Feb–Jun.

# Mountain Leaf-warbler

■ *Phylloscopus trivirgatus* (Cekup Daun Gunung) 11.5cm

DESCRIPTION Small warbler, olive-green above and dirty yellow below; central greenish crown-stripe, bordered by wide black lateral crown-stripes; yellow brow and black line through eye; no wing bars.
DISTRIBUTION Resident in mountains of Peninsular Malaysia, Sumatra, Borneo, Java, Bali and the Philippines to Lombok and Sumbawa.
HABITS AND HABITAT In lower and upper montane forest at 1,300–2,160m in the Malay Peninsula, and up to 3,300m on Mount Kinabalu, Sabah. Pairs or small groups glean insects from foliage. Builds a domed nest in a recess on banks or slopes, c. Feb–Apr.

# Everett's White-eye

■ *Zosterops everetti* (Mata Putih Rimba) 11cm

DESCRIPTION Several white-eyes are tough to distinguish, being green above with grey flanks and a yellow throat and belly. This species has a green forehead (not yellow), uniform with rest of crown, and the grey flanks and yellow of underside are richly coloured.
DISTRIBUTION Patchily from N Thailand through the Malay Peninsula to Borneo and the Philippines; not in Sumatra or Java. Resident in Peninsular Malaysia, Sabah and Sarawak; absent from Singapore.
HABITS AND HABITAT In hill and montane forest from a little above sea-level to at least 1,700m, replacing the similar **Oriental White-eye** Z. *palpebrosus* (with a yellow forehead), which occurs in coastal mangroves. In small, chittering flocks, frequenting the forest canopy, where it flies from tree to tree seeking small insects on the foliage.

# Black-capped White-eye ■ *Zosterops atricapilla*
(Mata Putih Kopiah Hitam) 10cm

DESCRIPTION Dark olive-green above and grey below; white eye-ring, emphasised by blackish surround that extends over forehead and much of face; throat and vent deep yellow, variably linked by line of yellow down centre of belly; lower mandible contrasting silver. Sexes are alike.
DISTRIBUTION Resident in the mountains of Sumatra and Borneo.
HABITS AND HABITAT Small flocks roam over the canopy of montane forest in Sabah and Sarawak, settling in small fruiting trees, and taking fruits of these and epiphytic mistletoes. Agile, probing among lichen and epiphytes, presumably for insects, and tearing small flowers apart to gain nectar. Its known altitude limits are *c*. 900–2,150m.

# Chestnut-crested Yuhina ■ *Yuhina everetti* (Burung Rimba Singgara) 12cm

DESCRIPTION Small, lively bird. White below and with white marks around eye, setting it off from foxy-chestnut ear coverts, crown and crest; upperparts grey-brown. Sexes are alike.
DISTRIBUTION Resident and endemic in Borneo, including Sabah and Sarawak.
HABITS AND HABITAT In the canopy and middle storey of lower and upper montane forest, usually at 900–2,800m, but also on hill slopes down to 150m in the lowlands. Flocks of 30 or more individuals move through the crowns of *Macaranga* and other roadside trees, taking small insects. They keep up a continual twittering contact call. Nest is built at ground level, in a niche on a slope or forested embankment; chicks are entirely black.

## Mountain Fulvetta
■ *Alcippe peracensis* (Burung Rimba Ranting Gunung) 15cm

DESCRIPTION Rounded grey head with a neat, long, narrow black eyebrow; paler grey underparts and grey-brown back, wings and tail – virtually nondescript if eyebrow is not noticed.
DISTRIBUTION Hill forest in Indochina, discontinuously to mountains of Peninsular Malaysia (not Singapore).
HABITS AND HABITAT Found in the middle and lower storeys of lower montane and upper montane forest, at 800–2,000m, including forest edges, old landslides and overgrown cultivation. Forages for invertebrates and some small fruits, and nests in Jan–May or Jun. Has a flamboyant song of 4–9 notes, varying across the scale, without which it would be noticed much less often.

## Grey-throated Babbler
■ *Stachyris nigriceps* (Burung Rimba Leher Kelabu) 13cm

DESCRIPTION Dark brown back, wings and tail; more ochre-buff cheeks, breast and belly; subdued pattern of white eyebrow and white malar-patch imposed over grey crown, grey throat, and blackish around and in front of eye.
DISTRIBUTION Resident from the E Himalayas through S China and continental Southeast Asia to Peninsular Malaysia, including Pulau Tioman but not Singapore; also in Sumatra, Lingga, the Natunas and Borneo.
HABITS AND HABITAT Busy groups of 4 or 5 work through the dense undergrowth, fern brakes and vegetation of forested roadsides and landslips, in lowland evergreen rainforest, and lower and upper montane forest, on slopes anywhere from just above sea-level to beyond 2,000m; never in extreme lowlands over level ground. Insectivore, breeding Jan–Jul. Continual tremulous reeling trills between flock members.

# Chestnut-rumped Babbler ■ *Stachyris maculata*
(Burung Rimba Rembah Besar) 18cm

DESCRIPTION Somewhat gawky appearance, with straw-yellow eye and narrow blue surround; grey head, shading to chestnut rump and tail; black throat, breaking up into strong black streaks on cream breast, and fading towards vent.
DISTRIBUTION From *c.* 8°N southwards through the Malay Peninsula, Sumatra and

Borneo. Resident in Peninsular Malaysia, Sabah and Sarawak; former resident in Singapore, now locally extinct.
HABITS AND HABITAT One of the more striking understorey forest babblers, seen in pairs and small family parties; cooperative breeding is probably assisted by previous young. Seeks insects among hanging clusters of dead leaves. In the group, noisy choruses with a melodious *wup wup wup…* are made by male, and harsh, scratchy notes by female, often several birds joining in.

# Chestnut-backed Scimitar-babbler
■ *Pomatorhinus montanus* (Burung Rimba Paruh Melengkung) 19cm

DESCRIPTION Impressive rufous-chestnut flanks and back; throat, breast and centre of belly pure white; wings and tail dark brown. Head black with a white eyebrow; bill long, downcurved and bright yellow with black upper base.
DISTRIBUTION Resident in southernmost Thailand and Peninsular Malaysia from 6°N (not Singapore), through Sumatra, Bangka, Java, Bali and Borneo.
HABITS AND HABITAT The middle storey and canopy of lowland evergreen rainforest, from the extreme lowlands up into lower montane forest to *c.* 1,350m, the upper limit varying locally. Nests down in the understorey, in a niche in an earth bank or roadside cutting. Found singly or in pairs, using the curved bill to probe for insects in bark, dead wood and epiphytes. Call is a loud, fluty *Po hoi* or *Po hoi hoi.*

# Fluffy-backed Tit-babbler

■ *Macronus ptilosus* (Burung Rimba Pong-pong) 16cm

DESCRIPTION Rich rufous brown, darkening from the bright crown towards back, wings and tail; throat black. Feathers of lower back and rump are elongated and stiffened, with reduced barbs giving a hair-like appearance, but this may not be visible unless birds are displaying. Skin on lores and around eye bright blue, and 2 blue inflatable throat-patches visible when birds are calling.

DISTRIBUTION Resident from S Thailand through Peninsular Malaysia to Singapore (now locally extinct), Sumatra and Borneo.

HABITS AND HABITAT In primary forest, disturbed forest and forest edges from near sea-level to a maximum 200m, including dense regrowth in the understorey and lower storey near old forest trails and the edges of old landslides and treefalls. Everywhere forages for insects in tangled thickets. Usually seen in pairs, and sometimes in family groups or mixed foraging flocks. Nesting in the Malay Peninsula occurs Dec–Aug. One member of the pair (the male?) gives a frequent *punk punk-punk-punk…* accompanied by soft churring by the other sex.

# Moustached Babbler ■ *Malacopteron magnirostre*

(Burung Rimba Bermisai) 17cm

DESCRIPTION Nondescript grey-brown above and off-white below, browner on tail and with dark brown crown and a dark moustache stripe; legs blue-grey. Juveniles duller, the moustache stripe less contrasting.

DISTRIBUTION From *c.* 12°N in Myanmar through the Malay Peninsula to Sumatra and

Borneo. Resident in Peninsular Malaysia, Singapore (confirmed records only in the period 1983–94), Sabah and Sarawak.

HABITS AND HABITAT In lowland forest from nearly sea-level to *c.* 900m, to a maximum of 1,200m in Sabah, in small parties or in pairs, and sometimes in mixed foraging flocks with other species. Gleans insects from the foliage, and may briefly chase flying insects. Song is a series of *c.* 3–6 spaced whistles, all on 1 pitch or slightly descending at the end.

# Scaly-crowned Babbler ■ *Malacopteron cinereum*
(Burung Rimba Tua Kecil) 16cm

DESCRIPTION Grey-brown above, and whitish below without any grey breast-streaks; secondaries, rump and tail more rufous brown. Crown blackish, with bright rufous forehead that has black feather-tips like scales; legs pink. The similar **Rufous-crowned Babbler** M. *magnum* has extensive rufous forehead without the black scales, faint grey breast-streaks and blue-grey legs.

DISTRIBUTION Resident from 11°N in Peninsular Thailand and Malaysia (not Singapore), through Sumatra, Bunguran and Borneo.

HABITS AND HABITAT In the lower storey of lowland evergreen rainforest, whether primary, logged or even secondary patches, singly, in pairs or in small groups joining mixed foraging flocks. Mostly in extreme lowlands, becoming scarcer up hill slopes so as to fade out by *c.* 300–500m. Song consists of varied range of notes, a series of 1 type followed by a series of another, in different combinations.

# Abbott's Babbler ■ *Malacocincla abbotti* (Burung Rimba Riang) 16cm

DESCRIPTION Dull rufous brown all the way from crown to tail, with more intense rufous flanks and vent, and buffy-white throat and belly. Brow and face are grey, but less distinctly so than in the very similar **Horsfield's Babbler** M. *sepiaria* in the same habitat, a species with a darker crown and obscurely streaked breast.

DISTRIBUTION From Nepal and NE India through Indochina and the Malay Peninsula to Sumatra and Borneo. Resident in Peninsular Malaysia, Singapore, Sabah and Sarawak.

HABITS AND HABITAT Favours the lower storey of forest and, especially, forest edges along rivers and swampy areas, including the landward edge of mangroves and palm swamps; less common in Sabah and Sarawak than in Peninsular Malaysia. Best located by its song, an alternating *wit chee chewee; wit chee chewoo*, with 1 phrase ending in an upturn and the next in a downturn. Other, more complex songs have been described from Borneo and Sumatra.

## Short-tailed Babbler

■ *Malacocincla malaccensis* (Burung Rimba Ekor Pendek) 14cm

DESCRIPTION Dark brown above and on its extremely short tail, darker on crown; very distinct grey sides of face, and white throat merging to peachy-buff breast and belly. Legs always pink. DISTRIBUTION Resident in Peninsular Thailand from 11°N through Peninsular Malaysia, Singapore, Sumatra, and the Anamba and Natuna islands to Borneo. HABITS AND HABITAT Favours ground level and the understorey of lowland evergreen rainforest, to 800–900m. Nest is a fibrous cup, built within a large, curled-up leaf on the ground, perhaps in Jan–Aug. Has a very clean appearance, hopping on the ground and giving a distinctive call: varied trilling notes, beginning softly before breaking into 5 or 6 down-slurred whistles and then another 5 or 6 deliberate steady whistles.

## White-chested Babbler

■ *Trichastoma rostratum* (Burung Rimba Dada Putih) 13cm

DESCRIPTION Dark brown upperparts, a little paler on crown, with pale buff on sides of face, shading to white underparts. Pink legs; slim, straight bill, dark above and blue-grey below. DISTRIBUTION Resident from *c.* 10°30'N through Peninsular Malaysia, some offshore islands of Singapore, and in Sumatra, Belitung and Borneo. HABITS AND HABITAT Favours the ground and understorey within lowland evergreen rainforest over floodplains, typically near water except where a few island populations lack competing babbler species, allowing limited upslope spread. Picks small invertebrates from the litter, roots and water's edge, and breaks off to whistle from 4 (rarely, Sabah and Sarawak) to 7 undulating notes, pure and cheerful. Nest is a fine leafy cup in waterside understorey.

# Streaked Wren-babbler ■ *Napothera brevicaudata*
(Burung Rimba Hujan Gunung) 14.5cm

DESCRIPTION Pale dusky brown all over, more buff below and more grey-brown above; entire underparts lightly streaked brown; crown, back and rump lightly scaled black.

DISTRIBUTION Resident from the easternmost Himalayas and S Yunnan through Southeast Asia to the mountains of Peninsular Malaysia, including Pulau Tioman but not Singapore.

HABITS AND HABITAT Thai populations are confined to lowland forest, but in N Peninsular Malaysia and Pulau Tioman it is found on middle slopes, and further S it occurs in lower montane forest at 750–*c.* 2,000m altitude. An insectivore, living on the ground alone or in pairs. Also nests on the ground Dec–Jun. Gives loud 2–4-note whistles.

# Black Laughingthrush
■ *Melanocichla lugubris* (Burung Rimba Hitam) 26cm

DESCRIPTION Plumage entirely unglossed black, with bare blue skin behind eye and orange-yellow bill, this perhaps redder in birds from Borneo, where adults (only) have bare greeny-yellow skin on crown and sides of neck.

DISTRIBUTION Mountains of Peninsular Malaysia, Sumatra and Borneo (including both Sabah and Sarawak).

HABITS AND HABITAT An insectivore of the middle and lower storeys of montane forest at 900–1,370m in the Malay Peninsula, but to 1,800m on Mount Kinabalu, Sabah. Found in pairs, often silent but wonderful when calling, a series of loud, frog-like gulps, followed by rich, bubbling laughter. Bornean populations have been split (as **Bare-headed Laughingthrush** M. *calva*) by some authors, but similar calls, mutual responsiveness to tape recordings, and scanty head-feathering of Peninsular Malaysian birds make the split equivocal.

# Spectacled Laughingthrush ■ *Rhinocichla mitrata*
(Burung Rimba Mata Putih) 22cm

DESCRIPTION Bright rufous-chestnut cap and face, with white ring around eye and on forehead; otherwise entirely ashy grey except for a white wing-panel and chestnut vent and thighs. Borneo birds have a buff mark only below eye (not entire ring), and slightly ochre tone to breast. Bill and legs bright orange-yellow.
DISTRIBUTION Resident in mountains of Peninsular Malaysia, Sumatra and Borneo, including both Sabah and Sarawak.
HABITS AND HABITAT At *c.* 850–2,000m in lower and upper montane forest, from the

canopy through the middle and lower storeys of the forest, but rarely on the ground. Also found in forest edges and secondary growth, including abandoned mountain cultivation and fern brakes. Call is a repeated 2-note whistle; breaks out into a great chorus when among flock members. Nests *c.* Feb–Jul.

# Sunda Laughingthrush ■ *Garrulax palliatus*
(Burung Rimba Lohui Puru) 25cm

DESCRIPTION Smoky blue-grey head, back, breast and belly, merging into chestnut-brown wings, rump, tail and abdomen. Sky-blue skin around eye. Sexes are alike. Resembles a giant version of the common, small, lower-storey bird, Chestnut-winged Babbler *Stachyris*

*erythroptera*, but that species is restricted to lowland forests, never montane.
DISTRIBUTION Resident only in Sumatra and Borneo, including the mountains of both Sabah and Sarawak.
HABITS AND HABITAT Small groups forage on the ground and in the lower storey up to the canopy in hill forest and lower and upper montane forest at *c.* 500–2,000m (but commonest around mid-point of this range), occasionally coming out to feed on open lawns at hill stations. A frugivore, also taking some insects. Birds keep in touch with cat-like mews and a raucous whistling chorus, 1 bird beginning with soft cooing notes and then others breaking into rattles.

# Malaysian Laughingthrush ■ *Trochalopteron peninsulae*
(Burung Rimba Kepala Merah) 27cm

DESCRIPTION Rich chestnut cap, throat, breast and belly; face grey, back grey-brown. Wing intricately patterned with chestnut greater coverts, black primary coverts, and golden fringes to flight feathers.

DISTRIBUTION In 2007, it was suggested that the species was endemic to mountains of Peninsular Malaysia, and it was thus split off from closely related forms from the Himalayas and S China through Thailand and Indochina (several were formerly grouped together under the name Chestnut-crowned Laughingthrush *Garrulax erythrocephalus*, but they have now been split into a variety of names and put in a new genus).

HABITS AND HABITAT The understorey and middle interior of dark lower and upper montane forest, at 1,050–2,000m; occasionally ventures out into old cultivation and edge vegetation. An insectivore and partial frugivore, nesting mainly in Jan–Apr. Usually in pairs, seldom larger groups, with cat-like mews and loud, jumbled, whistling duets.

# Blue-winged Siva ■ *Siva cyanouroptera* (Burung Rimba Siva) 15cm

DESCRIPTION Entirely light grey above with a white throat, underparts and sides of tail; light violet-blue sheen on wing feathers, this often hard to see in dull, misty conditions; distinctive pale iris. Females are slightly duller.

DISTRIBUTION Resident from the central Himalayan foothills through S China and discontinuously through Southeast Asia to the mountains of Peninsular Malaysia (not Singapore).

HABITS AND HABITAT Small flocks occur in the canopy and middle storey of lower and upper montane forest at *c.* 1,050–1,680m, passing through cultivation and clearings to forage in isolated large trees. Seeks small insects among the foliage, as well as taking small fruits.

# Silver-eared Mesia

■ *Mesia argentauris* (Burung Rimba Pipi Perak) 17cm

DESCRIPTION Very colourful with a black head; silvery-white ear coverts; yellow forehead, nape, collar and breast, and yellow in wing. Wings otherwise grey with reddish bases to flight feathers; rump and under-tail coverts reddish in male, yellow in female. DISTRIBUTION Resident from central Himalayan foothills through S China, discontinuously to the mountains of Peninsular Malaysia (not Singapore) and Sumatra. HABITS AND HABITAT Found in the canopy of lower and upper montane forest at 900–2,000m, and down into fern brakes and scrub in old cultivation. Small, noisy parties surge through the understorey, giving a whistled 8-note song, *tee-oo-wit, tee-oo-wit, tee-oo*, and other varied notes. There are regional differences between populations in Southeast Asia.

# Long-tailed Sibia ■ *Heterophasia picaoides*
(Burung Rimba Ekor Panjang) 29–32cm

DESCRIPTION Smooth, dark grey, this becoming paler on belly and under-tail coverts; shows a white flash at base of wing feathers and white tips to long, graduated tail. Iris red, feet and slim bill black. DISTRIBUTION E Himalayan foothills to S Yunnan, and discontinuously to Peninsular Malaysia (not Singapore) and Sumatra.

HABITS AND HABITAT At *c*. 1,000–2,000m in lower and upper montane forest, frequenting the crown and middle storey in small parties, including mixed foraging flocks. Groups move from tree to tree, quickly crossing open spaces at the hill stations, their long tails obvious in flight. A series of low notes is given (but no varied song; cf. Silver-eared Mesia, above) as they feed on insects and, especially, fruits. A nesting season of Feb–Jul is suggested.

## Oriental Reed-warbler

■ *Acrocephalus orientalis* (Cekup Paya Besar)
19cm

DESCRIPTION Large fawn-brown warbler,
creamy whitish below. Pale eyebrow runs from
bill to just behind eye, bordered below by short,
dark line through eye.
DISTRIBUTION Resident in NE and E Asia,
migrating S to Southeast Asia, Peninsular
Malaysia and Singapore, Sumatra, Borneo and
Java, through Wallacea as far as N Australia.
HABITS AND HABITAT Hard to see well, in
reedbeds, paddy fields and tall waste grassland in
the lowlands; occasionally a bird will pop up to
the top of the vegetation, may call briefly, and
then dive down again. In Borneo, it is recorded
from 25 Sep to 24 May; in the Peninsula from
28 Aug to 26 May; and in Singapore recent stay-
overs have remained into late Jun. Moult and
migration have been well studied in this species.

## Ashy Tailorbird

■ *Orthotomus ruficeps* (Perenjak Kelabu) 12cm

DESCRIPTION Crown, back, wings and tail
ashy grey; underparts ashy grey in male, paler
in female, nearly white in juvenile. Male has
extensive rufous sides of face, these more
restricted in female and absent in juvenile.
DISTRIBUTION Resident in southernmost
Vietnam, and from *c.* 8°30'N in Peninsular
Thailand through Malaysia and Singapore,
Sumatra, Belitung, Borneo and the N coast of
Java.
HABITS AND HABITAT Mangrove forests and
the landward side of mangroves everywhere, as
well as peat-swamp forest in Sabah and Sarawak.
Also increasingly invading inland habitats,
along rivers, through plantations and orchards.
In mangroves, it forages from the canopy
to the mud, taking small insects from the foliage as well as flying out to snatch insects
passing by. Nest is built within a 1–3-leaf stitched pouch, apparently in most months but
predominantly Jan–Jun.

# Dark-necked Tailorbird ■ *Orthotomus atrogularis*
(Perenjak Leher Hitam) 12cm

DESCRIPTION Green back, wings and tail; entirely chestnut crown extending down to eye, with grey cheeks and ear coverts; throat wth blackish streaks, these faint in female but broad and coalescing in male; rest of underparts creamy white. Beware: Common Tailorbird (below) can show black feather bases on throat.

DISTRIBUTION NE India and southernmost China through Southeast Asia to Singapore, Sumatra, the Anambas and Borneo.
HABITS AND HABITAT Favours the forest canopy from the extreme lowlands to montane forest at 1,100m, and especially the understorey along logging tracks and forest edges, riverbanks and dense, tangled secondary growth to 1,400m or more. Nest is built within a 1- or 2-leaf stitched pouch. Has a rising trill, this repeated and sometimes downturned.

# Common Tailorbird
■ *Orthotomus sutorius* (Perenjak Pisang) 12cm

DESCRIPTION Dark green wings, back and tail; chestnut cap darker, duller and merging more smoothly into back than in Dark-necked Tailorbird (above); light, variable streaking from above eye to sides of face and throat. Always with chestnut thighs. Juveniles lack the brown cap, but usually show a brownish tinge on forehead.
DISTRIBUTION Indian sub-continent and the Himalayan foothills through S China and Southeast Asia to Peninsular Malaysia, Singapore, Bintan and Java.
HABITS AND HABITAT The most common garden tailorbird, but also widespread in cultivation, plantations, scrub, roadsides and riverbanks. Originally confined to lowlands but has now spread to at least 1,700m with agricultural expansion. Nest is built within a 1–3-leaf stitched pouch, apparently in nearly every month. Call is a rapid, repeated *chik chik chik…* in monotonously prolonged bouts.

# Rufescent Prinia ■ *Prinia rufescens*
(Perenjak Belukar) 12cm

DESCRIPTION Grey head with short white brow and
faint eye-ring; grey-brown back and tail with pale tips
to tail feathers, and rufous tinge to wings. Underparts
cream with no trace of yellow. Sexes are alike, juveniles
browner than adults.
DISTRIBUTION Resident from E Himalayan foothills
and parts of E India, through S China and Southeast
Asia to Peninsular Malaysia, but not reaching Singapore.
HABITS AND HABITAT Found in rank grass and shrubs
along forest edges, riverbanks and forested roadsides,
from the extreme lowlands to a maximum of 1,500m in
the mountains; characteristic of hillier areas and denser
vegetation than the Yellow-bellied Prinia (below).
Nest is like a tailorbird's, between stitched leaves in a
bush. Pairs duet, 1 bird calling *chiep; chiep; chiep* while
its partner gives a series of 2- and 3-note calls, *chir-chir,
chir-chir-chir*.

# Yellow-bellied Prinia ■ *Prinia flaviventris* (Perenjak Kuning) 14cm

DESCRIPTION Grey head and ear coverts with trace of a pale eye-ring and a short white
brow (in females; obscure or absent in males); back and tail olive with white tips to tail
feathers. Throat white, merging to light yellow on belly. Much variation, including feather
wear and absence of yellow, causes continual confusion when using regional field guides.
DISTRIBUTION Resident from
Pakistan along the Himalayan
foothills through S China to Taiwan,
and through Southeast Asia to
Peninsular Malaysia, Singapore,
Sumatra, Nias, Borneo and Java.
HABITS AND HABITAT Widespread
throughout the rural lowlands, in
tall, unkempt grassland, especially
wet grassland with scattered shrubs,
including patches of such habitat at
forest or plantation edges. Presumed
to be entirely insectivorous. Males
give a short, rattling song, a cat-
like mew of alarm, and a sputter of
wingbeats that seems to be part of
their display.

## Symbols

R   Breeding or known to have bred; typically but not necessarily resident all year
X   Presumed locally extinct, formerly wild resident
M   Migrant, passage migrant, non-breeding visitor
V   Vagrant, fewer than about 5 occurrences
F   Feral
FX  Presumed locally extinct, formerly feral resident
?   Insufficient information available to determine status

## Global Status according to BirdLife International and the IUCN Red List 2008

LC  Least Concern
NT  Near Threatened
VU  Vulnerable
EN  Endangered
CR  Critically Endangered

| | | Peninsular Malaysia | Singapore | Sarawak | Sabah | Global Status |
|---|---|---|---|---|---|---|
| **Megapodiidae** | | | | | | |
| Tabon Scrubfowl | *Megapodius cumingii* | – | – | – | R | LC |
| **Phasianidae** | | | | | | |
| Long-billed Partridge | *Rhizothera longirostris* | R | – | R | R | NT |
| Dulit Partridge | *Rhizothera dulitensis* | – | – | R | R | – |
| Black Partridge | *Melanoperdix niger* | R | – | R | R | VU |
| Blue-breasted Quail | *Coturnix chinensis* | R | R | R | R | LC |
| Malaysian Partridge | *Arborophila campbelli* | R | – | – | – | LC |
| Red-breasted Partridge | *Arborophila hyperythra* | – | – | R | R | LC |
| Chestnut-necklaced Partridge | *Arborophila charltonii* | R | – | – | R | NT |
| Ferruginous Partridge | *Caloperdix oculea* | R | – | R | R? | NT |
| Crimson-headed Partridge | *Haematortyx sanguiniceps* | – | – | R | R | LC |
| Crested Partridge | *Rollulus rouloul* | R | – | R | R | NT |
| Red Junglefowl | *Gallus gallus* | R | R | – | F | LC |
| Crestless Fireback | *Lophura erythrophthalma* | R | – | R | R | VU |
| Crested Fireback | *Lophura ignita* | R | – | R | R | NT |
| Bulwer's Pheasant | *Lophura bulweri* | – | – | R | R | VU |
| Mountain Peacock-pheasant | *Polyplectron inopinatum* | R | – | – | – | VU |
| Malaysian Peacock-pheasant | *Polyplectron malacense* | R | – | – | – | VU |
| Bornean Peacock-pheasant | *Polyplectron schleiermacheri* | – | – | R | R | EN |
| Crested Argus | *Rheinardia ocellata* | R | – | – | – | NT |
| Great Argus | *Argusianus argus* | R | – | R | R | NT |
| Green Peafowl | *Pavo muticus* | X | – | – | – | VU |
| **Anatidae** | | | | | | |
| Wandering Whistling-duck | *Dendrocygna arcuata* | – | F | – | R | LC |
| Lesser Whistling-duck | *Dendrocygna javanica* | R | R | R | R | LC |
| White-winged Duck | *Asarcornis scutulata* | X | – | – | – | EN |

| | | Peninsular Malaysia | Singapore | Sarawak | Sabah | Global Status |
|---|---|---|---|---|---|---|
| Cotton Pygmy-goose | Nettapus coromandelianus | R | M | R | R | LC |
| Gadwall | Anas strepera | – | V | – | – | LC |
| Eurasian Wigeon | Anas penelope | V | V | V | V | LC |
| Mallard | Anas platyrhynchos | – | – | V | V | LC |
| Northern Shoveler | Anas clypeata | V | V | V | V | LC |
| Northern Pintail | Anas acuta | V | V | V | V | LC |
| Garganey | Anas querquedula | M | M | V | M | LC |
| Eurasian Teal | Anas crecca | V | V | – | V | LC |
| Tufted Duck | Aythya fuligula | V | V | V | V | LC |
| **Procellariidae** | | | | | | |
| Streaked Shearwater | Calonectris leucomelas | M | – | M | M | LC |
| Wedge-tailed Shearwater | Puffinus pacificus | M | V | V | V | LC |
| Bulwer's Petrel | Bulweria bulwerii | M | – | M | V | LC |
| **Hydrobatidae** | | | | | | |
| Wilson's Storm-petrel | Oceanites oceanicus | M | – | – | – | LC |
| Swinhoe's Storm-petrel | Oceanodroma monorhis | M | M | V | V | LC |
| **Podicipedidae** | | | | | | |
| Little Grebe | Tachybaptus ruficollis | RM | R | – | V | LC |
| **Ciconiidae** | | | | | | |
| Milky Stork | Mycteria cinerea | R | – | – | – | VU |
| Painted Stork | Mycteria leucocephala | F | – | – | – | NT |
| Asian Openbill | Anastomus oscitans | V | – | – | – | LC |
| Woolly-necked Stork | Ciconia episcopus | X | – | – | – | LC |
| Storm's Stork | Ciconia stormi | R | – | R | R | EN |
| Lesser Adjutant | Leptoptilos javanicus | R | M | R | R | VU |
| **Threskiornithidae** | | | | | | |
| Black-headed Ibis | Threskiornis melanocephalus | V | – | V | V | NT |
| White-shouldered Ibis | Pseudibis davisoni | – | – | X? | – | CR |
| Glossy Ibis | Plegadis falcinellus | V | – | V | LC | – |
| Black-faced Spoonbill | Platalea minor | – | – | V? | V? | EN |
| **Ardeidae** | | | | | | |
| Great Bittern | Botaurus stellaris | V | V | – | V | LC |
| Yellow Bittern | Ixobrychus sinensis | RM | RM | RM | RM | LC |
| Von Schrenk's Bittern | Ixobrychus eurhythmus | M | M | M | M | LC |
| Cinnamon Bittern | Ixobrychus cinnamomeus | RM | RM | RM | RM | LC |
| Black Bittern | Dupetor flavicollis | M | M | M | M | LC |
| Malaysian Night-heron | Gorsachius melanolophus | M | M | M | M | LC |
| Black-crowned Night-heron | Nycticorax nycticorax | R | R | R? | R | LC |
| Rufous Night-heron | Nycticorax caledonicus | – | – | – | R | LC |
| Little Heron | Butorides striata | RM | RM | RM | RM | LC |
| Indian Pond-heron | Ardeola grayii | M | – | – | – | LC |
| Chinese Pond-heron | Ardeola bacchus | M | M | M | M | LC |
| Javan Pond-heron | Ardeola speciosa | M | V | M | M | LC |
| Eastern Cattle Egret | Bubulcus coromandus | RM | FM | M | M | LC |
| Grey Heron | Ardea cinerea | R | R | M | M | LC |
| Great-billed Heron | Ardea sumatrana | R | R | R? | R | LC |
| Purple Heron | Ardea purpurea | RM | RM | RM | RM | LC |

| | | Peninsular Malaysia | Singapore | Sarawak | Sabah | Global Status |
|---|---|---|---|---|---|---|
| Great Egret | *Ardea alba* | RM | M | M | RM | LC |
| Intermediate Egret | *Mesophoyx intermedia* | M | M | M | RM | LC |
| Little Egret | *Egretta garzetta* | RM | M | RM | RM | LC |
| Pacific Reef-egret | *Egretta sacra* | R | R | R | R | LC |
| Chinese Egret | *Egretta eulophotes* | M | M | M | M | VU |
| **Phaethontidae** | | | | | | |
| White-tailed Tropicbird | *Phaethon lepturus* | – | – | – | V | LC |
| **Fregatidae** | | | | | | |
| Christmas Frigatebird | *Fregata andrewsi* | M | V | M | M | CR |
| Great Frigatebird | *Fregata minor* | V | – | V | M | LC |
| Lesser Frigatebird | *Fregata ariel* | M | V | M | M | LC |
| **Pelecanidae** | | | | | | |
| Great White Pelican | *Pelecanus onocrotalus* | V | V | – | – | LC |
| Spot-billed Pelican | *Pelecanus philippensis* | V | – | – | – | NT |
| **Sulidae** | | | | | | |
| Masked Booby | *Sula dactylatra* | V | – | V | RV | LC |
| Red-footed Booby | *Sula sula* | V | – | V | RV | LC |
| Brown Booby | *Sula leucogaster* | RM | V | M | RM | LC |
| **Phalacrocoracidae** | | | | | | |
| Little Cormorant | *Phalacrocorax niger* | M | – | – | – | LC |
| Great Cormorant | *Phalacrocorax carbo* | V | – | – | M | LC |
| **Anhingidae** | | | | | | |
| Oriental Darter | *Anhinga melanogaster* | XV | – | R | R | NT |
| **Falconidae** | | | | | | |
| Black-thighed Falconet | *Microhierax fringillarius* | R | M | R | R | LC |
| White-fronted Falconet | *Microhierax latifrons* | – | – | – | R | NT |
| Lesser Kestrel | *Falco naumanni* | – | V | – | – | VU |
| Common Kestrel | *Falco tinnunculus* | M | M | M | M | LC |
| Amur Falcon | *Falco amurensis* | V | V | – | – | LC |
| Eurasian Hobby | *Falco subbuteo* | V | – | – | V | LC |
| Oriental Hobby | *Falco severus* | V? | V | – | V | LC |
| Peregrine Falcon | *Falco peregrinus* | RM | M | RM | RM | LC |
| **Pandionidae** | | | | | | |
| Osprey | *Pandion haliaetus* | M | M | M | R?M | LC |
| **Accipitridae** | | | | | | |
| Jerdon's Baza | *Aviceda jerdoni* | R | V | R | R | LC |
| Black Baza | *Aviceda leuphotes* | M | M | – | – | LC |
| Oriental Honey-buzzard | *Pernis ptilorhyncus* | RM | M | RM | RM | LC |
| Bat Hawk | *Macheiramphus alcinus* | R | M | R | R | LC |
| Black-shouldered Kite | *Elanus caeruleus* | R | R | R | R | LC |
| Black Kite | *Milvus migrans* | M | M | – | – | LC |
| Black-eared Kite | *Milvus lineatus* | M | M | V | V | LC |
| Brahminy Kite | *Haliastur indus* | R | R | R | R | LC |
| White-bellied Sea-eagle | *Haliaeetus leucogaster* | R | R | R | R | LC |
| Lesser Fish-eagle | *Ichthyophaga humilis* | R | – | R | R | NT |

| | | Peninsular Malaysia | Singapore | Sarawak | Sabah | Global Status |
|---|---|---|---|---|---|---|
| Grey-headed Fish-eagle | *Ichthyophaga ichthyaetus* | R | R | R | R | NT |
| White-rumped Vulture | *Gyps bengalensis* | X | – | – | – | CR |
| Slender-billed Vulture | *Gyps tenuirostris* | V | – | – | – | CR |
| Himalayan Griffon | *Gyps himalayensis* | V | V | – | – | LC |
| Cinereous Vulture | *Aegypius monachus* | V | – | – | – | NT |
| Red-headed Vulture | *Aegypius calvus* | X | V | – | – | CR |
| Short-toed Snake-eagle | *Circaetus gallicus* | M | M | – | – | LC |
| Crested Serpent-eagle | *Spilornis cheela* | R | R | R | R | LC |
| Mountain Serpent-eagle | *Spilornis kinabaluensis* | – | – | R | R | VU |
| Eastern Marsh-harrier | *Circus spilonotus* | M | M | M | M | LC |
| Hen Harrier | *Circus cyaneus* | V | M | V | V | LC |
| Pied Harrier | *Circus melanoleucos* | M | M | M | M | LC |
| Crested Goshawk | *Accipiter trivirgatus* | R | RM | R | R | LC |
| Shikra | *Accipiter badius* | M | V | – | – | LC |
| Chinese Sparrowhawk | *Accipiter soloensis* | M | M | M | M | LC |
| Japanese Sparrowhawk | *Accipiter gularis* | M | M | M | M | LC |
| Besra | *Accipiter virgatus* | V | V | R | R | LC |
| Eurasian Sparrowhawk | *Accipiter nisus* | V | – | V | – | LC |
| Grey-faced Buzzard | *Butastur indicus* | M | M | M | M | LC |
| Common Buzzard | *Buteo buteo* | M | M | – | – | LC |
| Greater Spotted Eagle | *Aquila clanga* | M | M | – | – | VU |
| Steppe Eagle | *Aquila nipalensis* | M | M | – | – | LC |
| Eastern Imperial Eagle | *Aquila heliaca* | M | V | – | – | VU |
| Booted Eagle | *Aquila pennata* | M | M | – | – | LC |
| Rufous-bellied Eagle | *Lophotriorchis kienerii* | RM | M | R | R | LC |
| Black Eagle | *Ictinaetus malayensis* | R | – | R | R | LC |
| Blyth's Hawk-eagle | *Nisaetus alboniger* | R | M | R | R | LC |
| Mountain Hawk-eagle | *Nisaetus nipalensis* | R | – | – | – | LC |
| Changeable Hawk-eagle | *Nisaetus limnaeetus* | R | R | R | R | LC |
| Wallace's Hawk-eagle | *Nisaetus nanus* | R | | R | R | VU |
| **Rallidae** | | | | | | |
| Red-legged Crake | *Rallina fasciata* | RM | RM | RM | RM | LC |
| Slaty-legged Crake | *Rallina eurizonoides* | M | M | – | – | LC |
| Buff-banded Rail | *Gallirallus philippensis* | – | – | – | R? | LC |
| Slaty-breasted Rail | *Gallirallus striatus* | R | R | R | R | LC |
| Eastern Water Rail | *Rallus indicus* | – | – | V | – | LC |
| White-breasted Waterhen | *Amaurornis phoenicurus* | RM | RM | RM | RM | LC |
| Baillon's Crake | *Porzana pusilla* | M | M | M | M | LC |
| Ruddy-breasted Crake | *Porzana fusca* | RM | R | V | V | LC |
| Band-bellied Crake | *Porzana paykullii* | V | – | V | – | NT |
| White-browed Crake | *Porzana cinerea* | R | R | R | R | LC |
| Watercock | *Gallicrex cinerea* | RM | M | M | RM | LC |
| Grey-headed Swamphen | *Porphyrio poliocephalus* | R | R | – | R | LC |
| Common Moorhen | *Gallinula chloropus* | R | R | RM | RM | LC |
| Common Coot | *Fulica atra* | V | V | – | V | LC |
| **Heliornithidae** | | | | | | |
| Masked Finfoot | *Heliopais personata* | M | V | – | – | VU |

| | | Peninsular Malaysia | Singapore | Sarawak | Sabah | Global Status |
|---|---|---|---|---|---|---|
| **Gruidae** | | | | | | |
| Sarus Crane | *Grus antigone* | X | – | – | – | VU |
| **Turnicidae** | | | | | | |
| Small Buttonquail | *Turnix sylvaticus* | R | – | – | – | LC |
| Barred Buttonquail | *Turnix suscitator* | R | R | – | – | LC |
| **Burhinidae** | | | | | | |
| Beach Thick-knee | *Esacus neglectus* | X? | X? | R? | R? | NT |
| **Pluvialidae** | | | | | | |
| Pacific Golden Plover | *Pluvialis fulva* | M | M | M | M | LC |
| Grey Plover | *Pluvialis squatarola* | M | M | M | M | LC |
| **Recurvirostridae** | | | | | | |
| Black-winged Stilt | *Himantopus himantopus* | RM | M | M | M | LC |
| White-headed Stilt | *Himantopus leucocephalus* | – | – | V | M | LC |
| Pied Avocet | *Recurvirostra avosetta* | – | – | V | – | LC |
| **Haematopodidae** | | | | | | |
| Eurasian Oystercatcher | *Haematopus ostralegus* | V | – | V | – | LC |
| **Dromadidae** | | | | | | |
| Crab Plover | *Dromas ardeola* | V | – | – | – | LC |
| **Vanellidae** | | | | | | |
| Yellow-wattled Lapwing | *Vanellus malabaricus* | V | – | – | – | LC |
| Grey-headed Lapwing | *Vanellus cinereus* | M | – | V | – | LC |
| Red-wattled Lapwing | *Vanellus indicus* | R | R | – | – | LC |
| **Charadriidae** | | | | | | |
| Common Ringed Plover | *Charadrius hiaticula* | V | V | – | V | LC |
| Long-billed Plover | *Charadrius placidus* | V | – | – | V | LC |
| Little Ringed Plover | *Charadrius dubius* | M | M | M | M | LC |
| Kentish Plover | *Charadrius alexandrinus* | M | M | M | M | LC |
| White-faced Plover | *Charadrius (a.) dealbatus* | M | M | V | – | – |
| Malaysian Plover | *Charadrius peronii* | R | R | R | R | NT |
| Lesser Sand-plover | *Charadrius mongolus* | M | M | M | M | LC |
| Greater Sand-plover | *Charadrius leschenaultii* | M | M | M | M | LC |
| Oriental Plover | *Charadrius veredus* | V | V | V | V | LC |
| **Rostratulidae** | | | | | | |
| Greater Painted-snipe | *Rostratula benghalensis* | R | V | R | R | LC |
| **Jacanidae** | | | | | | |
| Pheasant-tailed Jacana | *Hydrophasianus chirurgus* | M | M | – | V | LC |
| Bronze-winged Jacana | *Metopidius indicus* | M | – | – | – | LC |
| **Scolopacidae** | | | | | | |
| Eurasian Woodcock | *Scolopax rusticola* | V | V | – | V | LC |
| Pintail Snipe | *Gallinago stenura* | M | M | M | M | LC |
| Swinhoe's Snipe | *Gallinago megala* | M | M | M | M | LC |
| Common Snipe | *Gallinago gallinago* | M | M | M | M | LC |
| Red-necked Phalarope | *Phalaropus lobatus* | M | V | M | M | LC |
| Grey Phalarope | *Phalaropus fulicarius* | – | – | V | – | LC |

| | | Peninsular Malaysia | Singapore | Sarawak | Sabah | Global Status |
|---|---|---|---|---|---|---|
| Black-tailed Godwit | *Limosa limosa* | M | M | M | M | NT |
| Bar-tailed Godwit | *Limosa lapponica* | M | M | M | M | LC |
| Long-billed Dowitcher | *Limnodromus scolopaceus* | – | – | – | V | LC |
| Asian Dowitcher | *Limnodromus semipalmatus* | M | M | M | M | NT |
| Little Curlew | *Numenius minutus* | – | V | V | V | LC |
| Whimbrel | *Numenius phaeopus* | M | M | M | M | LC |
| Eurasian Curlew | *Numenius arquata* | M | M | M | M | NT |
| Far Eastern Curlew | *Numenius madagascariensis* | M | M | M | M | LC |
| Terek Sandpiper | *Xenus cinereus* | M | M | M | M | LC |
| Common Sandpiper | *Actitis hypoleucos* | M | M | M | M | LC |
| Green Sandpiper | *Tringa ochropus* | M | M | M | M | LC |
| Grey-tailed Tattler | *Tringa brevipes* | M | M | M | M | LC |
| Spotted Redshank | *Tringa erythropus* | V | M | V | V | LC |
| Common Greenshank | *Tringa nebularia* | M | M | M | M | LC |
| Nordmann's Greenshank | *Tringa guttifer* | M | M | M | V | EN |
| Marsh Sandpiper | *Tringa stagnatilis* | M | M | M | M | LC |
| Wood Sandpiper | *Tringa glareola* | M | M | M | M | LC |
| Common Redshank | *Tringa totanus* | M | M | M | M | LC |
| Great Knot | *Calidris tenuirostris* | M | M | M | M | LC |
| Red Knot | *Calidris canutus* | M | M | M | M | LC |
| Sanderling | *Calidris alba* | M | M | M | M | LC |
| Spoon-billed Sandpiper | *Eurynorhynchus pygmeus* | V | V | – | – | CR |
| Little Stint | *Calidris minuta* | M | – | – | V | LC |
| Red-necked Stint | *Calidris ruficollis* | M | M | M | M | LC |
| Temminck's Stint | *Calidris temminckii* | M | M | M | M | LC |
| Long-toed Stint | *Calidris subminuta* | M | M | M | M | LC |
| Pectoral Sandpiper | *Calidris melanotos* | V | V | – | – | LC |
| Sharp-tailed Sandpiper | *Calidris acuminata* | V | V | V | M | LC |
| Dunlin | *Calidris alpina* | V | V | – | – | LC |
| Curlew Sandpiper | *Calidris ferruginea* | M | M | M | M | LC |
| Broad-billed Sandpiper | *Limicola falcinellus* | M | M | M | M | LC |
| Ruff | *Philomachus pugnax* | M | M | M | M | LC |
| Ruddy Turnstone | *Arenaria interpres* | M | M | M | M | LC |
| **Glareolidae** | | | | | | |
| Long-legged Pratincole | *Stiltia isabella* | – | – | V | V | LC |
| Oriental Pratincole | *Glareola maldivarum* | RM | M | M | RM | LC |
| Small Pratincole | *Glareola lactea* | – | V | – | – | LC |
| **Stercorariidae** | | | | | | |
| Pomarine Jaeger | *Stercorarius pomarinus* | M? | – | – | M | LC |
| Parasitic Jaeger | *Stercorarius parasiticus* | V | – | V | V | LC |
| Long-tailed Jaeger | *Stercorarius longicaudus* | M? | – | – | V | LC |
| **Sternidae** | | | | | | |
| Brown Noddy | *Anous stolidus* | R | – | M | RM | LC |
| Black Noddy | *Anous minutus* | – | – | V | V | LC |
| Sooty Tern | *Onychoprion fuscatus* | V | – | M | RM | LC |
| Bridled Tern | *Onychoprion anaethetus* | R | M | R | R | LC |
| Aleutian Tern | *Onychoprion aleuticus* | M | M | M | – | LC |
| Little Tern | *Sternula albifrons* | RM | RM | RM | M | LC |

| | | Peninsular Malaysia | Singapore | Sarawak | Sabah | Global Status |
|---|---|---|---|---|---|---|
| Gull-billed Tern | *Gelochelidon nilotica* | M | M | M | M | LC |
| Caspian Tern | *Hydroprogne caspia* | M | V | V | V | LC |
| White-winged Tern | *Chlidonias leucopterus* | M | M | M | M | LC |
| Whiskered Tern | *Chlidonias hybrida* | M | M | M | M | LC |
| Roseate Tern | *Sterna dougallii* | R | V | M | M | LC |
| Black-naped Tern | *Sterna sumatrana* | R | R | R | R | LC |
| Common Tern | *Sterna hirundo* | M | M | M | M | LC |
| Lesser Crested Tern | *Thalasseus bengalensis* | M | M | M | M | LC |
| Great Crested Tern | *Thalasseus bergii* | RM | M | M | RM | LC |
| Chinese Crested Tern | *Thalasseus bernsteini* | – | – | V | – | CR |
| **Laridae** | | | | | | |
| Heuglin's Gull | *Larus heuglini* | V | – | – | – | – |
| Laughing Gull | *Larus atricilla* | V | – | – | – | LC |
| Brown-headed Gull | *Chroicocephalus brunnicephalus* | M | V | – | – | LC |
| Black-headed Gull | *Chroicocephalus ridibundus* | M | M | M | M | LC |
| **Columbidae** | | | | | | |
| Rock Pigeon | *Columba livia* | F | F | F | F | LC |
| Silvery Wood-pigeon | *Columba argentina* | – | – | X | – | CR |
| Red Collared-dove | *Streptopelia tranquebarica* | R | F | – | – | LC |
| Spotted Dove | *Streptopelia chinensis* | R | R | R | R | LC |
| Island Collared Dove | *Streptopelia bitorquata* | – | – | – | V | LC |
| Barred Cuckoo-dove | *Macropygia unchall* | R | – | – | – | LC |
| Ruddy Cuckoo-dove | *Macropygia emiliana* | – | – | R | R | LC |
| Little Cuckoo-dove | *Macropygia ruficeps* | R | – | R | R | LC |
| Emerald Dove | *Chalcophaps indica* | R | R | R | R | LC |
| Zebra Dove | *Geopelia striata* | R | R | R | R | LC |
| Nicobar Pigeon | *Caloenas nicobarica* | R | – | – | R | NT |
| Cinnamon-headed Green-pigeon | *Treron fulvicollis* | R | M | R | R | NT |
| Little Green-pigeon | *Treron olax* | R | RM | R | R | LC |
| Pink-necked Green-pigeon | *Treron vernans* | R | R | R | R | LC |
| Orange-breasted Green-pigeon | *Treron bicincta* | R | – | – | – | LC |
| Thick-billed Green-pigeon | *Treron curvirostra* | R | R | R | R | LC |
| Large Green-pigeon | *Treron capellei* | R | – | R | R | VU |
| Yellow-vented Green-pigeon | *Treron seimundi* | R | – | – | – | LC |
| Wedge-tailed Green-pigeon | *Treron sphenura* | R | – | – | – | LC |
| Jambu Fruit-dove | *Ptilinopus jambu* | R | M | R | R | NT |
| Black-naped Fruit-dove | *Ptilinopus melanospila* | – | – | – | R | LC |
| Green Imperial-pigeon | *Ducula aenea* | R | M | R | R | LC |
| Grey Imperial-pigeon | *Ducula pickeringii* | – | – | V | R | VU |
| Mountain Imperial-pigeon | *Ducula badia* | R | – | R | R | LC |
| Pied Imperial-pigeon | *Ducula bicolor* | R | M | R | R | LC |
| **Psittacidae** | | | | | | |
| Blue-crowned Hanging-parrot | *Loriculus galgulus* | R | R | R | R | LC |
| Yellow-crested Cockatoo | *Cacatua sulphurea* | – | F | – | – | LC |
| Tanimbar Cockatoo | *Cacatua goffiniana* | – | F | – | – | NT |
| Blue-rumped Parrot | *Psittinus cyanurus* | R | R | R | R | NT |
| Blue-naped Parrot | *Tanygnathus lucionensis* | – | – | FX | R | NT |

| | | Peninsular Malaysia | Singapore | Sarawak | Sabah | Global Status |
|---|---|---|---|---|---|---|
| Rose-ringed Parakeet | *Psittacula krameri* | – | F | – | – | LC |
| Red-breasted Parakeet | *Psittacula alexandri* | – | F | – | – | LC |
| Long-tailed Parakeet | *Psittacula longicauda* | R | R | R | R | NT |
| Rainbow Lorikeet | *Trichoglossus haematodus* | – | F | – | – | LC |
| **Cuculidae** | | | | | | |
| Chestnut-winged Cuckoo | *Clamator coromandus* | R | M | M | M | LC |
| Large Hawk-cuckoo | *Hierococcyx sparverioides* | M | M | V | V | LC |
| Dark Hawk-cuckoo | *Hierococcyx bocki* | R | – | R | R | – |
| Moustached Hawk-cuckoo | *Hierococcyx vagans* | R | – | R | R | NT |
| Malaysian Hawk-cuckoo | *Hierococcyx fugax* | R | M | R | R | LC |
| Horsfield's Hawk-cuckoo | *Hierococcyx hyperythrus* | – | – | V | V | – |
| Hodgson's Hawk-cuckoo | *Hierococcyx nisicolor* | M | M | V | V | – |
| Indian Cuckoo | *Cuculus micropterus* | RM | M | RM | RM | LC |
| Eurasian Cuckoo | *Cuculus canorus* | – | – | – | V | LC |
| Oriental Cuckoo | *Cuculus horsfieldi* | ? | ? | M | M | LC |
| Himalayan Cuckoo | *Cuculus saturatus* | M | ? | M | M | LC |
| Sunda Cuckoo | *Cuculus lepidus* | R | – | R | R | LC |
| Banded Bay Cuckoo | *Cacomantis sonneratii* | R | R | R | R | LC |
| Plaintive Cuckoo | *Cacomantis merulinus* | R | R | R | R | LC |
| Rusty-breasted Cuckoo | *Cacomantis sepulcralis* | R | R | R | R | LC |
| Horsfield's Bronze-cuckoo | *Chrysococcyx basalis* | V | V | M | M | LC |
| Little Bronze-cuckoo | *Chrysococcyx minutillus* | R | R | R | R | LC |
| Asian Emerald Cuckoo | *Chrysococcyx maculatus* | M | – | – | – | LC |
| Violet Cuckoo | *Chrysococcyx xanthorhynchus* | RM | RM | R | R | LC |
| Square-tailed Drongo-cuckoo | *Surniculus (l.) lugubris* | R | R | R | R | LC |
| Fork-tailed Drongo-cuckoo | *Surniculus (l.) dicruroides* | M | M | M | M | LC |
| Asian Koel | *Eudynamys scolopaceus* | RM | RM | RM | RM | LC |
| Bornean Ground-cuckoo | *Carpococcyx radiatus* | – | – | R | R | NT |
| Black-bellied Malkoha | *Rhopodytes diardi* | R | X | R | R | NT |
| Chestnut-bellied Malkoha | *Rhopodytes sumatranus* | R | R | R | R | NT |
| Green-billed Malkoha | *Rhopodytes tristis* | R | – | – | – | LC |
| Raffles's Malkoha | *Rhinortha chlorophaeus* | R | – | R | R | LC |
| Red-billed Malkoha | *Zanclostomus javanicus* | R | – | R | R | LC |
| Chestnut-breasted Malkoha | *Zanclostomus curvirostris* | R | – | R | R | LC |
| Short-toed Coucal | *Centropus rectunguis* | R | – | R | R | VU |
| Greater Coucal | *Centropus sinensis* | R | R | R | R | LC |
| Lesser Coucal | *Centropus bengalensis* | R | R | R | R | LC |
| **Tytonidae** | | | | | | |
| Common Barn-owl | *Tyto alba* | R | R | F | F | LC |
| Eastern Grass-owl | *Tyto longimembris* | – | – | – | R | LC |
| Oriental Bay Owl | *Phodilus badius* | R | X | R | R | LC |
| **Strigidae** | | | | | | |
| White-fronted Scops-owl | *Otus sagittatus* | R | – | – | – | VU |
| Reddish Scops-owl | *Otus rufescens* | R | – | R | R | NT |
| Mountain Scops-owl | *Otus spilocephalus* | R | – | R | R | LC |
| Rajah Scops-owl | *Otus brookii* | – | – | R | R | LC |
| Oriental Scops-owl | *Otus sunia* | M | M | – | – | LC |
| Collared Scops-owl | *Otus bakkamoena* | R | R | R | R | LC |

| | | Peninsular Malaysia | Singapore | Sarawak | Sabah | Global Status |
|---|---|---|---|---|---|---|
| Mantanani Scops-owl | *Otus mantananensis* | – | – | – | R | NT |
| Barred Eagle-owl | *Bubo sumatranus* | R | M | R | R | LC |
| Dusky Eagle-owl | *Bubo coromandus* | R | – | – | – | LC |
| Brown Fish-owl | *Ketupa zeylonensis* | R | – | – | – | LC |
| Buffy Fish-owl | *Ketupa ketupu* | R | R | R | R | LC |
| Spotted Wood-owl | *Strix seloputo* | R | R | – | – | LC |
| Brown Wood-owl | *Strix leptogrammica* | R | – | R | R | LC |
| Collared Owlet | *Glaucidium brodiei* | R | – | R | R | LC |
| Brown Boobook | *Ninox scutulata* | R | R | R | R | LC |
| Northern Boobook | *Ninox japonica* | M | M | M | M | LC |
| Short-eared Owl | *Asio flammeus* | V | V | V | – | LC |

### Batrachostomidae

| | | | | | | |
|---|---|---|---|---|---|---|
| Large Frogmouth | *Batrachostomus auritus* | R | – | R | R | NT |
| Dulit Frogmouth | *Batrachostomus harterti* | – | – | R | R | NT |
| Gould's Frogmouth | *Batrachostomus stellatus* | R | – | R | R | NT |
| Blyth's Frogmouth | *Batrachostomus affinis* | R | – | R | R | LC |
| Bornean Frogmouth | *Batrachostomus mixtus* | – | – | R | R | NT |
| Sunda Frogmouth | *Batrachostomus cornutus* | – | – | R | R | LC |

### Eurostopodidae

| | | | | | | |
|---|---|---|---|---|---|---|
| Malaysian Eared-nightjar | *Eurostopodus temminckii* | R | R | R | R | LC |
| Great Eared-nightjar | *Eurostopodus macrotis* | R | – | – | – | LC |

### Caprimulgidae

| | | | | | | |
|---|---|---|---|---|---|---|
| Grey Nightjar | *Caprimulgus indicus* | M | M | M | M | LC |
| Large-tailed Nightjar | *Caprimulgus macrurus* | R | R | R | R | LC |
| Savanna Nightjar | *Caprimulgus affinis* | R | R | – | R? | LC |
| Bonaparte's Nightjar | *Caprimulgus concretus* | – | – | R | R | VU |

### Apodidae

| | | | | | | |
|---|---|---|---|---|---|---|
| Waterfall Swift | *Hydrochous gigas* | R | – | R? | R? | NT |
| Glossy Swiftlet | *Collocalia esculenta* | R | R | R | R | LC |
| Bornean Swiftlet | *Collocalia dodgei* | – | – | – | R | – |
| Himalayan Swiftlet | *Aerodramus brevirostris* | M | ? | – | – | LC |
| Mossy-nest Swiftlet | *Aerodramus salangana* | – | – | R | R | LC |
| Black-nest Swiftlet | *Aerodramus maximus* | R | R | R | R | LC |
| Edible-nest Swiftlet | *Aerodramus fuciphagus* | R | R | R | R | LC |
| German's Swiftlet | *Aerodramus germani* | R | – | R | R | LC |
| Silver-rumped Needletail | *Rhaphidura leucopygialis* | R | M | R | R | LC |
| White-throated Needletail | *Hirundapus caudacutus* | M | M | M | M | LC |
| Silver-backed Needletail | *Hirundapus cochinchinensis* | M | M | – | – | LC |
| Brown-backed Needletail | *Hirundapus giganteus* | RM | M | M | M | LC |
| Asian Palm-swift | *Cypsiurus balasiensis* | R | R | R | R | LC |
| Fork-tailed Swift | *Apus pacificus* | M | M | M | M | LC |
| House Swift | *Apus affinis* | R | R | R | R | LC |

### Hemiprocnidae

| | | | | | | |
|---|---|---|---|---|---|---|
| Grey-rumped Treeswift | *Hemiprocne longipennis* | R | R | R | R | LC |
| Whiskered Treeswift | *Hemiprocne comata* | R | XM | R | R | LC |

### Trogonidae

| | | | | | | |
|---|---|---|---|---|---|---|
| Red-naped Trogon | *Harpactes kasumba* | R | X | R | R | NT |

| | | Peninsular Malaysia | Singapore | Sarawak | Sabah | Global Status |
|---|---|---|---|---|---|---|
| Diard's Trogon | *Harpactes diardii* | R | X | R | R | NT |
| Whitehead's Trogon | *Harpactes whiteheadi* | – | – | R | R | NT |
| Cinnamon-rumped Trogon | *Harpactes orrhophaeus* | R | – | R | R | NT |
| Scarlet-rumped Trogon | *Harpactes duvaucelii* | R | – | R | R | NT |
| Orange-breasted Trogon | *Harpactes oreskios* | R | – | R | R | LC |
| Red-headed Trogon | *Harpactes erythrocephalus* | R | – | – | – | LC |

### Coraciidae

| | | | | | | |
|---|---|---|---|---|---|---|
| Indian Roller | *Coracias benghalensis* | R | – | – | – | LC |
| Dollarbird | *Eurystomus orientalis* | RM | RM | RM | RM | LC |

### Alcedinidae

| | | | | | | |
|---|---|---|---|---|---|---|
| Rufous-collared Kingfisher | *Actenoides concretus* | R | X | R | R | NT |
| Banded Kingfisher | *Lacedo pulchella* | R | – | R | R | LC |
| Stork-billed Kingfisher | *Pelargopsis capensis* | R | R | R | R | LC |
| Brown-winged Kingfisher | *Pelargopsis amauroptera* | R | – | – | – | NT |
| Ruddy Kingfisher | *Halcyon coromanda* | RM | RM | RM | RM | LC |
| White-throated Kingfisher | *Halcyon smyrnensis* | R | R | – | – | LC |
| Black-capped Kingfisher | *Halcyon pileata* | M | M | M | M | LC |
| Collared Kingfisher | *Todiramphus chloris* | RM | R | RM | RM | LC |
| Sacred Kingfisher | *Todiramphus sanctus* | – | – | M | M | LC |
| Black-backed Kingfisher | *Ceyx erithaca* | M | M | M | M | LC |
| Rufous-backed Kingfisher | *Ceyx rufidorsa* | R | X | R | R | LC |
| Blue-banded Kingfisher | *Alcedo euryzona* | R | – | R | R | VU |
| Blue-eared Kingfisher | *Alcedo meninting* | R | R | R | R | LC |
| Common Kingfisher | *Alcedo atthis* | M | M | M | M | LC |

### Meropidae

| | | | | | | |
|---|---|---|---|---|---|---|
| Red-bearded Bee-eater | *Nyctyornis amictus* | R | – | R | R | LC |
| Blue-tailed Bee-eater | *Merops philippinus* | RM | M | RM | RM | LC |
| Blue-throated Bee-eater | *Merops viridis* | RM | R | RM | RM | LC |
| Chestnut-headed Bee-eater | *Merops leschenaulti* | R | – | – | – | LC |

### Upupidae

| | | | | | | |
|---|---|---|---|---|---|---|
| Common Hoopoe | *Upupa epops* | M | – | V | V | LC |

### Bucerotidae

| | | | | | | |
|---|---|---|---|---|---|---|
| Bushy-crested Hornbill | *Anorrhinus galeritus* | R | – | R | R | LC |
| Oriental Pied Hornbill | *Anthracoceros albirostris* | R | R | R | R | LC |
| Black Hornbill | *Anthracoceros malayanus* | R | – | R | R | NT |
| Great Hornbill | *Buceros bicornis* | R | – | – | – | NT |
| Rhinoceros Hornbill | *Buceros rhinoceros* | R | X | R | R | NT |
| Helmeted Hornbill | *Rhinoplax vigil* | R | – | R | R | NT |
| White-crowned Hornbill | *Berenicornis comatus* | R | – | R | R | NT |
| Wrinkled Hornbill | *Aceros corrugatus* | R | – | R | R | NT |
| Plain-pouched Hornbill | *Aceros subruficollis* | R | – | – | – | VU |
| Wreathed Hornbill | *Aceros undulatus* | R | – | R | R | LC |

### Megalaimidae

| | | | | | | |
|---|---|---|---|---|---|---|
| Fire-tufted Barbet | *Psilopogon pyrolophus* | R | – | – | – | LC |
| Lineated Barbet | *Megalaima lineata* | R | F | – | – | LC |
| Gold-whiskered Barbet | *Megalaima chrysopogon* | R | – | R | R | LC |
| Red-crowned Barbet | *Megalaima rafflesii* | R | R | R | R | NT |

| | Peninsular Malaysia | Singapore | Sarawak | Sabah | Global Status |
|---|---|---|---|---|---|
| Red-throated Barbet | *Megalaima mystacophanos* | R | – | R | R | NT |
| Mountain Barbet | *Megalaima monticola* | – | – | R | R | LC |
| Golden-throated Barbet | *Megalaima franklinii* | R | – | – | – | LC |
| Black-browed Barbet | *Megalaima oorti* | R | – | – | – | LC |
| Yellow-crowned Barbet | *Megalaima henricii* | R | – | R | R | NT |
| Golden-naped barbet | *Megalaima pulcherrima* | – | – | R | R | LC |
| Blue-eared Barbet | *Megalaima australis* | R | X | R | R | LC |
| Bornean Barbet | *Megalaima eximia* | – | – | R | R | LC |
| Coppersmith Barbet | *Megalaima haemacephala* | R | R | – | – | LC |
| Brown Barbet | *Calorhamphus fuliginosus* | R | X | R | R | LC |

**Indicatoridae**

| | | | | | |
|---|---|---|---|---|---|
| Malaysian Honeyguide | *Indicator archipelagicus* | R | – | R | R | NT |

**Picidae**

| | | | | | |
|---|---|---|---|---|---|
| Eurasian Wryneck | *Jynx torquilla* | V | – | – | – | LC |
| Speckled Piculet | *Picumnus innominatus* | R | – | – | R | LC |
| Rufous Piculet | *Sasia abnormis* | R | – | R | R | LC |
| Sunda Pygmy Woodpecker | *Dendrocopos moluccensis* | R | R | R | R | LC |
| Grey-capped Pygmy Woodpecker | *Dendrocopos canicapillus* | R | X | R | R | LC |
| Rufous Woodpecker | *Micropternus brachyurus* | R | R | R | R | LC |
| White-bellied Woodpecker | *Dryocopus javensis* | R | R | R | R | LC |
| Banded Woodpecker | *Chrysophlegma mineaceus* | R | R | R | R | LC |
| Greater Yellownape | *Chrysophlegma flavinucha* | R | – | – | – | LC |
| Chequer-throated Woodpecker | *Chrysophlegma mentalis* | R | X | R | R | LC |
| Lesser Yellownape | *Picus chlorolophus* | R | – | – | – | LC |
| Crimson-winged Woodpecker | *Picus puniceus* | R | R | R | R | LC |
| Grey-headed Woodpecker | *Picus canus* | R | – | – | – | LC |
| Streak-breasted Woodpecker | *Picus viridanus* | R | – | – | – | LC |
| Laced Woodpecker | *Picus vittatus* | R | R | – | – | LC |
| Olive-backed Woodpecker | *Dinopium rafflesii* | R | X | R | R | NT |
| Common Flameback | *Dinopium javanense* | R | R | R | R | LC |
| Greater Flameback | *Chrysocolaptes lucidus* | R | X | – | R | LC |
| Bamboo Woodpecker | *Gecinulus viridis* | R | – | – | – | LC |
| Maroon Woodpecker | *Blythipicus rubiginosus* | R | – | R | R | LC |
| Bay Woodpecker | *Blythipicus pyrrhotis* | R | – | – | – | LC |
| Orange-backed Wodpecker | *Reinwardtipicus validus* | R | X | R | R | LC |
| Buff-rumped Woodpecker | *Meiglyptes tristis* | R | X | R | R | LC |
| Buff-necked Woodpecker | *Meiglyptes tukki* | R | X | R | R | NT |
| Grey-and-buff Woodpecker | *Hemicircus concretus* | R | X | R | R | LC |
| Great Slaty Woodpecker | *Mulleripicus pulverulentus* | R | V | R | R | LC |

**Eurylaimidae**

| | | | | | |
|---|---|---|---|---|---|
| Green Broadbill | *Calyptomena viridis* | R | X | R | R | NT |
| Hose's Broadbill | *Calyptomena hosii* | – | – | R | R | NT |
| Whitehead's Broadbill | *Calyptomena whiteheadi* | – | – | R | R | LC |
| Long-tailed Broadbill | *Psarisomus dalhousiae* | R | – | R | R | LC |
| Dusky Broadbill | *Corydon sumatranus* | R | X | R | R | LC |
| Silver-breasted Broadbill | *Serilophus lunatus* | R | – | – | – | LC |

| | | Peninsular Malaysia | Singapore | Sarawak | Sabah | Global Status |
|---|---|---|---|---|---|---|
| Black-and-red Broadbill | *Cymbirhynchus macrorhynchos* | R | XM | R | R | LC |
| Banded Broadbill | *Eurylaimus javanicus* | R | X | R | R | LC |
| Black-and-yellow Broadbill | *Eurylaimus ochromalus* | R | X | R | R | NT |

### Pittidae

| | | | | | | |
|---|---|---|---|---|---|---|
| Hooded Pitta | *Pitta sordida* | RM | M | RM | RM | LC |
| Fairy Pitta | *Pitta nympha* | – | – | M | M | VU |
| Blue-winged Pitta | *Pitta moluccensis* | RM | M | M | M | LC |
| Mangrove Pitta | *Pitta megarhyncha* | R | R | R? | – | NT |
| Giant Pitta | *Pitta caerulea* | R | – | R | R | NT |
| Rusty-naped Pitta | *Pitta oatesi* | R | – | – | – | LC |
| Banded Pitta | *Pitta guajana* | R | – | R | R | LC |
| Blue-banded Pitta | *Pitta arquata* | – | – | R | R | LC |
| Garnet Pitta | *Pitta granatina* | R | X | R | – | NT |
| Black-crowned Pitta | *Pitta ussheri* | – | – | – | R | – |
| Blue-headed Pitta | *Pitta baudii* | – | – | R | R | VU |

### Acanthizidae

| | | | | | | |
|---|---|---|---|---|---|---|
| Golden-bellied Gerygone | *Gerygone sulphurea* | R | R | R | R | LC |

### Eupetidae

| | | | | | | |
|---|---|---|---|---|---|---|
| Rail-babbler | *Eupetes macrocerus* | R | – | R | R | NT |

### Vireonidae

| | | | | | | |
|---|---|---|---|---|---|---|
| White-browed Shrike-babbler | *Pteruthius flaviscapis* | R | – | R | R | LC |
| Black-eared Shrike-babbler | *Pteruthius melanotis* | R | – | – | – | LC |
| White-bellied Erpornis | *Erpornis zantholeuca* | R | – | R | R | LC |

### Campephagidae

| | | | | | | |
|---|---|---|---|---|---|---|
| Large Woodshrike | *Tephrodornis gularis* | R | X | R | R | LC |
| Javan Cuckooshrike | *Coracina javensis* | R | – | – | – | LC |
| Sunda Cuckooshrike | *Coracina larvata* | – | – | R | R | LC |
| Bar-bellied Cuckooshrike | *Coracina striata* | R | X | R | R | LC |
| Lesser Cuckooshrike | *Coracina fimbriata* | R | R | R | R | LC |
| Pied Triller | *Lalage nigra* | R | R | R | R | LC |
| Rosy Minivet | *Pericrocotus roseus* | V | – | – | – | LC |
| Ashy Minivet | *Pericrocotus divaricatus* | M | M | M | M | LC |
| Fiery Minivet | *Pericrocotus igneus* | R | X | R | R | NT |
| Grey-chinned Minivet | *Pericrocotus solaris* | R | – | R | R | LC |
| Scarlet Minivet | *Pericrocotus flammeus* | R | R | R | R | LC |
| Bar-winged Flycatcher-shrike | *Hemipus picatus* | R | – | R | R | LC |
| Black-winged Flycatcher-shrike | *Hemipus hirundinaceus* | R | – | R | R | LC |

### Pachycephalidae

| | | | | | | |
|---|---|---|---|---|---|---|
| Mangrove Whistler | *Pachycephala cinerea* | R | R | R | R | LC |
| White-vented Whistler | *Pachycephala homeyeri* | – | – | – | R | LC |
| Bornean Whistler | *Pachycephala hypoxantha* | – | – | R | R | LC |

### Oriolidae

| | | | | | | |
|---|---|---|---|---|---|---|
| Dark-throated Oriole | *Oriolus xanthonotus* | R | X | R | R | NT |
| Eurasian Golden Oriole | *Oriolus oriolus* | V | – | – | – | LC |
| Black-naped Oriole | *Oriolus chinensis* | RM | RM | R?M? | R?M? | LC |
| Black-hooded Oriole | *Oriolus xanthornus* | R | – | – | R | LC |

| | | Peninsular Malaysia | Singapore | Sarawak | Sabah | Global Status |
|---|---|---|---|---|---|---|
| Black-and-crimson Oriole | *Oriolus cruentus* | R | – | R | R | LC |
| Black Oriole | *Oriolus hosii* | – | – | R | ? | NT |
| **Artamidae** | | | | | | |
| Ashy Woodswallow | *Artamus fuscus* | V | – | – | – | LC |
| White-breasted Woodswallow | *Artamus leucorynchus* | R | – | R | R | LC |
| **Aegithinidae** | | | | | | |
| Common Iora | *Aegithina tiphia* | R | R | R | R | LC |
| Green Iora | *Aegithina viridissima* | R | X | R | R | NT |
| Great Iora | *Aegithina lafresnayei* | R | – | – | – | LC |
| **Rhipiduridae** | | | | | | |
| White-throated Fantail | *Rhipidura albicollis* | R | – | R | R | LC |
| Pied Fantail | *Rhipidura javanica* | R | R | R | R | LC |
| Spotted Fantail | *Rhipidura perlata* | R | – | R | R | LC |
| **Dicruridae** | | | | | | |
| Black Drongo | *Dicrurus macrocercus* | M | M | – | V | LC |
| Ashy Drongo | *Dicrurus leucophaeus* | RM | M | R | R | LC |
| Crow-billed Drongo | *Dicrurus annectans* | M | M | M | M | LC |
| Bronzed Drongo | *Dicrurus aeneus* | R | X | R | R | LC |
| Lesser Racket-tailed Drongo | *Dicrurus remifer* | R | – | – | – | LC |
| Greater Racket-tailed Drongo | *Dicrurus paradiseus* | R | R | R | R | LC |
| Hair-crested Drongo | *Dicrurus hottentottus* | – | – | R | R | LC |
| **Pityriaseidae** | | | | | | |
| Bornean Bristlehead | *Pityriasis gymnocephala* | – | – | R | R | NT |
| **Monarchidae** | | | | | | |
| Black-naped Monarch | *Hypothymis azurea* | R | R | R | R | LC |
| Asian Paradise-flycatcher | *Terpsiphone paradisi* | RM | RM | R | R | LC |
| Japanese Paradise-flycatcher | *Terpsiphone atrocaudata* | M | M | – | V | NT |
| **Prionopidae** | | | | | | |
| Rufous-winged Philentoma | *Philentoma pyrhoptera* | R | X | R | R | LC |
| Maroon-breasted Philentoma | *Philentoma velata* | R | X | R | R | NT |
| **Corvidae** | | | | | | |
| House Crow | *Corvus splendens* | F? | F? | – | F | LC |
| Slender-billed Crow | *Corvus enca* | R | – | R | R | LC |
| Southern Jungle Crow | *Corvus macrorhynchos* | R | R | R? | R? | LC |
| Common Green Magpie | *Cissa chinensis* | R | – | R | R | LC |
| Short-tailed Green Magpie | *Cissa thalassina* | – | – | R | R | LC |
| Bornean Treepie | *Dendrocitta cinerascens* | – | – | R | R | LC |
| Racquet-tailed Treepie | *Crypsirina temia* | R | – | – | – | LC |
| Black Magpie | *Platysmurus leucopterus* | R | – | R | R | NT |
| Crested Jay | *Platylophus galericulatus* | R | – | R | R | NT |

| | | Peninsular Malaysia | Singapore | Sarawak | Sabah | Global Status |
|---|---|---|---|---|---|---|
| **Laniidae** | | | | | | |
| Tiger Shrike | *Lanius tigrinus* | M | M | M | M | LC |
| Brown Shrike | *Lanius cristatus* | M | M | M | M | LC |
| Long-tailed Shrike | *Lanius schach* | R | R | M | M | LC |
| **Nectariniidae** | | | | | | |
| Plain Sunbird | *Anthreptes simplex* | R | X? | R | R | LC |
| Brown-throated Sunbird | *Anthreptes malacensis* | R | R | R | R | LC |
| Red-throated Sunbird | *Anthreptes rhodolaema* | R | – | R | R | NT |
| Van Hasselt's Sunbird | *Leptocoma brasiliana* | R | R | R | R | LC |
| Copper-throated Sunbird | *Leptocoma calcostetha* | R | R | R | R | LC |
| Olive-backed Sunbird | *Cinnyris jugularis* | R | R | R | R | LC |
| Crimson Sunbird | *Aethopyga siparaja* | R | R | R | R | LC |
| Temminck's Sunbird | *Aethopyga temminckii* | R | – | R | R | LC |
| Black-throated Sunbird | *Aethopyga saturata* | R | – | – | – | LC |
| Ruby-cheeked Sunbird | *Chalcoparia singalensis* | R | – | R | R | LC |
| Purple-naped Sunbird | *Hypogramma hypogrammicum* | R | X | R | R | LC |
| Grey-breasted Spiderhunter | *Arachnothera modesta* | R | X | R | R | LC |
| Streaky-breasted Spiderhunter | *Arachnothera affinis* | – | – | R | R | LC |
| Streaked Spiderhunter | *Arachnothera magna* | R | – | – | – | LC |
| Little Spiderhunter | *Arachnothera longirostra* | R | R | R | R | LC |
| Thick-billed Spiderhunter | *Arachnothera crassirostris* | R | R | R | R | LC |
| Long-billed Spiderhunter | *Arachnothera robusta* | R | – | R | R | LC |
| Spectacled Spiderhunter | *Arachnothera flavigaster* | R | X | R | R | LC |
| Yellow-eared Spiderhunter | *Arachnothera chrysogenys* | R | R | R | R | LC |
| Whitehead's Spiderhunter | *Arachnothera juliae* | – | – | R | R | LC |
| **Dicaeidae** | | | | | | |
| Thick-billed Flowerpecker | *Dicaeum agile* | R | M | R | R | LC |
| Brown-backed Flowerpecker | *Dicaeum everetti* | R | – | R | R | NT |
| Yellow-breasted Flowerpecker | *Dicaeum maculatus* | R | X | R | R | LC |
| Crimson-breasted Flowerpecker | *Dicaeum percussus* | R | – | R | R | LC |
| Yellow-rumped Flowerpecker | *Dicaeum xanthopygius* | – | – | R | R | LC |
| Scarlet-breasted Flowerpecker | *Dicaeum thoracicus* | R | – | R | R | NT |
| Yellow-vented Flowerpecker | *Dicaeum chrysorrheum* | R | R | R | R | LC |
| Orange-bellied Flowerpecker | *Dicaeum trigonostigma* | R | R | R | R | LC |
| Plain Flowerpecker | *Dicaeum minullum* | R | X | R | R | LC |
| Black-sided Flowerpecker | *Dicaeum monticolum* | – | – | R | R | LC |
| Fire-breasted Flowerpecker | *Dicaeum ignipectus* | R | – | – | – | LC |
| Scarlet-backed Flowerpecker | *Dicaeum cruentatum* | R | R | R | R | LC |
| **Chloropseidae** | | | | | | |
| Greater Green Leafbird | *Chloropsis sonnerati* | R | R | R | R | LC |
| Lesser Green Leafbird | *Chloropsis cyanopogon* | R | R | R | R | NT |
| Blue-winged Leafbird | *Chloropsis cochinchinensis* | R | R | R | – | LC |
| Bornean Leafbird | *Chloropsis kinabaluensis* | – | – | – | R | LC |
| Orange-bellied Leafbird | *Chloropsis hardwickii* | R | – | – | – | LC |

| | | Peninsular Malaysia | Singapore | Sarawak | Sabah | Global Status |
|---|---|---|---|---|---|---|
| **Irenidae** | | | | | | |
| Asian Fairy-bluebird | *Irena puella* | R | R | R | R | LC |
| **Ploceidae** | | | | | | |
| Streaked Weaver | *Ploceus manyar* | – | F | – | – | LC |
| Baya Weaver | *Ploceus philippinus* | R | R | – | – | LC |
| **Estrildidae** | | | | | | |
| Red Avadavat | *Amandava amandava* | – | F | – | F | LC |
| Java Sparrow | *Padda oryzivora* | F | F | F | F | VU |
| Dusky Munia | *Lonchura fuscans* | – | – | R | R | LC |
| White-rumped Munia | *Lonchura striata* | R | R | – | – | LC |
| Javan Munia | *Lonchura leucogastroides* | – | F | – | – | LC |
| Scaly-breasted Munia | *Lonchura punctulata* | R | R | R | R | LC |
| White-bellied Munia | *Lonchura leucogastra* | R | – | R | R | LC |
| Chestnut Munia | *Lonchura atricapilla* | R | R | R | R | LC |
| White-headed Munia | *Lonchura maja* | R | R | – | – | LC |
| Tawny-breasted Parrotfinch | *Erythrura hyperythra* | R | – | R | R | LC |
| Pin-tailed Parrotfinch | *Erythrura prasina* | R | – | R | R | LC |
| **Passeridae** | | | | | | |
| House Sparrow | *Passer domesticus* | – | FX | – | – | LC |
| Plain-backed Sparrow | *Passer flaveolus* | R | – | – | – | LC |
| Eurasian Tree-sparrow | *Passer montanus* | R | R | R | R | LC |
| **Motacillidae** | | | | | | |
| Red-throated Pipit | *Anthus cervinus* | M | M | M | M | LC |
| Olive-backed Pipit | *Anthus hodgsoni* | M | – | M | M | LC |
| Richard's Pipit | *Anthus richardi* | V? | – | M | M | LC |
| Paddyfield Pipit | *Anthus rufulus* | R | R | R | R | LC |
| Pechora Pipit | *Anthus gustavi* | – | – | M | M | LC |
| Forest Wagtail | *Dendronanthus indicus* | M | M | M | M | LC |
| White Wagtail | *Motacilla alba* | M | M | M | M | LC |
| Grey Wagtail | *Motacilla cinerea* | M | M | M | M | LC |
| Eastern Yellow Wagtail | *Motacilla tschutschensis* | M | M | M | M | LC |
| Citrine Wagtail | *Motacilla citreola* | – | V | – | – | LC |
| **Fringillidae** | | | | | | |
| Brown Bullfinch | *Pyrrhula nipalensis* | R | – | – | – | LC |
| **Emberizidae** | | | | | | |
| Black-headed Bunting | *Emberiza melanocephala* | – | – | – | V | LC |
| Chestnut-eared Bunting | *Emberiza fucata* | V | – | – | – | LC |
| Little Bunting | *Emberiza pusilla* | – | – | V | V | LC |
| Chestnut Bunting | *Emberiza rutila* | V | – | – | – | LC |
| Yellow-breasted Bunting | *Emberiza aureola* | M | M | V | V | VU |
| **Sittidae** | | | | | | |
| Velvet-fronted Nuthatch | *Sitta frontalis* | R | M | R | R | LC |
| Blue Nuthatch | *Sitta azurea* | R | – | – | – | LC |
| **Sturnidae** | | | | | | |
| Crested Myna | *Acridotheres cristatellus* | F | F | – | F | LC |
| White-vented Myna | *Acridotheres grandis* | F | – | – | – | LC |

| Common name | Scientific name | Peninsular Malaysia | Singapore | Sarawak | Sabah | Global Status |
|---|---|---|---|---|---|---|
| Jungle Myna | Acridotheres fuscus | R | – | – | – | LC |
| Javan Myna | Acridotheres javanicus | F | F | F | – | LC |
| Common Myna | Acridotheres tristis | R | R | F | F | LC |
| Black-winged Myna | Acridotheres melanopterus | – | FX | – | – | EN |
| White-shouldered Starling | Sturnus sinensis | M | M | V | – | LC |
| Purple-backed Starling | Sturnus sturninus | M | M | V | V | LC |
| Chestnut-cheeked Starling | Sturnus philippensis | V | V | M | M | LC |
| Rosy Starling | Sturnus roseus | – | V | – | V | LC |
| Asian Glossy Starling | Aplonis panayensis | R | R | R | R | LC |
| Golden-crested Myna | Ampeliceps coronatus | X | – | – | – | LC |
| Common Hill-myna | Gracula religiosa | R | R | R | R | LC |

**Turdidae**

| Common name | Scientific name | Peninsular Malaysia | Singapore | Sarawak | Sabah | Global Status |
|---|---|---|---|---|---|---|
| Chestnut-capped Thrush | Zoothera interpres | R | – | R | R | NT |
| Orange-headed Thrush | Zoothera citrina | M | M | R | R | LC |
| Everett's Thrush | Zoothera everetti | – | – | R | R | NT |
| White's Thrush | Zoothera aurea | – | – | – | V | LC |
| Eurasian Scaly Thrush | Zoothera dauma | V | – | – | – | LC |
| Siberian Thrush | Zoothera sibirica | M | M | V | V | LC |
| Island Thrush | Turdus poliocephalus | – | – | – | R | LC |
| Japanese Thrush | Turdus cardis | – | – | – | V | LC |
| Eyebrowed Thrush | Turdus obscurus | M | M | M | M | LC |
| Fruithunter | Chlamydochaera jefferyi | – | – | R | R | LC |

**Muscicapidae**

| Common name | Scientific name | Peninsular Malaysia | Singapore | Sarawak | Sabah | Global Status |
|---|---|---|---|---|---|---|
| Lesser Shortwing | Brachypteryx leucophrys | R | – | – | – | LC |
| White-browed Shortwing | Brachypteryx montana | – | – | R | R | LC |
| Siberian Rubythroat | Luscinia calliope | V | – | – | V | LC |
| Rufous-headed Robin | Luscinia ruficeps | V | – | – | – | VU |
| Siberian Blue Robin | Luscinia cyane | M | M | M | M | LC |
| White-tailed Robin | Myiomela leucura | R | – | – | – | LC |
| White-throated Rock-thrush | Monticola gularis | M | V | – | – | LC |
| Blue Rock-thrush | Monticola solitarius | RM | M | M | M | LC |
| Northern Wheatear | Oenanthe oenanthe | – | – | V | – | LC |
| Eastern Stonechat | Saxicola maurus | M | M | V | V | LC |
| Pied Bushchat | Saxicola caprata | – | – | – | V | LC |
| Red-flanked Bluetail | Tarsiger cyanurus | – | – | – | V | LC |
| Chestnut-naped Forktail | Enicurus ruficapillus | R | – | R | R | NT |
| Slaty-backed Forktail | Enicurus schistaceus | R | – | – | – | LC |
| Southern White-crowned Forktail | Enicurus leschenaulti | R | – | R | R | LC |
| Northern White-crowned Forktail | Enicurus sinensis | – | – | R | R | – |
| Malaysian Whistling-thrush | Myophonus robinsoni | R | – | – | – | LC |
| Blue Whistling-thrush | Myophonus caeruleus | RM | – | – | – | LC |
| Bornean Whistling-thrush | Myophonus borneensis | – | – | R | R | – |
| Blue-and-white Flycatcher | Cyanoptila cyanomelana | M | M | M | M | LC |
| Pale Blue Flycatcher | Cyornis unicolor | R | – | R | R | LC |
| Hill Blue Flycatcher | Cyornis banyumas | R | – | R | R | LC |
| Large Blue Flycatcher | Cyornis magnirostris | M | – | – | – | – |
| Large-billed Blue Flycatcher | Cyornis caerulatus | – | – | R | R | VU |

| | | Peninsular Malaysia | Singapore | Sarawak | Sabah | Global Status |
|---|---|---|---|---|---|---|
| Bornean Blue Flycatcher | *Cyornis superbus* | – | – | R | R | LC |
| Tickell's Blue Flycatcher | *Cyornis tickelliae* | RM | – | – | – | LC |
| Chinese Blue Flycatcher | *Cyornis glaucicomans* | M | V | – | – | – |
| Blue-throated Flycatcher | *Cyornis rubeculoides* | M | V | – | – | LC |
| Malaysian Blue Flycatcher | *Cyornis turcosus* | R | – | R | R | NT |
| Mangrove Blue Flycatcher | *Cyornis rufigastra* | R | R | R | R | LC |
| White-tailed Flycatcher | *Cyornis concretus* | R | – | R | R | LC |
| Verditer Flycatcher | *Eumyias thalassinus* | R | – | R | R | LC |
| Indigo Flycatcher | *Eumyias indigo* | – | – | R | R | LC |
| Rufous-vented Niltava | *Niltava sumatrana* | R | – | – | – | LC |
| Large Niltava | *Niltava grandis* | R | – | – | – | LC |
| Yellow-rumped Flycatcher | *Ficedula zanthopygia* | M | M | – | V | LC |
| Narcissus Flycatcher | *Ficedula narcissina* | – | – | M | M | LC |
| Green-backed Flycatcher | *Ficedula elisae* | M | V | – | – | – |
| Mugimaki Flycatcher | *Ficedula mugimaki* | M | M | M | M | LC |
| Rufous-browed Flycatcher | *Ficedula solitaris* | R | – | – | – | LC |
| Snowy-browed Flycatcher | *Ficedula hyperythra* | R | – | R | R | LC |
| Rufous-chested Flycatcher | *Ficedula dumetoria* | R | – | R | R | NT |
| Little Pied Flycatcher | *Ficedula westermanni* | R | – | R | R | LC |
| Taiga Flycatcher | *Ficedula albicilla* | M | – | M | M | LC |
| Pygmy Blue Flycatcher | *Muscicapella hodgsoni* | R | – | R | R | LC |
| Ferruginous Flycatcher | *Muscicapa ferruginea* | M | M | M | M | LC |
| Grey-streaked Flycatcher | *Muscicapa griseisticta* | – | – | V | V | LC |
| Dark-sided Flycatcher | *Muscicapa sibirica* | M | M | M | M | LC |
| Asian Brown Flycatcher | *Muscicapa dauurica* | M | M | M | M | LC |
| Brown-streaked Flycatcher | *Muscicapa williamsoni* | R | M | V | RM | – |
| Brown-chested Jungle-flycatcher | *Rhinomyias brunneata* | M | M | – | – | VU |
| Fulvous-chested Jungle-flycatcher | *Rhinomyias olivacea* | – | – | – | R | LC |
| Grey-chested Jungle-flycatcher | *Rhinomyias umbratilis* | R | – | R | R | NT |
| Rufous-tailed Jungle-flycatcher | *Rhinomyias ruficauda* | – | – | R | R | LC |
| Eyebrowed Jungle-flycatcher | *Rhinomyias gularis* | – | – | R | R | LC |
| Oriental Magpie-robin | *Copsychus saularis* | R | R | R | R | LC |
| White-rumped Shama | *Copsychus malabaricus* | R | R | R | R | LC |
| White-crowned Shama | *Copsychus stricklandii* | – | – | – | R | – |
| Rufous-tailed Shama | *Trichixos pyrropygus* | R | – | R | R | NT |
| **Paridae** | | | | | | |
| Grey Tit | *Parus cinereus* | R | – | R | R | NT |
| Sultan Tit | *Melanochlora sultanea* | R | – | – | – | LC |
| **Stenostiridae** | | | | | | |
| Grey-headed Canary-flycatcher | *Culicicapa ceylonensis* | R | – | R | R | LC |
| **Alaudidae** | | | | | | |
| Eurasian Skylark | *Alauda arvensis* | – | – | V | V | LC |
| **Pycnonotidae** | | | | | | |
| Straw-headed Bulbul | *Pycnonotus zeylanicus* | R | R | R | R | VU |

| | | Peninsular Malaysia | Singapore | Sarawak | Sabah | Global Status |
|---|---|---|---|---|---|---|
| Black-and-white Bulbul | *Pycnonotus melanoleucos* | R | – | R | R | NT |
| Black-headed Bulbul | *Pycnonotus atriceps* | R | R | R | R | LC |
| Black-crested Bulbul | *Pycnonotus flaviventris* | R | F | – | – | LC |
| Bornean Bulbul | *Pycnonotus montis* | – | – | R | R | – |
| Scaly-breasted Bulbul | *Pycnonotus squamatus* | R | – | R | R | NT |
| Grey-bellied Bulbul | *Pycnonotus cyaniventris* | R | X | R | R | NT |
| Puff-backed Bulbul | *Pycnonotus eutilotus* | R | – | R | R | NT |
| Stripe-throated Bulbul | *Pycnonotus finlaysoni* | R | – | – | – | LC |
| Pale-faced Bulbul | *Pycnonotus leucops* | – | – | R | R | LC |
| Yellow-vented Bulbul | *Pycnonotus goiavier* | R | R | R | R | LC |
| Olive-winged Bulbul | *Pycnonotus plumosus* | R | R | R | R | LC |
| Streak-eared Bulbul | *Pycnonotus blanfordi* | R | – | – | – | LC |
| Cream-vented Bulbul | *Pycnonotus simplex* | R | R | R | R | LC |
| Red-eyed Bulbul | *Pycnonotus brunneus* | R | R | R | R | LC |
| Spectacled Bulbul | *Pycnonotus erythropthalmos* | R | – | R | R | LC |
| Red-whiskered Bulbul | *Pycnonotus jocosus* | F? | F | – | – | LC |
| Sooty-headed Bulbul | *Pycnonotus aurigaster* | – | F | – | – | LC |
| Hook-billed Bulbul | *Setornis criniger* | – | – | R | R | VU |
| Buff-vented Bulbul | *Iole olivacea* | R | R | R | R | NT |
| Hairy-backed Bulbul | *Tricholestes criniger* | R | – | R | R | LC |
| Finsch's Bulbul | *Alophoixus finschii* | R | – | R | R | NT |
| Yellow-bellied Bulbul | *Alophoixus phaeocephalus* | R | X | R | R | LC |
| Grey-cheeked Bulbul | *Alophoixus bres* | R | – | R | R | LC |
| Ochraceous Bulbul | *Alophoixus ochraceus* | R | – | R | R | LC |
| Streaked Bulbul | *Ixos malaccensis* | R | M | R | R | NT |
| Mountain Bulbul | *Ixos mcclellandii* | R | – | – | – | LC |
| Cinereous Bulbul | *Hemixos cinereus* | R | M | R | R | LC |
| **Hirundinidae** | | | | | | |
| Asian House-martin | *Delichon dasypus* | M | M | M | M | LC |
| Common Sand-martin | *Riparia riparia* | M | M | M | M | LC |
| Dusky Crag-martin | *Ptyonoprogne concolor* | R | – | – | – | LC |
| Barn Swallow | *Hirundo rustica* | M | M | M | M | LC |
| House Swallow | *Hirundo tahitica* | R | R | R | R | LC |
| Red-rumped Swallow | *Cecropis daurica* | M | M | ? | ? | LC |
| Striated Swallow | *Cecropis striolata* | – | – | M | M | LC |
| Rufous-bellied Swallow | *Cecropis badia* | R | – | – | – | – |
| **Cettiidae** | | | | | | |
| Yellow-bellied Warbler | *Abroscopus superciliaris* | R | – | R | R | LC |
| Mountain Tailorbird | *Phyllergates cucullatus* | R | – | R | R | LC |
| Sunda Bush-warbler | *Cettia vulcania* | – | – | R | R | LC |
| Bornean Stubtail | *Urosphena whiteheadi* | – | – | R | R | LC |
| **Phylloscopidae** | | | | | | |
| Plain-tailed Warbler | *Seicercus soror* | V | – | – | – | LC |
| Chestnut-crowned Warbler | *Seicercus castaniceps* | R | – | – | – | LC |
| Yellow-breasted Warbler | *Seicercus montis* | R | – | R | R | LC |
| Eastern Crowned Warbler | *Phylloscopus coronatus* | M | M | – | – | LC |
| Mountain Leaf-warbler | *Phylloscopus trivirgatus* | R | – | R | R | LC |
| Arctic Warbler | *Phylloscopus borealis* | M | M | M | M | LC |

| | | Peninsular Malaysia | Singapore | Sarawak | Sabah | Global Status |
|---|---|---|---|---|---|---|
| Pale-legged Leaf-warbler | *Phylloscopus tenellipes* | M? | V | – | – | LC |
| Two-barred Warbler | *Phylloscopus plumbeitarsus* | V | – | – | – | LC |
| Yellow-browed Warbler | *Phylloscopus inornatus* | M | M | V | – | LC |
| Dusky Warbler | *Phylloscopus fuscatus* | M | V | – | – | LC |
| **Timaliidae** | | | | | | |
| Oriental White-eye | *Zosterops palpebrosus* | R | R | R | R | LC |
| Black-capped White-eye | *Zosterops atricapilla* | – | – | R | R | LC |
| Everett's White-eye | *Zosterops everetti* | R | – | R | R | LC |
| Pygmy White-eye | *Oculocincta squamifrons* | – | – | R | R | LC |
| Mountain Blackeye | *Chlorocharis emiliae* | – | – | R | R | LC |
| Chestnut-crested Yuhina | *Yuhina everetti* | – | – | R | R | LC |
| Mountain Fulvetta | *Alcippe peracensis* | R | – | – | – | LC |
| Brown Fulvetta | *Alcippe brunneicauda* | R | – | R | R | NT |
| Black-throated Babbler | *Stachyris nigricollis* | R | – | R | R | NT |
| White-necked Babbler | *Stachyris leucotis* | R | – | R | R | NT |
| Grey-headed Babbler | *Stachyris poliocephala* | R | – | R | R | LC |
| Grey-throated Babbler | *Stachyris nigriceps* | R | – | R | R | LC |
| Chestnut-winged Babbler | *Stachyris erythroptera* | R | R | R | R | LC |
| Chestnut-rumped Babbler | *Stachyris maculata* | R | – | R | R | NT |
| Large Scimitar-babbler | *Pomatorhinus hypoleucos* | R | – | – | – | LC |
| Chestnut-backed Scimitar-babbler | *Pomatorhinus montanus* | R | – | R | R | LC |
| Pygmy Wren-babbler | *Pnoepyga pusilla* | R | – | – | – | LC |
| Golden Babbler | *Stachyridopsis chrysaea* | R | – | – | – | LC |
| Rufous-fronted Babbler | *Stachyridopsis rufifrons* | R | – | R | R | LC |
| Pin-striped Tit-babbler | *Macronus gularis* | R | R | – | – | LC |
| Bold-striped Tit-babbler | *Macronus bornensis* | – | – | R | R | LC |
| Fluffy-backed Tit-babbler | *Macronus ptilosus* | R | – | R | R | NT |
| Buff-breasted Babbler | *Pellorneum tickelli* | R | – | – | – | LC |
| Black-capped Babbler | *Pellorneum capistratum* | R | X | R | R | LC |
| Puff-throated Babbler | *Pellorneum ruficeps* | R | – | – | – | LC |
| Moustached Babbler | *Malacopteron magnirostre* | R | R | R | R | LC |
| Sooty-capped Babbler | *Malacopteron affine* | R | – | R | R | NT |
| Scaly-crowned Babbler | *Malacopteron cinereum* | R | – | R | R | LC |
| Rufous-crowned Babbler | *Malacopteron magnum* | R | – | R | R | NT |
| Grey-breasted Babbler | *Ophrydornis albogularis* | R | – | R | R | NT |
| Abbott's Babbler | *Malacocincla abbotti* | R | R | R | R | LC |
| Horsfield's Babbler | *Malacocincla sepiaria* | R | – | R | R | LC |
| Short-tailed Babbler | *Malacocincla malaccensis* | R | R | R | R | NT |
| Temminck's Babbler | *Trichastoma pyrrogenys* | – | – | R | R | LC |
| White-chested Babbler | *Trichastoma rostratum* | R | R | R | R | NT |
| Ferruginous Babbler | *Trichastoma bicolor* | R | – | R | R | LC |
| Bornean Wren-babbler | *Ptilocichla leucogrammica* | – | – | R | R | VU |
| Striped Wren-babbler | *Kenopia striata* | R | – | R | R | NT |
| Marbled Wren-babbler | *Turdinus marmoratus* | R | – | – | – | LC |
| Large Wren-babbler | *Turdinus macrodactylus* | R | – | – | – | NT |
| Streaked Wren-babbler | *Napothera brevicaudata* | R | – | – | – | LC |
| Eyebrowed Wren-babbler | *Napothera epilepidota* | R | – | R | R | LC |
| Black-throated Wren-babbler | *Napothera atrigularis* | – | – | R | R | NT |

| | Peninsular Malaysia | Singapore | Sarawak | Sabah | Global Status |
|---|---|---|---|---|---|
| Mountain Wren-babbler | *Napothera crassa* | – | – | R | R | LC |
| Collared Babbler | *Gampsorhynchus torquatus* | R | – | – | – | LC |
| Rufous-winged Fulvetta | *Pseudominla castaneceps* | R | – | – | – | LC |
| Himalayan Cutia | *Cutia nipalensis* | R | – | – | – | LC |
| White-crested Laughingthrush | *Garrulax leucolophus* | F | F | – | – | LC |
| Sunda Laughingthrush | *Garrulax palliatus* | – | – | R | R | LC |
| Black Laughingthrush | *Melanocichla lugubris* | R | – | – | – | LC |
| Bare-headed Laughingthrush | *Melanocichla calva* | – | – | R | R | LC |
| Spectacled Laughingthrush | *Rhinocichla mitrata* | R | – | R | R | LC |
| Chestnut-hooded Laughingthrush | *Rhinocichla treacheri* | – | – | R | R | – |
| Chinese Hwamei | *Leucodioptron canorus* | – | F | – | – | LC |
| Malaysian Laughingthrush | *Trochalopteron peninsulae* | R | – | – | – | LC |
| Bar-throated Minla | *Chrysominla strigula* | R | – | – | – | LC |
| Blue-winged Siva | *Siva cyanouroptera* | R | – | – | – | LC |
| Silver-eared Mesia | *Mesia argentauris* | R | – | – | – | LC |
| Long-tailed Sibia | *Heterophasia picaoides* | R | – | – | – | LC |
| **Acrocephalidae** | | | | | | |
| Black-browed Reed-warbler | *Acrocephalus bistrigiceps* | M | M | – | – | LC |
| Oriental Reed-warbler | *Acrocephalus orientalis* | M | M | M | M | LC |
| Clamorous Warbler | *Acrocephalus stentoreus* | – | – | ? | ? | LC |
| Thick-billed Warbler | *Acrocephalus aedon* | V | – | – | – | LC |
| **Megaluridae** | | | | | | |
| Rusty-rumped Warbler | *Locustella certhiola* | M | M | M | M | LC |
| Lanceolated Warbler | *Locustella lanceolata* | M | M | M | M | LC |
| Middendorf's Warbler | *Locustella ochotensis* | – | – | M | M | LC |
| Friendly Bush-warbler | *Bradypterus accentor* | – | – | – | R | LC |
| Striated Grassbird | *Megalurus palustris* | – | – | R | R | LC |
| **Cisticolidae** | | | | | | |
| Zitting Cisticola | *Cisticola juncidis* | R | R | – | – | LC |
| Ashy Tailorbird | *Orthotomus ruficeps* | R | R | R | R | LC |
| Rufous-tailed Tailorbird | *Orthotomus sericeus* | R | R | R | R | LC |
| Dark-necked Tailorbird | *Orthotomus atrogularis* | R | R | R | R | LC |
| Common Tailorbird | *Orthotomus sutorius* | R | R | – | – | LC |
| Rufescent Prinia | *Prinia rufescens* | R | – | – | – | LC |
| Yellow-bellied Prinia | *Prinia flaviventris* | R | R | R | R | LC |
| Hill Prinia | *Prinia superciliaris* | R | – | – | – | LC |

# FURTHER READING

Bowden, D. (2005). *Globetrotter Visitor's Guide to Taman Negara, Malaysia's Premier National Park.* New Holland Publishers (UK) Ltd.

Bransbury, J. (1993). *A Birdwatcher's Guide to Malaysia.* Waymark Publishing.

Cranbrook, Earl of (ed.) (1988). *Key Environments: Malaysia.* Pergamon Press.

Francis, C.M. (2008). *A Field Guide to the Mammals of South-east Asia.* New Holland Publishers (UK) Ltd.

Jeyarajasingam, A. and Pearson, A. (1999). *A Field Guide to Birds of Peninsular Malaysia and Singapore.* Oxford University Press.

Lim, K.S. (2009). *The Avifauna of Singapore.* Nature Society (Singapore).

MacKinnon, J. and Phillipps, K. (1993). *A Field Guide to the Birds of Borneo, Sumatra, Java and Bali.* Oxford University Press Inc.

Mann, C.F. (2008). *The Birds of Borneo: an Annotated Checklist.* British Ornithologists' Union.

Myers, S. (2009). *A Field Guide to the Birds of Borneo.* Talisman and New Holland Publishers (UK) Ltd.

Payne, J. (2001). *Wild Malaysia.* New Holland Publishers (UK) Ltd.

Payne, J. (2010). *Wild Sabah: the Magnificent Wildlife and Rainforests of Malaysian Borneo.* Beaufoy Books.

Phillipps, A. and Liew, F. (2000). *Globetrotter Visitor's Guide to Kinabalu Park, Sabah, Malaysian Borneo.* New Holland Publishers (UK) Ltd.

Phillipps, Q. and Phillipps, K. (2009). *Phillipps' Field Guide to the Birds of Borneo.* Beaufoy Books.

Robson, C. (2008). *A Field Guide to the Birds of South-east Asia.* New Holland Publishers (UK) Ltd.

Smythies, B.E. (1999). *The Birds of Borneo.* 4th edn. Natural History Publications (Borneo) Sdn. Bhd. and the Sabah Society.

Soepadmo, E. (ed.) (1998). *The Encyclopedia of Malaysia: Plants.* Editions Didier Millet.

Strange, M. (2004). *Birds of Fraser's Hill.* Nature's Niche Pte Ltd.

Strange, M. and Jeyarajasingam, A. (1999). *A Photographic Guide to the Birds of Peninsular Malaysia and Singapore.* Sun Tree Publishing Limited.

Strange, M. and Yong, D. (2006). *Birds of Taman Negara.* Draco Publishing and Distribution Pte Ltd.

Tan, H.T.W., Chou, L.M., Yeo, D.C.J. and Ng, P.K.L. (2007). *The Natural Heritage of Singapore.* Prentice Hall.

Wang, L.K. and Hails, C.J. (2007). An Annotated Checklist of the Birds of Singapore. *Raffles Bulletin of Zoology,* Supplement 15.

Wells, D.R. (1999). *The Birds of the Thai-Malay Peninsula. Volume One: Non-Passerines.* Academic Press.

Wells, D.R. (2007). *The Birds of the Thai-Malay Peninsula. Volume Two: Passerines.* Christopher Helm.

Whitmore, T.C. (1984). *Tropical Rain Forests of the Far East.* Oxford University Press.

Yong, H.S. (ed.) (1998). *The Encyclopedia of Malaysia: Animals.* Editions Didier Millet.

# USEFUL CONTACTS

**Borneo Bird Club**
http//:borneobirdclub.blogspot.com

**Malaysian Nature Society**
JKR 641, Jalan Kelantan
Bukit Persekutuan
50480 Kuala Lumpur
Malaysia
www.mns.org.my

**Nature Society (Singapore)**
510 Geylang Road #02–05
The Sunflower
Singapore 389466
www.nss.org.sg

**Oriental Bird Club**
PO Box 324
Bedford MK42 0WG
UK
www.orientalbirdclub.org
www.orientalbirdimages.org